Market Research
Handbook

5th Edition

Market Research
Handbook

5th Edition

ESOMAR WORLD RESEARCH PUBLICATION

Edited by

Mario van Hamersveld

Cees de Bont

John Wiley & Sons, Ltd

Other Wiley Editorial Offices

John Wiley & Sons Inc., 111 River Street, Hoboken, NJ 07030, USA

Jossey-Bass, 989 Market Street, San Francisco, CA 94103-1741, USA

Wiley-VCH Verlag GmbH, Boschstr. 12, D-69469 Weinheim, Germany

John Wiley & Sons Australia Ltd, 42 McDougall Street, Milton, Queensland 4064, Australia

John Wiley & Sons (Asia) Pte Ltd, 2 Clementi Loop #02-01, Jin Xing Distripark, Singapore 129809

John Wiley & Sons Canada Ltd, 6045 Freemont Blvd, Mississauga, ONT, L5R 4J3, Canada

Wiley also publishes its books in a variety of electronic formats. Some content that appears
in print may not be available in electronic books.

Anniversary Logo Design: Richard J. Pacifico

Library of Congress Cataloguing-in-Publication Data

Market research handbook. — 5th ed. / edited by Mario van Hamersveld, Cees de Bont.
     p. cm.
   Rev. ed. of: The ESOMAR handbook of market and opinion research / edited
by Colin McDonald, Phyllis Vangelder. 4th ed. c1998.
   Includes bibliographical references and index.
   ISBN 978-0-470-51768-0 (cloth : alk. paper)
   1. Marketing research. I. Hamersveld, Mario van. II. Bont, Cees de, 1964–
III. ESOMAR market research handbook.
   HF5415.2.H285 2007
   658.8'3—dc22   2007020425

British Library Cataloguing in Publication Data

A catalogue record for this book is available from the British Library

ISBN 978-0-470-51768-0

Typeset in 10/12pt Times by Aptara Inc., New Delhi, India
Printed and bound in Great Britain by Antony Rowe Ltd, Chippenham, Wiltshire
This book is printed on acid-free paper responsibly manufactured from sustainable forestry
in which at least two trees are planted for each one used for paper production.

Contents

Contributors

EDITORS

Mario van Hamersveld MSc

e-mail: ryamar@knoware.nl

Mario van Hamersveld studied economics and sociology at Rotterdam University. He is Director of van Hamersveld MC specialising in international marketing, management and research. Prior to his present role, he was Marketing Development Manager of the Consumer Electronics Division of Royal Philips in Amsterdam. He served as management consultant in the strategy team and was Manager Marketing Research and Support for the Consumer Electronics Division. He has also held other marketing and research positions with Philips at a corporate level over many years. He has been engaged in a variety of international management, marketing training and development activities and contributed to various international publications. He served on the board of a number of non-profit organizations and governmental bodies. He has been active in ESOMAR as Council Member, 1990–1996, President, 1996–1998 and Acting Director General (2001–2003). He is Editor-in-Chief of "Research World". In September 2005 he was awarded the ESOMAR Excellence Award for Standards of Performance in Market, Opinion and Social Research, the "John Downham Award".

Prof.dr. Cees de Bont

e-mail: C.J.P.M.debont@io.tudelft.nl

Cees de Bont is trained in economic psychology. He obtained an MSc from Tilburg University in 1987 and a PhD from the Delft University of Technology in 1992. The main subject of his PhD thesis was about generating and applying market feedback in the early stages of product development. After fulfilling his military obligations at the Royal Military Academy (KMA) and after working as an assistant professor at Tilburg University for two years, Cees joined Philips Design in 1995.

At Philips Design, Cees was the founder of the Human Behaviour Research Centre. This Centre aims at better understanding changes in society in order to provide a basis for (technological) innovation planning. A team was put in place, many projects were started on a wide diversity of topics, such as: mobility, generations (young and old people), and new methods were developed.

In 1997, Cees moved to one of the product divisions of Philips (Domestic Appliances and Personal Care) to become responsible for the discipline of market research and strategy. His main activities involved, among other things, strengthening the global team, defining ways of working, conducting consumer research (e.g. segmentation research and research on consumer satisfaction) and preparing presentations for senior management.

In 2002 Cees de Bont was appointed Professor of Marketing at the Vrije Universiteit in Amsterdam. Here he presented his inaugural speech on strategic consumer marketing. This part-time academic responsibility was combined with the professional work for Philips. In 2005 Cees de Bont moved to Delft to become the dean of the faculty of Industrial Design Engineering at the Delft University of Technology. This faculty is one of the leading academic design schools worldwide. In his role as Dean, Cees de Bont is integrally responsible for the faculty (340 employees).

AUTHORS

Ken Baker

e-mail: kc.baker@dial.pipex.com

Ken Baker graduated in Statistics and Economics from London University. He started his research career as an executive with British Market Research Bureau in the late 1960s, becoming BMRB's Chief Statistician in 1974, a position he held until leaving to form his own consultancy, Ken Baker Associates, in 1987. As a statistician he is perhaps best known as a pioneer of geodemographic systems, publishing with others the first commercial paper on the subject (1979) at The Market Research Society Conference. His subsequent interests have included data fusion. As part of a joint paper, he was presented with the David Winton Award for the best technical paper at the 1989 MRS Conference. This paper examined the strength and weakness of fusion techniques. He is a frequent lecturer on statistics, sampling and multivariate analytical methods on behalf of The Market Research Society and independent conference organisations.

Marco Bevolo

e-mail: marco.bevolo@philips.com

Marco Bevolo joined Philips Design in 1999, assuming responsibility for the cultural trend research programme. He was instrumental in the creation of CultureScan, an ongoing trend forecasting research project investigating cultures, aesthetics and design at regional and global level. He was promoted to Design Director in 2003, and now concentrates on communication and cultural trends as well as media relations. Prior to joining Philips Design, his work focused mainly on publishing and marketing communications. He was editor-in-chief for 'Intervista', an Italian lifestyle magazine. He then worked as copywriter with Armando Testa after experiences at Euro RSCG and Italdesign Giugiaro. Mr. Bevolo's work has been published in the Italian books 'the art of advertising' and 'Nuova Enciclopedia della Comunicazione', the Japanese design magazine 'Axis' and the Design Management Review of Boston. He is currently visiting lecturer at Domus Academy of Milan and at the International Institute for Journalism of the Donau University in Krems, Austria. Mr. Bevolo graduated in Psychology of Communication from the University of Turin.

Andrew Buckley

e-mail: abuckley@harrisinteractive.com

Andy Buckley is a Director of Employee Research at Harris Interactive and Deputy Head of the northern office of Harris Interactive in the UK. He has over 12 years' research experience, and in terms of employee research, his particular specialisms include employee engagement, internal communications, and measuring the impact of major change, such as mergers and acquisitions. He has conducted employee research across all industry sectors, but has specific expertise in retail, leisure, manufacturing, logistics and engineering. He is currently developing service profit chain models which identify the employee and customer engagement drivers of organisational performance. Andy started his career as a graduate trainee at GSR (now ORC International) where he specialised in financial research and syndicated tracking studies.

He has also worked for the specialist business-to-business and customer satisfaction agency, Customer Insight. He graduated with a degree in market research from Aston University and is an Associate Member of the Market Research Society.

Phillip Cartwright
e-mail: p.cartwright@gmail.com
Phillip Cartwright is Visiting Research Fellow in Marketing, Imperial College, Tanaka Business School, London. Previously, Phillip was Senior Director, Marketing Science Centre, Customer Intelligence, Research International. He has worked in the areas of marketing strategy, innovation and advanced quantitative methods. He has been a Senior Fellow in Technology and Operations Management at INSEAD, Fontainebleau, France. He was formerly a Principal in BearingPoint's (Andersen Business Consulting) Strategy, Process and Transformation team. Phillip has worked for Ernst & Young, ACNielsen and Dunn & Bradstreet. He has served on the Programme Committee for ESOMAR in 2003 and the advisory board of the Centre for Network Economy, London Business School. Phillip holds a doctorate in economics with specialisation areas in economics from the University of Illinois, Urbana-Champaign.

Pete Comley
e-mail: pete.comley@virtualsurveys.com
Pete Comley is the Chairman of Virtual Surveys, a company he started in 1998 to specialise in Internet and website research. Much of his initial work at Virtual Surveys concerned websites. However in recent years, running panels and conducting conventional research online has become a major part of his business. Pete has a Psychology degree. He started work at Research International in 1981. He then worked at both Nestle and Unilever. He was then a director at Simon Godfrey Associates (SGA), where he was responsible for Internet research and also worked on NPD research. Indeed, Pete has been heavily involved in developing the Internet as a method for data collection since 1995. He has presented numerous papers and run courses on this subject for ESOMAR, the MRS and many others.

Laurent Florès
e-mail: lflores@crmmetrix.com
Laurent Florès, PhD, is founder and CEO of crmmetrix, He is a frequent international speaker and writer on the topic of relationship marketing, WOM and social media effectiveness, new product development and marketing research at conferences such as WOMMA, AMA, ARF, IAB, Informs Marketing Science, ESOMAR, and IREP. He sits on the first elected Board of Directors of WOMMA, as well as the ESOMAR council. For his expertise in marketing and social media, he appeared in leading international journals such as The New York Times, the International Herald Tribune, Times of India, La Tribune, and Les Echos. Laurent started his career in marketing before moving to the market research industry, working for leading market research companies such as Millward Brown and Ipsos. He left Ipsos as Vice President, Director of Interactive, in 2000, to set up crmmetrix. His visionary perspective on the impact of CRM on market research was awarded the ESOMAR prestigious Fernanda Monti Award in 2001 and drove some academic collaboration with MIT and Columbia faculty members. After an initial computer analyst degree, Laurent studied business and marketing graduating from Rouen Graduate School of Business, he then received his PhD in Marketing from Grenoble University in France. Laurent is sharing his enthusiasm by teaching and writes frequently in both business and academic journals.

Kathleen A. Frankovic

e-mail: kaf@cbsnews.com

Kathleen A. Frankovic is Director of Surveys and a Producer for CBS News. She is responsible for all aspects of CBS News polling and manages the CBS News election decision team. She holds a PhD in political science and has been President of both the American Association for Public Opinion Research and the World Association for Public Opinion Research. She served on the ESOMAR Committee which recently revised the ESOMAR/WAPOR Guide to Opinion Polling.

Richard Goosey

e-mail: r.goosey@harrisinteractive.com

Richard Goosey is Senior Vice President of Marketing Science and Methodology at Harris Interactive. In a career spanning over 25 years he has been at the forefront of developing statistical modelling and analytical solutions for global organisations. His time in research covers both the agency and client side. He has held various senior positions on the supply side. He has published widely on survey design and methodology, and his paper 'It is Time We Started Using Statistics' was awarded the best methodology paper at ESOMAR 50th Congress. His paper on advanced methods of panel and server data integration was nominated for Best International Research Paper 2005 at the joint ESOMAR ARF Worldwide Audience Measurement conference. And his work on customer satisfaction research won awards for 'Best use of research in business and professional markets' and 'Best use of research for customer insight' at the 2005 Marketing Research Awards. Richard is a Fellow of both the Market Research Society, and the Royal Statistical Society, and is widely involved with the training of the next generation of researchers. He has chaired the Market Research Society Education and Training committee and sat on the Market Research Society Council, and the Royal Statistical Society Social Statistics Committee.

Andrew Green

e-mail: Andrew.Green@zenithoptimedia.co.uk

Andrew is Chief Marketing Officer of Ipsos Global Media. He was formerly the Head of Strategic Insights at ZenithOptimedia in London. Prior to this he was founding director of billetts connections, the research and analytics division of the billetts media consulting company. Other roles have included heading up the Global Research function for OMD in New York, Regional Managing Director of Zenith Media in South-East Asia, Director of Media and Syndicated Services at AC Nielsen Singapore and senior research positions at Carat and Saatchi & Saatchi. He left Oxford University in 1981 and has been in advertising since then. In 1998 Advertising Age named him as *Media Innovator* for his work setting up television audience research in China. He has written or contributed to two books on broadcasting in Asia including *Television in Contemporary Asia* (Sage, 2000) and *From Mao to the Millennium: Chinese Broadcasting in Transition* (BMRB, 2001). He sits on the editorial advisory boards of both *Admap* and the *International Journal of Advertising* and has been a member of the programme committee for the Worldwide Readership Symposium since 1993. Andrew's references on WARC include 45 published articles and conference papers.

Paul Harris

e-mail: paultharris@aol.com

Paul Harris runs his own statistical consultancy and is a consultant to a limited number of market research agencies. He had been the Chief Statistician of NOP Market Research Ltd for the past twenty six years. He was formerly with the Market Research Department of the Electricity Council and before that with the Central Electricity Generating Board, working on power station statistics. His interests include sampling methodology and the application of multivariate statistical methods to market research data as well as the use of computers in statistical analysis. He is widely experienced in the design and analysis of segmentation studies and has much experience in tradeoff and pricing studies. Among his published works is a Market Research Society Silver Medal paper on the effects of clustering on random sample surveys. He recently was awarded an MRS Conference Technical prize for a joint author paper on Data Fusion. He lectures widely on various topics for the MRS and other bodies and has contributed chapters to two published Handbooks of market research. He is a Chartered Statistician of the Royal Statistical Society. In 1996 he was awarded a Gold Medal from The Market Research Society for exceptional contributions to market research and the MRS over many years.

Nigel Hollis
e-mail: nigel.hollis@us.millwardbrown.com
In his 22 years at Millward Brown, Nigel has advised clients in a wide cross-section of industries, from alcoholic beverages and personal care products to the automotive and technology sectors. After 10 years leading a Client Service Group, Nigel took over the role of Director of Research and Development from company founder Gordon Brown. As the leader of R&D, Nigel was instrumental in developing Millward Brown's most successful research solutions, including TVLink^{TM} and BrandDynamics^{TM}. During that time, Nigel also set up Millward Brown's original interactive research business. While Nigel continues to help client service groups address the needs of global clients, in his current role he is responsible for developing and articulating the company's viewpoints on current issues of concern to marketers, such as the role of social networks, mobile marketing and gaming in the marketing mix. Nigel is a three-time winner in WPP's Atticus Awards for original published thinking in marketing services, and won the Grand Prix prize in 1997.

Dirk Huisman
e-mail: d.huisman@skimgroup.com
Dirk Huisman studied Economy and Business Administration at the Erasmus University Rotterdam. In his thesis he analyzed and described the development of the market research industry in the Netherlands. He is a specialist in and advocate of Conjoint Analysis and related methodologies. In 1979 he founded the SKIM Mc Ma, which has become SKIM Group, a group of 5 market research related business units, operating from Rotterdam (NL) and Newark (USA). He has presented at many conferences all over the world and published over 30 articles and monographs. The themes about which he has written various articles are: Pricing; Entrepreneurship; Conjoint Analysis; The role, future and development of market research; Research issues and solutions related to the Healthcare industry, the Automotive industry and the Telecom industry. He has received an Esomar award twice.

Véronique Jeannin
e-mail: v.jeannin@esomar.org
Véronique Jeannin started her professional career as an international law consultant in 1981. Since 1985, she has been engaged in a number of senior international marketing and multicultural management functions in major blue chip companies in Paris, London and Geneva focusing on various markets including Western and Eastern Europe, the Nordics and Africa. She brings with her a wealth of business, marketing and representation experience.

Véronique joined ESOMAR, The World Market Research organisation, on the 1st of March 2005 with the objective of meeting the challenges of the Market Research Industry in a rapid developing landscape, continuing the development of the organisation's leading position, enhancing effective industry facilitation and further strengthening ESOMAR's role in promoting high standards of industry performance. At ESOMAR she heads a 30-strong international team dedicated to the worldwide implementation of the organisation's strategy, in line with its mission and statutes.

Trilingual in French, German and English, Véronique possesses a Master's Degree in Business and International Law from the University of Paris XI. Truly international she has spent 20 years of her life living abroad.

The main companies that she has worked for include: Danone, Eden Springs Europe, R.J. Reynolds International, Gallaher Ltd, United States Tobacco.

C. Frederic John

e-mail: fred_john@mastercard.com

Fred John heads the intelligence team responsible for new product development research and evaluation for MasterCard International on a global basis. He joined MasterCard in 2001. Fred has been in the survey research field since 1978, holding senior positions with a number of leading suppliers, including Yankelovich Partners, where he managed the international network. His professional experience includes work across diverse sectors, with a strong emphasis on strategic and business-to-business initiatives. Fred is a recognized expert on international research and is frequently invited to speak or write on these topics, as well as on trends affecting the research industry itself. A paper presented to an ESOMAR forum that questioned the benefits of global supplier consolidation was named the best presentation of 2004 by *Research Conference Reports*. He is an active member of ESOMAR, serving on the Program Committee for the 2005 Congress as well as panels. Mr. John received his BA and MA from New York University, did graduate work at Columbia University, and received a grant for doctoral research in Europe from the German government.

John Kelly

e-mail: john@mdlresearch.com

Following a Business Studies degree, John has been in research for over 35 years. A lot of this time has been devoted to international research. He has spent a good deal of time outside the UK, and, during 1974–1978, he helped set up and then manage one of the first market research agencies in Iran. In addition, he has spent a lot of time working in the US – particularly in the late 70s and early 80s. John's international experience covers both B2B and Consumer markets, and all forms of Quantitative and Qualitative techniques. Work has been undertaken for clients from all over the world including: Allied Domecq, FedEx, Shell, UPS and Xerox. During part of his career, as well as working on international research projects, he was a partner in an agency that helped develop a number of DP packages that have gone on to become industry standard. John was also involved, in 1972–1974, in one of the first DP bureaus in London. In addition, he was associated with the early development and introduction of Computer Assisted Telephone Interviewing (CATI) into the UK. During his career John has visited over 50 countries worldwide, and researched in over 100. John has, for many years, been active in many industry bodies including ESOMAR where he was both President: 2001 and 2002 and Past President: 2003–2004.

Dieter Korczak

e-mail: info@gp-f.com

Dieter Korczak is Managing Director and Owner of the GP Forschungsgruppe, Institute for Basic and Applied Research, in Munich which he founded in 1985. Prior to that he was Head of the Illegal Substance Research Department at Infratest Health Research, Munich (1980-1984.) He has a Diploma in economics and a PhD in Sociology from the University of Cologne. Dieter's research interests are mainly in social research and health research. He is an international expert on social inclusion/exclusion, in particular in over-indebtedness research, and the use of illegal substances. Another of his special interests concerns the role and function of different health care systems. His work also covers sustainability and ecological justice and quality of life research. His most recent research deals with appropriate access to financial services, financial education, responsible lending and different credit cultures in Europe. Another main subject of ongoing research is cosmetic surgery. He is on the advisory board of *Research World* and has written and edited 17 books on different subjects. He has consulted for the European Commission and is member of the scientific expert group for the German government concerning the government's poverty and wealth reports. He has advised a number of Federal ministries in Germany and worked for major pharmaceutical companies.

Joël-Yves Le Bigot

e-mail: generation2020@noos.fr

Joël-Yves Le Bigot is the editor of "Researching Youth" – ESOMAR Monograph Volume 9 – and has conducted many seminars on the subject. As President of Institut de l'Enfant and the network of Youth Opinion International, he worked for the major international brands or institutions in many countries all over the world – for more than 30 years – concerning children, teenagers and young adults (from 0 to 35). With Generation 2020, created in 2001, he focuses on engineering long term "youth strategies" and setting up socio-economical models. He is author, or co-author, of several books: *Vive les 11-25 – Eyrolles – 2004, J'embauche un jeune – Dunod – 2006* and *Kid Marketing – E.M.S. – 2007.*

Gerard Loosschilder

e-mail: g.h.loosschilder@philips.com

Gerard Loosschilder is a Global Division Manager with SKIM Analytical in Rotterdam, The Netherlands. Before that, he was a Senior Director of Market Intelligence at Philips Domestic Appliances and Personal Care (DAP). In total, Gerard has 17 years of market research experience in various positions on the client and agency side, both in the Netherlands and the United States. Gerard holds a PhD in Market Research from the Delft University of Technology.

Catherine Lott-Vernet

e-mail: c.lott-vernet@junium.altavia.fr

Catherine Lott-Vernet is CEO of Junium, a french communication agency, specialised in addressing young people under 25. It has integrated the research institute "L'Institut de l'Enfant" created in 1978, pioneer in studies' methology adapted to children and young people. Junium research department develops original qualitative approaches, some of which combine ethnological studies and creative brain storming. It has recently delivered a study on young people aged between 15 and 25 and the new medias, to help brands and institutions choose appropriate and legitimate supports to talk to the youth in new face-to-face means. Junium meets young people at school on a daily basis through its pedagogical programs of communication developed for corporate communication strategies. Catherine Lott-Vernet drives the marketing consulting missions of the agency for banking companies, TV channels, phone operators, clothing brands, food services for school canteens, a transport public company. She gives frequent interviews to the French media on young people and money, brands, luxury attraction, addictive behaviours, illegal downloading, humanitarian, political and supported development commitments, health concern, etc. She gives lectures on similar subjects. She is co-author with Joël-Yves Le Bigot of *Vive les 11-25*, ed. Eyrolles. She graduated HEC in 1983.

Hy Mariampolski
e-mail: hy@qualidataresearch.com
Managing Director of QualiData Research Inc., Hy's PhD training combined sociology, social psychology and cultural anthropology. He has designed, directed and conducted numerous ethnographies and other qualitative research studies for major American and multinational companies. A pioneer in the application of ethnographic methods for marketing research, Hy is the author of two books for practitioners and research managers, Ethnography for Marketers: A Guide to Consumer Immersion (Sage, 2005) and Qualitative Market Research: A Comprehensive Guide (Sage, 2001). QualiData, along with its clients, the Moen Corporation and Design Continuum, received a 2005 Industrial Design Excellence Award from Business Week Magazine for a new product based on ethnography, the "Moen Revolution Shower". Hy recently has discussed ethnography during appearances on FOX-NEWS and ABC-TV. Hy serves as a member of the Board of Advisors of the Masters of Market Research program at the University of Georgia and on the Dean's Advisory Council at the College of Liberal Arts at Purdue University, his alma mater. He has taught courses in Research Methods, Qualitative Research and Focus Groups at Kansas State University, Yeshiva University and at Hunter College of CUNY. In June of 2006, Hy Mariampolski was elected to the Market Research Council, an honorary association of market research professionals.

John Marinopoulos
e-mail: john.marinopoulos@dvlsmithgroup.com
John Marinopoulos is a Director of DVL Smith Group. He has over 16 years of experience delivering business intelligence services within a number of fields of business. John's career expertise has been focused on the design and implementation of marketing and strategic intelligence both within organisations and in a corporate advisory capacity. John holds a Master of Science degree in Statistics from Monash University, Australia. He has spoken widely at conferences in Australia, Europe, USA and Asia on world's best practice models and methods in a number of areas such as strategic intelligence, brand and reputation management, and customer needs within financial services. John is an ESOMAR Council member, a National Council member of the Australian Market and Social Research Society, and was the ESOMAR Asia-Pacific Conference Programme Committee Chair in 2007.

Neil McPhee
e-mail: neil@nuance-research.co.uk
Neil McPhee is the Founder and Managing Director of Nuance Research Ltd (UK), a specialist Qualitative and Ethnographic Research provider. Neil has been a qualitative researcher for 34 years, and is a Certified NLP (Neuro Linguistic Programming) and Hypnotherapy Practitioner. He has presented papers on the use of advanced qualitative research and ethnography

at various events including MRS, ESOMAR, AQR/QRCA, ABMRC, AEMRI, BIG (Business Intelligence Group) and IMRA conferences. He has a degree in Politics, Sociology and Economics, and is a Chartered Institute of Marketing Diploma holder. Neil has been involved in Ethnographic research techniques since the early 1970's and before its formation he was Qualitative Research Director of MORPACE International Ltd. He spent 22 years forming, growing and then selling MSS Marketing Research, a full service agency.

Piyul Mukherjee
e-mail: proact@gmail.com
Piyul Mukherjee has been interacting with Indian consumers for nearly twenty years, tracing their evolving relationship with almost the entire gamut of categories and concerns. At ESOMAR, she has presented 'Hot Buttons that Trigger India', at the first Consumer Insights conference in Madrid, in 2003, and more recently, in February 2007, she presented 'Haggling, Bargaining and Fixed Price Policies – the changing face of Indian retail'. Her paper *No Goodbyes for Tata*, a case study related to life on university campus, received the Best Paper Presented award at the biennial AQR-QRCA qualitative research conference held in Dublin in April 2005. She is currently doing her doctoral studies at IIT Bombay on The Rapidly Changing Social Dynamics in India, and says "It is impossible to be a quiet observer with the churn taking place in the subcontinent, where over 50% of the population is below 30 years of age."

Elisabetta Osta
e-mail: elisabetta_osta@dunnhumby.com
Elisabetta Osta is Senior Director, Consumer Insights at dunnhumby in London, where she is working in blending shopper and consumer insights for actionable insights that can drive success in the commercialisation phase of innovation. Prior to dunnhumby, Elisabetta was European Consumer and Retail Research Manager at McKinsey & Co. in London for six years, where she was active in several knowledge initiatives in innovation, one of her main passions, consumer trends and shopper insights. Prior to McKinsey, Elisabetta worked for Gillette in market research, marketing and sales department in Kronberg, Germany, for L'Oreal and for GfK. Elisabetta holds a MBA from Kingston Business School and a Degree in Psychology from the University of Padua, Italy.

David Penn
e-mail: davidp@conquestuk.com
David Penn is Managing Director of Conquest Research Ltd, experts in brand tracking and communications research and one of the UK's largest independent companies. His career has spanned both client and agency: firstly with Lever Bros, from where he moved on to senior research roles in BP and United Biscuits. He then crossed the divide and joined Taylor Nelson as a director, before co-founding Conquest Research in the early 1990s. He has written and spoken widely on the impact of brain science on marketing research, and uses its principles to help frame Conquest's methodologies and analysis tools. He loves market research, but is frustrated by its failure to grasp some of the new thinking about the importance of the emotional unconscious. His paper: *How brain science can help us call a truce in the Recall Wars* was joint finalist for the 2005 ISBA award. David is a graduate of the LSE and lists philosophy, history and reggae amongst his interests.

Adam Phillips

e-mail: adam.phillips@realresearch.co.uk

Adam Phillips is a research consultant and Managing Director of Real Research. He is Chairman of the ESOMAR Professional Standards Committee. He is a Fellow of the MRS, past Chairman of the MRS and a former Council member of ESOMAR. He is also a member of the Press Complaints Commission in the UK and Vice Chairman of the Financial Services Consumer Panel, a statutory board which advises the Financial Services Authority on regulation of the banking, investment and insurance markets. His career spans media measurement, public opinion research, brand development and product research. He has been Managing Director of AGB Nielsen UK, the company which provides the TV audience ratings in the UK, the most complex TV broadcast environment in the world. He was Managing Director of Euroquest, a European research network which specialised in public opinion and media research and which carried out public opinion tracking research as part of the Eurobarometer series. He has also been Deputy Managing Director of BMRB, Managing Director of Mass-Observation, CEO of Winona Research in the USA and has worked as a market research officer in Unilever. He has won best paper awards for papers presented at the ESOMAR Congress on simulated test markets and pricing research. He has a degree in Mechanical and Electronic Engineering from Cambridge University.

Ray Poynter

e-mail: ray.poynter@virtualsurveys.com

Ray Poynter is Director of Virtual Surveys (a UK based market research agency specialising in the Internet) and principal of The Future Place. Ray has spent the last 25 years at the interface between research, technology, and innovation. Ray has held director level appointments with Millward Brown, IntelliQuest, The Research Business, Sandpiper and Deux, as well as acting as a consultant to many leading agencies. Ray is in regular demand as a conference speaker and workshop leader in Europe, US, and Australia – covering topics as diverse as brand tracking to the application of multi-variate techniques to choice modelling.

Jaideep Prabhu

e-mail: j.prabhu@imperial.ac.uk

Jaideep Prabhu is Professor of Marketing at the Tanaka Business School, Imperial College London. Prior to joining the Tanaka Business School, he was University Senior Lecturer in Marketing, the Judge Institute of Management, University of Cambridge (1999–2004); Assistant Professor and Fellow at the Center for Economic Research, Tilburg University, the Netherlands (1996–1999); and Visiting Assistant Professor at the Anderson School of Management, UCLA (1995–1996). He has a BTech degree from the Indian Institute of Technology, New Delhi, and a PhD from the University of Southern California. Jaideep's research interests are in international marketing strategy. In particular, he studies various cross-national issues concerning the antecedents and consequences of radical innovation in high-technology contexts. His most recent research is on the role of firm culture in driving innovation in firms across nations. He is on the editorial board of the *Journal of Marketing* and the *Journal of the Academy of Marketing Science* and his work has been published in numerous professional journals. He has consulted for the UK Government's Department of Trade and Industry for whom he co-wrote a white paper on innovation, and has taught and consulted with executives from ABN Amro, British Telecom, EDS, Egg, ING Bank, Oce Copiers, Philips and Xerox among other companies, in the US, UK, Netherlands, Germany, Switzerland, Portugal and Colombia.

Lucile Rameckers
e-mail: lucile.rameckers@philips.com
Lucile Rameckers is Senior Research Consultant at Philips Design, Eindhoven. She combines analytical, observational and creative methods to fully understand peoples' personal, cultural, and social contexts, then communicates her findings in as vivid a manner possible to multi-disciplinary teams in various innovation projects. Lucile graduated in Consumer and Business Studies (1993, Wageningen University) – as part of which she attended the Smeal College of Business (1992, Pennsylvania State University). Before joining Philips in 1999, she worked at Belgium's University of Leuven in Applied Economics, and as project manager of Market Research for SKIM Analytical, a Rotterdam-based international market research agency.

Maarten Schellekens
e-mail: maarten_schellekens@mckinsey.com
Maarten Schellekens is Vice-President of Market Intelligence at Royal Philips Electronics. Currently, he is responsible for all consumer and market intelligence in the Domestic Appliances and Personal Care division. Previously, Maarten held the same position in the Consumer Electronics division of Philips. In these roles, He was directly involved in the strategy processes by giving market intelligence support. Before joining Philips, Maarten gained extensive experience in strategic market research during his years at McKinsey & Company, where he was part of the Marketing Practice and involved in numerous strategic consultancy engagements.

Hans-Willi Schroiff
e-mail: hans-willi.schroiff@henkel.com
Dr. Hans-Willi Schroiff is Vice President Market Research at Henkel KGaA, Germany. Previously he held various academic positions, finally as Assistant Professor of Psychology at RWTH Aachen. He is the author of numerous publications – both in Psychology and in Market Research, and a frequent speaker at international business schools, business events and conferences. Dr. Schroiff is a member of the Executive Committee of the Marketing Science Institute (Boston). He is also Chairman of the Advisory Board for the German Internet Research Company Dialego (Aachen) and a member of the Advisory Board of ICW. Since 2003 he has lectured for MBA courses at the Marketing Department of RWTH Aachen.

Anjul Sharma
e-mail: anjul.sharma@synovate.com
Anjul joined Synovate (previously TRBI) in March 2000. She has over 10 years experience spanning new product and service development, advertising and branding taking in both a strategic as well as tactical focus. Anjul is an expert in a range of qualitative methodologies and techniques practicing these with both mainstream and ethnic audiences. She is recognised as a leading figure in ethnic research, advising a range of clients on how best to understand these audiences and meet their needs. Previously, she has been involved in research into their food and eating habits, media consumption habits, young peoples' identities and Islam, Islamic banking, international money transfer, exploring interest in 3G mobile devices, needs of ethnic

businesses, transport needs across BME and faith groups and perceptions of voluntary work. Anjul has presented at a range of national and international conferences and was awarded Best Contribution to the MRS Conference 2004 for chairing a session on ethnic research entitled 'Not All Black and White'. She also writes widely in this area as well as conducting training for clients and other researchers. A first class honours graduate in Sociology (with Social Anthropology), Anjul also holds an MA in Communication Studies.

Colin Shearer
e-mail: cshearer@spss.com
Colin Shearer is Senior Vice President of Market Strategy with SPSS Inc. From 1984, he has been involved in applying advanced software solutions to solving business problems. Previously with SD-Scicon and Quintec Systems, he was one of the founders of UK-based Integral Solutions Ltd (ISL) in 1989. A pioneer of data mining in the early 1990s, he was the architect of ISL's award-winning Clementine system, the first data mining tool aimed at non-technologist end-users, and led a team which tackled numerous successful data mining applications in areas including finance, broadcasting, market research and defence. In December 1998, SPSS Inc., the world's leading supplier of analytical solutions for the enterprise, acquired ISL, and Shearer became responsible for a worldwide team of data mining consultants and for SPSS's Advanced Data Mining Group. In 2002 he became head of SPSS's newly-formed Customer Analytics Business Center, a group formed to support SPSS products and solutions which apply predictive analytics to customer data for analytical CRM. He subsequently held global responsibility for product marketing at SPSS, before moving to his current position in April 2006.

DVL Smith
e-mail: david.smith@dvlsmithgroup.com
DVL Smith is a Director of DVL Smith Group, and a Professor at the University of Hertfordshire Business School. He is a Fellow, and former Chairman, of the UK Market Research Society and holds the Society's Silver Medal. He has won numerous awards from the Market Research Society, ESOMAR and other bodies. His Doctorate is from the Department of Organisational Psychology, Birkbeck College, University of London. He is a graduate member of the British Psychological Society, and a full member of the Chartered Institute of Marketing and also a full member of the Institute of Management Consultants. He is the author of *Inside Information - Making Sense of Marketing Data* and *The Art and Science of Interpreting Market Research Evidence.*

Helen Turner
e-mail: h.turner2006@btinternet.com
Helen recently left Synovate, the global agency, where she was Business Development Director, to become a freelance Consultant. She has over 30 years of experience within the Market Research industry, having worked within several major blue – chip companies (Gillette, Spillers, Van den Berghs and Kimberly Clark) before moving over to the agency side, working for The Sample Surveys Group, which then became part of Synovate. Helen joined Sample Surveys in order to widen their client base into new markets and developed various new areas as a result, including their Mystery Shopping offering. She encouraged the agency to follow the quality route, culminating in ISO 9001 and IQCS accreditation. Helen has been involved in many forms of research, across a wealth of markets; financial, FMCG, Government research

and service industries. She has particular experience of customer satisfaction surveys, product testing, hall tests, mystery shopping, international and self-completion work. She is an active member of the Research Community, being a Fellow of the MRS and a member of its Market Research Standards Board. She recently chaired a working party to review and update the MRS Guidelines on Mystery Shopping and was a member of a similar working party for ESOMAR, updating their Mystery Shopping Guidelines.

Dominic Twose
e-mail: Dominic.Twose@uk.millwardbrown.com
Dominic Twose is Global Head of Knowledge Management at Millward Brown. He has worked in market research for over 20 years – in statistics, client service and knowledge management – including 17 years at Millward Brown. He has worked on a variety of brands, specialising in financial services. He is the author of *Driving Top Line Growth* and *Remembering Serena*. He was one of the industry panel judges for the 2005 IPA Effectiveness Awards. He has a BSc (Hons) in Mathematics, is a full member of the MRS, and is an Associate of the Inner Magic Circle.

Stefanie Un
e-mail: stefanie.un@philips.com
Stefanie Un is a Senior Research Consultant at Philips Design, Eindhoven, the Netherlands. She joined the strategic research and design group in 2001. The focus of her work lies in the area of 'People and Trends', in which people play a central role in exploring the future of innovation. Applying research outcomes into the design and creation processes of innovation is a driving factor in her work: translating insights into different levels within the company and incorporating these into the various perspectives to ensure that research outcomes are meaningful for different audiences.

Stefanie graduated in 1999 in Social Sciences, specialized in the social aspects of new media, at the University of Utrecht, the Netherlands. Prior to graduation, she attended the school of Communication Arts and Journalism of the University of Wisconsin in Madison, United States (1998). Before joining Philips, Stefanie worked in the area of future research, strategic market research at KPN, a Dutch telecom company.

Virginia Valentine
e-mail: virginia@semioticsolutions.com
Pioneer in the use of semiotics in British market research, Virginia Valentine is the founding partner of Semiotic Solutions, the first and best-known British company to specialise in semiotic and cultural analysis. Since its inception 20 years ago Semiotic Solutions has worked for most blue chip companies, government and advisory bodies. Moreover, to Virginia's great pride, her pioneering work has now resulted in a thriving – and growing – international semiotic community stirring up cultural awareness throughout the global market research and planning scene. It is widely acknowledged that Virginia Valentine's work has dramatically widened the frontiers within which market research is able to investigate the meanings consumers attribute to product brands and communications. She is a fellow of the British Market Research Society, lecturer, broadcaster and regular speaker on the international conference platform, including leading ESOMAR'S popular workshops on semiotics. Her many industry awards include several for New Thinking and Methodological Advance, reflecting her passion for pushing the boundaries of understanding how the consumer mind works. In 2000 she co-authored a seminal

work entitled The 21st Century Consumer and her most recent paper, Repositioning Research, was a double winner at the 2002 Market Research Conference. This paper is now recognised as one of the inspirations for the development of 'new' market research and planning.

Raimund Wildner

e-mail: raimund.wildner@gfk.com

Dr. Raimund Wildner was born in 1955. After taking a degree in economics in Nuremberg, he was research assistant in the Department of Statistics in Nuremberg. He completed his doctorate in 1984. Since 1984 he has held various positions within GfK. Since 1988 he has been the Head of the GfK Group's Central Department of Methodology and Product Development. In 1996 he became Managing Director and then in 2005 also Vice-President of GfK-Nürnberg e.V. He is lecturer at the University Erlangen-Nürnberg, at the Nürnberger Akademie für Absatzwirtschaft (NAA) (Nuremberg Academy for Marketing) and also at the Bayerische Akademie für Werbung und Marketing (BAW) (Bavarian Academy for Advertising and Marketing) as well as being a Trustee of the Marketing Science Institute. He is author of a large number of publications on methodological issues in market research and on brand and pricing research. For a paper on pricing research he won the "Best Methodological Paper Award" from ESOMAR, the international marketing research organisation. Furthermore, he is the co-author of the book *Panels in Market Research*.

Foreword

Given changing business dynamics, the impact of new technologies (especially the internet) and new ways of working and demands in the market research industry – the time has come to publish a completely overhauled edition of ESOMAR's successful MARKET RESEARCH HANDBOOK.

The new 5th edition of the Handbook has a revised structure, reflecting today's actual business practice and enhanced content to represent the more strategic role which market research plays. This is completely different to the current edition which is more of a "how to" list. This makes the 5th edition Handbook far more strategic in its thinking and guidance increasing the perception of MR as a strategic tool.

As with earlier editions, the Handbook still remains at heart a pragmatic, "how to" guide of all the essential disciplines and skills needed by the modern research professional.

We're very grateful to our editorial team, Cees de Bont, University of Delft, Netherlands and Mario van Hamersveld, Van Hamersveld MC, Netherlands for their thoughtful and passionate commitment to this project. The board of ESOMAR's Developing Talent initiative provided their ideas and guidance to ensure that the publication lived up to the initiative's ideals and the objectives of stimulating the development of research skills for today's changing and increasingly demanding marketplace.

Finally of course – our thanks go to all the authors who allowed their work to be reproduced here.

I hope you'll agree that the MARKET RESEARCH HANDBOOK succeeds in offering tangible and creative solutions to today's business needs.

Véronique Jeannin
Director General
ESOMAR

Editorial

It has now been ten years since the fourth edition of this handbook was published. In that time the market research landscape has undergone sweeping changes. Technological progress has not only resulted in the rapid growth of the internet and hence of online market research, but has also had an impact on such areas as further digitalisation and advances in data capture. Intensive competition has led to the development of all sorts of new working methods, on both the local and international levels. In recent years, hundreds of scientists and thousands of practitioners have applied themselves in all sorts of ways to advance the professionalism of the discipline. The results of this incredible amount of activity can be found in the new products and services on the market, in contributions to symposia and congresses, in scientific periodicals and specialist publications.

The aim of this handbook is to outline state-of-the-art market research. Less emphasis is placed on the basics, as there is a multitude of other sources and publications available for these elementary points of departure. Rather, the aim is to present the most important working methods and noteworthy developments of recent years. In this way the handbook is an indispensable reference for professionals. At the same time it can be used for higher education – both scientific and professional - in which the emphasis is on management, product development, communication, marketing and related areas. The aim is to provide more in-depth information on the role of market research in improving decision making.

Earlier editions tended to be orientated towards the provider side of the industry, but we are now turning our attention to the client side. Our thinking is that activities in the field of market intelligence are ultimately aimed at supporting its contractors in making decisions and achieving their objectives. The handbook has therefore been designed to focus on how best to utilise research results and value creation.

Part One functions as an introductory section which places market research in the context of contemporary marketing intelligence. What is the scope of modern intelligence? When aiming for evidence-based decision-making, which angles need the most attention? What is the current world of market research? What are the performance standards for quality research? The market research process and its components are illustrated from various angles, with special attention given to one area in particular: data collection.

Modern market research is a dynamic profession which takes many divergent and fascinating forms. These vary by industry, by region and by country. It is therefore impossible to give a complete description of the current state of play in one volume, but we have endeavoured to give an overview of the mainstream of activities in the profession in Part Two.

Since the handbook aims both to cover a wide territory and at the same time offer practical handles, Part Three gives attention to specific applications for market research, eg for government, B2B, media research, opinion polling, mystery shopping and employee research, to name but a few. We have also given space to a more extensive description of topics that have grown in importance since the previous edition, such as online developments, semiotics, ethnography and data mining/data fusion. It is captivating to see that the scope of market research is widening and that the boundaries with other disciplines are gradually fading. The book concludes with a few select sections on the background building blocks – a research briefing, and contributions on statistics, ethics and classifications. Wherever possible we make sure that not only the "what" is described, but also the "how".

Naturally it sometimes happens that authors do not hold the same views about the added value of certain methods, and there are also different attitudes towards the value of new developments. For the most part we have left these differences alone, as they give a richly layered and colourful picture of the worldwide dynamics in the industry and the difference of opinions and approach in what has become a mature profession. Wherever possible we have included practical examples and illustrations. Each chapter includes references to literature or suggested readings for the interested reader who wants to learn more about the topics covered.

This book would not have been possible without the pioneering work done by John Downham, Robert Worcester, Colin McDonald and Phyllis Vangelder in earlier editions.

We thank Seán Meehan, Frank Wimmer, Laurent Florès, Paulo Pinheiro de Andrade, Peter Mouncey, Jaideep Prabhu, Fred John, Hubert Gatignon, Elisabetta Osta, Phillip Cartwright and KN Tang who acted as a sounding board for the content. Many thanks also go to the authors who contributed. Their hard work and tireless commitment was very much appreciated. Also to Anna Alú and Angela Canin as well as the entire ESOMAR team, we express our thanks. It was a pleasure for us to give shape to this book together – coming as we do from different backgrounds.

Theory meets practice? Market research is sometimes undervalued, but it remains a uniquely challenging discipline that has given all of us a lot of inspiration over the years. We have also enjoyed many constructive discussions and forged valued friendships in the industry. Through our work on this new edition, of what has become a renowned handbook, it is a privilege to be able to give a little back.

Cees de Bont
Mario van Hamersveld

Acknowledgement

Our thanks to the authors, we enjoyed working with and were inspired by all of you.

Cees de Bont
Mario van Hamersveld
Angela Canin

Part One
Market Research: The Context, Main Roles and Corner Stones

1

The Role and Changing Nature of Marketing Intelligence

DVL Smith

INTRODUCTION

It is helpful to open this book by providing readers with a definition of "marketing intelligence". The definition used in the last edition of this ESOMAR Handbook by Fredrik Nauckhoff stands the test of time. He described marketing intelligence as follows: "The purpose of marketing intelligence is to provide management with the facts, information and insights it needs to rapidly make the best, most efficient business decisions."

Later in this chapter we will elaborate on this definition when we describe the different types of marketing intelligence. But this top-line definition remains an informed one because it highlights the way in which these days, business effectiveness hinges, in large measure, on a supply of information from the market place.

Today, organisations, when making key decisions, are mindful of the importance of ensuring that they understand the views and opinions of current and potential customers and know what competitors are doing in the market place. They also need an appreciation of the views of other "stakeholders" involved in the business, including, for example, employees, the financial world and the media.

So, given the importance of using robust consumer and market place evidence to make informed decisions, it is not surprising that the market research industry, since its embryonic days in the 1930s, has gone from strength to strength becoming a vibrant industry providing business decision-makers with highly valued information and advice. Let us start by outlining the structure of this chapter.

STRUCTURE OF CHAPTER

We start by defining the scope of this chapter. Specifically, we look at the coverage of decision-making in the private and non-private sectors, and also review the issue of the degree to which it is possible to make broad generalisations about market research conducted across different cultures. Having put some parameters on the scope of this chapter, we expand on the above definition of marketing intelligence by looking at the different categories of market research, and comment on the respective strengths and weaknesses of each genre of research.

Next, we look at the way in which organisations are typically structured to deliver effective strategic and marketing plans, prior to reviewing the kinds of marketing information that these

Market Research Handbook, 5th Edition. Edited by M. van Hamersveld and C. de Bont.
© 2007 John Wiley & Sons, Ltd.

plans demand. Then we review the way that the market research industry is structured in order to meet these information requirements, highlighting the role played by internal client marketing intelligence departments, and also by market research agencies.

Following this, the different stages in the market research process are reviewed. We draw attention to the broad concepts and principles of which the reader needs to be aware in order to explore these issues in closer detail in later chapters of this Handbook. After this, we put the spotlight on the raison d'être for much market research, namely, effective evidence-based decision-making. We examine the way in which modern day marketing intelligence should be interpreted and applied in order to improve the quality of organisational decision-making.

This introductory chapter ends by reviewing some of the key changes that are taking place in the world of marketing and market research, before commenting on the implications of these major trends for the way market research is likely to change over the next decade. So let us now define the scope of this chapter: a look at what we will cover and to what depth.

SCOPE OF CHAPTER

Before looking in closer detail at the different kinds of marketing intelligence available to the decision-maker, we need to first tidy up three issues. First, there is the issue of what falls into the category of marketing intelligence, as opposed to related activities that also provide helpful customer information. Second, there is the question of the role marketing intelligence plays in both profit and non-profit making organisations. And thirdly, there is the issue of the extent to which it is possible to generalise across different cultures and make general statements about the market research craft.

What Falls into the Marketing Intelligence Category?

We have used the term "marketing intelligence", rather than "market research", to reflect the way in which today, organisational decision-making benefits not only from market research conducted with different stakeholder groups, but also from lots of other sources of marketing information. Thus, marketing intelligence includes: market research surveys; information about customers held within organisations' knowledge management systems; the analysis of market trends and developments from a host of sources; and competitor analysis.

In sum, most marketing decisions will benefit from the collation of information from a range of sources that we have labelled "marketing intelligence". Today, few decisions will pivot solely on the output from a solitary market research study. However, having said this, in this chapter, while discussing the issue of integrating market research with different information sources, we still make sure we alert the reader to the critical elements of the market research process.

Marketing Intelligence in Profit and Non-profit Making Organisations

The emphasis of this book is on using marketing intelligence for commercial decision-making. However, many of these principles apply to market research conducted in the public sector on social issues. Both profit and non-profit making organisations must keep in touch with the changing views of the different stakeholders. Thus, we expect researchers working in the non-profit sector to benefit from this book given the parallels and similarities between undertaking research for profit and non-profit making organisations.

These stakeholders could include: the organisation's customers or clients; employees; suppliers; those working in regulatory bodies; and individuals from a host of related areas. Without this feedback from the market place – whether this is for a profit or non-profit making organ-isation – it becomes difficult for an organisation to stimulate new ideas, ensure it keeps pace with change and make informed decisions between alternative projects competing for scarce resources. In addition, a flow of information from the market place is also a key part of the process of monitoring the effectiveness of different operations within any organisation.

It is true that commercial decision-making is different from decision-making in the non-profit sector. The commercial organisation can focus on what is the most profitable segment upon which to target its efforts. In contrast, non-profit making organisations invariably have a responsibility to deliver services across the community. So, there are clear points of difference in the way the output of marketing intelligence surveys conducted for profit and non-profit making organisations will be deployed. But many of the principles behind the way market information is collected, analysed and applied to the decision-making process remain the same.

And finally it should also be emphasised that the importance of marketing intelligence to organisations – whether they be profit or non-profit – is likely to continue to grow over the next decade and beyond. Both types of organisation will be under increasing pressure to make robust decisions based on the best possible understanding of their customers', and potential customers', needs and requirements.

Marketing Intelligence in Different Cultures

One further scene-setting issue concerns the extent to which it is possible to generalise about market research in a way that will apply to different organisations around the world, each with their own history and culture. And on this point, it has to be accepted that it is clearly impossible to catalogue all of the various approaches that different (commercial and non-commercial) organisations around the world will take in organising their affairs to deliver their end product or service.

However, at a high level of generalisation, it is possible to paint an overall picture of how, in broad terms, the typical client organisation is structured, and how market research agencies will respond to these needs, in a way that we believe will apply around the world.

Having briefly defined marketing intelligence, we now look in close detail at different types of research.

DIFFERENT TYPES OF MARKETING INTELLIGENCE

Having provided a working definition of marketing intelligence – one centring on the value of market information in decision-making – it is now helpful to categorise the broad types of marketing intelligence, pointing out which genres are more robust in comparison with others.

Evaluating the Past

The first distinction to make is the difference between research that is aimed at evaluating the effectiveness of what went on in the past, which could be described as hindsight, and research aimed at helping us better understand the future – foresight. We look at foresight in a moment. Fairly intuitively, the reader will understand that finding out what people think about products and services that they have been using for the past few months poses fewer challenges than attempting to speculate about what respondents think about new developments that are beginning to shape the future. So, asking Audi TT drivers, who have driven the car for a year, to comment on its strengths and weaknesses, is likely to be a more robust study than asking drivers to comment about whether they are likely to use an electrically powered Audi car in 10 years' time. In sum, evaluating what has happened in the past is a particularly powerful, robust and solid type of market research.

Predicting the Future

Clearly, in many scenarios, the expectation is that market research will provide some form of "foresight", or prediction for the future. At the heart of the prediction process is the need to focus on fully understanding the past and utilising this information to provide an interpretation of likely future events. But predicting inevitably takes market researchers into more challenging methodological territory. And we all know that there have been a number of celebrity prediction failures in the past that have been documented in the marketing literature. But the good news is that, year-by-year, market researchers are getting better at "predicting".

One reason why market researchers have improved in their ability to predict is that, over the years, they have learnt to frame questions in a way that makes it easier for respondents to better understand the nature of the new concept being presented. Today, if a respondent is being asked about a mobile phone with email facilities, text messaging, video photography and web services, we are now much more experienced in presenting fully worked up prototypes to make sure people fully understand what we are talking about.

Market researchers are also now much better equipped at painting a picture for the respondent of the likely future scenario in which a putative new product might be used than in the past. We have put behind us a reliance on rather weak, hypothetical questions along the lines of "How likely are you to buy this new product in the future?" which we know will provide sketchy predictions of likely take-up. And we are now, as an industry, much more able to anchor in the respondent's mind just how this product might operate in the future, thereby making this line of *hypothetical* questioning less vague, abstract and speculative.

Inevitably there will be some weaknesses in the ability of market researchers to spot winning upcoming ideas and trends, or to prevent organisations introducing products that have little potential. But, on balance, the market research industry now has reasonably sophisticated methods for attempting to screen out bad ideas, and for spotting and fostering ideas that find favour with the public.

Painting a Top-level Picture

Another important categorisation of marketing intelligence focuses on its breadth and depth. Is the research in question aimed at assessing people's attitudes in a fairly top-line way in order to build up a general impression of the views on a particular issue? For instance, this might be a study that seeks to build up a picture of the kinds of daily newspapers that people find accessible, friendly and of interest, without exploring individuals' purchase motivations in any great depth. This is in contrast to scenarios where there will be a call for research that seeks to drill down and explore in-depth the motivations behind different types of behaviour.

Exploring In-depth Motivations

On occasions, it will be necessary for informed decision-making to go beyond having a general impression of customer preferences. For example, we may want to find out why people favour, say, tabloid newspapers as opposed to the "quality press". This requires exploring attitudes in much greater depth. We will want to find out whether there are more deep-seated reasons why particular types of publications may be rejected as opposed to accepted. This latter type of investigation could involve exploring people's early family and social backgrounds, their political preferences (and prejudices), and other issues associated with an individual's level of intelligence and personality. And, not surprisingly, this process of establishing core motivations presents market researchers with more methodological challenges than simply measuring more top-line views.

Describing the World

Continuing with our categorisation of different types of market research, it is helpful to distinguish between market research that helps to *describe* the world, as opposed to research that seeks to understand the *causes* behind different behaviour as a platform for building models, frameworks and theories about how different consumers think and might behave. So, we can think of one type of market research as operating in a "descriptive" mode, where the aim is to describe the phenomena under investigation. Here we would find surveys to describe how people travel to work each morning, with detailed information about the numbers of people who travel by car, bus, bicycle, etc. Comprehensive pictures of how, in this example, people travel – coupled with accounts of the highs and lows of these travel experiences – would provide an important backdrop to decision-making on transport policy.

Building Theories About How the World "Works"

On occasion, the market researcher is expected to go further than just describing, and to map the linkages between different events. For example, market researchers may be asked to evaluate whether an increase in train travel is the result of a particular sales promotion and/or is due to the effectiveness of a particular advertising campaign and/or due to new pricing initiatives that had been introduced. And the reader will probably realise that the methodological challenges in linking different outcomes with prior events, and trying to build a "theory" that explains these cause and effect relationships, are greater than those in describing behaviour.

Monitoring Relative Change

Pursuing our classification of the broad categories of marketing intelligence we need to register the point that market research is particularly powerful when it is measuring *relative* movements, such as in brand awareness or market share. So, although a market research study may have fallen short of taking a perfect "absolute" reading of market share, it remains very robust when tracking, on a continuous basis, relative movements in market share. So, a market research survey may be slightly off centre in its *absolute* reading of, say, the level of satisfaction with a particular product or service, but it will be an extremely powerful way of monitoring, over time, whether customer satisfaction is improving or declining. Businesses are often less concerned with absolute measurements, and more focused on the relative changes that are taking place in the market place.

Triggering Creative Ideas

Another category of market research is less to do with providing objective, representative measures of what people think or do, and more to do with oiling the creative juices and helping generate "insights" about customers, or a market, that provides a "trigger" for innovative thinking. So, it has to be acknowledged that some market research will be less focused on taking an independent perspective and providing objective assessments of a situation, and used in a more subjective way in order to generate ideas.

For example, bringing together a group of business people who regularly use different hotel chains to take part in an idea-generating workshop to identify what is an "exciting" and "disappointing" hotel experience, while not following the rules of scientific representative measurement, can nonetheless throw up all sorts of interesting ideas. So, in sum, insights and critical observations that can provide a focal point for a successful strategy can often result from using "research" as the aid to the creative process, rather than thinking about it as part of a grounded investigative process (David Ogilvy called this "data rich creative thinking").

As we have introduced the word "insight", we should explain that this could either be the result of a "Eureka" moment – a flash of inspiration when a new idea or way of doing business is identified from a single observation at a focus group or when reading some customer correspondence. An "insight" could also be the product of a profound understanding, built up over time through clear, deep analytical thinking. Thus, a central point being made here is that market researchers use both analytical rigour and *also* their own creativity in finding solutions to business problems.

THE ROLE OF MARKETING INTELLIGENCE IN STRATEGIC AND MARKETING PLANNING

Having reviewed the nature of the different overall categories of marketing intelligence, we now look at the way organisations – across both profit and non-profit making sectors – broach the task of organising themselves to deliver their end product or service. We look at the kinds of frameworks that they have in place around which to develop the optimum strategy and plan their marketing activities. This review provides a backdrop for then looking at the areas where information collected from the market place by marketing intelligence professionals is instrumental in helping make that organisation more effective at a strategic and tactical level.

Corporate Strategy

Most organisations will develop a corporate strategy: an overall framework for clarifying at a high level what the company wishes to achieve. It has been argued that "strategic excellence" explains 80 % of all business success. This means that there is only a 20 % chance of achieving success through a misguided or inappropriate strategy that is then "retrieved" by tenacious, day-to-day, on the ground, tactical performance. Today, most would agree that developing a strategy and ensuring that the organisation stays on this course benefits from making use of marketing intelligence. To achieve strategic success, an organisation will need to ensure that it is constantly reading the "business radar", identifying key trends and developments, and having the information necessary to continually inform and adjust its corporate strategy in an effective way.

The Vision

To deliver strategic excellence many organisations will start the process by preparing some kind of *vision*. A "vision statement" is a description of the business as you want it to be in the future. It involves seeing the optimal future for the business, and vividly describing this vision.

This description might be centred around how you would like things to be, or how you will feel when this ideal is achieved. With a sharp, concise and focused "vision", it is possible to drive the organisation in a clear direction guided by a set of well-articulated values and standards. So John F. Kennedy's statement, "By the end of the decade we will put a man on the moon" could be seen as a vision for NASA, because it painted a clear picture of future goals. So in the world of business we find that the Ford Motor company vision is "To become the world's leading consumer company for automotive product and services". And Lou Gerstner's 1994 vision statement for IBM was "To be the world's most successful and important information technology company". And the Mayo Clinic has a particularly powerful vision: "The best patient care to every patient, every time".

The Mission

The vision statement will invariably be supported by a "mission statement". The mission statement is the organisation's vision translated into a precise statement of goals and priorities that will turn this big picture vision into practice. So we find that The Body Shop's mission statement has six elements, including, for example, addressing the issue of striking the right balance between the financial and human needs of stakeholders, employees, customers, franchises, suppliers and shareholders.

It is true that some organisations tend to blur the textbook distinction between *vision* and *mission*. But nonetheless, the discipline of having a clearly articulated vision and/or mission – an understanding of what the organisation stands for, where it is heading in the future, and how it wants to operate – remains at the heart of organisational planning.

In sum, today most organisations will have a concise, clear statement that demonstrates the future focus of the business, explaining what makes it distinctive, and thereby providing a basis for inspiring people to work towards this future. Successful organisations know that they must have a "vision" that is memorable, motivating, customer focused, and can be easily translated into strategy.

Business, Marketing and Operational Planning

Having in place an inspired corporate strategy – vision and mission – is a necessary, but not sufficient, condition of business success. Most organisations will then support these higher level strategic statements with detailed business and/or marketing plans that provide a focus for delivering different elements of the organisation's goals.

Business Plan

A business plan is a comprehensive planning document which clearly describes the procedures for identifying the markets, customers, expenditures and finances required to carry out the identified business objective. Put another way, this is the document that expresses the corporate vision and/or mission in concrete terms. It provides detailed information about target markets, competitive forces, distribution channels, the overall pricing strategy, and the strategy for positioning the company's image, and supporting communications, in the market place. This plan will also include detailed budgets and indicate the rate of expenditure in relation to forecasts of revenue and operating profits over the next year, together with highlighting any risks and opportunities associated with the venture.

Marketing Plan

Sometimes the business plan will be supplemented by a marketing plan. The marketing plan allows for more detail to be provided around what is a critical issue for most organisations – exactly how they will win profitable business. Typically the marketing plan will include detailed product-related issues, such as its policy for warranties. It will cover issues such as the trade discount policy, and also address factors such as the service levels to be provided, and a host of other detailed issues, ranging from merchandising to public relations. Many of these will require information input from marketing intelligence's dialogue with different stakeholders.

Operational Plan

To complete our broad review of the way organisations are structured, so we can see the role played by marketing intelligence within organisations, it should be pointed out that most organisations supplement their strategic business and marketing plans with a series of operational plans about the procedures that the organisation must follow to deliver their products and services. To a large extent, these operational plans will rely on internally generated information, rather than require the skills of the market researcher to conduct a dialogue with different stakeholder groups. However, even at this operational level, we still find marketing intelligence professionals being involved in supplying information. For example, a telecommunications company might want to conduct surveys with its suppliers to ensure that they are operating within the rules laid down by the telecommunication's regulator. And a clearing bank may wish to conduct a study amongst its employees to find out how easy it is for them to deal with customers, while implementing a new operational process or procedure.

Co-ordinating Corporate Objectives

Most organisations will also usually have an "organising structure" around which to coordinate its strategic and tactical goals as a basis for evaluating the performance of the organisation at the highest level. Different companies will use different approaches, but over the last decade an influential organising framework has been the notion of the "Balanced Scorecard", first developed by Kaplan and Norton in 1992. It gives managers a comprehensive framework for evaluating the performance of a business from a number of perspectives.

The Scorecard seeks to measure business performance from the financial perspective, the customer angle, the business process viewpoint, and from the standpoint of employees. Specifically, the "Scorecard" provides a focal point by: communicating the "vision" to staff and the outside world; translating the "vision" and "mission" into operational goals; linking this to individual performance; and also providing feedback so that the strategy can be adjusted accordingly on an ongoing basis (competitive renewal).

The critical measures included in the "Scorecard" are often the basis for developing a "dashboard" of key market and consumer metrics that management will access on a day-to-day basis to monitor their progress in achieving key targets. So it becomes important for marketing intelligence professionals to know, in the context of marketing planning, exactly what customer information – and in what form, and with what frequency – is pivotal to the "dashboard". It is these measurements that management will rely on most to successfully drive the business.

Transparent and Accountable Decision-making

So, in sum, organisations are now very much aware of the cost of making strategic errors and spending vast sums of money on developing products that people do not want. In addition, organisations are much more aware these days of the need to comply with the high standards of corporate governance. This includes demonstrating, in a transparent and accountable way, to shareholders that their strategic thinking is *evidence-based*, rather than based on the speculative whim of a small handful of individuals.

This is not to say that strategic decision-making and marketing planning is driven exclusively by market and consumer information. Strategic decision-making will, of course, also be informed by a host of information inputs, ranging from financial to sales data. In addition, organisational decision-making will continue, in part, to rely on instinctive, intuitive judgements made by senior management. But, in large measure, it is true to say that the strategic success of the modern organisation will depend on the professionalism and flair the organisation shows in collecting and interpreting the evidence collected from different stakeholders, and factoring this into the strategic thinking and planning process.

Marketing Intelligence Input into the Strategic Planning Process

Thus, in preparing a strategic plan, the marketing intelligence professional will first be called upon to paint a picture of the wider economic and cultural context. This will include searching out longer-term analyses of the trends taking place in society, together with financial commentaries on developments in key market sectors. Next, the marketing intelligence team will gather together information about key competitors, including their strategic positioning, together with an analysis of points of differentiation in competitors' product and service offering. This will also include an analysis of competitors' presence in different media.

Next, the marketing intelligence team will, for different markets and product categories, gather together available macro-level reviews of overall customer typologies and other information that allows an intelligent segmentation of the market place. The marketing intelligence team will also integrate into this picture internal knowledge that the organisation holds on its customers from loyalty card schemes and other direct marketing initiatives. In sum, marketing intelligence plays an important role in gathering together wider socio-economic and market data to feed into the strategic planning process. In addition, the marketing intelligence team will often conduct a meta-analysis of ongoing tactical market and product studies in order to identify whether there are any overarching trends that emerge from this ongoing research.

Having examined the importance of including cutting-edge market and customer evidence into an organisation's strategic, tactical and operational planning, we now look at the way in which the marketing intelligence function is structured within organisations, and explain how these internal client professionals then liaise with market research suppliers.

THE STRUCTURE OF THE MARKETING INTELLIGENCE PROCESS

In this section, we introduce the reader to the way in which the marketing intelligence process is structured to provide the kind of marketing intelligence that is needed by organisations to develop effective, strategic and tactical plans. We start by looking at the way in which marketing intelligence professionals working within client companies organise themselves to respond to the challenge of supplying the information required for business decision-making. We then look at the way that market research agencies are structured to work in partnership with professionals working in client organisations. This sets the scene for the next section in which we review the overall process that a typical market research project then follows.

The Marketing Function

In the early days of marketing, this was often a "central command and control" activity at the heart of an organisation. But, in today's fast moving dynamic, digital economy, where the company must respond quickly to the market place, the notion of the classic central command and control style marketing departments has, in many cases, given way to a more flexible organisational approach. Today, organisations favour flatter management structures. So, we often find the marketing function very closely aligned – that is to say, intertwined – with particular business units. There are a number of different models that companies might operate as they move away from the classic, top-down approach and respond to a world where marketing has to be even more responsive to, and be so closely in touch with, the consumer.

Today, we live in an era where "consumer-to-consumer" marketing is a powerful force. In this environment the fluid interchange of word-of-mouth product recommendations between customers has become equally as important in shaping the fortunes of a brand as the messages emanating from the organisation's central marketing function. In sum, there has been a big shift from the classic marketing approach that would have been typified by the way big FMCG giants would have promoted their soaps and detergents in the early days of marketing, and the structures now in place to handle the way today's leading brands – iPod, eBay and Google – are promoted.

The Internal Marketing Intelligence Function

Given the fact that it is hard to make general statements about the way the marketing function will be structured within any one organisation, it clearly becomes difficult to generalise about the various ways in which the marketing intelligence function within a company will be structured to support the marketing operation. But, notwithstanding the changing role of marketing, in simple terms, there will be two fundamental models for the way market researchers will support the marketing and wider business function.

- First, there will be a model whereby a specialist team of marketing intelligence professionals provide a service *across* all market sectors and brands operated by the organisation.
- The second fundamental approach will be one whereby marketing intelligence professionals are allocated to a different market sector(s) and/or brand(s) and become responsible for undertaking research *within* this particular niche.

Working on the Right Problem

One of the fundamental skills of the client marketing intelligence professional is their ability to define the precise problem confronting the organisation as a basis for then beginning to clarify how market and/or customer information might best help resolve this issue. These problem definition skills are a prerequisite of then beginning to shape the structure of the market research project best suited to address this issue.

The way the initial presentation of a problem is expressed may be unintentionally misleading. This is because the person explaining the problem might not make critical tacit knowledge explicit. It is also possible that an emotional knee-jerk interpretation of current events will initially dominate the explanation of the problem, thereby throwing the market research team off the scent of the real issue. Furthermore, the initial statement of the problem may show tunnel vision, rather than being based on an understanding of the broader context.

And, of course, the initial briefing about a problem may be only partially correct because of a hasty appraisal of a situation. And it also has to be accepted that the initial stab at trying to define a problem may show a lack of clear, deep, informed thinking. Thus, one of the key skills of the client-side marketing intelligence professional is to go beyond the presented symptoms of an issue and identify the *real* problem.

Thus, we may find that a problem is presented as being about an "unmotivated salesforce", initially steering us in the direction of a study to be conducted amongst the sales team when, in actual fact, the real problem may be that there are deficiencies with the product they are trying to sell. Another example might be that the initial problem is presented around customers' difficulties in understanding a new pricing policy for, say, a railway company, whereas the *real* problem is that customers are resentful of the new philosophy on pricing, rather than struggling to understand a particular pricing tariff per se. So, a key skill of the internal marketing intelligence professional is to ensure that they are working on the right problem. The old adage, "a problem well defined is a problem half-solved", is true.

Always Start at the End

A key problem definition skill is to always "start at the end" – obtain a clear understanding of the decisions that will need to be made by the company to address this problem. Then, having understood this, the researcher can work back to crystallise the research objectives, and establish what survey questions need to be asked. Thus, the key to success is making sure that, at the outset of the project, you have a clear understanding of the decisions that will be made based on your research.

There are a range of techniques to help with problem definition, including: making sure that you get a "360° view" of the problem by talking to all members of the client "decision-making unit"; fully understanding the wider marketing context to the problem being investigated; ensuring that you have teased out implicit knowledge that may be lurking below the waterline, but has never been made explicit; making sure that the initial research brief is always challenged, including cross-checking any statistics or arguments that are being advanced that are critical to the way the initial problem has been presented.

In sum, the experienced client researcher will learn to focus on the following "golden question": "At the end of the research project, what do you expect to be able to do with the data/evidence you are requesting?" The answer to this question should then guide the entire progress of the study.

The Boundary

Having pinpointed the "real" problem, the client market researcher then has an important role to play in deciding what "boundary" to draw around a particular topic before helping to decide on the optimum research solution. If a problem, and the subsequent thinking about the most appropriate research investigation, has been positioned on a pinhead, the failure to collect related contextual information could be fatal to understanding what is really going on. But if the researcher casts the net on a too wide canvas, the whole project can become unmanageable, with the result that lots of vaguely nice-to-know, but not mission-critical, information is collected.

Thus "delimiting" the study is another key client researcher skill. Is this a study that only makes sense if it includes, for example, all drivers – both of private and commercial vehicles – or can the study put the spotlight on private motorists and study the commercial issues later? In particular, the client market researcher needs to consider to what depth this particular issue needs to be investigated. This skill is critical in shaping the success of the entire project. It is easy for projects to either become too rambling in their scope, or to be set with too fine a focus, or even to be completely off-target in their emphasis.

The Register

The client market researcher also plays a vital role at the outset of the process on deciding the overall "stance" of the putative research study. It is important to ensure at the outset that the initial thinking about the upcoming research study is in the right "register". The agency, as we will be discussing, will take responsibility for fashioning the final research design. But the client researcher needs to set the process rolling by ensuring that the design chosen will be accepted by the user of the data. Clearly, some problems may just require more top-line overview. For example, a bank might want to know how many people may use a particular ATM cashpoint at different times during the day. But, on other occasions, the study will need to be set in a different register, requiring a much more in-depth assessment of the motives for using some, but not all, of the available services.

In sum, the client researcher is critical in ensuring that the agency who will carry out this project are fully aware at the outset of the investigation of the context – or boundary – within which this issue should be explored and the "register" in which this issue should be pursued. The client researcher will be the person who most understands the expectations of the end decision-makers and will communicate this to the agency.

Market Research Agencies' Role in Designing Research Studies

We have looked at the way organisations are structured in relation to their need for marketing and customer information, and examined the way in which the marketing intelligence department operates within the company. It is now time to briefly review the typical market research process that will be followed by agencies in responding to a client's internal statement of a problem (the research brief).

There is a thriving supplier industry, ranging from specialist independent consultancies through to large, full service agencies, which are often part of a PLC that operates a group of marketing services companies. And each agency will respond to a research brief in a different way. But, in most cases, the agency will respond with a document, usually referred to as the "research proposal".

The agency will start by building on the problem formulation stage of the project already initiated by the client researcher, by attempting to further refine the problem, and thereby add further clarity to the critical process of deciding on the optimum research solution. The agency will then embark on its key role of ensuring that the research design chosen to address a particular problem reaches an acceptable level of robustness, while also ensuring that the research will be delivered in a timely way, and will be in a form that will be listened to by senior management. Clearly, there is no point in having a perfectly engineered research study that is delivered much too late to help the decision-making process. Neither is it sensible to deliver research findings well ahead of schedule, if the content of the study is "thin", and thereby likely to make decision-makers feel nervous about using the data.

In sum, the role for the market research "team" – the client researchers working with the agency researchers – is to strike the golden compromise in providing sufficiently robust evidence, generated by methods that are understood by management, that management find reassuring, and that are delivered to a timetable that accommodates the decision-making process.

In preparing the optimum research design, the agency researcher will need to make a number of important trade-off decisions. First, there is the question of how much *precision* is needed from this study. Secondly, there is the issue of how much *depth of understanding* is required on the project. Third, what are the *practicalities* involved in undertaking the project (collecting the data and collating the findings). Fourth, there is the amount of *time* available. Fifth, is the question of the available *budget*. And there is also the issue of making sure that everything is done within the ESOMAR Code of Conduct.

A Research Design that is Fit-for-Purpose

So, let us take the example of deciding on the best way to assess the attitudes of customers towards the service they receive from a low budget airline. The typical design process is described below.

First, there will be issues about the *scope* of the study. Should this study be restricted to *existing* customers of the budget airline in question, or extended to include *potential* customers? Then decisions need to be made about whether the focus should be on *regular* or *occasional* travellers, and so on.

Next there are questions about the *structure* of the overall research approach. Is this to be an ad-hoc, one-off survey, or is it to be part of a continuous series of surveys that look at progress over time?

Third, there will be *sampling* issues to be addressed. There is the decision to be made about the size of the sample that will be needed. In part, this will be driven by the level of accuracy required for headline measures taken among customers, such as their overall satisfaction. But the sample size will also be decided by the extent to which it is necessary to put the spotlight on particular customer sub-groups, such as people travelling with young children.

Fourth, there will be *data-collection* issues to resolve. Should this study be conducted as a self-completion questionnaire administered to passengers on the plane, or be administered as an online web survey? Other alternatives include conducting a telephone study, or possibly interviewing passengers while they are at the airport. So the optimum choice of data collection method (or combination of data collection methods) needs to be resolved.

Fifth, there are issues associated with the *type of analysis* that will be conducted on the study. In some cases, a straightforward presentation of the findings, showing variations among different age and socio-economic groups, and so on, would be sufficient. In other cases, it may be appropriate to develop some form of customer segmentation, illustrating the different typologies of customer who travel on the budget airline.

In sum, the experienced agency professional will consider all of the above issues and undertake the trade-off process described above in arriving at a research design that is fit-for-purpose.

THE KEY CHARACTERISTICS OF THE MARKET RESEARCH PROCESS

We have built up a picture of the broad types of market research available to the researcher in solving a business problem and briefly reviewed the different data collection and analysis options available. We now look in closer detail at the key characteristics of the market research process. We look at the key tenets of acknowledged good practice that must be followed if robust results are to be obtained. This contextual review will put the reader in a good position to then study – in closer detail, later in this Handbook – particular aspects of the market research process.

Market Research Follows a "Scientific" Approach

Market research is a pragmatic process and, as such, cannot be considered to adhere to "pure" scientific method, but nonetheless most research projects do adhere to a quasi-scientific approach. This reflects the fact that market research developed out of adapting fundamental social science investigative principles developed in the 1950s. This rigorous school of thinking gave market researchers many of the critical tools they needed to operate.

These tools include the concepts of "validity". That is, is the evidence "true": is it free from systematic bias? It also gave us "reliability". That is, is the evidence that has been collected likely to hold good over time? There is also the issue of "sensitivity" of the method. For example, establishing whether very small changes in the fortunes of the company are due to a specific marketing initiative or the result of normal fluctuations in the market place is more of a challenge than measuring big shifts in performance. There is also the question of "generalisability". This is about the extent to which research findings can be applied to settings other than that in which they were originally tested. Thus, a research finding may be entirely valid in one setting, but not in another.

Thus, market researchers will attempt to follow, in a systematic way, the principles that we know will provide objective and robust evidence. But given the complexity of the commercial world, on many studies, market research will be characterised by high levels of pragmatism. Respondents will need to adapt to a range of methodological, practical and commercial challenges. These are the design "trade-offs" we reviewed in the earlier section. Importantly, the professional market researcher will know how to adjust for any shortfalls in the "perfect", or ideal, design, and factor this understanding into their interpretation of the evidence at the end of the project.

We can, therefore, think of market research as a process that starts with an understanding of the scientific principles that would define the "ideal" study. But then the process becomes subject to a series of pragmatic trade-offs necessitated by various practical commercial, and cost considerations. Thus, the experienced researcher knows how to *compensate* for the departure from the "ideal" study to the pragmatic research design trade-off that was eventually selected.

Building Up the Picture through Exploratory Research

Most market research projects start with someone in an organisation asking a question about something that they do not know about in the expectation that some form of information – rather than using guess work – may help shape a more informed decision. This questioning process may follow the "classic" form of setting up a working hypothesis, that will then be "tested" by the research. But more often than not researchers will respond by getting under way with a "working view" of the topic under investigation and use this as a starting point for the research. For example, if we were asked to improve customer service at a hotel, researchers will often get the investigative process under way by reviewing, from their own personal experience, the best and worst hotel experiences they have encountered. This initial "view of the world" will trigger the investigative process.

Looking for Clues

So, at the beginning of most studies, the researcher will assemble little clues and snippets of information. These will be obtained by reading various industry reports, checking available sources on the Internet, looking at past customer research reports, and informally talking to people about their own "anecdotal" experiences. It may also involve collecting more "archetypal" information, that is, feedback from senior people experienced on this topic who can talk authoritatively about the views of other experts in this field. This type of evidence will be subjected to "face validity", that is, do these preliminary "findings" ring true at a common sense level, and also, does this evidence square with existing "prior knowledge" – what we already know. Sometimes these kinds of clues and insights – drawn together into a formal summary of the strengths and weaknesses of the idea – will be sufficient to answer management's questions. But, usually the project will need to go forward into a phase of more "formal" qualitative research aimed at identifying the *range* of attitudes and behaviour that prevail on this issue.

Qualitative Research

Qualitative research tends to be – but is not always – conducted on a smaller scale, and its key strength is that it allows the researcher the flexibility of steering the research enquiry based on what is emerging from the interview, rather than having to follow a pre-ordained question structure. In short, qualitative research is a "response-led", not "question-led" methodology. Qualitative research can be progressed via focus group discussions, where groups of individuals share their experience, or though individual face-to-face depth interviews, and a range of other techniques described later in this book.

There are various theoretical underpinnings for qualitative research, but one that will be familiar to many researchers is the notion of "grounded theory". By grounded theory we are referring to a process of building up our understanding from observations made from the sampling process and relating this to our existing knowledge. Each piece of new evidence emerging from the research is evaluated in relation to what we already know about this topic. This theory tells us that you gradually refine – through a series of qualitative interviews – the overall picture of the issue under investigation, until you reach "saturation point". Here, subsequent interviews will add little to our *conceptual* understanding of the issue under investigation. We will, at this point – and this might be only 10 to 30 individuals – have identified all the key concepts and issues relevant to the investigation.

For example, if we spoke to 30 drivers of a particular brand of car, we would be confident that all of the major issues that characterise this car will have surfaced from this comparatively small number of interviews. Thus, if there were major problems with the steering, then this issue would emerge by the time we had interviewed 30 owners of this type of car. We would not need a large sample to confirm that the steering on this car is a problem issue, particularly if this finding squares with other feedback and knowledge the company has on this safety issue.

Identifying the Range of Attitudes and Behaviour

Qualitative research conducted with a comparatively small number of respondents is sufficient to map the *range* of behaviour and attitudes on that particular topic. However, it should not be used to precisely measure the existence of any type of behaviour or the presence of a particular attitude. In summary, grounded theory tells us that if we have identified the key issues from a small number of observations, provided this is consistent with our prior knowledge on this topic, then we can "rely" on this small sample to provide an indication of the *range* of customer attitudes and behaviour. But we should not rely on this research for a precise measurement of the extent of these attitudes.

On certain projects, management may feel that they can take an informed decision by using qualitative evidence, in conjunction with other sources of organisational knowledge and their own judgement. But in other cases, more quantitative information will be required. This will either be because measuring, not just identifying the range of attitudes on an issue, is critical to the decision, and/or possibly because the decision-maker knows that they must demonstrate a *quantified* business case for a new initiative.

Ensuring the Research is Representative

We now move on to the area of quantitative research and here, fundamental to the market research process, is the notion of being able to represent the wider population from the sample of people interviewed. Later in this book, we will be learning about the knowledge and skills needed to draw robust samples. But, in this introduction it is helpful to overview two broad sampling approaches open to survey researchers.

First, where precision is paramount, such as with certain Government sponsored studies, "probability sampling" methods will be followed. This is a procedure whereby everybody has a known or equal chance of being included in the survey sample. Specifically, a "sampling frame" needs to be constructed: all individuals who are in the universe to be researched must be included in this listing. Critically, with probability sampling, once the random sampling process has "chosen" an individual, then only this individual – not any other "substitute" – should be approached to take part in the survey. If they take part in the survey then this can be declared as part of the successful "response rate". If they do not take part, they are a "non-responder".

However, most market research studies follow a more pragmatic approach, often referred to as "quota sampling". Here, the age, gender, socio-economic, and other key characteristics of the target category of consumers to be researched are noted. Interviewers are then issued "quotas" that match this population profile. That is, interviewers will be asked to find people in a particular age, gender and socio-economic group. Then a "haphazard", but not truly random, process will be followed by interviewers as they approach people to establish whether they fit these "quotas".

Thus, a critically important difference between "probability" and "quota" sampling is that with probability sampling the interviewer must attempt to interview the "chosen" respondent, but with quota sampling, the interviewer does not have a designated person to interview, but can select any individual who meets the quota. However, we know from comparative methodological studies that have been conducted that, in the vast majority of cases, quota sampling roughly approximates the results achieved by more pure random sampling

Building Up a Picture of People's Profile Characteristics, Behaviour and Attitudes

Before looking in closer detail at the different data collection options open to the market researcher, it is helpful to reflect on what is at the heart of the market research process – understanding the relationship between who people are, what they do, and what they believe. Here it is helpful to review the three key types of information that will be collected in a market research study. These are: "classification" information (who people are); "behavioural" information (what people do); and "attitudinal" information (what people think about different issues).

Classification Data

When asking questions in order to *classify* individuals, market researchers are on fairly firm ground. So we know that when asking questions to identify a person's age, gender, income level, country of origin, and so on, we have some powerful tools in the tool-bag. But, absolute precision of wording, and an understanding of the context in which the question is framed, remain important.

For example, answers given by women to the apparently crystal clear issue of "Do you have any children?" are dependent on the exact way the question is contextualised and phrased. This is because in some cultures women, when answering the question about how many children they have, will include children who subsequently have been adopted, whereas for other cultures this is not the case. And in some cultures women may include stillborn children in the answer to such a question, whereas in other cultures it is not the norm to answer in this way. So, even in the heartland of obtaining classification information, absolute precision is required. But, asking about a person's basic characteristics remains a strong suit of market research.

Behavioural Information

In the next category, we have questions to map an individual's *behaviour*, such as how many times people go by car to the supermarket, as opposed to travelling on public transport. Again, on balance, this is comparatively straightforward territory for the market researcher. It is true that we have to take into account the accuracy of people's memories. Individuals may remember all the different houses they have lived in over the last 20 years, but not be able to remember a few weeks back about their travel patterns on a particular day. In addition, attention to detail is required in the framing of the question to avoid any ambiguity and/or lack of precision that could affect the responses. For example, in asking people whether they "go to a supermarket by car", it is necessary to define whether we mean as a "driver" or a "passenger". And there is the issue of how we classify trips made by taxis, and whether this includes using rented cars, and a host of other detailed points. But, by and large, assessing behavioural information is comparatively strong territory for market researchers.

Attitudinal Information

In the next category we have the more challenging task of attempting to assess people's *attitudes*. There are many different definitions of "attitude". A simple dictionary definition tells us that attitude is "a mental state of readiness prior to action". But market researchers' lexicon on the subject of "what is an attitude?" extends to more detailed definitions that entreat us to acknowledge important differences between "values", "beliefs", "needs", "wants", "feelings", "expectations", and more. But for the purpose of this introductory chapter, we can think of an "attitude" dividing into three elements. Let us describe these with an example.

If we want to know what someone thinks of the idea of banning fox hunting in the UK, in part, this person's "attitude" will be based on an *intellectually* derived assessment. It will be driven by what he or she knows about the way that people living in the countryside attempt to control the numbers of what they perceive to be "pests". But, this more rational, intellectual assessment could also be accompanied by a strong *emotive* element that perhaps includes our respondent associating "hunting with hounds" with the less attractive features of the British class system. And finally, there is the issue of the extent to which this mixture of the intellectual and emotive elements to our respondent's overall attitude to fox hunting, are related to his or her propensity to act (the conative element). Is our respondent just mildly annoyed by the idea of fox hunting, or are they motivated to join protest groups, and possibly run the risk of being arrested?

Going Beyond Limp Platitudes

Unless the acknowledged principles of how to assess attitudes are followed, we can end up capturing what we might call "platitudes", not true "attitudes". By "platitudes" we mean rather superficial, clichéd responses to a generalised issue that individuals repeat back to the interviewer as a response to a rather loosely worded, or ill thought-out question. So, this understanding of how attitudes are formed, and change, is a challenging part of the researchers' skill set. In sum, getting to grips with "why" people do what they do presents market researchers with their biggest challenge.

The Data Collection Options

Today, market researchers have a number of options when it comes to collecting information from consumers. These are discussed in detail elsewhere in this Handbook. But, in summary, these include face-to-face and telephone interviews, and, increasingly, online surveys. In addition, there is the option of observing respondents' behaviour, either in shops or in their homes. Moreover, with the arrival of the new digital age, there are now a host of opportunities to set up interactive dialogues with consumers via brand user sites and Blogs.

To illustrate the point about the range of data collection open to today's market researchers, let us outline the way today's researchers might assess customers' attitudes towards a new high quality camera that offers the best of leading-edge digital technology, together with the familiar and sought-after features of the traditional single-lens reflex camera.

Here, in building up a picture of customers' attitudes, the options would include a face-to-face, telephone or online survey, with users of the product. It could also include observation of individuals about to buy a camera in different shops. Further options include *usability* studies, where individuals are invited to attend an interview where they can use the camera. This process is then filmed, and then an interview takes place around the user's experience. There is also the option of collecting information from brand user websites, where different camera enthusiasts post their experiences on different message and discussion boards. In some cases, camera users may be sent a self-administered questionnaire, whereby they can record their experiences of using the camera in different photographic scenarios. Other data collection options may include contacting by phone camera users who we know are on holiday and getting them to report back, in an immediate way, their experiences of using the camera in a particular situation. In short, the data collection options are extremely varied, and the experienced market researcher will use a number of different methods to build up a rounded picture of the "total customer experience".

Can We Trust What People Say?

The majority of individuals welcome the opportunity to express their views on the range of products and services they use. Most individuals realise how their feedback, although helping give the organisation sponsoring the research a commercial edge in the market place, can also lead to an improvement in product quality and service that will benefit everybody. So it is important to register the point that most individuals are simply *not* in the business of being devious when asked questions. If someone asks you what car you drive, why not tell them, to the best of your ability, the truth, rather than mislead the interviewer? So, for the vast majority of market research we can rely on individuals who reasonably enjoy, and are cooperative in taking part in, research.

It is true that there are a few specialist situations where, when interpreting the evidence, one would need to be mindful of some form of "mendacity" creeping into the question and answer process. This essentially comes down to certain political election scenarios where, for various tactical reasons, someone who is, say, a lifelong supporter of Party X may tell the pollster that they will vote for this party, but know that, in reality, they are going to vote for another party because this "tactical voting" is the best way of dislodging the incumbent candidate. But this is fairly rare, and not relevant to most commercial or government-sponsored market research studies. So the bedrock of market research are individuals who we know will try to be as helpful as they can in giving their responses. But in return we must show respondents respect by setting up the interview as a "conversation" – a natural dialogue.

The Interview as a Conversation with the Respondent

The idea of an interview as a "natural dialogue" – a conversation – with the respondent is a very simple principle. But it is one that can often be overlooked by market researchers who perhaps think that respondents can just answer random questions that are fired at them in a staccato like way, with these being contextualised and presented without any form of order or structure. In these situations, respondents will give answers, but these will be much less robust than questions that are constructed as part of a structured dialogue that follows the conventions of a normal conversation.

Thus, a lot of poor research is the result of researchers not setting their questions in the appropriate context and, related to this, not ensuring that the questions are salient to the respondent. Clearly, it is difficult for people to answer questions that are outside of their frame of reference, and/or pitched at a far too generalised level, or alternatively are cast in a much too detailed way. Thus, a good questionnaire is not only about following the rules for scripting the questions, but also about developing some empathy with the respondent, and trying to construct a "vehicle" around which a dialogue – which is as close as possible to a normal conversation – can take place.

Looking to the future, with the opportunities opening up with the new Web 2.0 platform, this issue of developing a two-way dialogue with respondents will be even more on the agenda as researchers seek to use this interactive technology to "engage in conversations" with consumers, rather than hit them with a procession of pre-determined questions. In short, the new interactive technology is going to put the respondent at the centre of our research and give us a new window into the consumer mind-set.

People Do Not Always Say What They Mean and They Do Not Always Mean What They Say

If the researcher sets up a sound professional dialogue between interviewer and respondent, then people taking part in market research studies will be willing to discuss a wide range of often sensitive issues, including their sexual behaviour, or views on controversial religious or political topics. But it has to be accepted that the process of asking questions and listening to the answers in order to find out what people think is essentially a coarse instrument.

This presents market researchers with the enormous challenge of interpreting what people are trying to tell us in a survey. Here we are learning from the findings of neuroscience which, put simply, is confirming what many researchers have instinctively known for many years. This is that in a straight choice between reason and emotion, emotion usually wins. That is to say, there is a tendency in all of us to over-state the rational reasons for what we do, and underestimate, in our explanations, the emotional element. So we know that some individuals may give highly generalised, rounded out accounts of their behaviour that tends to flatter what they have done. For example, a person may realise that they have purchased the wrong product, but then may post-rationalise this by providing a different set of reasons for their purchase than was actually the case. But this is not done with any malevolence. It happens because individuals generally come to think that this "post-rationalised" account is the reason why they purchased the product. So being able to interpret *literal* survey responses is a key researcher skill.

Analysing the Evidence in the Context of What We Know about the Market Research Process

To help with the interpretation process, the market research industry has built up over the years an impressive array of normative evidence and insights into the research process that are critical in helping us to interpret the survey evidence we have conducted. Specifically, the market research industry has built up an array of "knowledge filters" through which analysts will pass their "literal" survey responses before arriving at a particular conclusion.

Thus, as we have seen, although well intentioned, some individuals, in giving responses to survey questions, may tend to accentuate the rational reasons for a purchase and underestimate the emotional factors. However, as researchers know about this tendency, it is possible to factor this knowledge into their interpretation.

Thus, the analyst will pass this data through a wide body of knowledge filters in interpreting survey data. These include: what we know about the accuracy of people's memories; what we know about how the context within which survey questions are presented might affect the results; the way in which small changes in wording could change the way people perceive the meaning of different ideas; and the fact that people, although trying to be helpful and honest in their replies, may tend to talk in more generalised "platitudes" and "clichés" rather than providing their "true" attitudes. In sum, past experience of how accurate our surveys have been can be factored into our analysis of the latest data. In addition, over the years, market researchers have built up a considerable body of knowledge about how well certain predictive market research models work, and so again, this understanding can be factored into the interpretation of the current survey.

The Statistical Analysis

In analysing market research data, the analyst has a number of different options. The analysis process starts with simply assembling and understanding the structure and pattern of the raw data. This will involve ordering raw data, applying various "data reduction" rules, and invariably introducing "cross-tabulation" to examine various sub-group variations. This type of elementary analysis would invariably also include using measures of location – mean, mode, median – to summarise the data, and also include various measures of variation to look at the variability of the data. The analyst may also apply certain statistical tests to look at whether or not the difference between different percentages can be seen to be as "statistically significant".

Building on this basic analysis, the analyst may then attempt to measure the relationship between two sets of data, and try to establish causative relationships through correlation analysis. This type of analysis may then be extended to visual mapping, using techniques, such as multiple correspondence analysis, to find ways of visually displaying the relationship between, for example, a business's turnover and the sectors in which it operates.

Going beyond this, certain market research studies will involve prioritising customers' needs by using various trade-off techniques, such as conjoint analysis, to establish which issues are more important to customers than others. Then, a further option in analysing the data is to identify discreet groups that share similar patterns of attitude in order to create customer segments and typologies that help us better understand a market.

In sum, the market research analyst will decide what is the most appropriate level at which to take the analysis for a study on a "fitness-for-purpose" basis.

Incorporating the Market Research Evidence with Other Internal and External Evidence Available to an Organisation

In the early days of market research, analysts would tend to analyse solitary data sets on a particular issue. Today, however, problems are invariably solved by looking at a whole host of different types of information sources. These days organisations, for instance, in the retail sector, will have a massive amount of customer information available from the data generated from participation in their customer loyalty card scheme. In addition, there will be lots of other information available from competitor analysis and various information sources available by searching the Internet. And, of course, there is lots of other feedback, including insights gleaned from correspondence with customers and dialogues conducted via website discussion forums and message boards. And, in addition, there is, of course, information to be incorporated from the financial world.

Thus, today, market researchers must know how to integrate their market research evidence into the massive jigsaw of information that is available to today's organisations. This is changing the face of market research because it requires the industry to develop analytical frameworks that can accommodate a mixed array of "formal" and "informal", and "hard" and "soft" customer evidence into the evidence-based decision-making process. Thus, as an industry we now urgently need techniques to analyse data in a more "holistic" way.

Understanding the Weight, Power and Direction of Evidence

One holistic framework that is helpful in drawing together hard and soft data from a range of different sources – thereby allowing us to examine its respective strength in shaping an evidence-based decision – is the notion of looking at the combined "weight", "power" and "direction" of a data-set.

Thus, in looking at the *weight* of evidence, we take each piece of evidence and inspect it on two dimensions. First, what is the numerical balance of support in favour of this particular issue? And secondly, what is the depth of feeling that is expressed on this topic?

Next we look at the *power* of the evidence. This also has two dimensions. First, to what extent does the latest survey evidence square with what we already know on this topic? Second, just how confident are we about this particular genre of research evidence based on our understanding of the knowledge filters?

And then there is the *direction* of the evidence. This again has two dimensions. What is the internal consistency within any one data-set? And secondly, how consistent is the data from one data-set to another?

Applying the Fuzzy Logic Principle

Applying the principle of fuzzy logic, we can use our concepts of weight, power and direction to establish whether a data-set has "high" or "low" actionability. Thus, we start by seeing if we have assembled a case that has strong numerical support, and firmly articulated emotional support. Then we see if the evidence squares with our prior knowledge, and is drawn from a reliable methodological category of research. We also check if the data is internally and externally consistent. If the answer to all these questions is "yes", we have highly actionable evidence.

And clearly, we would feel more confident about making a decision based on *high actionability*, than if the weight, power and direction of the combined data-sets told a confused story. That is, where the data that was not consistent, did not square with our existing knowledge, relied on methodologies with question marks over its wider track record of success, and which also showed limited numerical support, coupled with little firm expression of commitment to the product.

This is just one illustration designed to demonstrate the way researchers now need to develop holistic frameworks to make sense of "hard" and "soft" data arriving from lots of different sources.

THE ROLE OF MARKETING INTELLIGENCE IN THE DECISION-MAKING PROCESS

At the beginning of this chapter, we defined market research as being essentially about providing information to improve the quality of organisational decision-making. So it follows that we should end this introduction to the role and nature of marketing intelligence by looking at the contribution it makes to evidence-based decision-making. Let us start by looking at the conditions for sound evidence-based decision-making in organisations.

Conditions for Ideal Evidence-based Decision-making

In an *ideal* world, senior management – who accept, appreciate and understand, and value the role of market research – would be supplied with evidence generated through an independent, objective, systematic and rigorous process and that followed the tenets of good research practice. In addition, ideally this evidence would be a measure that was provided on a continuous basis over time so as to provide sound relative assessments of the issue under investigation.

Staying in this "ideal" evidence-based decision-making world, we would expect managers who have received this robust evidence to then evaluate it in a balanced and rational way. This would require managers to give equal weight to both *softer,* more impressionistic, qualitative data, and to *harder*, more technical, quantitative-based arguments. Moreover, decision-makers faced with this type of evidence would also not rush to judgement by selecting the more easily accessible, and more straightforward to understand, information, but instead make sure that they embraced the full gamut of different types of information.

In addition, decision-makers would ideally ensure that they did not fall into the trap of selectively picking evidence that supported their own prior position. And, of course, it would be *ideal* if decision-makers followed a rational process in the way they actually made decisions. This would involve developing clear, explicit decision criteria and prioritising the criteria upon which the final decision will be made. After this, the decision-maker would carefully review all of the alternative courses of action against these prioritised criteria, including looking at the consequences of following different decision outcomes, before making a decision.

But, of course, in practice, we know that in the hurly burly of commercial decision-making rarely is it possible to generate incontestable evidence, and to evaluate this highly robust evidence in the systematic way described above. The reality of everyday decision-making is that busy decision-makers must take decisions in a less than optimum way.

Framing the Choices for the Decision-maker

Because organisational evidence-based decision-making can be less than optimum – in some cases dysfunctional – it becomes important for today's marketing intelligence professionals to take responsibility for helping decision-makers make informed decisions. Today, market researchers are increasingly being asked to help reduce the gap between the ever burgeoning amount of available marketing data and the decision that needs to be made. This puts the spotlight on market researchers' ability to operate as "decision advisers" or "decision facilitators".

This is not to suggest that market researchers are involved with the final decision-making per se, but rather to make the point that marketing intelligence professionals now have an important role in making sure they – based on their analysis of the evidence – help frame the choices that are in front of decision-makers, and then advise on the "safety" of relying on different kinds of evidence to make decisions about the various choices.

So, with this in mind, let us now look at one of the key issues with which market researchers need to grapple in helping with the practical day-to-day decision-making process. This centres on the challenge of balancing the hard evidence against the intuitive gut feel of the experienced business decision-maker.

Balancing the Consumer Evidence with Management Intuition

Only a decade ago many market research professionals would reject the idea that they needed to factor management intuition into the evidence-based decision-making process. "Hunch" was largely seen by market research purists as playing second fiddle to the "hard" consumer evidence. But, in today's complex business environment, management intuition is now a much more accepted, and legitimate, part of the business decision-making process. Today, with the success of books, such as "Emotional Intelligence" by Goleman, and authoritative accounts of how intuitive thinking "works" by authors such as Claxton and others, we now need to respond to the challenge of combining the logic of the data, with the power of intuitive contributions from entrepreneurs and experienced decision-makers.

In the current climate, marketing intelligence professionals are constantly being encouraged to be "engaged" with, rather than being detached from, the business decision-making process. These days, there is an expectation that market researchers will put more of themselves into the analysis. As Virginia Valentine says, "In today's complex world, researchers must begin to think of themselves as admissible data." Thus, today the growing pressure on organisations to understand the complexity of the modern consumer requires market researchers not only to be sound methodologists, but also to apply greater levels of creativity in their attempt to unearth those key insights that are so important to shaping the fortunes of a business.

The Data May Be Dumb But Beliefs Can Be Blind

There is not the space here to review in detail the tricky issue of how, on the one hand, market researchers must draw out the power of intuition, while at the same time making sure we honour the robustness and legitimacy of the evidence. Inevitably, this activity is somewhat of an art form. On the one hand, market researchers want to respect "intuitive" contributions, but they must not let the pendulum swing too far in favour of the entrepreneur. When we hear Henry Ford's famous comment, "If I listened to my customers I would have invented a faster horse", we can be easily persuaded to ignore all of the consumer evidence, and go with the gut feel of the entrepreneur. But, if we lurch too far in favour of intuition, we are in danger of letting blind faith and prejudice dominate organisational decision-making, without giving sufficient weight to the voice of consumer reason in tempering these "judgements".

Providing tuition on how to strike the balance between embracing the best of (informed) intuition and learning from the hard consumer evidence is a big and complex topic. So all we can do in this introductory chapter is to provide a checklist of key questions that those associated with making an evidence-based decision might like to ask prior to making a judgement based on marketing intelligence evidence. These provide a focal point for two key checks. First, we need to be sure that the conclusions to a study are based on a full understanding of the robustness of the hard evidence. And secondly, we need to be sure that the conclusions have been through a process that sets the data in a wider context and has done justice to management hunch, intuition and instinctive feelings on the topic.

A 21 QUESTION GUIDE TO INFORMED, YET CREATIVE, EVIDENCE-BASED DECISION-MAKING

Below we provide a checklist of 21 questions that will firstly help the user of market research evidence ensure that they are making decisions that are based on an informed understanding of the robustness of the evidence. But, in addition, give them the confidence to know that they are making decisions that have benefited from going slightly beyond the "literal data" to embrace the wider implications of the evidence in front of us. So, in sum, the following 21 questions are designed to achieve the twin objectives of making sure you make safe decisions that are based on an understanding of the robustness of the data, while at the same time going beyond the immediate evidence in order to better understand the hinterland around the evidence that can help shape a better decision.

Question 1: Have we Assessed the Core Objectivity of the Source of this Evidence?

Thinking about the agency that conducted the research, is there any way they are linked with the need to produce a particular outcome for political, financial, or methodological reasons? In short, just how likely is it that this piece of evidence has been subject to systematic "spin" aimed at presenting a particular view of the world, including possibly the use of the technique of presenting "selected soundbites", thereby distorting the overall evidence in order to promote a particular point of view.

Question 2: Has the Detail of the Survey Evidence been "Tested to Destruction" to Ensure that it is Logical and There are not Stupid Howlers?

The next question to ask is whether the evidence and conclusions were based on logical reasoning. For example, this could include checking whether any of the original questions had a hint of ambiguity that could open the door for misinterpretation at the analysis stage. So, the start point for sound decision-making is to generate a checklist of where there might have been any possible opportunities for "error" creeping into the logical reasoning process.

Here, an important device is presenting the presentation (on a dry run basis) to a "Devil's Advocate" who has been instructed to "test" the robustness of each critical piece of the evidence to "destruction". That is, to scrutinise every aspect of the evidence that could be open to different interpretations given the way it has been collected and analysed.

A technique that helps us test to destruction the survey evidence is to take a particular recommendation and then role play the implications of the recommendation from the perspective of the "customer from hell". In addition, it is often helpful to take the interpretation of a piece of survey evidence and ask a dispassionate third party what they think of this particular "take" on the world.

Question 3: Understanding the Context in Which the Evidence was Conducted

At the time the fieldwork for the study was being conducted were there many major events happening on a worldwide, countrywide or local community basis that could have in any way influenced the thinking, and actions, of people taking part in the study? And a word to clients, if there is any vagueness in what the agency is saying, do not be too afraid at this point in the process to ask the agency for concrete examples of exactly what it is they are recommending based on this evidence. The effective client decision-taker will know how to "spar" with the supplier of the data in order to get to grips with the interpretation of data that has got no further than a glib initial narrow interpretation, as opposed to evidence that has been subject to clear, deep, logical and creative contextual thinking.

Question 4: How Does this Survey Evidence Square with Our Bigger Picture Understanding of this Issue?

What reliance would the team place on the consumer evidence (what would your score be out of 10, using a scale where 10 is total belief in the research evidence and 1 means you are extremely unsure about how much reliance to place on the meaning of the research evidence) given what else we know? Has any member of the research team been on to Google and pinpointed all the writers/"pundits" (from the business and academic communities) who have prepared models, frameworks or schemas that help explain how this particular phenomena "works"? And what were the key lessons learnt – how does this add power to our understanding of the current consumer research evidence? Has the evidence for this particular study been related to other studies conducted over the last six months by the agency/client company on this same market/product category/brand? What overall lessons have been learnt from this "meta-analysis"? What does this add to, or change, what we already knew from just looking at our (one) latest piece of survey evidence?

Question 5: How Far is this Study from the "Ideal" Study?

If the research team – with the benefit of 20/20 hindsight – was to (theoretically speaking) construct the "ideal" research solution to deal with this problem, just how far away from this ideal would be the research approach actually chosen? Here, it is particularly important to assess whether there are any fundamental omissions in the evidence that, in an ideal world, would have been collected to understand this issue. It is worth imagining just what this critically important missing data might have told you, and to weigh up the implications of taking a decision without this evidence. Should the decision then be delayed while we attempt to plug this missing gap, or do we feel that we are able to proceed with a decision even though there is a gap in our knowledge?

Question 6: Was a Fitness-for-Purpose Approach Adopted?

Was the method used to collect the data – online, telephone, face-to-face – appropriate? Specifically, to what degree, if at all, do the research team think they would have obtained different results with a different method? If different, would these be substantially different or slightly different? If substantially different, has this been factored into the current interpretation?

Question 7: Will this Survey Evidence "Travel"?

Here we are talking about the reliability of the evidence. Is it evidence that although collected about issue X in scenario Y, could nevertheless apply to different business situations and scenarios over a period of time? Specifically, when making decisions based on analysis like this, it is important to know whether the evidence collected related to a moment frozen in time, or whether it is the kind of evidence that will still be pertinent over a longer period. This is important as many decisions taken will go wrong because the evidence that was collected quickly becomes outdated. So, it is important to have a clear perspective on the extent to which the decision is grounded in a strategic understanding that holds good over time, as opposed to having a temporary insight into a changing phenomena.

Question 8: The Level of "Compensation" Required by the Analyst

It is important to recognise that literal survey evidence needs to be set in context and interpreted in light of what we know about how the survey process works (our "knowledge filters"). We need to be sure that the appropriate level of "compensation" has been applied to the evidence so that we can make informed, rather than naïve or unsophisticated, interpretations of the evidence. Specifically, we need to know exactly how this compensation process has been conducted. And it should have been made transparent and explicit to the client.

Question 9: What is the Success Track Record of the Method Being Employed?

How many times has the methodology/technique being employed in this particular study been used by the research team in the past, and what observations would the research team make about the past track record of the success and/or failure of this particular technique? And specifically, what do they feel about the past success of this methodology in relation to the current project? In sum, what do we know about the overall effectiveness of this genre of research and have we established the implications of this for our particular study?

Question 10: Do the Findings from this Latest Study Square with Our Prior Knowledge on this Topic?

Has this study, in essence, confirmed our initial thinking? If so, what extra thinking, fresh ideas and techniques have been applied to challenge this original viewpoint to reassure us that this is indeed the true position? Or has this study produced completely fresh insights on the problem? If so, what "checks and balances" have been put in place to ensure that these new observations truly reflect what is really going on in the market place?

Question 11: Is There Any Sample Bias, that is, are There People to Whom We Should Have Spoken that We Haven't?

If you were to compare the profile, the perfect/ideal target sample, of the respondents to whom we should have been speaking to in this study, with the profile of those we actually interviewed, are there any critical points of departure in these two profiles? If so, what implications do these points of difference have for the interpretation of the findings – and has enough been done to "compensate" for this discrepancy? Is it now "safe" to proceed with this off-target, less than ideal, sample?

Question 12: The Sensitivity of the Evidence to a Particular Technical Aspect of the Methodology Used

Thinking about the most critically important piece of evidence being presented in this survey, just how sensitive is this to a particular methodological approach or technical effect? What has been done to monitor the chances of a particularly powerful "technical irregularity" inadvertently steering the findings slightly off course? How do we adjust for this?

Question 13: Were the Survey Questions Asked in an Objective Way?

Did any member of the research team answer the questionnaire themselves, as if they were a respondent? Would this person say the interview has done justice to what they knew, and/or wanted to say, about this topic, or did the questionnaire only do partial, or little, justice to what they wanted to say? What does this mean for our results?

Question 14: Have We Attempted to "Stretch" the Literal Consumer Evidence – Within an Acceptable Boundary – to Extract the Maximum Creative Potential of the Evidence?

So far we have put the focus on testing the robustness of the evidence itself and ensuring that the way the decision-maker is evaluating the evidence is not based on any misunderstandings. But it is also important on certain projects to ensure that the decision-making process is also informed by a phase of what we might call "data stretching". We want to make maximum use of the creativity of the analyst.

What can happen with decision-making is that individuals get gripped with what we might describe as "corporate think", whereby they become risk adverse on behalf of their company. They become nervous of more ambitious interpretations of the data, given concerns about what this might mean for their career, and generally operate in a way that is away from their "gut instinct". So an ingredient within the optimum decision-making process is one that combines all of the above discipline and rigour with some techniques for getting individuals to lighten up and look at the opportunities within the data.

Some Ideas for Creatively Looking at the Decision-Making Process

Why not deliberately make the decision-making "personal" and ask people what they would do if they were making a decision that involved spending their own money? It also perhaps worth getting feedback on different ideas on an anonymous basis, thereby encouraging people to get in touch with their true feelings and provide "gut feel" responses, free from any corporate con-straints. Encouraging individuals to think more conceptually – to raise the level of abstraction with which issues are being discussed – can also be helpful. This helps decision-makers get out of the trenches of "win"/"lose" and "black"/"white" decisions, and look at issues from what we might call the *third corner*. Just how would this putative decision look from the perspective of different stakeholders?

Other techniques that can help liberate decision-makers include "visualisation" exercises. Get the decision-making team to cast forward five years in their mind and look at what different decision outcomes might look like from this standpoint. Related to this it is helpful to work through different "what if" scenarios, in terms of your company's own performance, and what competitors might do. Techniques, such as "game theory", that help individuals to grasp the bigger picture and better see what the competitors might do in relation to different decision scenarios, can be helpful.

Linked to this task, there is value in mapping out of some of the perceived uncontrollable factors that could affect this decision and reviewing closely the degree to which these are likely to kick-in and affect different types of decisions. Here, one technique is to work through the "nightmare" outcome scenario, and compare and contrast this with the "dream" outcome scenario.

In short, there are a range of techniques to get people out of their organisational comfort zone and go beyond their corporate "default" position. The purpose of this element of the decision-making process is to ensure that decisions are based on maximum strategic vision, and not just the result of short term, tactical consideration.

Question 15: Has a Balance Been Struck in Analysing the Different "Types" of Critical and Creative Thinking that Have Been Applied to the Analysis?

Firstly, have the facts been verified? Has the right level of critique and critical thinking been applied to the evidence? Then, have all of the feelings, hunches and emotions been drawn out from the facts? Have all the implications that flow from these facts and insights been explored? Have all of the creative possibilities, alternatives, new angles, perspectives, concepts, perceptions and lateral thinking been applied?

And has the right balance between all of these different types of cautionary, and creative thinking, been brought to bear in a balanced way in arriving at the final recommendation? In sum, did the analytical framework deployed to analyse the evidence achieve the appropriate balance between rigour and creativity?

Question 16: Do We Fully Understand the Role that the Survey Evidence will Play in the Context of the Decision to be Made?

If there was no consumer evidence available to make this decision, how much would the risk of making a wrong decision be increased? Would this take the decision to an "unacceptable" level of risk, a "manageable" level of risk, or hardly make any difference?

Question 17: How Generalisable is the Evidence Across Different Countries and Cultures?

In a scenario where, increasingly, findings of a study conducted in one particular country may be "generalised" out to wider parts of the globe, just how reasonable and sensible is it to do this? Why not ask someone who lives in another country to ask the equivalent of the UK's "ordinary man on the Clapham Omnibus" whether a one-line summary of your key research findings from one country would make sense in another, say China, Japan, or wherever?

Question 18: The Acceptability of the Genre of Your Research Approach to Senior Management

It is important to have an understanding of the acceptability to the "decision-making unit" of this genre of market research evidence. It is no good to naïvely assume that a quantitative-based set of actuaries who run an insurance company will warm to what they could perceive to be a rather "soft" presentation based *exclusively* on qualitative evidence.

And by the same token, "creatives" brought up in an advertising agency environment will not automatically engage with rather anonymous, bland, quantitative statistical evidence. So, have you done a "reality check" on the overall acceptability of your genre of evidence to your decision-making audience? That is, have you established what types of evidence are appropriate to what types of audience and managed this "fit"?

Question 19: Has Enough Been Done to Help the Decision-maker Navigate the Decision "Minefields" Associated with this Genre of Evidence?

What has the research team unearthed about this broad category of evidence-based marketing decision? What are the typical traps that individuals/organisations fall into when using this kind of evidence to make this type of decision? What are the top three lessons we have learnt over the years when applying this category of research evidence to this type of decision?

For example, we know that decision-makers often tend to reduce complex choices down to two simplistic alternatives, which can lead to naïve decision-making. We also know that certain decision-makers attach too much importance to the most accessible or easy-to-understand evidence, thereby taking some of the subtlety out of the decision process. Decision-makers also tend to talk up selective evidence that confirms their initial judgements, even in the face of other telling counter-statistics. Furthermore, we know that certain decision-makers will be overly influenced by powerfully delivered emotional messages, rather than concentrating on the wider, more representative, but dull facts.

Similarly, we know that decision-makers will be reluctant to let go of a project in which they have been heavily involved in the past, even though it is beginning to falter. This is called "anchoring". We also know that decision-makers might set up arbitrary benchmarks or criteria to making the decision that have no relation to the problem. For example, "let us go 50/50" seems a fair attempt at a resolution, but nonetheless, on certain issues, this may have no basis in logical reasoning.

The list of common decision-making flaws continues, but there is not the space in this chapter to review them all. But the above provides a flavour of what the professional market researcher will need to be aware of in helping with the decision facilitation process.

Question 20: Striking the Golden Compromise between "Reason" and "Emotion"

Our evidence needs to be, on the one hand, tested to destruction from the standpoint of its rigour and robustness. But at the same time, also set in the context of its compatibility with wider, more instinctive, intuitive observations. Given this, we now need to ask whether these two sides of the decision-making "equation" have been put together in a formal way and dispassionately evaluated in arriving at an overall judgement about the safety of different types of formal and informal qualitative and quantitative and other sources of evidence. Have we constructed the *balance sheet* of pros and cons in a considered way? So, for example, thinking about this decision, what are the three top pieces of evidence that most suggest that we should go ahead with this venture? And what are the top three pieces of evidence that suggest we should not go ahead, or proceed cautiously, or rethink the project? And, critically, which one piece of evidence do we personally most believe to be telling us the "truth"?

Question 21: Taking Personal Responsibility

The final ingredient of successful decision-making is about taking *personal responsibility* for ensuring the most effective decision is taken. Having ensured that sufficient rigour has been taken to evaluate the robustness of the evidence, and creative risks have been taken in stretching the meaning of the literal evidence, now is the time to make sure your views will be actioned. We know from the decision-making literature that it is quite common for individuals making a decision in a group to assume that someone else within the overall decision-making team will be making a key point and, therefore, do not bother articulating this point themselves. In addition, we know from post mortems of many bad decisions that individual members of the decision-making unit are often aware of potential problems, but think they should not raise their concerns because other members of the group do not seem so concerned about this issue. But later it becomes clear that *everybody* was thinking along the same lines, but nobody said anything!

We also know that it is common for members of decision-making teams to be aware of a potential problem but allow this issue, over time, to become "normalised". That is, the problem remains acknowledged as an issue, but without anyone actually rectifying this particular shortcoming. The most tragic example of this is the Challenger Space Shuttle disaster. Everybody realised that there was a longstanding problem with a particular O-ring in the rocket engine. But this had become "accepted" as a potential problem to the point where the rocket successfully "passed" numerous trials – with the qualification always being added that the problem with the O-ring must "one day" be sorted. This procrastination carried on until it was too late, when this tiny O-ring fault became the cause of a major disaster. So, in sum, taking personal responsibility for ensuring that all aspects of the problem have been, not only intellectually identified, but actioned, is important. The lesson should be not to leave things to others. Stand up and be counted. Always ensure that your voice is heard. In short, take personal responsibility for achieving successful outcomes.

FUTURE DEVELOPMENTS

We end this introductory chapter by reviewing the way in which the marketing intelligence industry is responding to the changing business environment, and seizing the various exciting opportunities being opened up by new technology. This provides a backdrop for then discussing the extent to which "new marketing intelligence" can be considered to be a modification of what market researchers have always done, or whether the changes that are taking place are so profound that we are now entering what we might term a different marketing intelligence "paradigm".

Finding Robust and Creative Solutions to Business Problems in an Ever More Complex and Fragmented Market Place

In response to the calls from business for faster, cheaper and better solutions, market research is responding by moving out of its technical "comfort zone", to work in a smarter and more creative way in order to meet its clients' changing needs and requirements. This reflects the way that products and services are now developed, distributed and advertised, in a market place that is becoming ever more complex and fragmented.

This change places heavy demands on market researchers whose role it is to understand the world and use this knowledge and insight to help take some of the risk out of business decision-making. Moreover, we also now live in an environment where the growing uncertainty in the way businesses operate has triggered a greater demand from different stakeholder groups for corporate decisions to be made in a transparent and accountable way. The confluence of these two trends creates a major challenge for market researchers. We have the relentless quest for customer insights that will generate profit for shareholders, coupled with the need for transparent evidence-based business decision-making.

Thus today, the call is for market researchers to be, on the one hand, objective, methodologically sound collectors and analysts of data, but at the same time, creative "interpreters" of what consumers are trying to tell us. In addition, market researchers need the added skill of being able to map out – in an impactful, credible way – the implications of their findings for busy decision-makers.

So, looking to the future, market researchers will increasingly be judged on their ability to help generate ideas that can be converted into profitable products and services. At the same time they will also be required to produce robust evidence and be the voice of reason and sound judgement. The future of marketing intelligence is about the industry's ability to develop its existing technical skill-set, while at the same time equipping researchers with the skills they need to be more creative and to operate as evidence-based information consultants.

The Pace of Technological Change

In responding to the need for more creative and actionable, yet still robust and evidence-based, insights, the marketing intelligence industry has been successful over the years in capitalising on changes in technology. The market research tool-bag has never been so full of exciting ways to find out what is happening in the world and how people feel about issues. There is not the space here to list all of the technical advancements that market researchers are now embracing. But the reader can see how market research is now increasingly relying on online surveys to gain access to busy respondents. In addition, it is an industry that is responding to the fantastic potential of the video mobile phone, with the opportunities this offers to sample large numbers of individuals at particular moments in time – possibly asking them to take photographs of what they are experiencing.

Instant and Interactive Interviews

In addition, in the world of qualitative research, market researchers can now "web-stream" what people are saying in focus groups conducted anywhere around the world to an HQ, where a client and agency brainstorming team can instantly analyse and action this information. And we have the re-emergence of photographic supported ethnography as a way of observing customers' behaviour. In addition, we have technologies that allow massive amounts of customer information generated by organisations' point-of-sale systems to be more readily integrated into other marketing intelligence evidence.

All of this means that market researchers have never been better placed to capture what is happening in the market place and establish what consumers think. And inevitably, market researchers will gradually be making more use of the interactive Web 2.0 platform, where respondents can feed their views to us when they want, rather than us relying on respondents to work to our subject, and timetable, agendas. This interactive technology gives market researchers a new and powerful window into the world of the customer.

The Changing Market Research Model

The changing environment and fast-moving technology provides challenges for the marketing intelligence professional. It means we are constantly trying to strike a balance between the application of our traditionally sound methodologies to generate rigorous and robust research, whilst at the same time responding to calls for innovative ideas and insights to be generated from new alternative, often less robust, approaches. So, the marketing intelligence professional is constantly, on the one hand, breaking new ground, but on the other, defending the faith with regard to what is safe evidence-based decision-making. This requires market researchers – in the spirit of being faithful to their objective roots for providing valid knowledge – to being totally transparent in the way they are now trying to blend its traditional new approaches.

Over the last decade we have seen a seismic shift in the way in which the marketing intelligence industry operates. The industry has moved away from just being seen as a quasi-scientific activity, providing hard quantitative measurement that is detached from the creative process and the complexities of intuitive decision-making. Today, it is seen as also embracing a much more pragmatic approach that requires high levels of creativity and imagination in order to tease out key insights.

The issue of whether these changes that have occurred in marketing intelligence over the last decade can be described as ongoing modifications to our existing modus operandi, or whether they represent a "fundamental shift of mind" in the way market researchers operate remains a moot point. It is true that our traditional market research methods are still in place to handle surveys that require objective measurement and description. But many would argue that as the industry now embraces so many creative approaches aimed at teasing out fresh insights, that this change warrants being described as a "paradigm" shift.

We accept that some feel uneasy about describing market research as now operating within a new "paradigm". They think that "paradigm" is an over-worked word. But whatever words we use to describe the overall framework, or model, that market researchers now operate to ply their craft, most would accept that our mode of operation has changed dramatically over the last decade. It is this changing role and nature of marketing intelligence that makes this edition of the ESOMAR Handbook so invaluable. It will help readers understand the journey that marketing intelligence has taken in recent years towards enhancing the quality of effective evidence-based decision-making. These are exciting times for marketing intelligence professionals.

REFERENCES

Barwise, P. and Meehan, S. (2004) *Simply Better*. Harvard Business School Press.

Bazerman, M. (2002) *Judgment in Managerial Decision Making* (5th Edn). John Wiley & Sons, Inc.

Buzan, T. (2001) *The Power of Creative Intelligence. 10 Ways to Tap into Your Creative Genius*. Thorsons.

Callingham, M. (2004) *Market Intelligence: How And Why Organisations Use Market Research*. Kogan Page.

Claxton, G.L. (1997) *Hare Brain, Tortoise Mind: Why Intelligence Increases When You Think Less*. Fourth Estate.

Davidson, H. (2002) *The Committed Enterprise: How to Make Vision and Values Work*. Butterworth Heinemann.

Dearlove, D. (1998) *Key Management Decisions: Tools and Techniques of the Executive Decision-Maker*. Financial Times/Pitman Publishing.

Gladwell, M. (2000) *The Tipping Point: How Little Things Can Make a Big Difference*. London: Abacus.

Gladwell, M. (2005) *Blink: The Power of Thinking Without Thinking*. Little, Brown and Company.

Goleman, D. (1997) *Emotional Intelligence: Why It Can Matter More Than IQ*. Bantam Books.

Gordon, W. (1999) *Goodthinking*. Admap.

Kaplan, R.S. and Norton, D.P. (2000) Having Trouble With Your Strategy? Then Map It. *Harvard Business Review*, September–October.

Karlöf, B. (translated by Gilderson, A.J.) (1993) *Key Business Concepts: A Concise Guide*. London: Routledge.

Mahmoud, O. (2002) The Operation was Successful but the Patient Died: Why Research on Innovation is Successful Yet Innovations Fail. Proceedings of the ESOMAR Congress.

Mahmoud, O. (2004) Market Research? Come on, This is Serious. Proceedings of the ESOMAR Congress.

Marinopoulos, J. and Laffin, D. (2006) *Integrated Customer Intelligence*. Excellence 2006. Amsterdam: ESOMAR.

Michaluk, G. (2002) *Riding the Storm: Strategic Planning in Turbulent Markets*. McGraw-Hill.

Palmquist, J. and Ketola, L. (1999) Turning Data into Knowledge. *Marketing Research*, **11**(2).

Porter, M.E. (1998) *Competitive Strategy: Techniques for Analysing Industries and Competitors*. Free Press.

Smith, D.V.L. and Dexter, A. (1994). Quality in Market Research: Hard Frameworks for Soft Problems. *Journal of the Market Research Society*.

Smith, D.V.L. (1998) Designing Research Studies. In *ESOMAR Handbook of Market and Opinion Research* (4th Edn), edited by McDonald and Vangelder. Amsterdam. ESOMAR.

Smith, D.V.L. and Fletcher, J.H. (2000) *Inside Information: Making Sense Of Marketing Data*. John Wiley & Sons, Ltd.

Smith, D.V.L. and Dexter, A. (2001) Whenever I Hear the Word "Paradigm" I Reach for my Gun: How to Stop Talking and Start Walking. Proceedings of the MRS Conference.

Smith, D.V.L. (2003) Factoring Intuition into the Analysis of Market Research Evidence. Proceedings of the ESOMAR Congress, Prague.

Smith, D.V.L. and Van Hamersveld, M. (2004) Research World, 3 Part Series (October, November and December). The new horizons – market research in 2010.

Smith, D.V.L. and Fletcher, J.H. (2004) *The Art and Science of Interpreting Market Research Evidence*. John Wiley & Sons, Ltd.

Smith, D.V.L. (2004) Consolidating The Role Of Market Research In Business Decision-Making By Extending Our Skill Set Into Business Consultancy. Proceedings of the ESOMAR Congress, Lisbon.

Smith, D.V.L. (2005) It's Not How Good You Are, It's How Good You Want To Be, Are Market Researchers Really Up For Reconstruction? Proceedings of the Market Research Society Conference.

Spackman, N., Barker, A. and Nancarrow, C. (2000) Happy New Millennium: A Research Paradigm For The 21st Century. Proceedings of the Market Research Society Conference.

Valentine, V. and Gordon, W. (2000) The 21st Century Consumer – A New Model of Thinking. Proceedings of the Market Research Society Conference.

Valentine, V. (2002) Repositioning Research: A New Market Research Language Model. *Journal of Market Research, Society*, **44**(2).

Van Hamersveld, M. (2005) Is the Future Today? *Research World*.

Wiseman, R. (2003) *The Luck Factor*. Century.

Zaltman, G. (2003) *How Customers Think*. Harvard Business School Press.

2

What is Market Research?

Adam Phillips

INTRODUCTION

This chapter is a general introduction to topics which will be discussed in much more detail in later sections of this book. It will cover what market research is and how it is defined, the basic types of market research, a brief overview of research methods and some comments on the effective communication of results. It will outline the development of market research as a distinct activity within the organisation and describe the character of the business today. There are specific sections on how to assess the quality of market research and the issues that influence quality and on maintaining access to representative samples. Finally, there are some conclusions about how the industry is likely to develop in the future.

The term market research will be used in this chapter to cover not only research into markets and consumer behaviour, but also social survey research and opinion research. All three types of research share the same core body of knowledge and skills and there is considerable overlap with some market research practitioners working in more than one type of research in much the same way that the medical profession includes both general and specialist practitioners.

WHAT IS MARKET RESEARCH?

Market research is a way of investigating and answering questions about human behaviour. Some of the tools in the market researcher's toolkit are exploratory in nature, some are descriptive and some are experimental. At the most basic level, the market researcher uses this toolkit to describe behaviour. However, the description of behaviour leads almost inevitably to a request for an explanation and a major activity for market researchers is, therefore, exploring the tactical and strategic options available to managers and making recommendations.

The key role of the market research function in an organisation is to provide reliable evidence which will help managers take better decisions. This sounds simple, but in practice involves not only the ability to collect information and analyse it, but also the ability to communicate and interpret the results in a way which helps others to use them.

An essential skill for the researcher is to be able to identify the core issue that lies at the centre of the question being asked and what evidence, if any, could help support a better decision. Another very relevant skill is the ability to make the trade-off between designing research to collect data which is sufficiently sensitive, valid and reliable to support the decision being

Market Research Handbook, 5th Edition. Edited by M. van Hamersveld and C. de Bont.
© 2007 John Wiley & Sons, Ltd.

taken, but which is no more costly in time and resources than the decision justifies. Finally, a good researcher finds a way to communicate the research findings in a manner which makes it possible for the organisation to engage with them and use them to take better decisions.

THE UNDERLYING THEORIES

Key disciplines used in market, social and opinion research are the social sciences – psychology, anthropology, sociology – economics and statistics.

The use of the sample survey as a way of describing the behaviour and attitudes of a much larger universe was the central element in the development of market research. The sample survey made it possible to collect reliable quantitative information at a much lower cost than doing a census. The disciplines of psychology and anthropology have nourished the development of market research by helping researchers understand the answers to questions, explain behaviour and develop insights. Another important element in the development of market research was the concept of experimental design, testing hypotheses and measuring the effect of different stimuli. Many of the advances made in the application of market research have come from conducting experiments with product or service design and publicity. Statistics has obviously been relevant in establishing that the results are sufficiently valid and reliable. Economics has helped to create a context for the results and explore scenarios.

A DEFINITION OF MARKET RESEARCH

As the diversity of information sources available to decision makers has increased it has become important for market researchers to differentiate and brand their services in relation to other information providers and consultants. A statement like: "market research provides reliable evidence which will help managers take better decisions" does not define market research as a unique activity, other functions also use evidence of people's behaviour to help organisations take better decisions.

Another important aspect of market research is that it relies on the widespread goodwill of the public to provide the information on which the whole industry is based. Market researchers need to be able to explain to respondents what market research is and reassure them about how the information they provide will be used, in order to get their agreement to take part in research. In addition, legislators are concerned that the public's goodwill is not abused by people who wish to collect individually identifiable personal information for other purposes while seeming to be carrying out market or survey research.

For these reasons it is important for there to be a widely accepted, clear and simple definition of market research. Examples of different definitions are given in the Appendix which highlight the difficulty market researchers have of explaining what they do in a concise and simple way. ESOMAR is in the process of revising the ICC/ESOMAR International Code on Market and Social Research Practice (Professional Standards). This revision incorporates a new and much shorter definition:

> Market research, which includes social and opinion research, is the systematic gathering and interpretation of information about individuals or organisations using the statistical and analytical methods and techniques of the applied social sciences to gain insight or support decision making. The identity of respondents the will not be revealed to the user of the information without explicit consent and no sales approach will be made to them as a direct result of their having provided information.

It is hoped that over time this definition will be adopted on a worldwide basis, when research associations and organisations update their self-regulatory codes and that, where appropriate, it will support the inclusion of market research in data protection, communication and other relevant legislation as a legitimate and distinct purpose.

TYPES OF MARKET RESEARCH

One of the commonest ways of classifying types of market research is to describe work as qualitative or quantitative research. At the simplest level, this differentiates work which uses large samples and structured questionnaires, which can be projected to a known universe, from those which typically use relatively unstructured interviews or discussion groups where it is possible to explore and follow up ideas. This latter type of work is constrained to use smaller samples because of the length of the interviews and the complexity of this type of analysis, hence the term qualitative. This division was important in the past because the limitations of computing power forced surveys that involved counting to collect relatively limited and very structured data. However, as computer technology has developed, this division has become blurred and the term qualitative is sometimes used to cover larger survey work where the data collection is extensive and the analysis allows for complex associations. "Qualitative quantitative research" is probably a better way of describing this work.

Traditionally, market research was bought in the form of individual projects. This is described by the industry as ad-hoc (or custom) research, as opposed to continuous research. Continuous research is, as its name implies, research which is regularly repeated in order to measure trends. This is done either by recontacting the same people who are members of a panel of respondents who have agreed to take part in research on a regular basis, or by recruiting fresh samples of people and asking them the same questions. This latter method is typically used for tracking the impact of advertising, since repeatedly questioning the same sample about the same advertising in a panel sensitises them to the advertising being evaluated which can make interpreting the results difficult. Virtually all qualitative work is ad-hoc whereas around 45 % (ESOMAR, 2005) of all quantitative research spend is on continuous research.

Multi-client or syndicated research is research where several clients who are interested in the same information get together to share the costs. This can be either for ad-hoc or continuous research. It is the approach used for most major purchasing and media measurement panels, since they are very expensive to run and all the participants in a particular sector need much the same data.

A variant of multi-client research is omnibus research. A research company commits to carrying out a survey on a regular basis and sells questions on the questionnaire to anyone who wants a small amount of information from the universe being surveyed. It is a very useful type of research, since it makes it possible to access a large high quality sample at relatively low cost. It is good for finding out basic information like: "how many", "how often" or "why". The issues to consider with omnibus research are that the nature of the questioning can be disconcerting to respondents because it can jump from margarine to toothpaste to book purchasing, for example, leading to poorly considered answers. There is also a risk that two companies can be asking slightly different questions on the same topic in the same omnibus questionnaire. This can influence answers by, for example, one client raising the awareness of certain brands before the spontaneous awareness question from another client in the same sector. Professional research agencies who specialise in this work try to avoid this happening, but sometimes the interaction is not obvious.

Finally there is desk research or database mining. Desk research, as its name implies, involves using existing information sources and reanalysing the information to answer a specific set of questions. Database mining is a more recent development and involves reanalysing a database, usually of individual consumer or respondent records, in order to provide answers to different questions from those for which the data was originally collected.

QUANTITATIVE MARKET RESEARCH

The development of quantitative market research was built on early social studies carried out in the second half of the nineteenth century. In 1899 Seebohm Rowntree surveyed 11 500 households in York, England using interviewers and published the results in a book entitled "Poverty: A Study of Town Life" (2000). In 1911, Charles Coolidge Parlin undertook to "gather information useful to businessmen". His first study of the agricultural implement industry in the USA resulted in a 460 page report and he subsequently produced a number of reports on different industries. Parlin called his operation "Commercial Research" rather than market research (Bartels, 1976). In the USA research into advertising was being carried out in the early twentieth century. In Europe the growth of commercial market research followed developments in the USA. The first recorded survey in the UK was some advertising research on Unilever's Pears Soap carried out by J WalterThompson, the American advertising agency, in 1925.

The practice of quantitative market research has continued to evolve since that time. The continuing growth in demand for market research and the increasing diversity of projects is evidence that understanding people's needs and expectations makes it possible to improve the products and services they are offered. Large organisations which have limited direct contact with their end users, whether commercial or governmental, need a formal mechanism for doing this. One of the pioneers in market research described it as "social feedback" drawing an analogy with the method of "negative feedback" used by engineers to stabilise complex systems.

In the early development of quantitative market research techniques there was serious discussion about the best way to collect data. Was observation better than asking questions, because the question might influence the response? What about the mode of interview – is the anonymity of the self-completion interview better than one where you have to confess your sins to an interviewer face to face? Does the rather formal style of the quantitative interview with a structured questionnaire lead to a different kind or response than an unstructured interview with no obvious record being made of the answers? Should a sample be recruited by random selection or is quota sampling more sensitive as well as more cost-effective, because the people taking part are more engaged and willing to answer questions?

An example of the way techniques of research have developed is that in the early 1950s researchers working on quantitative surveys for Procter and Gamble were required to memorise the questionnaire, do the interview without taking notes and write the responses down on the questionnaire afterwards out of sight of the respondent. It was thought that obviously recording the answers would make a housewife nervous and that her answers would therefore conform more closely to what she expected to be publicly acceptable than reflecting what she really thought. This is not an issue that is discussed much by quantitative researchers nowadays, which is perhaps a result of the commercial pressures on the industry and the trade-off between improved sensitivity and validity against cost. The way this particular issue is usually handled cost-effectively nowadays is that hypotheses are developed in qualitative work using an unstructured interviewing approach and then tested in quantitative research using a structured interview. However, this method does not actually eliminate the problem and, as will be discussed in later chapters, this is not always the best way to gain insight. An example of the limitations of this approach is in public opinion measurement, where the discussion of political issues among friends will be different from the discussion with a stranger, like an interviewer. The social context effect is much stronger in situations where opinion is changing rapidly, which is perhaps one of the reasons why politicians have become so reliant on focus groups.

Methodological questions are still discussed, but commercial practice, driven by some basic experiments and cost considerations, created pressure to standardise the mode of interview and the size of sample for the majority of research projects. The outcome by the 1970s was that most qualitative research was conducted using focus groups lasting 1.5 hours and most quantitative interviewing involved an interviewer asking questions from a questionnaire script where most responses were assigned to pre-coded answers by the interviewer.

With the development of powerful PCs in the 1980s and 1990s, the cost of analysis became negligible in relation to the cost of collecting the data, increasing the use of sophisticated statistical analysis. More recently, the development of the Internet and access panels has reduced the data collection cost by at least an order of magnitude.

In the future passive logging by various types of meters and scanners and the widespread deployment of radio frequency identification (RFID) chips will further reduce the cost of data collection, but at the expense of collecting answers to direct questions. The benefit of this development will be the ability to employ much larger samples and therefore increase the granularity of reliable data analysis. The risk is that behaviour will be misinterpreted as a result of poor research design.

A simple example of this risk of misinterpretation would be an attempt to increase the efficiency of telephone answering by reducing the number of operators and observing what happens to the average waiting time before the phone is answered by an operator. The call handling rate can be easily observed, what is more difficult and expensive to observe is the number of callers who get tired of waiting and hang up before the call is answered. However, with this method of observation at the organisation's switchboard, it is impossible to observe the number who cannot get through at all because all the lines are busy.

There will therefore continue to be a demand for skilled researchers to ensure the quality of data and interpret the results.

QUALITATIVE RESEARCH

The history of the development of qualitative research is not well recorded. Psychologists and anthropologists were enrolled by advertising agencies to explain behaviour and improve the effectiveness of advertising. Not many names have survived from that period. In the UK Mass-Observation in the 1930s and 1940s did some ethnographic studies and ran a large scale diary panel where people were encouraged to submit regular diaries about their lives and write short essays on topics of interest to the researchers. The results were published in books and reports. "The Pub and the People" (Mass Observation, 1987) is a good example of their work.

In the US in the 1950s Ernest Dichter developed "motivational research" which was demonised in Vance Packard's book "The Hidden Persuaders" (1957). However, it was only in the late 1970s in Europe that qualitative market research as we now know it began to be developed. This involved the use of qualitative research as a legitimate tool in its own right, rather than as an initial stage of exploratory work before quantification. The drive for this was the development of theories about branding and the importance of intangible emotional benefits in creating product difference and added value in a world where developments in manufacturing had made it possible to produce products of consistent high quality. Until that time most qualitative research had been fairly simple, aimed at understanding people's needs and designing advertising to communicate fairly tangible benefits. Nowadays the qualitative researcher uses a wide range of tools to explore and to try to understand. These will be covered in later chapters.

When using qualitative research it is important to be aware that the results usually appear less complex or "scientific" than quantitative results. This can lead to them being treated as unreliable in organisations which are very driven by numbers. The issues to be taken into account by the user of qualitative research are clearly set out in "Market Intelligence – How and why organizations use market research" by Martin Callingham (2004).

EXPERIMENTAL DESIGN

The basis of virtually all quantitative market research is sampling theory, however, a very important methodology used in quantitative market research has been the experiment and, in particular, the idea of testing something new against the existing product, device or service which is treated as a control. Experiments can be quite small scale; for example testing a new recipe for a beer against the current version, but they can also be large.

If we take beer as an example, a new formulation for a brand is likely to be first tested by the brewing team. If they think it tastes good and meets the specification, it is likely to be tested against control products (probably the leading brands in the sector) in a "blind" test (no visible branding, possibly even in opaque glasses or under coloured light if colour is an issue) by a small sensory testing panel, typically composed of people who work in the brewery or who live close to it. A number of formulations will be tested. The best ones will then be subjected to tests with a representative sample of drinkers – this could be a simple taste of a glass, probably a comparative test in which two different beers are compared, or a more sophisticated test where the drinking environment is replicated, either by giving the respondent the product to drink at home (if it is for home consumption) or by serving it in a bar situation. This testing could even involve getting the respondent to drink the new beer for a whole evening to make sure that the hangover experienced by heavy beer drinkers is no worse than that from the leading competitive brands. Further experiments can also be carried out with the advertising, packaging, pricing and display in the retail outlet before the product is launched. In some cases experimentation will continue after launch with different regions of a country being exposed to different levels of advertising or product promotion to establish whether the ROI of a big marketing campaign will meet the organisation's targets.

The design and execution of good experiments is central to a great deal of market research. The example given here is one of product development, but much experimentation is done in the area of advertising, promotion and pricing. At a more strategic level hypothesis testing and helping to predict likely scenario outcomes are important areas for market research experiments that are more qualitative in nature.

PANELS AND DYNAMIC DATA

A common misconception about market research is that it entirely consists of asking people questions about their behaviour, but one of the earliest commercial market research services was the retail audit developed by Art Nielsen in the USA in the 1920s. This involved selecting a representative sample of grocery stores and measuring the price of chosen products, the amount of stock in the shop, the amount that had been delivered since the last visit and whether it was on the shelves at regular (typically eight week) intervals. This retail audit provided manufacturers with information about what was happening to their product after it left the factory. In the days before the development of universal product codes and scanning checkouts, the Nielsen audit provided information on the performance of the company's sales force and logistics support. A whole management structure within consumer packaged goods companies was developed to use retail audit data and, until the development of the consumer panel, this was as close as anyone could get to tracking customer purchasing behaviour.

The weakness of the retail audit is that it measures sales, rather than purchases; it allows you to analyse what happens at the store level and understand the impact of distribution, display, promotion at point of sale and competition, but does not allow you to get close to the buyer. The development of consumer purchasing panels in the 1950s made it possible to begin to describe and understand consumer purchasing behaviour, at least as far as packaged grocery products were concerned. Since that time, there has been an explosion in the amount of panel based measurement, driven by the development of computer technology. In sophisticated retailers, not only is virtually everything sold from a store recorded in a database, but in grocery stores loyalty cards have created a situation where potentially every customer's purchases can be recorded along with demographic and attitudinal profile data, in order to build models of behaviour and improve customer service and targeting (Humby, Hunt and Phillips, 2006). These analytical techniques are now being extended into other sectors; automotive, banks, utilities, etc. A recent development is to merge the viewing information from the set top boxes of cable and satellite TV consumers with the purchase data from their loyalty cards (with their permission), in order to help understand the impact of advertising and publicity on the behaviour of store customers.

The importance of continuously collected data from a panel is that it provides a continuous record of individual behaviour which can be much more useful than a static snapshot. The difficulty with it is that the volumes of data are large, there are significant problems with missing or imperfect data, there are always sampling and non-response biases which need correction before the data can be projected to the universe and it is usually impossible to ask "why" questions directly of participants for fear of distorting their behaviour and rendering the panel unrepresentative of the behaviour of the universe. Nevertheless, the ability to observe dynamic behaviour and build models makes this one of the most important and sophisticated areas of market research.

A specific use of continuously collected multi-client research data is the concept of research as a "currency". The use of research currencies is most developed in media research where very large sums of money are traded using the viewing, listening and readership data produced by surveys. Advertising space in the media is priced on the size of the audience to which it is exposed. The only objective measure of media audience comes from survey data. In virtually all major media markets there is only one survey which is used to measure the audience. The audience figures from the survey therefore effectively have a direct monetary value and can be used as a currency for the purpose of trading advertising space.

Some social surveys play much the same role by creating a consistent set of data which can be used to provide an accepted context for the discussion of policy. The Labour Force survey in the European Union is used to provide detailed information about the characteristics and size of the workforce for the management of the European economy. The British Crime survey is used to provide an independent measurement of the level of crime in the UK as perceived by the public. The results are reconciled with the figures reported by the police, in order to provide a consistent and agreed set of information for public debate on the effectiveness of policing in relation to its cost.

TECHNIQUES

The basic types of market research described above can be used in many different ways. For examples for:

Size and description

- Market measurement
- Social surveys
- Opinion polls
- Behaviour
- Needs, attitudes and expectations
- Brand equity
- Exploring and explaining

Communication

- Advertising development
- Pre-testing advertising
- Advertising experiments
- Media research
- Media planning
- Advertising and communication evaluation

Product and service development

- Idea development
- Concept testing
- Sensory testing
- Product testing and optimising
- Pricing
- Promotion and packaging

Customer relations

- Customer satisfaction measurement
- Service delivery/mystery shopping
- Retail distribution measurement and auditing
- Store design and display

The use of these techniques will be covered in following chapters.

DATABASES AND DATA MINING

Market research started with the concept of collecting information using small samples to describe behaviour. However, there are now vast amounts of data arriving continuously in all organisations. Much of it is effectively census data. There is therefore legitimate pressure to use existing data and only collect additional data for specific purposes. Unfortunately, most of these data are not collected or held in a form which makes them easy to mine. The data are also often supplied by the organisation's information and computing division who do not want to put their systems at risk to produce ad-hoc analyses for market research purposes. Nevertheless, the cost of collecting survey data and the constraints on the level of granularity of analysis imposed by the limitations of sample size, mean that a researcher needs to know how to use this source of data.

Another very useful source of information is old market research reports and presentations. These can be very useful, especially for people who are new to the organisation or who are carrying out strategic reviews. Managing this information is difficult, because the title of the report usually does not accurately describe what is inside. It is well worth developing a good indexing system or arranging for all reports to be set up on an easily searchable database.

COMBINATION AND SYNTHESIS OF INFORMATION

The most important developments in market research in the recent past have been in ways to make better use of the data which is available. These can be loosely divided into combination and synthesis. **Combination** is where data from different sources is combined to create a database from which to extract more useful information, **synthesis** is where ideas and information are integrated, but without using a straightforward mathematical relationship. Combination seems more rational and "scientific" but many of the most important developments supported by research have come from synthesis. "Evidence based consulting" is a term which is frequently used when applying synthesis to market research information.

The simplest example of combination is where figures from a survey are combined with known behavioural data (e.g. cash flows through a bank account or purchasing from a store loyalty card) with the respondents' permission, to create a much more powerful market research database where customers' values, needs and attitudes can be related to behaviour.

Another simple example of combination is weighting survey results to put them into a form which will be more easily understood by the end user by, for example, weighting the sample up to the total population, so that instead of looking at percentages, there are also actual numbers of people. A slightly more sophisticated use of this approach might be to weight survey results so that the numbers are the same as the organisation's sales data. The Target Group Index (TGI)[1] uses this technique to produce a very powerful media planning tool by weighting the claimed readership of publications among participants in the survey to match the national readership survey, so that analysis of media consumption among target sub-groups of the population or of specific product brands and services can be related back to the standard media "currency" for campaign planning and costing purposes.

In the area of new product development, idea generation techniques and simulated test markets combine data from purchasing panels and company internal sources with product test results to create an accurate forecast of sales for new products and services. Product test results tend to be very hard for non-researchers to engage with, but a phased two year sales forecast with high, medium and low volume estimates speaks to the whole company's management. These product testing techniques regularly deliver forecasts which are better than $+/-15\%$ once the known market conditions are inserted. Unfortunately, predicting market conditions over a two year period is more difficult than testing a new product, so the actual error range on the initial forecasts can be significantly bigger, depending on the experience of the company and forecasters in a particular market.

A sophisticated example of combination is data fusion where two or more surveys are "fused" by a complex statistical method into a single database to create, for example, a database which incorporates readership, TV viewing and product purchase. The reason for doing this is that the data load on a single respondent with established recording techniques is too great to collect all the data needed to build the database. An example of fusion is Target Group Ratings in the UK, where the TGI data is fused with the BARB TV viewing data. Fusion works

---

[1] www.tgi.surveys.com

well for leading brands and programmes but there are serious theoretical concerns about the validity of fusion in relation to brands, programmes and publications with low penetration of the population.

Advances in data collection technology have recently reduced the data task for respondents significantly and this has led to the development of single source survey panels of which the best known is Arbitron and Nielsen's Project Apollo in the USA. The data collection task for the respondent is nevertheless significant, leading to some concerns about the representativeness of the sample and quality of recording by panel members. It also introduces an alternative set of audience figures which destabilises the established media currency. For this latter reason the IPA in the UK has developed a different methodology called "Touchpoints" which is designed to relate existing media currencies through the medium of a survey which effectively calculates an "exchange rate".

This is a brief summary of the kinds of data which can be developed by combination. Its use plays an important role in ensuring that users of market research data can engage with it, bring their experience to bear and extract full value from it. Synthesis is more complicated and emphasises the role of the researcher as interpreter and adviser. How this is done is covered in much more detail in following chapters. It is the most demanding and least developed area of market research. To massively oversimplify, the organisation has a great deal of knowledge about how its customers or citizens behave and some fairly solid hypotheses about the reasons for this behaviour. However, in the modern world there is a massive over supply of merely "good" value products and services, so to be successful a new product or service has to be perceived by some as "excellent" value. Similarly, in the public sector citizens are becoming ever more demanding of government and expect individually tailored services. This creates a serious challenge for every organisation and a major opportunity for the researcher.

Some organisations are lucky, like retail stores, banks or automotive manufacturers, in that they can collect information from all their customers at regular intervals at relatively low cost. The power of consumer relationship analysis has been commented upon earlier and is well described in "Scoring Points" (Humby, Hunt and Phillips, 2006). However, manufacturers and governments generally are distant from day to day contact with their customers and citizens. This limits the amount of information which can be collected for an acceptable cost. The researcher therefore has to start to combine information from different sources to help identify solutions. The ability to combine qualitative research with quantitative survey data and the organisation's internal information using the researcher's experience makes the modern market researcher potentially an extremely valuable member of any management team, whether dealing with tactics or more strategic issues. Synthesis really comes into its own for strategic decisions, where the questions are often higher level and more general and therefore not amenable to being reduced to a few simple dimensions for research.

EFFECTIVE COMMUNICATION OF RESULTS

The researcher does not exist in a vacuum; their findings need to be shared. Research findings used to arrive in vast books of reports and volumes of printout. These were largely superseded by PowerPoint presentations and volumes of electronic printout on the organisation's intranet. Quite a lot of research is now available in an interactive format and some key indicators summarising the volumes find their way onto the corporate dashboard for senior management to consider. Qualitative research reports are increasingly like mini documentaries with respondents speaking their own lines to highlight the key findings in a powerful way.

Large organisations frequently communicate key research findings on their intranets or internal TV stations, in order to ensure that staff are all working with the same tacit knowledge when taking decisions. One company I know of even used a regular audience measurement survey to ensure that the research findings were communicated in a way which meant that they were read by management.

It may seem that all this leads to more effective communication, but in many cases the distracting noise introduced by the style of presentation and the simplification necessary to get the attention of senior management means that the key elements are lost or obscured by the way they have to be communicated.

Two thoughts are important here:

- Why trust the messenger?
- OK, so what should we do?

Researchers are frequently concerned with trying to understand and explain difficult problems with imperfect data. They have lots of ways of deciding how confident they are in what they have found out. But why should they be trusted more than anyone else? Increasingly, people do not accept scientific research as correct just because it has been carried out by scientists.

Many researchers find it hard to communicate their findings and explain the appropriate level of confidence without seeming to qualify their findings. This lowers the confidence of the listener who is not an expert. Equally, over confidence is very disconcerting. For market research to be trusted and to be really useful to an organisation it is important for the researcher to be able to deliver the right amount of information in a way in which people with different experience can engage with it and build on what is "known". Some of this knowledge is likely to be information which is known by the organisation but which has not been directly derived from the research itself. Understanding how to build confidence and communicate effectively is the subject of numbers of books and training courses. It is a skill which is hard to develop but without it the researcher is simply a technician and has no significant role to play in managing a modern organisation.

Once we know what we know and have a fair idea about what we don't know, the question arises what should we do? Most researchers and accountants share a desire to base their decisions on firm foundations. However, no organisation continues to be successful without taking risks. Part of the job of the researcher is to help ensure that the scale of risk is known before the organisation moves. The role of scenario planning will be covered later in this book but it is the moment at which the organisation starts to move towards taking a decision that the researcher's job becomes interesting and rewarding. It is at this point that the researcher's unique understanding of the customer or citizen enables him or her to play a major role in helping the organisation take the best decision. It is not a risk free role, since the information available will always be partial and the future context uncertain, but the researcher should be better placed than anyone else in the organisation to appreciate and explain the scale of the risk and whether more information could be collected which will help to reduce it.

THE EVOLUTION OF THE MARKET RESEARCH INDUSTRY

The structure of the market research business has evolved as the use of market research has become more widespread. In the early days of market research, organisations regarded it as an important competence which was sufficiently unique to justify keeping the design and

	1960→	1970→	1980→	1990→	2000→
Business environment	○ Growth ○ Sellers	○ Stabilisation ○ Sellers/buyers	○ Stagnation ○ Tough battle place ○ Buyers	○ Turbulence ○ Low/no growth	○ Growth
Marketing concepts	○ Sales ○ 4 Ps (product, price, place, promotion)	○ Life cycle ○ Segmentation	○ Positioning ○ Competition analysis ○ Value added chain	○ Globalisation ○ Application of ICT ○ Integrated marketing (Customer, channel, competition)	○ Customer value solution ○ "One-to-one e-commerce" ○ Networking
Scope of activities	○ Market analysis ○ Local market ○ Single instrument ○ Short term ○ Consumer	○ Marketing research ○ Multi-domestic ○ Multi-instrument ○ Middle term ○ Consumer	○ Mkt research consultancy ○ International ○ Integral business ○ Short/middle term ○ Consumer/ retail	○ Market intelligence ○ Global ○ Decision support ○ Tactical/strategic	○ Integral business intelligence ○ Market/competitor dynamics
Methodological emphasis	○ Forecasting (time series) ○ Testing techniques ○ Small experiments	○ Models ○ Multi-dimensional ○ Innovation	○ Implementation ○ Standardisation ○ Exchange of expertise	○ Information management ○ Definition of information requirements, application, implementation ○ ICT, networking	○ Knowledge management ○ Interpretation/meaning

Figure 2.1 The evolution of market research (van Hamersveld and Smith, 2003)

analytic resources in house, only buying in data collection and, sometimes not even that. In the 1950s and 1960s (later in some countries with undeveloped independent market research agencies) Procter and Gamble, Philips and Unilever among others, had their own in-house market research units with interviewer forces to conduct interviews.

The high cost of face to face interviewing meant that a lot of research was conducted by mail. Research which needed a controlled environment was conducted in a central location facility like a mall or community centre. Until the 1960s the low level of penetration of telephones and the cost of calls made telephone an unattractive medium for market research, apart from specialist sampling and business to business work. Telephone is now accepted as the easiest way to contact a random sample in most developed countries. It is online research which is raising concerns about sample coverage and following the telephone research growth path, as the penetration of broadband continues to grow.

Much of the development of market research techniques was pioneered in this early period by companies for which market research was a cost centre, not a profit centre. Large corporations and advertising agencies invested significant sums in basic research into market research techniques and experiments in the 1950s, 60s and 70s.

Since then the understanding and use of market research by organisations has become almost universal, creating a significant industry and bringing about pressures to specialise and reduce costs. Most organisations for which MR is not a core activity disposed of their research field forces a long time ago, keeping only their analysts. Increasingly these analytical jobs have been outsourced as well to consultancies and research firms, so that what an organisation receives is likely to be an advisory presentation with supporting data, rather than a pile of printout or data tables. A similar change has occurred in qualitative research where for the most part long and rather academic analytic reports have been replaced by shorter more focused reporting, sometimes using video rather than the written word to convey the point in a more forceful way.

The most recent developments have been driven by information and communication technology. The development of computers facilitated the use of quantitative market research as a management tool, by enabling the cheap, rapid processing of large databases. More recent developments in the cost of computing and in particular, in the Internet, have enabled:

- the use of very large samples or near censuses;
- background real time processing to check answers and suggest questions;
- large scale qualitative surveys.

In this process of specialisation and deconstruction of the research production process, quality control of the process has become important, as this is no longer under the control of a single individual or even organisation.

QUALITY CONSIDERATIONS

Information quality is major concern for the professional market researcher. Essentially anyone can ask questions and, with the development of the Internet, the PC and access panel[2] sample providers, it is possible for someone to set up a global market research operation for very little capital outlay. This is a large topic and in this introductory chapter only the key issues will be covered.

---

[2] An access panel is a "sample database of potential respondents who declare that they will cooperate for future data collection if selected". ISO 20252:2006, International Standards Organisation, Geneva.

The high level quality concerns for researchers are reliability, validity and sensitivity. In simple terms reliability is the extent to which the results are repeatable and validity is the extent to which the results accurately reflect the dimension or variable the researcher is trying to measure. Sensitivity is, as the term implies, the extent to which the survey is able to extract small variations in the variable being measured from random "noise". For qualitative research these issues are not amenable to statistical analysis but are important nevertheless.

Reliability can be broken down into different types of reliability:

- Stability or test-retest reliability – are the results repeatable using a second independent sample or by repeating the measurement? For example, if the declared voting intention in two pre-election polls carried out at the same time is very different, it suggests that the measure of voting intention in one or both polls is inaccurate and unreliable. A special case of this test, where it is not possible to repeat the survey, is split-half comparison. A single sample is split into two randomly selected halves to check if the results of the analysis of the two halves are similar.
- Internal consistency – do members of the sample exhibit consistent response patterns? For example do people who do not like a product not buy it, whereas those who do like it buy it.
- Equivalency reliability – do the results of independent measurements using different techniques relate? For example, does my quota sample give the same answers as a sample selected using a random probability approach.
- Inter-coder reliability – do coders or analysts working independently on the same data give the same summaries? For example, in deciding what social grade to allocate to a person based on their occupation and education.

Reliability is a critical issue for researchers because there is no obvious way that someone looking at the aggregate results from a single survey can tell if they can be trusted. This is where the professional experience and training of the researcher are most important. An example of the problem is a continuous tracking study using Internet research. Internet access panels are typically constructed by recruiting people from a number of different websites. If the panel managers do not take steps to draw consistent proportions of the sample from the different sources this could render results unreliable between waves if, for example, some of the websites had been running advertising or a promotion for the topic being researched and others had not. The fluctuations observed over time could be a result of changes in sample sources, when in fact the underlying variables being measured had not changed at all.

This issue is of wider concern than just for Internet research; the difficulty of getting interviews with some classes of individual means that a good understanding of the detailed methodology used in any piece of research is very important in deciding on the reliability of the data collected. Tracking surveys and measurement panels are designed to keep the between wave variance as low as possible by using sophisticated matching and substitution techniques, while accepting that the absolute measurement may have a significant bias. However, since this bias is held constant it can be allowed for when using the results.

Validity of a measure or approach can also be broken down into a number of types of theoretical validity:

- Face validity – does the way we are doing the research seem sensible? Do I believe that it is measuring what I want to measure?
- Criterion related validity – does the variable I am collecting measure what I am interested in? For example, can I assume awareness of a unique attribute of a brand relates to sales of

the brand and use that to assess the success of a communication campaign, in a situation where a lot of other independent and uncontrollable variables will influence actual sales?

- Construct validity – does the variable I am collecting measure what I want to understand? For example is there an accepted definition of brand equity against which to test my brand equity scale?
- Content validity – am I measuring all the relevant variables? For example, are the customers who write in to complain representative of all my dissatisfied customers; we could be providing a poorer service than our competitors while generating fewer problems serious enough to cause a complaint.

Validity is a less difficult issue for market research than reliability, since it is more amenable to experimental testing and analysis. This does not mean that it should be taken for granted. An example of a type of research where validity could be an issue is once again in research using the Internet. The penetration of the Internet in the population in many countries is between 30 % and 50 %. Nevertheless, it is possible to select and weight samples to give a reasonably reliable measurement of voting intention for the whole population. However, the fact that voting intention can be reliably measured does not mean that these samples can be assumed to give an accurate measurement of fast food consumption or healthcare needs without further adjustment. The initial lack of representativeness of the underlying sample means that the results have to be treated with caution and validated using other survey techniques.

The fact that a particular measure has proved valid in one market sector is no guarantee that it will be equally valid in a different context. Brand awareness is an important measure of brand strength in many markets but in some markets advertising and promotion is so powerful that the measure is of no practical value; the market for cigarettes in some countries is a market where 100 % of smokers are aware of the leading brands and even a majority of non-smokers. Some car and toiletry brands are similar in this respect.

It may appear from the examples given above that Internet research is unreliable and not valid. This is not the intention. Internet research provides good examples because it is a relatively new way of interviewing and therefore methodologies are less established. There are also technical limitations with online surveys, of which the most important one is that certain types of people are very hard to reach online. Offsetting this sampling disadvantage is the ability to reach minority target groups cheaply and the amount of extra processing which can be applied to the administration of the questionnaire, making sophisticated trade-offs and more holistic interviewing possible. Online also has the advantage that the respondent is completing the questionnaire voluntarily at a time and speed which suits them rather than the interviewer.

Sensitivity is important because the more sensitive the measure, the smaller the sample that is needed to produce a result which can be reliably distinguished from the random noise in the survey sample. However, as always in market research there is a trade-off.

A direct comparison with two or three products is a more sensitive form of testing than a monadic approach, where the subject only tries one product and then rates it in comparison with their experience in the product field. However, if products are not normally used in a way which encourages direct comparison, the effect of appearance may become stronger than it will be in reality. Sometimes the tests for products are designed to emulate the way customers choose them. For example ensuring that a perfume is attractive on the initial sniff in comparison with leading brands, as well as being liked in actual use in a monadic test, where the comparison will be with the user's existing brands, will ensure that the perfume gets the best chance of being bought from the shelf and also bought again after extended use. One type of testing alone cannot cover both situations, but the in-use monadic approach is less sensitive to small differences in the product and therefore larger samples are needed to get statistically reliable measures of product difference.

In practice, ensuring that research is valid, reliable, sensitive and of adequate quality can be broken down into a number of areas covered by the following questions:

Research design – are the objectives clear and specific? Will research help the organisation make a better decision?

- Is the method appropriate for the objectives?
- If for decision support; are the criteria or thresholds for go/no go clear?
- For quantitative research; is the sample size big enough to provide results of sufficient statistical reliability to identify with confidence a difference which is material to the decision being taken?
- For qualitative research; will the sample contain all the types of people relevant to the objectives?

Respondent selection – are the respondents representative of the target group?

- Are the respondents who were approached typical?
- Are the ones who agreed to take part in the research the same as those who did not?
- Have they had different experiences, e.g. more exposure to market research or advertising in this sector?
- Are we confident that we interviewed the correct individual – a particular issue for Internet research, but also relevant for other modes.

Interview mode – how is the interview administered and in what surroundings?

- Is there an interviewer or is it self-administered, e.g. by mail or online?
- What are the surroundings, e.g. is it in the street, in a test centre or at home?
- If it is a product, concept or advertising test, how natural and realistic is the presentation to the respondent?
- Is there anyone else present who might influence the answers?
- How is the interview being recorded or observed?
- Are there a number of interviewers and locations to randomise any potential biases introduced by interviewer personality, local effects, the weather (for interviews in the street), etc?
- What controls are in place to make sure the interview is carried out in the agreed manner, or even carried out at all?

Interview – are the questions relevant, unambiguous, unbiased and comprehensive?

- Do the questions lead the respondent?
- Do they contain just one concept per question?
- Are the questions clear to the respondent – have they been pilot tested to check this?
- Do all the questions have precoded answers, or can respondents give their own answers?

Analysis – How is the integrity of the data maintained as it is processed or analysed?

- What checks are carried out on the consistency of the data after the interview?
- How many people are involved in coding or analysing the answers and how are they trained and controlled?

Reporting – Communication of the results

• Clear separation between hard fact, advice based on experience and speculation or opinion.

These are the questions to ask when trying to establish the quality of some market research. Making sure that they can be answered satisfactorily for a particular piece of research depends on the experience and organisational skill of the researcher. There are some tools available to help, in particular the new ISO 20252:2006 identifies key issues relevant to managing the research process and suggests areas which need to be taken into account in order to get a consistent and reliable research study executed. Any company certified to this International Standards Organisation standard should be able to answer the questions above. However, this standard is only about regulating the process of executing a survey and ensuring that the research provider does what they say they do, by checking their processes regularly by independent external audit. It still leaves the researcher with the responsibility of deciding what to do and how to do it. Also, at the present time this standard is new and is in the process of being implemented worldwide. It is still not widely available; however, there are other similar standards already in place in Europe, Australia and Canada. It is likely, but not certain that most large research agencies will adopt the ISO standard, but in the meantime the professional researcher needs to satisfy themselves that what they are receiving is of a suitable quality level. This means using a professional research agency and taking the time to establish that the project will be correctly executed. This could include attending briefing meetings, checking instructions and questionnaires and ensuring some basic quality checks are carried out on the fieldwork and data analysis.

Good quality does not have to be more expensive than poor quality, but in most cases it will be. The added value of the better quality will not be apparent to anyone without the necessary experience, but the result of a bad decision will eventually become obvious to others.

How to influence quality in practice is the subject of large numbers of books. A good summary of the issues for quantitative researchers is covered in "Measurement Errors in Surveys" (Biemer, Groves, Lyberg, Mathiowetz and Sudman, 2004).

THE MARKET RESEARCH INDUSTRY TODAY

The size of the commercial market research industry was around US$ 23Bn in 2005, as estimated by ESOMAR (ESOMAR, 2005b). Of this the great majority was in Europe and North America. However, there is quite a lot of market research which is carried out by organisations and consultants which does not involve commercial market research companies, so this figure almost certainly underestimates the total value of market research by a significant amount.

Table 2.1

Global MR revenues		
2005	US$Bn	Share
Europe	10.4	45 %
North America	8.3	36 %
Asia Pacific	3.3	14 %
Central & South America	1.0	4 %
Middle East & Africa	0.3	1 %
World total	**23.3**	**100 %**

Table 2.2

World's 5 largest research markets	
2005	US$M
USA	7722
UK	2411
France	2247
Germany	2185
Japan	1358

The market for market research is relatively mature, but it grew at 5.2 % nominal (3.2 % real excluding the effect of inflation) in 2005, slightly ahead of the growth of the world economy at around 4 % nominal. Over two thirds of global market research revenue is generated in the five largest markets: USA, UK, France, Germany and Japan.

It is interesting to examine the nations with the highest market research spend per capita. The top five are UK, France, Sweden, Germany and Norway. The USA which has led the market research world for most of its history comes in at sixth place in terms of market research spend per capita, although it is second after Hong Kong for advertising spend per capita. This is partly due to the strength of the Euro in relation to the dollar, but also reflects the impact of price competition in the USA and, in particular, the impact of the low cost per interview of Internet research in reducing prices.

The world of market research is changing in line with the development of the world economy. The five fastest growing countries in terms of market research spend are: China, Estonia, Lithuania, Thailand and Venezuela. If China maintains its 25 % real growth rate in 2005 it will join the world's top five market research nations in five or six years.

Manufacturing industry accounts for almost half the expenditure on market research, followed by the media and the public sector. Within manufacturing, consumer packaged goods account for slightly more than half the spend (56 %) followed by pharmaceuticals and healthcare (24 %) with automotive, durables and electronics each accounting for around 10 %.

Table 2.3

2005	MR spend per capita US$	Ad spend per capita US$
UK	39.7	414.6
France	36.0	205.7
Sweden	35.7	284.5
Germany	26.5	250.7
Norway	26.3	358.6
USA	26.0	523.5
Australia	25.6	369.9
Finland	23.4	307.5
Denmark	23.1	332.5
Switzerland	22.5	400.2

Table 2.4

Client sector

2005	Spend share
Manufacturing	48 %
Media	15 %
Public sector	8 %
Utilities	5 %
Wholesale and retail	5 %
Business to business	4 %
Financial services	4 %
Advertising agencies	3 %
Research institutes	3 %
Other	5 %

Quantitative research accounts for four fifths of the expenditure on bought in market research. Mail research is rapidly being replaced by online. However, the low cost of mail and online research per interview underestimates the volume of work this mode accounts for; it could easily be between half and two thirds of all quantitative interviews being carried out.

Looking at the type of research being carried out, half the money spent goes on ad-hoc (custom) projects, about a quarter is panel based continuous research and a further 10 % is continuous using independent samples (e.g. advertising tracking). Around 5 % is accounted for by omnibus research. Online research is exhibiting very rapid growth at the present time. In the US 30 % (US$ 1.2Bn) of ad-hoc research was carried out online in 2005. As the penetration of broadband rises in other countries it is likely that the share of research spend taken by online will grow sharply. Given that online research is much cheaper per interview, this is likely to exert a downward pressure on the revenue growth rate for market research.

The industry is also one which is quite concentrated. 25 firms accounted for 62 % of global research revenues in 2005 and 80 % of the spend came from around 1000 clients. However this conceals a more vibrant and innovative market than might appear at first sight. Although

Table 2.5

Research Method

2005	Spend share
Quantitative	**83 %**
Mail	6 %
Telephone	21 %
Face to face	24 %
Online	13 %
Other quantitative	19 %
Qualitative	**14 %**
Group discussions	9 %
In-depth interviews	4 %
Other qualitative	1 %
Other	**3 %**

Table 2.6

Type of research	
2005	Spend share
Ad-hoc	51 %
Panel	28 %
Other continuous	10 %
Omnibus	5 %
Other	6 %

global research firms account for two thirds of the market the other third is populated by hundreds of specialist companies, most of which are successful and provide an excellent service in their specialist sector. It appears that the large agencies are not increasing their share beyond the two thirds level and that this is because of successful competition from the smaller specialists.

Table 2.7

World top 10 (2005)	Home
VNU (Nielsen)	Netherland
TNS	UK
IMS Health	USA
Gfk	Germany
Kantar (RI, Millward Brown)	UK
IPSOS (Ipsos, MORI)	France
Information Resources Inc	USA
Synovate	UK
Westat	USA
Arbitron	USA

In 2005 the top 25 market research firms employed about 100,000 people full time world-wide. This does not include large numbers of part time workers who do interviewing or data preparation or who work for market research support companies.

MAINTAINING ACCESS TO REPRESENTATIVE SAMPLES

The core business of market research is asking people questions and tracking behaviour. Getting access to people who are prepared to take part in research is therefore vital to the continued existence of the industry.

Three relatively new types of work which use the techniques of market research and which could be confused with market research by the public are:

- Customer relationship management (where the responses from respondents in what appears to be a survey are used to directly influence the sales approach to the individual respondent).
- Consultation studies (government, local government or media polls where a self-selecting group can be presented as though it is a representative sample).

- Advocacy and word of mouth marketing (where consultation techniques that appear to be market research can be used to influence the thinking of the respondents with the objective of getting them to act as advocates for an idea, product or service).

One of the key roles of market research industry organisations and associations is to ensure that industry self-regulation is effective in differentiating market research from these activities. It is essential for the industry to ensure that taking part in a market research survey will never lead to any detriment to the public as individuals and to publicise the benefits for society of individuals being prepared to take part in properly conducted market research.

In order to reassure the public that they could trust market researchers with their personal information and encourage cooperation, the market research industry was one of the first to develop self-regulatory codes of practice (the first ESOMAR Code of Practice was introduced in 1948). Concerns about privacy and the explosive growth of direct selling which use similar techniques means that there is now considerable resistance to taking part in market research, especially among some target groups. This has also led to the development of legislation to control spam email, telephone selling (which has unfortunately included market research in some countries) and the movement of personal data across national borders. The modern researcher therefore has to be aware of the requirements imposed by legislation and self-regulation. These are largely common sense, given the danger of identity theft and the need to reassure people about how their personal data is going to be used. Nevertheless they impose considerable restrictions on the freedom of the researcher and are likely to become more onerous in the future. Ethics and standards are covered in detail in a later chapter.

CONCLUSIONS AND FUTURE OUTLOOK

Market research is no use if it does not help organisations take better decisions. This means that the researcher has to engage in the management debate using their knowledge and experience, rather than just providing information for others to use. But also market research cannot function if the public is not prepared to cooperate by providing their personal information to market researchers. This means that in doing their work researchers must ensure that they maintain public confidence in market research and do nothing to abuse the trust placed in them.

The cost of collecting information from good quality samples is going to continue to rise. The Internet may help to moderate this trend for a time, but people are becoming much more resistant to providing personal information, unless compensated for their time. This trend is going to change the character of market research.

There is going to be pressure to avoid collecting unnecessary information by using panels and holding individual respondents' answers to earlier surveys on the database. There is also going to be a very significant increase in the use of observation, metering, passive data collection and invisible processing, so that people can provide information without the load of answering questions. There will still need to be lots of surveys; it is hard to see how an observational opinion poll could work, but much more effort is going to be directed at the effective use of existing data, combined with holistic qualitative research.

The critical role of the researcher from the organisation's perspective is evolving from an information technologist into an adviser, but one whose advice is firmly grounded on solid evidence. This is reflected in the fact that in commercial organisations the market research department has evolved into the consumer insight unit.

A key role for the researcher in future will be to ensure that the quality of non-financial information used by the organisation is fit for purpose. This role receives a higher profile in the public sector, think of the debates around the quality of census data in both the USA and UK, but access to high quality information is vital to the success of all large organisations whether operating in the commercial or public sectors.

There will continue to be a requirement for market research, since responding to the needs of the individual is fundamental to the functioning of a democratic society. Well executed market research meets this requirement, but poor market research can be misleading and more damaging than no market research at all.

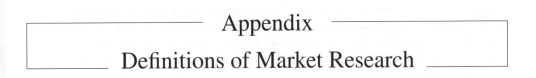

Appendix
Definitions of Market Research

ESOMAR – PROPOSED NEW DEFINITION FOR REVISED ICC/ESOMAR CODE

Market research, which includes social and opinion research, is the systematic gathering and interpretation of information about individuals or organisations using the statistical and analytical methods and techniques of the applied social sciences to gain insight or support decision making. The identity of respondents will not be revealed to the user of the information without explicit consent and no sales approach will be made to them as a direct result of their having provided information.

ESOMAR – CURRENT DEFINITION

Marketing research is a key element within the total field of marketing information. It links the consumer, customer and public to the marketer through information which is used to identify and define marketing opportunities and problems; generate, refine and evaluate marketing actions; improve understanding of marketing as a process and of the ways in which specific marketing activities can be made more effective.

Marketing research specifies the information required to address these issues; designs the method for collecting information; manages and implements the data collection process; analyses the results; and communicates the findings and their implications.

Marketing research includes such activities as quantitative surveys; qualitative research; media and advertising research; business-to-business and industrial research; research among minority and special groups; public opinion surveys; and desk research.

In the context of this Code the term marketing research also covers social research where this uses similar approaches and techniques to study issues not concerned with the marketing of goods and services. The applied social sciences equally depend upon such methods of empirical research to develop and test their underlying hypotheses; and to understand, predict and provide guidance on developments within society for governmental, academic and other purposes.

Marketing research differs from other forms of information gathering in that the identity of the provider of information is not disclosed. Database marketing and any other activity where the names and addresses of the people contacted are to be used for individual selling, promotional, fund-raising or other non-research purposes can under no circumstances be regarded as marketing research since the latter is based on preserving the complete anonymity of the respondent.

AMERICAN MARKETING ASSOCIATION

Marketing research is the function that links the consumer, customer, and public to the marketer through information – information used to identify and define marketing opportunities and problems; generate, refine, and evaluate marketing actions; monitor marketing performance and improve understanding of marketing as a process. Marketing research specifies the information required to address these issues, designs the method for collecting information, manages and implements the data collection process, analyses the results, and communicates the findings and their implications.

MARKET RESEARCH SOCIETY – UK

Research is the collection and analysis of data from a sample or census of individuals or organisations relating to their characteristics, behaviour, attitudes, opinions or possessions. It includes all forms of market, opinion and social research such as consumer and industrial surveys, psychological investigations, qualitative interviews and group discussions, observational, ethnographic, and panel studies.

ACADEMIC DEFINITION – NARESH K. MALHOTRA

Marketing research is the systematic and objective identification, collection, analysis and dissemination of information for the purpose of improving decision making related to the identification and solution of problems and opportunities in marketing.

REFERENCES

Bartels, R. (1976) *The History of Marketing Thought*. Grid.

Biemer, P., Groves, R., Lyberg, L., Mathiowetz, N. and Sudman, S. (2004) *Measurement Errors in Surveys*. John Wiley & Sons, Ltd.

Callingham, M. (2004) *Market Intelligence – How and why organizations use market research*. Kogan Page, Chapter 7 – Qualitative information and its relationship to quantitative information, pp. 98–112.

ESOMAR (2005a) "Global Market Research 2005 – ESOMAR Industry Report".

ESOMAR (2005b) All data in this section comes from "Global Market Research 2005 – ESOMAR Industry Report".

Humby, C., Hunt, T. and Phillips, T. (2006) *Scoring Points: How Tesco Continues to Win Customer Loyalty*. Kogan Page.

IPA Touchpoints: www.ipatouchpoints.co.uk.

ISO 20252:2006 – Market, opinion and social research – vocabulary and service requirements. International Standards Organisation, Geneva.

Malhotra, N.K. (2006) *Marketing Research – An applied orientation*. Prentice Hall.

Mass-Observation (1987) *The Pub and the People*. Ebury Press.

Packard, V. (1957) *The Hidden Persuaders*. Random House Inc.

Professional Standards, Codes and Guidelines: www.esomar.org.

Project Apollo: www.project-apollo.com.

Rowntree, S. (2000) *Poverty: A Study of Town Life*. Centennial edition. Bristol: The Policy Press.

van Hamersveld and Smith, D. (2003) *Responding to clients' changing market research needs: the road map for a successful future*. Research World, October 2003, ESOMAR.

3

Data Collection: Key Stone and Cornerstones

John Kelly

He who has not laid his foundations may be able, with great ability, to lay them afterwards, but they will be laid with trouble to the architect and danger to the building.

Machiavelli

INTRODUCTION

In this chapter, the fundamental importance of the data collection process to the efficacy of market research will be discussed. Whilst a whole range of data collection techniques have evolved over the years in response to client requirements and developments in communications and technology, this chapter will mainly focus on those that are generally used in ad hoc market research. The chapter will look at: the role of data collection per se, various types of data collection, and the techniques that are used, with specific reference to the international research context. In addition, reference will be made to the components of the research process that have an impact upon data collection, such as sampling and questionnaire design, and also those that follow the data collection phase to convert raw data into information: coding, data processing, etc. It is the intention to provide an overall background to the data collection function and to provide some insights into the key components that will allow the researcher to deliver data of whatever form that will facilitate the transformation from data to information to insights.

Building Block of the MR Process

We have seen in the earlier chapters the vital importance of market research to decision-making in business, industry, government and society. Naturally, for market research to be able to play this pivotal role it must be based upon the surest foundations.

It is, without doubt, acknowledged that market research can only be truly effective where the objectives of any project or programme of research are clearly understood by all parties. However, once this has been established, perhaps the next fundamental element is the existence of a cost effective, efficient and robust data collection stage. The use of the word "robust" might appear incongruous, given that in some cases we may be talking about research that does not rely upon a quantitative approach, rather upon other forms of data collection which – although not necessarily featuring the collection of vast arrays of data – can still, with the appropriate methodology, provide data and thus information and insights that will bear rigorous scrutiny.

Market Research Handbook, 5th Edition. Edited by M. van Hamersveld and C. de Bont.
© 2007 John Wiley & Sons, Ltd.

There is both a potential dilemma but also a positive feature within the research process, given that in some instances there may well be no absolute right way to satisfy stated objectives. However, the beauty and utility of market research takes this apparent failing and turns it into a positive benefit: this is where the innovation and flexibility of the market research industry and its practitioners come to the fore. There are, indeed, any number of tried and tested techniques to deliver all forms of data, but that does not stop researchers from developing new measures to satisfy "old" problems or, indeed, from developing new methods for new problems being posed on an almost daily basis. We will see later in this chapter the scope of the data collection methodologies and techniques that have been designed to answer any number of data collection scenarios.

Currently in market research it is possible to categorise the main data collection formats that have evolved over time into five main categories: Face to Face, Mail/Postal, Telephone, Online and Observation. It is true to say that research, wherever it is conducted in the world, uses these main techniques. However, local conditions may mean that variations to a specific technique may be used but, in essence, the data that are delivered by these variations will be of a similar nature.

However, in the new economic climate, market research must deliver quality data and information at a speed that accords with the decision-making cycle demanded by data users, but, as in the past, the emphasis must be on quality, irrespective of the time or cost constraints imposed upon the research process.

This chapter does not seek to provide a complete toolkit on how and when to use specific data collection techniques; this is addressed in other chapters later on. It is intended to be more of a compendium of the many approaches available and the considerations that surround the data collection process.

The Market Research Industry's Response to Changing Requirements

Before embarking upon an explanation of the current data collection facilities available to market researchers, it is worth dwelling for a short time on how the industry got to where it is today in terms of the two major forms of data collection: quantitative and qualitative methods. One immediately obvious conclusion, given the current plethora of methods, is that the market research industry has shown itself to be not only adaptable, but also resilient over time. Market research has had its own version of the Kondratiev wave phenomenon.

Quantitative Research

Looking overall at quantitative data collections methods, which will be discussed in more detail later in this chapter, there are a number of key events that have led the industry from its infancy in the 1930s to the current day. In the early days, data were collected face to face according to scientific strictures, although it is true to say that other more revolutionary methods were also being used: observational techniques in the United Kingdom in the 1930s and 1940s (one of the first UK companies was called "Mass Observation").

However, it was not until the post Second World War era that market research truly started to play a fuller role in the business and economic environment – the establishment of ESOMAR in 1948 is a testament to the increasing influence of the discipline.

No doubt the increase in market research activity was then, as it has been for many years, spurred by manufacturers and others, government included, wishing to get closer to their clients, customers and citizens. Client demands have now moved on from their initial requirements, and now not only require a fulsome array of data, but at a cost-effective price – such that there is demonstrable value for money, given the squeeze on market research budgets. Naturally, data are now to be delivered at speeds that would have been thought unimaginable in the early days of market research and even one or two decades ago.

Without question, the impact of various forms of technology has been manifest in the market research process. This was particularly evident with regard to the increased use of the telephone as a data collection medium for research among consumers which started in the US in the 1970s, and then in Europe and elsewhere in the 1980s and 1990s. The telephone had, it is true, been a more significant data collection medium in the B2B environment for a number of years. However, the key issue in the use of the telephone related to the penetration of telephone ownership and when it would reach a sufficient proportion of the population to provide representative or near representative data. At one point it was felt that the telephone might, as it had in the US, become the dominant means of data collection in the consumer environment throughout the rest of the world. It did, for a time, take share away from other methods but today, despite the establishment of numerous large and small scale call centres is still not dominant in many of the major research markets. What happened was that it developed a revenue stream of its own that added to the overall turnover of the research industry. Generally researchers realised that it was not the panacea that it had been made out to be, and that it had a role to play in many research circumstances, but not in others.

There are some parallels here with the way that the Internet has come to be used in market research. However, it is likely that, for various reasons, the Internet will become the dominant means of data collection in many countries if the current increase in its usage continues apace. That is not to say other means of collecting data will be discarded, rather they will be used when the online space does not provide the depth of data required for a specific research problem.

The way that market research has developed over the last number of years in response to client demands and technological advances has led to a degree of divergence in the data collection methods used when addressing audiences in the consumer (B2C) environment and business/commercial (B2B) environment. It is possible to say in a general statement that B2B audiences are more often addressed using technological means: telephone and online ap-proaches. In many major markets, however, the majority of B2C respondents are still contacted and interviewed using face to face methods, though all methods of quantitative data collection are used, when appropriate, for both sectors.

It would not be possible to leave any overall discussion of quantitative data collection methods without re-affirming an earlier statement that the Internet is likely to become the dominant data collection method in the future. Indeed, evidence in the last five years in the US and other markets, where the Internet share of data collection continues apace, would suggest that the day of Internet domination in data collection is nearer at hand than many may realise.

Qualitative Data Collection

As with quantitative data collection, the qualitative discipline has seen significant changes over time – probably at a slower rate than in the quantitative arena.

The methods used now include projective techniques of all forms, brainstorming sessions, etc but probably the most significant advance has been in the provision of viewing facilities that allow non-participants to view proceedings without impinging upon the group structure and dynamic, but which enable interaction with moderators should the need arise. Focus group facilities are now available in most markets throughout the world.

Another development in qualitative research could be labelled "In with the *old*" as they are adaptations of old methodologies, some now enhanced through technology e.g. Ethnography, Semiotics, etc. Some of these techniques, e.g. ethnography, can actually straddle the line between qualitative and quantitative methods, but are none the less effective. Each of these approaches and others are discussed in more detail later in this volume.

Globalisation

It would be impossible to talk about any changes in the use of data collection methods without acknowledging the impact that globalisation of trade has had upon economies, societies and thus market research.

End users of data, who gather data from a number of worldwide markets and thus provide information for consistent marketing and other business strategies, wish to ensure that any data collected are, as far as possible, comparable: this has led to a commonality approach throughout the world with modifications in some markets to account for prevailing conditions.

There is a discussion later in this chapter of data collection developments in selected regions in the world.

TYPES OF DATA COLLECTION

There are a myriad of ways in which data can be collected to provide input to the market research process, but they do essentially divide into two distinct types: Primary data collection methods and Secondary methods.

Secondary Data Collection (Also Known as Desk Research)

Although labelled as secondary, this method is, more often that not, undertaken prior to the commencement or during the initial stages of a market research exercise. In essence, the activity involves consulting any existing data or other sources of information that might be pertinent to the subject of research.

Secondary Data Sources

As with many other activities in business and society today, the existence of the worldwide web has revolutionised the way in which secondary data can be and are collected. The emergence of a variety of search engines and the pre-eminence of brands such as Google has made the task of collecting secondary data that much easier.

Indeed, it might be suggested that the Internet now provides access to untold information and the key, in secondary data searches in the modern era, is to determine which data are useful and usable and will inform the current project, and which should be discarded, ignored or treated as "good to know". This is quite a contrast to the lot of a secondary researcher of even a few years ago, when there was a paucity of available data and they would have had to consult a variety of published resources. The volume of available data in the public domain could also be limited on particular subjects.

The availability of seemingly untold data on the Internet need not be as daunting as it might seem, as there are now a variety of specialist secondary data search companies who will, at relatively reasonable rates, undertake specific searches to satisfy almost any requirement.

There are, for those who may wish to undertake these searches on a "Do-it-yourself" basis, any number of portals that can be visited. These portals and individual websites will allow access to Government statistics, company reports and ranges of useful sites about population, usage statistics, etc. Indeed, the volume and value of these secondary data that are available should not be underestimated by researchers as they can add value both at the planning, data collection and analysis stages of projects.

Data Mining

Although the Internet does provide unrivalled access to secondary data sources, it is possible for market researchers to derive additional data from previously existing data sources that have either been constructed as part of a market research exercise, or are in the form of extant databases that are either proprietary or in the public domain.

Data mining is the process which involves sorting through large amounts of data and picking out relevant information, generally in the form of patterns, etc. It is a relatively new discipline but applies many older computational techniques from statistics, information retrieval, machine learning and pattern recognition. It has become a more prominent secondary data approach because of the increased power that the new generations of computers afford.

Data mining has been defined as "the nontrivial extraction of implicit, previously unknown, and potentially useful information from data and the science of extracting useful information from large data sets or databases".

Data mining relies to a great extent on "Metadata", or summary data that can be used to describe or search a given set of data. These metadata are often expressed in a condensed data mineable format, or one that facilitates the practice of data mining.

Although the term "data mining" is usually used in relation to analysis of data it is, like "artificial intelligence", an umbrella term with varied meanings in a wide range of contexts. It differs from traditional data analysis because it is not based or focused on preconceived existing models.

A subsequent chapter in this volume goes into the subject of data mining in more detail.

Primary Data Collection

In the simplest sense, primary data refers to data that have been gathered for a specific investigation or task, as opposed to secondary data which are already in existence and can be found as part of a data search exercise. The value of primary data is in its newness and freshness and the fact that it has, for the most part, been collected with the intention of answering a specific question or questions: will represent a set of data that was not previously available to the researcher.

Quantitative and Qualitative data collection comprise the two main disciplines that deliver primary data in market research. Primary data collection involves collecting data from the general public, consumers, those in business, etc., as opposed to consulting secondary data sources. All forms of data collection can be used to furnish data in a market research study.

Quantitative Research

Quantitative research is numerically oriented, requires significant attention to the measurement of market phenomena and involves statistical analysis. Quantitative data collection is generally evaluative and should have a degree of statistical reliability attached to it.

It will involve contacting and interviewing a large sample, however defined, that will be representative of the target population that it is to replicate. However, in some instances a sample may be skewed or biased for a particular reason.

The main rule with quantitative research is that every respondent is asked the same series of questions.

Quantitative surveys can be conducted by using post (self-completion), face-to-face (in-street or in-home), telephone, email or web techniques.

Quantitative data collection can be used for the largest range of data collection applications, some of which will include:

Data Describing Markets and Their Trends

- Usage and attitude surveys
- Market sizing
- Market segmentations
- Diary-based projects
- Tracking studies (with the same respondents over time if desired)

As Part of the Concept/Product Development Process

- Concept testing
- Product testing

Providing Consumer Insight

- Brand profiling
- Customer satisfaction
- Customer relationship management

Qualitative Research

Qualitative research provides an understanding of how or why things are as they are. It will provide impressions, views, theories, responses to proposed concepts, products, advertising, etc. It can be exploratory in nature and can often be used as the precursor to a quantitative data collection phase, helping to determine what should be quantified. Compared to quantitative methods, it usually involves a small number of respondents. Unlike quantitative research there is no fixed set of questions but, instead, a topic guide (or discussion guide) is used to explore various issues in-depth. The discussion between the interviewer or moderator and the respondent is largely determined by the respondent's own thoughts and feelings.

As with quantitative techniques, there are also various types of qualitative methodologies. Research of this sort is mostly done face-to-face, although there have been "on-line" groups using the Internet or the telephone to conduct depth interviews. Perhaps the best-known and most used technique is the focus group or group discussion. These are usually made up of a small number of targeted respondents, a research moderator whose role is to ask the required questions, draw out answers, and encourage discussion, and an observation area, usually behind one way mirrors with video and/or audio taping facilities.

In addition, qualitative research can also be conducted on a "one on one" basis, i.e. an in-depth interview with a trained executive interviewer and one respondent, a paired depth (two respondents), a triad (three respondents) and a mini group discussion (four to five respondents).

Discussion of the Main Quantitative Data Collection Methods

Quantitative data collection may be characterised into a number of separate activities:

- **Ad hoc or custom data collection** – to answer a specific research question.
- **Continuous data collection** – to collect data on a continuous basis either as part of a tracking study, omnibus study, consumer panel or other means. These data may be elicited, as in the case of tracking studies and omnibuses, from different respondents for each "wave" or from the same panel of respondents over time.

A more detailed discussion of the individual methods, which can be used in all research environments for B2C and B2B (a specific chapter devoted to research in B2B environment appears later), follows:

Personal Interviewing (PAPI/CAPI)

In this form of data collection, the interviewer generally contacts and then interviews the respondent face-to-face. It is the most traditional form of interviewing. Personal interviews can take place in almost any environment, but are typically undertaken in the home, at a mall or other central location, on the street, outside a venue or polling place, etc. They can be recorded on paper (PAPI), be computer assisted (CAPI) or collected using other hand held devices (PDAs).

Main Advantages

- A very flexible approach.
- Does not necessarily rely upon the availability of sampling frames.
- Provides the respondent with the ability to see any selection and variety of stimuli whether these are related to products, concepts, advertising, etc.
- Respondents can feel/taste/test products in a controlled environment.
- Interviewers can contact and interview respondents while they are undertaking or just have undertaken a specific activity or in a specific location: after shopping, at an entertainment venue, etc.
- Interviewers are able, by establishing rapport, to achieve longer interviews than with non face to face methods.
- Provides the opportunity to include a variety of questioning approaches including open-ended questions as the interviewer can undertake probing according to visual clues as well as verbal.
- The interviewer can pick up on non-verbal clues and provide these as additional, if anecdotal, data.

Main Disadvantages

- Personal interviews can cost more per interview than other methods.
- May involve a complex sampling and contacting procedure.
- Depending upon the data collection medium – paper, etc. may involve a number of administrative stages that can add to the overall timescale of a project.

Telephone Surveys (CATI)

- Has been the most popular method in the B2B environment for many years, and has been an effective method for B2C research in the last two decades, specifically with the establishment of dedicated "call centres".

Main Advantages

- People can usually be contacted faster and more easily over the telephone than with other methods.
- The use of a CATI (computer-assisted telephone interviewing) system provides a number of benefits:
  - Short time delay between interviewing and delivery of results.
  - Complete standardisation of the interview content.
  - Interview administration is automatically handled (skips, internal consistency, etc.) allowing the interviewer to concentrate on the interview itself.
  - Sample and contacts are provided automatically to the interviewer.
  - Easier to schedule and undertake appointments and any recalls.
- Call centres facilitate the monitoring of interviewer performance on a constant and consistent basis.

Main Disadvantages

- Can be subject to problems of non response as the potential respondent may not immediately recognise that they are being asked to participate in a market research study, and may confuse the approach with those of others who use telephone contacts as a means of sales and marketing.
- The interviewing "window" for a variety of target populations may be limited, e.g. those who are at work.
- Difficult to use stimulus materials as part of the interview process.
- May not be possible to obtain the depth of information required from open-ended.

Mail/Postal Surveys

Advantages

- Among the least expensive of market research data collection methods.
- Can be used when other means of contacting a target population are not possible, e.g. names and addresses of the target population are available, but not telephone numbers or e-mail addresses.
- Can involve the use of stimulus materials.

- Not as intrusive as other data collection methods as respondents can respond at their leisure and when it is convenient to them.

Disadvantages

- Can take longer than other data collection methods.
- May be difficult to obtain responses from less well-educated target populations.
- Additional costs are incurred as a result of a follow-up mailing to improve response rates.
- May need to offer some form of incentive to generate response.
- The initial mail out may need to be extremely large to ensure a reasonable number of returns – this will add to the cost.
- Not necessarily sure that the correct respondent has completed the interview.
- May not be appropriate to collect certain types of data: spontaneous awareness, probed open-ended responses, etc.
- Issues of non-response: information from those who do not respond is often as important, and sometimes more important, than information from those who do.

Computer Direct Interviewing (CASI/CAWI)

With this data collection method, respondents enter responses directly into a computer that has been set up at a specific venue: work places, shopping malls, trade shows, entertainment venue, hospital, health centres, etc. The interview and data storage software may be contained internally on the computer that is in situ as it is for CASI (Computer aided Self-completion Interviewing) or the computer may be linked to a dedicated website where the questionnaire resides and data are stored as in Computer aided Web Interviewing (CAWI).

Irrespective of which of these methods are used, the outward presentation to the respondent is very similar.

Advantages

- Target populations provide answers in the immediate context.
- There is direct data entry.
- Can derive more honest and accurate answers to sensitive questions.
- In employee research there is often a greater willingness to give more honest answers to a computer than to a person or on a self-completion paper questionnaire.
- Can eliminate interviewer bias.
- The flow of the interview is handled by the software.
- Response rates are usually higher – the process is still new enough to encourage respondents to undertake interviews.
- If interviewer recruited, can set quotas.

Disadvantages

- Placement in the chosen location must be carefully considered.
- May not be suitable for certain sections of the target population.
- These are self-selecting respondents.
- Can be open to multiple responses by the same person.

Email Surveys

Using email data collection can be very cost-effective and accomplished in a short space of time. Currently, more people have email than have full Internet access, but this is changing very quickly.

Advantages

- Can be undertaken extremely quickly.
- The vast majority of the cost is taken up with the set-up procedure.
- Both pictures and sound files can be attached, as can other forms of stimuli.
- Can achieve higher response rates than other data collection methods.
- Can be used effectively where faithful representation of the target population will not be a disadvantage to the use of the data collected.

Disadvantages

- Types of questions and, therefore, data that can be collected are limited.
- Depends upon the existence of a suitable sampling frame.
- Little or no control over who is actually responding.
- Must overcome the reticence of people to responding to unsolicited emails.
- Difficult to extrapolate findings to the population as a whole as the available sample may not totally reflect the characteristics of the general population.
- Cannot be used throughout the world.
- As with mail/postal methods there is no control to ensure the "right" person responds.

Internet/Intranet (Web Page) Surveys

Web surveys are rapidly gaining popularity. They have major speed, cost, and flexibility advantages, but also significant sampling limitations and may restrict the groups that can be reached using this technique.

Advantages

- Data collection can be extremely fast. A request inserted on a popular website can gather several thousand responses within a few hours.
- The majority of the cost is associated with the set up of the survey.
- There is no real disadvantage whether collecting data from a large or a small sample.
- Picture and sound files can be used.
- Complex questionnaires with rotations, randomisations, etc., can be completed.
- Can take advantage of all the features associated with text formatting including colours, fonts and other formatting options.
- Can deliver data on sensitive subjects.
- Can generate fuller responses to open-ended compared to other self-administered methods.

Disadvantages

- May not be able to reflect the population as a whole, certainly true for the B2C environment.
- No guarantee that respondents will complete the interview.

- Have to ensure that a respondent can only complete the questionnaire once.
- No guarantee that the respondent is who they say they are.

Omnibus

Omnibuses have been used as a means of data collection for over 40 years. An omnibus survey is a method of collecting quantitative data on a wide variety of subjects as a part of the same interview. Usually, a number of clients will request proprietary data from the survey, while sharing the common demographic data collected from each respondent.

The advantages to client include cost savings (because the sampling and screening costs are shared across multiple clients) and timeliness (because omnibus samples are large and interviewing is ongoing and are reported relatively quickly).

An omnibus survey generally uses a stratified sample and can be conducted either by mail, telephone, or Internet.

They can be used for a number of research tasks, from exploratory research to continuous tracking among a particular population. They are particularly useful when undertaking incidence checks and gathering data from lower-incidence groups.

Consumer Panels

Large scale panels of consumers that are used to track and report on various behaviours, e.g. TV viewing, Radio listening, Consumer Goods purchasing, etc.

Retail Audits

Retail audits involve the collection of various observations at the point of sale in retail environments, e.g. measurements of sales volumes/values, market share, price points, number of facings, shelf position, etc., and can be used to derive a variety of metrics related to consumer purchasing activity.

The retail audit is based upon samples of retail outlets which are to represent the importance of various categories of outlets. A consumer panel will aim to provide representation either at a household or individual level.

Data for either of these data collection methods are now collected electronically. In the case of the retail environment this has been facilitated by EPOS (Electronic Point of Sale) and AN (Article Numbering), and in the household environment by means of electronic data collection.

Retail and consumer panels provide highly accurate information down to the level of individual items. These data allows decision-makers to analyse their product structure, pricing and distribution policy, and their position in relation to competitors.

Internet Access Panels

With CATI response rates dropping and Internet technology becoming more widely used, online access panels are a major growth area in the market research world. It is relatively easy to start building an online panel, and many agencies are doing this. They can provide an efficient means of selecting and interviewing representative samples of target populations which will generate greater confidence in the accuracy of any data collected.

In the more traditional methods of data collection, "broad" quotas such as age, gender, or socio-economic groupings, etc., are used in an attempt to provide representative samples. An access panel can deliver very tightly targeted samples through the use of known interlocking quotas.

Where matched samples are required in the research process, access panels can deliver a high level of accuracy, as it is possible to selected identically matched groups of households or individuals where there can be confidence in the comparability of the cells. This is facilitated because, as part of the sign-up procedure, panelists supply details about the demographics of all individuals in the household, as well as a range of other ownership and usage information.

At the highest level, Access Panels can be representative of the national population. Access Panels can offer a good solution as they can avoid the costs associated with random recruitment and the unpredictability of other databases. This is particularly true where respondents have completed a double opt-in process, thus agreeing to be part of the panel set up for market research purposes and agreeing to participate in market research.

The effectiveness of the recruitment and management of a good access panel is indicated by the response rates that are achieved. The response rate reflects the number of people actually completing the survey as a percentage of those who were originally approached.

Undoubtedly, strict panel management and developing a relationship with panel members will generate greater loyalty and a willingness to complete surveys when asked.

Qualitative Methods

It is not the intention here to provide a full explanation of focus or discussion groups, brainstorming sessions or one on one depth interviews, as they will be readily known to all who are involved in the market research process. What will be provided is a brief description of some of the techniques that are used as part of the qualitative data collection process.

What might be useful, however, would be a short summary of the advantages and disadvantages of each method.

However, it is worth bearing in mind that initially these methods were adopted as means of exploring motivations, attitudes, etc., and to derive hypotheses that could be subjected to more rigorous validation through any of the number of forms of quantitative research. Often, the true value of the qualitative process is only demonstrated when it is followed by a robust phase of quantitative research. If there is no follow up, "results" from qualitative approaches can be subject to discussion and mixed interpretation – this does not help end clients, researchers or, indeed, the process itself.

Focus Groups/Group Discussions

Although these terms are now used to describe the same activity, they did, in fact, spring from separate beginnings. The Focus Group was originally a US-based research method involving, as it does, more of a leaning towards measurement and a degree of quantification within the qualitative environment, whereas the Group Discussion was essentially a European research tool which relies upon investigation in depth of motivations, behaviours, etc. However, Focus Group has now become the more common descriptor.

Main Advantages

- The ability to discuss per se.
- Interaction between group members to develop ideas, etc.
- Participants feel less "exposed/threatened" than in a one to one environment.
- Can cover a range of subjects in a relatively short time frame.
- Can view any form of stimuli.
- Ability to use projective techniques.
- Client can observe the proceedings.

Main Disadvantages

- Potential for domination of the group by a few members.
- Not always possible to discuss "sensitive" subject matter.
- Group "view" may override or suppress individual attitudes, etc.
- Spontaneous awareness and views cannot be captured.
- Over-hyping of views/feelings to fit in with others.

Depth Interviews

These can take a number of forms (Mini, Semi-Structured, Telephone, etc.) and may involve more than one individual (Paired, Peer Group, Partner, etc.).

Main Advantages

- Can explore individual behaviour and attitudes in great detail.
- The views and beliefs of the respondent can be assessed free from pressure of other participants.
- Ability to discuss "sensitive" subject matter.
- Can be easier to recruit than would a group.
- Possible to modify topics as interviews progress.

Main Disadvantages

- Time consuming compared to groups.
- Can be costly.

Some Projective Techniques

These are indirect techniques in the form of unstructured prompts or stimuli that encourage and help respondents to project and give voice to their underlying motivations, beliefs, attitudes, or feelings.

Some examples of projective techniques include:

Word association – respondents are asked to say the first word that comes to mind after hearing a word or phrase. This will often take the form of a disguised approach as not all of the words used as prompts may be "test" words. Word association is useful in testing brand names – variants include chain word association and controlled word association.

Sentence completion – respondents are given incomplete sentences and asked to complete them.

Story completion – respondents are given part of a story and are asked to complete the story.

Cartoon tests – pictures of cartoon characters are shown in specific situations and with dialogue balloons – one of the dialogue balloons is empty and the respondent is asked to insert the words the character is saying.

Thematic tests – respondents are shown a picture (or series of pictures) and asked to make up a story about the picture(s).

Role playing – respondents are asked to play the role of someone else – researchers assume that subjects will project their own feelings or behaviours into the role.

Third-person technique – a verbal or visual representation of an individual and his/her situation is presented to the respondent – the respondent is asked to relate the attitudes or feelings of that person.

Collages – respondents are asked to use a variety of pictures/images (cut from newspapers, magazines, etc.) to construct a collage to express their feelings.

Brand personification – respondents are asked to image what sort of person (could also be a car, animal, etc.) a brand might be.

Online Qualitative Research

It is worth noting here that some qualitative techniques have migrated in some form to the online environment.

Some Other Techniques

Mystery Shopping/Travelling, etc.

This form of data collection is generally undertaken as an independent assessment of service or performance standards (Airlines, Hotels, Food outlets, Banks, Car dealers, Government Departments, etc.).

The skill in this discipline lies in the recruitment and use of a panel of "shoppers" that will be appropriate to the specific task to be undertaken. In the early days companies tried to use existing fieldforces for this task with less than satisfactory results.

Observation

Observation as a data collection technique has grown in usage in the last few years although, as indicated earlier, it was one of the early methods used in market research.

The main advantage of observational research is flexibility as researchers can, if they choose, change approach as needed. It also has the significant advantage that it measures behaviour directly, as it happens, unlike other forms of research that offer reports of behaviour or intentions. One of the main disadvantages of the technique is that it may be difficult to extrapolate any data that are found.

Generally, there are three types of observational research:

Covert observational research – Here the data collector does not identify themselves to the subject: data are collected undetected, or from a distance. This method has the advantage that the respondent's behaviour will not be contaminated by the presence of the researcher. However, there can be some ethical issues with the deceit involved in this approach.

Overt observational research – The data collectors identify themselves and explain the purpose of their observations. Whilst this approach is undoubtedly ethically sound, some feel that respondents may tend to modify their behaviour when they know they are being watched and portray an "ideal" rather than their true self.

Researcher participation – The researcher participates in what they are observing – this may help them to obtain a finer appreciation of the activity under observation, but there are concerns that as a result of participation a degree of objectivity is lost.

The most frequently used types of observational techniques are:

Personal Observation

- Products in use
- Influence of packaging
- The purchase decision
- Social interaction

Mechanical Observation

- Eye-tracking
- On-site cameras in stores
- Measuring television watching behaviour

Audits

- Retail audits

Tachistoscopes (T-scopes)

These are a mechanical means of projecting images for very brief periods of time.

T-scopes continue to be used in market research, where they are generally used to compare the visual impact, or memorability of marketing materials or packaging designs. T-scopes used for this purpose are typically still based around slide projectors rather than computer monitors because they can display a truer image and have the facility to display large or life-size images.

Eye Tracking/Scanning

The most widely used current designs are video-based eye trackers. A camera focuses on one or both eyes and records their movement as the viewer looks at the target stimulus.

Two general types of eye tracking techniques are used, Bright Pupil and Dark Pupil.

Eye tracking setups vary greatly; some are head-mounted, some require the head to be stable (for example, with a chin rest), and some function remotely and automatically track the head during motion.

Brain Science/Semiotics/Ethnography

These are techniques that have been available to researchers for some time, but are now coming to the fore. Each of these is discussed in more detail later in this volume.

Practical Examples

The research industry has, over the years, developed dedicated tools to answer questions raised by particular industry sectors or marketing and advertising activities. These will include pre- and post-testing of advertising, collection of data in the retail environment, product testing and pricing studies, etc. Whilst data collection methods for all of these activities are conducted by the widest range of supplier companies in the research industry, they use their own variations of the techniques and their own associated vocabulary. Indeed, there is no agreed industry standard for either terminology or prescription of techniques to be followed. However, practical examples of many of these techniques will be found later in this volume.

DIFFERENCES IN DATA COLLECTION APPROACHES BY REGION/COUNTRY

Cultural Considerations in International Research

When undertaking multi-country research, the influence of local culture and practice must be factored into any analysis and interpretation of resultant data. Generally, these differences are exhibited in the consumer research environment more so than in the business sector, although some will apply here as well.

The local differences that will require consideration are the impact or influence of language, faith/religion and consumption and behaviour patterns.

Language

The major consideration is to ensure that all significant languages in a country or region of a country are covered, and where countries share a common language that local idiom and usage are observed.

Faith/Religion

Researchers must always ensure that they show the utmost respect for religious observances in any country under research.

Consumption and Behaviour Patterns

These can vary from country to country, and it is essential for researchers to ensure that any survey documentation allows respondents to answer in the manner most appropriate to their behaviour.

Other Cultural Considerations

Researchers should be aware of the desire to please on the part of some respondents in certain countries. This may lead to a tendency to select "positive" answers on agreement scales and similar questions.

Respondents can sometimes give answers they feel will reflect well on them; there is sometimes a desire not to lose "face" in front of an interviewer.

Some respondents may exhibit a general tendency to exaggerate answers. In other instances, if respondents are unsure of the status of the survey, they may give what they perceive to be "correct" answers rather than what they really believe. This may continue to be the case even though the questions are not overtly political and deal purely with commercial products or services.

Methods do Travel

Whilst is possible to conduct research in almost any country in the world using almost any data collection method or technique, it is advisable for researchers to ensure that any interpretations made as a result of consulting the data are done with the knowledge of local idiom and custom. It should be borne in mind that employing the same techniques may not always deliver exactly the same form of data.

Description of Data Collection Activities and Trends in Selected Regions

General Environment

International and local researchers are now fortunate, unlike their predecessors, that they are able to employ the widest range of research techniques, both qualitative and quantitative, in almost all countries where research is conducted.

Figure 3.1 shows the proportions of the worldwide spend in 2005 on market research accounted for by each data collection method. What will be immediately obvious is the way in which online data collection is continuing to increase in volume and also to take "share" from other methods.

Indeed, if we look at Figure 3.2 we can see that online data collection in Japan is now rivalling face to face as the dominant data collection method: face to face was, by far, the favoured method in Japan. Looking at Australia we can see that online is now the most popular data collection method, having eclipsed the telephone – the previous "market leader". It is possible to surmise that, in the not too distant future, online data collection will be the dominant medium in most major markets.

Current Data Collection Methods and Trends for Certain Regions

Africa

The level of development in most African countries is very low and means that, for many countries, the research industry is still in its infancy. The advent of information technology

Research methods	Spend by research method (%)	Variance 2004 (%)
Quantitative	83	−1
Postal	6	−1
Telephone	21	+1
Face-to-face	24	−7
Online	13	+2
Other quantitative	19	+4
Qualitative	14	−1
Group discussions	9	−2
In-depth interviews	4	+1
Other qualitative	1	0
Other	3	

Figure 3.1

Japan

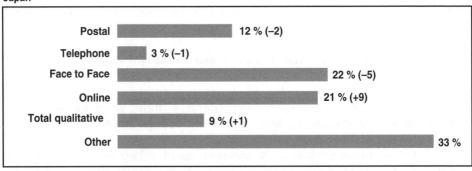

Australia

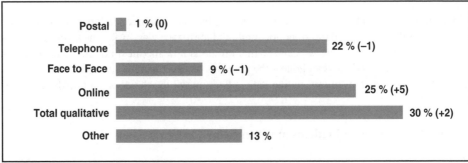

Changes from 2004 are provided between brackets

Figure 3.2

and communication is fast catching up the rest of the world in certain countries: South Africa, Nigeria, Egypt and Kenya. The speed of development in other countries is still some way behind. Overall the information and communications infrastructure is being built throughout the continent, albeit at a slow pace.

Political pressures can create difficulties for the research community in a number of countries, as do the high levels of inflation in others, making the cost of most things prohibitive.

Culture is also an issue in certain countries, where national characteristics can lead to the research process being viewed, at best, with suspicion even in some of the more developed markets.

For quantitative research, paper-based face to face research is the dominant quantitative methodology, although the telephone can be used for the B2B community. However, it is possible to undertake most forms of data collection.

All forms of qualitative methods can be undertaken, but focus group viewing facilities are not always available. One method that is starting to gain in popularity is Ethnography.

Asia Pacific

Quantitative Methods

With the exception of Japan, the market research industry in Asia is highly globalised – the top 10 global market research companies generally account for 50 %+ of each country's market. As a consequence, local market research companies tend to follow the established pattern set by the global companies. This means that Retail Audits, Consumer Panels, specialist business solutions and other techniques are much the same in Asia as in the rest of the world. In general, it is in the speed of implementation of new techniques and methodologies where the region may fall behind.

The quantitative share and absolute value is increasing due to a move towards syndication, large scale tracking and consumer panels. Syndication has always been available particularly in Retail Audits and Media Measurement.

Most Asian countries have now switched from manual TAM diaries to people meters. There is also a change in the format of consumer panels, which have switched from manual diaries to home scanning as a result of the improvement in bar codes across Asia.

In most of Asia, consumer data collection has been accomplished using in-home interviews. CATI, as in other regions, is the key medium for B2B interviews in most countries. It is also now being used more for consumer interviews in the past few years.

Managed Access Panels are taking over from CATI in a number of key markets: Japan, Australia, New Zealand, Singapore, Hong Kong, Korea and Taiwan. This is an area where leading Asia Pacific countries are moving faster than those in Europe. Even in China, Internet interviewing for consumers will overtake CATI as the method of choice – 100 m Chinese can be connected online: the 100m that advertisers/marketers are targeting.

Whilst more research in Japan, Australia, Hong Kong and Korea is probably moving to online data collection, the rest of Asia is likely to be much slower to adopt online consumer interviewing.

In Japan there has been a large increase in research recently, and the use of very sophisticated mobile phones that can read bar codes makes interviewing easier for people "on the go".

Central location interviewing has always been popular for concept/product and ad tests, and this method is also moving towards online panels very rapidly in the more advanced Asian countries – offering in particular speed rather than merely cost advantages.

Centralising CATI interviewing for B2B is another trend. These hubs are more likely to be found in Hong Kong or Singapore, where a wide range of nationalities are found, as calls can be made into 10–15 countries. However consumer CATI interviewing is still conducted locally in most cases.

Trends in Qualitative Research

There has been a move away from pan-regional studies to those involving individual countries. This was helped by the strengthening of local market research facilities and the development of small boutique agencies offering research at lower cost. This led to a reaction from mainline agencies who began to introduce less common techniques to provide differentiation and to add value to the qualitative offering.

These tools included: projective techniques, ethnography, accompanied shopping, NLP, semiotics, etc. – all offering ways of studying the Asian consumer with more in depth dimensions. This trend has waned as most of these techniques were easily copied and perhaps did not deliver substantially enhanced added value.

Online groups have been conducted sporadically but there does not seem to be a discernible trend in this direction yet.

Europe

Quantitative Methods

As with other regions, online methods are starting to account for a greater proportion of research undertaken.

Qualitative Techniques

Ethnography is undergoing a renaissance in Europe at the moment, although not generally in any new way. In fact, customer immersion methodologies of all types are gaining in usage and are being used to describe almost anything that involves an in-home or in-situ visit, where an interview is undertaken and video recorded. This is a slightly different usage of an old technique, as ethnography has at its core the extended observation, in natural habitat, of the respondents/subjects, rather than simply visiting and filming an interview. This is probably because, just like qualitative research in the 1970s and 1980s, bigger/mainstream agencies were seeking to maintain a competitive edge and invest in a methodology that was more often practised by smaller specialist agencies.

The range of consumer immersion techniques continues to grow, including:

- in-home observation;
- accompanied shopping, etc.;
- diaries;
- online (virtual) ethnography.

Semiotics is currently another "hot" topic as is **NLP (Neuro Linguistic Programming)**, though again, it is not a new technique and first emerged in the early 1980s in UK research.

There is also a strong movement towards online groups, blogging, web-based qualitative information/research gathering.

Middle East/North Africa

The market research industry in most of the Middle East and North Africa is relatively young – Egypt is the leading country in terms of market research.

In Saudi Arabia (KSA) and United Arab Emirates (UAE), market research activity has been increasing rapidly since the 1980s as a result of the evolution in the clientside from being purely product driven towards being marketing driven. However even now, the MR industry faces many constraints:

- Insufficient co-operation from Government in terms of obtaining legal licenses and permissions, extensive bureaucracy and a lack of published statistical information, etc., including Census data.
- Difficulties in securing respondent participation: distrustful of the process and cultural inhibitions.

USA

The USA continues to lead the way in the adoption of online data collection methods as confirmed by the prominent industry newsletter *Inside Research* which suggests that just under 30 % of survey research volume is now collected online.

Apart from the seemingly all-pervasive use of the Internet, there is a move to undertake passive measures not only to collect data in the media sector using PPM (portable People Meter) technology, but also online.

In the qualitative arena the use of ethnography is gaining significantly in popularity.

Central America

Quantitative Methods

The preferred quantitative method in the region continues to be door to door, although the telephone is now starting to become a viable option for research: CATI studies are particularly popular in Mexico, which is the most developed market in the region.

Qualitative Methods

For qualitative research, focus groups are still the most common qualitative method by far in Mexico, Central America and the Caribbean. There has been some use of ethnography but this is relatively new in the region.

Emerging Trends

Almost all major research firms have offices already in the region, particularly in Mexico and Central America. Consumer panels have been established. Online data collection is still largely in its infancy.

SAMPLING

Once the method of interviewing to be undertaken in quantitative research has been decided, the next decision to take concerns the sample to be interviewed, its size and composition. Sample considerations in qualitative research revolve around a different series of considerations and will not be discussed here.

In general, it is true to say that market researchers will recommend the minimum sample necessary to answer any problem at hand. However, the size of the sample may well be determined not only by the desired precision of any found data, but also by the magnitude of sub-samples that will be required at the analysis stage.

Statisticians in market research are well aware that a small, representative sample will reflect the group from which it is drawn. Indeed, a larger sample per se may not, of itself, provide any greater confidence in data derived as the rate of improvement in the precision decreases as the sample size increases. It is necessary to quadruple a sample size to halve the error associated with it, e.g. increasing a sample from 250 to 1,000 only doubles the precision. Decisions about sample sizes to be used are more often determined by the available budget and any time constraints that may be imposed upon the duration of the research.

It is also worth stating that any sample interviewed as part of a research exercise should be representative – however that is defined – of the population that it is designed to represent. What should be avoided, at all costs, is a biased sample. Bias occurs where the selection of respondents is, in some way, unduly influenced by human choice, or where a sampling frame may not totally encompass the target population or parts of it, or finally, if the correct population cannot be found or refuse to co-operate.

Ultimately, when all relevant considerations have been taken into account, the researcher will be faced with the choice between probabilistic sampling methods (which are mathematically superior) or the more pragmatic non-probability methods. However, both methods do have their place, with more pragmatic methods having come to the fore in the past two decades in response to client demands in terms of budget and speed of response.

Summary of the Main Sampling Methods

Random Sampling

Random, or as it is also known, probability sampling, is a sampling system that affords each member of any specific target population an equal and known probability of selection.

Systematic Sampling

Systematic sampling is a modification of random sampling. In systematic sampling researchers calculate the desired sampling fraction, and, thereafter, go through the available sampling frame selecting every nth contact to arrive at the desired number of contacts. It is true, as far as purists are concerned, that this method does not provide a true random sample. The sampling frame may have been constructed using some form of classification and this could affect the chance of any member of being selected once the sampling fraction is calculated. However, generally all practitioners would treat a systematic sample as though it were a true random sample.

Stratified Sampling

It is possible using stratification as part of the sampling method to improve the precision and efficiency without the need to increase a sample size.

Stratification does not necessarily mean that the principles of randomness are abandoned: what is involved, before sample selection takes place, is the classification of the target population into a number of strata using known population characteristics, e.g. age, gender, etc. It is also possible to undertake stratification after the selection of individuals. Random stratified sampling is more precise and more convenient than simple random sampling.

When stratified sampling designs are to be used, there are number of questions to be asked of the sampling regime, of which the three key questions are:

(a) On what basis is the stratification undertaken i.e. what are the characteristics that are used to subdivide the universe/population into strata? It is desirable to construct strata such that any sampling units within strata are as similar as possible.
(b) How many strata should be constructed and what stratum boundaries should be used? Generally, the advice is that as many strata as possible should be used.
(c) What sample sizes are required within each stratum? This will generally be determined by non-statistical concerns: budget, time constraints, etc.

Cluster Sampling

This is the process of sampling complete groups or units rather than the target population as a whole. One of the benefits of cluster sampling is that data collection can be completed within a smaller budget than would be the case if a true random sample were undertaken, thus providing reliability of data for a reduced cost: this can go some way to countering the argument of reduced statistical efficiency.

Multistage Sampling

This is a complex form of cluster sampling. It involves stratifying by sub-groups within the overall target and then, within those sub-groups, sampling using another known criteria. The technique is used frequently when a complete list of all members of the population does not exist.

Probability-Proportional-to-Size Sampling

This is a type of multistage cluster sampling. In this method, the probability of selecting an element in any given cluster varies inversely with the size of the cluster.

Quota Sampling

At its simplest, quota sampling is, indeed, a method of stratified sampling, but one in which the selection within strata is non-random. Interviewers are provided with specific quotas of respondents to interview without having to approach them according to contacting procedures that follow random means.

In quota sampling, individual samples are designated for specific sub-groups. Attempts are made to set overall quotas that ensure that the sample reflects, with relative accuracy, relevant sub-groups in the target population.

Quota v Random Sampling

There has been often heated debate about the advantages and disadvantages of quota sampling when compared to probability sampling. Some practitioners still maintain that the potential unreliability of the quota sample method and the possibility for bias make it a very poor substitute for methods that rely on a random approach.

Others, whilst admitting that it is theoretically not as rigorous as probability sampling, maintain that it can be used with safety in certain circumstances, especially where adequate safeguards can be imposed. In these instances, where "reliability" can be attached, quota sampling can serve a valuable purpose and deliver data at a lower cost than that associated with probability sampling.

The researcher's art is founded upon delivering data at a reasonable cost with the smallest acceptable sample, which is where quota sampling methods can come to the fore. There is, as has been recognised from the very birth of research, a desire on the part of researchers not to over-engineer samples and increase cost for the sake of it.

Main Arguments Against Quota Sampling

It is generally thought that it is difficult, if not impossible, to provide estimates of sampling errors with quota sampling because of the lack of randomness. There is a school of thought that believes that not being able to estimate errors is not an issue as these are relatively small compared to other errors and biases that are associated with most surveys.

Sample selection is left too much at the discretion of the interviewer and it is not always possible to exert as much control over the fieldwork process as it takes place – although this can be remedied through validation and back-checking.

Main Arguments for Quota Sampling

In most cases, quota sampling can provide a more cost-effective research solution, enhanced by the fact that quota sampling approaches are easier to administer and implement in the field.

Unlike other probabilistic methods, quota samples can be achieved without the need to use or consult sampling frames

PROCESS/PRACTICALITIES ASSOCIATED WITH THE DATA COLLECTION FUNCTION

Questionnaire Design

The fundamental role of data collection to the market research process is acknowledged, but it can only be accomplished to any satisfactory degree and furnish data that are useable if the vehicles that are used to collect data are fit for their tasks.

This vital aspect of the research process is so broad in scope that there are numerous volumes devoted to this alone. It is therefore the intention in this chapter to concentrate upon the key considerations to be borne in mind.

Whilst data can be collected in the quantitative and qualitative environment, the need for the effective design of data collection instruments is more acute when collecting quantitative data and, for that reason, the remainder of this sub-section will concentrate upon quantitative data collection in its various forms.

General Considerations

It is of paramount importance that data collection vehicles are appropriate for the method of data collection and are mindful of the environment in which data collection will take place – this may well have a bearing upon a respondent in a number of ways, and influence their views on what questions mean and how they should respond to them.

Questionnaire design is a highly skilled craft given that everyone is an expert in asking questions: it happens so frequently in everyday life. Added to this is the fact that errors in questionnaire design cannot always be measured, unlike some of those that may creep inadvertently into the design of a sample. Any bias due to question wording can be potentially greater than those from any other source.

It is all too easy to unwittingly introduce bias as a result of the format and wording, and also the order in which questions appear.

Whilst the questionnaire as the main survey document is typically administered by an interviewer to a respondent, there are others who should be considered when questionnaires are designed – coders, DP departments, etc.

What should always be considered is how a questionnaire can capitalise upon a respondent's willingness to answer questions and allow them to do so.

Questionnaire Design Specifics

The first rule is to design the questionnaire to fit the medium. What will be possible in the face to face environment will not necessarily work with other data collection media: telephone, online, etc. This will be particularly true regarding the use of stimulus materials and in the interactions between interviewer and respondent.

When considerations imposed by the medium have been taken into account, the next stricture that it is wise to observe is to keep the questionnaire as short and as simple as possible. It is a useful exercise for researchers to ask themselves how they will utilise the information collected from each question. If a satisfactory answer is not forthcoming, then there would be a good case to omit the question. Researchers should not give in to the temptation to add a few more questions just because you are doing a questionnaire anyway. It is helpful to classify prospective questions into three groups: must know, useful to know and nice to know. If there are any concerns about the length of a questionnaire then it would be advisable to consider discarding the final group, before compromises are made concerning the other two categories of question.

Generally, the longer the questionnaire the less likely it will be for a respondent to participate in the survey. However, of at least equal importance is the subject matter and question content. A potential respondent is more likely to respond if they have some involvement and interest in the research topic.

A short but informative introduction to the questionnaire will be of immense value to the interviewer and respondent.

Ensure that the questionnaire contains all necessary information for the interviewer so that they are not put in the position where they have to make decisions about what should or should not be asked.

It cannot be stressed enough that perhaps the most important element of the questionnaire is the clear reassurance for the respondent that any responses will not be individually identified, but only combined with many others to form aggregated data. Also, the respondent should be left in no doubt that they are not participating in any form of sales exercise in another guise; and that they will not, as a result of participation, be the subject of any unsolicited subsequent sales activity.

One way to make respondents feel valued is to ask them a question that will interest them, or make a provision for them to express their opinion: they will have answered any number of questions, but may not have been asked the specific questions that they wanted to answer.

It is also dangerous to assume understanding on behalf of the interviewer and respondent – questions must be intelligible to both.

Finally, it will help all concerned if the interview experience can, as far as possible, resemble a "conversation" between the interviewer and the respondent. In this context, the pace and flow of the interview will be of significant aid – and abrupt transitions of subject should be avoided.

Question and Answer Choice Order

Two key considerations are to be observed when resolving question order and answer choices. The order of questions should be such that it encourages respondents to continue with the survey and provides not only a rewarding but enjoyable experience for them. Question order should also recognise the states of mind that the respondent will pass through: from being wary to being interested, to a wish to end the interview as quickly as possible.

The other issue is how the order of questions or the order of answer choices could influence or bias the data that result.

Ideally, initial questions should encourage respondents to continue with the interview and should not be too difficult to answer, as they will help to establish rapport between the interviewer and the respondent.

Whenever possible, it would be advisable to structure the questionnaire so that sensitive or difficult questions are included near the end of the questionnaire, as the rapport that has been built up will make respondents more inclined to answer these questions.

The way in which answer choices are ordered can make individual questions easier or more difficult to answer. It is generally considered good practice, when there is a logical or natural order to answer categories, that it should be used. However, the way in which responses such as "agree-disagree" scales and numerical scales are presented may be dictated by specific circumstances in the questionnaire or survey context. Often, in an attempt to obviate the potential for "order bias" it may be appropriate to rotate the order in which these scales are presented to the respondent. However, there has been lengthy debate about the efficacy of "rotation" which will not be entered into here.

Question order should also be considered so that the respondent is not alerted to information that may be the subject of later questioning, thus depriving the researcher of the ability to obtain spontaneous responses.

Where there is a series or a repeated series of questions that all have the same answer choices, it will help to avoid respondent fatigue and encourage them to consider each statement or attribute on its merits if the answer choices are presented in a different way from time to time.

Some Comments on Question Wording

Questions must make sense for both the interviewer and the respondent: if it helps understanding, use colloquial language.

It will be very difficult to decipher responses, if provided, to a question which is, in reality, two questions in one.

Similarly, ambiguous or imprecise questions or words and vague concepts will make it difficult for respondents to answer.

A sensitive approach must be adopted for any potentially "taboo" or personal subject matter, but with a careful approach these subjects can be covered.

Asking the respondent to indulge in feats of memory will not provide truly valuable data.

Try to avoid wording that favours one answer choice over another; this will also apply to the inclusion of leading questions.

Emotionally charged words can also present problems if not set in the correct context or introduced in such a way that the respondent can see the relevance to the questionnaire.

The use of technical terms and acronyms can be problematic unless the researcher can be confident that respondents will know what they mean, as will the use of unfamiliar words.

Double negatives and other complex questions can also cause confusion.

Generally, the shorter the question, the better the response.

It is often sensible to leave your demographic questions (age, gender, income, education, etc.) until the end of the questionnaire as the interviewer should by this point have built a rapport with the interviewee that will allow honest responses to such personal questions. However, an exception to this general rule occurs where there are demographic questions that help to qualify a contact for inclusion in a survey – these questions must appear as early in the interview as possible.

Questionnaire Pre-Testing/Piloting

The final, and vitally important stage of the questionnaire design procedure is to test a questionnaire with a small number of interviews before it is signed off. Ideally, the test should be with similar respondents to those that are the subject of the study in hand. Pre-testing the questionnaire will be invaluable as it will highlight any unforeseen problems with question wording, answer categories, interviewer instructions, etc. It will allow interviewers to test the mechanics of the interview, and this can help researchers to deliver an improved set of data from the research exercise.

Coding

The activity of coding is primarily used in quantitative research to help to make sense of "freeform" data that are collected as part of an interview in an attempt to add some flesh to the bare bones of the quantitative data. It should be noted that, in general, data resulting from semi-structured one on one interviews, whether purely qualitative in nature or within a quantitative context, are treated in a different fashion.

In its simplest sense the process of coding entails grouping the same or similar responses, depending upon the words used or the sense conveyed so that they can be analysed as part of the process that converts the raw data into aggregated information.

The Cinderella or forgotten child of the research process – the post coding of responses to any form of open question – should be treated with the attention that it deserves. Researchers in their various guises, be they client, supplier, data collector, etc., pose and ask questions to elicit open responses for very specific reasons and any resultant responses need to be treated sensitively so that they will enhance any data derived and add to the "story" that any particular piece of research is trying to tell.

Of paramount importance to the listing and coding process is a briefing by the researchers who have established the methodology for the project, to ensure that the objectives and desired outcomes are explained to those who will be undertaking the coding process: without an understanding of the nature and focus of the research, it would be difficult for them to know what should or should not be drawn out from the verbatim responses provided.

This briefing will be invaluable when coders are undertaking the listing phase, which is the precursor to the establishment of the eventual codeframe. Listings should be undertaken on as many completed questionnaires as is feasible, such that any responses from specific sub-groups within the overall sample are adequately represented.

The coding process in multi-country research must be treated with the utmost care: what researchers will be trying to achieve is consistency of codeframes without losing any real differences by market/region or culture that may have been unearthed. A thorough listing phase is of major importance in an international context.

Data Entry

The facilities and procedures that are now available are a far cry from the days when the punched card was the medium of choice for market research data entry.

However, irrespective of the method of data entry, whether it is direct entry as part of a computer assisted or other direct entry method, or following on from paper-based face to face interviewing or another paper-based approach, appropriate data entry verification procedures must be in place. For any direct entry system, thorough pre-testing must be the watch word to ensure that routing/branching or skips are doing their intended job. For paper-based data entry, the ideal would be to undertake 100 % verification, i.e. re-entry of all the data.

Data Processing

General

It is not the intention here to go into the full intricacies of data processing and analysis in market research, more to confirm that it is still more of an art than a science, but now ably supported by a multitude of excellent products and systems that can render raw data into a myriad of aggregated forms; from fairly straightforward tabular presentations to the most complex multivariate, mapping, segmentation and other analyses.

What is, however, without dispute is that no matter how sophisticated the data processing or analysis system or exponent, it is impossible for them to improve the quality of the base data with which they are working. This only confirms the importance of the original data collection process: how it was developed, set up, managed and monitored.

Multivariate Analysis

Generally, multivariate analysis techniques are employed to describe the relationships between sets of variables. In the simplest sense, these analyses will help to inform the researcher about correlations and similarities within the data set, and whether data can be summarised in particular ways and, more importantly, if the data can lead directly to any conclusions about behaviour, attitudes, etc., that can be used as predictors for behaviour.

Traditionally, multivariate analyses have been classified into two groups.

In the first group, which deals with the interdependence of variables, analysis techniques such as: Correlation, Factor and Principal Component analysis, Mapping, etc., are designed to determine the relationships between variables. Other techniques, Cluster analysis for example, look at the "distance" between respondents across a series of variables, and attempt to unearth groups that show the greatest similarity and to produce groups that show the greatest differences. However, whilst these techniques show similarities, they do not shed any light on the ability of any one variable to influence another.

It is the second group of techniques that measure the dependence of variables on each other. One of the oldest of these methods is AID (Automatic Interaction Detector) which attempts, via data trees, to explain the importance of each "branch" of the tree. Other methods in this group include: CHAID (Chi Square Automatic Interaction Detector, which provides greater statistical reliability than AID), Multiple Regression and Discriminant Analysis.

The use of the multivariate techniques has also led to specific research applications such as Conjoint Analysis, which essentially looks at the trade-offs made between sets of items.

Given the popularity of Conjoint Analysis, it is probably worth describing the methodology in a little more detail.

Today it is used in many disciplines apart from market research: social sciences and applied sciences including marketing, product management, and operations research. The overall objective of conjoint analysis is to determine, from a limited number of attributes, what combination is most preferred by respondents. It is used to good effect in testing the acceptance of new products and other concepts and their attributes. It can also be effective in assessing the overall appeal of advertisements and other marketing collateral. Once the features of the product or concept under test have been chosen, data are collected by means of showing unique combinations of features to respondents who rank, rate, or choose between these. Combinations are presented so that they are seen as potential substitutes, but dissimilar enough that respondents are able to indicate preferences between them. Resultant data may consist of individual ratings, rank-orders, or preferences among alternative combinations. The latter is referred to as "choice based conjoint" or "discrete choice analysis". Analysis latterly has centred around Hierarchical Bayesian procedures that operate on choice data. The analysis determines utility functions that indicate the perceived value of each product or concept feature and how sensitive consumer perceptions and preferences are to changes in these.

The approach has a number of key advantages:

- It determines the psychological trade-offs that are made when respondents evaluate several attributes together.
- Preferences can be measured at the individual level.
- It is possible to use physical stimuli.

It does also, however, have some potential disadvantages:

- Data collection process can be complex.
- Generally, it is better to use a limited set of features as the number of combinations increases considerably as more features are added.

In addition to the traditional forms of multivariate analyses there are now newer techniques that are being increasingly used and these are based upon Artificial Intelligence (AI) and use Neural Networks, Fuzzy Logic, etc.

As with many other things in market research and life in general, it is now possible to adopt any number of analysis techniques. What is important is for the researcher to understand the advantages and disadvantages of each method and what data and information are likely to be delivered. Also, it is imperative to be aware of the principles underlying the techniques to be used.

Significance Testing

In English, as in other languages, "significant" generally equates to important. However, in the statistical sense the meaning of "significant" can be defined as being "probably true" i.e. not due to chance. It is perfectly possible for a research result to be true and statistically significant without actually being important. It is essential to bear in mind that when a statistician pronounces that a result is "highly significant", what they are actually saying is that the result is very likely to be true, and not, as might be interpreted, that it is highly important.

Therefore, significance levels tell the researcher how likely a finding is the result of chance. Generally, researchers use the 0.95 (or 95%) confidence level to denote that a result is reliable.

It is possible, on occasions, to over-state the importance of the 95% level. The 95% level comes from the world of academia, where a theory usually has to have at least a 95% chance of being true to be considered plausible. However, in the wider economy it may well be the case that a 90% chance of being true, although it cannot be proven, would be sufficient evidence to embark upon a specific course of action. Therefore, the level at which to set action standards must be set with a degree of pragmatism in mind, but this will naturally be tempered according to the likely financial investment that is dependent upon any decision. However, in many cases, researchers are looking for "direction" rather than absolute "truth" and can live with a lower level of confidence.

What is important when undertaking any test of significance is to be aware of the basis upon which the test data were collected – generally it is advisable to avoid bias in the data collection process, as most significance tests assume that data have been collected as the result of random sampling methods.

A fuller explanation of various significance tests is contained in a later chapter.

STANDARDS/QUALITY

The question of the quality of market research data has been a significant topic in the industry for a number of years. It is true to say that all sides of the industry have, since its inception, been clear that for market research data to be used effectively and the resultant information to be taken seriously it should be based upon a sound footing emanating from an appropriate design, with data collection executed to the highest standards followed by tutored analysis, interpretation and, where required, recommendations.

The policing of "quality" was for many years within the domain of the research industry itself – although the existing codes of conduct or ethics that were developed, some of which have existed since the late 1940s, did not necessarily specifically feature quality as an aspect.

It is probably fair to say that quality, which had been taken for granted within the realms of market research, became a requirement in the 1980s with the involvement in the market research purchasing sphere of procurement or purchasing departments, and the development of international standards that could be applied to the market research industry – although they were not specifically designed for the industry. These international standards were actually aimed at regulating various processes and, given that a great deal of market research is concerned with process, became a surrogate for an industry standard.

However, whilst these standards were not exactly embraced by the industry many companies, principally suppliers, have become accredited to them (ISO 9001 being a prime example) in response to clientside prompting.

One of the first attempts to inject an objective assessment of quality into the whole of the market research process was in the UK in the late 1990s, which led to the establishment of a British Standard that not only looked at the quality of the process but also at the "fitness for purpose" of the design of a specific project within market research. This forerunner has been used in some measure to develop an international standard that was approved and launched in early 2006.

The continuing importance of international research made it desirable that there was some agreed standard to which researchers could refer when conducting a survey across many markets. In addition, the research industry in individual countries and worldwide has come to the realisation that, as a mature player with vital role in the economy and society, there would need to be an independent arbiter of the way in which the process of research is conducted.

ISO 20252

ISO 20252 is the worldwide market research industry's answer to the oft stated requirement by users of market research for the specification, establishment and implementation of at least minimum common standards for those elements relating to process components of market research activity.

As indicated earlier, this demand, which had been latent for a number of years, has been hastened by the globalisation of the activities of many of the major users of survey research. There was a perceived need for consistent and comparable research to be delivered from countries throughout the world which led researchers to realise that even best local practice and controls would not provide the framework within which comparability and consistency could be guaranteed. Hence, there was a recognition that an agreed set of common and clear standards should be devised, and this has been met by the provision of this new standard.

The Process

Naturally the standard did not materialise overnight, and took a great deal of discussion over a five-year period and, as might be expected, was detailed and consultative. The drafting process for the standard was driven by a working party composed of members from 20 countries from all regions of the world, among them: Australia, Brazil, Canada, France, India, Japan, Mexico, Russian Federation, South Africa, UK and the USA. In addition, there were a number of observer countries and there was liaison with a number of pan-industry bodies (ESOMAR included). The drafting process took as its starting point existing standards from Spain, Germany and the UK and the recently developed pan-European standard.

Countries involved in the working party were represented by one or more professional industry experts supported in some cases by an expert in standards. Participants from the profession were there to represent a number of different disciplines and experiences: research suppliers, academics, official statistics organisations, trade and professional association officers or elected representatives.

The Standard

It will be evident to those who read the standard that is primarily concerned with Process Quality. It was agreed at the beginning that the standard would not attempt to cover any of the design quality issues in market research. This decision was reached for two reasons:

- It was recognised that it would be a hard enough task to get agreement from researchers regarding the requirements of a standard and that it would be perhaps impossible to achieve a consensus on what would constitute acceptable levels of design quality.
- It was felt inappropriate to address the issue of design quality and establish a global standard where, for a variety of reasons, there is availability of different interviewing and other research resources. In addition, budgets can often be limited and these would dictate specific research approaches. Inevitably, in these conditions, researchers would have no recourse but to make certain trade-off decisions that could involve design, cost, and project timelines, etc., to render an acceptable response to a client's research requests.

The complete standard is a lengthy document so a summary of the main sections is included here.

Quality Management System Requirements

For those aspiring to be accredited to ISO 20252 there must be evidence of some form of quality assurance procedure being in place. This condition would be satisfied if, for example, an organisation has already undertaken ISO 9001. However, not all companies may, for legitimate reasons, wish to go through the process of accreditation to ISO 9001 – as it is not appropriate for some of their activities. This section of the standard shows how they can do so without the need to be certified to ISO 9001.

Within this section are details of organisation and responsibilities, documentation, record keeping, training and competency, the use of sub-contractors, error resolution and analysis, and problem resolution.

Managing the Executive Elements of Research

In this section the various elements in the research process are itemised – starting from the initial request from the user through all stages until the ultimate outcome. It states the procedures that should be instituted to ensure that the requirements of the standard are understood and primarily requires that all relevant resources, expertise and procedures are brought to bear in a timely fashion to deliver satisfactory performance for each aspect of the survey process. What is clearly defined is the "ownership" of each aspect of the process.

Data Collection

All aspects of data collection, especially fieldwork, are discussed in this section. Specific rules are communicated covering all the components of the fieldwork activity from the recruitment and training of different types of interviewers, interviewer appraisals, validation of interviews undertaken – including some minimum levels.

Given that the data collection function lies, as described earlier, at the very heart of the research offering, this aspect of the research process is discussed in more detail in the next part of this chapter.

Data Management and Processing

Here all processes from data entry to the provision of analysis, presentations and recommendations are covered. For each activity, there are standards relating to clear instruction, the various levels of verification (for such aspects such as data entry and coding), documentation and, very importantly, error resolution.

Project Documentation

The standard requires the complete recording of all aspects of a project.

ISO Benefits

The research industry, having taken the step to institute worldwide standards following a thorough consultative and drafting process, is convinced that the outcome will be of immense benefit to all those involved in market research from whichever side of the industry. The value of the endeavour is confirmed by the relative speed with which the standard was taken from initial concept and drafting to ultimate enactment as an ISO.

The benefits of the ISO can be summarised as follows:

- It is a transparent specification having been openly drafted with scrutiny throughout, and consultation along the way. There are no inherent barriers to participation – all those who wish to can seek accreditation. It is also a "living" system not set in stone as it is a requirement that it must be inspected regularly to ensure that it is itself "fit for purpose".
- A consistent approach and comparability of process are enshrined in the clearly stated audit requirement.
- It provides independent objective assessments of service standards, vetted by an independent third party, which can be the basis of contracts between suppliers and clients. These are facilitated by the inclusion of minimum standards supported by a clear audit trail for verification purposes.
- The standards call for research suppliers to identify and define the processes involved. Importantly it requires ownership to be established that generates a state of staff involvement and understanding of the process and, more importantly, their place in the process which may have been missing previously.
- The system has, as a key component, the ability to unearth and remedy errors which, by its very nature, will improve the performance of all concerned.
- Implementation of the system makes all aware of the inherent benefits of improvements in quality, and leads to continual striving for better quality.
- For users, the commissioning process, particularly, can become more transparent as it possible for them to be able to compare a number of responses to a research brief in a like for like manner.

The Future

The publication of ISO 20252 is a key step in satisfying the demand for commonality of research processes in the international context.

It could be hypothesised that existing standards represent a base level. It is probably inevitable that these will be strengthened over time as they are exposed to a greater number of organisations – this will provide greater opportunities for the strengths and weaknesses of the system to be assessed and augmented as appropriate.

Whilst the standard has been formulated from the experiences in many countries around the world, it is not possible as yet to for it to be totally encompassing. It should be regarded as "work in progress" with the system evolving as best practice is modified over time.

Approach to Fieldwork Management

When looking at data collection that involves the use of interviewers irrespective of the medium (primarily Face to Face or Telephone methods), it has been recognised for many years that for fieldwork to take its true role in the research process, the activity must be subject to thorough and transparent management. However, until the mid-1970s there were no specific standards established for the management of the fieldwork process. However, this changed in 1974 with the advent, in the Netherlands, of the "Your Opinion Counts" campaign. This was followed by the establishment, in the United Kingdom, of the IQCS (Interviewer Quality Control Scheme) which has gone from strength to strength and is still in rude health to this day.

The IQCS was set up to ensure that those involved with the fieldwork process were offering a "good product" that could be assessed by means of agreed standards – many of these were used in the initial drafting phase of the ISO 20252 standard.

Fieldwork Standards

The concept behind the standards that are now within the ISO 20252 were established to ensure the maintenance and development of all aspects of the quality of fieldwork/data collection using comprehensive, clearly defined and actionable standards that can be subject to independent inspections to ensure compliance, such that clients can be certain that basic standards of administration and fieldwork are being maintained.

The standards, irrespective of the medium of data collection should cover: Head Office Management and Administration, Project Management and Administration, the role of Supervisors, Training and Appraisals and validations.

Looking specifically at each of these elements in turn:

Head office management and administration involves, among other things, the keeping of records for each type of fieldworker: interviewer, recruiter, auditor, etc., including details of:

- application
- references
- recruitment
- training
- assignments worked
- appraisals
- validation

Project management and administration should ensure that all individuals working on a project must be adequately briefed (by post, telephone, tape, video, electronic means or in person). In addition, details of briefings undertaken and interviewing documentation with details of the validations undertaken with full records of interviewers used and samples achieved must be kept.

All supervisory staff should be adequately and appropriately trained for all supervisory tasks allocated to them. In most cases, interviewing supervisors will have been interviewers themselves and will have knowledge of what is required of the role.

Approaches to **training and appraisals and validation** can vary by country, but are all necessary activities to ensure that fieldwork and data collection can provide quality data within the research process.

Other Aspects of Fieldwork and Data Collection

Interviewers, and those involved with data collection, are often the "face" of the market research industry as far as the general public are concerned and the industry is often judged by their performance. It is therefore important for interviewers to be allowed to be ambassadors for the industry. For this to happen, they need to be engaged in the process which can stem from effective briefings on specific projects including a clear outline of the research objectives. They should also be made to feel part of the research team. Ideally, researchers should themselves, as part of their training process, undertake the role of an interviewer for some time – this will provide them with first hand experience of the environment in which interviewers operate!

But it should be remembered that no matter how good the interviewer – he/she cannot deliver useful data from a poor questionnaire.

PROTECTING THE RESPONDENT

It has been a feature in the data collection sphere that response rates have been falling for some time. Market research has also suffered from the behaviour of those in other commercial spheres whose activities, as far as the general public are concerned, encroach upon market research or blur the image of market research.

Market researchers have always wished to ensure that the protection of their respondents is of fundamental importance in any contact with them and subsequent use of data and information that they supply.

In this regard, researchers have long understood the value of self regulation not only to ensure that researchers in all disciplines behave ethically towards respondents, clients and their colleagues, but also as clear evidence to those outside the industry whether in government, the legislature or wherever that this industry understands that it must be self-policing. There have been various codes of conduct and other ethical codes in existence.

One of the first such codes was published by ESOMAR in 1948. This was followed by a number of Codes prepared by national marketing research societies and by other bodies such as the International Chamber of Commerce (ICC), which represents the international marketing community. In 1976 ESOMAR and the ICC decided that it would be preferable to have a single International Code instead of two differing ones, and a joint ICC/ESOMAR Code was therefore published in the following year (with revisions in 1986).

Subsequent changes in the marketing and social environment, new developments in marketing research methods and a great increase in international activities of all kinds including legislation, led ESOMAR to prepare a new version of the International Code in 1994. This new version sets out as concisely as possible the basic ethical and business principles which govern the practice of marketing and social research. It specifies the rules which are to be followed in dealing with the general public and with the business community, including clients and other members of the profession.

ESOMAR and the ICC keep the code under constant review to ensure that it is in line with current legislation as well as prevailing business practices.

There are numerous other local codes that mirror the ESOMAR code promulgated by members' societies or bodies that represent the agency side.

WHAT DOES THE FUTURE HOLD?

Digital is Everywhere

In theory, it should be quite easy for a market researcher to predict what will happen to the data collection process in the next few years. However, given the way that the process has changed within the last decade it would be a foolhardy person who would make predictions with any degree of confidence.

However, it is possible to say with certainty that current and future advances in technology will continue to impact and dictate how data, both quantitative and qualitative, are collected in the future. The web is already the major source of secondary data collection and this will only increase as even more pages are added to the worldwide store of information.

What is likely to happen, is that there will be a reliance upon opt-in and carefully managed panels as opposed to some of the "looser" panels that exist today.

More and more data will be collected and reported in "real time", with "Blogs", "Chatrooms" and "Word of Mouth" being mined for data of all types. This could essentially be an unstructured approach, although "threads" could be inserted to generate the appropriate discussions.

Another consequence of the advent of technology could be the move from "Broadcast", i.e. large sample with less depth of questioning/information gathering to "Narrowcast" where a smaller number of subjects are explored in much detail: online video diaries and the like.

However, in a paradoxical twist, the greater use of online technologies may see the increased use of additional and different modalities to satisfy all the data requirements for a particular study – perhaps data from a real time online study helping to formulate the approach for one on one or group qualitative approaches, recognising that digital data collection may not, by its very nature, be able to provide required depth or research environment to elicit all forms of data.

Whilst, at present the Web appears to be all pervasive and without barriers, there are indications that the Internet could one day be broken up into separate networks around the world, according to a warning given by one of the leading lights in the development of the net. If we look at the net in five years from now it is estimated that there are going to be many more Internet users in Asia than Europe or America, with more Chinese web pages than English pages. Indeed, the Chinese government is concerned that users still have to type web addresses using Latin characters even when the pages are Chinese – a large proportion of the Internet users in China do not know the Latin alphabet, as is also the case in India.

This issue of the net becoming unconnected may well come to the fore and have a significant say in how research develops in what will be the economic powerhouses of the future – the CRIB or BRIC economies: China, Russia, India and Brazil.

How the Web develops will have consequences for research among the B2C and B2B communities alike.

New Business Models

Whilst the way in which the Web will develop and finally settle into a stable network is likely to have a disproportionate effect on market research and the data collection process in the future, there are indications in the industry that there is a re-structuring on the supply side in response to technological developments, client demands and the globalisation of trade. The last 10 years has seen a spate of mergers and acquisitions – sometimes involving large companies who might appear to have been unassailable – that have seen the largest companies move even further away from the small and medium size agencies who, in theory, inhabit the same industry.

This means that there are now a few very large data collection concerns that have the ability to invest in the latest technologies – where some of the smaller players would find it difficult to match them and must continue to work with older methods.

Changes on the buying side of the industry quite naturally have shaped responses by suppliers; one of the manifestations of this can be seen in the number of partnerships that have been forged between some of the largest buyers and the largest suppliers. This in turn may well have led to the number of clientside companies that downsized their internal departments – relying more upon "tied in" suppliers to provide lower, mid and, sometimes, senior level cover.

Outsourcing

Another phenomenon that has been evident in the last decade or so has been the recourse to offshore third parties, many in India, for many back-office functions, primarily data collection and data processing – this trend is likely to continue, given the continued pressure on market research budgets.

Speed

There will be no escape from the need for increased speed particularly where data are required for sectors and categories that are themselves subject to change in response to market conditions.

The General Data Collection Environment and Society

Not only has the business landscape changed as far as the data collection process is concerned but so has the general data collection environment for both B2C, B2B, quantitative and qualitative research.

Researchers are now dealing with consumers that are far more sophisticated than their counterparts of some years, and this has meant that not only data collection techniques themselves but forms of questioning have had to be tailored to adapt to these new conditions.

In addition, given the variety of stimuli that beset respondents in their everyday lives it is now becoming important to set market research exercises in their correct context, for example accompanied shopping, where those under research can be observed and questioned at the point of contact with brand, service, etc.

This greater consumer sophistication can be discerned in other developments, many are now putting themselves out of reach of some research activities by registering with "Do not Call/Do not Spam" registers.

This has had an impact on what were already falling response rates: it is an issue that the industry must address before this starts to create concerns about the validity of data that are collected. One solution, which has for many reasons been anathema until now is the necessity to pay people for their data. It is true that this has been part of the business for qualitative research and web survey participation, but it has not, to date, proved necessary for most quantitative research projects – particularly in the B2C sector.

One other cloud on the horizon could be the threat of respondents providing data, possibly at a cost, exclusively to a specific entity – manufacturer or data collection agency or whatever.

What is also being witnessed now with the increase in online research is a move away from traditional sampling techniques with greater reliance upon panels to access respondents.

The use of online research will create "a distance" between researcher and respondent which will mean that other means of data collection will need to be utilised to provide data that cannot be easily captured by the medium.

Finally, in the B2C environment there is now greater awareness of the value of personal data and the need to protect it for a variety of reasons.

This might be mirrored among B2B respondents who may refuse to divulge company or other data by sheltering behind legislation such as the Sarbannes Oxley Act as enacted in the US or similar. This may be the recourse of a number of respondents in the heavily researched sectors of IT, Finance, etc.

The Market Research Industry in the Future

Ultimately what will the future hold? Will it see the market research industry backed into a corner or being consigned to being a bit-part player in an information-saturated world? Or could it be that our salvation may lie in the industry in general remembering, cherishing and broadcasting what was initially valuable and unique about what we do and not focusing totally upon process, cost of provision or any of the other stock market-led shibboleths.

Yes, we must provide cost effective data. But perhaps we should take heart from the fact that all the data in the world is as nothing if it is not weighed and analysed with expertise, intelligence and common sense such that data are turned into information and insights and presented with clarity and, lest we forget, personality. For whatever the medium, the world will not heed a mass of data, but those with a message.

REFERENCES

Brace, I. (2006) *Questionnaire Design.* Viva Books Private Limited.
Crask, M., Fox, R.J. and Stout, R.G. (1995) *Marketing Research Principles & Applications.* Prentice Hall.
Crisp, M. and Wright, L.T. (1995) *The Marketing Research Process.* 4th Edn, Prentice Hall.
Malhotra, N.K. (2006) *Marketing Research – An Applied Orientation.* 5th Edn, Prentice Hall.
Roe, M. (2004) *Market Research in Action.* Thomson Learning.

4

The Market Research Process

Hans-Willi Schroiff

INTRODUCTION

To many outside observers, Market Research seems predominantly an "ad hoc" type of service. Apart from regular "water level measurements" in terms of market shares, distribution percentages, etc. coming from syndicated suppliers, it is a commonly held belief among users of research services that occasional aspirations of the consumer or the client are sufficient to keep their business moving at the right pace and at a profitable level. Every now and then – e.g. when innovation pipelines seem to dry up, when no internal agreement on the forthcoming ad campaign can be reached, the research function is called to the boardroom to do magic and, e.g. reveal immanent and unmet consumer needs, confirm personal views about an advertising campaign and unveil the reasons why market shares rise or fall.

The underlying belief is that Market Research can be accomplished by a rather short-term, low and discontinuous effort, it is believed that a flashgun aimed at consumers and markets is sufficient to reveal their dynamic, unfathomable, and interwoven nature, it is believed that a sort of "still life" flash allows us to reconstruct the storyline of a whole movie with all its complexity.

Basically it is believed that isolated pieces of market information will allow us to develop a valid and full market understanding which in turn should allow us to make better business decisions than our competitors.

This continues to be one of the major judgmental fallacies of corporations today. Having the finger at the pulse of your consumer is essential for corporate health and differentiates winners from losers in whatever market.

It is not the topic of this contribution to meticulously identify the various reasons why companies fail or succeed. What we will do, however, is closely examine the potential contribution that the Market Research function could make if properly and continuously used.

The most essential precondition for truly obtaining a value-added "return on investment" (ROI) from Market Research funds is to subscribe to a systematic Market Research *process* with dedicated procedural and decisional hygiene. Then – and only then – will corporations be able to benefit from connecting to consumers via the research function.

Focus in this chapter is on our experience in the "fast-moving consumer goods" (fmcg) sector. We acknowledge that, e.g. "business to business" models work under slightly different settings. Nevertheless, we seriously believe that the basic structures described here do apply to other business contexts as well.

Market Research Handbook, 5th Edition. Edited by M. van Hamersveld and C. de Bont.
© 2007 John Wiley & Sons, Ltd.

ORGANISATION OF THE CHAPTER

We start out with a brief description of the main responsibilities of the Marketing and the Market Research function and their mutual interactions.

We then continue with "process hygiene" as an essential precondition that must be met in order to truly benefit from research investments in total. In that regard we are going to differentiate between a "macro process" and a "micro process" of research activities which must be viewed in close correspondence to each other.

The *"Macro Process"* refers to the basic steps of value creation from a corporate perspective and how research can actively support this. It consists of carefully designed steps between assessing a relevant consumer need, developing a respective product and observing the launch success in the real market up to the point where we have built a loyal consumer base – guaranteeing sales and sustainable profits. As we will point out below, this process needs to be entertained in its entirety in order to really extract value from investments in Market Research. Any partial use of the research function may well sustain a certain business perspective, but improving your business track record in a systematic and continuous way only results from the systematic and continuous use of Market Research. Like every chain, this value creation chain of activities tends to break at its weakest link, thus lowering the added value of the activities in general.

The bridge between the "Macro Process" and the "Micro Process" is provided by the "Research Plan". The "Research Plan" defines for each Marketing project which studies are to be conducted, at what time, and at what kind of costs, with which decision points – leading to a clear-cut pattern of activities which is adapted to the relative risk of the activity.

The *"Micro Process"* refers to the single steps within a single project (e.g. Lachmann and Schroiff, 1998). We are now looking at a single piece of research within the general cycle of activities making up the Macro Process. Again we will argue that the Micro Process also consists of a systematic chain of value added activities which in their entirety are decisive for the value of the whole project. We will differentiate between the intellectual quality of the research briefing of the client, the translation effort of the research partner to design a study set-up properly reflecting the needs to answer the research question, the sampling quality to truly capture the appropriate structure of the respondents' base and – last but not least – the retranslation of the findings into an operational recommendation. A research project can fail on any of these single steps – rendering the whole research effort practically useless. A sloppy field organisation with superficial recruiting tactics can spoil the validity of the final recommendations in an instant.

In order to derive value from research, we now begin to understand that it is the *underlying research process* in its macro and micro orientation that needs to be managed adequately in order to gain a competitive advantage with the help of Market Research. Surely it is the quality of the individual research effort, but this is just one piece of the mosaic. In the following we will elaborate on this simple basic idea of " … getting the processes right".

BASIC ISSUES OF THE MARKETING FUNCTION

Let us first take a brief look at some fundamental business processes since it would obviously matter to tie the ongoing research support to the basic business processes: Although our background is largely in "fast moving consumer goods" (fmcg), the major steps underlying a successful corporate business performance tend to be governed by similar issues in almost any type of business where you sell something to a consumer, customer or client.

We all have seen zillions of books about the Marketing function and its (changing) role within the corporation (e.g. Homburg and Krohmer, 2003; Steffenhagen, 2004). We believe that the core activities for the Marketing function can be roughly divided up into the following three activities.

(Consumer-centred) Innovation

At the forefront there is a clear requirement for continuous consumer-centred innovation. Innovation has turned out to be the key driver of business success in any type of sustainable business. Particularly in recent times, we have seen the rise of so-called "Private Label" products, i.e. dealers' own offers. As empirical evidence shows, the only weapon against these type of products is a clear market orientation and a continuous innovation programme (see, e.g. Bruhn and Steffenhagen, 1989; Deshpande, 1999). But innovation just does not happen all by itself. Being constantly innovative requires an ongoing effort within the organisation to constantly change and re-invent itself to a major degree. Besides this attitudinal issue corporations need to ask themselves what they do in order to safeguard a continuous interface with the changing consumer.

The crucial question becomes "What Do We Say ?". What kind of new exciting offer do we present to the consumer/client? What are you going to tell her/him about what the product does, what kind of problem solver does it represent, what do you tell her about the brand as the "icing on the cake", what does the brand stand for in terms of psychological associations or connotations?

So at one point in time a branded products corporation needs to really understand what the consumer *product proposition* is. At the same time you need to decide on the *brand as a psychological carrier system* for the product proposition. One also needs to understand how these two propositions interact and whether they really fit to each other. The final result is the "branded product" that you propose to the consumer.

Market Research is the only way to help you understand the two cornerstones of your branded offer from a consumer's perspective. Research activities take you through a couple of exercises sustaining the consumer-centred innovation process. At the end of these activities you will be able to select a couple of truly sharp consumer-centred branded offers ready for concept-testing. With the help of Market Research the corporation creates a branded offer *with* the consumer, not *for* the consumer.

(Consumer-centred) Development

Interacting with consumers does not stop after having secured the fundamental branded product idea. A consumer-centred corporation strives to also develop the offer with the consumer in the subsequent product development phase.

Developing a blueprint for a branded offer will not be sufficient – you need to turn your concept into reality. This means that you need a product and a brand, but also a package, a commercial, a set of product aesthetics, an idea about how the branded offer should be priced, an idea about its potential vs. a couple of competitors, etc. – in other words "How Do You Say It?" becomes a set of questions aimed at the single contribution of each marketing mix factor towards total persuasion of the consumer. Therefore a section of Market Research called

"Pre-testing" will provide tools and algorithms to let you know more about the perceptual impact of your package, the attractiveness of your price, the persuasion of your commercial, etc. Finally, we will even provide a total evaluation of the whole marketing and communication mix including a kind of sales forecast for the first year in the market.

(Consumer-centred) Market Observation

A promising sales forecast does not imply a guarantee that the prediction will actually come true. The more dynamic, the more interrelated the respective marketplaces, the more it will be required to continuously observe their dynamics via sophisticated monitoring systems. After the product has passed all internal decisional hurdles and has been introduced to the market, there is no justification for leaning back and waiting for success.

Now is the time for intensive monitoring of the new offer in the real marketplace and taking corrective action if required. Basic Market Research activities in that phase have been traditionally divided into "observation" activities and "analysis" activities. Observational systems, tools and procedures will tell you *what* happened, analytical tools will give you an idea *why* it happened. The latter will finally lead to the right set of indicated actions to keep the project on track or get it back there.

As a result of all the previous steps, an informational base will build up that accumulates knowledge about learnings from fact-based decisions across time. These Meta-Learnings (e.g. about the rules of distribution build-up, how to communicate an emotional concept, etc.) will enable you not to re-invent the wheel every time, but base your decisions on proven facts in the history of your and other's projects.

BASIC ISSUES OF THE MARKET RESEARCH FUNCTION

Let us now take a look at a basic "characterisation" of Market Research for a better understanding. We use the following definition which provides a set of statements about the required features of the research function:

> *Market Research is the fundamental resource for business insights, measurement, knowledge, and tools that are systematically used for achieving higher levels of market performance and stakeholder value.*

Market Research is meant as an overall intelligence filter between the Marketing function and the Marketing environment. While we speak to our consumers via advertising and products, the consumer feeds back her behaviour, her opinions, her desires, her evaluations, etc. to the organisation via Market Research. Organisations who wish to maintain a thorough and continuous market orientation, generally achieve this via intensive Market Research activities. Market Research captures, filters, focuses the multiple responses of consumers and tries to construct an objective and complete mental model of the total marketing environment. The more objective, the more complete this model is, the more the corporation is likely to understand and react upon consumers' feedback. Being a *"Fundamental Resource"* implies that we look at this function as a basic asset that mediates the consumers' response to the organisation.

Providing *"Business Insights"* relates to the fact that Market Research can no longer be viewed as a simple logistic interface providing data. Data need to be merged into information which then transforms into insights. Deriving the right insights from data is one of the major secrets of business success – not the availability of data per se.

Being based on "*Measurement*" means that our reports do not reflect our subjective opinion, but are strictly based upon sound measurement procedures, designed to capture the respective aspects of the consumers' minds and their behaviour. We do not back up decision making based on individual beliefs and gut feeling, but strive to collect consumer feedback by professional data collection and interpretation.

Accumulating "*Knowledge*" refers to the fact that our findings are not elusive, but are made available in horizontal information flow systems to everyone who wishes to capitalise on the findings. Besides that, we aggregate knowledge pieces in our data banks and transform them into actionable meta-learnings, yielding ready-to-go marketing know-how.

Enabling "*Higher Levels of Market Performance*" signifies our mission to provide actionable information to marketers, helping them to drive both baseline and topline results. It is our objective to do research as a means to support marketing actions, not as "nice to know" story-telling. "Top-Line Growth" is the core topic here.

Based on these premises, the Market Research function interacts closely with the Marketing function on each of these deliverables.

SUMMARY

This first part has set the stage for the content to follow. We have understood who the main players are, and we have identified the main business topics that govern successful corporate performance today.

Figure 4.1 summarises it all by showing the continuous flow of research activities which spans from pro-active to retrospective – the whole is totally centred on the consumer. It is

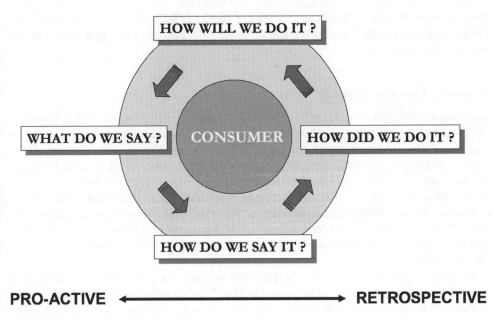

Figure 4.1

an ongoing activity cycle with basically no beginning and no end. Taken together, there is a simple, yet powerful way to address basic marketing issues via a consolidated research process. The cycle constitutes a kind of value chain where knowledge about the consumer is turned into company profits.

The four questions remain essential. We will address in greater depth at least two of them ("What Do We Say?/How Do We Say It?"). For each of these questions the Market Research function provides a broad set of sub-processes, each of them connected to a set of respective research tools.

Traditionally, books on Market Research have focused on the tool side (e.g. Green et al., 1988; Hamann and Erichson, 1989; Tull and Hawkins, 1987). This contribution focuses on the macro and micro processes of the research function.

THE "MACRO" PROCESS

A Complete Market Research Portfolio

In the following we will develop a basic view on the Market Research service structure by maintaining that value from research only arises for each of these basic business issues if a business-oriented and structured *process* is paired with a set of appropriate *tools*. Focusing either on the process or on the tools seems feasible, however this bears the risk that the end result of whatever activities will fall short of expectations.

Thus we will describe for each of the basic business issues a simple, yet valid process structure and suggest a couple of tools that are closely linked to them. We are not pretending that this is the *only* process structure or the *only* tools that make sense in that context, but we are very confident that it is only via the combination of a systematic process and valid tools that value can be derived from investments in research.

Each process moves from a *relatively vague start towards a relatively certain end* – investments in research help to identify basic topics of consumer interest, narrow down and refine the potential opportunities and help select those action streams that lead to more promising results in the real market.

Process I: "Consumer Insights"

As discussed earlier, it seems vital for a consumer-oriented company to entertain an ongoing and close relationship with their client base – thus ensuring to be able to anticipate changes in consumers' lifestyles, needs, wants, etc. (see, e.g. Barabba and Zaltman, 1991; Zaltman, 2003).

Innovations are basically of two types: either of the "*make and sell*" type or of the "*sense and respond*" type. "Make and sell" innovations are typically generated by R&D via process or ingredient innovations – it is the task of the marketing function to create concepts and communication to stimulate consumer interest. "Sense and Respond" type of innovations start out with a valid consumer need derived from a close interaction with future clients – the actual making of the product follows at a later stage including the respective marketing activities (Haeckel, 1999).

Recently the notion of "Consumer Insights" has emerged as a common heading for a set of research *tools*. We tend to look at "Consumer Insights" as the *function* within Market Research that establishes a continuous interface to consumers, their desires, their habits, their attitudes, they way they live, the way they shop, their worries and their joys. "Consumer Insights" also is a synonym for a value creating *process* of creating consumer-centred innovations by selecting the right product innovation for the right brand equity:

1. *Product Innovation* – Consumer Insights efforts provide the basics that help us to define sharp *product* concepts. Consumer Insights are available through many sources residing inside the corporation. These sources need to be aggregated in a meaningful way, the core issues need to be distilled from the sea of information, in a directed semi-creative process. We need to derive which products might hopefully address those needs better than existing products or come up with totally innovative suggestions.
2. *Brand Equity* – Besides that, we are assessing how people value our biggest assets in a company – our brands. We are looking at brands as psychological carrier systems, powerful mechanisms to establish and maintain the emotional relation to the buyer and to provide a meaningful face for a meaningless product body (e.g. Aaker, 2004; Arnold, 1997; Esch, 2004; Keller, 2002).

A consumer-centric product concept in combination with a psychological carrier system in the form of a mighty brand – these are promising ingredients for the magic formula of marketing success, particularly when paired with the extra sparkle of creativity. How can this be accomplished under the stewardship of the Market Research function?

Figure 4.2 shows a schematic (i.e. not comprehensive) representation of how a first process model could potentially look (see also Schroiff, in press). The essence of the chart describes a refinement process where we start with a very broad set of bits and pieces of information about the consumer and conclude with a set of sharp product concepts. This is something general and basic that we will encounter throughout the text: a systematic market research process is always moving the corporate perspective from a relative vague start to a very certain end by constantly working on the refinement of the consumer perspective.

In this case we migrate from a variety of consumer knowledge towards a "sharp" product concept (where "sharp" means both *precise* and *intelligent*).

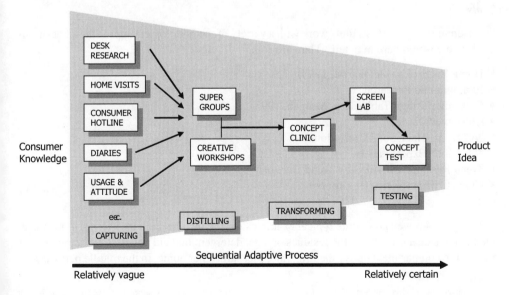

Figure 4.2

The process is sequentially adaptive and comprises the following stages:

- Hunting and Gathering
- Distilling
- Enriching
- Transferring
- Testing

In the following we will refer briefly to the various stages and to a selection of tools that would typically be used at the respective stage.

Hunting and Gathering

It is assumed that in the beginning we are exposed to a huge variety of potential insights, learnings, or facts about consumers, their preferences, their environment, their habits, their needs, etc. This "front end" is entirely unstructured and fuzzy, it does not bear a sign of what is important, of which elements belong together, etc., the fuzzy front end provides no information about temporal patterns, it may contain hard facts and soft guesses. The first task is to collect multiple informational facets about consumers and to avoid zooming in on one or a few of them in a premature fashion.

This is exactly what is commonly observed with companies who all pretend to be consumer-focused. Either only few informational sources are considered in mapping out the consumer and/or managers quickly focus on a restricted couple of insights that confirm their expectations or are vulnerable to other traps of selective perceptual bias.

Thus the first stage of any Consumer Insights exercise is the comprehensive collection of informational sources and arranging them in a non-overlapping way. In other words, if you do not collect all the stones of a mosaic, you will never be able to (re-)construct the full picture.

Tools

"Consumer Insights" (C.I.) units work with a variety of methodological approaches that simply cannot be covered here in detail.[1] Here are some:

- Home Visits (e.g. McQuarrie, 1998)
- Ethnographic Research
- Consumer Round Tables (e.g. Morgan, 1993)
- Consumer Diaries
- "A Day In The Life" Descriptions
- "On Line" Expert Panels
- Trend Research provided by Trend Bureaus
- Cynic Clinics (Non-User Groups)
  etc.

In Figure 4.3 we show some typical examples for the insights collected from Home Visits. On the left side a user shows the residues of a gel detergent that did not dissolve completely in the dosing compartment due to the low water pressure at her home. In the middle part we see a

---

[1] I am very much indebted to Sonja Kuch and Jens Bode for all the methodological approaches they have pointed out to me in recent years.

Figure 4.3

user applying a coloration product. On the right side, a user is speaking about the unexpected colour result of a coloration product – she hides her hair under a hood while talking to the interviewer.

The unifying element of all approaches is to capture mental models of consumers about markets and brands in these markets, about general needs, trends or perceived deficits with existing products, etc. It is important to note that C.I. never addresses single products/brands and never researches individual product features like fragrance. It rather strives to provide you with a bird's eye view of the market from a consumer's perspective. This will enable you to look at your marketing arena from a strategic point of view, not from the tactical angle of a single marketing-mix factor.

The results from the various approaches can best be compared to provide pieces of a complex mosaic which (when completed) shows you a perfect image of the marketing landscape from a consumer's perspective.

Distilling

What follows then is another critical stage – how do you arrange the various pieces of the mosaic in such a way that at least the shape of a meaningful picture emerges? Having collected the single stones is a necessary prerequisite, but how do we put them together? Here we must extend the analogy also to the artist him/herself: a meaningful picture can only be created by someone who already has a conceptual idea of what to paint. In other words – if *"distilling"* is the next critical task after "hunting and gathering", the distilling process can only be done by someone who has a (neutral) concept of the category. The purpose of this stage is to condense the various informational pieces towards an emerging pattern which finally constitutes an approximation of a comprehensive mental model about the consumer. It is of crucial importance to depict a holistic image of the target group instead of selectively cherry-picking a couple of insights that by chance match our technological possibilities. We have "... to walk in her shoes" in order to have her walk in our shoes finally.

Tools

It would be a little far-fetched to speak about "tools" in that context. The requirements are clear: structure and order have to be generated for the myriad of bits and pieces of information. This demanding and tedious task provides a major value-addition in the whole process since it defines the big topics.

This task can be dealt with in different ways: (a) it can be outsourced to an outside service, (b) it can be dealt with internally by a neutral function – e.g. Market Research; (c) it can be located inside a Strategic Business Unit (SBU). Whatever model is chosen in the end, does not matter specifically. The decisive point is that at the end of this distilling phase we have a structured and cross-validated model of consumer beliefs.

Enriching

In the next stage we will go on an *"enriching"* process of our distilled factual knowledge. This stage is arbitrary, but we wish to emphasise the rich body of implicit knowledge that resides within an organisation. So why not make use of additional comments by internal experts in order to build more factual knowledge around the building blocks that came out of the "distilling" phase?

Tools

The "enriching" stage is nothing but an additional step to make sure that the corporation actually includes everything that is known – both explicit and tacit (implicit) knowledge must be made available to the innovation task. The best way to guarantee the inclusion of all kinds of knowledge is to tap into the respective resources. Each company is filled to the brim with experts who again are filled with implicit knowledge about their area of expertise. By means of *structured expert interviews* it is possible to tap into this knowledge and make it available to the innovation process.

Transferring

The following stage is the most critical – here we are focused on *"transferring"* the mental model about the consumer into innovative product ideas. Creative performance matters most in this stage when trying to find answers to the question: "Where do we go from here?" This represents the key issue behind our exercise – what are the product offers that spring to our mind when we walk in our consumers' shoes? What would be an immediate consequence of the findings in terms of new products or offers? The main advantage of this procedure is that we start from a consumer's perspective of the market and thus make it easier for him/her in the end to connect to the product offers made.

Tools

Creative Workshops – usually in the form of an "off site" event, taking several days to present the distilled findings, identify clusters of opportunities and work on them with the "creative support" from respective agencies and/or trainers who specialise in leveraging creative potential.

Creative Groups with Consumers – an alternative form of a "Creative Workshop" where (creative) consumers are among the participants; usually lasting about a day or two; ideas oscillate between corporate participants and consumers: first rough ideas, e.g. are presented to consumers and continuously refined in a kind of "back and forth" interaction.

Testing

The final stage in the Consumer Insights process model is the "concept testing" stage. *Concept screening* tools helps to separate the wheat from the chaff by narrowing down the broad number of suggestions to those who are prone to truly generate consumer interest. Final concept tests benchmark the idea in terms of consumer acceptance (usually with reference to a database) and provide further guidance for improvements.

Tools

Screening
Screening filters are applied to narrow down the result from the creative overflow of dozens of concepts and filter out those which seem more promising than others. A first selection of a vast number of concepts can be achieved via a number of tools that are provided by almost any research supplier. Other than a concept test the consumer is confronted with a broad number of concepts (mostly in the form of a simple concept board) and have him/her rank them on a couple of evaluation dimensions. So what one gets in the end is a ranked order of conceptual priorities.

A winning concept in a concept screening, however, may be the "one-eyed among the blind" – i.e. one would have to fine-tune the winning concepts and benchmark them against other concepts. This is done in a concept test.

Selecting
In a concept test one usually presents a single concept to the consumer and have her/him evaluate this concept along a few basic dimensions like buying intention, credibility, relevance, newness, and "fit to the brand". On top of this she/he has to come up with some reasoning why she/he gave certain evaluations, but the results are evaluated mainly based on comparisons to empirical benchmarks. In general, we are able to sort out the good concepts from the bad and ugly, and to provide first explanations why the concept does (or does not) fly with consumers. A concept test is not suitable for extrapolating market potential – it merely shows a kind of disposition towards the idea of the branded offer, not more and not less.

However, we will also work on those which did not pass the consumer acceptance test right away – maybe it was just the wording or the visual or whatever that made consumers reject the concept. We are well advised to retest these after working on the perceived deficits. Finally, we will subsume all ideas in a kind of "concept library" in order to periodically screen those again that were not suitable at a certain point in time. But that does not mean that they should be dropped forever.

The major purpose of this process stage is to screen, optimise, and finally select those candidates that create consumer interest and which are now ready to be developed on their multiple facets of marketing and communication mix.

Concept testing at this early stage with the intent to provide a volume forecast seems irrational and misleading – as many factors may intervene on the road to final success.

Illustrative Business Case: Creating a New Beauty Concept

The Unilever advertising campaign for their body care brand "Dove" has apparently been a tremendous success, as claimed by the advertising industry – both creating direct impact, and

Figure 4.4   The "Dove Campaign"

also initiating a general kind of hype about a new body-consciousness for women. This success was largely based on extensive research activities by Unilever to generate consumer evidence for the acceptance their worldwide campaign.

Here is a shortened version of the "Dove Report" about the underlying research process for a new beauty concept which illustrates perfectly how Market Research contributes to the generation of a major business opportunity by listening to the "voice of the consumer"

> ...In order to generate truly significant findings, Dove and The Downing Street Group, a research consulting group, created a rigorous, four-phase research process that resulted in "The Dove Report: Challenging Beauty".

First, in order to determine the subject and scope of the study, The Downing Street Group gathered and reviewed all the literature regarding women and beauty, including other studies, surveys, media reports and academic literature. The goal was to try and figure out what research had not been conducted previously.

Second, Dove identified and commissioned a panel of experts to further review existing research and literature, and provide guidance on untapped opportunities on the topic of women and beauty. Advisors agreed that existing research had examined the many problems that the subject of beauty causes women – from eating disorders and self-esteem issues, to jealousy and feelings of worthlessness. But there was an emergent and novel opportunity to research the solutions and strategies that many women are already using to combat the negative feelings that beauty often can elicit. The research set out to test the hypothesis that American women radically underestimate their own beauty. The hypothesis proved to be incorrect.

Third, The Downing Street Group conducted intensive qualitative research to gain a better understanding of the real beauty issues women face, and how they speak about them. More than 200 women were interviewed in their homes – individually or with friends and family. They were taken on beauty excursions, and were asked to keep journals, take photographs and gaze in the mirror, all while being observed and questioned by The Downing Street Group. The goal of this phase was to ensure that the quantitative questionnaire contained the proper content, and was contextualised in a way that captured how real women talk about beauty.

Fourth, a quantitative questionnaire was created and administered to 1 600 women across the country. The results of the research have led to "The Dove Report: Challenging Beauty." (Source: the "Dove Report")

Process II: Pre-testing

Those concepts which have passed the filtering process are ready for the following process stage: developing the offer via a series of pre-testing procedures where the various facets of the marketing and communication mix are refined in order to achieve maximum synergies for obtaining a favourable consumer acceptance.

The pre-testing stage tries to minimise marketing risk by systematically checking and improving the single factors of marketing/communication-mix until they have reached maximum compatibility with a previously defined strategic/tactical objectives.

The main challenge in this area is to achieve predictive validity – i.e. the "ex ante" prediction in the lab should match closely to the "ex post" verification in the real market.

Again we refer to a process model in Figure 4.5 that bears similar characteristics to the one we have seen in one of the previous paragraphs: here we start with the "product idea" and move through the stages towards the final offer for the "market introduction". But again we move from a vague start towards a "certain" end product by refining its single features and holistic proposition together with consumers. We, e.g. might want to check the product performance, the advertising execution, the price positioning and other factors of the marketing and communication mix.

All these tests are *selective* at first, i.e. they are directed towards a single marketing-mix factor. A subset of methodologies called "test market simulations" are tools that attempt to

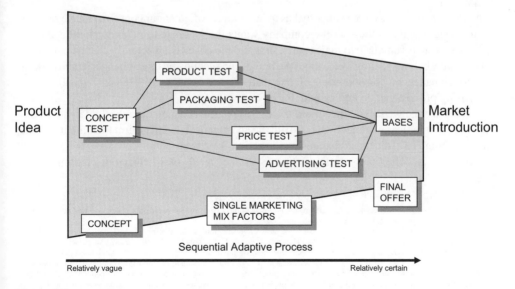

Figure 4.5

make a prediction on the total volume or market share for the first year after the introduction of the product. These are *holistic* tests – i.e. they seek to assess the integral of effects of all marketing mix factors on future market performance.

Advertising Evaluation

As we cannot cover all the various marketing mix factors (see e.g. Moscowitz, 1996, on product testing, and Simon, 1992, or Brzoska, 2004, on price assessment), we are going to focus on one of the most important categories within the pre-testing stage: the evaluation of advertising.

Not surprisingly, the advertising budget still accounts for the majority of the marketing budget in fmcg companies. Surprisingly, it still remains a sort of matter of debate how to decide whether this money has been spent wisely or not.

Ad Testing[2] is a quite complex issue that cannot be covered completely in a contribution like this one (e.g. Steffenhagen, 1996). However, we must introduce a few basic distinctions in order to classify the methodologies and to make you aware of the various steps of persuasion via mass market advertising.

The Advertising Evaluation Process

Not surprisingly, the evaluation of adverting within the general process of developing the product also follows a logical sequence of events as shown in Figure 4.6.

We generally assume that the development of advertising is based on a sound and complete vision of what the *product* (innovation) does in terms of functional and emotional benefits and what the *brand* as a psychological carrier system is contributing to the persuasion process. The "intended message" (i.e. what in the end the consumer should see, feel, believe, etc.) is laid down in whatever form of "*Ad Briefing*" document. The Ad Briefing represents the foundation for the work of the creative ad agencies which have to transfer the vision into a 30 second commercial.

An *advertising pretest* consequently has to let us know whether our consumers have received the message exactly in the way the company wants the message to be understood and acted upon. This usually entails two major parts: first, did the advertising actually change or confirm existing/new beliefs, feelings, etc. about the brand, and second, did these changes/confirmations lead to a change or corroboration of intended buying behaviour? This is basically all an advertising pre-test can do and should do.[3]

In other words, we tackle three main issues: (a) did the consumer playback indicate a close fit to our communication objectives?, (b) did the ad content change/confirm their mental model about the brand?, (c) did these changes/confirmations lead to attracting new users or confirming existing buyers? The "brut message" thus is the net result of whether our communication

---

[2] We are indebted to my colleague Ludger Gigengack for years of discussion around advertising testing and to Andrea Fliss and Christiane Reuters for providing the Vernel "Aromatherapy" case.

[3] We are not supposed to provide an extensive overview on ad pre-testing tools and will refrain from giving any recommendations on which method to use under which circumstances. However, it seems safe to conclude that the majority of paradigms are either more *diagnostic* or more *evaluative*. "Diagnostic" means that the main intention of the test procedure is to understand how well the intended advertising message is perceived and played back by the consumer. The main criterion is "fit to the intended message". "Evaluative" means that the main intention of the ad testing procedure is to measure the extent to which the commercial drives sales. While diagnostic tests tend to be non-evaluative, the opposite is true for evaluative tests – they mostly do not bear a major diagnostic component.

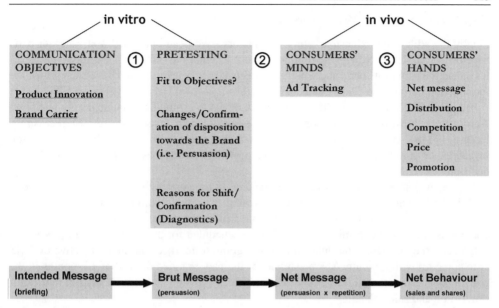

Figure 4.6

intentions will lead to a more or less probable behavioural disposition and why this occurs. It shows which effects the ad produces "in vitro".

Next follows the airing of the advertising. The number of airings (often measured in "opportunities to see", OTS, or "gross rating points", GRP) indicates the probability that a member of the target group actually had the chance to see the advertising (which definitely does not guarantee that it was fully processed). Evidently it is a function of the characteristics of the brut message and the number of repetitions how the ad content is rooted in consumers' minds. This memory trace (i.e. what we call "net message") is measured via a Market Research procedure called "Advertising Tracking". Ad Tracking reports what traces the advertising campaign has left "in vivo" – i.e. under real life conditions.

The "net message" now competes with other marketing mix factors like, price, distribution, promotion activities, etc. – its strength relative to other influential factors finally determines whether the consumer's hand reaches out in favour of the advertised product at a set price despite the intervention of massive competitive reactions in the market.

The logic of the simple process also demonstrates that whenever the value chain is interrupted or badly executed, the result of the entire process is at stake.

First, there could be a major disconnect between the briefing and the execution. Or there could be an inadequate briefing in general – e.g. pairing a products innovation with an inadequate brand carrier. Second, there could be a major discrepancy between brut and net message transfer due to insufficient "share of voice". Or there could be a "masking" of our ad message by a concurrent competitor ad with the same content. Third, a great campaign cannot produce sales because the distribution build-up is lagging behind or the price points have been set independently of what the brand equity can justify.

In other words, between an innovation and its commercially successful advertising lies a series of major steps which need to be completed and adjusted in a continuous way.

Test Market Simulations (Volume Forecasts)

Finally the ad and the other marketing-mix factors have been optimised – all relevant parts have been completed. Now is the time to find out whether the offer in its entirety is more (or less) than the sum of its parts and whether it meets the sales levels which have been set for the introduction period (see Clancy et al., 1994; Schroiff, 2001a; Urban and Hauser, 1980).

Traditionally local test markets have been employed to estimate the national sales response. Across time, however, their importance has gone down in favour of "Test Market Simulations" (TMS). However, across time test markets have proven to be either too slow, too revealing, or simply too unreliable in order provide a sound basis for a corporate launch decision.

Several available research paradigms at the present time use different ways to estimate, e.g. the brand's market share or sales volume one year after its introduction based on the results of a controlled buying simulation in a test studio and a subsequent trial period under normal usage conditions. Test Market Simulations (TMS) are scheduled for the very end of all pre-testing activities – they represent the final step before going to market. The final objective of TMS is to come up with a volume/share estimate of the new branded offer after 12 months in the market. This estimate will further confirm the launch decision and provide helpful figures for production and sales planning.

What is the "dark side of the moon"? All TMS are based on the "ceteris paribus" principle; predictions are valid only as long as no changes occur in the marketplace during the validation period. In today's marketplaces with their ongoing dynamics it seems quite unreasonable to assume that nothing is going to change across a period of one fiscal year or even longer. That is why recently the long-established validity claims of TMS suppliers have been severely challenged.

If major changes occur in the marketplace, a re-forecast has to be initiated taking the variations into account and incorporating them in a revised forecast. In order to accommodate the frequent changes of today's marketing environment, corporations have moved to pursuing a procedure based on several re-forecasts as the launch progresses. This helps to adjust marketing activities much earlier and more cost-effectively during the total launch period. In a typical setting each forecast will automatically be followed by three re-forecasts, e.g. after 4, 8, 12 months together with suggestions for respective adjustments of the marketing mix factors.

Illustrative Business Case: Evaluating an Advertising Campaign

A case study should highlight a few of the things we have outlined above. In our case, we are referring to Vernel, a fabric softener brand in Germany. The category is characterised by intense competition –focusing mainly on its core benefit "softness" as its basic functional benefit and in recent years particularly on fragrance as a further (aesthetic) product feature.

In 2005, the Vernel Brand Management decided to move one step up the benefit ladder and suggested a communication approach that was centred on "well-being", "indulging yourself" and the like, using the topic of "Aromatherapy" as a core theme for the new advertising campaign. In line with the launch of three new Vernel variants ("sensual", "relax", "energy") the ad agency proposed an execution for the "sensual" variant that was clearly emphasising the theme by showing a stressed-out woman who visibly pampers herself by having used Vernel "Aromatherapy" on her bed linen.

The results of an advertising pre-test clearly not only confirmed the communication objectives laid down in the ad briefing. Furthermore they suggested that the new proposition for Vernel not only appealed to current users of the brand, but also helped to move the proposition into the "relevant set" of users of competitors' brands – e.g. a total of 25 % current non-considerers now included the brand in their relevant set.

Having met the action standards for airing, the commercial was put on air in two waves (one massive, one pulsing) over an extended period of time. Already during the airing period it could be observed by means of continuous ad tracking that the ad and its underlying propositions were gaining ground in the mind of the consumer. The difference in the brand's image profiles between "viewers" and "non-viewers" suggested that both the core message and its persuasive implication could be attributed solely to the advertising (and not to price or promotion effects).

Not only did the subjects of the ad tracking exercise reveal their changed attitudinal disposition towards the brand, they also pointed out their willingness to include the brand in their relevant set for the next purchase occasion – purchase intention rates grew by about one third versus the period before the ad was on air.

A closer look at the respective panel data (both trade and consumer panel) helped us to verify whether respondents were just paying lip service to an interviewer or whether they were really serious about trying Vernel "Aromatherapy".

The comparison of purchase acts and market shares in the German IRI trade panel disclose an increase of 2.6 % of Vernel value market share in a year-to-year comparison as a result of the Vernel "Aromatherapy" TV ad.

The Vernel case study again shows that advertising evaluation must not necessarily be a mysterious operation – built entirely on managerial gut feeling and/or sophisticated models about unconscious consumer motives. If conducted continuously and with procedural rigour, the value chain from communication intent to advertising-induced net sales becomes subject to scientific analysis, professional judgment, and profitable decision making.

Again – this chain also tends to break at its weakest link: once an essential piece of information is missing, the doors are wide open for subjective beliefs and educated guessing. That is one of the reasons why we continue to advocate a data-driven route to corporate decisions about huge budgets; the costs of wrong decisions seem to outweigh the investments, e.g. in ad tracking.

Process III: Market Observation and Analysis

The product has been finally launched and has to prove itself in the real market. There is a clear set of expectations derived from the test market simulations under which conditions the activity will yield the respective return. A service within Market Research – the "Business Intelligence" function – observes the new launch specifically and includes the findings in their general observation and evaluation of the markets (e.g. Blattberg et al., 1994; Curry, 1993; Schroiff, 2006).

Business Intelligence functions currently undergo a major change, as markets go transnational, paper reporting goes to web-based portals, the traditional "one-source" focus of analyses is replaced by integrated databases and multi-source queries and the classical "What is happening?" questions are more and more followed by detailed answers on the "Why is it happening?" issue.

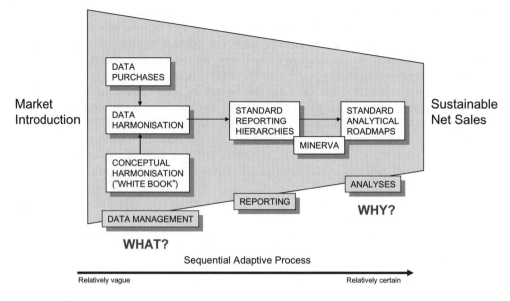

Figure 4.7

Process Model: From "Market Introduction" to "Sustainable Net Sales"

The "Business Intelligence" process model again follows the same basic principle we have already encountered – migrating from a very vague starting point towards a clear-cut evaluation, e.g. of a launch or a business case. Market Observation follows a systematic process between market data and corporate decision making based on insight patterns (see Figure 4.7).

As a consequence, the function comprises the following basic value-added contributions:

Integrated Data Management (Across Businesses and Geographies)

Valid insights about the performance in the market can only be based on highly standardised transnational databases residing in large-sized data warehouses. Here data from different suppliers and regions are harmonised according to corporate specifications ("White Book" standards). The effort guarantees meaningful aggregations beyond the country level as well as multi-source analytical operations on a basic and advanced level.

Basic Reporting/Standard Analytics

Basic reporting tasks usually start out with national/international *standard reporting* e.g. like company shares, SBU shares, national brand shares and move on to *standard analytical templates* analysing distribution, price, advertising, etc. Specific analytical modules are focusing on new product success, pricing, portfolio/assortment evaluation (see Farris et al., 2006).

Advanced Analysis

Finally we end up with *advanced analytics* like marketing mix modelling where we provide insights on the relative impact of several marketing mix factors on total sales or "return on investment" calculations, where we try to give you an impression on the financial return of marketing expenditures.

Illustrative Business Case: Analysing Market Share Losses

In the late 90s a major decline of market share was observed for one of the leading brands in one of our categories. While the waning share was clearly visible at the surface, it was largely unknown in the beginning why this apparent continuous erosion of consumer interest was occuring: there was no *single* factor that obviously went along with the negative development.

The Business Intelligence function performed a thorough evaluation based both on syndicated data from multiple integrated databases (e.g. trade scanner data, bi-monthly audit data, consumer panel, advertising tracking data, media data, shipments) as well as discrete events in the respective market (e.g. competitor launches) – trying to establish a meaningful pattern of valid cause–effect relationships.

Transnational integrated reporting and analysis portals like "MINERVA"[4] made this a manageable task within a relatively short period of time. Among other issues it was found among for the major sales-oriented parameters that:

- The brand was suffering from both a *quantitative and a qualitative distribution problem* which was worsening across time: e.g. more and more variants were introduced at a faster and faster pace to compensate the declining net sales. As a first consequence, full distribution levels for the new variants were never reached. As a second consequence, the brand appeared differently to consumers in its portfolio – dependent on the fragmented distribution level that was reached in the respective outlet. The major competitors had a smaller number of variants, a higher distribution and thus a more consistent shelf image.
- The brand had higher *promotion levels* compared to competition, yet was not able to convert these high promotion levels to respective promotion-based sales. This again had to do with the quality of the promotions (e.g. share of price promotions vs. other promotion types like second displays), their timings and the distribution of promotion efforts on the different outlet types.
- The brand had moved itself into a *price positioning* that proved to be untenable given its perceived brand equity. Slipping into a price gap that a competitor opened up due to their price reductions, the brand quickly lost buyers due to an unfavourable price perception.
- Finally, the market moved away from the benefits which were making up the core positioning of the brand. Its major functional proposition to the consumer quickly became outdated. Furthermore, the advertising reflected worlds that today's consumers could no longer get emotionally attached to.

There were many more findings that the Business Intelligence function provided to the Brand Management. Most of these conclusions could be drawn on an international basis by analysing in different geographical contexts. The synopsis of all bits and pieces led to a general

---

[4] The MINERVA portal is a joint development of Henkel KGaA and ACNielsen.

set of indicated actions which were transformed immediately into corrective measures. Today the brand is enjoying a healthy market share again.

THE "RESEARCH PLAN" AS A BRIDGE BETWEEN MACRO AND MICRO PROCESSES

Until now we have referred to three different stages of the research process and what potential interactions with the consumer they enable. The next issue on our agenda is how to sequence the respective studies in a formal programme for each and every major research project – thus using "research planning" as a sound basis for optimal Market Research process hygiene.

"Research Planning" basically means to adjust the investments behind a project in a meaningful relation to its entrepreneurial risk. Although feasible, it seems odd to run a full test market simulation study in order to assess the incremental market share for the 25th colour nuance of a hair coloration product. The relative risk would not at all be related to the projected costs of the study.

On the other hand – introducing a new product under a new brand in a new geography represents a major risk for a corporation. Thus all potential candidates for failure should be checked and adjusted. According to the perceived degree of risk Market Research develops a "Research Programme" in close conjunction with the respective SBU.

In many corporations the "Research Programme" has become an integral part of the catalogue of documents that need to be submitted for major "decision gates", like e.g. an "investment gate" after concept testing or a "launch gate" after the full development of the branded product.

The "Research Programme" may take different formats. The most obvious format is simply a list of projected studies in their sequential order, establishes an upfront plan of the various research activities summarised under a marketing project. Figure 4.8 shows an example. The listing includes basic information about the research issue, the tools to cover the questions, costs and timing. Ideally the programme covers all potential market research activities including the various steps for Market Observation (which have been omitted here).

In the above case the hypothetical corporation intends to introduce an existing product in a new geography. As quite common in the food category, even international brands undergo slight modifications both in the product and the communication to cater to the local tastes of consumers. The "Research Plan" is thus reflecting properly the basic research activities that are needed to mould the offer to the new market: besides a general check on the concept, the packaging (only for shelf impact) and the possible adaptation of taste parameters of the product itself, there is clearly a major concern with the TV communication which is checked in three iterative steps (focus groups, in-depth interviews, quantitative ad test) in order to tweak locally the advertising message/execution.

Corporations use different forms of "Research Plans" which may go beyond the straightforward listing of the process elements. Quite common is a more complex version which rather takes on the form of a "Research Protocol". It exhibits the activities and results of the Research Plan (including benchmarks, and comments).

Furthermore, elements like decision rules or action standards are included for each of the projects, thus introducing a more pronounced decisional hygiene as a major element of process hygiene. Others include a track record of which studies have actually been skipped or cancelled

Marketing Scen.	Existing brand, new geography
SBU	Baby Foods
Brand	Brand X
Project	Brand Extension: **"Project X"**
Objective	Determine the potential for Project X in new geography

	Issue	Programme	Cost Estimate	Timing
Background				
Concept **– qualitative** **– quantitative**	Fine tuning	Focus Groups Concept Test		
Mix Facets **– Packaging** **– Formula** **– Communic.** **– Price**	Pack stand-out Taste Evaluate TVC No issue	Packaging test Taste test Focus Groups In-Depth Interviews Ad test		
Complete Mix	Check sales volume	Test Market Simulation		
TOTAL				

Figure 4.8

in order to call attention to the remaining decision risk that has not been covered appropriately by Market Research.

In sum, procedures like the "Research Plan" provide a powerful yet simple tool to decide about the scope of Market Research investments upfront and adjusting them to the underlying entrepreneurial risk. More elaborate forms even include a normative decision component for a higher degree of decisional hygiene.

The (corporate) Market Researcher is responsible for shaping the "Research Plan", advocate it and discuss it with Senior Management.

"Research Plans" and "Research Protocols" can be tied closely to existing decision gates – like, e.g. the "Go 1" gate (decision to develop a project) or "Go 2" gate (decision to launch a project).

The "Go 1" usually presents the product idea (e.g. derived from Consumer Insights) and the brand carrier – both as an empirically-backed plan, suggests early executional approaches for the main marketing mix factors and confirms the feasibility of the project in terms of R&D, production, etc. The "Go 1" would typically include a *Research Plan*. It provides content, timing, and costs for developing the project until the launch.

The "Go 2" typically presents the concrete realisation of the plan in the form of a project with finalised mix and financial plan. The "Go 2" would come along with a *Research Protocol*. The Research Protocol exhibits the actually performed activities and results of the Research Programme (including benchmarks and comments). It represents the input for the final launch decision.

"Research Plans" and "Research Protocols" are a fundamental exercise to establish both process hygiene and decisional hygiene within the overall Market Research process. The consistent use of these tools help the corporation to develop an upfront perspective of its research investments, tailor it better to the current knowledge deficits and adjust the research budget properly.

THE "MICRO" PROCESS

The "Micro" Process – Designing the Study

So far we have discussed a "Macro" process which provides an overarching frame for the research activities. Furthermore, we have seen how to choose from a broad range of potential studies those that make sense for a given research question under a given risk level.

We will now turn to the "Micro" level, i.e. the *process level of the individual study*. Lachmann and Schroiff addressed this issue back in 1998 (Lachmann & Schroiff, 1998) under the general discussion heading of what constitutes "quality" in Market Research.

For Lachmann & Schroiff (1998) the "quality" of a Market Research study was rooted in a variety of influential factors that require tight control by different players in this process. In the end, the quality of a project is reflected in the quality of business decisions that the research enables. The focus of their "quality" concept thus is clearly on generating a superior *intellectual* contribution to facilitate optimal decision making.

We are updating this point today due to recent developments that focus increasingly on "logistic" features of a Market Research study by emphasising delivery times and prices. Although favourable cost–quality relationships are also of importance in our discipline, we must recognise that the result of a Market Research project is predominantly a *single intellectual contribution* and not a *physical mass product*.

In other words, users of research should be reminded that the policies of a corporate purchasing department can be applied successfully to crude oil or office supply, but might not be fully appropriate when applied to intellectual property. The traditional notion of "quality" that is so deeply connected to error-free industrial mass production, does not seem applicable in a case where several parties are trying to generate business insights tailored to changing business decisions.

The 1998 paper by Lachmann & Schroiff was built on two causal factors for "quality", (a) the *division of roles* in a typical market research project and (b) the *various process steps* of a typical market research project.

The "division of roles" relates directly to the organisational context in which Market Research departments are typically embedded. We recognise different organisational models where, e.g. the function may be reporting directly to the CEO or the CMO (Chief Marketing Officer). On the other hand, Market Research departments are deeply rooted in the various businesses – reporting, e.g. to the head of a strategic business unit (SBU). Other models again emphasise a central Market Research department located at the Headquarters while others prefer to have the research function locally spread in a decentralised function to be near to the local consumer.

Whatever the organisational form is – in the end it matters whether the "division of roles" can exist as a form of conceptual independence between the Marketing and the Market Research function.

Why is the "division of roles" critical? Let us take a look at a research process in academia and a market research. In an *academic process* of knowledge generation, different roles are typically pooled in the same person. The scientist develops a working hypothesis based on her/his prior knowledge or insights, draws up an experimental plan for investigation, runs the study, collects the data, applies tons of statistics and maths to the data, and sooner or later comes up with some findings which either corroborate or overthrow her/his prior conjectures.

In a typical *Market Research project*, one commonly finds a division of roles. In most cases the process is divided up between three parties: the business manager, the corporate market researcher and the research supplier. Although we are personally opposed to a strict division of roles in that context, the classical division of responsibilities can be regarded as follows:

The *Business Manager* defines the nature of the research problem, the *Corporate Market Researcher* translates the knowledge deficit into a testable design, while the *Research Supplier* is mostly involved in the actual conduct of the study, the data reduction, etc.

In that case we find a challenging set-up of roles which bears both opportunities and risks. Obviously it matters how tight the interface is between the three parties in order to truly create operational value by answering the right question with the right design and the right procedure.

Figure 4.9 provides an overview of the "Micro" process by pairing the individual roles with a typical sequence of procedural steps that usually make up a research study.

It is assumed that the majority of research projects follow the simple path outlined here. Let us take a brief walk through the various steps before identifying the major problems associated with the sequence of events in this typical order.

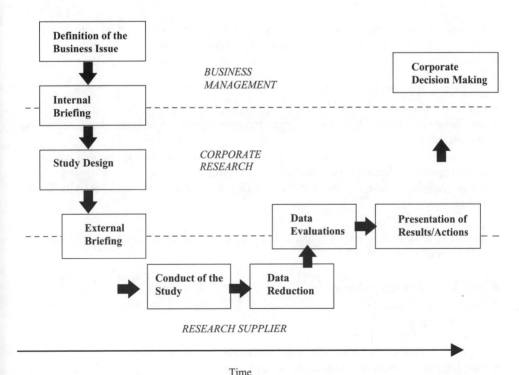

Figure 4.9

Definition of the Research Question

In the most ideal case, a specific piece of information is missing to arrive at a major business decision. This means that at the very beginning of the research process it is already crystal-clear what type of information needs to be collected in order to obtain the required insights, which expectations the respective business manager has regarding the potential set of outcomes of the study and which conditional actions are taken as a consequence of the actual research results.

In most other cases, however, the fundamental research objective needs to be thoroughly prepared. The "return on investment" (ROI) of a study can fail right at the start: once badly conceived, all subsequent professionalism is unlikely to bring about a usable result. "We have to test my TV spot" is not a sign of a very precise problem formulation. *Vague problem descriptions* have led to many procedural and interpretational mistakes in the past.

Another fundamental mistake in the research process is the mixing *of problem and method*. "We have to test my TV spot in a standardised test" is a striking example of this mistake. In that case the method dictates the problem formulation – something which is clearly against the rules of empirical sciences and must lead to faulty decisions.

The precise description of the problem or the lack of knowledge not only facilitates the design of an appropriate market research experiment but also has an impact on the evaluation of the results and the resulting actions. If a problem has been clearly defined hypotheses can be derived which can be tested empirically.

There are a couple of other major problems such as:

- Methods dictate problems – the "easy way out"! The problem is not "I have to do a commercial test" – that is a *means* (tool) and not a *problem*/objective.
- Zooming in too early on one hypothesis, dictated mainly on the basis of past experience.
- Often, decision makers take too narrow a focus – concentrating on the short-term, tangible, quantitative type of problems.
- Decision makers spend too little time on specifying their problem.
- Insufficient coverage of hypotheses – you can never explore a hypothesis that you have not considered!
- Do not rely on "proven hypotheses" – they may guide you in the exploration, but can be extreme pitfalls. Challenge the constraints of the given . . .
- Create hypotheses first – evaluate them later (e.g. by means of Market Research). Do not restrict yourself!

What can be of help in such a situation is to ask oneself a set of very basic questions (see also Hammond et al., 1999).

- What is my decision problem?
- What are my objectives?
- What are my alternatives in this problem?
- What are the consequences of the various alternatives?
- What are the trade-offs between the consequences?
- How uncertain/certain are these consequences?
- How high is the risk tolerance of myself/my organisation?
- What other issues are linked to this decision?

- What types of information do we need to take that decision?
- How much do they cost – how much are they worth?

Another major issue is to think of potential outcomes of the study plus the indicated actions following each of the various outcomes. Therefore at the beginning of the research process the actions following the various outcomes have to be described as precisely as possible. Only then can the interpretation and evaluation of market research data become clear and operational.

A typical set of standard questions in order to provide the required input quality would include:

- What is the marketing problem?
- What are the hypotheses on the cause of this problem?
- What will be the operational outcomes of a study?
- What are the conditional actions under each outcome?

Step 1: Isolate Your Problem

In general, problem analysis is started by the inspection of market data. The data might indicate a number of problems. We differentiate between the *general* marketing problem (decrease in sales) and a number of *specific* marketing problems.

Specific marketing problems result from a more detailed analysis of the general marketing problem. Examples of specific marketing problems are price problems, distribution problems, awareness problems, etc. – i.e. factors related to the various components of the marketing mix. Sources for the general marketing problem might be found in more than one of these factors.

Step 2: Develop Causal Hypotheses

The next step consists in the development of causal hypotheses for the specific marketing problems. Questions such as "Why do we have an awareness problem with product X?" should be considered. Possible answers to these questions lead to the formulation of causal hypotheses such as "We probably have awareness problems with product X because my share of voice in the last 12 months was considerably below average". Another hypothesis might be "We probably have awareness problems with product X because my spot has an insufficient impact" or "We probably have awareness problems with product X because my communication is interchangeable with spots from other brands". Each of these hypotheses can be tested empirically.

Step 3: Point Out Which Possible Actions Should be Taken as a Result of the Various Outcomes of the Study

It should be pointed out clearly in the request what the possible actions under the various outcomes are. The reason for this step is best illustrated by the following examples.

A request was made to test a particular spot in an advertising test. In the briefing it was mentioned that the spot would probably not go on air in this particular country for some legal reasons. It was supposed to be tested only because other countries were testing the spot. Under these circumstances an advertising test made no sense because the outcome of the test would be of no decisional value – obviously the decision had already been made.

A similar event occurred when a request was made to test a particular fragrance in a sniff test. By chance market research learned that the perfume would never be used in the formula because of its costs. Nevertheless the fragrance was incorporated in the test because one simply wanted to know "how good we would be if we had the money". Again the decisional value of the results is zero, the research has no operational consequences. Therefore it is extremely important to specify which actions should be taken as a result of the various outcomes.

Internal Briefing

Ideally the marketing problem is described by a formal research request before a certain methodology is chosen. The research request is the market research brief given by Marketing to Market Research. It describes the problem which needs to be addressed by market research in a qualified way. At the same time it is a documentation for all individuals involved in the research process why a piece of research was initiated. It defines the criteria of decision making. It describes in advance "how" the research will answer a question and avoids disappointment in final presentations. Let us now look at the various steps more closely.

The research request and the briefing typically help market researchers to grasp the scope of the problem, the expected key findings and their decisional implications. A tight briefing bridges the critical gap between a client and a researcher by spelling out precisely the context in which the problem is embedded.

Consequently, major problems may arise in case this "meeting of the minds" is not taking place. Unfortunately many research investments do not yield an appropriate ROI because clients interact with researchers in a kind of "throw it over the wall" mentality: essential aspects of the problem are not mentioned, the full scope of the problem situation remains in the dark and the decisional implications are left open. This may happen even in the case of a well worked-out initial problem setting. Nevertheless the consistent mapping of the study's objectives to a Marketing context are crucial for a researcher to develop a research approach.

Besides the written research request it thus seems advisable to conduct formal briefing talks where both Marketing and Market Research interacts closely against the background of the actual research project.

Study Design

After the research request has been completed it is submitted to Market Research. The design of the market research study, the selection of test persons, etc. is entirely the responsibility of Market Research. Basically the researcher provides a format that translates the abstract problem into a set of concrete marketing actions. The key issues here are:

- Design a study that answers the research question.
- Maintain an acceptable cost–benefit ratio.
- Point out the limitations (e.g. the constraints on internal and external validity of the data).
- Convert the empirical data into a decision-oriented format that provides an answer to the research problem.

We cannot go into detail regarding the various aspects that need to be covered in this translation process, but it is definitely more than converting marketing questions into a "paper and pencil" questionnaire. Study design involves a professional treatment of many issues and questions in order to guarantee a scientifically sound approach to the research questions. Here are a (non-exhaustive) couple of issues that are crucial from our perspective:

Study Design

How should we design the study? With what properties of the systems to be studied must we reckon? How shall we choose experimental treatments?

Information Value

In what setting and by what overall strategy shall we gather evidence? What resources does this require? What amount and kinds of information can we gain?

Target Group

How shall we select events (actors, behaviours, contexts) from among a population and how shall we apportion them to be observed?

Dependent variables

From what sources (subjective report, direct observation, or other) shall we seek evidence about each property which is to be measured? What comparisons among objects shall we ask of the actor?

Experimental Control

How shall we carry out manipulation and control procedures?

Turning Observations Into Data

How shall we convert observational records into data? What kind of data will we generate? What assumptions do we wish to make about the data?

Data Analysis Questions

How shall we organise the data for analysis? What kinds of questions do we want to ask of the data? What kinds of analytic models are available for my questions, given my data and assumptions?

External Briefing

What follows now in most cases is the involvement of an (external) research supplier. Usually a pre-selection is made by the corporate Market Researcher since many research suppliers have specialised in certain topic areas. What was mentioned above regarding the "meeting of the minds" between corporate Marketing and Market Research units also holds true for the next intellectual transfer phase: the briefing of the research supplier about the study design, its origins in the respective business context, and its implications for the operational details of the planned research.

The research supplier adds to the ROI of the study by acting as a sounding board and pointing out relevant opportunities for further research or constraints to the original briefing content.

Major problems do always arise in case this translation of the study design into the actual procedure or questionnaire is not absolutely "waterproof". Relevant aspects of the study are skipped, not precisely reflected in the questionnaire, etc., if the interaction is not managed professionally from both the corporate researcher and the research supplier.

A major risk to an adequate translation of a research question into a suitable questionnaire represents the "standard" character of many research efforts today. In order to minimise time and costs, research issues are either bundled or addressed in a standard type of approach. This may make sense in some cases (e.g. for benchmarking reasons), but usually ignores the fact that most research projects tend to be unique due to the specific business settings under which they are commissioned.

Conduct of the Study, Data Reduction, Data Evaluation

The research supplier is responsible for the professional conduct of the study – e.g. the precise sampling according to the sampling frame, the correct assessment of the subjects' responses, etc., based on a universal and well-conceived coding frame, for the correct use of data reduction algorithms and statistical inference and for the appropriate evaluation of the resulting patterns in the light of the original research questions.

Again we would like to point out that each research project tends to be specific and addresses a set of questions which should not be subject to standardisation – neither in terms of asking patterns, data reduction, nor particularly evaluation.

Presentation of Results/Indicated Actions

This step is concerned with the communication of the research findings and the respective business recommendations to the client. It is probably one of the most ignored steps, nevertheless it is a truly important one. What actually is happening here can be summarised as the perceived value of Market Research in general. A sloppy presentation by an untrained presenter (who for whatever reason shoots past the main targets of the study) will kill the best planned and thoroughly conducted study.

The presentation is the Market Researcher's "moment of truth" where one has to take a position about consumer reality based on accumulated facts and knowledge. This mental aggregation may be difficult per se, it is even thornier to stand up in front of a corporate audience and defend the findings against all forms of criticism. We actually saw more projects fail in the final presentation than at any other stage of the research cycle.

This clearly must have implications for the selection and training of Market Research staff – both at a corporate research department as well as with outside suppliers. The data nerd hiding behind his/her computer print-outs might be great for the trickiest jobs at the back office, but no good for speaking publicly to the board and recommending certain business directions convincingly.

The most common problem in presentations is thus what we call "decision fright" – a set of observations is not bundled in an insight which then again entails a clear course what to do next. At times Market Researchers tend to hesitate and not point out the managerial consequences of the findings in order not to get between corporate firing lines. "Decision fright" basically destroys one of the major objectives of a study – to seek clarification among conflicting views within a group of decision makers. If this crucial benefit of research is not delivered, the value of the total project is seriously diminished. It ends up with a quite common form of "cherry picking" where different parties seek confirmatory evidence for their opinion among the informational debris that the presentation has left behind.

Corporate Decision Making

The final stage is to take a *corporate* decision about what to do next. The emphasis here is truly on "corporate": insights and indicated actions must now be viewed within a general corporate decisional context. For example, despite negative evidence the corporation might decide in the end that the product is going to be launched in order to be strategically present in a specific market. It further means that the decision cannot be delegated entirely to the consumer. Too often, we hear as an ex-post excuse ". . . the consumer has told us in a study not to launch this product". In fact, it is the corporation that has a final say in weighing the empirical evidence in favour of or against a decision. Market Research reflects the actual consumers' perspective in the best possible way.

Market Research is an aid to decision making; it is not the decision itself. So use Market Research in order to establish a skin-tight relationship to the consumer, but take it as an input for managerial considerations. The manager's job starts when the insights are available.

CONCLUDING REMARKS

Market Research represents a great opportunity for any business – but only when properly used. One of the most critical preconditions for proper use is the corporate commitment to view Market Research as an *ordered process*.

We hope that this chapter has adequately described that value from investment in research can only be expected where a company subscribes to a continuous interfacing with consumers. Anticipating consumer needs, developing products that meet those needs and monitoring the preconditions for sales-development closely represent the value drivers for successful corporations these days (see Deshpande, 1999).

It is the task of Market Research to provide updates on mental models about consumers continuously – how they think, how they feel, how they act. This chapter has provided a blueprint of how this can be accomplished in principle. Naturally, our general outline may require additional tweaking under specific corporate circumstances, but we are firmly convinced that the processes described here help to create both procedural and decisional hygiene in the Market Research processes.

REFERENCES

Aaker, D. (2004) *Brand Portfolio Strategy*. Free Press.
Arnold, D. (1997) *The Handbook of Brand Management* (2nd edn). Addison-Wesley.
Barabba, V. and Zaltman, G. (1991) *Hearing the Voice of the Market*. Harvard Business School Press.
Blattberg, R., Glazer, R. and Little, J.D.C. (eds.) (1994) *The Marketing Information Revolution*. Harvard Business School Press.
Bruhn, M. and Steffenhagen, H. (Hrsg.) (1998) *Marktorientierte Unternehmensführung* (2. Aufl.). Gabler.
Brzoska, L. (2004) *Die Conjoint-Analyse als Instrument zur Prognose von Preisreaktionen*. Kovac.
Clancy, K.J., Shulman, R.S. and Wolf, M. (1994) *Simulated Test Marketing*. Lexington.
Curry, D.J. (1993) *The New Marketing Research Systems*. John Wileys & sons, Inc.
Deshpande, R. (ed.) (1999) *Developing a Market Orientation*. Sage Publications.
The Dove Report, www.campaignforrealbeauty.com/uploadedFiles/challenging_beauty.pdf
Esch, F.-R. (2004) *Strategie und Technik der Markenführung* (2. Aufl.. München: Vahlen.
Farris, P.W., Bendle, N.T., Pfeifer, P.E. and Reibstein, D.J. (2006) *Marketing Metrics: 50+ Metrics Every Executive Should Master*. Wharton School Publishing.
Green, P.E., Tull, D.S and Albaum, G. (1988) *Research for Marketing Decisions* (5th edn). Prentice Hall.

Haeckel, S. (1999) *Adaptive Enterprise – Creating and Leading Sense-and-Respond Organizations*. Harvard Business School Press.

Hammann, P. and Erichson, B. (1989) *Marktforschung* (2. Aufl.). Fischer Verlag.

Hammond, J.S., Keeney, R.L. and Raiffa, H. (1999) *Smart Choices. A Practical Guide to Making Better Decisions*. Harvard Business School Press.

Homburg, C. and Krohmer, H. (2003) *Marketingmanagement*. Gabler.

Keller, K. (2002) *Branding and Brand Equity*. Marketing Science Institute.

Lachmann, U. and Schroiff, H.-W. (1998) Marktforschungs-Qualität – ein Begriff der Buchhaltung oder der Geisteshaltung? *Planung and Analyse,* **2**(98), *14–18*.

McQuarrie, E.F. (1998) *Customer Visits – Building a Better Market Focus* (2nd edn). Sage Publications.

Morgan, D.L. (ed.) (1993) *Successful Focus Groups.* Sage Publications

Moscowitz, H.R. (1996) *Consumer Testing and Evaluation of Personal Care Products*. Marcel Dekker.

Roleff, R. (2001) *Marketing für die Marktforschung*. Gabler

Schroiff, H.-W. (in press) Marktforschung. In: *Enzyklopädie der Diagnostik*. Hogrefe.

Schroiff, H.-W. (2001) Durchführung des Markttests. In: Pepels, W. (Hrsg.). *Launch – Die Produkteinführung*. Kohlhammer.

Schroiff, H.-W. (2006) Marketingcontrolling durch Marktforschung. In: Reinecke, S. and Tomczak, Th., (Hrsg.) *Handbuch Marketingcontrolling* (2nd ed.). Gabler.

Simon, H. (1992) *Preismanagement* (2. Aufl.). Gabler.

Steffenhagen, H. (1996) *Wirkungen der Werbung*. Augustinus Verlag.

Steffenhagen, H. (2004) *Marketing – eine Einführung* (5. Aufl.). Kohlhammer.

Tull, D.S. and Hawkins, D.I. (1987) Marketing research (4th ed.). Macmillan.

Urban, G.L. and Hauser, J.R. (1980) *Design and Marketing of New Products*. Prentice Hall.

Zaltman, G. (2003) *How Customers Think*. Harvard Business School Press.

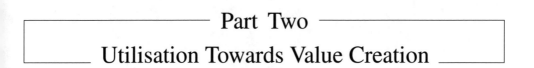

Part Two
Utilisation Towards Value Creation

5

Developing a Company Strategy

Gerard Loosschilder and Maarten Schellekens

INTRODUCTION

A corporate strategy is about the fundamental choices that a company makes: How to grow? In which markets and categories do we wish to play? How do we position ourselves to win, relative to competition? What capabilities do we build and invest in? These fundamental questions have to be answered while crafting a corporate strategy. The American Marketing Association defines Corporate Strategy as "The overall plan that integrates the strategies of all the businesses within the corporation. It usually describes the overall mission, the financial and human resource strategies and policies that affect all businesses within the corporation, the organisation structure, the management of the interdependencies among businesses, and major initiatives to change the scope of the firm such as acquisitions and divestments."

Marketing research can play many roles to help define the company strategy, such as providing the inputs to describe the market and competitive environment in which the company operates, help define the marketing strategies and tactics to conquer a market, or help to optimise the execution. The key word is "help"; market research is a supportive function in many organisations, but also a pivotal one in providing a vision on the outside world. In this chapter, we describe the role of market research in many aspects of strategy development. We will explore the nature of corporate strategy first. Then, dissect the various steps of strategy definition and provide examples of the role market research can play. The steps are: landscaping new markets to discover new opportunities, then the decision where to play, and finally developing new strategic propositions in the new territory. Then we will move on to the question of how market research can support merger and acquisition processes as an alternative to organic growth. We finish this chapter with a critical note addressing the role of market researchers in the corporate strategy development process.

THE STRATEGY PROCESS IN LARGE CORPORATIONS

In smaller companies (SMEs), there is usually no formal strategy process. The strategy is implicit in the choices that executive management makes over time. Once in a while, and often issue-driven, the company reflects more fundamentally on where it stands, and what direction to take, redirecting the company strategy. In larger companies (e.g., Fortune 500), there is a formalised strategic process. The need to formalise the strategy process increases with the size of the company, because there are often more divisions or business units that need to be aligned, the number of stakeholders involved in strategic decisions explodes, and the external

Market Research Handbook, 5th Edition. Edited by M. van Hamersveld and C. de Bont.
© 2007 John Wiley & Sons, Ltd.

environment is more complex. Often, a dedicated person leading a small team of professionals is put in place to lead the strategy process. The focus is heavily on ensuring that the strategy process runs smoothly, but especially if this person is at a senior level in the organisation, she will also drive the discussion with regard to content. A formal strategy process is often carried out at fixed times in the year, with a meeting-structure set in place between relevant stakeholders. Usually, there is a fair balance between top-down deployment, in which senior management sets the overall direction, boundaries and targets for its divisions or business units, and a bottom-up contribution, in which the individual divisions and business units communicate their commitment within the current constraints and competitive environment. The time horizon is often three to five years. The series of meetings result in strategy documents and presentations, up to the Board of Management. Their final approval concludes the strategy process, after which execution starts.

Market research may support strategy definition in many ways. The most formal and structural is when it assumes a predefined role in the strategy process. Most strategy documents use a *situation-complication-resolution* framework to frame strategic issues.[1] Irrespective of level (company, division or business unit), one first needs to understand the current "status quo", or the situation one is in, including the overall context, e.g., the competitive landscape. The scope needs to be broad in order not to overlook opportunities and threats. Markets are often broadly defined. There is a focus on macro-trends impacting our industry: What happens in the world out there? How will demographic trends impact our business? What technological advancements are expected over the next decade? Which geographic markets are emerging? What happens in the retailer landscape? What consumer trends do we see? What opportunities does this provide, and what is our ability to successfully leverage them? These questions are complex and require expertise in relevant areas, if only because they are interwoven.

Let me give an example (see also Figure 5.1). A fixed-line telecom operator faces a "situation" that is rapidly changing and that poses threats to its current business. First of all, mobile telephony is rapidly penetrating, cannibalising the fixed-line business. Secondly, there is the emergence of Voice-over-IP (VoIP), a new technology that allows consumers and companies to use the Internet for making phone calls, replacing the need for fixed-line telephony. But there are also other technical developments that provide threats but also opportunities, such as "Triple Play": the conversion of TV, telephone and the Internet. It implies that the competitive environment becomes increasingly complex, and players in all three areas (mobile phone, cable and fixed-line phone operators) have to determine how to compete in the future.

This fixed-line operator needs market research to get a fact-based understanding of developments in the outside world. Examples of questions on these outside developments where market research is able to make a contribution, are: How are the different market-segments developing (fixed line, mobile, Internet, VoIP, cable, etc.)? What are the technological developments in these areas? Who are the players in the market? How will the consumer respond to the new technologies? What new business models are likely to emerge? What are differences

---

[1] The Situation-Complication-Resolution is a framework that is often used for storytelling and originates with Aristotle in the time of Ancient Greece. A plot (like a strategy document) needs to have a beginning, middle and an end. The Situation sets the stage, and is needed to fully understand the next part that builds the tension in the story: the Complication. This is the element that needs to be resolved, like a septime chord in music. The final part, the Resolution, releases the tension through a satisfactory conclusion that continues logically from the storyline. In a strategy document, this is the part where the real strategic direction will be specified.

We believe it is very helpful to organise a strategy document (like a market research document, for that matter) in accordance with the ideas about good storytelling. A strategy document needs to be acted upon, so it is better to organise it in a way that helps readers to grasp the important information quickly and to navigate through the document easily. Strategy is often seen as an interruption of our busy day-to-day job, so people will read it in haste and pick out the information relevant to themselves, asking three elementary questions: "so what", "where does this come from" and "how does this affect me?"

Situation ↓	**State the condition at point of problem and the probable cause**
	A major telephone company active both in landline and mobile connections states:
	− Compared with the same period last year, we have lost 15 % of our fixed-line subscriptions and 25 % of our call volume.
	− Telephone services via VoIP and MSN Messenger are booming. Industry reports tell us the call volume has grown with 500 % versus last year.
Complication ↓	**Flesh out barriers to come to solution**
	Consumers rely more on their cell phones even for calls at home (explaining the loss of fixed-line subscriptions) and on calls through VoIP and MSN Messenger. A complication is that we are involved in both fixed-line and mobile connections. So we cannot do anything that may hurt either part of our business (cannibalisation), for example by discouraging home calls from a mobile phone. Also, our fixed-line business benefits from high-speed Internet connections, so we can't discourage VoIP. But, it is unclear how the business model behind calls through VoIP and MSN Messenger can deliver us sustainable revenue.
Resolution	**Lay out possible solutions and the solution path**
	Possible solutions to better address the new dynamic may involve:
	− Actively promote home calls from a cell phone with special rates, and offer an upgrade package from fixed to mobile connections.
	− Actively promote upgrade of fixed lines to high-speed Internet connections, including a VoIP package to drive acceptance.
	− Offer a total package for mobile, fixed-line and VoIP, that optimises cost and choice-options for consumers (e.g. VoIP isused when possible, but fixed-line option is still available).
	A monitoring programme will be initiated to see if the loss of fixed lines is stopped, converted into a growth of high-speed Internet connections, or of mobile connections andcall volume including home calls.

Figure 5.1   Situation-Complication-Resolution Framework: a simplified example

across geographies (e.g., USA versus Europe)? Questions like these require a high level of market research involvement, with high leverage of relevant providers of data, information and consultancy. Given the high need for expertise in telecom, specialised providers are often selected, and there is a high reliance on existing, secondary data sources.

This example indicates that market research plays (or should play) a significant role in times when the landscape is rapidly changing, and especially in the case of "paradigm shifts". These changes may impact the company significantly, and therefore one needs a thorough understanding of their drivers to deal with them. Most changes can be attributed to two drivers: (1) the presence or emergence of latent consumer needs and (2) the launch of disruptive innovations that appeal to these latent consumer needs.[2] A paradigm shift can change the competitive landscape dramatically. Incumbents lose their position and new entrants emerge. Examples are (1) Apple that has taken over leadership in the portable audio category from the Sony Walkman, (2) Canon who made the switch successfully to digital imaging whereas Kodak failed to do so, and (3) the success of the Blackberry in creating a multi-functional PDA that allows accessing and sending email anytime anywhere.

The problem with these rapid changes in the competitive landscape or "paradigm shifts" is that they are hard to set off, it is difficult to predict if they will be successful, and they are hard to react to (correct timing is key). The emergence of the mobile phone is an example. From the onset it has been a disruptive innovation appealing to latent consumer needs, creating a paradigm shift in interpersonal communication. But the failure of the industry to create demand for the third generation (3G) mobile telephony illustrates how hard it is to shift the paradigm. Many telecom companies made huge losses by making large investments in 3G licences and having no return on investment. Another example is the supersonic jet (e.g., the Concorde), which never turned into a profitable business. Two conditions have to be met in order to create a paradigm shift: (1) There has to be a latent demand that is big enough to create a sufficient revenue stream at sufficient margin levels within a reasonable time after entering the market, and (2) one also has to find the right go-to-market strategy to trigger and activate it. Both challenges offer a great opportunity for market research to contribute.

To conclude, strategic analysis doesn't happen in a vacuum; but results from close collaboration among various stakeholders, often including dedicated strategists and sometimes market researchers. Typically, a senior company executive is responsible for the strategic analysis, and when the effort is really important, the CEO is directly involved. Strategy processes are very dynamic, interactive and iterative. The result is a story-telling document: it tells the story about what is happening in the marketplace, where we stand as a company, what future developments are likely to be, and what potential issues and/or opportunities we face as a result. It concludes with options: potential courses of actions that the company can undertake, including the trade-offs and risks involved. Market research tends to get less involved when it comes to outlining potential resolutions, and the reason is that in practice market research is more seen as a source for facts (the "situation" and to some extent the "complication"), than as a source of solutions (the "resolution").

A ROLE FOR MARKET RESEARCH IN CORPORATE STRATEGY

Developing a cohesive company strategy is a major intellectual and political challenge. Not only does the strategy impact the future choices within the company significantly, the

---

[2] Schellekens, M.P.G. and Laurentius, A., Turning threats into opportunities in times of paradigm shifts, Presentation for the conference "The New Competition: Challenges and Opportunities", Marketing Science Institute, Lisbon, 2006.

development of a strategy is also full of ambiguity. There is no "one size fits all"; each company has a unique position requiring a unique, custom-made strategy. In the end, a strategy is based on a number of premises and belief-systems that can never be fully validated but merely be disputed. In the science of company strategy, paradigms emerge and are over time superseded by other paradigms. Figure 5.2 provides an overview of influential paradigms, attempting to outline their implications for market research contributing to company strategy.

Influential strategists are often considered "gurus", their paradigms undisputable truths. However, their value is not so much in the frameworks they provide but their underlying message. Although their work is usually based on careful research among a broad sample of companies, their conclusions can vary significantly. Consequently, their work should be considered a source of inspiration, not the absolute truth and an off-the-shelf strategy. Executives should take the frameworks into account, but then assess them on their relevance to their own situation (i.e., the company's profile and the environment it operates in) and then adapt and apply them to their best knowledge. It is precisely for this reason that a thorough, fact-based underpinning of strategic choices is vital. Market research plays an indispensable role in this.

The gurus and their paradigms typically do not pay explicit attention to the role of market research, but – interpreting the different paradigms – we can infer how the role may vary by paradigm. The paradigms differ in their *focus*: either outside-in (market intelligence focuses on the outside world to monitor trends and developments presenting them back to the business as opportunities and threats) or inside-out (market intelligence works with the business to maximise the value of the company's intangible assets, e.g., turning technologies and other competencies into products and services). From the description of the different frameworks in Figure 5.2, it is clear that the different points of departure (outside-in and inside-out) can coexist.

LANDSCAPING NEW MARKETS

The Situation-Complication-Resolution framework may offer a neat rational framework for analysing and setting a strategic direction, it also has a blind spot: it is by its nature reactive, and to some extent deterministic. What it misses is imagination, intuition, creativity and the sense that one can shape markets. That is why we also actively need to engage in, what we call, landscaping new markets. The purpose of opening up new markets is to drive top-line growth. The very first exploratory step is to landscape the market, which is very much a discovery process, in fact. We may wonder if landscaping the new market is the right word, because essentially, the new market is not there yet, or only – and hardly visibly – emerging. To complete the analogy with landscaping, one way to see it is to describe a yard by describing the lawn, the deck, the terrace, the border with plants and trees, and the fencing. However, in our situation it is more accurate to describe the yard if it is just a bare piece of land, perhaps with some plants rooting. Landscaping is truly a discovery process, in which one tries to visualise what is not there yet, but what, with a little work, could be there.

It is arguable if market researchers will play a significant role in the landscaping of new markets. Landscaping is seeing a market that does not yet exist and leveraging its opportunity when it has not materialised yet. Entrepreneurs are better at this than market researchers. Market researchers are better at describing an existing market and its current size, growth and other dynamics in painstaking detail. Landscaping new markets is *not* describing the current

Influential Strategists	Key Message	Focus	Implications for Market Intelligence
Michael Porter "Competitive Strategy" (1980)	Five forces of competitive strategy place the market, the customer, the competitive environment, and the supplier base at the starting point of a strategy.	Outside-in	Focus on building intelligence around the five forces: customers, suppliers, current competitors & new entrants, and adjacent categories & substitute products.
Hamel and Prahalad "Competing for the Future" (1994)	Companies should focus on core competences, as long-term competitiveness is derived from the ability to develop core competences more efficiently (lower cost, higher speed) than competitors.	Inside-out	Find new markets and applications for existing competences (e.g., technologies, products, service delivery, organisational capabilities).
Treacy and Wiersema "The Discipline of Market Leaders" (1994)	Companies compete best by focusing on one dimension of value to excel in (operational excellence, product leadership or customer intimacy).	Based on choice	Depends on chosen value dimension: support performance claim development to claim best total cost or best product, or develop customer understanding to deliver the best total solution.
Reichheld "The Loyalty Effect" (1996)	Companies can achieve sustainable profitable growth by focusing on adding value to its customers and in this way deserving their loyalty, not by exploiting customers.	Outside-in	Focus on customer loyalty and relationship intelligence, supporting retention of the current customer base rather than recruitment of new customers.
Foster and Kaplan "Creative Destruction" (2001)	"Older" companies are more risk-aversive than newer companies, making them relatively un-innovative and process driven. New entrants see gaps in market and create propositions to fill gaps. The information age will expedite this process, forcing incumbents to become more innovative and make strategic leaps.	Outside-in	Strategic, creative and insight-driven market intelligence to identify business opportunities. Creative business intelligence to timely spot new trends, business models paradigms and new ventures leveraging or building these trends to follow, leap frog, partner or acquire them.
Jim Collins "Good to Great" (2001)	Great strategies are based upon a deep understanding of the intersection of three key-dimensions (What can we be best at in the world? What drives our economic engine? What are we deeply passionate about?), and translate this to a simple concept (the "Hedgehog")	Inside-out	Support of a relentless execution against the company s competencies, economic engine and passions, and by that, being a loyal passenger of the "bus", the set of company employees with the highest potential.
Barwise and Meehan "Simply Better" (2004)	Strategy should be focused on delivering consistently better than competition on generic category benefits, as customers usually choose the brand, which they think will most reliably deliver the basics.	Inside-out	Focus on what it takes to be ahead in category benefits, and support performance claim development on these benefits.
Chan Kim and Mauborgne "Blue Ocean Strategy" (2004)	Instead of battling competitors within the confines of existing industries/categories, companies should create "blue oceans" of uncontested market space ripe for growth. Such strategic moves ("value innovations") create powerful leaps in value for both the company and its customers, rendering rivals obsolete and unleashing new demand.	Outside-in	Focus on identifying white spaces (unmet or latent needs not being met yet) and support product concept development in this space.

Figure 5.2   Strategy paradigms and the role of market intelligence in corporate strategy

user base and their satisfaction with current products, as it will only result in incremental innovation. All bets are off; we are looking for an opportunity for breakthrough innovation, shifting the paradigm of product purchase and usage fundamentally, and changing consumer consumption patterns. For example, the launch of the microwave changed the way people had dinner with the introduction of microwave-able TV dinners to be consumed in front of the television.

It is a discovery process in which one does not know what one does not know; we are looking for something that is not there, at most just emerging. This requires some special skills and tools that market research could master and offer back to the company.

1. Landscaping requires market structure analysis – identifying all stakeholders in the market, and the policies, strategies and tactics that define market positions, and drive change in this market.
2. Landscaping requires patience – take your time for discovery and give meaning to what you see. That's because one needs to reach beyond the obvious – reach beyond what is already there. It may well be that staring out of the window is your strongest tool.
3. Landscaping requires "new eyes". It is not without reason that ethnographic research and cultural anthropology are now so popular – it becomes harder to innovate and come up with new-to-the-world ideas. Ethnography has taught us to immerse ourselves in the subject we are trying to understand (e.g., the tribe of "young mothers"), to go beyond the material culture of what they do and consume, and look for a deeper meaning. Only when we are fully immersed, we may deduce the latent needs that are fundamental to one's behaviours, and induce new ways to better address these latent needs. Market researchers can introduce new techniques to their business enticing the business to look with "new eyes".
4. Landscaping means exploring new ways to immerse with the target group. Here, market research could learn from creative entrepreneurs in entirely different fields such as the tourist industry. For example, this industry offers urban jungle tours that could compete with our ethnographic methods as a way to immerse with a specific target group and participate in its daily life.
5. Landscaping requires new thinking styles found typically with owners of creative thinking (e.g., Bono's Thinking Hats). Market researchers are typically analytic thinkers, good at deduction and induction, whereas landscaping also requires creative and lateral thinking, and finding analogies.
6. Landscaping requires the stamina to ask, and answer, the "so what" question. Typically, landscaping requires trend and foresight information, but this is dead information if we cannot answer the question "so what"? So what if the globe is warming, if the population is aging, or if people live second, virtual lives on the Internet? What does it mean to my business and me, and how can I turn this into an opportunity? Apart from just delivering the trend and foresight information, market researchers can become facilitators of business-thinking by organising "so what" workshops and becoming more provocative and daring.
7. But also, landscaping means that market research must not only aspire to provide the ultimate answer, but just to inspire, and facilitate others to come up with the answer.

Of course there are also more analytic roles market research can take in the landscaping process – roles that are more in our comfort zone. Anobvious one is by answering the brand extension question: how far can we stretch our brand while entering new product and service categories before we will lose our credibility (in the old and new space), and will no longer be able to command the premium we were used to in our current product category.

CHOOSING WHERE TO PLAY

We landscape a new market by having a fully external orientation. It does not address the major strategic question for a company of where it wants to play in this newly identified landscape. What does the brand or company want to be to whom? What does it want to stand for? Who does it intend to attract and sell to? The company's mission and vision already imply the answers to these questions, but they still require translation into the company's brand identity guidelines. In this section we will discuss the role market research can play in this translation. The choice where to play is a management decision, but the decision is probably based on insight into the white spaces in the market and the competitive environment, which is a market research topic, as is how the brand is performing against its aspired identity.

The model (Figure 5.3) consists of interplay between four components across two axes. The vertical axis makes a distinction between reality (the actual situation) and aspiration. Typically, there is a gap between the two, most easily imagined as between brand identity (the aspired situation) and brand image (the actual situation), but also between target group (who people are) and target mindset (who people aspire to be). The horizontal axis distinguishes between the brand and the consumer, two identities in a communication process.

Brand image is how the consumer (or target group) perceives the brand. Most relevant is the gap between brand identity and image, e.g., the gap between consumer-brand perception and the brand's aspirations. The larger the gap, the more dramatic the corrective action required.

The Brand

Suppose the brand wants to become a major player in consumer healthcare solutions. Consumer healthcare solutions will then become a major theme in the brand identity and the brand

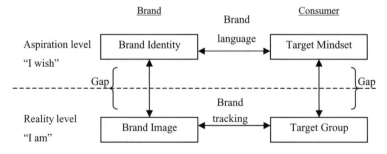

Figure 5.3   The gap between reality and aspiration[3]

[3] The model originates from the authors, but similar definitions can be found with thought-leaders in brand management (e.g., Paul Temporal (2002), Advanced Brand Management). "Brand identity" stands for the aspired brand (everything the brand wants to be seen as), to be distinguished from the perceived brand (the totality of consumer perceptions about the brand, or how they see it). The two may not coincide. We have stretched this distinction to also describe the possible gap between target group and mindset, indicating the difference between the reality of people's existing and their aspiration of what they would like to be. The key area and challenge is to connect the aspired brand (brand identity) with the aspirations of the consumer (target mindset) in a powerful way.

language. The brand language will be enriched with words to further underline and emphasise the brand identify, for example "clinical", "credible" or "empathetic" – adjectives to describe how the brand will deliver on its promise. This will be translated into brand identity guidelines that will be implemented across all touch points with the end consumer, e.g., ATL and BTL, packaging and point of sale communication.

The brand identity will also translate into the product portfolio, and which products in the portfolio will be considered image carriers; hero products providing evidence of the brand promise. What matters here is what the product can contribute to the brand, and which products will contribute to establishing the brand identity; not what the brand can contribute to the product. For example, if the brand wishes to be perceived as a major health player, it will communicate around products with a health association, e.g., power toothbrushes, blood pressure meters, medical equipment. Or it will emphasise the health aspects of products that are not immediately associated with health, e.g., domestic appliances.

Market research will play a role in the white space analysis if there is room for a brand focusing on health, and how that will help the brand positioning itself in the competitive environment and against market trends. Market research will also play a role in the definition of the gap between identity and image, i.e., how far away the brand is from being associated with "health". This will apply to the brand image in qualitative terms, e.g., how the brand performs on image statements such as "clinical", "credible" or "empathetic", and how much the brand is associated with health products. For example, Philips would like to be associated with health products such as hospital equipment and blood pressure metres. Yet, it is more associated with entertainment products such as televisions and DVD players.

It is the role of brand management to define the products they wish to identify the brand with. Market research's role is to determine how successful the brand is in creating this link, and measure with which products the product is *actually* identified. For this purpose, market researchers can include questions in their brand tracking instrument such as "which products do you know of this brand"? Other questions we can include are:

- Which companies do you know that are active in this category?
- Do you know this brand offers the following products?
- Which products would fit this brand? Which do not fit with the brand?
- Which of the following products would you expect this brand to offer? Which would you expect them not to offer?
- How much would you trust these products if they were offered by this brand?
- How likely would you be to buy this product if it was offered by this brand?

Brand image is a blend of associations consumers have with a brand through a history of exposures and experiences. But if we limit it to the product component, the results of a brand tracking study can help define the gap between brand identity (e.g., the products brand management wants to be associated with) and brand image (the products that the consumer associates the brand with). A tracking instrument can also help set direction for the future, by supporting:

- Product development. A tracking study can suggest to which product categories the brand can be extended, by showing which products a consumer can and cannot imagine with the brand. For example, perhaps consumers may be able to imagine a fruit-based soft drink but not an alcoholic soft drink (e.g., a Breezer) with Coca-Cola.

- The identification and filtering of merger and acquisition candidates. For this purpose, market research can show if consumers perceive or can imagine a target brand and its products as a natural extension to the acquirer's brand.
- Marketing communication. Based on the gap analysis, we may decide to display certain products more prominently to build a clearer link between a product and the brand. Over time, the tracker may show if the attempt is successful.

The Consumer

So far we have focused on the brand only, but we have deliberately depicted the consumer in the same figure, because they need to be assessed in conjunction – if only because the gap analysis between "reality" and "aspiration" can be applied to the consumer just as much as to the brand. Let's explain by means of an example of a Philips health business, to describe the gap between target mindset and the actual characteristics of a target group.

In our health business, we always talk about the Life Achiever as a person with a preventative mindset with regards to health. The person aspires to take preventative measures to ensure good health, and is willing to pay a premium for effective measures. This suggests the image of a healthy person who exercises, maintains a healthy diet and is generally in good shape. However, in reality, the Life Achievers have a medical/clinical history with more than their share of health problems (e.g., hypertension, a high cholesterol level, diabetes, oral health problems and so on), which has resulted in this increased involvement in oral care and willingness to pay a premium. There is a solid gap between the aspiration and reality.

Another example: at a target group level, we often use the persona of "Jenny" to describe a sleep-deprived, 32-year-old mother of two young children, whose partner takes a passive role in the household, who has a stressful job and who is slightly overweight due to her pregnancies and having no opportunity to exercise. But her target mindset is very health-oriented, and that is what she looks for in the brands that she uses, the magazines that she reads, and television programmes that she watches. It would be a cardinal mistake to address Jenny by referring to her reality; it is better to address her mindset. This is also why we define the brand language at the level of the link at the aspiration level: between the brand identity and the target mindset. We see this as an approach with a general appeal, as we assume that anyone can have the target mindset – it will just be more prevalent in some people than in others (the persona of "Jenny" will resonate with some people more than with others, or some women will look more like Jenny than others).

It is useful to make the distinction between aspiration and reality, both in brand strategy and in product development. For example, in product development the product promise described by the concept (insight, benefit and reason to believe) will typically address the gap between aspiration and reality. The dilemma addressed by the insight can be the gap itself (e.g., "you want to be slim but you aren't") or the inability to address the gap (e.g., "you aspire to be slim but you don't find the opportunity to diet"). The brand communication, of course, has to be a little more subtle than that.

To summarise, the question of where to play, can be answered by answering the following questions:

1. Will the product help the brand accomplish its goal? What is the aspired brand identity, and how will this product help to accomplish the goal set forward by this identity, and the gap between image and identity?

2. Does the product address the aspired consumer need of an aspired target audience? Who is the target audience, what is their current situation (reality, behaviours, socio-economic and demographic data, clinical or medical situation, housing situation, etc.) and what is their aspiration? Are there any dilemmas to be found between reality and aspiration that are not sufficiently addressed by current products?

SEIZING THE OPPORTUNITY

Once we have landscaped the market and discovered some opportunities for new product/market combinations, we may want to move on by assessing the market potential of these new ideas, as well as by identifying possible market entry points and barriers. Market potential is the maximum penetration a brand, product or service can achieve across a population under ideal circumstances (e.g., a perfectly compelling proposition, full awareness so a perfect marketing plan, and availability, so perfect distribution). There are three areas that need careful consideration when engaging in market sizing: (a) the definition of the target group, (b) the geographical scope and (c) barriers that may affect adoption.

Defining the Target Group

The definition of the right target group is essential for a market sizing assessment. Not only do we need to understand which part of the population may be susceptible to the proposition, we also need to put the right boundaries around it. In the consumer package goods market potential is typically defined against a Gen Pop universe (general population), the largest common denominator. It's fair if one wants to maximise an opportunity. Common restrictions are to only look at "housewives" (e.g., for detergents or other household goods for which the female partner in the household is considered the main decision maker and user). Whilst archaic, a brand may stick to it to maintain compatibility with earlier studies. Another limitation is to only involve a current user base (e.g., all dishwasher users to test a new cleaning solution). Of course there are reasons to deviate from the previous, "broad" definitions, for example if one wants to make a clear distinction between "retention" (of a current user group) and "recruitment" (of a new user group).

Suppose that the dishwasher market is not saturated yet, and a brand of cleaning solutions has discovered that dissatisfaction with currently available cleaning solutions is a major purchase barrier. The trick is then to develop a cleaning solution proposition that triggers consumers to switch from their current manual dishwashing. The assessment focuses on triggering switching behaviour and estimating switching potential to drive deeper market penetration.

Another example is the Philips Coolskin electric shaver with a pre-shave emulsion. The markets of electric shavers (e.g., Braun, Remington and Philips) and blades (e.g., Schick and Gillette) are stale in that it is hard for electric shavers to attract blade users. Philips positioned Coolskin against dissatisfied blade users and, by that, tapped into the vast potential of blade users, competing directly with Gillette.

Another reason for deliberately limiting the "universe" definition is because one wants to define (identify or verify) the Bull's Eye target group. The Bull's Eye is our key target group, and those who can be expected to be among the first to accept and buy the new product. The question is of course if the Bull's Eye target group is large enough, and if the proposition yields sufficient appeal to warrant the investment. Of course, the "universe" definition can deliberately be extended to test if the proposition also yields appeal at the fringes outside of the Bull's Eye.

Geographic Expansion

Geographic expansion is a specific subset of market potential. For example, many companies look into entering the BRIC countries (Brazil, Russia, India and China) because of their vast population sizes and rising prosperity. But there are many pitfalls, such as:

1. Propositions (products, services and brands) may not bear the same relevance across markets. For example, many health products such as massage chairs and sticks that have proven to be successful in Asia, have failed to yield consumer demand in Europe. Hence the suggestion is to have local insights drives local proposition development and adaptation.
2. Not all may have the disposable income to buy the product. Income differences in emerging markets are higher than in established markets limiting the population that can actually afford the product. To adopt a right price level, one may benchmark price levels against the PPP (purchasing power parity).
3. A lack of infrastructure or retail structure may limit the ability to reach the consumer and tap into the market potential. So the trick is only to project expectations against the portion of the population one can reasonably reach, e.g., in metropolitan cities and urban areas. We can call the combination of 1 and 2 a "pocket approach", e.g., only projecting expectations against an adjusted potential.
4. Marketing strategies that work in one market may not work in another. For example, Philips Sonicare is successful in the United States with its marketing strategy of having dental professional recommendations influence consumer purchases. However, for this strategy to work, conditions must be right. The consumer has to visit the dentist regularly, preferably for preventative rather than curative reasons, the dentist needs to have a service attitude to actively pass on the recommendation, and the consumer has to be receptive to receiving it and following up. If one condition is lacking, the strategy fails.

Barriers and Constraints

Landscaping potential new markets does not only involve demonstrating the upside potential; it also involves managing expectations, and addressing possible reasons why an opportunity may not materialise. To mention some:

1. Markets can be capped due to rules and regulations. For example, healthcare solutions are often subject to reimbursement schemes with strict criteria. Either one is eligible or not, or the amount that will be reimbursed is capped. The brand then has a choice: either stay within the constraints of the reimbursement schemes, or develop the opportunity associated with out-of-pocket payment.
2. Competition may provide an access barrier. In the landscaping phase, it comes mainly down to assessing the risk of competitive actions, and assessing the effects on top and bottom line.
3. Limitations to switching potential. For example, users of competitive products, solutions and brands may be very loyal to their current solution, which may slow the adoption curve of the new solution. Also, the purchase of the new product may compete with other expenses.

This will particularly be true for products with a high initial purchase price, such as a home defibrillator. Consumers will usually not deny the risk of a cardiac arrest (the number one cause of death in the US) which usually happens at home. But that's not the same as forking out the money to purchase a home defibrillator, which typically has the same cost as a quick vacation.

4. Slow adoption/diffusion of new technology. In many high tech markets, the adoption of a new category (e.g. DVD-Recorders) is highly dependent on the acceptance of new technology standards (DVD-R, DVD+R, DVD-RAM). Only when it becomes clear to the consumers which standard will "win", are the consumers willing to make the investment. This also applies to high-tech categories for which there is a high dependence on content, whether it be games for game-consoles, high-definition TV-channels for HD-TV or the right applications for 3G mobile telephony. For market research to be able to contribute effectively in these areas, it should focus strongly on learning in the area of game theory.

The Role of Market Research in Landscaping and Sizing a Market

Landscaping and subsequently sizing the market is typically not the domain of traditional market research firms such as Ipsos, RI, TNS or Synovate. Consultancy firms such as McKinsey, Bain and Kurt Salomon & Associates dominate this world. They have specialists in this area, have existing frameworks to conduct these exercises efficiently, have the back office capability to host desk research and process huge amounts of information in a short period of time, and have the library and repository function to have much information already available or easily accessible from external sources. The information used is usually a mix of existing, publicly available data, and custom research by means of expert interviews or larger-scale surveys. If time allows, there will usually be a first phase in the process based on existing information, because it is fast and cheap. This is used to identify gaps in the information and assess the risks associated with the gaps. A second phase of custom market research will fill the gaps.

Although traditional market research firms are usually not in charge of the process of landscaping a market, they will be invited to do bits and pieces for either their direct client or for a consultancy working for one of their clients. The work usually involves:

- Providing a more detailed description of the target market by means of a custom survey. Not all questions can be solved based on publicly available sources, either because specific data/variables are not available, or because the analyst does not have access to the original data so that it is impossible to make new crossings between variables, and focus on specific details.
- Doing volume projection and forecasting. Once the brand starts preparing a market entry, they may want to have an indication of the appeal of their products and a prediction of the year·1 and 2 sales it will yield. Instead of just depending on a single volume projection, the outcome will typically be triangulated with historic data or data from similar situations, e.g., other launches.

ASSESSING NEW STRATEGIC PROPOSITIONS

By strategic propositions we mean strategic product/market combinations that should contribute significantly to the top and bottom line, not just product improvements within the current portfolio. Developing strategic propositions is the logical next step in the landscaping exercise. Choices have been made on where to play in this landscape, and the business case based on a first market-sizing exercise has been validated initially. The point of departure is that the company's mission, vision and scope have been defined, and so has the target audience. These are the constraints within which we work. Essentially, the process of assessing new strategic propositions consists of the following steps or elements:

1. Defining the insight. An insight can be defined as a not yet obvious discovery about the consumer that enables us to establish a connection between our brands and consumer's lives and elicits the emotional consumer reaction of "you obviously understand me". The insight is a deeper understanding of what the consumer aspires to and wants to accomplish, but currently can't, resulting in an unmet need.

The complicating factor about insights is that the consumer is often not fully aware that she wants something she cannot get, which is why traditional market research by means of asking questions in focus groups and interviews may not be sufficient. In the discovery process of finding an insight, we typically observe consumers in their "natural habitat" (to refer back to language more common to ethnographers and cultural anthropologists), and may even engage in participant observation.

To give a better understanding of what we mean by observing people instead of asking questions, one of the authors was once involved in a strategic product development project in which we were aiming at capturing the "kick of a game". Gambling machines were, due to new legislation, being banned from bars and cafés, and gambling companies were about to lose an important source of revenue. Games based on skills, however, were still allowed (e.g., pinball machines), so we suggested replacing the gambling machines with skill-based machines provoking the same kind of "kick". We used participant observation to understand the kick of games, in both gambling and skill-based games. Our observers went to gambling houses to observe and play together with gamblers in their natural habitat. They played together with the gamblers to immerse in their world and identify with their aspirations, and to experience the game the same way an experienced player does. Our observers accumulated this knowledge in an experiential way, and used it in creative sessions to generate ideas for new and exciting skill-based games.

This knowledge is not the insight itself; it is more a set of facts. Different from "knowledge" or a set of facts, an insight includes an unmet need: the consumer wants to solve a problem or aspires to reach a certain desired end-state but cannot reach it with the current set of measures. The unmet need in our example could have been that future consumers want to retain the kick of playing the gambling machines yet they could no longer do that in the comfort zone of their local bar. This is then followed by a "wish", e.g., "I wish I could have the same kind of kick as I get it while playing the gambling machines in my local bar".

2. Defining the benefit. The benefit addresses the insight in that it promises to deliver against the "I wish", and brings the user closer to the desired end state.

Defining the benefit is pretty straightforward once the insight has been defined. For example, in our example, the benefit could have been that we offer a product that offers the same kick as a gambling machine but is in fact a skill-based game so it can be played in a bar. The other way around, we could also have promised a new environment that does not qualify as a bar so it would still be allowed to play the gambling machines. The ultimate benefit is of course one that can be used as a discriminator, in that it can claim to be the *only* solution that offers this opportunity.

3. Defining the reason(s) to believe. The benefit statement defines what we promise to deliver; the reason to believe describes how we expect to deliver it.

Typically this is where the company innovates: a new "technical" solution to address the benefit, hopefully in a superior way to existing solutions. This is where it can become tricky – we don't want to over-promise yet the new product needs to be compelling and credible. So this is where the innovation and product development process needs to focus, warranting the decision to invest in, develop and launch this new product and position it as a superior alternative to existing solutions.

MERGERS AND ACQUISITIONS

A merger or acquisition[4] is a fast way to deliver growth and to create a foothold in a market. A company may look for a merger or acquisition if organic growth and development takes too long, or if there are significant barriers barring a company from entering a market or growing organically.

Market research can be involved in various stages of an acquisition process:

- Defining, through the company's vision and mission, in which market it wants to grow, and how it wants to grow.
- Identifying potential targets or acquisition candidates to deliver the growth.
- Assess if targets are the right candidate, and assess their price or acquisition value in the (pre) due diligence process.

Market research's involvement in the first point is not any different from other types of strategy research discussed before, so we will not repeat this here. Instead, we describe the activities market research may support in the latter two stages.

Identifying a Target

Earlier we described how market research can help identify a market opportunity by investigating trends and doing fore-sighting work. Market research will also be engaged in competitive intelligence to better understand the competitive landscape. Intelligence work to identify an acquisition candidate or target is slightly different. The trick is to define which target would create the best market entry point, and what is the best spot to conquer a market from.

Suppose, for example, that we're looking to create a foothold in the elderly healthcare market. The population is aging, people's life expectancy is on the rise, and the post-war baby boomer generation is approaching or entering retirement. Healthcare costs are rising and governments are or will be happy to offload this burden to private enterprises. Philips has identified this trend and has set itself the mission to become a major healthcare player. Now, Philips can do this by means of organic growth, but acquisitions would provide a much faster entry. This is why, for example, Philips has acquired Lifeline, the US market leader in Personal Emergency Response Services (PERS). PERS is a combination of a call-centre service and a set of enabler products. PERS is typically used by elderly people, women of 75 years or older and living alone. They carry a panic button, and when pushing it, it will automatically connect them,

---

[4] In this section we address acquisitions, i.e., a larger company taking over a smaller one, rather than mergers, i.e., two equal partners joining forces, although the principles are the same. The acquiring company is called the "acquirer" and the acquired company or candidate is called the "target".

through a telephone line, to a service dispatcher in a call centre who will check what's wrong with them. Sometimes the event is a serious medical one requiring emergency follow up, e.g. a fall resulting in an injury; more often the event can be directly addressed by the dispatcher over the phone.

Lifeline has been discovered by a process in which a vision and mission were matched with opportunities, and the availability of acquisition candidates. With hindsight we may ask if Lifeline was the right entry point or foothold in the healthcare-for-the-elderly market. On first sight it may look odd: Philips entering the service business. But we claim it is a right move, because:

- It matches Philips's vision and mission to become a major healthcare player.
- It is consistent with the market trend towards independent living – people wanting to live in the comfort of their own home for longer, sustaining a higher quality of life.
- The acquisition is in a healthy spot, not a dead spot of the healthcare business. For example, appliances businesses are often commoditised, suffering from low margins, and service businesses are in better shape from a margin point of view. In addition, the value of many healthcare markets is capped by reimbursement schemes – rules defining who is eligible to a service and who is not. Markets that are defined by consumers paying for themselves, out-of-pocket, are more subject to the rules of consumer pull. We believe that a business such as Lifeline may position Philips well to enter the consumer self-pay market, once it takes off. And many think it will have to take off, as governments will need to cut back on healthcare expenses.
- The PERS market is far from saturated so there is high upside potential and opportunity to recover the acquisition cost, and Lifeline is well positioned to penetrate deeper into the US market.

Assessing the Target's Value – Stand Alone and Upside Value

Next we assess the target's acquisition value, which consists of two components, the stand-alone value and a mark-up. A company's stand-alone value is its intrinsic value based on its current assets and activities, and its future outlook, driving the return on investment if one were to acquire the company. The mark-up is what one has to pay on top, because the target is desirable, e.g., because the "market" "thinks" that the future outlook is much better than the stand-alone value expresses. Especially in a situation where the mark-up is significant, the acquirer must be very confident in its ability to create return on the investment, and in the value drivers to help create this return.

Value drivers are the levers the acquirer can employ to create return on investment by driving top and bottom-line results. Cost savings due to synergies between acquirer and target are among the first value drivers to be sought to drive bottom-line result. After the acquisition, market research can contribute to this by joining forces and merging departments and knowledge bases. Prior to the acquisition, market research is typically involved in identifying value drivers that have to do with leveraging the target's assets or synergies between the two companies:

- The current business portfolio of brands, products, distribution channel access and presence in geographic markets, as well as the existence of a loyal customer base providing recurring sales and extended life-time value.
  - o Value drivers are then opportunities to scale up the current portfolio, and leverage their untapped potential.

- Future business potential, consisting of:
  - Technology – the shared (portfolio of) technologies or IP (intellectual property) that can be commercialised through new product development. For example, the promise of bio-technology is a reason for large companies to seed money in bio-tech start-ups, or take stock in them.
  - Competencies – the acquirer is looking for something the target does well, and that is scalable to other situations and markets. For example, Lifeline is an expert in operational excellence – the art of running a call centre or crafting response protocols that minimise the number of false alarms to third parties (e.g., ambulance services).
  - Insights – a superior understanding of consumer need or needs of other stakeholders in the value chain, resulting in innovation opportunities because of not-yet tapped potential.
  - Access – sometimes the acquirer is interested in a target because it would provide access, e.g., to a retail channel (e.g., pharmacies in Europe), to decision makers (e.g., industry purchasers) or to exclusive rights or intellectual property barring entry.

Differences with Market Research in an Organic Growth Process

Some differences between market research to support mergers and acquisitions compared with processes supporting organic growth are:

- The speed with which we do our research is of essence. The lead time of organic product development is typically measured in months or years. Merger and acquisition projects often run much faster. This is particularly true if a company is sold by auction. So, whatever market research we wish to do, we need to do it fast. Instead of doing custom market research, as we would do in organic development, we tend to rely on information that can be collected fast: syndicated data, desk research and expert interviews. Implicity, we accept the risks of having blind spots or basing our decisions on incomplete information.
- The acquirer does not have access to information about the target other than what is available in the public domain. This means all parties involved, including market research, must be creative and visionary.
- Because of the capital investment in an acquisition, there is a high level of risk and uncertainty. This means that there must be a lot of justified trust in the results of a study, projecting back on the maturity of the research team involved.

A CHALLENGE TO MARKET RESEARCH

Predicting future demand in categories that are new or rapidly changing, is probably the biggest challenge to market research while at the same time offering a great opportunity for making an impact. The impact market research can make here goes far beyond the impact of the more accepted forms of operational and tactical market research, which, unfortunately, is very much the comfort zone of many market researchers. *Strategic* market research is vital to a company's success or failure, yet we don't find many market researchers in the strategic echelons of a company. Why is this?

The dilemma may be that strategic market research means, essentially, dealing with a high level of ambiguity and risk, requiring seniority and maturity, e.g., an ability to look at situations from a perspective of 30,000 feet, whereas market researchers tend to be project managers, working from a fixed assignment and with a preference for well-defined questions, methods, facts and figures.

For example, imagine that one has to recommend to the telecom industry whether or not to make the investment in 3G-mobile telephony. Most market researchers would be extremely hesitant to step in and actively advise the company on the market potential of 3G. The decision to enter this business is a major one, and it involves answering fundamental questions such as: is there a substantial latent consumer need to be addressed by 3G mobile telephony, and what products and services would we be able to offer that we do not offer now but would offer the consumer a significant benefit over current solutions? Seeing the success of 3G (or the lack thereof), we believe that these questions have not been answered sufficiently. We can only conclude that the role of market research in the decision whether or not to invest in 3G must have been minor. If market research was involved, it had not sufficiently acted as the conscience of its business, assessing the risk and preventing the business from failure.

We believe that the market research industry has not been able to show sufficient leadership and vision to make its way to the management table on strategic topics. This place is taken typically by consultancy agencies such as McKinsey, Bain or Swander Pace – which tend to do their own market research. Instead, market researchers are still viewed as "people who run the market research projects delivering data" instead of "thought-leaders on relevant content areas delivering insight and vision" (e.g., forecasting consumer acceptance for new technologies). As a result, unfortunately, market research is not given sufficient opportunity to weigh in on strategic topics, and vice versa, companies do not use market research to its full potential.

REFERENCES

Barwise, P. and Meehan, S. (2004) *Simply Better, Winning and Keeping Customers by Delivering what Matters Most.* Harvard Business School Publishing Corporation.

Chan Kim, W. and Mauborgne, R. (2004) *Blue Ocean Strategy: How to Create Uncontested Market Space and Make Competition Irrelevant.* Harvard Business School Publishing Corporation.

Collins, J. (2001) *Good to Great, Why Some Companies Make the Leap . . . and Others Don't.* Harper-Collins Publishers, Inc.

Foster, R. and Kaplan, S. (2001) *Creative Destruction, Why Companies that are Built to Last Underperform the Market – and How to Successfully Transform Them.* Doubleday

Hamel, G. and Prahalad, C. K. (1994) *Competing for the Future.* Harvard Business School Press.

Porter, M. (1980) *Competitive Strategy, Techniques for Analyzing Industries and Competitors.* The Free Press.

Reichheld, F.F. and Teal, T. (1996) *The Loyalty Effect, The Hidden Force behind Growth, Profits and Lasting Value.* Harvard Business School Press.

Temporal, P. (2002) *Advanced Brand Management.* John Wiley and Sons (Asia).

Treacy, M. and Wiersema F. (1994) *The Discipline of Market Leaders, Choose Your Customers, Narrow Your Focus, Dominate Your Market.* Perseus Books.

6

Research for Innovation: Defining Market Propositions

Elisabetta Osta, Phillip Cartwright, Jaideep Prabhu and Marco Bevolo

ABSTRACT

Radical innovation is about market creation. The process for market creation (innovation) can be ascribed to three dynamic phases: see, act, launch. "See" is about recognising a disruption or white space in the market place, "act" is about testing ideas pre-market launch and launch is about commercialisation of innovation. Research and insights play a very important role in the innovation process and three research objectives mirror the three innovation phases: explore, test, monitor. This chapter focuses mostly on those. Several techniques are available, key success factors include the integration of several insights (within each innovation phase) and the operationalisation of the insights. The innovation arena is fertile with new developments (the case study for Philips design in the context of new trends is detailed in this chapter). Researchers and providers should fit the most appropriate portfolio of techniques to the specific needs of the situation to avoid the barriers that typically occur in the research for innovation.

INTRODUCTION

Innovation – the successful commercialisation of new ideas – lies at the heart of success in business today. New products and services generate new sources of revenue for organisations, helping them to reach new customers or to satisfy existing ones better. In the process they offer long-term advantages over competitors. Indeed, the battle cry "innovate or die" has never before seemed so compelling or urgent. Yet innovation, rarely an easy thing to do, is now even tougher. Despite a voluminous and ever expanding literature on the subject, the outstanding question still remains: how can organisations innovate systematically?

This question is particularly vexing in the context of radical innovation – the creation of "new to the world" goods and services that open up whole new markets rather than incrementally leveraging existing ones. Given the complexity of contemporary markets, triggers for radical innovation can come from many sources: consumers, competitors, regulators or changing technology. Each of these triggers, if pursued, could lead to costly failure or long-term competitive dominance. Moreover, they could lead to a complete change in the structure of a market by eliminating current incumbents and elevating new entrants, or they could deepen the status quo by enhancing the dominance of incumbent firms. The stakes for everyone involved are high, but so is the accompanying uncertainty.

Market Research Handbook, 5th Edition. Edited by M. van Hamersveld and C. de Bont.
© 2007 John Wiley & Sons, Ltd.

As a result, the critical business challenge is systematically to identify new market opportunities, create products and services for these opportunities, and then commercialise them successfully. With each of these issues dealing with market constituencies such as consumers and competitors, which are the natural domains of marketers, radical innovation is fundamentally a marketing problem. It engages all marketing roles, from market researchers to manufacturing product managers.

This chapter deals with the challenges posed by radical innovation, with a particular focus on the role of market researchers and marketing managers. Specifically, it lays out a framework (See-Act-Launch) for thinking about radical innovation. Using this framework, we elaborate on the different stages of finding ideas for radical innovation, developing them into finished products, and then bringing these products successfully to market. We identify the major challenges that firms face at each stage and discuss a range of tools and approaches for dealing with them. These are presented so that companies can adapt and vary their use according to their own specific needs.

Given the central role that consumers play in the eventual success or failure of a radical innovation, we emphasise those tools and approaches particularly suited to gaining customer insight at each stage. A particularly critical factor in successful radical innovation is finding a *language* that effectively communicates the relevance of the innovation to the market. This communication may appeal to rational or emotional levels. Ultimately it must effectively translate what the product does ("what's new") into conscious or unconscious benefits for the new market ("what's in it for me"). This binds the innovator with the user (in the case of market driving applications) or the user with the innovation (in the case of market driven innovations). Accordingly, this chapter examines how marketers might go about developing this language through the three stages of See-Act-Launch. There is no agreement on whether radical innovation is in essence a market driving or a market driven process, and by extension, whether one approach is likely to be more successful than the other (see Christensen and Bower, 1996; Narver, Slater and Maclachlan, 2004; Slater and Narver, 1998, 1999). Each view is likely to be right for different reasons and in different contexts. Here we assume the market driven approach to discuss tools for gaining customer insight. We also draw on the market driving approach by discussing the process of creating an effective language and context (see Hargadon and Douglas, 2001) for communicating the benefits of an innovation to customers.

WHAT IS INNOVATION?

Definitions

Following the most recent European Community Innovation Survey (CIS, 2004), we define innovation as "the market introduction of a new or significantly improved good or service". Innovations in manufacturing and distribution processes, new organisational forms or business models are beyond the scope of this chapter.

We recognise that innovation in goods and services can be of varying degrees of novelty: new to the world, new to the market, new to the enterprise; significantly improved or only marginally modified. Accordingly, we define radical innovations as those goods or services that are new to the world rather than merely new to a market or to an enterprise. Given the vast literature on innovation from different authors across many disciplines, there has been a proliferation of terms to describe what we call *radical innovation*. These include: disruptive, discontinuous, revolutionary, competency destroying and radical innovation (see among others Christensen, 2006; Freeman, 1974; Garcia and Calantone, 2002; Tushman and Anderson, 1986). As has been recently noted, however, many of these terms are open to the charge of prejudging the outcomes of the innovation because they define the innovation in terms of its effects rather than its attributes (see Sood and Tellis, 2005; Tellis, 2006). To avoid this charge and to ensure uniformity we use the more neutral term "radical innovation".

See-Act-Launch: A Framework for Radical Innovation

Buisson, Cartwright and Silberzahn (2006) propose that a framework for successful understanding and management of a radical innovation is: first, being able to recognise the disruption (See); second, being able to act on this recognition and create a radical innovation (Act); and third, being able to launch corresponding radical products successfully (Launch). The process can be related to that set forth by Utterback and Abernathy (1975) in the context of Incubation, Take-off, Mass-Market. See-Act-Launch is a comprehensive process for managing disruptions and successfully introducing radical products that is based on these ideas. It is summarised in Figure 6.1.

Research and insights are crucial in the innovation process. Mirroring the innovation phases, the research process for innovation consists of three iterative phases: exploration, testing/forecasting and monitoring – which run parallel to the See-Act-Launch phases of innovation.

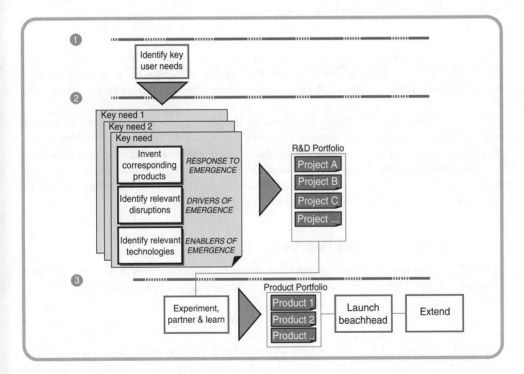

Figure 6.1   See-Act-Launch: a framework for radical innovation

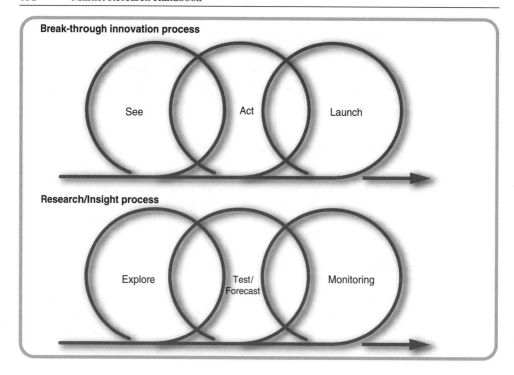

Figure 6.2   Research and insights vs. innovation phases

Exploratory research/insights are prevalent in the "See" phase – either the innovation is not there at all and consumer needs and market opportunities have to be understood, or a new technology market creation potential needs to be assessed and the landscape scanned for disruptions.

Coincident with the Act phase, Test/Forecast insights require accuracy for the positive economics of market creation – several good techniques and methodologies (Nielsen Bases, IRI, and others) are available for forecasting mainstream consumer markets. True technology disruptions have been so far more difficult to tackle. As concerns the product launch, monitoring is essential when the product is available in the market, particularly in the very early phases of launch to enable a successful commercialisation of innovation.

SEE-EXPLORE: Identify Key User Needs

The See phase of the innovation process is where a collective frame is constructed to make sense of a major change in an organisation's environment – a change significant enough to ensure a response (Cartwright and Silberzahn, 2006) or to determine a white space, an opportunity determined by consumer needs. Here, ideas about the marketplace are collected and compared to understand consumers' needs and the consequent business opportunities. This is frequently the most difficult phase of the process. It is frequently referred to in the context of ideation and many research suppliers, of all sizes, have developed techniques for developing and collating new ideas (see, for example, Research International's Innovation Journey). Idea generation involves the application of qualitative research techniques such as recording the ideas generated by the interaction between internal company researchers and outside experts. In the case of "hard to reach" consumers, techniques of ethnographic research may be employed where trained experts are employed to understand the needs of consumers by observing their everyday lives. The collation of research findings allows insights to be refined and focused toward the development of new products by working with "professional consumers" trained in ideation techniques.

Fundamental to a consumer-centric "see phase" is to determine and analyse end-users' fundamental needs. This is critical, particularly in the area of technology-based innovation where firms must recognise the demand-pull side as well the supply-push side favoured by R&D and marketing. A possible fundamental need may be to access personal data anytime, anywhere (e.g., iPod). This identification phase must balance gut feel, creativity and research. There is often a tendency to rush toward quantitative research. Both qualitative and quantitative research is necessary, but qualitative assessment early on drives creativity. Quantitative research and execution follow. The environment of most industrial sectors can be described by about twenty fundamental needs. The objective at this stage is not to be exhaustive, but rather to make sure not to miss the one that corresponds to a fundamental shift in the firm's environment.

Deszca et al. (1999) highlight six different types of methodologies relevant for radical innovation which can be ascribed mainly to the exploratory phase:

- diffusion models
- visioning techniques
- lead user analysis
- information acceleration
- empathic Design
- customer Immersion

Diffusion models are different forecasting methods that predict the diffusion of a specific new technology. They differ in structure, in their assumptions, data and estimation procedures. The weakness of diffusion models lie in the fact that the several variables that can influence a new market creation are unknown.

Visioning techniques can be approached either from projecting historical experience or visioning the future. The Delphi Method involves using a panel of experts for sales forecasts of a new technology. Backcasting asks experts to build future scenarios and define the specific requirements needed to achieve them.

Lead users analysis (mentioned in other sections of this chapter) involves lead users to assess future needs for radical new products in categories characterised by rapid change. A weakness of this method lies in the fact that there is often a gap between lead user and normal user that cannot be accurately predicted.

Information acceleration involves the use of virtual reality to simulate behavioural responses. These techniques are widespread, for instance in shopping insight generation, pricing research, with the advantage that variables can be easily controlled and changed.

Empathic design focuses on product creation based on understanding consumers' non-articulated needs. Product designers, product developers, trained anthropologists and ethnographers observe potential customers in their own environment and analyse their behaviours.

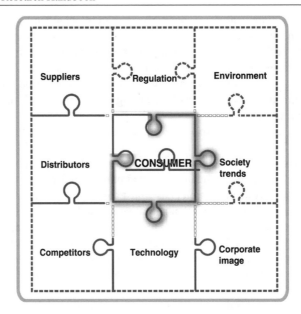

Figure 6.3   The nine sources of insights

Customer immersion sessions involve face-to-face contact between customers and product developers. The weakness of this approach resides in the possibility of contamination between the product developers and the consumers. Researchers should constantly question the relevance of the methods in use, in relation to the context and situation, and should approach the context of a potentially radical innovation very differently from a non-disruptive one.

The consumer and the shopper must be at the heart of insight generation and a consumer insights team should consider all relevant tools to integrate consumers into the process, both marketing driven and technology driven organisations. Within this context we consider the crucial element of shopper insights as part of the consumer insights arena.

In the exploratory phase, in order to detect white spaces of threats/disruptions in the environment, there are eight other non-consumer sources of insight (with the consumer/shopper at the centre) (Figure 6.3).

Technology

Insights into latest technological developments can be crucial to identify potential new disruptions or new opportunities opened up by the latest external innovations. For technology companies it is vital to be on top of the latest discovery or breakthrough.

Society

Insights into the latest developments in society are extremely relevant in order to be aware of macro-trends that will affect consumer decisions in future. In Europe, the aging population, immigration, obesity and increasing income disparity are examples of long-term sociological trends likely to affect consumer choices for a number of years.

Competition

A good overview of the competition, beyond a thorough assessment of their market position in terms of sales, can be a useful source of insights. For example, competitors' strategy for growth and innovation, distribution and supply, and their creation of consumer value can be of interest. This should be complemented by what is happening at the periphery, with small emerging companies usually at the leading edge of innovation. Tapping into the knowledge of what is happening in other parts of the world can also be a source of useful ideas, and help to detect potential disruptions or threats.

Regulation

Regulatory changes can create disruptions and threats, or they can become opportunities. For instance, the regulation of online gambling in a few countries could make or break several million dollars worth of market capitalisation for current leading online gambling providers.

Distribution

The strategies of the main retailers and distributors of own products are crucial, as well as spotting disruptions in the landscape. A combination of technology and e-tailing has had a major impact in the music industry. Anderson (2006) believes that the phenomenon of online distribution systems fuelled by the i-Pod are changing patterns of consumption as consumers have access to "niche" music closer to their personal taste.

Supply

Shifts in supply are very relevant in certain industries, such as energy, where changes in the strategy of suppliers or new entrants into the market can have disruptive effects.

Corporate Image

More recently, insights into the environment and community, and "corporate image" are very important to enhance company image or to avoid potential pitfalls.

Financial Markets

Particularly for new start-ups or companies seeking funding it is crucial to understand trends in financial markets as well as the financing landscape of investment banks and venture capitalists. Technology driven companies or start-ups newly formed around a new technological idea (biotech, nano-tech) can profit significantly from deriving ideas on market creation by looking at these nine sources. However, regular scans of all of them – integrated, for instance, in an annual company review – can prove extremely valuable for *any* company in detecting discontinuities as well as potential opportunities. Business intelligence (desk research) and internal knowledge from several departments (sales, purchasing, R&D, marketing) can be useful in harvesting insights from sources peripheral to the consumer.

The case studies below provide two examples pertaining to the sources of insights, and more specifically the necessary innovation for research to enable anticipation of future developments in culture and systems thinking. The first example, Culture Scan is a programme focused on the exploration, analysis and roadmapping of trends within global and regional cultures, with the deployment of techniques ranging from field observation to opinion makers and leaders interviews. The second example, after the Culture Scan case history, Ambient Experience Design, illustrates the pragmatic outcome of design research at visionary level.

CASE STUDY: PHILIPS

Example: Culture Scan

Mixing academic theory with design pragmatism, Culture Scan focuses its research on emerging aesthetics, communication and cultural concepts in Asia Pacific, Europe and the USA. Culture Scan offers an annual forecast that feeds into "new solutions roadmaps" and into concrete projects. The programme operates by maintaining an overview of "weak signals" in art, fashion, new media, pop music and other cultural "pillars", including more conceptual domains like literature and philosophy. Through the years since its conception in 1999, it was feasible for Culture Scan researchers to develop models and approaches that gained a rich, dynamic (not static) understanding of the cultural context where people experience product, services and messages. Philips Design teams, with input from external experts, regularly detect change and track the evolution of trends in cultures of relevance, from China to Brazil, from New York to Antwerp.

Of course, the main challenge is not so much to access content: after all, this is the age of Google! The real challenge is to make research actionable as a true asset for innovation. All the analysed manifestations and subsequent future concepts disseminated through workshops and other ad hoc internal channels and activities. Dissemination is performed in parallel while the analysis is conducted, resulting in a co-creative mode that guarantees acceptance by research users, e.g. designers. Hence, with a unifying effect, the results are actionable throughout the organisational regions and across different design accounts reporting to the different Philips business units.

Another key feature of Culture Scan is its openness to an external network of experts, who offer continuous insights to internal analysts in a true peer-to-peer dialogue. The role of external experts and the crucial management of the networks were tested, assessed and formalised in a number of fast paced, challenging projects. These included both internal research, as part of the New Solutions Development, which is established in the company as the most experimental practice, and customer delivery to Philips divisions. But how did it really work?

From time to time, advertising, media, luxury retail, luxury hospitality and architecture were analysed. Besides the review of available scanned content, the most effective methodologies to define the scope and identify change dynamics were explored and piloted. However, when working in paradigm changing domains, like advanced new media or the evolution of luxury, the conventional approaches to research might not have been sufficient to support future explorations into such unknown territories. Hence the question: what are the best techniques to nurture content and to validate conclusions?

The prototyping of trend analysis tools was performed using various sources as reference: from the practice of reportage and journalism, to the theory of action research, from the developing art and science of managing informal networks of "knowledge gatekeepers", to plain database management techniques. A great variety of sources indeed, and sometimes unconventional as compared to classic market research. And the most unconventional, the most interesting too!

The core learning was that when addressing highly innovative domains, innovating in research methodologies and theories is crucial in order to maintain the necessary edge in the research itself. Of course, this seems particularly necessary when operating in the context of paradigm-changing and/or radical innovation, where research participants cannot always give rational feedback on unknown products or services. However, isn't the world in general moving towards a faster and faster speed of change, from paradigm to paradigm?

Example: Ambient Experience Design

Born out of earlier explorations of creative teams at the highest conceptual level, Ambient Experience Design provides a good example of how the challenge of the "fuzzy front" of innovation can be met, addressing those areas where new paradigms kick into the actual product service mix.

Based on the principles of the Nebula visionary concept for a 2020 bedroom operated by means of ambient intelligence, Ambient Experience for Healthcare, a dedicated approach for the clinical context, was launched as an advanced system solution for hospitals in 2004. The delivery of this service requires highly integrated coordination across all Philips Divisions, from medical systems to lighting, from consumer electronics to domestic appliances, and beyond: IT consultants, software specialists and more high tech expertise. Within the Ambient Experience approach, content and applications are diffused in 3D and digital environments that operate in an anticipatory, seamless and pervasive fashion. The result is a new way to deliver high tech based benefits, creating environments around people's needs; a truly humanistic revolution that translates into new opportunities for the high tech industries on long term, macro level.

Of course, research played a key role in defining the framework for Ambient Experience. Primarily as the approach itself was born out of the freedom of design research explorations towards white spaces and unknown territories where traditional categories converge and meet, or do not matter at all. Secondly, because only the discipline of deep ethnography and the innovation of new tools can enable the scoping of solutions in a domain that simply does not exist: how could a hospital room we tested that nobody has actually ever even seen, not to mention experienced?

In the healthcare arena, Ambient Experience has achieved excellent results in patient satisfaction and clinical performance. The intention here was to address a more general dimension of personal and social sustainability, in the widest sense. The CT suites for the General Children's Hospital in Chicago were based on research addressing the needs and values of multiple stakeholders. Such fundamental research translated into concrete benefits for every person in the value chain. This meant that direct users (e.g., radiologists), as well as indirect users (e.g., the families of examined children) and business stakeholders (e.g., DMUs and CEOs of private hospitals) were offered a superior experience. As an example, it recorded a reduction of children's sedation rates of 30 %–40 %, with greater quality of both operations and customer relations, and increased family and staff satisfaction rates.

Although these examples may not fit other industries' immediate – and therefore less long-term – contexts, it appears crucial and strategically critical that both mature and emerging organisations aim to improve research techniques beyond how they explore future opportunities. The conclusion seems to be very simple and demanding at the same time, as this requires putting people at the centre of their strategic and creative processes, by leveraging research through constantly renewed foresight techniques.

ACT-TEST – FROM IDEAS TO PRODUCTS

For each fundamental need identified, an organisation must invent corresponding products, and identify possible disruptions and related technologies:

- *Invent corresponding products*: conduct creative work to imagine products and services that could be associated with the need. In our example, one could imagine a mobile phone with a storage system that is synchronised in real time with a corporate server, maintaining duplicates of files when no connection is available, etc.
- *Identify the disruptions likely to contribute to the emergence of the need and select the most significant*. In our example, it could be the increased mobility of executives, the availability of high-speed connection everywhere or the falling cost of data storage.
- *Identify the related technologies that can be used to create products*. Most importantly, companies should understand the limitations of the technologies that might jeopardise the creation of products. Example technologies could be storage systems, synchronisation, high-speed connection, or miniaturisation of computers. Expertise and some distance from the analyst are crucial in this step.

"Acting" consists of all the initiatives taken by the company outside its value network to establish a growing presence where a disruption has allowed interesting opportunities to be created or simply where white spaces exist. The final step before actually launching the product may be the simulated test market (STM) in order to understand the sales potential of new products and the ability, through sophisticated diagnostics, to fine-tune marketing programmes and target the right consumers in the right way. Traditionally, the questions behind research into the sales potential of new products are simple. How many people will try a new product, how many will continue to buy it, how often, and in what quantities? The answers are critical to determining whether to proceed.

The basis for STMs is a diffusion model (see, e.g., Bass, 1969), the objective of which is to capture the distribution of a new product introduction among a defined set of adopters. The relationship is expressed in terms of a mathematical function of time that has elapsed from the point of introduction for the purpose of estimating the number of adopters and predicting the development of the diffusion process. In the end, the models are applied to predict the acceptance of an innovation or new product from the point of manufacture to end user.

A new product represents a risk not just for the supplier, but for the consumer too. Many barriers, real or perceived, may discourage people from trying and adopting new products, even if the concept is attractive. The impact of these initial barriers varies considerably between categories, and individual consumers are affected by them in very different ways. Obtaining trial is a prerequisite, but sustained success requires loyal, regular users. Product features play a key role – if people dislike the flavour or fragrance they will not continue to buy – but so does the communication of the underlying concept, as discussed earlier. Consumers' expectations must be matched by their actual experience. STMs show that companies can achieve this by modifying the positioning rather than the product itself.

Past experience of categories and products are relied upon to demonstrate how the consumer base develops for different types of product. For some packaged goods (non-durables), initial purchases are made over the very short-term, while for others (durables) trial continues over an extended period. For truly innovative products – such as the first wireless communication applications – penetration may build slowly from a base of early adopters until the product is more widely understood and sales take off.

Traditional research techniques used particularly in the "Act" phase of innovation such as focus groups, concept testing, and quantitative and qualitative surveys rely heavily on verbalisation and imply a degree of rationalisation from the respondents. However, from neuropsychology (the study of the human brain) we can infer that these are less effective for assessing responses to the completely new concepts of radical innovation. When confronted with the new, our brain tends to search back in memories and habits and tries to link the new knowledge or information to previous existing knowledge. If the new concept, or perceptive pattern, cannot be related to previous knowledge, there is the likelihood of it getting discarded as "noise" rather than linked back to a known knowledge "pattern", while in successful cases a new knowledge pattern is created (Zull, 2002). From this we can assume that consumers participating verbally in interviews or focus groups can be very effective in calibrating an innovation with a moderate grade of newness (incremental innovation), but it would be likely for the same respondents dealing out of the blue with a completely new concept (radical innovation) to reject it, therefore researchers should be analysing insights and devising new methodologies very carefully.

Crucial to the success of the "Act" phase is the creation of a language that translates the key USP of the product in a language that is understood by consumers. Many launches fail as the language does not cover the gap between the intrinsic technology of the product and the consumers. Early adopters can be important ambassadors of the new technology in the incubation phase, creating an intuitive language that links the product with other consumers. If a product has early adopters with wide networks (described by Malcom Gladwell as "connectors" (Gladwell, 2000)) it can easily reach the "tipping point" and become successful. Von Hippel (2005) advocated the importance of "lead users", core consumers at the forefront who drive the innovation forward. Having used the product they can best articulate the link between their needs and the technology.

When the language linking the product to the consumer is not established, it can lead to the technology dying without being adopted. WAP technology struggled in early 2000. It continued to have low adoption rates and failed to take off, despite the technology being ready, major investments from several companies, and good levels of consumer subscriptions. Users did not like the protocol, and the language failed to link the technology to their needs.

For less radical innovations, the common language between technology and consumers is less of a challenge as the gap is narrower – there is widespread understanding of the technology and its benefits. Products launched can be kept flourishing by a constant flow of new versions, improvements and range extensions. The challenge here lies in leveraging all the white spaces within the existing core technology, defining appropriate life cycles, and developing good forecasting methods for the adoption of the incremental innovation. Several insights methodologies have been crucial to the success of brands and products. For example, the launch of P&G Kandoo Baby Wipes built existing strong knowledge of mothers' and babies' needs gained with products that were precursor of Kandoo. P&G underwent a major insights-generation project in several countries, using several research methodologies, from mothers' participation to virtual reality for testing the new product and packaging in-store. The insights generated were very important for steering the

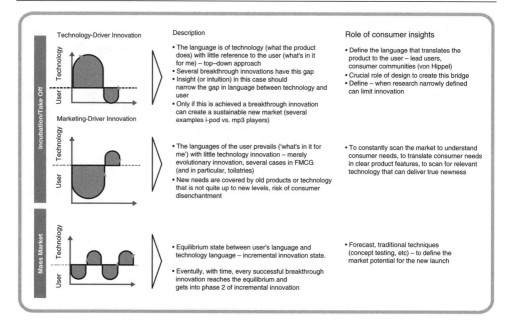

Figure 6.4   Dynamics of market creation: the language that connects users to innovators (technology)

product towards success. In short, insights plays a crucial role along the entire innovation spectrum (from disruptive to incremental) to fine-tune the language that will connect the product or service to the consumers, leading to the creation of a new and sustainable market.

LAUNCH-MONITOR – THE COMMERCIALISATION OF INNOVATION

Experiment, Partner and Learn

As disruptions are about market creation, marketing must learn about the emerging structures of the market itself, as well as about customers' needs. Without being able to ask customers directly about their expectations, market research has to be more actively involved with those who are creating the potential market.

In particular, it must engage in market learning in parallel with product development. Given the high uncertainty about clients, products and usage at this stage, this "last mile" to the market must be highly interactive where design, testing and learning steps are conducted in short cycles. As Chesbrough (2003) notes, no amount of planning and research can reduce the uncertainty at this stage: not only is the best path to market unknown, it is unknowable. Instead, marketing must experiment, adapt and adjust in response to early feedback. This can only be achieved by close interaction between the R&D team, the marketing team, and the target users that have been identified as the beachhead to larger segments. Given the amount of learning at stake, and the fact that this learning often will be about domains that are totally new to the firm, a solution will often be to develop partnerships with other firms that have the required knowledge. This "Experiment, Partner and Learn" phase is crucial. Marketing must play the leading role, as it is really about driving the learning of the firm into its new territory. For that, marketing must become engaged in the radical innovation business: from passive readers of clearly established markets to proactive participants in learning about the disruptive market.

Discover the Beachhead Segment

By now, the organisation has progressed towards a working product based on its view of the emerging market. Commercialisation has started in an unfocused way, with limited investment, to learn about the market. After some time, it is likely that there will be a few successes with some early adopters. This has allowed further tuning of the product. More importantly, if the market experiment phase has been properly conducted, it has suggested a few candidate target segments. As suggested by Moore (1991), this is the stage when the organisation will have to stop and pause to select the target segment that will be the beachhead. This segment must be chosen using the following two criteria:

- It must be small enough to allow the firm to take leadership quickly and easily. This is counter-intuitive, but crucial. We have seen why going for large segments is a sure recipe for failure. To use Christensen's expression, one must be patient for growth, but impatient for profits (Christensen, 1997).
- The organisation must already have some credible experience in that segment. once the segment is chosen, all resources must be used to invade it and take it over.

Extend Through Adjacencies

Once the beachhead segment has been captured, the process can be repeated, i.e., select another small segment, and invade it. The next segment should be adjacent to the first one. Otherwise, there will be no leverage between segments. Adjacencies can be in terms of industries or functions. The process is repeated from adjacent segment to adjacent segment. The success of the launch is dependent on both the manufacturer and the retailer(s) understanding its objectives and being prepared to do what they need to achieve them.

The immediate post launch phase is very critical to the commercialisation of innovation and in this context two elements are of crucial importance:

- The speed with which learnings occur in the very early phases of the commercialisation of innovation.
- Appropriate marketing adjustments to steer the new product carefully towards success.

Blending shopper insights with consumer insights is critically important in this phase. Linking consumer to shopper and calibrating marketing activities to make sure that initial difficulties of the new product in the market are overcome is crucial to success.

Monitoring is not just a matter of taking a look at what has happened. It is very much a matter of using information with an eye toward improving immediate future performance.

Moreover, monitoring should provide in-depth insights at the speed of light: is my product relevant to my target group? Who is buying? What are their characteristics? What triggers repeat buys? Is the conversion rate from triallist to repeat purchases good enough? And at later stage: what are the differences from my early adopters to my main users? Should I change my marketing techniques to reflect the differences?

RESEARCHING FOR INNOVATION

Choosing Techniques

Researchers involved in the innovation process should rely on a portfolio of techniques, and even more importantly stay abreast of new emerging techniques that may be better suited than familiar ones.

There is no definitive answer on which technique to choose. Here we hope to build understanding (including methodological biases) of the available tools, to help make the most appropriate choice and to encourage experimentation. The tools range across verbal, active and observational. Each of these three approaches has drawbacks – observations rely entirely on the analysis and conclusion of the researcher; verbal participation may lead to rationalisation in the respondents and answers may not fully reflect unconscious habits; and active participation may enact a special relationship with the product that can bias the results. Moreover, non-lead users may have difficulties in interacting with a radical new product. Each of these drawbacks may also become strengths according to the problem at hand. It is very important that not only the potential usage and satisfaction is monitored (consumer insights) but also that shopping habits are taken into consideration – what factors can facilitate the purchase of the product or service? Shopper insights are becoming more and more crucial to ensure success in the commercialisation of innovation.

Here we use the See-Act-Launch framework as a context for categorising the usefulness of different techniques and tools (Figure 6.5). Technical details on each tool can be found in Bond and Debacq (1998).

	Observation	Verbal participation*	Active participation
Explore (See)	• Anthropological research • In-store cameras • Mystery Shopping • Empathic design	• Focus groups • In-depth interviews • Shops alongs	• Lead users • Delphi • Backcasting techniques • Customer immersion
Forecast / Test (Act)	• Forecasting models (diffusion models) • In-store observations	• Diaries • Concept testing • Some forecasting techniques	• Product testing/ Usage test • In home tests • Information acceleration
Monitor (Launch)	• Retail Panels • (Household panels) • In-store observations	• Surveys • Shopper insights	• Usage satisfaction • Consumer clinics • Accompanied in-store visits

* Rationalisation distorsions may apply

Figure 6.5   Choice of relevant research technique can be made according to type of innovation phase – some examples

As pointed out by Leifer (2000), existing research is based on incremental innovation rather than radical innovation (The contributions of Christensen, Anthony & Ross, 2004; Utterback, 1994 & von Hipple, 1986 provide notable exceptions). Matters are further complicated by the fact that in reality, See-Act-Launch is non-linear and dynamic. For opportunities to become markets, they require an interlinked combination of vision ("Seeing") and marketplace involvement ("Acting"). Companies that see tend to do, and companies that do, tend to see. As Donald Schön wrote, "the marketing process is a reflective conversation with consumers" (1983).

Insights providers should be familiar with the type of company they are working with, as not all companies operate in the same space and therefore not all have the same needs.

Companies can pursue radical innovation in all three of the innovation phases (See-Act-Launch) or they can focus their efforts on a particular phase.

Revolutionary companies (mostly technology-based) often focus on the "See" (incubation) phase, for example nanotech and biotech. However, only a few or them are able to create a new sustainable market with their innovation and grow into large corporations. The majority are likely to sell their inventions at early- or mid-phase to larger corporations with distinctive capabilities to bring products to the market, or in the worst case they will exit unsuccessfully.

The main difficulty in creating a market for radical innovation is the wide gap between the technology driven innovation and the consumers they are trying to reach. Consumers simply don't understand the "what's in it for me" proposition of the new product or service. Ideally the "what's in it for me" benefits should be relevant in at least one of the following: rationally, emotionally or socially.

However, large corporations may also face difficulties in finding this common language during the "See" phase of a potentially radical innovation. Often it takes years and several iterations of the product before a new product or service is successful, even in cases not involving complex biotech or high tech.

Success Factors in Consumer Insights

Independent of any one phase of the innovation process, the success of consumer insights, regardless of the phase of innovation or innovation context, depends on four critical elements:

- Flow of insights that generate actions
- Integration of insights
- Compelling communication
- Avoidance of organisational silos

The Importance of Flow of Insights

Insights-driven organisations have a constant flow of insights, with the relevant learnings leveraged both at strategic and operational levels. Tesco, the UK retailer, has a constant flow of consumer insights, with the relevant information incorporated into the company strategy reviews discussed by the Board and developed into action plans. The retailer is able to integrate transactional data, loyalty card data, customer surveys and in-store observation in a constant flow of metrics. These are actioned by stores, headquarters and the Board. Such a constant flow of insights has been pivotal to Tesco's success in driving innovation in retail (new formats, services and categories) and products (its own label range). Companies that build and act on a constant flow of insights, develop a rock-solid knowledge base over time, capitalising on a positive learning spiral.

Integration of Insights

Integrating different insights is crucial to radical innovation. It is often complex, as integration is meaningful across different dimensions: the present, with a wide spectrum of other consumer-centric insights; the past, enriched by learning from past experience and research and the future. The integration of insights is particularly complex in the See or "Exploring" phase where the number of dimensions to be taken into consideration is exponential. A strictly analytical approach may be too narrow, while a holistic approach with some use of "intuition" and "pattern recognition" can be more fruitful. As Grogan and Banerj (2006) point out: "(integration) requires the development of new skills". Building a data integrator resource may necessitate retraining and often recruitment of different profiles. Researchers must be comfortable piecing together data from different sources, often piecing it together iteratively to build up a complete picture of the consumers' world. A company should aim to integrate a portfolio of insights into a system that generates a constant flow of insights that can be acted upon. Several research institutes offer a "system" approach, while some companies have developed their own tailored systems.

Compelling Communication

The inherent complexity of the insights and of the analyses required for results often poses the challenge of conveying the main message in a simplified form. Communication style also has to be adapted for each audience. Each decision-maker must understand the key results and be able to explain them throughout the organisation.

Avoiding Organisational Silos

McKinsey research on idea generation has pointed out the importance of cross-functional teams and the pivotal role played by the consumer insight professionals in generating successful innovations. An organisation maximises its impact through having networks rather than silos, enabled by cross-functional teams actively engaging and exchanging insights and knowledge. This facilitates the formation of one common language spoken within the organisation, centred on the consumer. These cross functional teams benefit from being "immersed" in the life of the consumers and developing a thorough understanding of their needs, habits and use of products (Grogan & Banerj, 2006).

New Trends in Research for Innovation

A lot is happening in the research for innovation landscape – and this chapter does not aim at giving a comprehensive overview.

In the "Exploring" phase, a lot of work is done in understanding the trends in a comprehensive way that allows not only to plan for the long term in terms of strategic direction for innovation but also to embed the findings in the company operations, thus making companies much more reactive and proactive towards changes in the landscape. Several companies have done work in this arena, the case study from Philips gives a very good example of development in this arena.

In the area of concept testing a lot is happening, across the spectrum, new methodologies are entering the space giving the marketeers wider choices – from lead users, to applications of neuropsychology, to leveraging virtual reality and online. The main trend is in the authors' view set by von Hippel's followers who leverage consumers' co-creation.

In the area of commercialisation of innovation, several new developments are in the landscape, that allow marketing departments to have a very close steer of the early phases of launch with a in-depth understanding of the consumer and shopper early adopters and the possibility to steer closely the marketing and in-store activities.

Obstacles to Research for Innovation

Clearly, not all innovations are successful. In a different, yet relevant context, Evgeniou and Cartwright (2005) build on the literature relating to judgment, uncertainty, bias and heuristics (e.g., Kahneman, Slovic & Tversky, 1982) to understand barriers or obstacles to successful information management. While the original context is different, some of the obstacles are relevant to understanding frictions in the contextual framework of See-Act-Launch (Cartwright & Silberzahn, 2006). Setting out a typology of barriers, Evgeniou and Cartwright focus on:

- Behaviour
- Process
- Organisation

Behavioural Obstacles

Significant behavioural obstacles are *confirmatory bias* and the inability or *difficulty of balancing creativity* and *hard market data*. Confirmatory bias arises when the choice is made to confirm existing beliefs using existing data despite other relevant information. The difficulty in balancing creativity and empirical evidence arises from a misalignment between intuition, prior beliefs, and what the data reveals. It is particularly prevalent in emerging markets where data is scarce. This explains why vision and creativity drive innovators often beyond reason. Examples of this include Microsoft's BOB user interface, supposedly designed to simplify the use of computers and Webvan's online credit and delivery grocery business that went bankrupt in 2001. Unlike confirmatory bias, this imbalance does not imply a deliberate neglect of data or information. It's really a matter of preserving creativity in the face of hard evidence. Clearly these sources of bias can lead to misjudgments concerning innovation in terms of needs and relevance.

Discussed in terms used by Kahnemann, Slovic and Tversky (1982), the heuristic of representativeness seems especially relevant. Representativeness refers to cases in which people are asked to judge the probability that an event (object) belongs to a particular class. Given something they have never seen before, they try to relate it to something they have seen before. Based on their recollections, they attempt to assess usage. Depending on the extent of the departure from their knowledge base (especially important for innovations) this might be quite difficult. Individuals confronted by that which is new are likely to engage in a classification exercise. Users trying to classify the new product or service as belonging to a particular known class are likely to arrive at a confused understanding. They fail to integrate the information they receive from the communication to market process with prior probabilities that would they would apply in the absence of such information.

Process Barriers

With respect to process barriers Evgeniou and Cartwright (2005) refer to *unsuccessful problem definition*. This amounts to unsuccessful concept definition. While failure to define concept falls largely on the supply side (innovator-entrepreneur), the consequence is that poor or weak signalling to the market results in users failing to understand the innovation. The process breaks down owing to failure in the knowledge transfer interaction or feedback loop. Apple's Lisa, the first commercially available computer equipped with a graphical user interface (GUI) falls into this category as Apple failed not so much to sell the computer as the concept itself that a GUI was the way to go. Apple made the mistake again in 1984 with the Macintosh but this time, the product was saved by the laser writer, which helped potential users identify the machine with a well-defined use: desktop publishing.

A second process barrier is that of research rigidity. This concerns failure to recognise that the supply–demand interaction is dynamic and iterative. Kahnemann, Slovic and Tversky (1982) refer to availability giving rise to a need for iterative learning associated with reliance upon available instances or scenarios for assessing the probability of a particular development. In the process of assessing usage of the new product, users are dependent on imagination. A good example is the launch of third generation (3G) mobile phones for which users are still trying to figure out what they could be used for beyond trivial examples of football video on a stamp-sized screen. In this case, the learning failure is owing to a misalignment between the imagined usage and the actual likelihood of use.

Organisational Barriers

Information asymmetries are a source of organisational failure. In the simple case where the innovator and entrepreneur are the same person, the likelihood of information or learning asymmetries seems low. As the organisation becomes more complex, more people are involved across business units, so the probability of a learning failure owing to asymmetries increases.

ACKNOWLEDGEMENTS

The Authors wish to thank Helena Wilson and Aunia Grogan, McKinsey & Company, London 2006.

REFERENCES

Anderson, C. (2006) *The Long Tail*. Random House.
Andrews, A. and Bevolo, M. (2003) "Understanding Digital Futures". *Design Management Journal*.
Bass, F.M. (1969) "A New Product Growth Model for Consumer Durables", *Management Science*, **15**, January.
Bass, F.M. (1980) "The relationship between diffusion rates, experience curves and demand elasticities for consumer durable technological innovations", *Journal of Business*, **53**.
Bevolo, M. and Brand, R. (2002) "Brand Design for the long term". *Design Management Review*.
Bond, J. and Debacq, J. (1998) "Research in new product development", in *ESOMAR Handbook of Market and Opinion Research*, 4th edn, eds. McDonald, C. and Vangelder, P., pp. 775–802. ESOMAR.

Buisson, B., Cartwright, P.A., and Silberzahn, S. (2006) "Early Warning Systems and Firm Survival, the Role of Market Research in the Face of Major Market Disruptions", Excellence 2006, ed. D.S. Fellows, pp. 145–158. ESOMAR World Research Papers, 2006, Amsterdam: ESOMAR.

Cartwright, P.A. and Silberzahn, S. (2006) "A Dynamic Model of disruptive innovation in the space of market recognition: a high-tech perspective", presented at ESOMAR, Innovate 2006, Miami Beach, FL., May.

Chesbrough, H. (2003) *Open Innovation, the New Imperative for Creating and Profiting from Technology*. Harvard Business School Press.

Christensen, C. (1997) "The Innovator's Dilemma, When new technologies Cause Great Firms to Fail", Boston: Harvard Business School Press.

Christensen, C., Anthony, S.D., and Roth, E.A. (2004) *Seeing What's Next, Using Theories of Innovation to Predict Industry Change*. Harvard University Press.

Christensen, C.M. (2006) "The Ongoing Process of Building a Theory of Disruption," *Journal of Product Innovation Management*, **23**(1), 39–55.

Deszca, G., Munro H. and Noori, H. (1999) "Developing Breakthrough Products: Challenges and Options for Market Assessment", *Journal of Operations Management*, **17**, 613–630.

Evgeniou, T. and Cartwright, P. (2005) "Six Barriers to Information Intelligence", *European Management Journal*, **23**(3), 293–299.

Freeman, C. (1974) *The Economics of Industrial Innovation*. London: Pinter.

Garcia, R. and Calantone, R. (2002) "A Critical Look at Technological Innovation Typology and Innovativeness Terminology: a Literature Review", *Journal of Product Innovation Management*, **19**(2), 10–32.

Gladwell M. (2002) *"The Tipping Point"*. Little, Brown & Company.

Gladwell, M. (2005) *Blinking*. Little Brown & Company.

Grogan, A. and Banerj, V. (2006) "Harnessing Consumer Insight to Drive Innovation", ESOMAR.

Kahneman, D., Slovic, P. and Tversky, A. (1982) *"Judgment Under Uncertainty: Heuristics and Bias"*. Cambridge University Press.

Hargadon, A.B. and Yellowlees, D. (2001) "When Innovations Meet Institutions: Edison and the Design of the Electric Light", *Administrative Science Quarterly*, **46**(3), 476–502.

Leifer, C.W.L. et al. (2000) *Radical Innovation: How Mature Companies Can Outsmart Upstarts*. Harvard Business School Press.

Marzano, S. and Aarts, A. (2003) *"The New Everyday – New Visions of Ambient Intelligence"*. OIO Publishers.

Moore, G. (1991) *Crossing the Chasm: Marketing and Selling Technology Products to Mainstream Customers*. HarperCollins, research for radical innovation.

Narver, J.C., Slater, S.F. and Maclachlan, D. (2004) "Responsive and Proactive Market Orientation and New-Product Success", *Journal of Product Innovation Management*, **21**(5), 334–347.

Schön, D. (1983) *The Reflective Practitioner – How Professionals Think in Action*. Basic Books.

Slater, S.F. and Narver, J.C. (1999) "Market-oriented is More than Being Customer-Led", *Strategic Management Journal*, **20**(12), 1165–1168.

Sood, A. and Tellis, G.J. (2005) "Technological Evolution and Radical Innovation", *Journal of Marketing*, **69**(3), 152–168.

Tellis, G.J. (2006) "Disruptive Technology or Visionary Leadership?", *Journal of Product Innovation Management*, **23**(1), 34–38.

Tushman, M.L. and Anderson, P. (1986) "Technological Discontinuities and Organizational Environments", *Administrative Science Quarterly*, **31**(3), 439–465.

Utterback, J.M. (1994) *Mastering the Dynamics of Innovation*. Harvard University Press.

Utterback, J.M. and Abernathy, W.J. (1975) "A Dynamic Model of Process and Product Innovation" *Omega*, **33**, 639–656.

Vissers, B. (2006) *"From Aesthetic trends to new value signs"*. ESOMAR.

von Hippel, E. (1986) "Lead users: a source of novel product concepts", *Management Science*, **32**(7), 791–805.

von Hippel, E. (2005) *Democratising Innovation*. MIT Press.

Zull, J. (2002) *The Art of Changing a Brain: Helping People Learn by Understanding How the Brain Works*. Stylus.

7

Refining Market Propositions

Nigel Hollis and Dominic Twose

INTRODUCTION

This chapter focuses on what research should be done to check whether or not a brand is healthy and how best to refine and refresh its proposition to better appeal to its target market(s).

The chapter is divided into five sections:

1. A review of the issues involved in maintaining the health of an established brand.
2. Understanding the competitive environment.
3. Identifying whether your brand needs refinement.
4. Steps to take in ideating/refining the existing strategy.
5. Specific research approaches required to deliver on the strategy.

MAINTAINING A HEALTHY BRAND

Existing brands are the life-blood of the company. While new products and innovations attract much of senior management attention, the risk attached to new product introductions is very high. Existing brands, on the other hand, typically represent a secure future revenue and profit stream, provided they are kept healthy.

The Status Quo Trap

Market shares for established brands are remarkably stable over time (Farr, 1998). Most product and service categories exhibit little change from year to year, and for much of its life an established brand will exist in a stable environment. Even in the most fiercely contended categories, competitive activity will tend to cancel out, as one brand's actions are counteracted by others.

This fact can often lead companies to develop a myopic view of the brand and its category. The prevailing assumption is that the status quo will prevail. This often results in established brands being ill-prepared to meet a new challenge or losing relevance to their target market and having to take drastic measures to recover lost ground (Twose, 2005).

The first task in ensuring the health of an established brand is to create a monitoring system that will allow you to understand whether shifts are taking place in the market that might require a change of strategy.

Market Research Handbook, 5th Edition. Edited by M. van Hamersveld and C. de Bont.
© 2007 John Wiley & Sons, Ltd.

The Lure of Change

Equally as damaging as a failure to invest in change when it is needed, is change for change's sake. In this age of revolving door CMOs and brand managers new incumbents often seek to make changes to an existing proposition in order to justify their existence or claim a success before moving onto their next position. All too often these changes actually dilute the brand's equity because they create a lack of clarity regarding what the brand stands for.

Executing the Same Positioning Differently

Most successful brands do not change their strategy without very good reason. Consistency is typically a major factor in brand success. Established brands will have a loyal following of existing consumers or customers. They have established expectations and beliefs about the brand that ensure their continued loyalty. Any change that aims to appeal to new customers but risks alienation of the existing customer base is potentially self-defeating (see New Coke case study).

Recent findings from the world of neuroscience point to the importance of maintaining a clear and balanced brand positioning over time. Page and Raymond (2006) suggest that people use "representations" to understand, make decisions and interact with the world around them. Representations are made up of little bits of information drawn from externally perceived, remembered or imagined items. According to Page and Raymond brands which quickly and easily form strong representations have the best chance of being chosen in a cluttered environment. Critically, however, the strength of those representations depends on people having a balanced understanding of the brand – one that includes its physical cues, its functional benefits and the emotions evoked by it.

While all marketers should seek opportunities to disrupt the category status quo in their favour, for most established brands the ongoing challenge is to find ways to refresh an already established brand positioning.

Case Study: New Coke, What Not to Do

In 1985 The Coca-Cola Company introduced a new product formulation of its flagship Coca-Cola brand. Intended to counter the growing strength of Pepsi "New Coke" was launched with the tagline "The Best Just Got Better". While most consumers continued buying the brand, a minority overtly resented the change and lobbied for the old formula to be reinstated. Less than three months after the introduction slow sales performance and growing negative publicity convinced Coca-Cola executives to announce the return of the old formula under the name Coke Classic.

The New Coke debacle is a classic example of misinterpreted and misapplied market research.

The true reason for Pepsi's growing success was misinterpreted. Influenced by the apparent success of the "Pepsi Challenge", which purported to show that more consumers preferred Pepsi to Coke in a blind sip test, Coca-Cola executives focused on the product formulation, ignoring other potential reasons for Pepsi's success. In fact, two other factors played a part. Pepsi had worked to establish a youth-oriented brand identity since the 1960s and was starting to reap the rewards of people growing up loyal to the brand. The merger between Pepsi and Frito-Lay also enabled the new PepsiCo to leverage Frito-Lay's highly developed retail distribution system to gain increased distribution and shelf space.

Given the nature of the brand, the research conducted to test the new formulation was also inadequate. While survey results indicated that the new formulation was preferred to both regular Coke and Pepsi the tests did not include extended use of the products and were conducted blind. Sip tests conducted in a mall often produce different results from extended use at home because flavours, sweetness and carbonation are appreciated differently with continued exposure. Further, the product is just one aspect of a brand. Particularly with an established brand where users have expectations triggered by the brand name and packaging, branded testing can lead to very different conclusions from blind testing. In the case of New Coke respondents were only asked if they would drink the new product if it was Coca-Cola after tasting the new formulation. Their expectations were essentially side-lined.

Finally, it is reported that while the product tests results were positive overall, a minority of respondents were incensed by the thought that the formulation might be changed. This warning signal was ignored and little thought given to the pressure that hard-core brand loyalists might bring to bear.

In the case of new Coke, the outrage at the idea that the product had been tampered with was so strong because of the strength of attitudinal loyalty and nostalgia people had for the brand. Many brands with weaker loyalty would not even get a second chance as buyers become disillusioned and find alternatives they prefer. This lesson does not apply just to a product or service, but packaging and positioning too; people need to be able to recognise their brand and continue to identify with it. Change for change's sake is rarely desirable. Rather the brand manager should seek ways to refresh or refine the brand's proposition over time unless there is a well-founded reason for a more fundamental change.

What to Worry About and Why

There are a broad range of things that a brand management team needs to monitor in order to understand if the brand's proposition is still relevant and competitive. The following list reviews the most likely factors which might require a brand's proposition to be refreshed:

Change in the Target Market

Peoples' needs, habits and beliefs change over time. The established brand cannot afford to assume that things will stay the same and should assess its relevance periodically and appeal to the target market.

- What changes might provide opportunities/threats?
  - Are their rational and emotional category needs evolving?
  - Are their consumption habits changing?
  - Is the way they shop the category changing?
  - Are their beliefs about the category evolving?
  - Are their lifestyles changing?

Weakness in the Product Offer

A great product or service experience is the platform on which a great brand is built. Assessment of the existing product against new competitive products and testing of new formulations should be conducted as needed.

- Does the current product or service offer stack up?
  - Does it meet target group expectations?
  - Does it offer a competitive advantage?

Poor Packaging or Design

For some brands packaging and design is integral to the product, e.g. automotive and computer hardware. In others like consumer packaged goods it offers a separate but equally valuable aspect of the brand. In both cases consumer tastes may change or new competitive offerings result in the existing design looking dated or lacking functionality.

- Is the existing packaging/design competitive?
  - o Does it meet target group needs?
  - o Is the design still appealing and distinctive?

Changes in Brand Image

Perception is reality. Consumer beliefs about the brand and its benefits will be based on partial knowledge of it and the competitive brands. While your marketing activity will be directed to supporting the existing positioning, competitors will be working to strengthen theirs. There are two risks, (a) that your marketing activities are not successful or are outweighed by the competitive pressure, (b) that the competitors find a new angle that weakens your brand's positioning in the eyes of the consumer.

- How does your brand awareness and image compare to competitors?
  - o Are target consumers aware of your brand? Does it come readily to mind when a relevant need arises? Is the brand promise understood and motivating?
- How does your brand compare to competitors on the functional and emotional attributes/benefits known to be category drivers?
  - o Are these beliefs changing for better/worse?

Distribution Weaknesses or Opportunities

A brand needs to be available when and where people need it, or think to look to buy it. Are there weaknesses that need to be addressed?

- Is the brand available where people might look for it?
  - o Is the retail partner/distributor satisfied?
  - o Is the brand visible and attractive in the retail environment?

Pricing Problems

Price is a double edged sword. You can sell more volume by dropping the price but margins will be eroded and profit may fall. In the longer-term reliance on price as a volume driver may erode brand equity as consumers are taught to buy on price. You need to know whether the price is competitive and justified by the brand's equity.

- Does the current proposition justify the price asked?
  - o Is the pricing competitive?
  - o Is the price below key thresholds?

Promotion Competitiveness

Consumer promotion can provide a means to add some "new news" in the absence of other brand differentiating activities. You need to monitor whether or not your promotions are supporting brand equity as well as attracting new buyers.

- Are the brand's current promotions attractive to existing buyers and prospects?

Communication Issues

Evidence from tracking research by Millward Brown (Twose, 2005) suggests that a brand is likely to prosper if it has an effective share of voice greater than its market share. Effective share of voice relates to the brand's advertising saliency more than just its weight of spend and is the end result of the creative, weight and media used.

- Is your brand punching its weight in market?
- Is the media mix effective?
  - o Does it reach the right people at the right time?
  - o Do the different communication channels work synergistically?
  - o Is the weight in each communication channel sufficient?
- Is the current creative execution effective?
  - o Is it on strategy?
  - o Does it communicate effectively?
  - o Does it evoke the desired response?

Internal Branding Problems

In many industries a company's own staff is its face to the consumer. They may be disillusioned or dissatisfied resulting in a less than compelling brand experience.

- Are the staff/dealers/resellers satisfied?
- Are they aligned and enthused by the existing proposition?

UNDERSTANDING THE COMPETITIVE ENVIRONMENT

The competitive environment facing brand marketers today is complex and fast-paced. They must have a robust, holistic view of what is happening over time in order to make the right decisions in a timely manner. Obviously not every single aspect of the brand's proposition can be monitored on a continuous basis. The following would represent a reasonable research programme for a large brand.

Continuous or standard monitoring would include two basic types of research:

1. Research to understand *what* is happening to sales over time. This data would be collected from a variety of sources, backed up by information on distribution, pricing, promotion and media spend.
2. Research to explain *why* those changes in sales are taking place. This data would be collected from consumers active in the product category and include awareness, brand consideration and imagery, awareness and response to marketing programmes.

Monitoring research will periodically need to be augmented by ad hoc research, e.g. competitive product testing, and investigation of specific issues, e.g. why is a competitive brand launch stealing share?

This section will review the type of research standardly conducted to monitor a brand for signs of weakness or threat.

Research to Monitor *What* Is Happening to Sales

Consumer packaged goods industries in developed markets usually have access to scanned retail sales data that provides weekly tracking of volume, share, regular price, temporary price reductions and displays, overall and by retail outlet type. In less developed markets this type of data will still be available but collected by a physical audit of stores. Standard analysis will report key trends and often separate sales into incremental volume due to price and display activity and base sales sold at full price.

Retail sales data is often complemented by panel data focusing on purchasing patterns at the household or, in some cases, the level of the individual. Key measures are penetration (what percentage of households buy the brand), repeat purchase (how many times they buy in a specific time frame), and what other brands are bought.

Manufacturing companies outside the packaged goods industries will obtain similar data from alternative sources. In some cases they will supply ex-factory data to an industry body that consolidates the information from a number of manufacturers to give share data. In others specific companies, like NPD in North America and Europe, will create panels specific to an industry to track purchasing behaviour. Failing these sources of information companies may set up surveys to track claimed purchasing over time or make do with ex-factory shipment data and sales force reporting.

Service companies will have access to statistics on acquisition and retention, churn rates and individual customer records on usage, services bought, etc. Provided the customer database is in good shape, service companies can interrogate the database to gain a detailed understanding of the current state of their business. Are they losing more customers than they are gaining? Is there an opportunity to up-sell existing customers to premium services?

Whatever the source of data on sales, the key questions to be answered as part of an ongoing situation assessment are as follows:

1. Where does the current revenue and profit come from: distribution channel, product line or consumer/customer group?
2. What is the current status? Improving, static or declining?
3. What are the sources of improvement or decline: specific brand activities or competitive actions?
4. How does your pricing compare to that of the competition and are there any psychological price barriers?

If time series sales or share data is available, Market Mix Modelling can be employed to understand the quantitative impact on sales of short-term marketing activities. Market Mix Modelling uses statistical techniques to identify relationships over time between sales or share and causal data like pricing, distribution, and weight of advertising and sales promotion.

Research to Monitor *Why* Things Are Changing

Behavioural data like scanned sales data or customer records do not give a complete picture of what is happening on their own. They do not provide an understanding of consumer motivations and they do not measure all the touch points that drive those motivations and subsequent behaviour. Brands are assets that derive their value from what people think of them. As a result most companies use survey research to provide insight into what people think about their brands relative to the competitive set.

Tracking Study Methodology

A tracking study must provide insight in a consistent manner over time in order to highlight changes in awareness and attitudes and the causes of change.

   Tracking studies can be conducted by phone, online, face-to-face or by mail. Surveys are either conducted continuously (a few each day), or waves conducted at regular intervals or around specific brand activities, e.g. relaunch or new advertising campaign. Continuous is considered the gold standard because it allows the data to be plotted over time in relation to potential causal data, e.g. media or promotional spend, in order to identify cause and effect. A typical continuous tracking study graph is show in Figure 7.1. Wave tracking studies will yield only a partial picture of what is happening over time and may cause the brand team to react slowly to a trend or misinterpret the cause of a trend. In either case the research supplier should aim to complete equal numbers of interview per day across the week in order gain a representative picture and avoid potential bias from unexpected events. A tracking study

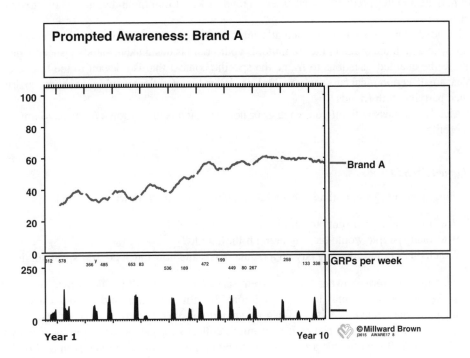

Figure 7.1   A typical continuous tracking study graph

should be designed to give a representative picture of the health of the competing brands but depending on the relevance to your product or service category. Data should be collected for competing brands (usually those representing 80 %+ of category volume) since people would usually consider buying from a repertoire of competing brands. The sample definition for a tracking study should match that of people expected to buy the product category or segment in which your brand competes. If the category is growing or the inter-purchase interval long you may need to consider sampling people who might buy it in future. If service is a key component of your brand offering then consider monitoring staff attitudes over time.

The tracking study must focus on the likely indicators of success or failure for the brand. These need to be identified based on information from attitude and usage studies, segmentation studies and other sources. The following topic areas will be most relevant.

Brand Health

Key measures of amount spent on the category, unaided and aided brand awareness, current brand usage and consideration, brand experience and imagery should be included as standard but customised to meet the needs of your brand and category.

Brand Awareness and Familiarity

The unaided and aided awareness will tell you whether your brand suffers from a lack of visibility compared to key competitors. In more considered purchase categories brand familiarity may be a better predictor of whether a brand makes it into the individual's consideration set.

Unaided awareness will be particularly important in impulse categories since it reflects the ease with which the brand comes to mind. If your brand is designed to satisfy a specific need, phrase the unaided questions to frame the specific context that is relevant to the brand, e.g. What small, economical cars can you think of? What brand of beer would you choose to drink when partying with friends?

Aided awareness will tell you whether or not the brand is well-known or needs to improve its profile.

Claimed Brand Usage

Existing brand usage and brand consideration help answer the following questions:

1. How loyal are my current buyers (a surrogate for panel data)?
2. How many people would buy my brand if they could?
3. Which other brands do they buy on a regular basis and how much do they spend on them?

In solus use categories, ownership or current service provider will be the primary measurement. Service providers may have the additional benefit of tapping into customer databases to integrate true behaviour with claimed usage and consideration to identify individual customer value. For other companies it is useful to collect surrogate information on sensitivity to price, how different brands are perceived to be in the category and interest in trial of new offers.

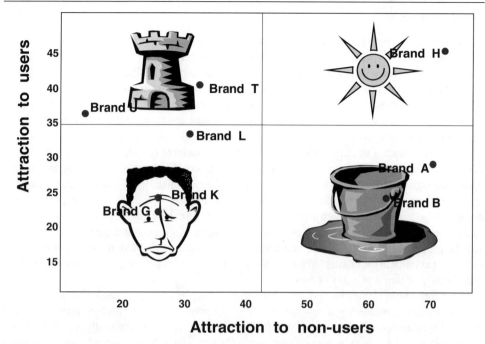

Figure 7.2 Brand attraction map

By comparing the degree of consideration to a brand within users and non-users we can gain insight into the relative strength and attractiveness of your brand compared to its competitors. Interpretation of the brand attraction maps (Figure 7.2) is relatively straightforward.

Top right: This is the strongest position any brand can be in; its current users are likely to remain loyal to it AND it is attractive to users of competitor brands.

Top left: Given the importance of existing users to a brand, this is still a relatively strong position to be in, this is especially true for bigger brands and in markets where consumers have longer term relationships with brands. Current users are likely to remain loyal to the brand. However it is not likely to attract users of competitor brands and the marketing team need to focus on how best to do so.

Bottom right: This is a relatively weak position for a brand to be in. Its current users are not likely to remain loyal to the brand; however, the brand proposition is attractive to users of competitor brands (which is important for smaller brands and brands in repertoire markets). The marketing team need to focus on why existing brand buyers are not loyal.

Bottom left: This is the weakest position any brand can be in. Current users are not likely to remain loyal to it and it is not likely to attract users of competitor brands.

In each case you should be seeking to identify strengths and weaknesses versus the competition and check whether the brand's competitive position is strengthening or weakening over time.

Brand Experience

Critical to future brand consideration is how existing users experience the brand. A good experience may bond people to the brand making them immune to competitive offers. A bad experience may cause them to seek alternatives or become dissatisfied and an active brand detractor. Measuring brand experience is particularly important for more considered and long inter-purchase goods, like cars and cameras, and services, like banking and health care. If your brand competes in a service industry then separate customer satisfaction studies will likely be needed to track the customer experience over time, e.g. call centre or service satisfaction.

At the very least a tracking study should include measures of satisfaction with the brand experience asked of existing users and potential purchasers. This may need to be augmented on a periodic basis to investigate the different stages of experience, from initial brand contact to ongoing transactions. Particularly important is to ensure that all aspects of the experience are considered, e.g. monitoring both the experience of driving a car and the service experience. Even in a consumer packaged good category topline measures of shopper and consumer experience will help identify potential issues and problems. How does satisfaction among brand users compare to competitive brands? What are the trends? Do shoppers report that they can find the brand easily or that it stands out on shelf?

Note: Reichheld (2003) has promoted the use of the Net Promoter Score (NPS) – positive recommendations minus negative – as a simple measure of likely brand performance, obviating the need for more complex customer satisfaction research. While undoubtedly a useful, simple statistic, care still needs to be taken – in particular, an understanding of attitudes to competitors is likely to be valuable. For example, in the developed countries, many people complain about their bank, but a feeling that "they're all as bad as each other" results in far fewer account switches than might be expected. When choosing a measure of customer satisfaction it is important to ensure that it is tailored to your specific category and ideally would be validated against subsequent behaviour to prove that it is a leading indicator of sales.

Brand Imagery

These questions should be designed to understand the brand's positioning and its relative strength on key drivers of consideration. A tracking study should cover only the key attitudinal statements for the brand and category. Ideally these will have been identified as the drivers of consideration and leading indicators of brand performance.

Brand imagery data can be used to answer the following questions:

- How do people think my brand compares to the competition?
- Are the brand perceptions that lead people to consider my brand changing?
- What are the relative strengths and weaknesses of my brand versus the competition? Among my current buyers? Among prospects? How are things changing over time?

A correspondence map is one of the simplest ways to understand the relative positioning of brands. The example in Figure 7.3, from the bath/shower category, highlights four key categories:

1. A sensitive, mild, kind category, typified by Brand F.
2. A moisturising category, typified by Brand B.
3. A sector for all the family, with Brands I and E being good examples.
4. Brands offering invigorating fragrances; such as Brands J and K.

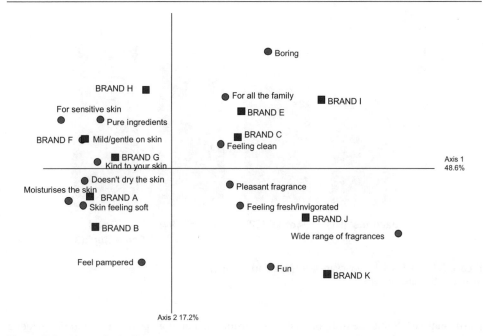

Figure 7.3   Shower/bath category

Correspondence maps are superb at painting a broad picture of the market, but are weak at identifying precisely how strong a brand is on a particular dimension, because of the compromises required to portray a mass of complex information in a two dimensional format. It is worth noting that in this case the two axes only portray 66 % of the variance in the data. Further exploration might demonstrate an important third dimension.

A "driver" analysis will help you understand the relative importance of each attribute in driving consideration and behaviour. There are a number of statistical techniques which can be used of varying sophistication. Be aware, however, that all rely on identifying correlation and do not necessarily give insight into causation. For example, high share brands are often perceived as popular, but which is the chicken, which the egg? Do people buy the brand because it is popular – ubiquity and herd instincts are important drivers of sales in impulse and conspicuous consumption categories – or is it seen to be popular because it is well distributed?

As well as conducting the driver analysis to identify drivers for the category overall, you should also conduct the analysis for your specific brand. Particularly if yours is not the major brand in the category, aspects that differentiate your brand from the general pattern may be hidden because the larger brand has an overwhelming influence on the general relationships identified.

Volumetrics

Tracking is not a replacement for volume sales data but it can fill in gaps when there is no other source. For instance, how well does your brand perform in kiosks and handcarts? What is your brand's share of wardrobe? How much snack brand volume gets sold though gas or

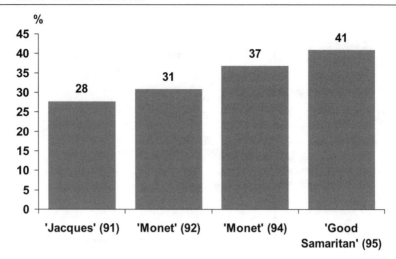

Figure 7.4   Claimed TV ad awareness (peak during burst)
Source: Millward Brown.

petrol stations? Some measure of category consumption and/or spending should be included so that respondents can be classified by category importance.

Quality of Marketing Communication

Market mix modelling will tell you whether or not your communications are driving sales directly. However, you also need to know whether your ad expenditures are working to build and support the underlying demand for the brand.

There are three main aspects that need to be measured:

1. Awareness of advertising for the brand will tell you whether or not your marketing communication is linked to the brand and is leveraging media spend efficiently. A good example is the "Reassuringly Expensive" TV campaign for Stella Artois (Figure 7.4). TV advertising began for the brand in 1991, with the execution "Jacques". Tracking highlighted that branding and cut through were a problem for that execution. People remembered the ad but many could not identify which brand it was for. Building on this finding and from pre-testing results, the agency improved subsequent ads, improving branding and optimising ad length. As a result cut-through improved (Source: IPA case study).
2. Recall of what people remember about the advertising can give useful insight into whether the communication is on strategy and which executions are driving response. For Stella, communication of the key messages improved over time too.
3. The correlation with changes in brand awareness, image and consideration will provide evidence of whether the communication is having the desired effect. Brand empathy for Stella Artois improved in line with the improvements in the advertising response (Figure 7.5).
4. There will be cases in which there is little change in the brand data, either the communication is intended to re-enforce an existing positioning or because the communication is ineffective. In order to diagnose the reason you need to ask people for their self-reported reaction to

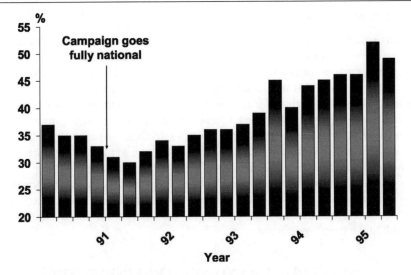

Figure 7.5   Stella brand empathy
Source: Millward Brown.

the advertising. If this data is needed for specific executions then use of a visual prompt is desirable.

Monitoring Word of Mouth

An unsolicited recommendation has always been the best advertisement a brand can have, but the advent of the Internet and mobile phones has dramatically increased WOM's reach and speed of dispersion.

Many companies monitor Internet chatter on message boards, blogs and social network sites to identify which topics and brands are being talked about and to highlight changing trends and emerging issues. The detailed and granular data collected from these sources can be used to give insight into potential problems and issues with your brand, identify new unmet needs and provide ideas for more formal marketing communications.

While it is useful to know what is said online it is important to remember that this is only a fraction of the day to day communication that takes place and that consumers often regard online sources of information as less trustworthy than offline. For these reasons monitoring WOM on a tracking study can be a very good way to understand the likely influence of this communication channel on your brand. Measuring the proportion of people who have talked about your brand or recommended it, and whether or not the import was positive, neutral or negative will give you a good understanding of the influence of WOM in general. It can also be helpful to profile the brand advocates and the brand critics, to see if they have particular profiles, or hold particular images of the brand.

Nature of the Consumer

By tracking key demographics and attitudes marketers can check whether the target audience is changing or not. As with brand imagery, questions should be limited to criteria previously identified as leading indicators of change or useful in analysing sub groups.

Leading Indicators of Brand Health

The modern marketer has access to a vast amount of information, internal and external to their company, online and offline. At times this can prove overwhelming for the insight analyst, never mind senior management. As a result most companies are seeking to develop a portfolio of key indicator measures that will identify developing trends and issues.

These measures should be drawn from both behavioural and attitudinal data sources to give a 360 degree view of brand health using a "less is more" principle. You want to identify the smallest number of measures to track brand health effectively. Apart from removing over-lapping measures from the portfolio, analysis should be used to identify measures which are leading indicators of future brand performance, e.g. lead/lag correlation.

Once a set of leading indicators has been identified updates can be distributed to the relevant parties by the appropriate communication channels. Many marketers have chosen to create a portal or "dashboard" on their intranet to ensure easy and timely access to the latest information on the health of the company's brands.

DOES YOUR BRAND NEED REFINEMENT?

In some cases the answer to this question will be obvious.

If the market for the brand is growing, share is increasing, the product is competitive and equity strong, then the brand should stay the course. If any of these basic building blocks indicate weakness then adjustments will need to be made to address the problem. The next section outlines various actions that might need to be taken to revitalise the brand.

In some cases, however, the signals that something is not right may be less obvious. Particularly when sales performance is good attitudinal early warning signals may be discounted or ignored. The following analyses can help identify potential issues before they have a significant impact on sales.

Sales and Equity Trends Are Inconsistent

Brand consideration or demand may not translate directly into sales. Much can be learnt from studying differences in trend or absolute scores between the two. If sales are flat but equity declining, then you need to understand the source of the sales volume. Is the brand buying sales through price or volume promotion? Are sales coming from existing loyal customers or new, price shoppers who are bargain hunting? If so, then the brand risks entering a downward spiral where demand for the brand weakens and increasing discounting is required to maintain volume.

If equity appears strong, but sales are weak, then consider whether there are structural issues that need to be overcome. Is the pricing consistent with that of the equivalent competitive brand? Is there a problem with distribution or in-store visibility?

In one example, tracking data showed that brand health for a petfood was declining. However, sales for the brand were growing. Further investigation highlighted that sales were being driven by price promotions. Sales modelling reinforced the analysis; base sales were in decline, and more recent incremental sales were attributed to the promotional activity.

The brand proposition needed to be refreshed, if they were going to break out of this cycle of selling on promotion. This simple example serves as an excellent illustration of the dangers inherent on relying on sales data alone as a measure of brand health.

Brand Equity and Product Quality Are Not Aligned

A big risk for established brands occurs when product quality falls behind brand perceptions. If a programme of cost reduction pushes too far, the brand might find itself in the position that sales and equity are good but blind testing of product performance is weaker than the competition. If so the brand is at risk. Trial of competitive brands, or worse still cheaper store brands, may reveal the shortcoming of the established brand to its users, resulting in people switching away from the brand on a permanent basis.

Occasionally it may be that the product provides a competitive advantage that consumers do not know about. Publicising the benefit can provide grounds for a brand to significantly improve its competitive position.

STEPS TO TAKE IN IDEATING/REFINING THE STRATEGY

Monitoring brand health is an important safety programme but it is unlikely to identify significant new opportunities. Research and development and market research will typically combine to achieve the following objectives:

1. To identify opportunities to disrupt the status quo for competitive advantage before the competition or a new entrant does so.
2. Provide deeper diagnosis if things are not going well and identify ways to refine the existing proposition or find new ways to communicate it to the target market.

Identifying New Ideas

Growth can come by identifying new needs that the brand might serve among an existing or new user group or new ways to re-state an existing position. A variety of research techniques are appropriate at this stage, starting with traditional qualitative and ethnographic research.

Ethnographic research is now a popular way to identify unserved needs. Ethnographic research is the direct, first hand observation of daily behaviour. The behaviour is related to the product category, e.g. cleaning the floor, cooking a meal for the family, shopping for clothes. The research seeks to observe phenomena as it occurs in real time and allows the researcher to understand the influences and beliefs behind the behaviour. New opportunities often come from observing someone using a product for something it is not designed to do or hearing them complain about what it does not do well.

One risk to consider in ethnographic research is that the observed respondents may act in a manner that's different from normal due to the presence of the observer. Whether new opportunities arise from traditional focus groups of ethnography a quantitative phase of research should be implemented to confirm the substance and scale of that opportunity.

An additional source of ideas and feedback are your company's own staff. Ideas can be generated from brainstorming sessions with internal staff which are later concept tested with consumers. Sometimes it can be beneficial to include consumers in the process, i.e. allowing staff to view focus groups as part of the brainstorming or interacting with consumers as part of a break out team. New positioning, service offerings and ad campaigns might need to be tested with employees to gain insight into whether they are motivated by the change or not.

How far ahead you need to extrapolate from the research will also vary. The redesign of an established car brand may take three to four years and involve significant investment in new equipment. The risk attached to the decisions involved is far greater than for a soft drink, not just because of the money involved but because it requires the marketing team to anticipate the changing environment over a longer time frame.

All successful companies should be constantly identifying a broad range of ideas and then filter out those without the potential to survive and identify those with a spark of potential. At these early stages of the research process the research is as much to provide food for thought for the marketing team rather than setting a specific direction. The emphasis is on new ideas (rooted in the existing proposition).

Defining New Innovations

The preceding section describes the typical approach of a research-led development agenda, often pursued by companies in traditional consumer packaged goods and services. By contrast, technology firms may be innovation-driven, relying on their Research & Development investment to provide a stream of new innovations which may be relevant to an established brand or be introduced as a new brand.

For companies like these the role of research changes from identifying unmet needs to gaining an understanding of the likely demand and uptake for the new innovation. To provide direction for subsequent product and creative development, it is necessary to provide a clear description of the proposition in terms of benefits, target group and brand alignment (if appropriate). This enables affected team members to operate from the understanding while encouraging all parties to preserve the integrity of the value proposition.

Research can play a pivotal role in refining/optimising the language of the proposition while building alignment among contributing parties.

Qualitative research is typically the best forum in which to begin this type of research. The objective is to refine the description of the offer in question to ensure it is readily understood by the target audience, and in the process identify "power language" that can be used at a strategic level or possibly in promotional materials.

Following exposure to a (typically written) concept description, respondents are encouraged to play back what they think the product does and what the benefits might be. Misunderstandings are identified, and respondents are encouraged to provide alternative descriptions. Often, respondents are asked to identify specific text within the concept statement that they consider to be compelling, persuasive, weak, disappointing, or confusing. This can be accomplished with simple tasks using highlighters or underlining – thus giving the moderator tangible "take away" evidence to help him/her draw conclusions (beyond just the discussion in the room). Armed with this evidence, marketers are in a better position to clearly express the target-specific benefits of the offer in question.

This type of research is often followed by quantitative value proposition research, wherein a number of "surviving" statements are carried forward for further testing. As part of the evaluation, it is not uncommon to ask respondents to rate the impact of specific phrases within each concept statement. This gives marketers even greater (certainly more precise) direction in terms of which phrases should be emphasised, cut, or reshuffled – not only among broadly defined markets but also on a segment-specific basis.

Repositioning Your Brand

In general, brands which grow big and stay big do so by staying consistent to their positionings. As an example, in the UK, the retailer Sainsbury's pursued a consistent strategy over six years using the chef Jamie Oliver in over 100 ad executions.

However, there may be times when repositioning is required. Examples from the UK IPA Effectiveness award winners include:

- Explosion in competition: Stella Artois faced thirty new competitors.
- Own-label challenges: Olivio was the first olive oil spread in the UK, and was selling well – until the own label brands recognised its success, and produced their own olive oil spreads.
- Social changes: reduction in consumption of home made sandwiches was damaging sales of Marmite and Dairylea sandwich spreads.

Under such circumstances, repositioning may be essential.

Identifying new positionings generally requires qualitative research to gain a deeper understanding of consumer need and brand context. Such research may be in the form of depth interviews or group discussions, ethnographic research, or diary keeping.

The areas explored tend to fall into three main groups:

Understanding Attitudes to the Category

A thorough understanding of the car-buying market showed how, even during the "passive" phase when people were not thinking about what car they wanted to buy next, in practice they were forming a mental short list – and it was at this stage that Volkswagens were being rejected, at least in part through high price expectations.

Understanding the Product

Group discussions highlighted that Stout beer tended to be drunk as a leisurely, relaxed and sociable pint.

Understanding Surrounding Social Issues

While a quantitative Usage & Attitude (U&A) study identified that there was a small group of young adult users of Batchelors Supernoodles (traditionally aimed at the children's market), it took group discussions to identify why. Throwing together whatever was in the kitchen was the norm for this group. The food had to be tasty and substantial, but, above all, quick.

Quantifying the Opportunity

In the case of Batchelors Supernoodles the U&A study preceded the qualitative work. More common would be to conduct quantitative research after the qualitative in order to confirm the attractiveness of the new opportunity or proposition.

In the case of a new usage opportunity for an established brand then a U&A study is appropriate. These broad scale surveys focus on consumer needs and beliefs, brand usage and attitudes, with the objective of quantifying the scale of an opportunity. When refining the existing brand proposition then you may need to test the new idea. This research may take a variety of forms but it is essential to make sure that respondents realise that it is the idea not the execution that is important. If ideas are well-differentiated then a sequential monadic approach works well, exposing people to one concept at a time. When ideas are very similar then a multi-cell approach is less prone to respondent fatigue. The objective should be to identify which proposition is most appealing, relevant and differentiating.

Once the opportunity has been confirmed the need for research will focus on specific aspects of the marketing mix.

RESEARCH TO IMPLEMENT THE STRATEGY

What research needs to be conducted will vary on a case by case basis, depending on the category, brand and scope of refinement. While the different research techniques are treated separately by subject matter a primary consideration should be to identify what objectives can be combined in order to minimise the investment of time and budget and to gain a more complete understanding of the consumer response. The refinement may end up affecting multiple and interlocking aspects of the brand. Map out your research plan ahead of time to identify which research needs might be combined into one project to provide findings faster and more cost effectively.

Advertising Development

Having identified what you want your refreshed positioning to be, you need to communicate it to both your existing customers and your potential customers. This ought to be reflected across every aspect of the marketing mix. But since advertising commands such a major part of the marketing budget, the development of it is an area that commands substantial time and financial investment.

It is also an area that relies on the input from the advertising agency. The creative team(s) will develop a number of concepts to illustrate the positioning that has been drawn up for the brand. Creative Development work will then be carried out to produce the optimal route.

A major input here is qualitative Group discussions but the task is a complex one, and demands the skills of a specialised moderator. The concepts will generally be expressed in a very rough form; frequently drawings on a board. Respondents will be unlikely to have seen such things before, so will need to be introduced to their task carefully, and encouraged to use their imaginations in ways that may be unfamiliar. Additionally, while it can be easy to criticise ideas, one of the key parts of Creative Development work is to identify aspects that do work, those that show potential and those that do not. The overall objective is to explore how to maximise the potential of an idea and to overcome negative reactions. There is little value in debriefing at this stage with a string of negatives; the moderator's task is to find routes forward.

There are two main tasks for the research; the first is to identify the most promising route(s); the other is to help refine the preferred scripts. Sometimes this can be achieved in the same discussions, but it is as well to recognise these are two different tasks, and to accept that two different stages are required.

The need to explore and develop ideas is the key reason for interviewing people in groups rather than interviewing individuals. Within groups, particularly groups that have been warmed up and are interacting well, it is possible to brainstorm ideas. It can also be helpful for the moderator to have a good relationship with the agency creative team, to help ensure that politics and personality clashes to do not interfere with the debriefing process, and the creatives have a clear idea of what needs to be done, and a positive attitude to the task. For these reasons, it is common for the moderator to be employed by the advertising agency.

Quantitative Pre-Testing

Once an ad has been through one, or several, stages of Creative Development, there are usually time, and budgetary, pressures to produce the agreed upon script and put the ad on air. While Group discussions serve a valuable role, however, there are some aspects of successful advertising that cannot readily be assessed within groups.

Understanding of an ad can be overestimated in groups. A moderator is there to explain what the ad is about, and if a couple of people in the group get the idea quickly, it can be difficult for the remainder to own that they had problems understanding it. There is also the issue of benchmarks. Out of a bunch of weak concepts, one idea may emerge as the best, and be greeted with consequent enthusiasm; but in reality it may still be a below-par idea. Additionally, it is notoriously difficult in qualitative research to identify how well an ad is linked to the brand it is meant to benefit. For these reasons, and more, it is generally advisable to add into the process a quantitative pre-test.

There are a number of major research companies who offer proprietary quantitative pre-tests. There are also a number of smaller agencies who offer largely ad-hoc approaches to pre-testing. The reason that several potential solutions exist is the lack of consensus about how advertising works – and hence a lack of consensus about which are the best measures to use to assess it.

There are two main tasks for quantitative testing:

1. Predict the likely effect of the advertising on the brand.
2. Provide guidance for improving the ad.

The emphasis placed on the two objectives varies according to the research company philosophy.

Historically there have been some fundamental disagreements within the research and advertising industries about which pre-test measures relate to sales. Today most pre-tests include measures designed to assess "Recall" and "Persuasion".

Recall aims to predict how well advertising will be remembered by the target audience. The use of recall in pre-testing dates back to the 1920s when Daniel Starch used a system based on recognition of print ads. In the 1930s Gallup introduced a system based on respondent's ability to describe advertising they had seen. With the advent of continuous tracking, recall measures gained popularity because of the proven link between ad awareness and sales (Hollis, 1994). Perhaps the most persuasive argument as to why this linkage existed was propounded by Gordon Brown. He stated that it was important for advertising memories to come to consumers' minds after exposure when they later thought about the brand – either when choosing it or when experiencing it.

Today, recall is measured in two basic ways: memory test or predicted branded impact based on attitudes to the ad. Memory test systems involve showing the ad in a reel of around 10 other ads, placing the ad in programme content on a tape or airing the test ad on TV. Respondents' ability to recall the test ad following exposure is taken as a predictor of its likely impact on air (recall intervals vary from a few minutes up to 24 hours). The alternative to literally testing peoples' short term memories of the ad is to predict the likely on-air impact from respondents' attitudes to the advertising (Brown, 1990). Both measurement approaches are widely used and proponents of each have demonstrated that these measures relate to in-market sales effects.

Popularised by research systems corporation Persuasion Shift testing saw widespread use in the US from the 1980s onward. In a typical approach respondents are recruited to a central location, ostensibly to view a TV programme. Before watching the programme they are asked to choose one or a number of brands (usually this is in the context of choosing a reward for taking part in the research). The respondents then view the programme, which has one or more ad breaks in it. Following this, they are asked a few questions about the programme and are then asked again to choose brands from a selection. Brands advertised during the programme are included in the list for selection. The stronger the shift in brand choice to the advertised brand, the more successful the ad.

Persuasion Shift appeals on a number of levels. It offers a reasonably natural environment for exposure to the advertising (an alternative approach used, is to send videos to people's homes with the programme and adverts recorded on it – this is regarded as even more natural). When conducted well, respondents have little idea of the real nature of the test. Since, for many, advertising is meant to increase consumer's likelihood to choose the advertised brand, the approach is intuitively sensible. And the major agencies offering this approach have validated their measures against sales. Alternative approaches which rely on asking respondents whether the ad made people more likely to buy the brand have been benchmarked against purchase shifts (Farr, 1993) and later validated against sales (Farr & Gardiner, 2000).

There is little doubt that knowing how successful the ad has been in making consumers want to choose or buy the brand is useful but persuasion shift testing has its proponents and opponents. The opponents tend to suggest that it is biased to more rational messages. By contrast, recall is not. So when choosing a pre-test it makes sense to select one that measures both recall and persuasion, since both have been shown to have a relationship with sales effects and measure different things (Hollis, 1994). Relying only on one measure or the other could be highly misleading. One further word of warning, however, advertising does not act in isolation, so no pre-test will accurately predict sales effects in every case.

Linked with predicting sales effects is the issue of norms. Most major providers maintain extensive databases that are used to help understand whether a persuasion or recall score is a strong or weak one. It is highly beneficial to be able to put specific test results into the context of other advertising – preferably among a similar target, in the same category, and in the same country.

The other main role of quantitative pre-testing is to provide further guidance for improving the ad. For this reason, it is useful to have a bank of diagnostic questions within the questionnaire, as well as a series of open-ended questions, to help understand respondents' reactions to the ad. Only in this way can weaknesses be identified and overcome. Were aspects of the ad misunderstood? Was attention diverted to another part of the screen when the brand was introduced? Was one of the characters off-putting? Were people so focused on one section of the ad that they failed to appreciate a key point that followed?

While the bulk of the advertising development budget continues to be spent on TV, in these days of media fragmentation it is increasingly useful to be able to test advertising for other channels too; as well as overall campaign tests. Some of the major agencies have developed tests for these too, but, for testing non TV media, there is a difficult balance to be struck, since the cost of testing the ad may be relatively high in relation to the cost of airing the advertising. However, when contemplating a major, long running campaign, it is likely to be worth considering testing all the main elements.

Regardless of which agency or which technique you use, there are some factors that are common to all good pre-testing. There needs to be a clear brief and set of objectives, and an environment needs to be created whereby the client, ad agency and research agency feel they are partners working in a collaborative process. This is often best achieved through pre-meetings involving all key players. That way, the research agency can best understand exactly what the ad is meant to achieve and how it is meant to achieve it, which should result in the right questions being asked within the survey, and the right emphasis being put in the interpretation and recommendations.

A good example of this process can be seen in advertising for San São, from the Coca-Cola Beverage Company, launched in Scandinavia in 2003. A relaunch was planned, with a focus on the brand's Brazilian heritage. An ad was developed, and quantitatively pre-tested. Results were disappointing; the ad failed to engage viewers, and enjoyment and branding were only average. However, the research identified some clear potential in the ad; the music was enjoyed, and stimulated thoughts of carnival, and the way the bottles were integrated into the music was appreciated. A meeting between client, researchers and ad agency personnel agreed a way forward, identifying visual elements which needed to be better exploited, and aspects of the communication which needed to be stressed. The resultant finished film was vastly improved. Engagement was improved, and the ad was considered immensely enjoyable, and much better branded. As a consequence the branded impact of the ad doubled, message communication improved, and the finished ad was found to be very persuasive. The level of brand appeal achieved was the highest ever recorded in Denmark. The ad was aired, and won a diploma in the Danish Arnold awards, the most prestigious awards in the Danish advertising industry.

Packaging Research

The word "packaging" summons up images of the crowded shelves of the grocery store or supermarket. While packaging is critical to packaged goods brands it also applies in the wider context of appearance and design. For a petrol station the "packaging" can be thought of as the forecourt design – does it portray a modern, clean look, or is it tired-looking, smelly and dirty? For a car the "packaging" can be thought of as the design of the vehicle – is it contemporary and stylish? For a telecom company it will extend from the logo to the vast array of sales and informational literature. For this reason it is extremely difficult to generalise about the research methodologies that should be applied.

Packaging is a crucial element in the marketing mix. It communicates with potential customers as they consider a purchase. It also communicates post-purchase; there are few forms of marketing that consumers are happy to not only keep in their homes, but regularly interact with. Packaging can command attention, convey basic product information, and when the consumer has no other information, it can be viewed as the sole sales representative for the product, particularly in larger retail environments or on the street. It can also be part of the product experience; was it easy to open? Did it keep the product fresh? Did it feel comfortable to sit in? Was it easy to navigate?

Even simple packaging changes can change the way a product is viewed. One brand of cheese which had been wrapped in clear plastic changed its packaging to waxed paper. This improved the brand's quality connotations and facilitated a price increase. A soft drink manufacturer in Australia brought out a new flavour variant. The flavour was unique, but so too was the packaging, due to the vibrant colour of the product (visible through the clear plastic bottle) and the striking label. Sales modelling showed that, unlike the mainstream flavours, the high in-store awareness, fuelled by the distinctive packaging, was a significant factor driving purchase.

Increasingly, for consumer goods brands the requirements of retailers need to be taken into account in packaging design; they want packaging that can be loaded and unloaded onto shelves as quickly and with as little effort as possible.

There are two main roles for packaging research:

1. To ensure you have an understanding of your current packaging: knowing which elements are found attractive, which work well, which require improvement, etc.
2. To pre-test new packaging before launching it into the marketplace.

There are a number of aspects to cover when researching packaging;

- Does it stand out? Is it distinctive? Is it attractive?
- Is it functionally suitable, in terms of protection, portability, storage, and usage?
- Does it convey the required information on ingredients, usage, storage, nutrition, etc?
- Does it imply an up-to-date and contemporary image, and the right brand personality?
- Does it fit with current consumer attitudes in terms of bio-degradability, fuel consumption and re-use potential?

Understanding reactions to current packaging is an area that used to be a regular part of most brands' research programmes, but has become less common of late, in the face of pressure on research budgets. This is unfortunate given the importance of packaging in the marketing mix. Marketers are generally keen to learn whether their advertising is wearing out, and the same should apply to packaging. Additionally, the role of packaging to support messages conveyed in other parts of the marketing mix can be a valuable one. In the UK, Velvet toilet tissue adopted a new positioning, summarised in the slogan "Love your bum". However, there was some confusion about which brand of toilet tissue loved your bum, typified by the comment "I love that new Andrex ad with the bottoms". Adding the line prominently to Velvet's packaging helped ensure the proposition was associated with that brand and not the brand leader.

One cost effective route to monitoring the effectiveness of your packaging is to add a packaging question to a tracking study on a periodic basis; this will allow a top line view of whether more in depth investigation is required. However, this in no way substitutes for detailed, tailored research.

When assessing new packaging, there are two opposing requirements that need to be balanced. To fully assess the practicality of a new design, respondents need to handle the packaging, to use it as they would normally. This requires the packaging to be made up to a finished form. But, on a restricted marketing budget, this can seem a costly process to do this on the small scales required for research, particularly when it is difficult to prove the return on investment of revised packaging.

There are two main forms that packaging research can take:

1. Respondents can be exposed to the product in its new packaging in a central location and asked for their opinion (this is the only practical way to assess the physical properties of durable goods although virtual designs do allow the assessment of issues of style). Where the usage is complicated, or involves several stages, it can be helpful to record respondents' comments verbatim as they go through the process, rather than relying on their memory at the end.
2. Tachistoscope tests assess recognition. Respondents are exposed to the new pack design in a central location or on the web. The length of exposure is controlled, starting with a very brief exposure, and then increasing the length of exposure until the brand is recognised. Normative data can put the findings into context. A Tachistoscope approach can also be applied to a "shelf test" with the respondent being exposed to an entire mocked-up supermarket shelf. Self reported questions can substitute for the direct measurement method if necessary.

Whatever the format of the research, which will depend on the requirements of the product category and packaging type, it is common to compare the new packaging with the current packaging, in a paired comparison test.

A word of warning, while there are clear advantages of using mocked-up designs in mocked-up situations it is always worth building in a final real-life test. In the UK, one building society launched a new branch design, which, properly, spread over all points of contact, including the "For Sale" signs posted outside properties. It took some time to realise that, at night and under street lights, the writing on the boards was rendered invisible.

One newer form of research which is set to grow as the required technology becomes cheaper and smaller involves micro-cameras. These cameras can now be incorporated into a pair of glasses or hidden buttonholes. Respondents are asked to conduct everyday tasks, including shopping for specific products or services, and the resulting video allows researchers to follow respondents around a store or service outlet to understand what catches their eye and query the respondent about specific aspects of their experience.

Packaging research cannot be viewed in isolation. A milk product producer in Mexico was considering introducing new packaging, centred on an easier-opening proposition. Research was conducted to evaluate two versions of the new design, against the existing design using a sequential monadic design. 750 housewives took part in the test. They were given three identical packages to use in home. They were later recontacted, asked to evaluate the packaging, and then given three more packs with one of the alternative designs. One of the new designs was clearly preferred across every attribute. However, the cost of producing the new packaging would have meant charging a higher price for the product. So, as part of the research, a Brand Price Trade Off exercise was also conducted (see section on Pricing, below) to assess consumer willingness to pay extra for the packaging. The outcome showed that launching the preferred packaging at the higher price would result in no more additional sales than launching the other new design at the regular price. Even though the new design was preferred, the benefits of launching it to market were not enough to justify the necessary investment.

Pricing

No other controllable marketing lever has the same immediate financial impact as a pricing change. And yet assessing the impact of a pricing change is far from an exact science.

Successful marketing allows brands to support a price premium. Looking at IPA Effectiveness Award Winners, a number of the papers specifically refer to the supported brands increasing their relative prices; brands such as Clean & Clear, Lurpak, Stella Artois, Felix, Skoda, the Guardian, Hovis, Honda, Bounty and Pampers. But how does the brand team decide what an appropriate price should be?

The most basic pricing question is how demand for the brand will change as pricing changes. Increasingly, this is becoming a harder question to answer. Consumers are rarely faced with standard pricing as marketers seek to alter their perception of value through price promotions, extra volume free, free financing, and the like. And in today's Internet-fuelled world, consumers can make detailed price comparisons from home very simply, particularly for high ticket items. As a result of all these factors a price identified as optimal in research may be difficult to achieve, or its value perception changed as a result of new information.

Pricing research requires careful consideration of a number of issues:

You will be asking respondents to respond to an artificial situation with limited information. Sometimes you will be asking people to anticipate what they will do in real life under very different conditions. How can you make the research as realistic as possible?

When assessing likelihood to buy at different price levels, you are likely to be drawing particular attention to the product's price; more notice than the consumer may pay in-store. This drawback can be overcome to some extent by using a standardised proprietary approach, where the research output has been modelled and validated against subsequent market behaviour.

Lastly, there is another important difficulty. No research can anticipate how competitors will react to your price change. Testing alternative scenarios and war gaming with the results is the best way to be prepared.

The most reliable approach to answering issues related to pricing is by analysis of historical data on actual purchases, since it is grounded in real customer behaviour. Econometric modelling is the most widely used tool to assess this. However, there are drawbacks; because, of necessity, the data is historic, one needs to be aware of the possibility of a change in market conditions. For instance, constant price wars may have resulted in the market becoming more price sensitive, or the introduction of a "premium" range may have produced a less price sensitive market. Another disadvantage to the use of historical data is that it is not always possible to reliably disentangle the effect of pricing changes from other marketing activity. And one further problem is that it can only estimate likely responses to conditions that have previously occurred. It will not be reliable at extrapolating the effects of new pricing levels.

Econometric modelling allows you to fine tune pricing based on prior experience. If you need to research new price options then you need either a real-life test or Brand Price Trade Off.

Brand Price Trade Off analysis is a statistical approach to exploring the effects of price changes on brand choice. The technique can be used to estimate the likely market share among a list of brands for a particular price level for each brand. So it can be used to estimate whether increasing the price of a brand will have an adverse effect on sales, or if it is possible to increase it a certain amount before sales decrease significantly.

In summary, the technique involves selecting a number of brands – generally your brand and its key competitors – and setting up a number of price levels for each. The actual prices can differ across the brands, but the number of price levels needs to be the same. To start with all the brands are set at their lowest price, and respondents are asked which brand they would choose at the set prices. The price of the brand they choose is then increased to the next level, keeping the prices of the other brands constant. The question is repeated. The respondent may continue to choose the same brand, or switch to an alternative. The process continues until the respondent chooses one of the brands at its highest price level, or until he decides that he would not choose any of the brands at the current price levels. The output usually consists of a simulator, allowing the user to estimate likely market shares for different price levels.

The basic Brand Price Trade Off approach can be extended to include other variables apart from price, i.e. different combinations of features. In each case it may be desirable to include explanatory questions to help understand what drives brand choice.

While the elements involved in pricing research can be straightforward, in market studies can be complex, particularly when the purchase decision is not straightforward. A study was conducted for a homeopathic pharmaceutical manufacturer to deliver recommendations on the pricing strategy for a medicine aimed to relieve joint pain. The price for the product had remained fixed for several years, and the client was considering raising the price, and needed input to help assess the optimal level. The task was complicated due to the fact that there is more than one decision maker in the process of choosing the product:

1. The patient – the final buyer.
2. The doctor – who recommends a product.
3. The pharmacist – who can influence the purchase decision.

The research consisted of several stages. The first stage involved interviewing doctors, to assess their role in the decision process, their awareness of current prices, and their tolerance towards price rises. Then purchasers of the medicine were interviewed, to assess to what extent they consulted doctors, and to what extent the doctors' recommendations were followed, as opposed to seeking out cheaper alternatives.

Then a market experiment was conducted in eighteen pharmacies around the country. In each pharmacy, new, higher prices were introduced for the medicine being tested. This experiment lasted four weeks. A comparison of sales data from the test pharmacies with the sales data from the "control" pharmacies, where the prices remained stable, allowed an estimation of the product's price sensitivity curve. During one month almost 380 purchases were recorded in the "test" pharmacies.

A statistical model was produced, based on inputs from all these aspects of the research. The output was clear; the price could be raised by 15–20 % with little risk of loss of sales. In practice, the client raised prices by 10 %. Demand did not fall, and the client's value share increased accordingly.

Product Refinement

There are two broad ways products can be refined. Changes can be made to the materials or the design of the product, and variants can be produced. Variants can range from simple flavour variants, to launches of the brand into new categories.

The balance between whether R&D drives the innovation agenda – by producing new, better performing hardware or software for instance – or consumer research will vary from industry to industry. Additionally, sometimes product changes are forced on the marketing teams, through raw materials becoming harder to source, or the availability of cheaper alternative raw materials. Sugar alternatives are now often significantly cheaper than sugar and, in certain recipes, hard to tell apart, so it is not surprising that many non-diet soft drinks use them.

The tasks involved here is, in essence, the same as new product development. But in this case, some additional factors are key, which can fundamentally affect the research design. Most established brands will be focused on protecting the existing franchise, ensuring that existing users are satisfied with the product and seeking ways to extend usage.

Key questions are as follows:

- Who should the product be tested among? Is the intent to revitalise the brand among its existing user-base or extend its penetration to new or lapsed buyers?
- Is the intent to increase purchase rate? Existing users will be best able to comment on whether or not the product offering might change their behaviour.
- Is the objective to target users of specific competitive brands? If so, ensure you can read the response of these people separately but also check the product out among existing brand users to ensure the offering does not alienate them.

The fundamental objective is to find out if the new formulation/package/design offers a competitive advantage. Three aspects may need to be tested:

1. Improved benefit delivery.
2. New benefit delivery.
3. Cheaper formulation.

Improved Benefit Delivery

If the decision is made to improve the established brand the new formulation should be tested against the existing product, and if identified as an improvement should then be tested against the competition to ensure that the advantage is detectable and is perceived to offer an advantage that is likely to result in an increase in profits.

The research translation of this would be:

> To determine whether the proposed new formulation significantly improves overall acceptability against competition compared with the current product.

If necessary, iterate concept and product refinement until there is significant win versus a current benchmark.

New Benefit Delivery

If the new product formulation is being designed to address a need which is recognised by consumers and is not adequately satisfied by other brands or products then the research company will simply ask the respondents to test the brand as directed. Where the product is being extended to a new need it may be necessary to highlight the reason why the product is beneficial before testing can commence using a concept board. This will help frame the evaluation and ensure people judge the product's performance in the right context. An understanding of whether the product exceeds, matches or falls short of expectations set-up by the concept can be gained by comparing data on overall opinion, likes, dislikes and likelihood to buy from the concept stage, with data from the same questions asked after the product is tried.

Cheaper Formulation

If the objective is to improve margins by introducing cheaper product formulations then the new options should be tested against the existing formulation. The test design should prove that the new formulation is indistinguishable from the old.

(The risk here is that a series of cost reduction exercises may not be significant in themselves but overall lead to a cumulative decline in product quality that is detected by the consumer. It is always useful to maintain a "gold standard" formulation against which new ones can be tested to ensure that this has not happened.)

Brand Extension

These days it is relatively common to find a master brand which has been leveraged across many different product categories. This can be a very successful route provided the overall equity of the brand name is not diluted. Dove started as a soap alternative, but has now extended to shampoos, deodorants and body wash.

With most established brands finding it difficult to continue to grow market share, it is not surprising that the concept of extending into other areas has strong appeal to marketers. Additionally, the more facings you have in a supermarket to cover all your variants, pack sizes and flavours, the less space will be available to the competition.

However, there are a number of pitfalls to avoid when considering launching variants:

- There is the potential to alienate existing users by making the brand seem less special.
- Diverting resources and attention from the core product range to launch the new variant may leave the core brand vulnerable to competitive activity.
- There is the potential for the variants to dilute the core product meaning.
- There is also the issue of whether the company has the capacity to produce new products outside of the main product ranges in a cost efficient way.

Overall, it is easier for a brand to stretch into a functionally similar category, but brands with appropriate images, personality and values may also find it possible to extend into new areas. One brand which has successfully extended itself is Disney. While starting – and continuing today – with making films, it successfully extended into Disneyland theme parks, TV programming, and even Disney Stores. These all fitted within its clear brand identity of offering "magical" family entertainment.

Key areas to research among consumers are the usual ones covered in the new product development chapter. In addition it is helpful to investigate how suitable consumers consider it for the brand to extend into the new area, what their concerns might be, how the product would be used, and in place of what? If the variant is going to simply cannibalise the parent brand it may not be worth launching.

The concept of a new and faster absorbed pain reliever within the Panadol umbrella was first concept tested in Denmark and Sweden in 1998 using focus groups. As a result of these groups, GlaxoSmithKline decided to launch the product in the Nordic markets. The next step was the development of the name and packaging. Six focus groups were conducted in Denmark and Sweden in 2000, and the consumer insights were used in the development of the name, packaging and Communication. GlaxoSmithKline launched the new pain reliever Panadol Zapp in Denmark and Sweden in 2001. The consumers' response to the Panadol Zapp launch was positive, and the brand was successfully launched in Finland and Norway in 2002.

(NOTE: Panadol is marketed as Panodil in Denmark, Sweden and Norway.)

Given that excessive extension within a category has the potential to dilute brand equity it is desirable to check that all offerings do indeed add incremental volume to the franchise rather than cannibalise existing offerings. The application of TURF analysis (Miaoulis, Free and Parsons) will provide information on three important criteria:

1. How many consumers will use each offering in the product line?
2. The likely volume of usage for each offering.
3. The degree of overlap in usage among the offerings.

This information will allow the marketing team to identify the most efficient and profitable coverage of potential buyers in the face of economic, technological and manufacturing constraints.

MAINTAINING FOCUS AND ALIGNMENT

The process of revitalising a brand proposition is a long one. Hence, the importance of maintaining internal alignment against shifting goals is important.

Potential disrupters may include: new management, supply chain variables, legal concerns, competitive threats, raw material prices, changing commercial priorities, environmental concerns, and emerging consumer trends. As a result there are many opportunities for the brand team to lose focus and either make changes that dilute the brand's equity rather than enhance it. Timely and relevant market intelligence is the best way to reduce risk and maintain alignment.

Last, but by no means least, is the need to ensure that colleagues in other departments are aligned and enthused by your plans. Fulfilment of a new brand promise usually requires contributions from groups beyond the brand and advertising functions. Gaining alignment from production and/or operational units can be the key to delivering a customer experience that matches a brand promise – so it is important to gain input and buy-in from those parts of the organisation when you are in the development process.

When GTE and Bell Atlantic came together to form a corporate positioning for the new telecom brand, Verizon, multiple business leaders were involved in the development process – from ideation sessions through qualitative and quantitative proposition testing and interpretation. When a diverse set of affected parties/business leaders collaborate in the construction project, it is much easier to gain C-level approval and then implement the new brand strategy successfully.

REFERENCES

Brown, G. (1990) "Copy Testing Ads for Brand Building", 7th Annual ARF Copy Research Workshop.

Farr, A. (1998) "Is Size all that Matters?", *Admap*.

Farr, A. (1993) "Persuasion Shift Testing – Putting the Genie Back in the Bottle", *Admap*, January.

Farr, A. and Gardiner, S. (2000) "Creative enough for the Financial director?", *Admap*, October.

Hollis, N. (1994) "The link between TV ad awareness and sales: new evidence from sales response modeling", *Journal of the MRS*.

Miaoulis, G., Free, V. and Parsons, H. (1990) "Turf: A new planning approach for product line extensions", *Marketing Research*, March.

Page, G. and Raymond, J. (2006) "Cognitive Neuroscience, Marketing and Research: Separating Fact from Fiction", ESOMAR Congress Proceedings.

Reichheld, F. (2003) "The One Number You Need to Know", *Harvard Business Review*, December.

Twose, D. (2005) "Driving Top Line Growth", *WARC*.

RECOMMENDED READING

Qualitative Research

Gordon, W. (1999) "Goodthinking: a guide to qualitative research", *Admap*.

Robson, S. (1990) "Group Discussions", *A Handbook of Market Research Techniques*. Kogan Page.

Sampson, P. *"Qualitative research and motivation research". Consumer Market Research Handbook.* McGraw-Hill.

Willis, K. (1990) "In-depth interviews", *A Handbook of Market Research Techniques*. Kogan Page.

Packaging Testing

Klimchuk, M. and Krasovec, S. (2006) *Packaging Design: Successful Product Branding from Concept to Shelf*. John Wiley & Sons, Ltd.

Lewis, M. (1991) *"Brand Packaging" Understanding Brands*. Kogan Page.

Schlaeppi, T. (2000) "Packaging Research", *Handbook of International Market Research Techniques*. Kogan Page.

Schlackman, W. and Chittenden, D. (1986) "Packaging Research", *Consumer Market Research Handbook*. McGraw-Hill.

Concept and Product Testing

Bond, J. and Debacq, J. (1998) "Research in new product development", *ESOMAR Handbook of Market Opinion Research*, ESOMAR.

Davis, J. (1986) Market "Testing and experimentation", *Consumer Market Research Handbook*. McGraw-Hill.

Haig, M. (2003) *Brand Failures*. Kogan Page.

Advertising Development

Brown, G. (1991) *How Advertising Affects the Sales of Packaged Goods Brands: a working hypothesis for the 1990s*. Millward Brown.

Cowley, D. (1991) *Understanding Brands*. Kogan Page.

Du Plessis, E. (2005) *The Advertised Mind*. Kogan Page.

Franzen, G. (1994) *Advertising Effectiveness*. NTC.

McDonald, C. (1992) *How Advertising Works*. Advertising Association.

Advertising Work's volumes 1–14 IPA/WARC.

Advertising Pre-testting

Ambler, T. and Goldstein, S. (2003) *Copy testing: practice and best practice*. Advertising Association.

Feldwick, P. (1996) "A brief guided tour through the copy-testing jungle", European Advertising Effectiveness Symposium ASI.

Haley, R. and Baldinger, A. (1991) "The ARF copy research validity project", *Journal of Advertising Research*, 40(6).

Hedges, A. (1974) *Testing to Destruction*. Institute of Practitioners in Advertising.

McDonald, C. (1997) "Pre-Testing Advertisements", Admap Monograph.

White, R. (2000) "Pre-Testing Advertising", WARC Best Practice.

Tracking Studies

Feldwick, P. (1998) "Tracking Studies", *How Advertising Works: The role of Research*. Sage Publications.

Hollis, N. (2004) "The Future of tracking Studies", *Admap*.

McDonald, C. (2000) "Tracking Advertising and Monitoring Brands", Admap Monograph.

White, R. (2005) "Tracking ads and Communication", *Admap*, April.

8
Launch and Monitoring of
In-Market Performance

Raimund Wildner

THE ROLE OF NEW PRODUCTS FOR MARKET SUCCESS

There is strong evidence about the vital role of product innovations for market success. Wübbenhorst and Wildner (2002) identified 22 highly successful brands out of 95 fast moving consumer goods (fmcg) categories in Germany from the years 1998 to 2001. These were defined as those which either rose to one of the top three ranks in the market or improved their market position in these ranks in terms of market share volume. For 13 out of these 22 brands the market success could be attributed to the introduction of new products. Even more: Other factors such as ongoing brand management and broadening the distribution base regularly resulted in smaller increases in market share than if the increase was due to new product introduction.

Geis and Wildner (2005) analysed the growth of 1 140 fmcg manufacturers' brands in 69 categories depending on the launch pressure defined as the number of product launches per million Euro turnover. The result was non-ambiguous: the third of brands with the highest launch pressure grew 7.5 % faster than the average of the brands, the third with the medium launch pressure grew 1.4 % less and the third with the lowest launch pressure grew 5.6 % less.

Not only brand growth depends heavily on innovations, but also the development of total markets: Out of 69 markets those 23 with the highest launch pressure grew from 2001 to 2003 on average by 2.9 %, those 23 with medium launch pressure shrank by 1.4 % and those with the lowest launch pressure shrank by 5.0 % in terms of category turnover (cf. Wildner, 2004). The reason is obvious: because of product life cycles those categories (brands with no or few innovations) lose in the market whereas brands with a steady flow of innovations can make up for the losses of the existing products and win market share.

This is true for fast moving consumer goods but even more for technical goods like household appliances or consumer electronics. GfK analysed 177 categories in these fields in Germany for the years 2003 to 2005. In total four categories grew more than 100 % in value per year. These were flat TV, MP3-players, USB storage sticks and car navigation systems. All these categories were driven by innovation. On the other side there were three categories which shrank by more than 50 % in value per year. These were categories which were replaced by innovations: mini-disc players (replaced by MP3-players), still film cameras (replaced by digital cameras) and TV recorders (replaced by DVD recorders). So in this product field fast growth and fast decline are both driven by innovation.

Market Research Handbook, 5th Edition. Edited by M. van Hamersveld and C. de Bont.
© 2007 John Wiley & Sons, Ltd.

So new product launches are necessary both for brands as well as for total markets. But on the other side there are many indicators that about two thirds of all product innovations go awry, damaging the financial base and the image of those companies that introduce them into the market place. In 1996 there were 55 600 EAN-Codes that showed up for the first time in German grocery shops, 48 % of them were wiped out one year later (source: Madakom). So it is a vital question for manufacturers how new products are to be developed and introduced into the market in order to avoid failure.

SELECTING A STRATEGY FOR MARKET INTRODUCTION

Overview

From a strategic standpoint, innovations can be looked at from different perspectives:

- Concerning the degree of innovation from the manufacturer's perspective: is it a new market for the manufacturer, an average improvement or a small improvement?
- Concerning the degree of innovation from a market perspective: is it a new market, a significant, an average or a small improvement?

If the innovation is to be introduced into the market, there are additional strategic decisions to be made:

- The timing and market entry order of the innovation: the company that introduces the innovation first is the pioneer which is followed by the early and late followers.
- The branding of the innovation: is it a line extension (offered under a brand name which already exists in the respective market), a brand transfer (offered under a brand name which already exists in another market, but not in the respective market) or a new brand that did not exist before?
- The pricing of the innovation: is it in the premium, in the consumer or in the low tier range?
- The communication: is there advertising for the innovation, what kind of execution, how much and in which channels?
- The distribution strategy: how fast should the build-up be and in what channels should it be started?

Which of these strategies are to be preferred? Geis (2003) offers at least partial answers. He analysed 869 new products from 31 categories in the fmcg area that were introduced into the market between 1998 and 2001. These were categorised by market experts of the market research company GfK Panel Services according to three classifications:

- Order of market entry: Pioneer vs. early follower vs. late follower.
- Degree of innovation from a corporate perspective: new market vs. average change vs. low/very low change.
- Degree of innovation from a market perspective: New market, average change, low/very low change.

Figure 8.1 shows examples for this rating.

Furthermore, all innovations were classified according to market success as measured in the consumer panel: Those 25 % of new products gaining most revenues were classified "top", those 25 % with the least revenue were classified "flop" and the remaining 50 % in the middle as "average". The results are shown in Geis and Wildner (2005).

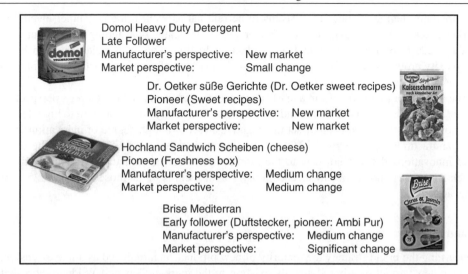

Domol Heavy Duty Detergent
Late Follower
Manufacturer's perspective: New market
Market perspective: Small change

Dr. Oetker süße Gerichte (Dr. Oetker sweet recipes)
Pioneer (Sweet recipes)
Manufacturer's perspective: New market
Market perspective: New market

Hochland Sandwich Scheiben (cheese)
Pioneer (Freshness box)
Manufacturer's perspective: Medium change
Market perspective: Medium change

Brise Mediterran
Early follower (Duftstecker, pioneer: Ambi Pur)
Manufacturer's perspective: Medium change
Market perspective: Significant change

Figure 8.1   Examples for classification of new products
Source: Geis, G. and Wildner, R. (2005).

Timing and Degree of Innovation

Concerning the timing of an innovation it is preferable to be the first in the market. The pioneer has a 57 % chance of being in the most successful 25 % of the innovations. For the early follower this figure reduces to 33 % and for the late follower to 20 %. This is not surprising: The pioneer occupies the segment in the mind of the consumer. He is the one who sets the rules. Followers have to share market shares with him.

Despite numerous examples shown by Schnaars (1994) and others, the finding that followers to market have a smaller change of success holds true. In 1979 Wordstar was the Pioneer in Word Processing but later lost ground to WordPerfect (1982) and Microsoft Word (1983). In 1952 the de Havilland Comet 1 was the pioneer in commercial jet aircraft but latecomer Boeing won the game with the 707, which came in 1958. Examples like this simply show that there are numerous possibilities for pioneers to make mistakes.

From a manufacturer's standpoint it is better to realise a low or very low degree of innovation. If a new market is created, the chance of being top in terms of market performance is a mere 11 %. If there is just a medium innovation for the manufacturer, the chance of being top increases to 30 % and it becomes 35 % for a low or very low degree of innovation. The reason for this is quite understandable: the newer the market for the manufacturer is the less experience he has concerning technology and market conditions and the higher the risk is for failure in the market.

From a market standpoint it is different: If there is just a low degree of product change, the chance of being top is 20 % only. In this case the new product is not seen as something novel and the interest of consumers keeps low. If there is a high or very high degree of product change, the chance of being top in the market increases to 36 %. So it has a considerable chance of success. But on the other hand those rare innovations that create a new market very often require substantial communication efforts and/or a change in consumer behaviour which lowers their chance of success. So it is not surprising that those innovations offering a medium product change have the highest chance of success: 54 % of those innovations are in the top tier of new products.

A medium degree of innovation seems to be optimal as well in the consumer electronic markets. Research by Mukherjee and Hoyer (2001) indicates that adding new features to products can have a negative effect on product evaluation. This is especially true in high-complexity products like PCs. The reason is the investment of time anticipated in learning to use the new features.

The degrees of innovation from a market perspective and from a manufacturer's perspective are not independent. Geis (2003) found for fmcg goods that as a rule a medium to high degree of innovation in the market can offset the negative effect of a high degree of innovation from the manufacturer's perspective. 33 % of such innovations are in the top tier. On the other hand innovations that are not new to the market but to the manufacturer are exactly those which have nearly no chance to succeed: only 1 % of them is in the most successful 25 % of innovations.

Brand Strategy

Concerning the brand strategy the majority of new products is introduced as a line extension, i.e. as a new variant of a brand already existing in the market. Geis and Wildner show that 36 % of them are in the top tier concerning market success. Brand transfer (using a brand that already exists in another market) and using a totally new brand are generally less successful strategies (17 % respectively 15 % top). This is not surprising: An existing brand in the same market lends competence and image to the new variant in the perception of the consumer. This is less true for an existing brand in another market, whereas a new brand has to build awareness and image from scratch. As research shows, the line extension strategy is followed by about two thirds of the new products.

But there is a potential shortcoming to this strategy: Research on 256 innovations of fmcg products in the years 2003 to 2005 by Twardawa (2006) shows that 51 % of the existing products of those brands under which an unsuccessful innovation was launched lost value market share in the following 12 months, whereas only 30 % of those were where a successful innovation was introduced. The damage of an unsuccessful line extension for the mother brand was especially significant if the mother brand was a strong one with many loyal customers.

For some innovations a further question is whether an innovation should be offered within the existing assortment of products or whether a new line extension should be launched. So a detergent brand introduced a form-keeping factor and launched a new product. Another possibility would have been to bring this feature in the existing products. Research not yet published shows that this is mainly a question of the position of the brand in the market: If the brand is the market leader or a premium brand, the brand may be strong enough so that launching a new product may be the right decision. But if the brand is neither the market leader nor premium it is better to bring the innovation about within the existing products.

Communication Strategy

The effect of advertising spending was analysed by Geis and Wildner (2005) with a data base of 219 fmcg brands out of 69 categories for which Nielsen Media Research delivered advertising data for the years 2002 and 2003. One hundred and thirty-three out of these 219 brands had a product launch in those years, 86 had not. Furthermore, we distinguish between those 50 % of the brands with higher advertising spending (average 14.8 Million. Euros per year) and those 50 % of the brands with lower advertising spending (average 1.7 Million. Euros per year).

The isolated effect of

- high advertising vs. low advertising: +5.2 percentage points in sales growth,
- new product vs. no new product: +11.2 percentage points in sales growth shows that on average a product launch is about double as effective as high vs. low advertising.

If we combine the effects of advertising and innovation, the effects do not just add up but have an additional increasing effect. Compared to those brands with low advertising spending and no launch

- brands with high advertising spending but no launch grow 2.9 % faster,
- brands with low advertising spending and with a launch grow 9.2 % faster,
- brands with high advertising spending and with a launch grow 14.6 % faster.

That means: without a product launch the effect of higher advertising spending is 2.9 %, with a product launch it is 14.6 % − 9.2 % = 5.4 %. So the launch of a new product almost doubles advertising effectiveness. In short: those who have a relevant innovation have something to say! Those who have something to say will be heard!

This corresponds with results from BehaviorScan test markets in USA as well as in Germany: 58 % of the advertising tests for new products in USA showed a significant increase in sales volume whereas only 46 % for established products. In Germany the figures are 55 % vs. 50 %. Even more: If there is a significant effect it is higher on average if there is a new product compared to an established product (cf. GfK, 1995).

Concerning Media strategy, Twardawa (2006) shows that successful innovations have higher shares in electronic media, as well more campaigns with mixed media. In terms of execution they stress the newness of the product, show a rational product benefit and use a key visual. It is especially important to inform those consumers that are innovators. Innovators can be identified by tracking in the consumer panel how many out of a set of innovations a consumer buys and how early he does so. The innovators are those who generate the early volume that is necessary to develop and keep distribution.

For consumer electronics the greater part of the advertising is done by the retailer (and paid by the manufacturer) in connection with promotions. So the key for advertising is the distribution of advertising materials to the retailers.

Distribution Strategy

For the success of a new product it is essential that there is a fast and coordinated build-up of awareness and distribution. If distribution is high but awareness is poor, too few consumers know about the new product. So sales in the shops are low and there is the risk that the retailers take the product off the shelf. On the other side, if there is a high awareness level but the product is not distributed enough, the advertising fizzles out.

Distribution should start in the big shops that are preferred by innovators and which have the most space on the shelf. It is easier to distribute there than to the smaller shops. As a rule of thumb for fast moving consumer goods, the weighted distribution within hypermarkets should be 70 % six to eight weeks after launch. For consumer electronics the distribution build-up normally is slower: successful innovations had a 40 % weighted distribution after one year and 60 % after three years.

Several authors have investigated retailers' decision making concerning distribution decisions (cf. Hultink, et al., 1999): for fmcg products the labelling as private label products, lower relative costs, higher potential in category volume and higher degrees of newness are factors that enhance acceptance. Furthermore, the pioneer and the early follower get a higher acceptance than the late follower.

For consumer electronics the situation is different. Here it is even more important to sell the product to the retailer. Since there are so many different models in the market the retailers have more possibilities to choose which products are to be distributed and which not. In the field of consumer electronics there are 24 400 different products, 5 300 of them newer than one year (Winkler, 2003). Furthermore, recommendations by the sales people are much more important than in the fmcg area. So the retailer has an especially powerful gatekeeper position. To sell the product to the retailer, it is important that the new products have the right characteristics. Hultink et al. (1999) carried out and analysed 291 interviews with 291 Dutch retailers about the importance of 26 criteria in seven durables categories. Overall the financial aspects "price/quality ratio", "price" and "contribution margin" were on the three top ranks. "Durability", "hype in market", "sales in units", "warranties" and "newness/innovativeness" were on ranks four to eight. But between the categories there were significant differences: For example for PCs it is especially important to minimise the risk of a product problem. So "durability" is first together with "price/quality ratio", followed by the "contribution margin". The ranking of the criteria for tyres is very different: first is "contribution margin" and "sales in units", followed by "supply reliability" and "delivery speed".

In the area of consumer electronics very often it is important that complementing components (e.g. DVD players and movies on DVD) are available at the same time. One reason for the great success of the Apple iPod was the fact that hard- and software were offered at the same time in an integrated way. And the reason why in the 1970s the video system VHS won against the competing – and according to experts' judgment technically superior – systems Betamax and Video2000, was that there were significantly more movies available in VHS format than in the other formats.

To accomplish a fast and joint distribution build-up of all necessary components, it is important that a wide range of devices are available. Normally this cannot be done by just one company (Apple's iPod being an exception). Two years after the launch of Video Recorders consumers were able to select out of 87 models from 32 manufacturers, as for DVD players it was 102 models from 30 manufacturers. So it is necessary to forge alliances and cooperations. The CD player (introduced in 1983) was successful because the patent holder Philips made it possible for other companies to produce CDs and CD players (and gets a steady flow of income from the royalties since then).

Pricing Strategy

Concerning the price, the results by Geis (2003) indicate for fmcg goods that it is best to offer the innovation at a price that is a little bit (index 106) above market price. But the relationship between launch price and market success shown by him are weak. A more clear result is shown by Twardawa (2006) analysing 265 new product introductions.

He distinguished the following groups of innovations:

- Over-promising: offering a minor product improvement for a medium or a premium price or offering a medium product improvement for a premium price.
- Under-promising: offering a medium product improvement for a low price or offering a major product improvement for a medium or low price.

- Quite right: all other combinations, i.e. offering a minor product improvement for a low price or a medium improvement for a medium price or a major improvement for a premium price.

A first result: innovations tend to be in the over-promising region. 58 % of all new products belong to this group. 30 % were quite right and only 12 % were under-promising.

The reason for this pattern becomes obvious if you have a second look at the data. The vast majority of the new products were line extensions, i.e. they were introduced under the name of an existing brand. Very often those brands are premium brands and therefore the new product is sold under a premium price. But often the innovation does not keep the promise given by the premium brand and the premium price. For example, under the name of a German premium brand known for High Duty Detergents a new Low Duty Detergent was introduced. There was nothing special with this Low Duty Detergent, except the premium name and the premium price. The product failed to generate enough repeat purchasers and flopped.

Analysis shows that 66 % of all flops were over-promising compared to only 40 % of those products that were successful. This means: two thirds of all failed products failed because their price–performance-ratio was poor. So price matters a lot but only in relation to the performance of the product.

Whereas fmcg goods show a high degree of price stability over time this is totally different in the consumer electronics markets. Successful innovations lose in the first six years after market introduction an average 44 % in price, unsuccessful innovations lose even more (56 %) (cf. Winkler, 2003).

THE RESEARCH PROCESS BEFORE THE LAUNCH OF A NEW PRODUCT

Overview

So if innovations are indispensable on the one hand, but on the other hand often go wrong, it is very important to select the right products for market introduction and to select the right options for the introduction strategy. To answer these questions a large assortment of market research instruments are available. Figure 8.2 gives an overview of them.

How to generate ideas and how to test them in concept and product tests is dealt with in another chapter. The same is true for possibilities to test the advertising and the price. So this chapter explains in detail how the complete marketing mix can be tested.

Concept and product tests, communication tests and price tests check certain aspects of the innovation: The product or its aspects like taste, packaging, etc., or certain marketing variables like price or communication. But even if the concept and product testing, the advertising test and the price test got excellent results, this is no guarantee that the product will be successful in the market. Finally it has to be tested whether these aspects fit together. As an example an advertising for a confectionery showing young women dancing in the morning mist on a landing stage at a lake and thus communicating lightness and freshness can be very motivating; if the product itself is sticky, heavy and sweet this does not fit to the advertising and will cause disappointment which will cause a low repurchase rate.

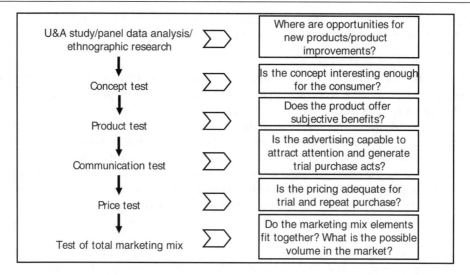

Figure 8.2   Market research instruments for generating and testing new or improved products

Basically there are four classes of tests that combine different aspects of the marketing mix:

1. Store test based on sales data of a sample of retail outlets.
2. Electronic micro test markets based primarily on purchase data of households in a special test region.
3. Regional test markets.
4. Simulated test markets based on simulated purchase acts of consumers.

Each of these methods has its pros and cons.

Store Test

A store test is a sale of test product(s) under controlled conditions in selected retail outlets on a trial basis.

It allows (within limitations that are discussed later) volume forecasts. Moreover, it is possible to test the new product(s) under different conditions as long as these refer to marketing variables that are realised in the shop. So it is possible to test different prices and different placements within the shop as well as different promotions. This is done in different test groups of shops. Very often the "matched samples"-design is used to do that: Test groups of shops are equally structured in terms of size, region and type of retail outlets. In most cases an additional control group of shops is added. In the outlets of the control group the test products are not introduced in the market. They are used to deliver those figures to which the figures of the test group(s) can be compared. Figure 8.3 shows an example of such a test design, where different prices for the new product are tested.

Originally store tests were organised by market research companies. Lately the retailers urge the manufacturers to do a store test in the retailer's shops that is organised by him before they accept the product for distribution. Some manufacturers prefer to organise their store tests themselves. A typical store test has a pre period of six to eight weeks and a test period of 12 to 16 weeks.

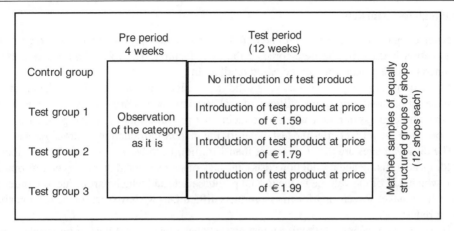

Figure 8.3   Example of test design to test a new product with different prices

Organisation of a store test means distribution of the new product, doing the promotions that are foreseen in the test plan, noting all occurrences that might influence the sales figures of the test product and ensuring that the relevant data are collected.

Store tests have the advantage that their results are based on thousands of purchase acts done in perfectly biotic situations with purchasers using their own money to buy the product. Furthermore, the results are expressed in sales shares and goods turnover figures which are criteria that can be readily communicated to retailers when introducing the product into the market.

This is accompanied by cons that are equally important. Firstly, store tests are only suitable for those introductions into the market that do not use TV, radio, print or Internet advertising. Awareness for the new product can only be built by in-store promotions or leaflets/samplings distributed within the catchment areas of the shops.

Secondly, store tests traditionally do not give any information about how much of the volume is due to trial and how much is due to repeat purchasers. Especially for fmcg products this is important because it is repeat purchases that make fmcg products successful in the long term. This gets clear if the forecasting procedure from a store test is reflected in more detail. To make it short, reference products are taken and their volume in the test is compared to the national volume after adjustments for distribution. By this, correction factors are derived that are applied to the sales of the test product. If additionally, distribution and aided awareness are taken into account, a volume forecast can be estimated. But this is based on the volume sold in the test market. If it is a product with a high trial purchase act and a low repeat purchase act, the initial volume of the test will be too high. This very often is the case with confectionery, where a novelty peak at the beginning delivers high sales volume but comes down quickly after a relatively short time period. If the initial trial purchase volume is low, but most of those who try the product buy it again, the initial volume of the test may be too low.

There are ways to overcome this disadvantage at least partly, if store card data are used. Of course store card holders are not representative to all consumers. But at least the store card data can give hints about repurchase figures as an indicator for long term product success.

Finally the secrecy of the test is low. This gives the competition the possibility to save time for the development of a similar product.

Regional Test Markets

In essence regional test markets are the introduction of a new product in a whole region. The introduction is done by the field force of the manufacturer. The role of market research is confined to collect data from an increased retail audit.

As a pro this type of test delivers very valid results. Its results are based on a data base that is made up of thousands if not millions of real purchase acts. Furthermore, it is possible to use the whole marketing mix when introducing the product. Finally, if the product is to be introduced in the market after the test, a part of the market introduction is already done.

The disadvantages are the costs (more than 1 million Euro because of fees for distribution build-up, advertising and production costs), the lack of secrecy and that there is no information as to which part of the volume is due to trial purchase acts and which part is due to repurchase acts which makes forecasting for fmcg products difficult, as we have seen in the section about the store test.

These are the reasons why regional test markets have lost a great deal in importance since the early 1980s. If a test market is done at all, it is normally only used as the last test for a product that was already tested successfully elsewhere.

Micro Test Markets

Micro test markets were first developed in the 1970s in France (ERIM), and were then adopted in Germany by GfK and A.C.Nielsen. IRI in the US added the possibility to test TV advertising. The Micro test markets existing in Europe are based on IRI's BehaviorScan test markets. They are run by GfK in Germany and MediaScan in France. In the following the BehaviorScan test market in Germany is described in more detail (See Figure 8.4).

BehaviorScan is located in the village of Hassloch in South-Western Germany. Hassloch had a combination of characteristics that made it the best possible choice. Firstly, it was big enough so that a household panel of 3 000 households could be recruited. Each of the panel households gets an identification card with a household number printed on it as bar code. Secondly, it was not too big so that cooperation with nearly all important retailers could be installed. Today seven retailers in Hassloch and a town nearby are cooperating. They are all equipped with scanner cashiers. The panel households show their identity card and the shopping basket is registered in the computer system together with the household number. These data are transferred to the market research company for analysis. Thirdly, the population of Hassloch is representative for Western Germany in terms of household characteristics. Despite being a village, there are many employees from a big chemical company in nearby Ludwigshafen. Fourthly, Hassloch is located in the area of one of the early cable pilot projects. Because of this it had a very high cable penetration which was important for the testing of TV advertising with the split cable technology.

The split cable technology consists of:

- A micro-computer for every household that is to be addressed by test advertising. 2 000 out of the 3 000 households have this micro computer. These are connected with the main TV set of the household.
- A central office in Hassloch with a control computer that is connected to all micro-computers. They are programmed to switch the attached TV sets to a special GfK channel, if the micro computer gets the command to do so and the TV set attached is switched on the channel where the test advertising is to be sent.

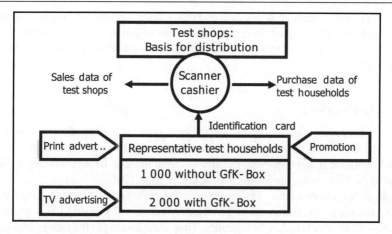

Figure 8.4   Overview of the BehaviorScan test market system
Source: GfK.

The switching takes place if there is a command that is triggered by pressing a button in the central office. In effect, a commercial is replaced by another commercial of the same length. By this it is possible to test the introduction of a new product that is introduced with TV advertising.

So if a new product is to be introduced with TV advertising and the main purpose of the test is to learn what will be the overall volume of the product, all 2 000 households with GfK box get the advertising to have the maximum data base for analysis. If the main purpose of the test is to learn about the effect of TV advertising, a procedure is applied that is called matching: it starts with a random attribution of all households to test vs. control group. Now the programme looks for possible switches of households between test and control group that makes the buying behaviour in the relevant category in a pre period more similar. In the end there are two groups whose buying behaviour in the pre period is nearly identical. After this, the test group gets the advertising, the control group does not. By comparing the buying behaviour of the two groups the market researcher gets the effect of the TV advertising.

As an incentive the households receive a weekly programme guide for free. It is equally possible to insert test advertising in a part of the copies and to evaluate the effect of the print advertising by comparing the purchase behaviour of those who got the print advertising with the purchase behaviour of those who did not.

The results of a BehaviorScan test of a new product are:

- Purchase rate: does the new product trigger trial purchase acts?
- Repeat purchase rate: is the quality of the product in comparison to its price so convincing that it is bought again?
- What is the influence of print advertising, TV advertising, promotions?
- Volume forecast that proved to be valid within $+/-$ 12 % in the past.

The advantages of micro test markets like BehaviorScan are their reliability which is based on the absolute biotic test situation and the nearly complete set of marketing mix variables that can be tested. So within one test a lot of questions can be answered. The disadvantages are that the new product cannot be kept secret and that it takes a relatively long time to test it. The length of a test should be at least three purchase cycles within the category. In practice it varies between 16 to 52 weeks. Owing to these disadvantages micro test markets are used less today than a decade ago.

Simulated Test Markets

Simulated test markets essentially are a combined concept and product test with a model attached. The unrivalled market leader in this field is Bases from A.C.Nielsen. Novaction, Research International and GfK offer slightly different models. In the following TeSi which is offered by GfK, is described in more detail (cf. Erichson, 1996).

The data collection procedure can be described as follows: 300 to 500 category users are invited to a temporary central location. Firstly, they get some money which is a little bit more than the most expensive brand in the category. They are asked to put the money into their purse. Secondly, they are asked in a preliminary interview about their characteristics as well as about their purchase behaviour in the category (purchase quantity, size and composition of relevant set and the most preferred brand; shares of requirement within the relevant set are gained by a chip game).

Thereafter, in an advertising simulation the test persons are shown TV commercials or other advertising for the test product, as well as for other products in the category. By this, 100 % awareness for the test product is achieved.

Then there is a buying simulation. The test persons are led to a shelf and are asked to buy a product with the money they received at the beginning. They are told that they will be given the product to take with them. After the product is paid for they are asked which product they would buy if the product bought first would not be available. This is repeated as long as the respondent selects as many products corresponding to the size of her/his relevant set.

Then they are given two products: first they are given the product they bought. If this was the test product, the second product is the one preferred by the respondent as noted in the preliminary interview, if not, the second product will be the test product. They are asked to use both products and to come back to the central location for another interview at a date about three to four weeks from then.

After the home use phase they are invited to the central location again. (Other simulated test markets like Bases do the following interviews by phone.) Here they are asked about their share of requirement with a chip game, now including the new product. Furthermore, they are asked about their product experience, the strengths and weaknesses of it compared to the product preferred so far. Now the data collection is finished.

In an analysis phase thereafter the following quantities are computed:

- Penetration, i.e. share of trial purchasers among category users from the buying simulation in the first central location visit.
- Share of requirement, i.e. in how many out of 10 shopping trips with a purchase act in the category she/he will buy the product: from the chip game in the second central location visit.
- Buying intensity index: from the information about buying quantity at the first visit. The buying intensity index is defined as the average category quantity of a buyer of the brand divided by the average category quantity of a category buyer.

Using the well known Parfitt-Collins formula:

$$SoM = P \times SoR \times BI$$

with:

SoM: Share of market
P: Penetration
SoR: Share of requirement
BI: Buying intensity index

you get a market share estimate under the condition of 100 % distribution and 100 % awareness.

To take into account realistic distribution and awareness figures, a reach factor is computed with:

$$R = w \times D + (1 - w) \times D \times A$$

with:

R = reach factor
w = weighting factor with w being between 0 and 1 denoting the share of turnover that is generated at the shelf without advertising. Normally w is set 0.3.
D = weighted net distribution
A = aided awareness.

The market share computed with the Parfitt-Collins formula is multiplied with the reach factor. The result is the market share after one year.

There are further modifications to take into account promotions, to estimate awareness development from a given advertising quality and the advertising spending.

The main advantages of a simulated test market are its speed (about three months), that the new product is kept secret and that the forecast of the market share is based on trial and repeat purchase acts. Disadvantages are the limited testing possibilities for promotion and the fact that simulated test markets work best for new products that belong to well defined categories. In total the advantages outweigh the disadvantages. So simulated test markets grew during the last 20 years.

THE RESEARCH PROCESS AFTER THE LAUNCH OF A PRODUCT

After the product is launched, its success has to be controlled by the tracking instruments, namely the different panels (cf. Günther et al., 2006) and the advertising tracking. Here only some suggestions can be given as to how these instruments can be used.

Using the Consumer Panel

For fast moving consumer goods in the core of these instruments is the consumer panel, since this is the only instrument to track repurchase figures that are important for the long term success of the new product. Figure 8.5 gives an overview of the possible situations and their share of all innovations.

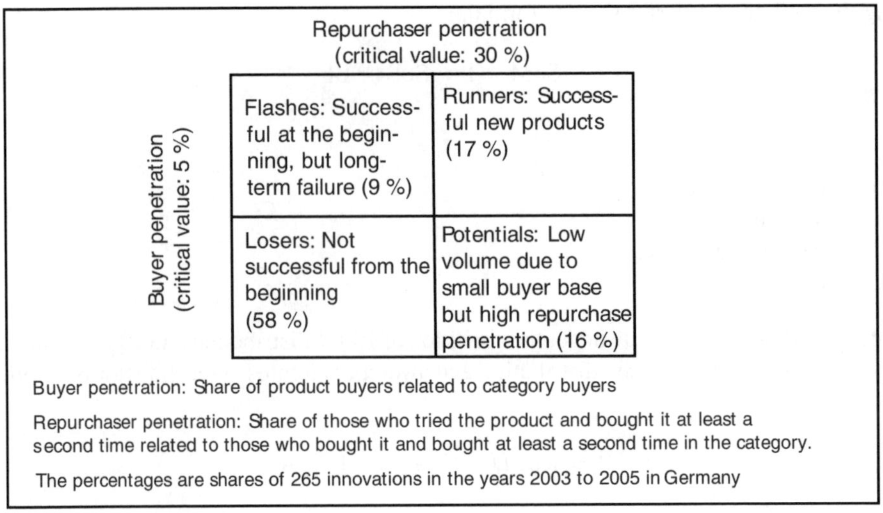

Repurchaser penetration (critical value: 30 %)	
Flashes: Successful at the beginning, but long-term failure (9 %)	Runners: Successful new products (17 %)
Losers: Not successful from the beginning (58 %)	Potentials: Low volume due to small buyer base but high repurchase penetration (16 %)

Buyer penetration (critical value: 5 %)

Buyer penetration: Share of product buyers related to category buyers

Repurchaser penetration: Share of those who tried the product and bought it at least a second time related to those who bought it and bought at least a second time in the category.

The percentages are shares of 265 innovations in the years 2003 to 2005 in Germany

Figure 8.5   Classification of new products according to their success
Source: Twardawa 2006.

What is important for marketing management is that each of the four possible situations has different consequences for the marketing manager:

- Losers: unsuccessful products with poor buyer and repurchase penetration. If there are no specific shortcomings of the product that could be addressed, the project should be dropped.
- Flashes: they are successful at the beginning due to a strong buyer penetration but they lose volume when the target group is exhausted and repeat purchasers are too few. This points to disappointed expectations which can have three causes:

1. Quality is poor. This can be tested by a product test.
2. Price is too high. This can be tested by a price test.
3. Communication is over-promising or describing the product wrongly.

Research shows that the most frequent cause is the wrong quality–price relation. In these cases lowering prices is the remedy to make a flash long term successful. 40 % of the flashes of one year increased market share in the next year due to lowering of prices (cf. Twardawa, 2006).

- Potentials generate enough repeat purchases but too few trial purchase acts. This can have the following causes:

1. Poor distribution: This can be checked by retail audit data.
2. Poor communication, which can be seen by an advertising tracking.
3. The product is meant to serve a niche.

If the lack of trial purchasers is due to poor communication and/or distribution, there is a significant danger that another manufacturer copies the product. So it is essential to increase marketing support. 72 % of the potentials of one year were successful in the following year due to increased marketing support (cf. Twardawa 2006).

- Runners are successful products. Nevertheless, their long term success is not a given fact. Their biggest risk is that marketing support is taken away from them. 34 % of the runners of one year lost market share in the following year due to this fact.

The figures shown so far were figures after one year. To get earlier information on how well a new product is accepted, it is important to pay special attention to the innovators. Innovators in the consumer panel can be defined by their effective purchase behaviour, i.e. they bought far more of a given set of innovations in the past than the average households. It is important that these households buy the product early in order to generate the sales volume that is necessary to keep and build further distribution.

For durables the distinction between trial purchase acts and repeat purchase acts is less important. Furthermore, these products are bought less frequently. So the number of purchases in a consumer panel are very often too small to allow detailed analyses. Therefore, market development of these products normally is tracked in retail audits, not by consumer panels. An exception is the textiles market, where retail audits do not exist. Here consumer panels are used.

Using the Retail Audit

For durables as well as for fmcg products the retail audit is important to track the distribution build up for the new product. The main figures are the unweighted (which percentage of the stores sells the product?) and the weighted (which percentage in category value sell those shops that sell my product?) distribution. The relation between those figures show in which type of shops the product is sold: if the weighted distribution is greater than the unweighted distribution, on average the product is sold in bigger stores and vice versa. Normally for new products in the introduction phase, the unweighted distribution should be smaller than the weighted distribution since the distribution build up should start with the big, not with the small shops to get a sufficient distribution fast.

A second important figure is the sales value per shop with distribution. This should be compared to other products in the category. If the figure is at the lower end of comparable products, there is the risk that the retailer will stop distributing the product.

Finally, the development of the price of the new product should be tracked as well. If the prices are reduced beyond what was planned, this can be an indicator that the value perception of the product is poor.

If available, the promotion figures should be checked as well. Promotions with a small price reduction can help significantly in building up trial purchases. But if the price reduction gets too high, there is the risk that the value perception of the product is damaged and the customers are no longer willing to buy the product at the normal price.

For new products which need complementing products (like DVD players and films on DVD) it is important to check all these figures of the complementing products as well.

If the analysis reveals problems, the following instruments offer the possibility for further insight:

- If distribution is low, a study based on interviews with retailers may reveal the problems from the retailers' side.
- If sales per shop with distribution are low, the promotion figures should be checked. In the durable sector it might be that the retailers do not recommend the product. A study among retailers can check this and if necessary reveal reasons. But in most cases this is due to problems with consumers, for which data from advertising tracking can give additional information.

Using Advertising Tracking

Advertising tracking studies are wave surveys where the same questions are asked regularly to form wave to wave equally structured samples consisting of different respondents of 300 or more category users. The main purpose is to check whether the advertising campaign for the new product works.

For this the following questions are asked for the new product as well as for the existing products:

- Awareness questions:
  - Unaided and aided advertising awareness
  - Contents of the advertising
  - If applicable: Awareness of slogan, jingle etc.
- Image questions:
  - Certain image dimensions like quality, specific quality dimensions etc.
  - Which products are in the relevant set, which product is preferred?

The first analysis step compares the performance criteria of the advertising, e.g. the aided awareness with the advertising costs. What is analysed for each performance criterion is the level of the criterion (low or high), the trend (up or down), the sensitivity to changes in advertising money spent (does the criterion react to it?), all in relation to the advertising costs. Figure 8.6 shows a campaign that is successful in generating aided awareness and one that is not. For new products the aided advertising awareness is a key performance indicator for the success of the advertising.

In the second step the relationship between the image dimensions and the preference of the product is analysed. A possible way to do this is to build a logistic regression between the answers to image dimension questions and whether the product is preferred or not. By this it is learnt what are the relevant image dimensions that drive the preference for the product.

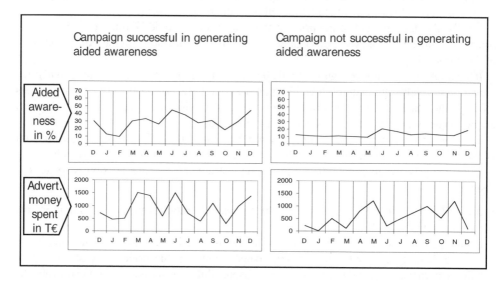

Figure 8.6 Comparing a successful with an unsuccessful compaign in advertising tracking

FINAL REMARK

Product innovation is risky, expensive and absolutely necessary. So it is not surprising that there is a whole bunch of instruments to test the several aspects of the product and the marketing mix before market introduction and to track the innovation after the product is introduced into the market.

Recent developments show that simulated test markets grow in importance. But they are more and more transformed by choice based models that reflect the consumers' decision making process better than the methods used so far like chip games (like in TeSi) or rating questions like in Bases.

REFERENCES

Erichson, B. (1996) "Methodik der Testmarktsimulation" (Methodology of test market simulation), *Planung & analyse* **2**, 54–57.

Geis, G. (2003) *Management der Markteinführung von Konsumgütern* (Management of the market launch of consumer goods). Diss. St. Gallen, Switzerland.

Geis, G. and Wildner, R. (2005) "Market success through innovation" *Yearbook of Market and Consumer Research*, **3**, 5–21.

GfK (Publisher) (2005) *Ökonomische Werbewirkung* (Economic advertising effect). Nürnberg.

Günther, M., Vossebein, U. and Wildner, R. (2006) *Marktforschung mit Panels* (Market Research with Panels). Wiesbaden.

Hultink, E.J., Jürg, T.M. and Robben, H.S.J (1999) Retailers Adoption Decision of New Consumer Durables, *Journal of Product Innovation Management*, 483–490.

Mukharjee, A. and Hoyer, W.D. (2001) "The Effect of Novel Attributes on Product Evaluation", *Journal of Consumer Research*, **28**(3), 462–472.

Schnaars, S. (1994) *Managing Imitation Strategies*. The Free Press.

Twardawa, W. (2006) *Innovation als Weg aus der Stagnation* (Innovation as a way to overcome stagnation) GfK (editor): Konsumlust statt Konsumfrust.

Wildner, R. (1988) Application of Models to Improve Sales Prognoses, ESOMAR Seminar on New Methodologies in Test Marketing, Amsterdam (The Netherlands), 205–228.

Winkler, W. (2003) Innovation bei Consumer Electronics: Technik Top – und was bringt der Markterfolg? (Innovation in the Field of Consumer Electronics: Technological advanced – but what shows the market success?), in: GfK-Nürnberg e.V. (editor): *Innovationen Top oder Flop: Der Konsument entscheidet*, Nürnberg.

Wübbenhorst, K.L. and Wildner, R. (2002) "Die Schwäche der Marke ist die Schwäche der schwachen Marke" (Brand weakness stems from the weakness of having weak brands), *Planung & Analyse*, **2**, 17–21.

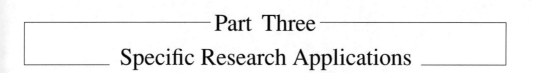

Part Three
Specific Research Applications

9

Media Research

Andrew Green

DEFINITIONS

Media research provides estimates of the number and type of people using different media – for example how many people are watching specific television programmes or reading particular magazines. Media research is employed by marketers to help them direct their advertising messages through these vehicles to the people they want to reach, at the time they want to reach them.

In addition, the media themselves utilise audience research to help them select and schedule editorial content, as well as to put a value on the space they sell to advertisers.

As well as estimating audiences, the media research business is generally held to include other activities such as the monitoring of commercial activity (adex) and provision of analytical models and software with which to manipulate the data. These do not, however, involve survey or panel research and so will not be covered here.

STAKEHOLDERS

In most countries, the media are by far the largest funders and therefore stakeholders in media research. In the UK, Germany and France for example, between 80 % and 90 % of media research funding comes from the media.[1] The remaining share is mainly generated from the media agencies, with advertisers chipping in directly in Germany. In Spain, the media contribute around two thirds of media research finance.

Each of these stakeholders have different and sometimes competing sets of commercial goals and priorities. Such differences can have a considerable impact both on the final form of the audience data published and of any attempt to develop or change how this data is generated over time.

The Media

The media are concerned both with valuing their audiences for advertising sales purposes and with scheduling programmes and editorial in a way that maximises the audience to their stations or publications.

Programmers and writers need to keep an eye on audience trends to ensure that people are watching their programmes and reading their publications.

---

[1] ESOMAR (2006). Draft Guidelines for the WFA Blueprint (unpublished).

Market Research Handbook, 5th Edition. Edited by M. van Hamersveld and C. de Bont.
© 2007 John Wiley & Sons, Ltd.

Generally speaking, the higher the number of people watching a programme, the higher the amount advertisers will be prepared to pay to buy a slot in that programme. But simply attracting more people is not the only thing that matters.

Those who buy advertising space from the media are also concerned with the *type* and the *quality* of the audience.

People with higher incomes or, sometimes, younger people with less entrenched brand preferences are often favoured as target audiences. In this case, the price charged for reaching (say) 1000 people with a given advertising spot can be pushed higher if more of these people fit into the desired demographic category being targeted by the advertiser.

Audience "quality" is harder to define or to measure than demographics. But advertisers are obviously interested in achieving a higher impact for their messages. If a magazine or television salesperson can produce evidence that shows how particular pages or programmes are more likely to be attended to closely than others – and that this attentiveness will carry over to the advertising as well – they may be able to charge premium prices for these slots.

Syndicated audience research services (i.e. those paid for jointly by the media, advertisers and agencies) are often supplemented by proprietary subscriber or other studies which delve into more qualitative aspects of the relationship between the audience and the media.

Marketers

Marketers need to reach as many as possible of their target consumers at the lowest possible cost. They also ideally want to reach people when they are in an attentive and a receptive state of mind.

Audience research helps them to choose from amongst the various media outlets. It can also be used to analyse how competitors use media – from simple estimates of the amount they have spent on advertising to diagnosis of their scheduling strategies.

Media Agencies

The bulk of the work of selecting and scheduling media is done by media agencies on behalf of their advertiser clients. Again, the requirement is for data on how many and what type of people watch, listen to or read the various media. Agencies – like the media – also need software that helps them to manipulate the audience information in various ways.

Many media agencies like to supplement syndicated audience research data with additional insights into people's attentiveness to the media and their receptivity to advertising. They usually do this by commissioning special studies from research companies that they can then use to help differentiate themselves from competitive agencies.

Regulators

Regulators like Ofcom in the UK, the Conseil Supérieur de l'Audiovisuelle in France and the Federal Trade Commision in the United States are responsible for monitoring the output and performance of the broadcast media in these countries.

In doing this they have to be aware of what people are watching and how. For example, in the UK there is a so-called "watershed" from 9.00 pm after which more sensitive material (both programming and advertising) can be broadcast. This clearly only makes sense as long as children are not watching in great numbers after this hour – as the regulation is designed expressly to prevent them from being exposed to such material.

In many countries, for example, advertising codes prohibit the targeting of young people by the manufacturers of alcoholic spirits. One way in which conformity to this code can be monitored is through analysis of the types of publication in which advertisements are carried, to ensure that no more than a certain percentage of readers are under the legal drinking age.

Organisational Frameworks

Various structures exist under which the media research business operates in different companies. The primary ones are the pure commercial structure, funded by subscriptions; Media Owner (MO) surveys funded and controlled by the media; and the Joint Industry Committee (JIC) structure.

In the United States media research is operated as a standard commercial business with companies free to offer research services to anybody who wants to subscribe to it. No pre-agreement from any industry organisation is required for a company to enter the market; all are theoretically free to do so.

Media Owner contracts enable the media to control a survey in its entirety without (what they might consider to be) tiresome intervention from other commercial interests.

Under the JIC or Joint Industry Committee model, representatives of the key stakeholder groups (i.e., the media, media agencies and advertisers) jointly agree on exactly what they want to research and how they would like the research conducted and reported. They then invite research companies to tender against a detailed specification drawn up by the stakeholders and award contracts for specified periods of time.

In most European countries where the JIC approach predominates, there are also commercial surveys which exist side-by-side with and complement the JIC-sponsored research. Good examples of this are the Target Group Index (TGI) surveys in over fifty countries which collect product consumption information and combine it with media exposure data, allowing users to ascertain, for instance, which newspapers are favoured by new car buyers or heavy consumers of air travel.

The claimed advantage of the JIC approach is that media audience estimates assume the status of a "currency" – acceptable to both sides of the buyer/seller equation and directly

Country	Television	Magazines	Newspapers	Radio
France	MO	MO	MO	MO
Germany	MO	JIC	JIC	JIC
Italy	JIC	MO	MO	JIC
Netherlands	JIC	JIC	JIC	MO
Spain	Subscription	JIC	JIC	JIC
UK	JIC	JIC	JIC	JIC

Figure 9.1 Media research structures: leading European countries

translatable into a monetary value. It also prevents monopoly research suppliers becoming entrenched in a business with very high costs of entry.

The opposing argument is that markets like the US have also successfully created currency media research under their more freely competitive, commercial model.

It is further pointed out that JICs are dominated by the media (as the majority funders) and change is very difficult to achieve, while in the US research companies really do become entrenched (e.g. Nielsen has measured television audiences as an effective monopoly there for more than fifty years, easily fending off several major competitive challenges).

Under US law JICs are considered to be a restraint on trade in the sense that buyers of research are effectively ganging up or "colluding", thereby unfairly discriminating against the commercial interests of the sellers of research services.

The idea of asking research companies to re-pitch for a monopoly audience measurement contract every five to seven years is, for JIC supporters, an opportunity to continually refresh services and keep them up to date. They would argue that developments in audience research technology have been much faster in JIC markets than in markets like the US which, until the early part of the 21st century, was far behind most of its European and Asian counterparts in the basic technology of audience research adopted and in what was reported.

To US incumbents however, JICs are an opportunity for buyers to gang up and put them out of business and are not compatible with the proper operation of a free market.

RELATIVE IMPORTANCE WITHIN MARKET RESEARCH

The 2005 ESOMAR Industry Report estimated the global market research business that year to have been worth approximately US$ 23.3 billion of which media research revenues represented some 15 %. In 2004 the equivalent share was 16 %.[2]

Due to the syndicated nature of much of the media research business (i.e. products and services purchased by a large number of buyers), it is often a relatively high margin business compared to customised (ad hoc, single buyer) research.

Investment bank Merrill Lynch has summarised the characteristics of the various types of market research and their impact on research company profits (Table 9.1).[3]

Another contribution made by the media research business to the overall market research industry has been in the development of new techniques. The peoplemeter and portable peoplemeters for measuring radio and television audiences are two examples of this (see later in this chapter). The development of 'double-screen CAPI' (Computer-Aided Personal Interviewing) by Ipsos for the French magazine readership survey AEPM is another.

RESEARCH QUESTIONS/ISSUES

The commercial media are as much delivery vehicles for advertising messages as they are of content to readers, viewers and listeners. Many make all or most of their revenues from advertising. For these companies, media research is ultimately about determining the value of their audiences, which then allows them to put a price on the space.

Marketers want to know what media exposure to their messages can contribute to their own bottom line.

---

[2] ESOMAR (2005 & 2006). *Industry Study on 2004; Global Market Research 2005.*
[3] Merrill Lynch (July 2006) *European Market Research: The Importance of Data.* www.ml.com.

Table 9.1 Types of market research

Market Research Discipline	% of Market	Characteristics	Examples
Syndicated	25 %	• Concentrated: dominated by 1–2 players • Monopolistic market conditions: created by prohibitive costs of entry • Long-term contracts (can be rolling) • Mainly quantitative data collection and repackaging	• Audience measurement • Sales tracking
Continuous	15 %	• Fairly concentrated • Barriers to entry can be significant • More driven by economic cycle vs. syndicated; less vs. customised • Can be quantitative and qualitative	• Access panels • Consumer panels • Ad tracking
Custom	60 %	• Very fragmented • Low barriers to entry • Highly competitive	• One-off research projects

Source: Merrill Lynch.

Non-commercial media also need to attract subscribers or, in the case of taxpayer-funded broadcasters, to demonstrate sufficiently broad appeal to justify their call on public funds.

Targeting

One of the first steps a marketer takes is to determine who the most profitable target audience for his particular product is likely to be – which segment of the population, in other words, is most likely to respond positively to marketing stimuli.

Some targeting decisions will be fairly straightforward: for example the target audience for feminine hygiene products, men's shoes or children's toys. Others are less clear cut but still intuitively obvious, like targeting youth fashion items to younger people or expensive financial products to high net worth individuals.

At a more complex level, advertisers will want to examine a consumer's demographic and household characteristics (e.g. Do they already own multiple electronic gadgets? Have they got a garden? Are there children living in the household?).

They may also look at product usage and general attitudes (known as psychographics) or at specific types of neighbourhood (known as geodemographics). If possible, the information gleaned from this process is then linked to data on media consumption. This helps marketers make the optimal choice of media for reaching their target audiences.

Audience Measurement – Eight Steps

Media performance can be measured at a number of levels and the data used to help marketers plan better campaigns and media owners to correctly value their advertising space.

The Advertising Research Foundation in the US has classified the media performance measurement task into a hierarchy of eight levels taking measurement from a pure media one to something as close as possible to the business needs of marketers. These are as follows[4]:

1. *Vehicle Distribution.* This is the foundation of any audience measurement system. It is a count of the number of units in which advertising will appear, such as how many television or radio sets are switched on, the number of copies of a magazine or newspaper being distributed or sold, the volume of poster panels available, the number of households connected to the Internet and so on.

   In many countries, newspaper circulation is audited by independent organisations (like OJD in France and Spain or ABC in the UK). These bodies offer a third party validation of the net number of copies of a publication distributed minus those unsold. They can often also supply breakdowns of how many are sold at full price, at a discounted price or given away free.

   Media planners and buyers may take the view that a newspaper or magazine that is given away or otherwise discounted does not have the same value to the reader as one bought and paid for by them. It may be read less intensively than one for which the full cost has been paid. Audited circulation data can therefore be used as a measure of circulation quality.

   Television tuning information is generally supplied as a by-product of the standard audience measurement services. A "set meter" is attached to every television or set-top box in the households of participants in a TV audience measurement panel. This monitors whether the television is turned on or off and, if on, to which channel it is tuned. No such device is currently available for producing this information on radio tuning levels.

   Poster contractors can supply detailed map co-ordinates on the location of every panel they own as their measure of distribution. Sometimes this data can also be cross-referenced with population statistics and other data enabling both the contractors and marketers to place higher or lower values on particular locations.

   In practice, even detailed location maps are not available in many countries where ownership of sites is spread amongst a large number of small companies, let alone more in-depth information about the locations. Many have yet to computerise this data, let alone make it available to advertisers.

2. *Vehicle Exposure.* The next step up the hierarchy of measurement is a count of the number of people potentially exposed to the media being distributed. It is obviously possible for a switched on television set to be watched by more than one person or for an individual copy of a newspaper or magazine to be read by several people.

   For this reason, media research surveys make estimates of these audiences that generate higher numbers than the vehicle distribution count described above. They will also tell us something about the composition of these audiences: the age, sex and income of the audience, for example, or information about their product purchasing or lifestyle.

   Standard television and radio ratings services as well as print readership surveys provide exactly this and represent the main activities of the media research business.

   This measure of potential vehicle exposure is often expressed as a Gross Rating Point or GRP: a GRP represents the percentage of a given population seeing the vehicle. Across a series of advertising insertions and over time, it is likely that the same people will have an

---

[4] Advertising Research Foundation (2003) *Making Better Media Decisions.*

opportunity to see or hear ads more than once – hence the number of GRPs achieved by an advertising campaign can easily exceed 100 (100 %).

If a marketer wants to know how many out of a given population had a potential opportunity to see his message at least once (counting them just one time) this is expressed as audience *reach*.

Dividing the GRPs by the reach will yield an estimate of the average number of times or frequency with which the message has been seen by the target audience.

As an illustration of this, audience research may tell us that 80 % of all men had an opportunity to see a television ad over the course of a month. But adding each spot without considering duplication may have come to 400 % (or 400 GRPs). On average, therefore, each of the 80 % who saw one or other of the programmes where the ad ran will have seen the ad five times ($80 \times 5 = 400$).

3. *Advertising Exposure*. Ideally, of course, marketers want to go beyond vehicle exposure and to estimate how many people actually saw their advertisement.

In the United States it has long been the practice to plan and buy television advertising according to the programme audience – even though the audiences to different commercials within and around a programme can vary quite substantially.

A report by media performance monitoring company MPMA[5] showed that individual commercial break audiences could vary by an average of 5 % either way around the average programme audience – a significant difference in a market where a single 30-second commercial can be priced in hundreds of thousands of dollars.

In most of the rest of the world advertisers pay according to the audiences to individual commercials so this is a non-issue.

In the print media however the standard audience measurement surveys tend to measure audiences to the publication only. To get a handle on likely audiences to the individual pages where ads appear marketers must rely either on commissioning their own custom studies or on the handful of general services which offer estimates of average or magazine page exposure (known as APX or MPX studies).

Ad exposure and vehicle exposure are the same thing as far as the poster industry is concerned. The standard way to measure this is via some kind of count of the number of vehicles and/or pedestrians passing by particular panels and sometimes adjusting these counts by factors which affect the visibility of the panels.

This is carried out in the UK, for example, in three stages:

1. Each roadside poster panel (and some transport, supermarket/shopping mall and bus shelter sites) are identified and mapped;
2. Road traffic surveys from government authorities (which are updated regularly) alongside some surveys into pedestrian traffic are used to estimate the gross number of people passing by each panel;
3. A "Visibility Adjustment" is calculated for each site dependent on how far it is from the road, its height, whether it is illuminated and a number of other physical factors that affect the likelihood of the poster being easily seen. The factors are agreed within an industry organisation and applied consistently across all sites.

This level of sophistication is not applied in most countries, although several are now moving in this direction.

---

[5] MPMA (2004). *Optimizing Media Placement Through Better Placement*. www.mpma.us/.

Internet advertising exposure – both to simple banners and to paid-for Search advertising – can be measured through analysis of the number of "click-thrus" to individual web pages.

4. *Advertising Attentiveness*. The fourth level of measurement aims to focus in on the factors affecting whether people are likely to be attentive to the advertising they are exposed to. There is plenty of evidence to suggest, for example, that advertisements placed differently in the same publication or within the same television programme will be recalled differently as a direct result of the placement.

Premiums are usually charged by television stations for early positions in advertising breaks because attention to them is likely to be higher[6] than those appearing in the middle of a series of other commercials.

Several media research studies have addressed these areas, some as one-off, individual snapshot surveys and others as continuous services. In Belgium, the Stop/watch study[7] has been carried out on behalf of publisher Sanoma Magazines and its sales house Medialogue since 1996. It offers a series of benchmark indices on the effectiveness of different magazine advertising formats, positions and sizes based on studying several thousand individual advertisements in the period since then.

In the United States, Affinity LLC's VISTA Print Effectiveness Rating Service[8] markets a continuous series of measures indicating whether people are engaged with particular advertisements and whether they have taken any action as a result of seeing them.

As with the Stop/watch report, the findings from this study and those like it can be used as directional help in determining the likely value to marketers and publishers of certain placements and formats.

Many studies have also been carried out into the relative attention likely to be paid to advertising in different television programmes. Differences have been identified according to the position of advertising in a break, whether the break is itself within a programme or between programmes and the type of programming being broadcast.

5. *Advertising Communication*. Continuous tracking of advertising effects was popularised in the 1970s by Millward Brown, a company founded in 1973. At its most basic level this involves asking samples of consumers whether they can remember seeing or hearing advertising for particular brands or products recently. If this is done daily and weekly over a lengthy period of time, a picture can be built up of how marketing efforts and other factors affect what is going on in consumers' minds.

"Awareness" can be defined and asked about in several ways. For example, the brand may not be mentioned in the question ("which car brands have you seen advertised recently?"); or it may be revealed ("have you seen any advertising for the Toyota Yaris recently?"). It might also be media specific – asking people if they can remember where the advertising was seen or heard.

A range of other Key Performance Indicators (KPIs) can be tracked in this way, all of which can be used to monitor the on-going effectiveness of creative executions and media plans.

---

[6] See, for example, a US study carried out by Nielsen Media Research for the Cable Television Ad Bureau in April 2000. The study identified the different recall levels to television advertising according to placement in long or short breaks, to the position of advertising and to the number of ads in the break. Billetts Commercial Break Ecology report (1998) in the UK delivered similar findings.

[7] www.ppamarketing.net/public/downloads/Stopwatch_everything_on_magad_impact.pdf.

[8] www.affinityresearch.net/vistaratingservice.html.

Although not strictly speaking media research, marketers often base the weight of advertising they choose to run or even their media mix on the level of awareness or "cut-through" they see their advertising achieving in the marketplace over time.

6. *Advertising Persuasion.* Similar sorts of approach can be made to measure whether the advertising is actually changing the way people feel about brands – by increasing their "intention to buy" or "willingness to consider". This can be continuously tracked or asked before and after advertising campaigns run to gauge their effectiveness in breaking through.

As with Advertising Communication measures, these kinds of metric are not normally considered to be in the domain of media research as such. Marketers often attempt to gauge the communication value of particular creative executions – particularly on television, where the cost of mistakes is very high – by pre-testing ideas or half-finished advertisements with groups of people. Some have found this to be a good predictor of how well an advertisement will communicate with or persuade a target audience.

7. *Advertising Response.* Ultimately, persuasion needs to be turned into action. The ARF defines this level of performance data as "response short of sales" to isolate such behaviour as calling a toll-free telephone number, clicking on an Internet banner or returning coupons. These are relatively easy to measure and are the primary business of direct response agencies, rather than survey research companies.

8. *Sales Response.* Purchase of a product in response to advertising is the ultimate goal of a marketer though this obviously depends on a large number of influences in addition to media effects. Below top-line sales it is also possible to get information on the proportion of the sales represented by loyal, occasional and new buyers via either single source panels or analysis of store loyalty card data.

In summary, the business of media research is involved in responding to a large number of questions and issues. To do this, a range of techniques and measures are employed.

RESEARCH APPROACHES

Survey Measurement

All the traditional research methods are used, including face-to-face, telephone, online and mail surveys. Focus groups, continuous panels, neuroscientific experiments, ethnography and other techniques are also employed.

In recent years, there has been a global decline in the share of interviewing carried out face-to-face. Security concerns, people leading busier lives and a general reluctance to respond to surveys have driven response rates down and research costs up.

ESOMAR reported that face-to-face, personal interviewing was down from 31 % to 24 % of expenditure on data collection globally between 2004 and 2005. Over the same period telephone interviewing increased marginally from 20 % to 21 % of the total while online increased from 11 % to 13 %.[9]

Yet while the media research profession has not been isolated from the financial and response rate pressures affecting the rest of the market research business it has, to date, been slower to change.

---

[9] ESOMAR (2006). *Global Market Research Report 2005.*

Table 9.2   Summary of readership studies, 2005

	Region	Country	Annual Sample Size	Survey Name
1	Africa/Middle East	Bahrain	1,000	National Media Analysis (NMA)
2	Africa/Middle East	Egypt	2,000	NMA
3	Africa/Middle East	Ghana	3,000	All Media and Product Survey (AMPS)
4	Africa/Middle East	Iran	10,000	TGI
5	Africa/Middle East	Iraq	2,700	NMA
6	Africa/Middle East	Israel	10,000	TGI
7	Africa/Middle East	Jordan	2,000	NMA
8	Africa/Middle East	Kenya	2,000	AMPS
9	Africa/Middle East	Kuwait	2,500	NMA
10	Africa/Middle East	Lebanon	2,500	NMA
11	Africa/Middle East	Oman	1,900	NMA
12	Africa/Middle East	Qatar	1,300	NMA
13	Africa/Middle East	Saudi Arabia	3,500	NMA
14	Africa/Middle East	South Africa	12,400	AMPS
15	Africa/Middle East	Syria	2,500	NMA
16	Africa/Middle East	Tanzania	2,000	AMPS
17	Africa/Middle East	Uganda	1,800	AMPS
18	Africa/Middle East	United Arab Emirates	2,400	NMA
19	Africa/Middle East	Zambia	1,000	AMPS
20	Asia	Australia (1)	55,000	Roy Morgan Readership Survey
21	Asia	Australia (2)	35,000	Panorama
22	Asia	China (1)	81,100	China National Readership Survey (CNRS)
23	Asia	China (2)	70,000	China Marketing and Media Study (CMMS)
24	Asia	Hong Kong	6,000	Media Index
25	Asia	India (1)	262,900	National Readership Survey
26	Asia	India (2)	242,118	Indian Readership Survey
27	Asia	Indonesia (1)	13,300	Media Index
28	Asia	Indonesia (2)	24,000	Roy Morgan Readership Survey
29	Asia	Japan	12,200	Audience & Consumer Report (ACR)
30	Asia	Malaysia	10,000	Media Index
31	Asia	New Zealand (1)	12,752	Roy Morgan Readership Survey
32	Asia	New Zealand (2)	15,000	National Readership Survey
33	Asia	Philippines	2,000	Media Index
34	Asia	Singapore	4,200	Media Index
35	Asia	South Korea	8,000	Media Index
36	Asia	Taiwan	7,000	Media Index
37	Asia	Thailand	8,000	Media Index
38	Europe	Austria	17,750	Media Analysis
39	Europe	Belgium	10,500	CIM Survey Press and Plurimedia
40	Europe	Croatia	41,975	MEDIApuls
41	Europe	Czech Republic (1)	29,170	Media Projekt
42	Europe	Czech Republic (2)	16,133	TGI
43	Europe	Denmark	45,000	Index Danmark/Gallup
44	Europe	Finland	28,120	Kansallinen Mediatutkimus

(*Continued*)

Table 9.2   (Continued)

	Region	Country	Annual Sample Size	Survey Name
45	Europe	France (1)	20,100	L'Audience de la Presse Magazin (AEPM)
46	Europe	France (2)	25,500	Audience de la Presse Quotidienne et de la Presse Hebdomadaire Regionale
47	Europe	Germany (1)	21,121	Allensbacher Markt Analyse/Werbeträger Analyse
48	Europe	Germany (2)	38,904	Media-Analyse
49	Europe	Greece	26,520	BARI/National Readership Survey
50	Europe	Hungary	31,320	Media Analysis
51	Europe	Ireland (1)	7,000	Joint National Readership Survey
52	Europe	Ireland (2)	2,941	TGI
53	Europe	Italy	36,000	Audipress
54	Europe	Netherlands	24,000	NOM Print Monitor
55	Europe	Norway (1)	29,882	Forbruker & Media
56	Europe	Norway (2)	21,000	Norsk Medieindeks Riksundersøkelsen
57	Europe	Poland	36,000	PBC General
58	Europe	Portugal	15,120	Bareme-Imprensa
59	Europe	Romania (1)	10,000	TGI
60	Europe	Romania (2)	17,000	National Readership Survey
61	Europe	Russia	97,000	National Readership Survey
62	Europe	Slovakia	6,776	TGI
63	Europe	Slovenia (1)	8,030	National Readership Survey
64	Europe	Slovenia (2)	8,812	TGI
65	Europe	Spain	43,000	EGM
66	Europe	Sweden	48,000	Orvesto Consumer
67	Europe	Switzerland	23,500	MACH Basic
68	Europe	Turkey	48,000	Biak
69	Europe	UK (1)	36,097	National Readership Survey
70	Europe	UK (2)	27,000	TGI
71	Europe	UK (3)	10,000	Roy Morgan Readership Survey
72	Europe	Ukraine	34,000	National Readership Survey
73	Latin America	Argentina (1)	10,250	Target Group Index (TGI)
74	Latin America	Argentina (2)	14,000	Estudio General de Medios (EGM)
75	Latin America	Brazil	53,385	Estudos Marplan/EGM
76	Latin America	Brazil	16,000	TGI
77	Latin America	Chile (1)	12,000	Estudio Nacional de Lectoría
78	Latin America	Chile (2)	11,350	EGM
79	Latin America	Colombia	4,096	TGI
80	Latin America	Costa Rica	12,000	EGM
81	Latin America	Ecuador	2,000	TGI
82	Latin America	Guatemala	12,000	EGM
83	Latin America	Mexico (1)	12,400	TGI
84	Latin America	Mexico (2)	55,200	EGM
85	Latin America	Peru	3,000	TGI
86	Latin America	Puerto Rico	5,000	TGI
87	Latin America	Venezuela	4,000	TGI
88	North America	Canada (1)	12,300	Print Measurement Bureau (PMB)
89	North America	Canada (2)	24,800	NADbank
90	North America	USA (1)	26,000	Mediamark Research (MRI)
91	North America	USA (2)	10,000	Roy Morgan Readership Survey
	GRAND TOTAL		**2,176,122**	

For example, of 91 magazine and newspaper readership surveys in 71 countries listed in a compilation for the Worldwide Readership Symposium in 2005,[10] no fewer than 73 were either fully or partly conducted face-to-face, with a further 15 by telephone and the rest by a mixture of online, diary and self-completion techniques (see Table 9.2).

Controversy raged in the UK industry during 2006 after the National Readership Survey proposed addressing particularly severe response rate declines in London by moving part of the survey online.

It was also mooted that hard-to-reach respondents might need to be paid for their time – this is the solution that has long been adopted by the US readership research supplier MRI. Face-to-face interviewing is rarely used for commercial market research purposes in the US these days; however, by paying respondents, the survey has managed to achieve relatively high response rates in excess of 60 %.

There are many reasons why change – especially fundamental change – has been so hard in the media research business. The most important of these is the use of media audience data as a currency of transactions between buyers and sellers – and the consequent need to ensure all sides of the transaction have full confidence in the accuracy, consistency and credibility of the measure. Because buyers and sellers have different interests and perspectives, this often legislates against major change.

Electronic Measurement

While face-to-face interviewing continues to play a prominent role in the media research world, another distinguishing feature of the business is its extensive use of panel-based approaches to measure television viewing. Electronic "peoplemeters" began replacing the dominant diary technique in the early 1980s and now operate in 74 markets globally (see Table 9.3).

It has always been important in the measurement of television audiences that a continuous approach is used in order that analysis can be carried out of audience behaviour over periods of several weeks or even months.

Advertisers need to know how many people are likely to see one or more of their spots in a campaign that might last anything from a week to several months. Television stations may wish to examine, as well, how many people sample a new programme and then either continue watching future episodes or try other programmes. They also look at data on how long people tune into individual programmes, where they switch to when they stop viewing a given show and so on.

Radio measurement still mostly uses a diary-based approach. Respondents are recruited then asked to maintain a diary of all their radio listening, indicating whether they are listening and to which stations by 15 or 30-minute periods throughout the day.

Diaries allow a picture to be drawn of how listeners switch between stations over a period of time and also permit advertisers to gauge people's likely exposure to one of their commercials over a period of up to a week. Modelling can stretch this analysis period up to four weeks.

In some countries[11] an electronic device known as the PPM^{SM} (Portable People Meter) is being used to measure audiences to either radio, television or both. Users of PPM research

---

[10] Meier, Erhard (2005). *Summary of Current Readership Research*. Proceedings of the 12th Worldwide Readership Symposium, Prague.
[11] For the latest list of countries that have adopted or are testing the PPM approach see www.arbitron.com/international/ home.htm.

Table 9.3 Peoplemeter countries, September 2006

	Region	Country	HH	Research Contractor
1	Africa/Middle East	Israel	460	TNS
2	Africa/Middle East	Lebanon	400	Ipsos
3	Africa/Middle East	South Africa	1,510	AGB Nielsen
4	Asia	Australia	6,050	AGB Nielsen
5	Asia	China (1)	9,500	AGB Nielsen
6	Asia	China (2)	11,700	CSM
7	Asia	Hong Kong	600	TNS/CSM
8	Asia	India (1)	4,555	IMRB/Nielsen Media Research
9	Asia	India (2)	7,000	amap
10	Asia	Indonesia	1,795	AGB Nielsen
11	Asia	Japan	5,000	Video Research
12	Asia	Kazakhstan	700	TNS
13	Asia	Malaysia	1,000	AGB Nielsen
14	Asia	New Zealand	500	AGB Nielsen
15	Asia	Pakistan	50	Gallup PK
16	Asia	Philippines	2,200	AGB Nielsen
17	Asia	Singapore	750	TNS
18	Asia	South Korea	1,900	AGB Nielsen
19	Asia	South Korea	2,000	TNS
20	Asia	Taiwan	1,800	AGB Nielsen
21	Asia	Thailand	1,200	AGB Nielsen
22	Europe	Austria	1,500	GfK
23	Europe	Armenia	120	TV MR AM
24	Europe	Azerbaijan	400	TV MR AZ
25	Europe	Belgium	1,500	GfK
26	Europe	Bulgaria	750	GfK
27	Europe	Bulgaria	560	TNS
28	Europe	Croatia	660	AGB Nielsen
29	Europe	Cyprus	450	AGB Nielsen
30	Europe	Czech Republic	640	Mediasearch
31	Europe	Denmark	1,070	TNS
32	Europe	Estonia	250	TNS
33	Europe	Finland	1,000	TNS/Nielsen AGB
34	Europe	France	3,150	Mediametrie
35	Europe	Georgia	300	TV MR GE
36	Europe	Germany	6,800	GfK
37	Europe	Greece	1,300	AGB Nielsen
38	Europe	Hungary	870	AGB Nielsen
39	Europe	Ireland	670	AGB Nielsen
40	Europe	Italy	5,100	AGB Nielsen
41	Europe	Latvia	300	TNS
42	Europe	Lithuania	350	TNS
43	Europe	Moldova	350	TV MR MLD
44	Europe	Netherlands	1,220	GfK
45	Europe	Norway	1,000	TNS
46	Europe	Poland (1)	1,650	AGB Nielsen
47	Europe	Poland (2)	1,100	TNS
48	Europe	Portugal	1,000	Markdata
49	Europe	Romania	1,150	TNS AGB International
50	Europe	Russia	1,650	TNS

(Continued)

Table 9.3   (Continued)

	Region	Country	HH	Research Contractor
51	Europe	Serbia (1)	890	AGB Nielsen
52	Europe	Serbia (2)	400	TNS
53	Europe	Slovakia	800	TNS
54	Europe	Slovenia	450	AGB Nielsen
55	Europe	Spain	3,800	TNS
56	Europe	Sweden	1,500	AGB Nielsen
57	Europe	Switzerland	1,870	GfK
58	Europe	Turkey	2,200	
59	Europe	UK	5,100	BARB
60	Europe	Ukraine	1,200	GfK
61	Latin America	Argentina	1,321	IBOPE
62	Latin America	Brazil	3,459	IBOPE
63	Latin America	Chile	450	IBOPE
64	Latin America	Colombia	900	IBOPE
65	Latin America	Costa Rica	300	IBOPE
66	Latin America	Dominican Republic	310	AGB Nielsen
67	Latin America	Ecuador	500	IBOPE
68	Latin America	Guatamala	220	IBOPE
69	Latin America	Mexico	2,650	IBOPE/AGB Nielsen
70	Latin America	Panama	220	IBOPE
71	Latin America	Paraguay	270	IBOPE
72	Latin America	Peru	450	IBOPE
73	Latin America	Puerto Rico	465	Mediafax
74	Latin America	Uruguay	330	IBOPE
75	Latin America	Venezuela	500	AGB Nielsen
76	North America	Canada	2,600	BBM
77	North America	USA	10,000	Nielsen Media Research
	GRAND TOTAL		**140,685**	

can, with the appropriate software, carry out all the kinds of analysis available to users of peoplemeter-based audience research. However in most countries diaries remain the main way of monitoring radio audiences[12] with a far lower level of analysis possible than for television.

As with print audience measurement, the television and radio industries have often been slow to embrace any changes which any one of the major customer groups for the research may consider detrimental to their commercial interests.

At first, peoplemeters were resisted by television stations because they generated lower audiences (ratings) than the old diary technique had recorded. Advertisers, on the other hand, liked the fact that electronic measurement left less to the imagination of the respondent and could pick up smaller stations and dayparts which people could easily forget having watched. Both the broadcasters and the advertisers were concerned with the significantly increased cost of an electronic solution.

The debate reared its head recently in the United States when ratings supplier Nielsen Media Research proposed replacing diary measurement in the ten largest cities with a

---

[12] In the United States diaries are still used for measuring audiences to television stations in almost 200 local markets.

Figure 9.2   Portable peoplemeter (PPM)

peoplemeter system. Despite protests, all ten cities have now been upgraded to a peoplemeter service.

Many radio stations have been faced with similar issues as Arbitron attempts to push its PPM out to as many markets as possible. As with the change from diaries to peoplemeters for television, parallel runs of the diary and PPM have shown the latter improving the shares for smaller stations and dayparts and dampening the highs for the larger stations and more popular dayparts.

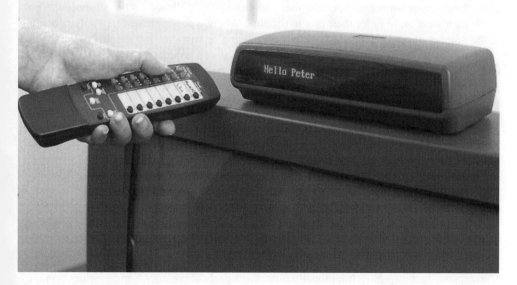

Figure 9.3   Peoplemeter

In addition, the PPM service is considerably more expensive to set up and run than a diary system.

The Internet has emerged as the fastest growing advertising medium globally for several years now, with a number of different approaches used to measure the potential audiences to advertising pages or banners.

Web page owners are able to access detailed information on how many times their web pages are loaded (known as page "traffic" or "views"). They also know in many cases when pages are viewed by the same PC user on multiple occasions via use of "Cookies". Cookies are pieces of information generated by a Web server (where a user goes to find information) and stored in the user's computer to speed up future access. They may also be tagged with various items of information on which exact pages a user accessed, etc.

Industry measurement organisations like Nielsen's NetRatings and comScore offer "people-centric" rather than "site-centric" data. By attaching devices to a panel of Internet users, they can track the sites visited, time spent online and so on, exactly as they would a panel of television viewers or radio listeners. This enables advertisers using the data to calculate the reach and average frequency of exposure to their messages. It also ensure that the visits of web robots (also known as spiders or crawlers) which trawl the web constantly retrieving data for indexing or search sites, are not counted.

This approach brings Internet audience measurement broadly into line with the measures used for other traditional media – allowing buyers and sellers to talk the language of audience impressions, reach and frequency and opportunities to see advertising.

But because the Internet effectively has an in-built audience measurement mechanism, companies like Omniture in the United States have created businesses based on their ability to offer real-time analysis of web traffic to Internet site owners. The behaviour of all those who click on a given site can be tracked in great detail, allowing reports to be generated on which pages are the most popular within a site, the typical path somebody might take from page to page, where the most responded to banner ads are placed and so on.

Advertisers, for their part, can access information about how many people visited sites or pages where their banner ad ran, how many of those people clicked on the ad itself and how many then went on to order their products online. Many web advertisers pay only according to the number of clicks generated by their advertising or, in a growing number of cases, on a pay-per-acquisition basis – i.e. when the customer orders a product.

Banner advertising is however a declining part of the Internet advertising business, having been superseded by Search advertising – where marketers bid for keywords on sites like Google or Yahoo. In return, the Search site will place advertisers bidding the largest amount for a word high on the first page of results generated by a user search. There is then a further charge for the number of times the link is clicked on.

Either way, the way audiences are measured on the Internet is far closer to the ARF's 7th level of audience measurement – Advertising Response – than any of the traditional media can offer. As a result many feel that the medium does not need to revert back to "Opportunity to See" metrics along the lines of the older media forms. Instead, it can offer marketers an instant snapshot of how much return they are getting from their investment in the medium.

BENEFITS AND LIMITATIONS

Currencies – money – have traditionally oiled the wheels of commerce in the wider economy through their role as both a means of exchange and as a store of value. In the advertising world, media research often fulfils the same purposes. For example, readership surveys and peoplemeter services, each in around 75 countries, play this role. With the Internet, no single measurement approach has yet achieved the status of a currency, with different metrics being used by different marketers.

Media research has proven its value by helping media owners quantify their audiences and offer a measurable product to advertiser customers. From the advertiser side it helps to place a value on the potential audiences to their messages.

But syndicated media research necessarily has limitations. Not every marketer's target audience can be precisely identified on a broad survey, meaning that certain generalisations need to be made – for example, a broad demographic description (e.g. women aged 25–44) may have to suffice when the people the advertiser really wants to reach are heads of household responsible for grocery purchasing.

In addition to this, the definition of an "audience" varies considerably between surveys and cannot usually be exactly matched to advertisement exposure. The typical definition of an audience to a television commercial, is somebody who presses a button on his or her peoplemeter control panel to indicate that they are present in a room with a television set tuned into a given channel.

The meter cannot know whether in fact the person has forgotten to press his button or, while in the room, is actually watching what is on the screen with any degree of attention. A reader, according to many of the surveys, is somebody who has an "opportunity" to read or look at a publication. It does not usually specify a particular issue and rarely a given page – which is where an advertisement will be placed.

The advertiser needs to take these varying definitions into account when planning advertising campaigns.

A third major drawback with the currency surveys is that they usually only deal with a single medium. This is because the major financial backers of the research – the media owners – do not have an interest in helping to promote competitive media. Television stations do not feel the need to burden their panels with questions on magazine or newspaper readership, while magazine publishers care little about how their users interact with radio.

Most research has shown, however, that media work better together than separately, due both to their ability to reach more people in combination and due to advertising impacting people in different and complementary ways.[13]

The two main approaches offered to marketers whose focus is their target consumer rather than audiences to individual media, are single source research and data fusion.

The first approach – adopted for example by the Target Group Index (TGI) surveys in more than 50 countries – is to ask the same group of people questions about consumption of several media on the same survey and to offer cross-media analysis (e.g. how many people have seen a brand message in any one of, say, three media where campaigns have been running).

Many print media surveys also offer broad coverage of peoples' consumption of other media like television and radio which can be used by media planners.

The second approach is to mathematically link different surveys together. To do this, a number of common variables are extracted from each survey – for example, the age, sex, occupation and location of respondents from surveys are usually known.

In its simplest form, this demographic data can then be used to link two or more surveys together: one survey becomes the "hub"; others play the role of "donors". A donor readership

---

[13] See for example Smith, A. (2002) *Take a Fresh Look at Print*. 2nd edn. Federation of International Periodical Publishers.

survey will contain information on what, for example, women aged under 35 working at home read. This readership information can then be attached to a television hub survey where the viewing habits of this same group are tracked. We can then estimate both what they read and what they watch.

Much more sophisticated versions of this basic process have been developed in many countries, allowing marketers to gauge the reach of their advertising campaigns across several media, rather than them having to work with different and incompatible sets of results from each medium.

Caution must, of course, be exercised in using such data.

DO'S AND DON'TS

Despite the limitations of media research, there are always steps which can be taken to ensure the best possible research for a given purpose – and most of these steps are those that should be taken in designing and executing any market research survey. For example:

DO:

- Carry out proper sample selection, using probability methods where possible; in the case of online surveys, as close a representation of the people being targeted as can be achieved.
- Insist on transparency in all fieldwork operations – e.g. properly calculated response rates (i.e. detailing how many respondents were not at home when contacted, who refused or who were otherwise ineligible); for online surveys, full details of how panels are recruited, screened and maintained and how many responded to the survey out of those initially contacted. Some kind of quality control of how respondents answer questionnaires should also be in place to indicate the time they spend answering questions (to verify whether or not they are they just racing through giving random answers or properly considering each question).
- Ensure proper ordering and rotation of questions to avoid any response bias. A good example of where this might occur is in a readership survey where titles asked about earlier in a questionnaire often generate higher readership numbers than titles asked about later.
- Agree on proper reporting standards and conventions. It is not uncommon for different software packages to read and report media research results in slightly different ways, which can cause confusion in markets where the research is used as a "currency" (see above).

DON'T:

- Overburden respondents with too many questions or an over-complex task. If this happens, the quality of the answers may suffer. For example, answers to questions near the end of very long surveys may be skipped, rushed or simply made up. Panellists asked to wire up all the televisions in their homes and then to press buttons every time they enter and leave a room with the set switched on should not be asked to carry out too many additional tasks, despite the desire of hungry marketers to attempt just that.
- Assume that the results of the research represent the Holy Grail. Research, as the old adage goes, should be used as a lamp to illuminate the tasks you are undertaking, not as a lamppost to lean on. For example, the fact that people have an *opportunity* to see an advertisement cannot be precisely equated with an actual exposure – there are many intervening factors which will affect the relationship between the two such as the position the ad appears in a magazine or programme, its size or length and the quality of the execution.

- Compare GRPs from different surveys without considerable care. Using the most widely prevailing methodologies to measure magazine readership and television viewing, an opportunity to see a television advertisement is more likely to equate to potential advertising exposure than an opportunity to see a print advertisement. Receptivity and attentiveness are separate questions.

CURRENT DEVELOPMENTS AND THE NEAR FUTURE

The future of the media research business is both exciting and worrying. Exciting because of all the change and innovation already being pioneered in the sector; worrying because some of the trends in the media business may move faster than the media research business can keep up with.

To pick on just three of the most promising technologies:

- *Set-top boxes*. Many millions of television sets are now connected to set-top boxes, which enable digital signals from satellites, cable or terrestrial transmitters to enter the home and be distributed according to which services the customer has paid for. In the UK, 70 % of households had at least one set-top box in their homes at the end of 2006.

  The opportunity exists for the data from these very large numbers of households to be collected and aggregated, giving vastly more accurate estimates of the number of sets tuned to individual programmes and advertisements. This opportunity may be thwarted if data control regulations are tightened or consumers object *en masse* to being tracked – however, financial incentives may overcome some of their fears.

  There are a few examples of this kind of work being done at the end of 2006. TNS Media Research, for example, is working with satellite television provider DirecTV to measure the daily viewing habits of 250,000 subscribers in the United States. Digital Video Recorder company TiVo, also in the United States, offers advertisers a service based on detailed tracking of viewers equipped with their boxes.

- *Passive, Portable Meters*. Arbitron's Portable Peoplemeter, Telecontrol's MediaWatch, Eurisko's Media Monitor and Ipsos's MediaCell smart phone are just four examples of this technology. The idea is that people carry some sort of device on their persons throughout the day which automatically detects which radio or television station signals they come into contact with or (in the case of Eurisko) which poster panels they pass.

  The technologies used vary. Arbitron's meter relies on an encoded, inaudible signal sent out by participating broadcasters being picked up by the meter as people go about their daily business. Telecontrol's MediaWatch actually records snippets of television and radio sounds and then "matches" them in a laboratory with the audio tracks of what radio and television stations were known to have been playing at given times.

  Eurisko's Media Monitor also uses a sound matching methodology and has demonstrated a system for pinpointing when people wearing the meter pass individual poster sites, using UPS positioning technology.

- *RFID Chips*. Radio Frequency Identification Devices are used by manufacturers and retailers to tag goods so as to monitor where they are at any point in time. This enables logistics managers to follow them through the distribution chain from factory to store and isolate any inefficiencies in the supply chain. They work by sending signals to radio receiving devices located at strategic points such as at the factory despatch point, wholesale and supermarket warehouses.

The smallest such devices measure 0.15 mm × 0.15 mm, and are thinner than a sheet of paper (7.5 micrometers). The lowest cost RFID tags, which are the standards chosen by Wal-Mart, DOD, Target, Tesco in the UK and Metro AG in Germany, are available today at a price of US$ 0.05 each.[14]

It may be possible at some point to sew these into the clothes or place them at some other point on a respondent's person in order to monitor when they come into contact with certain media, eliminating the need for them to carry pager devices or other bulky appendages.

There have been a number of other initiatives looking at measuring media consumption from a consumer rather than a media vantage point.

In a pilot for The Apollo Project in the United States in 2006, 11 000 people aged 6 and over in 5,400 households were equipped with technology to scan household product purchases and to combine this with information on exposure to media (collected by means of Arbitron's Portable Peoplemeter (see above).

Advertisers will use this data to match product purchase and media exposure, helping them to understand how the two may be linked.

A different kind of initiative pioneered by the Institute of Practitioners in Advertising in the UK involved a survey of how people spent their time with media over the course of a week, divided up into half-hour segments.

The Touchpoints study is now being used to fuse (see above) several of the UK's currency surveys covering, for example, audiences to television, print media, radio, posters and cinema – as well as product purchase information. These are run as separate surveys currently. Touchpoints enables users to run analyses covering people's consumption of all these media simultaneously so, for example, they can assess how many people had an opportunity to hear or see messages for a given product or service across any or all of these media and how many times they were likely to have been exposed to it.

This second approach is clearly not as accurate as the first, but involves considerably less expense and upheaval to an industry accustomed to using particular media surveys to measure audiences.

---

[14] http://en.wikipedia.org/wiki/RFID.

10
Institutional and Social Research

Dieter Korczak

Public sector research is very different from market research. It does not deal with questions like how to get the biggest market share for products or how to identify the hyper-consumer. Instead it aims to find solutions to problems such as the unequal distribution of wealth and the growing rate of unemployment, the best relation between the development of the economy and environmental issues, the construction and funding of the health care sector or social exclusion issues.

Whereas market research focuses on consumers to increase sales and profits usually as part of *short term* strategy, public sector research seeks to understand people's needs and behaviour to establish what will best serve the public interest as part of a *long term* strategy. Very often it is used to provide an independent perspective, based on the will of a civil society and taking into account people's interest, to counterbalance competing lobbies.

The background of social research is sociology and sociological theory. The major societal questions have been topics of sociological approaches, research and theory like family, role, socialisation, group, organisations, institutions, systems or change, movements, modernisation, transformation, revolution. The specialisation within sociology led to sub-divisions which deal with specific subjects like economical sociology with economics, cultural sociology with migration, family sociology with families. One citation undermines very clearly the importance of sociology for social research: "Economics is too important to be left to the economists" (Coleman, 1990: 57).

DEFINITION AND DESCRIPTION OF THE SUBJECT OF INTEREST

According to Mouly, research is "a method or study by which, through the careful and exhaustive investigation of all the ascertainable evidence bearing upon a definable problem, we reach a solution of that problem" (cited by Powell, 1997: 2).

The subjects of *social* research are the *social actions and interactions of people, their values, attitudes and norms as well as the impact and power of social organisations and institutions (see Max Weber, Emile Durkheim)*.

Institutional and governmental research is part of social research. It is normally aimed at reaching solutions to problems identified and therefore mainly orientated on state of the art and status quo analysis and on future perspectives: where are we now and where and how do we have to go?

Market Research Handbook, 5th Edition. Edited by M. van Hamersveld and C. de Bont.
© 2007 John Wiley & Sons, Ltd.

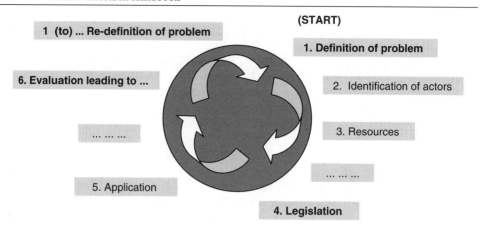

Figure 10.1   Policy process
Source: FES-Project group, 2006

Governments need information about ongoing trends whether it is the needs of the overall population or specific groups. They need to evaluate administrative and political programmes, control and adjust action plans and this usually happens at the city, regional, state, central government and the international level.

It is obvious that institutional or governmental research is needed for policy making. The policy process follows its own rationality. It usually starts with the awareness and definition of a problem. The next step would be the identification of the relevant actors and target groups. When they are clearly identified e.g. by number, social milieu, social strata or value orientation the process continues with a potential estimation of resources available and resources needed. Subsequent to this part there can or will be a discussion in the administration and in the parliaments on the need for regulations or legislation. After the implementation and application of either programmes, regulations or legislation, ideally an evaluation of the application follows. Then the policy process restarts again by a (re)-definition of the problem (see Figure 10.1).

CUSTOMERS

The customers of social research are local bodies as well as national and international institutions (see Figure 10.2).

Public customers can be categorised by their vertical hierarchy. The vertical distribution starts with specific local oriented studies ordered by the municipalities. The next level would be studies with a broader focus contracted by regions, counties or states. A more general and in most cases nationwide approach is the aim by governmental bodies, ministries and the government itself. On top of this hierarchy we find international bodies and organisations like the European Commission and the United Nations and their sub-divisions.

Apart from the public customers there are non-governmental and private customers as well that order social research. The horizontal distribution covers foundations and non-governmental organisations (NGOs), media, political parties, universities and investors, on a national and international level.

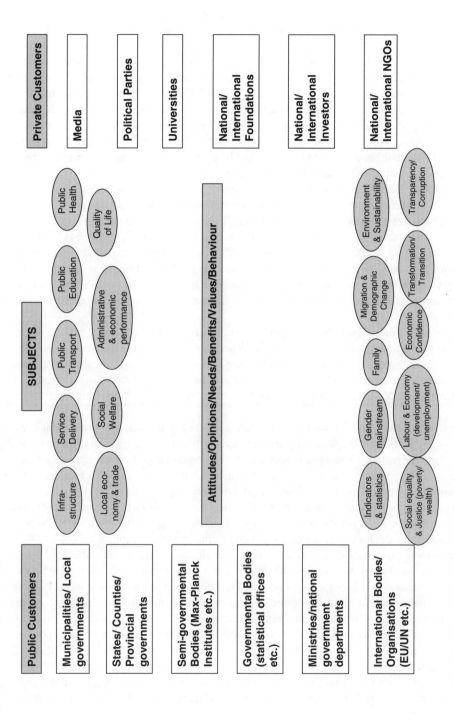

Figure 10.2 Social research: customers and subjects

SUBJECTS

The list of subjects which are covered by social research and research for institutions and governments is long and related to the political purpose and duties of the administration (see Figure 10.2).

Big cities and municipalities, for example, have to organise construction, buildings, traffic and use of land, economy and trade, energy and waste, public education and public health care, sport, social security and safety, migration and cultural diversity. There is a public interest in a good administration of all these topics and there is a municipal bureaucracy with specific responsibilities to cover it. The development of a city is measured by different indicator systems and statistics, often in comparison to other cities or areas. Nevertheless, each activity is as well regarded by the public, commented upon by public opinion and honoured or punished by the next elections of the city parliament and the mayor.

The same philosophy is valid for states, governments and the international bodies. In modern societies with different states like Germany, Switzerland and the USA, the average number of state ministries per state is around nine to ten. Their subjects of interest are interior safety, justice, finance, science, research, technology, economy, infrastructure, energy, labour, social affairs, family, youth, women, seniors, health, school, education, culture, environment, consumer protection and agriculture. What makes the overview difficult is that there is no common organisational structure for each state and the shape of the ministries. Each state can arrange and combine the responsibilities in its own way – that means in a specific tailored ministry.

On the government level the catalogue of topics is completed by foreign affairs, defence and economic cooperation and development. Whereas research on the local and state level is focused on the needs of the local population, the national bodies and ministries are already interested in a broader and international perspective. In Europe this is mainly a result of the legislative power of the EU which forces national law to adapt to EU-law within a certain time frame.

The UN and their sub-divisions are taken into account for research questions because they define on a global level the forward-looking research programmes, e.g. *Earth Summit 1992, Kyoto Conference 1997, Millennium Summit 2000, Johannesburg Summit 2002 and Renewables 2004*. There is a broad international acceptance that it is essential to agree upon common goals and strategies to face the challenges of the future.

These common goals are sustainability, reducing poverty, fostering democracy, building peace, safeguarding Human Rights, promoting education, safeguarding food, saving lives and promoting public health and promoting equitable forms of globalisation.

International experience demonstrates that these goals cannot be reached without the support and cooperation of the private sector. The private sector plays an active role in shaping people's social situation and conditions of employment. Furthermore, it penetrates into areas that states and governments cannot reach for political, economic or logistic reasons. Therefore in many cases a Public-Private-Partnership is needed and done.

For example, the Johannesburg Declaration on Sustainable Development and, more specifically, the Monterrey Consensus call on the private sector to step up its commitment to the development process and to abide by the principles of good corporate governance. More and more companies are taking on this responsibility, for example by participating in the United Nations Global Compact Initiative on the issue of Human Rights, labour, environment and anti-corruption.

RELATIVE IMPORTANCE IN CURRENT MARKET RESEARCH

The scientific approach of social research needs specific skills. Most research institutions focus on FMCG (fast moving consumer goods) and/or product oriented research and are not prepared and organised to conduct social research. Governments around the globe appreciate the importance of research to a growing extent. In South Africa for example research is identified as one of the "Ten Commandments" of government communication: "In working out campaigns and programmes, there should be a deliberate effort to understand the communication environment, including target groups, appropriate media platforms, messages and forms of interaction. In this regard, communication research is a critical element of the trade. Communication is an art form, but it should be based on science" (Netshithenzhe, 2003).

The worldwide total revenue of social and public research is around 8 % of the total sales of the market research industry, clearly demonstrating that social research is still a niche or boutique product in this market.

RESEARCH QUESTIONS AND ISSUES

Public money is tax money. The way public money, given for research, is spent by a research institute is therefore under severe scrutiny. Each single expenditure has to be proved, gets controlled and has to be accepted by the financial administration of the public customer. Reputation, experience in the field and trustworthiness is therefore of great importance for research institutes.

The research issues and questions addressed are extensive and differ between developing and transitional countries and modern societies.

They include, for example, opinion polls for government and political parties to estimate social and political change, value and attitude studies, monitoring of demographic change, analysis of the effect of policies and programmes concerning all the areas of governmental activities (see Figure 10.2 for examples).

To give a brief impression: cities order studies about the local quality of life or how to attract companies to the area. State administration need reports on the economy, environment or the social situation in their region, often in comparison to competing regions.

At the governmental level, each ministry contracts studies for their specific purpose whether it is the ministry for technology funding research on new technologies or the ministry for consumer protection contracting studies on the consequences of BSE. Another ministry is studying the situation of single parent families, the growth of racism among the youth, or the perspective of senior citizens.

In transitional or developing countries the fact and change analysis is very important, e.g. how many households have electricity, how many have got it in the last few years and how many have to receive it in the next few years?

RESEARCH APPROACHES AND WAYS OF WORKING

Social research has to be funded. Research institutes gain funding either by developing a proposal and looking for customers or by competition with other institutes in tenders (see Table 10.1). For all these studies, there is huge competition between consultants, market and social research agencies and university institutes.

Table 10.1   Research approaches and type of studies

Ways of ordering/contracting	Type of studies
• Proposal by research institute	• Scientific evaluation of programmes
• Direct contracting by government institution	• Action/implementation research
• Limited tender	• Research to get basic knowledge
• Call for tender	• Preparation of Law/policies
• Legal obligations of a governmental institution	• Comparative research
• Selling of/subscription to unique research products	• Opinion polls
	• Communication research
	• Tracking studies
	• Panel research

There are also national and international networks of researchers who cooperate on projects and who are knowledgeable about mainstream legislative and political activities and social ideas. They watch national and international developments very closely to prepare for future projects.

There are different ways to the realisation of a research project. One way is to develop a research proposal which can be initiated by the researcher's own thought, his watchfulness concerning societal trends or on the suggestion of his customer. This is usually a difficult way which costs a lot of preparatory (unpaid) work, convincing work that is quite often not successful in the end. A lack of success is caused in most cases by the fact that public money can only be spent if it is budgeted. Budget discussions are done for the coming year, the need has to be negotiated within the institution and between the other organisations of e.g. a ministry. Finally, the proposed research project needs a precise position in a public household plan to be commissioned.

If the research projects cost a smaller amount of money or can be declared either as pilot projects or as follow-up projects then in most cases the administration and the project responsible on the customer side are allowed to contract a project directly with an institute.

Another type of research is ordered by a *limited* call for tender. If a customer has a very specific research question and knows exactly which research institutes have the equivalent expertise, then he gives a limited call for tender to these institutes only. Studies worth more than Euro 200,000 are usually announced by a public call for tender and researchers are often involved in the political and administrative process which has led to a call for tender.

Concerning the calls for tender, it can be said that an average success rate is getting one project out of 10 proposals. A very good success rate is getting one project out of three to six proposals.

Quite a lot of social research is done by the legal bodies themselves or by semi-governmental institutions, e.g. statistical offices, German Institute for Youth Research, US National Institute for Mental Health.

Government institutions are funded to achieve their specific objectives, and the funding can include an allocation to conduct or outsource social research. Government institutions can either fund social research as a single institution, in cooperation with other government institutions, or as part of a public-private partnership.

As these institutions are totally or mainly dependent on state or governmental money their independence and objectivity is sometimes limited.

Projects can be short term/ad hoc or long term (e.g. longitudinal or tracking). On the international level, there are great statistical inventories which investigate many different aspects of life, e.g. the OECD Pisa-study investigating educational success, the EUROSTAT/SILK investigating the living conditions of the population in the European Member States or the African Media Barometer investigating freedom of the press and independence of the media, the International Social Survey Programme which has investigated in the last 20 years, e.g. social inequality, role of government, environment, family and changing gender roles.

Some research institutions provide the opportunity to subscribe to the findings of social research products available on a regular basis (e.g. twice a year) or to buy the findings of ad hoc research projects.

Social research projects can be primary (qualitative or quantitative) or secondary in nature.

Quantitative methodologies might be quite challenging to apply in developing countries. The challenges include inappropriate data to draft a proper sample, infrastructure (e.g. roads and transport to reach respondents), socio-economic conditions, access (e.g. affordability of telephones and cost and availability of access to the Internet) and security (e.g. crime and/or war in Africa and the Middle East).

BENEFITS AND LIMITATIONS

The benefits of social research can be seen in the broad range of subjects: improvement in the scientific process; impact on improvement of policies, programmes, products and services; meeting the needs of the population, and the increase in the number and duration of the research projects. Social research projects can be conducted to address objectives regarding one or various government policies, projects, products or programmes.

To give a number: Most of the social research projects in Germany, Switzerland and Austria last 1–3 years.

An evaluation of the FORIS data bank (including 19573 research projects from 1995 to 1999) showed that 16 % of the projects were interdisciplinary, 16 % economic projects, 15 % sociological projects, 12 % educational projects, 9 % political science projects, 8 % (social) psychological projects and 6 % concerning the arts and humanities.

Limitations may be imposed by the long planning phases, uncertainties of financing, limited funds, bureaucratic procedures, activities to influence the research results (legitimacy research) and non publishing or non sharing the results.

CURRENT DEVELOPMENTS AND NEAR FUTURE

Researchers in this field need to understand the mentality of administrators and bureaucrats and the reporting style required by the public sector. In contrast to companies which want to have their reports as concise as possible, public sector clients need a thorough understanding and comprehensive explanations as they are accountable to the public. This means they want researchers to provide very complete reports which can be published.

Market researchers in consumer companies focus on one product or service. If they want to broaden their experience, they have either to move up or out of the company, often taking their knowledge with them. Research administrators in the public sector have a broader knowledge base and stay in the position for a longer time. This means that research is part of an ongoing strategy, they can build up more expertise over time and have more consistent ways of working.

What the private and the public sector do share in common is that every department must compete for budgets, and there is always a question mark about finding the resources to fund the next study.

The effects and results of transformation, modernisation and globalisation result in more social research all over the world. The growing importance of social research will continue due to the increasing amount of problems.

One major subject of research which has been and will be of further importance, is the transformation process in the countries which belonged before 1990 to the communist hemisphere. Many of them have changed to capitalism. The social fractures in these countries – including China – are enormous. It includes a change of institutions, a change of values, a change of patterns of everyday life. The transformation opens new possibilities and chances but increases, on the other hand, risks, uncertainties and the gap between wealth and poverty.

There are many other questions of similar importance which are craving answers and solutions.

How do societies deal with migration and immigration? Many European countries experience a change in their population structure with around 20 % foreigners in their country, many of them illegal, many of them working in low-paid jobs or even in the black market.

What do European countries do about low birth rates and the increasing proportions of seniors (60y+) within their populations? This demographic change provokes a lot of yet unanswered questions concerning the growing need for care and the financing of the health care systems, housing conditions, retirement insurance and the general situation of retired people.

How does the digitalisation of life influence people's activities? For example, the Internet is open to everyone to organise chat-rooms and blogs, to show private pornography, to sell books, cars, to build up networks of professionals, self-help groups, alumni, pederasts and terrorists.

Is there a common and world-wide understanding of human living and working conditions? How do companies take on their social responsibility? What does it mean for the organisation of societies when some people are extremely rich and many are extremely poor?

What answers enable the world community to prevent a "real" climate change, to ban terrorism, to support and stabilise democracy? There are many consequences of the globalisation of everything (brands, work, money flow, travel, information, terrorism, etc.) which touch privacy, quality of life and human rights.

The list could be continued endlessly. There is much work to be done and a huge amount of research money for social research needed. But it is more or less a matter of political will whether this money will be planned, budgeted and spent.

The way social research is done by a municipality, a state, a federal government or an international body shows the real face of these institutions.

ILLUSTRATIONS/MINI-CASES

"Sustainable City"

An environmental foundation, the "Deutsche Umwelthilfe", conducted in the midst of the 1990s a competition between cities to elect the best environmental city in Germany. More or less at the same time, the GP Forschungsgruppe, a social research institute, published a "Quality-of-Life-Map" of Germany. In this map 54 indicators for environment, wealth, health, infrastructure, culture and safety were presented for each of the 534 municipalities in Germany.

Combining all these different indicators, Tübingen was crowned as the city with the highest quality of life in Germany.

After the Rio conference on sustainability the local agenda 21 was promoted, and the two above named institutions (plus two others) decided to develop an instrument for a new competition between the German municipalities to choose "The Sustainable City". A project design was developed, a proposal put to the "German Federal Environment Foundation". It was accepted and financed and the competition was conducted from 2002 to 2004. Besides the effect of the competition on the administrative work of the statistical and environmental departments in the cities the final result was a commonly accepted set of 21 indicators to measure sustainability in cities. The winning cities are happy to promote their results in order to attract companies and families to their area.

"The Dutch Chipcard"

The Dutch public transport companies considered the introduction and operation of a national chipcard in 2002. The aim was to make public transport market oriented, to improve service and to decrease costs. The activity was influenced by demand from customers for a better service and by the improved technological performance of contactless cards. With the chipcard as a nationally accepted instrument of payment, the customer can use with ease all means of public transport, and will find few barriers when getting on and off, between modalities and around travelling. Public transport companies can be evaluated and rewarded according to their performance and customers and personnel feel secure because of controlled access to public transport. Before the realisation and introduction of the concept the Dutch Ministry for Transport financed an investigation on the overall economic impact on Dutch society as a whole. The roll out of the system is planned from 2006 through successive tenders and realisation phases.

"Change of Environmental Consciousness"

Since 1996 the German Federal Agency for the Environment has conducted a representative population survey on environmental consciousness on a bi-annual basis. The scientific analysis is done by a university institute, the fieldwork by a market research institute. The tracking study is mainly used to evaluate the political importance of environmental attitudes and topics and to measure the reactions of the population to political regulations. Some results of the survey in 2004 were, e.g. that the topic of the environment was de-dramatised and de-emotionalised and there was a tendency to delegate responsibility from the individual to the government. Environmental justice was found to be a new important concept because poor people, especially ethnic minorities, had a much higher burden of environmental pollution and damage than the average population. As one consequence the environmental justice concept will be integrated in the poverty and wealth reporting of the Federal German government.

"Peer Review Social Inclusion"

The Lisbon European Council of March 2000 asked Member States and the European Commission to make a decisive impact on the eradication of poverty by 2010. Member States co-ordinate their policies for combating poverty and social exclusion on the basis of a process of policy exchanges and mutual learning known as the "Open Method of Coordination"

(OMC). Peer Reviews are a key instrument of the OMC. A peer review is an event where a host country presents a policy or institutional arrangement (good practice) or a policy reform to a selected group of decision-makers and experts from other countries (peer countries) and to stakeholders' representatives and European Commission officials. In addition to the host country presentation a thematic expert presents an evaluation paper on the subject under discussion based on secondary analysis. The aim of the peer review is to create mutual learning processes based on existing evaluation or monitoring data. Peer reviews have been taking place since 2004, financed by the European Commission. Subjects of interest were, for example, over-indebtedness, homelessness, reconciliation of work and family life, social exclusion of families, integration of immigrants, eradication of shanty towns and citizens' social support networks.

"Corruption Perceptions Index"

Transparency International is a global NGO-network, funded by various governmental agencies, international foundations and corporations. It was founded in 1995 in Berlin and its aim is the fight against corruption. The annual Corruption Perceptions Index (CPI) is the best known of TI's tools. It has been widely credited by putting the issue of corruption on the international policy agenda. The CPI ranks more than 150 countries by their perceived levels of corruption, as determined by expert assessments and opinion surveys. The CPI uses nine sources: the World Bank, the Economist Intelligence Unit, the Freedom House, the World Competitiveness Centre, the Merchant International Group, the Asian Intelligence Newsletter, the Africa Governance Report, the World Economic Forum and the World Markets Research Centre. The CPI is based on perceptions because it is regarded as difficult to assess the overall levels of corruption in different countries based on hard empirical data. In the results of the CPI 2006 a strong correlation between corruption and poverty is evident. Guinea, Iraq, Myanmar and Haiti have the highest levels of perceived corruption, Finland, Iceland, New Zealand, Denmark and Singapore the lowest levels.

REFERENCES

Adorno, Th.W. (1970) *Gesammelte Schriften.* Frankfurt A.M.: Suhrkamp.
Berger, P.L. and Luckmann, Th. (1966) *The social construction of reality.* Garden City, New York: Anchor Books.
Böschen, St. (2004) *Handeln trotz Nichtwissen. Vom Umgang mit Chaos und Risiko in Politik, Industrie und Wissenschaft.* Campus.
Bourdieu, P.-F. (1979) *La distinction. Critique sociale du jugement.* Paris.
Coleman, J. S. (1990) In: Swedberg, R. (Ed.) *Economics and Sociology: redefining their boundaries: conversations with economists and sociologists.* Princeton, 47–60.
Durkheim, E. (1961) *Die Regeln der soziologischen Methode.* Neuwied, Luchterhand.
Etzioni, A. (1988) *The moral dimension. Towards a new economics.* Free Press.
Evers, A. and Olk, Th. (Ed.) (1996) *Wohlfahrtspluralismus. Vom Wohlfahrtsstaat zur Wohlfahrtsgesellschaft.* Opladen, Westdeutscher Verlag.
FES-Project group (2006) Report. Conference on Financial Education. Charleroi.
Giddens, A. (1994) *Beyond left and right. The future of radical politics.* Polity Press.
Habermans, J. (1981) *Theorie des kommunikativen Handelns – Handlungsrationalität und gesellschaftliche Rationalisierung.* 2 Bde. Frankfurt a.M.: Suhrkamp.
Hug, Th. (Ed.) *Wie kommt Wissenschaft zu Wissen?* Band 2: Einführung in die Forschungsmethodik und Forschungspraxis. Band 3: Einführung in die Methodologie der Sozial- und Kulturwissenschaften.

Band 4: Einführung in die Wissenschaftstheorie und Wissenschaftsforschung. Baltmannsweiler. Schneider Verlag.

Lindblohm, Ch.E. (1959) "The Science of Muddling Through". *Public Administration Review*, **19**.

Netshitenzhe, J. (2003) *Challenges of government communication: the South African experience.* [Presentation at a workshop on improving public communication, Bagamoyo, Tanzania, 18 March 2003] Available online: http://www.gcis.gov.za/media/ceo/030318.htm cited on 27 November 2006.

Popper, K. (1976) *Logik der Forschung.* Mohr.

Powell, R.R. (1997) *Basic research methods for librarians* (3rd edn.): Ablex.

Sen, A. (1989) *On ethics and economics.* Blackwell Publishers.

Weber, M. (1972) *Wirtschaft und Gesellschaft. Grundriß der verstehenden Soziologie.* 5. revidierte Auflage. Mohr.

www.fesmedia.org.na
www.issp.org
www.peer-review-social-inclusion.net
www.transparency.org
www.uba.de
www.un.org

11

Business to Business Research

Neil McPhee

WHAT IS B2B RESEARCH?

Business-to-Business research (B2B) is characterised by its involvement with targets other than domestic/retail/members of the public buying/using, etc., on their own behalf.

This is an important distinction, as it paints a very broad picture of the territory inhabited by B2B research and researchers. As we will see in this chapter, these characteristics pose some very specific challenges for any research project or researcher, and involve some different skills.

There is no ideal definition, but something along the lines of the following will probably encapsulate the essence of what it is, in the modern world.

> the investigation of any market, whether by secondary (published) means, qualitative or quantitative research, where the targets or markets being examined are deemed to act in their capacity as commercial, business or organisational terms, as opposed to in and for their own personal, domestic requirements.

This is of course imperfect, but it is intended only as a guide and not an absolute. There are many grey areas in B2B nowadays, where, for example, the growing body of employment is in very small or solo enterprise forms. Experience shows that many sole business people, acting as craft or service providers (plumbers, software/hardware engineers, etc.), may act as commercial operations, in a practical sense, but think in a domestic way, and often behave accordingly.

Take for instance the growing body of the self-employed. Many put a volume of business related purchases quite properly through their business accounts, computer equipment, printers, cartridges and so on. Where do they buy them? Often from exactly the same places, and using the same criteria as they would/do, if they were buying for a home requirement. Equally, they may in fact be buying for "home" use, but put the purchase through as a business expense, with attendant tax advantages. Should these purchases be treated as domestic or business?

Again, there is no single answer, but it serves to illustrate the increasing complexity of the sector, and we will return to this later in the chapter.

IS IT DIFFERENT?

Doing B2B research, it is often asked if it is different from Consumer research, and implicitly whether any different skills, techniques and so on are necessary. The answer is a qualified

Market Research Handbook, 5th Edition. Edited by M. van Hamersveld and C. de Bont.
© 2007 John Wiley & Sons, Ltd.

"Yes", B2B is somewhat different, but in a way which places a premium on experience rather than specific knowledge.

One key difference is in the area of sampling. While it is possible to make some general points about differences, and indeed these are made below, the real issue is that of experience in researching these markets, as there is no absolute answer to sample differences. So too with actual B2B interviews, and again, experience leads to expertise, rather than any definable differences, per se.

Sample

The B2B sample is comprised of people who make or contribute to decisions, buy goods and services, view advertising and so on, as a part of their own employment. This means that they span a very wide range of constituent elements, literally from the owner/manager/sole employee, through mid-sized businesses, through the "shop floor" up to CEO, CFO and the other C-Suite inhabitants in larger enterprises, and on to Global HQ decision-makers. This is very different in look and feel from the much simpler structure (and limited roles) of the typical domestic structure, but in essence is still composed of those who fringe the decision/usage, those who use the product of the decision and those who make and pay for the decision.

Outlook

The outlook in B2B is often seen as different from FMCG research, but this is one of the Great Myths, and should be consigned to the scrap heap, where it belongs. Rationality is also often assumed to be inherent in the B2B arena, where steely eyed, hard-nosed business people make rational, calculated judgements, purely on logic, facts and figures, not so. Moreover, we have innumerable pieces of evidence to illustrate that business people make just as emotion-based judgements and decisions as do consumers. This can hardly be a surprise, as these business people are ordinary consumers when they leave their offices!

So the key point must be, for B2B research, do not forget that the target respondent is just a human being, and makes both rational and irrational decisions, and that research approaches must recognise this.

Accountability

One big difference between B2B and Consumer research is in the scale and complexity of accountability for decisions and actions. In a small company this may be quite limited to the organisation itself, the family of the owners, the Bank, etc., but with a larger or Multinational concern, the implications can be enormous, and the network of fall-out inherent in a decision vast. This means that to be realistic in its coverage, research should seek to represent a very wide frame of contextual reference and may well involve several countries, regions and layers of management for it to be truly representative. All this adds to cost, timescale and complexity.

Stakeholders

So too with stakeholders, internally. In any decision there are likely to be a wide range of interested parties, ranging from marketing and sales functions through to senior management, finance and so on. This width again poses problems for the B2B researcher, especially for the internal research manager and the external agency provider, in terms of ensuring that while all views are taken into account (and all parties feel they get a share of the research cake), the research itself is not constructed in a haphazard way where it ends up as an incohesive mass of individual questions and objectives, with no real sense of direction and purpose. Besides being a recipe for a really confused and unappealing prospect for any respondent in terms of interview design and content, it will almost by default mean that no one internally will be satisfied with the results, feeling that their key nugget has been watered down/not covered/not given enough time and space, etc.

Who Wants What?

There is also a major issue in many B2B surveys with details and expectations, and it is paramount that the internal researcher, commissioner of research and all other relevant parties acknowledge that certain requests and expectations cannot be fully met. In particular, it has been many researchers' experience that Sales functions wish to have direct, attributable feedback from respondents such that they can follow these up for sales purposes. This is (currently) completely outside the ESOMAR Code of Practice, and no reputable agency would comply with such disclosure. There are opportunities for asking up-front for permission to disclose, but Sales departments in particular tend to see all such conditions as unnecessary barriers to sales and put significant pressure on the research function to provide sales lead information. This is to be avoided as, at best, it prevents full disclosure of views by respondents, and at worst is likely to put respondents' views of market research, per se, at severe risk. Similarly, other functions want a different style of research ranging from the micro-level details up to the big picture, overview. Clearly, for the researcher providing a report or presentation this poses severe problems.

An increasingly useful approach here is to allow, post research, for several presentations and maybe a workshop style presentation to different departments and functions, such that elements of the research findings can be tailored to specific audiences. This will allow, for example, an overview of a multi country study to be presented to senior management, giving only top line findings, "big picture" views and without much detail, where for individual countries or other functions, a presentation directly relating to their own territory can be produced.

Again, beware of extra costs and time scales, as such separate reporting can generate quite a lot of work and time to prepare.

Researcher as Gatekeeper

In a very real way, therefore, the internal researcher has a critical role to play as Gatekeeper for these internal pressures and pressure groups. It is up to him or her to take appropriate soundings from all concerned, before the research is commissioned, in order to manage all expectations and requirements, such that when the external researcher or actual research process begins, there is common agreement on what is being sought, how it is being sought and what will be delivered as a result.

It is not an external agency's role to manage this internal trade-off process, but often it will be the external agency who shoulders at least some if not all the blame, if individual parties feel short-changed.

Uses and Abuses

Research is a vital tool for bridging the gap between the B2B provider of goods, services etc., to the market and those on the receiving end. It is said with increasing frequency that some B2B client organisation teams, especially in Sales & Marketing do not want the restrictions offered by various market research Codes of Practice. They believe that their markets are perfectly capable of accepting their anonymity being abandoned, in favour of a much more direct exchange between buyer and seller, facilitated by the research process. This is contrary to all established market research practice and should be avoided: if respondents know that their every response to questions will be transmitted, and identified, back to sellers, they will inevitably withhold or feed spurious results back into the system. It is the anonymity that is inherent in the exchange, along with very specific craft skills (i.e. asking questions in the "right" way) that makes the current model work.

There are a number of very definite areas for research, and some that are inappropriate.

Research as an Aid to Decision Making

This is the prime role and the one for which it is ideally used, the ability of well-conducted market research to inform and enhance decisions about virtually any aspect of the B2B mix. It is not there to be misused or abused: some of these abuses and misuses are highlighted below.

Research as PR Fodder

Research surveys, usually quantitative, are often seen as good public relations material and here samples of not much more than 100 are often found, many undertaken by remote means (online, for example), or telephone. Sometimes these have some deeper significance, but the key point to remember is that they have been conducted for a reason: and that is to promote the specific company/organisation/product in the media. While there is no suggestion that any of the results are wrong, very often, the rigour of a "proper" survey may be missing and the sample size will tend to be on the small size.

Research as a Reactive or Defensive Act, to Justify a Decision

Among the main reasons for research, survey research tends to be conducted with the purpose of confirmation. This may be to endorse an advertising campaign execution, to check out reactions to a new product, to validate strap line usage, or to check out a new product idea. This is either qualitative or quantitative research but the purpose is to validate something that is already in place or exists. This is in contrast to the usage of research to guide an upcoming but unformed decision, whether this be new product development, advertising development or the like. The key difference is in the approach, the former using a framework, intellectual and methological, which is premised on an existing scenario. The latter uses a much more intangible, open structure, seeking "new/uncharted" waters and requires a more flexible approach, this is especially important in the form and format of questions and questioning, and very often includes at least a stage of qualitative research.

Here the skill of the interviewer is to probe into unknown or less concrete areas, and this needs an advanced level of skills in interviewing and certainly (should not) rely on a structured approach to interviewing.

Research to Avoid a Decision

Some research is conducted with the aim of using the research in place of executive decision-making. While research information certainly illuminates the decision process, it is only to illuminate it and certainly should never take the place of experienced management or of industry/sector knowledge.

Research to Explore New Product/Service Development

This is (or at least should be) a major usage of research. Finding what actual or potential customers really want is a major plus point for the research process, but is not one without its pitfalls. Simply asking an engineer, *"what new products do you want?"* will be unlikely to provide much benefit, but using the researchers' craft skills it will be possible to tease out what problems are currently presenting themselves and what longer term needs the user/respondent has.

Research to Sell Something

While it is obviously tempting to obtain the responses of individual companies/people in a B2B survey, to aid the selling process, this is totally contrary to the letter and spirit of the research model and should remain so. Equally, using research to promote the sales of a product will only result in bringing the research process into disrepute, and must not be allowed to happen.

Often B2B clients, new to the process, ask basic questions about the process, and so too do respondents. Some of the more common are shown here, with answers to the queries.

B2B RESPONDENT FAQ'S

Respondents in B2B qualitative surveys frequently raise queries regarding the survey. The following represent the likely queries to be raised by the target audience.

Why is a third party conducting the interviews/Why doesn't (Client) contact me directly?

The response here focuses on the strengths and weaknesses of in-house vs. out house market research interviewing and these critical points are:

- A third party is independent, neutral and objective.
- All parties want an honest "warts and all" answer.
- It does not have any "contaminating" commercial dealings that might prevent an open exchange.
- A third party has resources that are specialist (interviewing, analysis, etc.) and expensive. In house resources may seem lower cost as they are "hidden", but are often more expensive in reality, and also using these often adversely affects internal operations by taking time and focus from the individual's real job.
- A third party has sampling skills to ensure that a representative and unbiased sample is drawn.
- A third party can report the good and the bad without worry.

But specialist sector knowledge is vital, isn't it, to the interview?

- All interviewing personnel are thoroughly briefed before starting the project, and are skilled in the interview techniques needed to encourage and interpret respondent's views.
- Sometimes it helps to obtain a fresh view of an old situation.

How can we be sure that the researcher won't disclose our views without our permission?

- Use an Agency that is bound by the Code of Conduct of our Professional Bodies, the national Market Research Society, ESOMAR, AQR, etc.
- Ensure that they always ask permission before even contemplating releasing attributable quotes, and will always honour a refusal.
- The findings go to make up a whole picture of opinions about the Client company, not just individual respondents' views.

How long will the interview take?

- The aim is to be as honest as possible. If it is an hour's interview, say so. Frequently it is found that respondents often claim only to be able to spare (say) 30 minutes, but in the event, often spend an hour with the researcher.
- This is especially true when it is clear they have travelled from another country to see them. This also frequently encourages many respondents to participate, suggesting that a personal visit presents the research as "serious" enough to warrant the trip/cost.

What will the interview be about?

- Aim to give the respondent a basic subject area at the initial letter of introduction stage, as this often answers this question before it can be raised.
- It also allows the respondent to consult with colleagues about basic information, if needed.
- It is (usually) presented as the Client wanting to evaluate how it needs to adapt to changing market conditions, and/or to ensure that its new service or services are being developed in the right way to meet customer needs.

Can't you interview me by phone?

- Researchers usually would rather meet respondents face-to-face, as Non Verbal Communication is a vital part of the interview process, but rather than lose an interview, it will offer a tele-depth interview.

RELATIVE IMPORTANCE IN CURRENT MR

Small but Misdiagnosed

In recent years B2B Research accounts for around 15–20 % of research turnover, according to ESOMAR figures. This is a small part only of the total research cake but is nonetheless vitally important and involves major decisions. B2B is not easily distinguished from industrial research.

Some Big Myths

1. Rationality: B2B respondents/decision makers are rational . . . absolutely not true! See above for further explanations.

2. Ability to verbalise: because many are very well educated, they are good communicators in an interview. Just as many consumer respondents may be inarticulate or able to answer our questions, so too with B2B respondents. This is especially true of some very specialised functions where technical language (techno-speak) or a highly introspective personality (see techno-speak!) makes communications about their jobs, requirements, attitudes and so on, very hard for them to achieve. Frequently, this is compounded by the design of the questionnaire wording or design, where really only the writer understands what was meant or required by a specific question. Be very careful of this area: it can lead to real problems.

3. Knowledgeable: They have the answers you want . . . not true, not all respondents (actually very few in larger companies/organisations) know all about what happens in their management structures. It is often necessary to interview at several points in a single organisation in order to obtain a realistic view of what actually happens.

4. Straightforward: B2B respondents are straightforward, simply ask them questions, and they will (can) answer: see above for Knowledgeable and Rational and Able to verbalise.

5. Ease of interviewing: the myth is strong that B2B interviewing is easy. As many a consumer researcher has found the conventions of the B2B environment are very different and can be hard to manage.

RESEARCH QUESTIONS/ISSUES

Response Rates

One of the major problems facing B2B research (and indeed all research) is a declining response rate. This is especially important in view of the relatively limited number of potential respondents in any given target sector. If you wish to interview the CFO of Top 100 companies, clearly there are only . . . 100! If you get a 20 % response rate, you have talked to only 20 of them. This makes it especially important to ensure that every opportunity is taken, and there are some essential points here.

Over-demanding Length

While there are no absolute limits for interviews, common sense and practical experience shows that there are some guidelines that are usually best to follow, to avoid harm to the survey itself or to the research industry itself.

- Telephone interviews – usually no more that 20–30 minutes.
- Online/self completion – 30–40 minutes (MAXIMUM).
- Depth interviews – 1–2 hours.
- Group discussion – 2–3 hours.

It is important to remember that there will always be exceptions, and a really interesting and involving questionnaire/interview can extend times, but the use for example, of extended attitude batteries, requiring scale (1–10, very strong to not very strong) type responses is extremely tiring and dull for the respondent. So too will be an interview where there is a lot of monosyllabic responses or factual information. Involvement comes from a dialogue and this can extend the interview if the respondent sees a sequence that makes sense and engages them in what should effectively be a conversation.

Time Pressures

This is a major area, with downsizing, travel/meeting pressures, etc. on all businesses. Respondents have precious little time to make available to the researcher and this situation will not improve. It is incumbent on all of us to limit the time pressures on the respondents and to ensure that they see the research as valuable and worthy of their attention. This is especially true for sectors where there are clearly only a few potential respondents (IT, physicians, for example) and where these respondents will be asked repeatedly for interviews by a number of research bodies and clients. Remember they owe us nothing: it is by persuasion and incentivisation skills that we get any of their time, and this should be respected.

Confidentiality

One of the foundations of the research industry is the guarantee of confidentiality. Without this, the research risks moving out of its zone of professionalism into areas where research findings are routinely passed onto client sales teams for follow up and this would surely spell the end of the nature of research as it is now. There are frequent calls from certain client sectors for a more open exchange, with attributable findings passed onto client teams. This is often on the grounds that the respondents know the client well and have direct dealings with them, and if research suppliers are to meet the needs of clients they must acknowledge these closer relationships and bend to the inevitable. This is to be avoided. The assurity that information will not be passed on without permission is a fundamental part of the research process and should not be weakened.

Codes of Practice

The latter point is enshrined in a range of Codes of Practice, primarily that of ESOMAR, but also individual, national parallel bodies. These are very important and should form the spine of all research purchases. Do not ever buy from a non-adhering supplier.

There are other codes and quality marks, which are of less value, and where these only refer to procedures, these may be taken with some judicious scepticism. It is perfectly possible in B2B research to follow all stated procedures but to fail to deliver quality research.

Critical questions should be: Who does the work? Allied to this, what standards do you expect/need in order to achieve your goals?

Brands across the seas: how to research brands in several different countries? This problem was overcome by using an initial series of IDIs (individual depth interviews) conducted face to face, followed by a larger programme of telephone interviews all with senior managers in the Oil industry, including on oil rigs. By using only native language speakers, and working from a central UK telephone unit, working up to 20 hours a day, to cover different time zones, the client obtained the required information. Critical to the success of the work were: 1. a clear statement of information needs, 2. a quantitative questionnaire developed from the qualitative depth interviews and piloted to ensure wide usability in different languages, and 3. a very specific debrief agenda.

RESEARCH APPROACHES, METHODS AND WAYS OF WORKING

Writing the Brief

Writing the brief is a major component of a successful research piece. The brief is the core source, along with a personal briefing, on which the researcher designs the form and content of the research, and certain elements are vital.

- Clarity: be very clear as to what you want, from whom you expect/need a survey response.
- Realism and Timing: set/seek realistic goals, not simply what the CEO says he wants.

> **Sorry, we've changed our minds.** Client briefed an agency on a particular piece of work, but at the moment of the commissioning, internal management decided that the budget was unavailable. Having had the client researcher spend considerable time and effort, the project had the proverbial rug pulled, as he had not been given sufficient money to achieve objectives.

Asking for focus groups with senior IT Directors across Europe within a two-week period including debrief is simply not realistic. Neither is getting them all to fly into a single venue so that the groups can be viewed in a single studio by remote client observers.

- Budget: low budgets mean restricted research. There is no such thing as thorough, high quality but cheap research. Cutting the budget means cutting something in the research mix, and this is perfectly reasonable. Smaller sample sizes, shorter interviews, single debrief, telephone rather than face to face . . . all are realistic ways of cutting back on costs. But there are consequential cuts in content, coverage, accuracy and length. You get what you pay for, and the trade-offs are shown here.
- Qualitative: one of the under-used approaches in B2B research is qualitative research. B2B qualitative research is more than a topic guide and a tape recorder, and the increasingly understood nature of decision making and human communications show that the B2B quali-tative research process can sometimes fail to fully understand or access the realities of human beings, in the corporate context, and therefore fail in the very goal it sets for itself – estab-lishing and developing a true and valuable understanding and model of corporate/human behaviour for our clients/projects.

There is an increasing body of evidence that, for example, the different brain wiring and emotional make-up of men and women have very real implications for their outlook, behaviour and response to stimuli, not least of all, in the research exchange. The research industry tends to treat gender, however, just as a quota control for Consumer research and probably not at all in B2B research, and too often fails to differentiate between the sexes in terms of the different approach each requires and the different feedback each gives, and thus does not give full opportunity to the huge contribution of Qualitative research to understanding human interaction. B2B respondents are only human.

However, there is a tendency amongst some researchers and clients to think of business respondents as somehow less fully human when they are interviewed at work than when they are consumer respondents. Certainly they are constrained by their corporate circumstances, and have "rules" by which they are governed to a greater or lesser extent, but they are just people,

	FACE-TO-FACE	TELEPHONE	SELF-COMPLETION
Recruitment	Controlled	Controlled	Self-selecting
Response Rate	Fixed	Fixed	Variable
Speed	Moderate	Fast	Slow
Administration of interview	Controlled	Controlled	Uncontrolled
Use of Stimulus	Unlimited	Limited	Limited
Interaction	Very Good	Good	Poor
Complex interviews	Present	Limited	Not possible
Mood	Enjoyable	Formal	Self-discipline needed

Figure 11.1

and react as people everywhere do, emotionally and semi-rationally, even when they are at work. An increasing thrust of B2B qualitative research today is about seeking to understand, capitalise on, and affect the non-rational response mechanisms in a business setting.

Let's play, Doctors: previous Qualitative interviews with Physicians across Europe and USA had failed to provide any satisfactory explanation/theory as to why Client drug brand had been losing sales share to a major competitor. Research had followed traditional, rational grounds and had asked rational questions about drug efficacy and so on. New approach used a range of projective tools and personality analogies, drawing exercises and word/image association techniques and identified a major brand personality difference.

Who said Doctors would not take part in that type on interview (in groups)?

Sorry, the budget's secret . . . you might want to spend it all. Client approached an agency with a brief for research in the grocery store management arena. After three versions of the proposal, agency was told that there was insufficient budget for the project at the level proposed. Had client been honest at the outset about how much was available, agency could have modified approach in line with this, but client did not want to commit to a level believing that the agency would simply recommend that maximum.

This applies to both internal and to external relationships, and it has always been the case that decision-making units and criteria have been more complex than in domestic markets, simply because the number of people involved is often so much greater and the relationships harder to identify and pin down.

In practice this means that before the interviewing, at the sampling stage, we must be aware of the potential scope of the decision making, allowing for different people's and function's inputs, and multiple interviews in one organisation are increasingly used to triangulate corporate responses.

However, there are other implications and these concern both the conduct of the interview itself, and the post interview analysis. Certainly the approach to an effective B2B interview has to be more than reading out questions and taping/noting the answers. It also means that the analysis stage has to focus on interpretation as well as reportage, and that presentations should be more than clever PowerPoint slides.

Self-completion/Online

Self-completion has always been a standard technique in B2B and is still so, though more on-line than postal, probably, and certainly in the USA, where the tradition of self-completion has been greater than many other areas. The benefits are still theoretically lower costs and speed of response, but equally, the negatives are of fairly standardised questions, seeking factual and superficially attitudinal questions/answers. There are many proponents for Online Qualitative research, and the reader must engage all critical faculties in order to validate the real impact and value of such a tool. Certainly it can be done. Whether it can ever be truly qualitative research, in the sense that we understand the technique is debatable, but the argument still goes that without peer or face-to-face pressure, respondents will offer up real and useful insights. For some subject matter and some respondents, this may be true, but for many interview issues the ability to engage a respondent face to face or at least have the opportunity of telephone dialogue, will surely outweigh any time or cost benefits.

We should expect online interviewing especially where multi country projects involve significant time zone variations, to continue to be an increasing part of the research mix, but it is to be hoped that users (and suppliers) will engage this tool with some circumspection in order to ensure that it is applied only to those subjects/tasks where it is truly suited.

Telephone

For many B2B subjects the standard choice, for quantitative and for many qualitative research projects, will be for a telephone interview. There are many advantages for this:

- Automatic sample frame (assuming the business has a phone entry in a directory).
- Ease of calling/recalling.
- Well-proven technique.
- CATI software, assisting routing, processing, etc.
- Well established telephone facilities/quality standards.
- Relative ease of contacting the desired person (this does not mean it is easy!).

However, we know that response rates are falling, and we also know that the reputation of telephone inbound calls is not always helpful and that many people find it hard to understand the distinctions between a research and a sales call. Telephone research will continue, and though there are increasing pressures on the timescales and costs (it is in danger of becoming a commodity purchase, which it is not), this method will be a staple for some time yet. This equally applies to qualitative research, where telephone depth interviewing continues to be a fairly popular approach. The downsides here are in terms of the relatively limited duration given to an interview, and while it is possible to engage the respondent for 30–60 minutes, it is extremely hard work on both parties, and a much more likely time duration is 20–30 minutes, hardly much of an in-depth interview, and one which is entirely devoid of any clues or feedback from non-verbal sources.

For those who are sceptical about the contribution of Non Verbal Communications, consider the parallel of telephone and face to face selling, and imagine the differences in sales style and subject matter when using the two approaches. A good salesperson can indeed sell in any medium, but typically major sales are made face-to-face, and tele-sales seeks multiple, smaller sales, using a scripted approach. This is equally true of telephone research, thus it can work acceptably well where a dispersed/hard to get at target group is concerned or where costs prohibit face-to-face, or where the information sought is simple/factual, but whenever the stakes are higher, a face-to-face route is to be advised.

Face-to-face

Though more expensive and time consuming, and often involving an incentive payment, face-to-face interviews, frequently qualitative in nature, are an essential tool for B2B research. They allow the greatest opportunity of achieving an in-depth interview understanding, and require a much more extensive knowledge of interviewing skills, techniques and people communications.

Analysis or Reportage: to Count or to Understand

The commissioning client should be aware of the requirements from the supplier/agency for the eB2B research. Is it for a simpler version: the "report" of what was found, factual with summaries, or for the "analysis and interpretation", as in what actually does it mean to the company? The requirements are not only a necessary precursor to commissioning the research, but are also essential in the selection of an agency supplier. It will also have a significant influence on costs, as the ability and experience to perform analysis and interpretation tasks are clearly more expensive than simpler reporting. It is also an issue that will impact the client researcher, as in absence of an interpretive report, this task will fall in-house, on someone.

DO'S AND DON'TS

There are a number of basic do's and don'ts!

Follow these!

Don'ts

1. Ask for proposals, but do not commission.
2. Ask for the universe on Friday afternoon.
3. Ask more than 3–5 agencies.
4. Ask for the universe but be unable to pay.

Do's

1. Tell all agencies the truth.
2. Give budget guidelines.
3. Know/agree the objectives before the start.

Now what is it I want? A client rang and asked for some Customer Satisfaction research among Financial Intermediaries. He had no objectives, no preferred target groups, no timescales, no budget indicators and indeed wanted the agency to offer a complete plan in a vacuum, with no clues at all.

The agency that won the work proposed . . . a cheaper budget! Hardly the mark of a professional – or indeed, ethical – Client researcher.

RESEARCHING B2B MARKETS – FUTURE CHALLENGES

Time Famine

Fewer people, doing more jobs, and with more and more requests for research interviews. A scenario likely to get more extreme in the future, and one that is already very familiar to many B2B researchers.

The reality of a "leaner, meaner" staffing policy, with fewer layers of management, and a greater use of non-personal communications, poses a real challenge to the research community in terms of securing time and commitment for a B2B face-to-face interview. Recent work within the research community has shown us the worrying trends in response rates, and time famine will not assist in securing a slice of an increasingly scarce resource – respondents.

The problem of getting into a respondent's diary at all, and then getting appropriate time for the interview, will be increasingly difficult. This places emphasis on time-beneficial approaches (online, telephone) but equally these are not always satisfactory for the objectives, and have severe limitations for what can be achieved.

What will it be? Shortfall in data or greater costs of project?

Client Profile and Needs

There is anecdotal evidence that the research buyer is, within the B2B context, increasingly a non-researcher, and this will undoubtedly have an influence on the relationship between, and requirements of, both sides. It is also apparent that with the prevalence of new trading formats (increasing outsourcing, part-time, freelance and contract employment) that the nature of the commissioner-supplier-respondent-user continuum will be altered.

Researchers will need to be alert to this. It means that B2B research commissioners will either have to rely more on the advice of trusted partners or get onto a very steep learning curve. Or be disappointed, more often.

There is NO SUCH THING as good, cheap research. Have one or the other. By all means have low cost research, but do not expect it to be full and true. Something has to give. Maybe it's the experience of the researcher who does the work. Maybe it's the amount of analysis time. Maybe it's the incentive payments for respondents (that ensures a realistic and representative profile is achieved). But somewhere, someone has reduced the input to make a project cheap.

Do you really want to take the risk?

Travel

The costs and time usage of travel are an increasingly tough part of a B2B qualitative research project, clearly even more so with an international project, but bad enough with a single country one. Congestion, delays and cancellations and closures make scheduling and completing the research driven travel a problem, and there may well be a drive for non-face-to-face interviews, or briefing and debriefing meetings, using videoconference style tools. This will place on a different footing the nature and exchange of qualitative research, and must be resisted as much as possible.

This also raises the question of risk territories. With B2B research increasingly global in nature. And with many war or terrorist zones present, the risks to personnel increases. As do costs.

Role of Incentives: Over Researched Targets – What's in it for Them?

Notwithstanding the respondent or client company views regarding payments to respondents individually, the true cost of a respondent's time will at some point have to be taken into account. This is particularly important where senior level, and thus higher cost, individuals are concerned, and the basis of engaging their interest, as a basis for interview may not hold up as the commercial and time pressures mount up.

Take the true cost of one hour's interview with the Manufacturing Director of a multi-national. Assuming the salary is £70,000, and that the hourly charge-out rate is around £100–£125. The true cost to the respondent company of the hour's interview is closer to £150+, taking account of disruption of other people, and meeting-scheduling. What would happen to the cost of the interview were these costs to be reflected in the incentive payment? It may well be that in the future, to achieve the target respondent sought, the incentive becomes part payment, to cover the true cost of time, but with additional information supplied, in the form of Summary reports. This does occur at the moment, but the likelihood of this basis becoming more common is high and with the increase in importance of a Knowledge Management approach, it is not hard to see respondent companies becoming more demanding with their requirements for more detailed information exchanges.

New Targets: Future Employment Models – Whom to Interview, Where and When?

Outsourcing, contract or part-time employment are all offered as the way forward in the future, and if this is to be the case research may have to take account of an acceleration in what is already seen, that is a shorter term, and less defined target group for interview, and a less homogeneous one, too. Researchers may end up interviewing three or more different companies to obtain responses essentially from one enterprise.

Imagine a target respondent company. It has three contract suppliers for call centre, manufacturing and distribution, but has a design marketing and admin function of its own.

For a customer satisfaction or corporate image survey, who is to be targeted for interview? What does this do to the analysis framework?

Clearly many issues are involved here, and no one solution or approach will satisfy every situation, but this does give real food for thought for the qualitative B2B researcher.

So too for the research supplier. Increasingly, time and cost are the de facto criteria for awarding research project contracts, not craft skills and knowledge. If speed and costs are so important, how long before research suppliers must charge for their preparatory work (i.e. preparing proposals that are subsequently unsuccessful)?

It is for the commissioners of research to weigh their short term gains against longer term loss of relationship, and find a much more hard-nosed time vs. cost equation used against

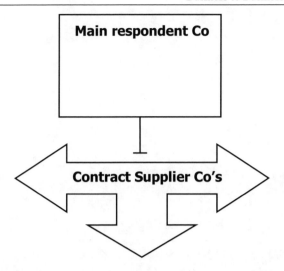

Figure 11.2

them, just as they would/do to their customer base. Imagine for a moment the implications for a research project undertaken on the same basis as their legal advisors. "Sorry, the project was harder/took longer than we planned. The bill is therefore 50 % bigger than we thought."

Or, "Due to increases in fieldwork rates, the final bill shows an increase of 20 %": just as Energy suppliers across Europe (and elsewhere) are currently doing to their B2B customers.

Now that would be interesting!

FURTHER READING

Zaltman, G. (2003) *How Customers Think*. Harvard Business School Press.
Smith, D.V.L. and Fletcher, J.H. (2001) *Inside Information*. John Wiley & Sons, Ltd.
Bandler, Grindler (1990) *Frogs into Princes*. Eden Grove Editions.

12
Research in Specific Domains: Healthcare; Automotives and Telecom

Dirk Huisman

INTRODUCTION

The healthcare, automotives and telecom domains have in common that fundamental changes in the industries are primarily technology driven and consumers can be intensely involved in the usage or choice of the products. A common characteristic for these domains is that technology related decisions condition a company's room to manoeuvre and its commercial limitations and opportunities for many years. Consequently in these domains decision makers often have a long term perspective.

The fact that the usage of the products in these domains impacts and re-shapes the daily lives of the users and the intense and often emotional involvement of the user makes in-depth consumer understanding in these domains imperative in order to transform technology into appealing solutions and products. This means that in these organisations often there is a wealth of insights and consumer understanding. However compared to the mainstream market research industries these insights are embedded in a domain specific frame of reference. To provide new insights one has to know and understand these frames of reference.

In these technology driven domains long term commercial success[1] and a high and consistent ROI are on the one hand based on break through innovations and on the other hand on the implementation of the consumer insights. Although the domains are technology driven the leading companies in these industries spend more on marketing than on R&D.[2]

What does it mean for research in these domains?

The technological/clinical focus and the academic background of these domains and the complexity of products, in particular in healthcare, provide a fertile ground for more advanced and complex types of market research.

DOMAIN: HEALTHCARE

Introduction to the Healthcare Domain

In 2002 in the 30 OECD countries on average 8.5 % of the Gross Domestic Product was spent on Healthcare.[3] The difference between the countries is big. The USA being on top

---

[1] Lieshout, K. and Huisman, D. QFD Integrating Technique and customer orientation, Esomar seminar BtoB marketing: Re-engineering of traditional market research seminar, London, 1994.

[2] Manchanda P. et al (2005) Understanding Firm, Physician and Consumer Choice behavior in the Pharmaceutical industry. *Marketing Letters* 16:3/4; Springer Science and Business media.

[3] OECD Health Report 2004.

Market Research Handbook, 5th Edition. Edited by M. van Hamersveld and C. de Bont.
© 2007 John Wiley & Sons, Ltd.

with 14.6 % of the GDP compared to the bottom countries Mexico and Turkey with 1.5 % of the GDP. The costs for healthcare are rising faster than in any other domain. In 2004 in the USA only the total expenditures had grown to $ 1.9 trillion which equals 16 % of GDP. Of these huge expenditures in the US 11 % is spend on pharmaceuticals, but this percentage varies by country: in countries like the UK and Germany this percentage is lower, 9–10 %, and for the 30 OECD countries the expenditures on pharmaceuticals vary between 9 and 39 % of the total healthcare expenditures. In order to counter and control the increasing expenditures on healthcare the cost control is moving from public organisations to private organisations (private hospitals, private insurance, etc.). Currently in the USA 45 % is spent by public organizations and 55 % by private organisations and the move to private is impacting the market and the choice processes.

Concentrating on healthcare as a research domain we have to realise that by far most market research is contracted or spent by the pharmaceutical industry and the related industries (medical devices and equipments industries and the biotech industries). In line with the privatisation one can see that research initiated by private healthcare organisations (hospitals, health insurers) is on the rise, but still it is only a fraction of the research initiated by the pharmaceutical industries. Apart from that it is the type of research (patient satisfaction, optimising health schemes) which is less domain-specific.

The ESOMAR industry report[4] indicates that 24 % of the global research expenditures by manufacturers is spent in pharmaceutical and related industries. But the healthcare domain is wider than manufacturers only. Based on available turnover data and industry feed back we estimate that 3 billion Euro, or 16.3 % of the total global market research expenditure, is spent on healthcare market research.[5] Comparing the 16.3 % share of healthcare in the global research expenditures with the average 8.5 % healthcare share of GDP we see that the healthcare domain is very research prone. This sensitivity to market research is even more striking when we realise that the research dollars are mainly spent by the pharmaceutical and related industries that are responsible for only 11 % of the total healthcare costs. The high research spending is explained by the high risk–high revenue character of the pharmaceutical industry. According to IMS Health[6] only 1 out of 10 000 compounds are a success, the development costs of a successful drug are greater than $ 800 million, with an average development cycle of 12 years and a limited (8–10 year) patent protection and related capitalisation period. According to the US Government Accountability Office the R&D spending by pharmaceutical companies has been increasing from 1993 to 2004 by 147 % to $60 billion per year. The new drug filing grew over the same period of time by only 38 %. The difference underlines the opinion of the PhRMA that "developing new drugs has become more challenging, risky and expensive than ever before".[7] Market research is spent to reduce these risks (identify and track the potential for new drugs and define benchmarks resulting in clinical end points during the development phase); maximise the chance on high revenues after launch and help to extend the product lifecycle.

---

[4] ESOMAR Industry report: Global Market Research 2005, Amsterdam 2006.

[5] The third largest global research organisation (IMS) concentrates only on healthcare and represents 12 % of the global research revenues of the top 25 global research agencies. The large pharmaceutical spend is 40–50 % of their budget on continuous research (mainly IMS). The 25 global research companies represent two-thirds of total global market for market research.

[6] Manchanda, P, et al, op cit.

[7] Pharmeceutical Research and Manufacturers of America, PhRMA statement on GOA report, www.pharma.org/new_room/press releases.

Market Research in the Healthcare Domain

In the healthcare domain the researchers in pharmaceutical industry are well organised[8] and have created the right conditions to compare results. Virtually all pharmaceutical products are grouped into categories according to the Anatomical Classification System. This system has been harmonised by the WHO (World Health Organisation) to meet the needs of the WHO. Today virtually all audits, sales, medical and promotions around the world are based on this system. This means that most research data is comparable and can be benchmarked or validated across the world.

Bearing in mind the high risk–high revenue character of the pharmaceutical industry and the main reasons to conduct market research the product life cycle concept is very important in the healthcare domain and most research is product life stage specific. It is of particular relevance to understand the various pre-launch phases, because a significant and most essential part of research is conducted before a drug is launched. After testing in computer models and animals the following phases are defined[9]:

- Phase 1: the first exercise is to test a drug on human subjects, normally volunteers to test safety as well as the tolerable dose-range and regimen.
- Phase 2a: pilot clinical trials intended to test the efficacy and safety in selected human groups with the index disease
- Phase 2B: rigorously designed well-controlled trials to evaluate efficacy and safety. It is the most valid evidence of clinical efficacy of a new drug
- Phase 3a: studies in large number of patients in order to generate further evidence of efficacy and safety under controlled and uncontrolled conditions as well as in special patient groups (e.g. those with renal insufficiency or liver dysfunction). This takes place before the submission of the New Drug Application (NDA) to the regulatory authorities to register a new drug.
- Phase 3b: a trial initiated after the submission of an NDA, but before approval in order to substantiate efficacy based on other end-points such as subjective sense of improvement, quality of life and resource utilisation.
- Phase 4: sometimes referred to as post marketing or post launch surveillance studies, these are designed to provide additional information on the safety and efficacy profile of the drug in the real world.

Market research starts in phase 1 to establish possible opportunities for the compound in development. End of phase 2 and during phase 3 the critical market research studies in customer needs, treatment algorithms, attitudes, market potential, segmentation and product profile sensitivities are initiated. Often these studies are initiated twice: first to investigate the area. The role of these investigative studies is twofold. In this phase the results are used to identify the potential for the new compound. The potential varies with the possible product specifications. In order to feed go/no go decisions the potential is estimated for the alternative product specifications that might be the outcome of the clinical trials. Research is used to set benchmarks or the clinical end points that the trial results should meet. The second role of the investigative research is to underpin pre-launch marketing activities. Clinical trial results are published and

---

[8] In the USA the industry researchers are organised in the Pharmaceutical Business Intelligence & Research Group; in Europe in the European Pharmaceutical Marketing Research Association. The European based pharmaceutical companies collaborated in 1968 to create a classification scheme.

[9] EphMRA: *Research Through the Product Life Cycle*, 3rd edn and EphMRA: *Lexicon, a Pocket Guide to Pharmaceutical Marketing and Marketing Research Terms and Definitions*, 5th edn.

help to create the frame of reference of the new drug in development. Positioning the new drug starts with the publications about the clinical trials and in particular the clinical trial results. It is important to tune the communication about the trials to the improvements and the parameters the physicians are looking for or sensitive to. When the compound passes the test in phase 2b the investigative studies are repeated, fine tuned and extended in order to define the positioning, the product profile and product claims and the segmentation.

Other pre-launch studies consider trade mark and brand name research, packaging and handling studies. End of phase 3 the tactical studies: communication, detail aid testing, sales force focusing and tracking research are initiated.

When designing, interpreting and comparing studies in the pre-launch and post-launch phases one has to realise that context differences condition expectations and reactions from physicians as well as from decision makers:

- In the pre-launch phases the product is a "virtual" product, often a dream product and expectations are high. For the physicians the product is virtual and still a promise, but they want to know the unknown clinical details and consequently they react much more sceptically. In this phase it is critical to map in detail the current treatment algorithms and practices. This means mapping the consecutive decisions for the different patient types and conditions and identifying in each step what are the drivers and barriers of the choices made by the physician. The drivers and barriers of choice are related to the various product performance characteristics: what types and levels of improvements is the physician aiming for. Knowing the impact of all product characteristics on the choices made it is possible to simulate the choices made and predict the impact the product in development may have at the alternative product profile definitions. Choice based conjoint analysis is the most often used methodology to measure sensitivities and build the simulations models. The simulation models have to be flexible because one wants to simulate alternative product definitions, and one has to be able to include other new competitor products as well. Besides one has to realise that in the pre-launch phase one predicts and forecast the product potential in the maturity phase, 6–8 years later.

  Apart from the conjoint analysis studies in the pre-launch phase the studies are often qualitative in nature. Qualitative research in healthcare differs from qualitative research in other domains because understanding why physicians make certain choices requires that the researcher understands the clinical arguments. Typical for the pre-launch phase is that the products are evaluated based on "facts" provided and rational benefits offered: what are the efficacy data; what are the side effects; for which patients, etc? This clinical mind set reflects the initial phase when the new drug is introduced. When a product is introduced the physician reacts primarily to the clinical facts and not (yet) to the brand promises.

- In the post launch phase the physicians react based on their experiences, habits and emotions and they are far less sensitive to the "clinical facts" provided by the pharmaceutical companies. If for instance a physician had a very bad experience, which really struck him emotionally the perception of anything said about the drug will be based on that traumatic experience. If on the other hand the experiences are positive the physician will prescribe the product because (s)he can rely on it, the promise is proven. The nature of the marketing initiatives is changing. The focus is now on reinforcing the promise, stimulating loyalty and extending the use of the product by introducing new adjoining indication areas and introducing new modes of administration. The focus of the market research studies is changing as well. It is much more tracking and communication focused. Throughout the life cycle of a

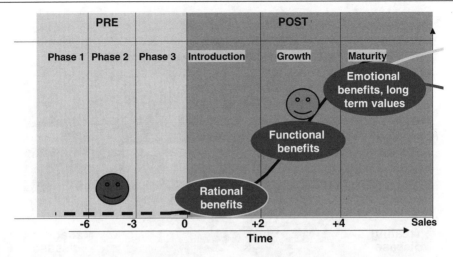

Figure 12.1   The changing marketing and research context of a drug throughout the lifecycle
Note: In the pre-launch phase expectations are high; communication mainly regards the clinical facts and one has to predict potential in the maturity phase 8 years later. In the post launch phase the dream is replaced by reality and by the physicians' own experiences. Marketing and communication is moving from the clinical facts to the brand promise.

drug the benefits looked for and the related communication and marketing initiatives evolve from being focused on the rational facts and benefits to the functional benefits and finally to the emotional relation between the physician and the product.

Complexity of the Healthcare Domain

The healthcare domain is not homogeneous at all. From a marketing perspective, a health economics perspective and a consumer need perspective the domain can be mapped along two dimensions[10] the *"illness-wellness"* dimension and the *"acute-chronic"* dimension, resulting in four smaller domains for which the business context and the consumer needs are completely different.

In the two wellness domains choices are mainly made by consumers/patients and marketing is more like consumer package goods/fast moving consumer goods marketing. The large multinationals, particularly those rooted in the food and beverages industries, are becoming more and more active in these domains, because a health related claim adds value and differentiates products and as such are enabling higher margins. For the pharmaceutical companies the wellness domain offers opportunities, but mainly threats. The threats are based on the fact that the business model, the critical success factors and the risks are different from the pharmaceutical markets. The opportunities are based on the fact that pharmaceutical companies are R&D driven and consequently generate a lot of new insights and innovations, which sometimes can be better capitalised outside the clinical environment.

An important difference between the wellness related domain and illness related domain is that the product claims in the illness related domain have to be substantiated and proven in

---

[10] Simon, F., 'Redefining healthcare", key note speech presented at Esomars' Global Health Conference, Miami 2002.

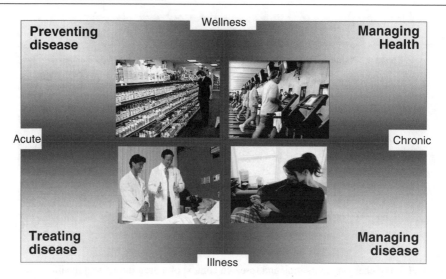

Figure 12.2   Mapping the Healthcare domain along the two consumer needs related dimensions

clinical trials. In the wellness related domain the justification of a claim is far less rigid and more marketing based. The consequences of the strict requirements in the illness domain are that before approving a new drug the investments and time needed before launch are huge compared to the wellness domain. As specified before the development costs involved in a successfully developed new drug are more than € 500 million. Another important differentiator between the wellness related domain and the illness related domain is the key role of healthcare professionals in the decision making process. It is in particular the clinical context which makes healthcare marketing and healthcare market research a specialty, because the clinical context adds a dominant extra layer to the required insights. To successfully launch or market a (new) drug you have to understand medicine, the treatment options and the treatment algorithms.

The relevance of the acute-chronic dimension, particularly in the illness domains, is based on the difference in clinical context and perspective. In the treatment domain the healthcare focus is on intervention and decision making in order to solve an issue. With the correct diagnosis and correct decisions the healthcare professional can have a direct and significant impact on cost (savings) and quality of life creation. In the treatment phase the potential of a medication to create value is highest, which is why healthcare marketing and healthcare marketing research is concentrated on the treating domain. Another reason to focus on the treating domain is that treatment decisions and choices made in the treating domain have a huge impact on product usage and the choices made in the managing disease domain.

An example of the impact of the treatment choices in the acute phase on chronic prescription can be found in the treatment of schizophrenic patients. In schizophrenia patients suffer from positive symptoms like hallucinations, hearing voices and other stimulations leading to psychoses: the schizophrenic patient loses control over her/himself, go out of her/his mind and can be very aggressive. In the acute phase the primary treatment objective is to tranquilise the patient and to get control back. Consequently efficacy of the medication on positive symptoms and the onset to action, or the time between administration and the first signs of the effect of the medication, is driving the choice for a medication. Apart from the positive symptoms the patient is also suffering from negative symptoms. Negative symptoms are, amongst others, withdrawal, social isolation, feeling depressed. These negative symptoms are in the chronic phase or maintenance phase as important if not more important than the positive symptoms, because they have a significant impact on the patient's quality of life. Research among patients and among psychiatrists has shown that in the maintenance phase the patients have learned to cope with the positive symptoms but not with the negative symptoms. Consequently one would expect that in the maintenance phase medications that are more effective on negative symptoms or, which have fewer side effects (negative impact on quality of life) would be chosen. Analyses of treatment patterns over time as well as analyses of the sensitivities for product features show that the sensitivity for product features in the acute phase still dominate the product choice. In other words in order to be prescribed new medications, which might be more effective on negative symptoms or which might have fewer side effects, must perform in the acute phase as well as the current treatments. The importance of the focus of marketing and market research on the acute phase becomes even more evident when we realise that a significant proportion of the medications prescribed in the maintenance phase result from choices made in the acute phase.

The technique used to measure the feature sensitivity for different patients in different phases is choice based conjoint analysis. To measure the sensitivities to product features the physician is asked to choose one out of four different medications for a specific patient, which are defined as a combination of product features (efficacy scores and side effect scores). Analysing the choices made by all physicians for each patient reveals which features and feature specifications are driving the choices of the physicians in case of each of the patients.

In the managing disease domain cure or intervention is less of an issue. Managing disease often means chronic product usage and helping patients to live a normal life. Because managing disease is often a long term process the healthcare professionals are still involved to monitor progress and sometimes to take a decision to adapt medication. Consequently the healthcare professional is still the primary marketing target, but in the managing disease domain the role of the patient in the decision making process is becoming more important. First in the mind of the physician, who is more inclined to consider other than pure clinical criteria (like convenience) or who is focusing more on the impact of decisions on the patients "daily" quality of life. Apart from the other focus from the physician the patient is also more actively involved in the decision making: as influencer providing feedback or asking questions; or as initiator suggesting alternatives for treatment; or as co-payer. Consequently the marketing initiatives from the pharmaceutical industries in managing the disease domain are also more patient focused. However the room for direct to consumer (dtc) marketing differs by country. In the USA dtc advertising is allowed, in most European countries not, which does not mean there is no room for dtc marketing. Via the Internet, public relations and information brochures about diseases or products it is very possible to communicate with the consumer and to try to build a relationship.

Although the treating disease domain is of vital importance for the pharmaceutical industries in order to get (new) products accepted and prescribed, the managing disease domain is of vital importance to capitalise the investments in new products. In the managing disease phase repeat prescription or repeat buying generates the cash flow needed. The importance of repeat prescription explains why in healthcare almost 50 % of the market research expenditures are spent on tracking prescriptions and tracking the perception of and attitude towards specific brands. It also explains why in the healthcare domain so much attention and money is paid to life cycle management and extending the prescription of a patented drug.

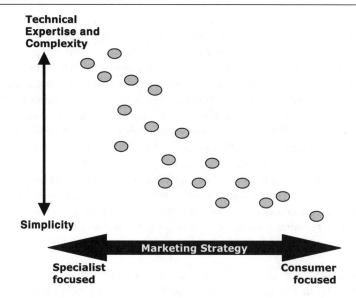

Figure 12.3   The product markets in the healthcare domain can be mapped along two dimensions: A, The complexity and technical expertise needed when using/prescribing the product and B, the focus of the marketing strategy

Apart from mapping the healthcare domain in four sub domains we can map the different product markets or indication markets along two dimensions: A. The complexity and technical expertise needed when using/prescribing the product B the focus of the marketing strategy.

Examples of products requiring a lot of technical expertise or treatments that are complex are transplantation related products. In these product markets the marketing efforts are mainly aimed at the transplantation specialists, which conditions the marketing activities and marketing communication. Products that are relatively simple to prescribe/use and where marketing is much more consumer focused are, for instance, in the erectile dysfunction indication area and the female contraceptive area. In these markets the marketing effort is spread over the physicians and consumers. Pain-relief products or markets have become completely consumer focused and as a result these products moved from prescription drugs to over the counter products.

Comparison of the various product markets over time shows that there is a clear trend towards more consumer focused marketing strategies. The component of consumer aimed communication is becoming more important and also in healthcare market research one can see that the consumers/patients are more often invited to participate in a survey and they are becoming important as respondents.

The complexity of market research in the healthcare domain is the consequence of the heterogeneity in healthcare markets and the consequence of the extra layer of the clinical insight needed. The third and most likely the most complicating phenomenon is the multi layered and diffuse character of decision making in the healthcare domain.

On top of the pyramid of decision layers are the national or regional healthcare policy organisations like the Federal Drug Administration (FDA), the National Institute for Clinical Evidence (Nice) and the Ministry of Health. These policy makers accept and condition the use of medications. Payers are sometimes part of the national healthcare policy makers, but nowadays payers are more often independent institutes or insurance companies. Also the payers

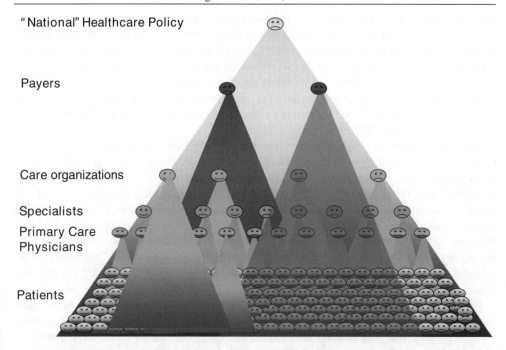

"National" Healthcare Policy

Payers

Care organizations

Specialists

Primary Care
Physicians

Patients

...The "market" is the result of decisions by different players at various layers ....

Figure 12.4   Decisions in the healthcare domains
Note: These are influenced by many "players" in the industry who are acting at different layers. A decision higher up in the pyramid might condition the choices made or the decisions, which could be made by a number of players lower in the pyramid.

decide whether or not a medication is included in the formulary and whether or not it will be reimbursed. Also, hospitals and care organisations decide if and how far new drugs are accepted and included on the formulary. Depending on the indication and the country new medications are first discussed and initially prescribed by the specialists and later prescribed (follow up prescription) by the primary care physicians, but in some indication areas the primary care physician takes the initiative her/himself as well. At the bottom are the patients who in the Internet era are sometimes quite well informed and ask for a specific medication. All the players in the various layers interact with each other and influence each other. When marketing drugs or when conducting market research in the healthcare domain one should bear in mind that the study results can always be changed due to the "external effects" or the players who were not included in the survey (the ceteris paribus clause).

AUTOMOTIVES DOMAIN

The automotive industries are responsible for 10 % of the global market research expenditures by manufacturers, compared to 24 % which is spent by the pharmaceutical industries. This partly reflects the fact that the automotive industry is smaller than the healthcare industry. But the market research intensity in the automotive industries is less as well. The lower research intensity is connected with a number of product and market characteristics. The automotive market is a saturated market compared to a growing healthcare market. Another difference which is related to the structure of the industry regards the concentration and consolidation of the automotive industries. The global automotives market is dominated by less than 10 conglomerates. Another important difference is that an innovation in the automotive industries is not introduced as a new product, but as one of the many *components* of existing products, which are renewed, re-launched or launched as a new concept.

Although the automotive industries have the long term perspective and the innovative focus in common with the healthcare industries the context in which to design and conduct market research is completely different.

The conglomerates in automotives are extremely secretive and competitive, but on the other hand they are cooperating actively in collecting market data. Consequently there is a wealth of up to date insights about the historic development of the market and the market segments (tracking data). These historic trends are combined with future focused cultural, social and psychological trend-analyses. The framework (structure, segmentation and development of the market) within which the main marketing decisions are taken is updated continuously, but it also functions as a corset that conditions the information and answers looked for and limits receptivity for new solutions and insights. Apart from the tracking studies, the brand image research and the feature sensitivity studies, most research conducted is model specific: car clinics and positioning research.

In line with the consolidation and the market saturation the corporate culture in the automotive industries is quite conservative and inflexible. At the same time there is an enormous technology push resulting in many innovations and many decisions when, how and whether or not to integrate the innovations. At the demand side there is a very strong consumer involvement, which is loaded with emotions. Managing these emotions is essential in order to create a strong and long lasting profitable relationship with the customer. The complexity in the automotive industries is based on the fact that a car is a bundle of many innovative technical features in combination with the fact that consumer choices are individual specific and emotionally loaded. These two drivers make the industry dynamic and they have to be managed within the conservative corporate culture and within a saturated market.

Supporting Product Design and Product Development Decisions

The automotive industries have to deal continuously with questions like *which new technologies and innovation projects should be pushed; which features or feature packages will be driving the choice of the consumer in the future and will the consumers be willing to pay for these features?* The complexity in answering these questions is based on the large number of features the manufacturer as well as the consumer must deal with and on the fact that the features are new and unknown to the consumer.

Previous studies[11] show that the future importance of a new feature is a function of the current feature awareness; the estimated current value of the new feature and the benefit the consumer is associating with the feature. In order to become an appealing feature in the future the consumer should have already, in the current situation, assigned an above average value to that feature. That current value is often based on the benefit the consumer associates with the feature. And for certain benefits, e.g. safety, it is known that when the awareness of the related feature increases the value of that feature will increase as well. On the other hand it is also known that in case the current value of the future feature is low and the benefit association is

[11] Huisman, D. Simulate to create a winner, Esomar annual congress, Paris, 1999.

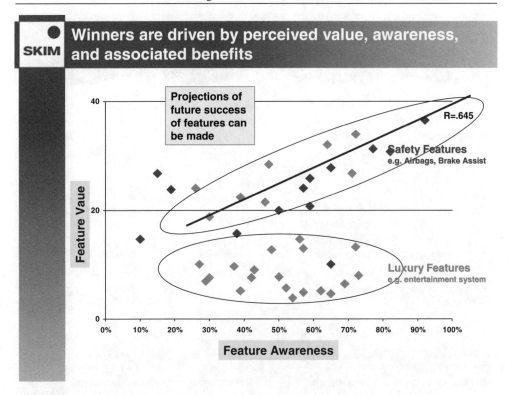

Figure 12.5 Relationship between the feature value of (future) features and the awareness of these features

Note: Only if current feature value is above a specific threshold, increasing the awareness will lead to a higher value. This relation is in particular strong when the feature is also associated with a choice driving benefit (e.g. safety).

with benefits that are not "driving" choice (in this case luxury) increasing awareness will not lead to a higher feature value.

When measuring future feature value one has to cope with the fact that new features are not always known. In the case of unknown features the features have to be described in simple terms specifying the function without specifying the technical details and without specifying the benefit for the consumer. The latter is of relevance because to identify the potential to increase in value the consumer has to specify the associated benefit him/herself.

Another issue specific for the automotive industries regards the large number of features to be taken into consideration and in addition to that the willingness to pay for the feature. A way to cope with the many features is to group them (i.e. engine related features in one group of features) and measure the feature value within that group. In a next step it is possible to measure the sensitivity of features across the group to make one file with all feature values. Feature value can be measured in various ways. Choice based conjoint analysis is the advisable technique if one is looking for the monetary value of the feature, but other techniques are applicable as well, like Max Diff analysis, ranking techniques and distributing points.

Features are part of different decision making processes. This is of relevance when measuring the feature value and the willingness to pay. For a number of features the consumer preference

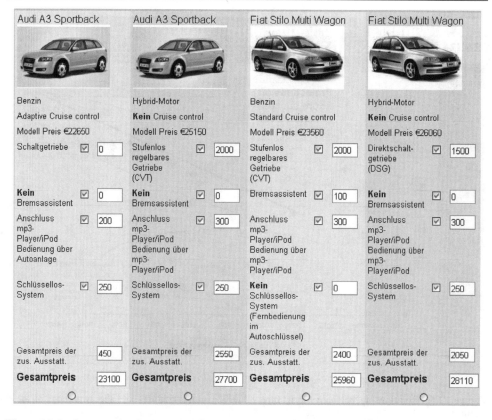

Figure 12.6   An example of a choice task in a build your own adaptive choice based feature value model. Consumer choose within their short list
Note: Within the short list they have the option to choose between two cars of their preferred models, with different standard specifications and they can optimise the chosen model.

is a conditioning element for the remaining choices made, like "I always drive diesel". That consumer does not trade off diesel against a lot of other features, but he/she is making the choice knowing he/she is buying a diesel. These conditioning elements should be considered when designing a study or should be included in the choice process. A technique which is becoming more popular when dealing with many features is the "build your own" approach. The consumer is able to create his/her ideal car and in the programme to build their own ideal car the exclusion rules (i.e. big engine not possible with best fuel economy) and the financial consequences are programmed so the consumer is forced to adapt his/her ideal to create his "feasible ideal" car. The appealing element of the "build your own" method is the involvement of the consumer, who likes the interaction and being taken seriously. Apart from the overview of preferences in the market in particular the insights into the lessons about the willingness to trade in preferred features are valuable. To learn something about the market one needs many respondents and in the analysis it is hard to identify the feature value for each individual. An elaboration of the build your own method is the adaptive choice based feature value modelling.[12] Out of a large list of features the consumer selects the ones he/she would

---

[12] Bannink, M. P.Im.P. my ride, the car buyers preference, Esomar Automotive Conference, Lausanne, 2006.

like. In addition he/she identifies the shortlist of preferred make-models he/she would take into consideration when choosing a new car. Within the shortlist of preferred models and preferred features he/she is asked to optimise the "model-feature package-price combination".

From the analysis of the choices made it is obvious that a choice for a car or a feature package is never just a matter of simply adding up preferences for features independently, but a complex interaction between price, features, competition and many other items. Consumers often adapt their choices and even switch models. One lesson is that consumers seem to be driven by the total price of the car. They select a feature as long as it fits in the total price of the model, irrelevant of the originally stated willingness to pay a certain amount for a feature. In addition the willingness to select a feature appears to be driven by the underlying benefit, which is consistent with the results of the future feature value studies.

Product Launch and Positioning Research

Most research in the automotive industries is organised around the (re)launch of new models. Very specific for the automotive industries are the car clinics. Car clinics are surveys to evaluate new models amidst their direct competitors. The conditions to show and evaluate the models are very strict (placing, lighting, order) and the sample criteria are also very detailed and strict. The learnings from the car clinics are very detailed and model specific and they are used to position the model; to identify the perceived strengths and weaknesses according to the various target groups and to identify the drivers of the perception. The drivers include the total impression from the model, which differs from the side view, front view or rear view and often the drivers can be small details, the rear light; the cockpit; the seat, etc.

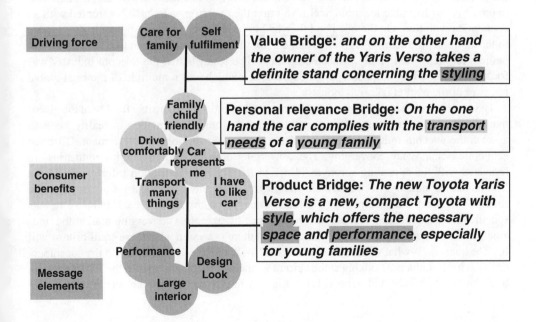

Figure 12.7   Example of a positioning study linking differentiating car elements to the underlying drivers of choice
From Paresi, F. and Ramackers, L., op cit.

These model related drivers of the perception are important just like the car features are important, but they are only the triggers that are processed in the mind of the car buyer. When positioning the model these triggers are used to link the differentiating model elements to benefits and emotions that are rooted in the mind of the consumer. The binding relationship between the car and the car buyer is emotional. When positioning a new model the aim is to intrigue; take advantage of the differentiating elements and strengthen the emotional relationship with the model. This approach is based on the means-end relation theory and the research technique used to identify the link between the differentiating car element and the benefits and the emotional drivers is laddering.[13] During the interview the positive drivers differentiating the new model are identified for each individual. The car buyer is asked to state why these preferred car elements are important for him, in addition he has to state why these specified benefits (of the preferred elements) are important or of relevance to him. The aim is to bridge the car features to benefits, situations and emotions that are important to the individual car buyer. This information is used to position the new model. Positioning implies identifying targets for the new model, identifying how to differentiate the model; which elements of the new model to stress; identifying how to link these elements to benefits and drivers of choice and how to execute this.

TELECOM DOMAIN

The telecom domain is special, because it was clearly a technology driven industry, which has been taken by surprise by technological innovations it did not foresee. Traditionally telecom operators existed in a protected market, enabling them to capitalise their huge investments in infrastructure and technology. However their analogue technology became obsolete when the telecom industry was digitalised, with the introduction of Internet, VoIP and mobile telephony.[14] Apart from the technological revolution the operators were also confronted with an economic revolution. On the one hand they had to bid billions of Euro on licences to operate in the new and promising UMTS environment, on the other hand they had to accept new competitors on their traditionally protected markets. The result is that the telecom industry was forced to write off an amount as extra depreciation which was a multiple of the total global turnover of the market research industry.

The survivors in the telecom industry are recovering and are responsible for 7 % of the global market research expenditures. However this figure is a misrepresentation of reality, because as such the telecom industry does not exist any more, as an independent domain. Different economic domains are converging. The converging domains and converging industries are indicated with the appealing acronym TIME, or the Telecommunication Information Media Entertainment industry. In this domain the players from the four industries are at the same time co-operating and competing with each other. Each market and each industry has its specific rules, specific key success factors and specific pace. In a converging market the rules amalgamate and new equilibriums will result, but there is no sign what these equilibriums will be. The question is what will be driving success? Will it be the connection with the consumers or will it be the content? Looking at the current winners or success-stories in the TIME domain, like Google, You Tube and Second Life, it is puzzling to see that the consumers don't have

---

[13] Paresi, F. and Rameckers, L. Emotional information in strategic decisions, Esomar Automotive Conference, 1998.

[14] Emmerson, R.D., Parsons, S. and Rutkowski, R. Voice over Internet Protocol (VoIP), Impacts on communications carriers and consumers, Esomar Telecommunications Berlin, 2000.

to pay for services and "the winners" have others to pay for their investments, it seems all virtual.[15]

What is the Role of Market Research in a Domain in Turmoil?

It is obvious that the role of market research during the decline of the industry was marginalised, creating room for suppliers of syndicated research. As the business model is changing dramatically, without a clear indication what the model will be there is a strong need for research providing insight into what propositions will generate revenue. In order to answer this question it is crucial to identify what propositions will generate value to the consumer and which elements in these propositions are driving choice. Knowing which elements of the propositions generate value the operators can identify whether or not their cost structure and technology enables them to push the value generating proposition. This approach (multi layered discrete choice modelling) resembles the techniques used in the automotive industry to identify feature value and it is proving to be very successful.[16] However the TIME markets are very volatile and in general the effect of offering winning propositions does not last long as they are copied by competition. This means that in the TIME industries there is a constant need to create and adapt winning propositions. The frequency of change requires that there is a constant evaluation of what elements generate consumer value. This data is uploaded in simulation models used to predict consumer reactions under various conditions and under various competitive reactions. It looks almost like playing war games. Because in the TIME industry there are no dominant suppliers of panel data, like Nielsen in the fast moving consumer goods industry and IMS in the healthcare industry there is no consumer based insight into the development of the markets. Therefore internal sales and traffic data is used to validate the simulation results. This is one of the reasons underlying the increasing demand for database analyses and for the merger of secondary (internal) and primary research data in the TIME industries.

In the TIME industries more future focused studies are revitalised as well. To understand the consumer we need to observe consumers in their daily life, to identify how they act and what is really driving them. The observer should be completely open minded and while observing should not try to categorise or qualify what (s)he is observing.[17] A traditional anthropological methodology "participative observation" is suitable to identify consumer needs and consumer behaviour. The lessons from these studies provide in depth insights into what people need and what is driving people.[18] It provides a relevant framework for the development of new products and services and that is what is required in an industry in turmoil.

---

[15] Jenzovsky, S. Examples presented during the Esomar Telecom Conference Consumers in the converged world, Barcelona, 2006.

[16] Warnecke, et al.: Pushing the right buttons, Esomar Telecom Conference Consumers in the converged world, Barcelona, 2006.

[17] Kirah, A. Key note Esomar Telecom Conference Consumers in the converged world, Barcelona, 2006.

[18] Öhrfelt, F. et. al: Converging Technology, Diverging Families, Esomar Telecom Conference Consumers in the converged world, Barcelona, 2006.

13

Youth Research

Joël-Yves Le Bigot, Catherine Lott-Vernet and Piyul Mukherjee

I prefer the dreams of the future to the history of the past

Thomas Jefferson

WHAT IS YOUTH ALL ABOUT?

In many markets, not just for toys or food and drinks as in the former times, but also for entertainment, clothes, cosmetics, even cars, banking, travel – young people can be "deciders" (what they buy with their own money) or "influencers" of purchases or selection of brands (their prescription power, what they ask for).

The "youth market" is huge and fast-growing; "Kids and teens are now the epicenter of American consumer culture. Their tastes drive market trends and their attitudes shape brand strategies" (Juliet B. Schor).[1] They command the attention, creativity and money of advertisers. Billions of "marketing dollars" are directed towards children, teenagers and young adults; James McNeal, probably the best estimator of the size of the US children's market, has calculated that in 2004, total advertising and marketing expenditures directed at children reached $ 15 billion, a stunning rise from the mere $ 100 million spent on television advertising in 1983. The US child population – 12 and under – amounts to 52 million.

Manufacturers are advertising because young people are buying. New marketing concepts have appeared: "skippies" (school children with purchasing power), "six pocket children" (getting money from the two parents as well as their four grandparents)... Children's purchasing power has risen rapidly. McNeal reports that children aged 4 to 12 made $ 6.1 billion in purchases in 1989, $ 23.4 billion in 1997 and $ 30 billion in 2002, representing an increase of 400 % in less than 15 years. Teenagers spend even more; they account for $ 170 billion of personal spending in 2002, i.e. a weekly average of $ 101 per person. The teen market is crucial because the children's market tracks it. Trends and styles are migrating quickly from adolescence to kids. Young people are becoming shoppers at an earlier stage; first with parents and later going solo or with friends. The world's first mall catering exclusively to children opened in Alpharetta, Georgia in 1996. It has been enormously successful and "kids' villages" are opening around the USA. One single country accounts for nearly one fifth (18.7 % precisely) of the world youth population. India is a very young country with 350 million under the age of 15 and 220 million in the 15–24 age group.

---

[1] *Born To Buy*, New York: Scribners, 2004.

Market Research Handbook, 5th Edition. Edited by M. van Hamersveld and C. de Bont.
© 2007 John Wiley & Sons, Ltd.

France is an exception in Europe concerning demography. Due to the high birth rate at present this country is the second most populated one out of "the 25" and will be first in 2020. Research conducted by Institut de l'Enfant in 1979, demonstrated that 43 % of the expenditures of a family with children were influenced by these boys and girls. This figure is now considered as a "reference" by business, media and politicians!

For the future, "kid-fluence" (Juliet B. Schor) implies all kinds of investigations and serious research on "the purchasing decision process". This is especially true because children, tweens, teens and even "adUlescents"/young adults are:

- more vulnerable than adults; less aware of economics;
- not financially independent; they usually do not spend money they have "earned".

In this context, the word "young" – whether applied to marketing, communication, research or management – should be applied to any person who is not yet an "autonomous adult" (from birth to 18 years old, and even in many countries up to 25 years old). Educational situations define the boundaries; babies before schooling, children through pre elementary and elementary schools, adolescents (or teenagers) during secondary education and adUlescents after.

STAKEHOLDERS

The growing "economic socialisation" of youth concerns six parties, with different interests and views.

The Youth Population

Everywhere in the world, specialists from different fields mention that "kids are getting older younger" and refer to that evolution as the "KAGOY phenomenon": young people are asking for more freedom and more power, earlier in life. There is nothing wrong about that since "youth" is the normal time for young people to be ambitious and to question, both their lives and the world around them.

Another evolution is taking place in many countries. Professional and social insertion is more difficult than it used to be: the young are becoming adolescents earlier BUT adults later. Such is the case in France, Southern Europe and even now in the USA ("boomerang kids").

Parents

They are unquestionably the prime educators of their children, specially mums! What the vast majority of them want for their kids is a better life than theirs and they are ready to do a great deal to make provision for a promising future. Sometimes they are not at ease with the pace of evolution and fear not being able to cope with possible setbacks.

They are quite often considered – wrongly according to us – as having a major responsibility for their children's quest for "more" (products) and "immediately" (instant satisfaction).

Teachers

In all countries, instruction is mandatory up to a specific age, depending on the level of development of the country (usually 16). Large amounts of money are allotted to this mission. The major part of this investment is devoted to the acquisition of basic academic skills (reading, counting, writing . . .) rather than evolutionary know-how for the future (consumer socialisation, lifelong education . . .)

Work Environment

Due to a quick and permanent transformation of their markets – new products, increasing competition – companies are interested in young customers (new needs to tap, additional financing . . .).

In addition to the three traditional short-term facets of the "youth market" (buyers, prescribers and pioneers of new habits and brands), employers are becoming more and more interested in securing future associates with whom to work. Some youngsters get "small jobs" from 16 onwards.

Media

The media have contributed largely to the disappearance of boundaries between adult and youth markets – concerning both products used and communication – to effectively target them. They also tend to speak more about "Youth as a Problem" – drugs, alcohol – than "Youth as a Resource" – new opportunities, different approaches . . . They practise "hot coverage" – spectacular events, violence, sex – instead of encouraging critical thinking.

Institutions

Parents, teachers, business people and journalists are represented by associations whose preoccupations are more concerned with the short-term and defending their members than with future generations and significant issues. Politicians should be more inclined to prepare the way for future opportunities and challenges for young people.

"Youth Market Research" was initiated in the United States more than 40 years ago with the objective of creating better products and services for young people. For similar reasons, Institutes specialising in researching children and teenagers started operating in Europe at the beginning of the 70s. The Institut de l'Enfant was created in 1972. Due to the great interest in the subject, as early as 1979 ESOMAR organised the first international seminar on "Researching Children" in Aarhus, Denmark, home of Lego!

The impressive development of Junior Marketing – creating products and services totally adapted to this age group in terms of function and design – Junior Communication – not only "addressing young people", but establishing "authentic and long term dialogue" – and Junior Management – how to motivate and acknowledge young associates without discouraging long time employees – is clearly explained by five trends in our "world society".

The first one is undoubtedly "profusion of information" of all kinds, through multiplying media, which implies:

- quick obsolescence of knowledge concerning a large number of subjects and permanent renewal of certitudes;
- new sources of information and new routes for dissemination;
- different control of flows of information; what is good or bad for young people, at what age, from whom, under what provisions . . . ?

The second factor is the general questioning of traditional "gatekeepers" – parents, teachers, justice, church, business, media, who used to control the information passed on to young people. Evaluation of quality of information is now based on its "authority" – meaning functionality and reliability – much more than on the transmitters' status. Good and honest gatekeepers are questioning themselves as much as they are questioned by young people!

A third reason explains why children and teenagers occupy such a crucial position in our society: they master technology and communication, so important these days, much better than the adults. This is true for computers, the Internet, mobile phone, as much as for changing techniques in marketing and advertising. They are much more savvy than one may think!

The fourth explanation is the decisive contribution of research which accords greater attention and favourable reception to the "Psychology of Development": Dr Benjamin Spock (*Baby and Child Care* – Penguin Books – 1946), Berry Brazelton (*Theory and Research on Behavioral Pediatrics* – Plenum Publishing Corp – 1982), Jean Piaget (*The Origins of Intelligence in Children* – International Universities Press – 1992), Erik Erikson (*Childhood and* Society – Norton & Co – 1964), William Crain (*Theories of Development* – Pearson – 2005), Howard Gardner (*Frames of Mind* – Basic Books – 1985), and Deborah Roedder John ("Consumer Socialization of Children" – *Journal of Consumer Research* – University of Chicago Press – 1999)...

The fifth and final justification, the one which, in our minds, constitutes the true origin and legitimate territory of "youth power", is their role in the future. Children, teenagers and adUlescents are the "coming players" in an open-ended situation. They "have the right" to design the opening century – mainly in terms of attitudes and behaviours rather than opinions – and forge different concepts to cope with new challenges. It is not only the responsibility of adults to make provisions for them ... it is also in our best interest!

RELATIVE IMPORTANCE IN CURRENT MARKET RESEARCH

While it is impossible to give a figure – accurate and worldwide – about exactly what share of global market research concerns the Youth Population, the global children and youth consumer industry can be used as a surrogate. An estimate was available on Internet at the end of August 2006: "anywhere between $ 200 to $ 400 billion"!

Youth Market Research is no more only a "niche"; it is big business, considering the "Lifetime Value" of consumption of products, services and brands. Strategic Consumer Relationship Management implies, almost mandatorily addressing children, teenagers and AdUlescents.

The "Young" population is highly valued everywhere, regardless of the demographic situation. It is just as important in countries with few babies like China, Japan, Scandinavia, Italy, as in those others with a high birth rate such as India, France or the USA. The "few babies" will, in the space of a single generation, carry the future of their economies on their shoulders, and the youth in high growth nations are already bringing about sweeping reforms in the global marketplace, with a combination of independence and initiative.

Because of the difficulties involved, youth research is more innovative than working with adults.

- There are so many co-educators that determining the proportional influence of each is very difficult. These go beyond the usual parents, teachers and local experts. Role models in the media – not necessarily alive, have a distinct influence, in today's connected world. Gandhi, for instance, has recently been resurrected as an all-pervasive icon amongst the youth in India.

- We deal with anticipation of the future and not lessons of past or present situations. "I don't use experience to theorize about the future, I bet on it": says Bill Gates in *The Road Ahead*.[2]
- It is sometimes hard for young people to express what they think/like and want to get. Said differently, perhaps it is hard for the generation that is *not* young to understand them! Apart from the traditional "gatekeepers", this entails the need to co-opt the neutral "fence-sitters" – observers of the same age or slightly older, who belong to similar psychographic profiles, to explain and interpret youth research even while the process of collection of data is in progress.
- We now deal with a generation that is at ease with living in a single global "virtual" world, as well as one that proudly wears its local culture as its identity, in the multi-civilisational world of the future. "Young consumer insight" implies challenges, ambition and expertise.

Usually the development of the size of the market follows two patterns:

- First, it focuses on publics in a certain order: children first, teenagers second, then babies and, finally, young adults.
- Secondly, it follows a set succession of techniques: qualitative initially, followed by the addition of quantitative procedures, and, finally, multi-annual barometers.

The amount of investment in Generational Market Research – concerning juniors, seniors – is a good criterion to evaluate the economic maturity of a country, and this has been increasing across the board globally.

RESEARCH QUESTIONS/ISSUES CONCERNING YOUTH

Researching Youth, an Ambition Without Limits

Dealing with youth means permanent evolution and a quest for excellence.

- During the last 40 years we have progressively discovered different facets of the youth market: initially as buyers, after as prescribers on products and brands, later as pioneers for new products or services, and, more recently, as future associates.
- At the beginning of this century, unfamiliar challenges are arising and the new generation is facing different opportunities. Taking advantage of the changing environments implies mobilising specialists from a wide spectrum of disciplines and permanent team-working. As a symbol of openness – for the sake of youth – the three contributors of this chapter represent a synergy of experience and perspective.

Pester Power is Dead. The Aspirational Approach is the Issue!

Health problems of youth are becoming a major issue in many countries, already developed or developing, and we, as professionals, should understand and share that concern and behave responsibly. We fully endorse what Neil Samson, from Kids and Youth, said at an ESOMAR Conference in 2005 ("Is pester power dead? Diet, health, obesity" – Age Matters).

---

[2] *The Road Ahead* (1995) New York: Penguin Books.

Dependable research has proved that reposing on concepts like "child as a king" or "nagging factor" is:

- not very effective: aspirational attitudes and positive and lasting behaviours result from complicity between parents and children;
- short-term oriented: negotiation is much better for improving "family time";
- politically dangerous: justifying limitations for food industry and advertising.

Building a long-term partnership is strategic. Meanwhile, gatekeepers are more concerned about reproduction of the past, business and young people should work together on "projects for the future".

The Horizon is Wide Open for the Youth Population, but the Future Could be Insecure

Logically, most professionals (marketers, advertising people) are in favour of a "free market economy" rather than the constraints of an "organised economy". We agree on the idea that consumer socialisation of youth should encourage a durable attractiveness for life and create a calling for adulthood rather than producing fashion addicts and brand victims. There is little doubt about the fact that the vast majority of young people in every country will be richer than their parents. Are we sure they will be happier?

Serial Youth: Becoming an Adult!

Adulthood – being an adult – is not a matter of age or status. It is a question of autonomous and responsible behaviours resulting from a dynamic progression; from infant to child, teenager and so on. Any child experiences two births, the first one at delivery and the second when entering adolescence perhaps more challenging than the first one.

The purchasing decision process changes over the period of development, from 0 to 25! Professionals should know exactly what is relevant for each stage and mobilise around the synergetic dynamics involved in each (new steps in the flow!). This is why segmentation is so important, to the degree that it is relevant (age, level of schooling . . .).

Priority Should be Given to the Attitudes and Behaviours of Youth rather than their Opinions

Young people are repositories of consumer knowledge and awareness. They are the first adopters and avid users of many of the new technologies. They are the household members with the most passionate consumer desires, and are the most closely attached to products, brands and latest trends. For us, it is quite dangerous to construct anything solely on young people's opinions (what they think or want for tomorrow) because they face a double concern; changes within themselves as well as the constantly evolving environment.

All strategic decisions – marketing, communication – should always be based on facts and not on assumptions, judgements or prejudices.

The World Youth Population; Think Global and . . . Act Global

Today's young people resemble the times more than they do their fathers and mothers! They are essentially the product of the present era and the world culture (fashion, music, sport, technology...) and sociology (family, religion, work, environment...). World culture is more and more conditioned by Globalisation; in manufacturing, communication and distribution. World Brands – Coca-Cola, McDonald's, Nike, Sony, Apple, MTV, L'Oréal, Microsoft – are appraised by young people everywhere as common language and shared values.

For Youth, the Major Challenge is Time

Children, adolescents and young adults have no real problem with reality vs. virtuality, mastering of space (here and there), dealing with private life and public exposure ("extimacy"!). Time is the major challenge (old enough to be allowed to, time to..., day and night, multi-tasking, weekly schedules, school time vs holidays...). Now many families are "cash rich but time poor". Young people have a specific vision of time compared with adults and they are also looking for different priorities between work, leisure, family.

Directly Initiating Young People to Products/Services and Brands

Because of their decreasing control of flows of information, in the future, traditional gatekeepers will be less active in passing on their behaviours and/or attitudes to young people. In practice, this means that manufacturers will have to convince new consumers of the "the need" (for cosmetics, cars...) and convey a "positive service" with their products or brands. As we often say "whoever you are, you'd better consider that people under 20 don't know you"!

For dynamic youth the major value is to be "cool." Products and brands should play up to the "aspirational" image – initiating an authentic and balanced dialogue – and be packaged as "fun-ctional".

Looking for "Youth Adhesion"

Responsible selling to young people implies recruiting them first and making them loyal after! Coaching – anticipation, proposal – is basic for any partnership between business and the young public (never say target). Marketers should set up a fair "customer relationship management" nurturing it constantly: in order to go beyond pure material satisfaction by making possible progressive experiments of emotional accomplishment.

Effectiveness and Ethics Come Together on Matters of Junior Marketing and Communication

These two concerns should be considered through a prospective dimension – within five to twenty years from now, and not be addicted to the past (value judgements referring to "good old days").

ESOMAR has been very active for many years in both directions:

- *Effectiveness* via the organisation of specialised seminars and the publication of a monograph entitled "Researching Youth" with contributions from the world's finest specialists on the subject.
- *Ethics* via two guides, one on "Interviewing Children" (with the International Chamber of Commerce) and the other one on "Research Online".

RESEARCH APPROACHES, METHODS AND WAYS OF WORKING

In researching children, we are all talking a foreign language
Paul A. Mayes (2002) *Researching Youth* ESOMAR

Researching Youth, irrespective of the method decided, requires humility and passion. Young people are not miniature adults. Methodologies and materials for investigation – questionnaires, animation and observation plans, the kind of face to face meetings to be put in place – are much more demanding, requiring an edge-of-the seat pace tailored to each stage-of-life, to match the mood amongst the youth segment that is one of infectious optimism and enthusiasm.

For the young population under investigation, the follow-up of information is in the structuring. These age cohorts need to be accorded the respect justified by their high self-confidence and information-processing ability, fuelled by ambition and an achievement orientation. As professional adults, lifelong relationships between themselves, the product and the brand would constitute the ultimate jackpot. This induces a kind of *obligation for results.*

"Junior Marketing Intelligence" and *"Control Panels"* aid to optimise the information flow concerning young people, serving and taking on the role of a permanent observation tower scanning the environment. This is usually via a combination of techniques: qualitative, ethnographic, quantitative, involving a variety of "experts" such as the "gate keepers", as well as the "fence-sitters", also called the junior consultants such as expert teens. It helps to meet those slightly older than the age cohort being studied, that the younger ages *really* look up to; and recognised opinion leaders of own age milieu. In these scenarios, "designing tomorrow" workshops are conducted, with the targeted age cohort; putting adult specialists in situations with young participants. For instance, creative directors of TV programmes sit down every three months, with prep school children (along with the research facilitator and even the parents in case required), and ideate/weave future story ideas, is the direction currently running popular children's programmes could take. This entails a regular communication and creation back and forth, more like a series of research exercises, each with limited objectives.

The Appropriate Usage of Gatekeepers. Sometimes they are the only way to "listen to" and "understand" children. Parents and teachers can tell you each child's particular leaning – what is concentrated on, and what is distracting; their sense of reality versus the oases of fantasy created in daily lives; conformity versus attention seeking behaviour. With the younger children absorbing everything seen and heard, it is the gatekeepers who are the best judges of how this would translate into long term behaviour. In qualitative studies, simultaneous sessions with parents watching and commenting on the children's focus group in progress, become more insightful, than meeting them separately. Children are well aware of the role of a gatekeeper as disciplinarian – what a mum, dad or a teacher "says" to actively dissuade – behaviour/purchase/TV viewing, etc. Obtaining a parallel perspective, on the ideas of discipline – as well as activities enjoyed participating in along with the gatekeepers, will provide cues to their motivation.

Parents, grandparents, teachers as well as historical "heroes" in school text books and movies are looked up to. The traits adored in these role models, can provide the key to values culturally sought: Fun loving? Looks? Humour? Achievement orientation? High self worth? Helpful nature?

The influence of research situations and locations. The closer to the real lives of the children is the location, the more relaxed the environment. These could be akin to bedrooms (living rooms, in space starved Indian homes!), college canteens or even, the coffee shops, for older youth. Even a statement "there are no right or wrong answers" may serve to remind the child of the classroom, and is best avoided. Sometimes, the question "why" is seen to imply criticism. However, giving marks out of 10 often works, and it is not unusual for children to rate as 11 out of 10, or 20 out of 10, to indicate their complete endorsement of something.

Stage-of-life, such as recruiting in school year works better than age bands. We cannot mix developmental milestones – say, those in "primary" or prep school with those in "secondary" or high school, even if both are at the cusp 10 years of age. The sense of community amongst children tends to be really high. Peer group, family – each is key. Important to identify and meet within the frames of reference, making the interaction less abstract. Inviting friendship pairs helps to break shyness barriers. This keeps the children rooted (less likely to posture) and works especially well in mixed gender groups across ages. Modifying the venue for child specific studies – posters, balloons, lights, the right snacks, multiple "going home" presents is important. Pokemon cards and collectibles had been very successful with younger children, in the last few years, and have left a vacuum that is currently waiting to be filled.

Input of Data Using Additional Qualitative Techniques

Alternative "tools" would include an inventory – of pockets, closets, toy chests, latest promos collected, their favourite web sites (and blogs, if aware), collection of wallpapers and screen savers, their private internet and gaming devices (indicating the level of ease with the simulated world). Discussing Reality Shows, an intrinsic part of the times, serves as an excellent and animated warm up. Can provide additional layers of understanding regarding the role played by the media, the distinction between fiction and the non-fiction realm of everyday life, as well as the value systems within their sphere of experience today. Online blogs also work well.

Buying simulation provides a good indicator to spontaneous likes and dislikes, and is an aid to understand merchandising and accessorising. Sometimes, this has been seen as rather inconsistent in the prediction of sales that is better understood from gatekeepers. Promotions need to be rated in terms of potential playground currency as well as "how will children justify its purchase to parents". Picture or video reports – taken by participants beforehand, or by an observer later, also work well. Collages, scenario building, story telling via comic book formats, bubble drawings usually bring a safe third person angle in. These aid in the recreation of fantasy, that continues to be important to children. Apart from triggers, we need to locate the signs of drudgery, anxieties and stress perceived in their perpetually busy lives.

A basket of surrogate indicators may be used to secure the conditions for a sincere dialogue between young people and marketers and advertisers. The amount being spent on the child's education as a part of the household budget. The parents' wishes and ambitions for the child, especially in emerging markets. For example, the "extra-curricular" activities participated in, apart from school. The amount of time spent in the "virtual" versus the "real" world (TV, 'net, gaming) in a day/week. Whether enrolled in "English speaking" schools, in the new global world, is also an indicator of the ambitions of the family. Who the child shares his/her room with, is a signal of the sharing of a lot of other products also – such as personal grooming. Monitoring the daily schedule, such as time to go to bed: in South Asia, it is quite often, along with the parents' bedtime – past 11 pm.

Creating Products or Communications; Validating and Optimising Results with the Young Participants

Action/fast edits make sense – often even within the longer time frame of a pre-test. Concepts, prototypes, foods, smells and tastes, advertising, need a lot of visual and tactile stimuli. Sending a participant out of the room at the venue, then having the others describe/enact/draw the stimulus just seen, to this "live" person, away from the presence of the moderator brings in an evocative layer. This audience would otherwise have merely glossed over some details, as being too obvious and not to be stated to the "moderator adults". We need to understand the "WOW" factor of catch phrases, and body signs (high five, salute, etc.). Youth and children love to process words, especially those that add to their choice of adjectives . . . *Horrid, brilliant, fabulous, awesome, yuckiest, ghastly.* Contradictions, incongruities, youth as well as younger children, love them all. Also, within the context of multiple entries and exits, as is real life, communication would need to be developed and researched – not just in totality, but in bits and pieces, starting and ending anywhere. This would capture the reality of distracted attention spans and multitasking behaviour of the current times.

Accuracy of Measurement Through Quantitative Techniques, Questionnaires: wording, structure, is critical, as is the length. The need to pre test final questionnaire with vocabulary matching is very important. The younger the age, the more "short" and "varied" it needs to be. A lot of "doing" different things work better than a single funnelling of thought, that may bore the audience. To a 6 year old, 15 minutes is a long time, while a 17 year old could be coaxed into a two hour interview, provided it is made interesting enough. Smiley scales – with degrees of *"liking a lot"* and *"liking slightly"* may look good as substitutes to the more adult five point scales, but invariably get top-boxed responses from children, due to their *black* or *white* nature of processing. The thought of *"what will others say"* plays a critical role in collective cultures, and it is important to include questions that help capture this "impression on others", as much as the more self actualized "I love it myself".

Specialised staff in youth research studies would mean that academic background is sometimes as important as training. More so, is the team's attitudinal openness. Rather than relate to those dressing young, this audience loves people with transparent and mobile facial expressions that indicate nuances of alarm, excitement, wonder and so on. This is seen as being indicative of spontaneity and an "ageless", happy and vibrant personality they like to associate with.

The presentation of results would need a lot of skill and analysis by the researcher, especially in the building of attitudinal and behavioural models. *Nurturing and sharing in youth dynamics* is far more important than gathering ad-hoc information about young people. Mobilising them – actively and for the long term – needs to take precedence over seducing them (one shot). Young people opinions are versatile, attitudes are steady, and behaviours adaptable. Value systems take shape when people are young. Often things that are relevant when you are young (e.g. environmental issues), become part of your lifelong value system. Few elderly people are concerned with the environment, for example, if it was not an issue when they formed their identities. By being alert, we can be active participants in these historic epoch-making moments of the early 21st century.

To foretell is nothing, to devise is crucial – Anatole France

BENEFITS AND LIMITATIONS

Benefits

Most of the dynamic international brands – Coca-Cola, McDonald's, Nike, Microsoft, L'Oréal, Sony – express growing needs especially in emerging countries: Indian teens alone buy nearly 60 % of the fizzy drinks, chocolates and jeans sold in their country! "Many marketers believe that they haven't captured the tip of the Indian youth iceberg yet" – P. Mukherjee (2006) Proact.

Young customers represent easier business; convincing new targets and apprentice consumers is less difficult than making experienced ones change their habits and suppliers. Children, teenagers and young adults constitute very reactive publics; they are "consumer born" and they influence the usage and attitudinal patterns of mainstream society! Addressing them is a functional process to recruit early adopters.

Reliable segmentation means successful marketing plans through strategic targeting and intense partnership with these very demanding partners; the "more generation" is challenging professionals. Since they master new technologies and they look for renovated design, it is easy to embark young people on the course of simulation/implementation of marketing plans (from product to usage, communication, pricing and distribution). "Marketers who befriend today's young people are actually building relationships with the movers and shakers of tomorrow!" – D. Morrisson – TwentySomething Inc.

They have also developed an immense potential for creativity, because of their long "inurement" to dreams (during childhood) and "worlds of possible". As adolescents they imagine projects for the future involving matching, adapting/customising or transgressing present reality.

In addition to what precedes, working for/with young people is a practical way of pioneering the irreversible evolution of the "consumer of the future". As D. Rushoff says in his book *Playing the future: What we can learn from digital kids*[3] "children are today what we should be ... and shall be later".

Limitations

"Details" about the research situation are essential when working with young people (caring attitudes from adults; attention span, wording, openness, reaction to conformist/provocative answers ...). They can be difficult to integrate for non-specialists.

Traditional "market research recipes" are not always adequate. For example it is very difficult for young people to foresee their personal transformation in the years to come and the evolution of the environment they share with the rest of the population. This means that what they ask for should be "redesigned" before being considered as authentic expectations to build products and/or communications platforms.

This ever-changing clientele implies permanent recruitment and follow-up. Nothing is to be taken for granted for long but it is not a question of fickleness or dishonesty. Loyalty is earned in as much as marketing and advertising "solutions" are renewed otherwise they see/feel "the tricks").

---

[3] (1996) New York: Harpers.

DO'S AND DON'TS

A hundred years from now ... the world may be better because I was important in the life of a child.

Joël-Yves Le Bigot

Do's = Seek Out "Active Adhesion of Young People"

Researchers should be irreproachable dreamers even militant (ambitious, dreamers, action-oriented. . .) AND rigorous (secure, humble, careful, systematic in double checking . . .).
  We must fight for:

- working on reliable products (good for the public, significant input . . .) and transparent communication (real dialogue, fair service . . .) and responsible marketing strategies and distribution network: for both young people and gatekeepers who care;
- promoting high ambition in terms of research objectives; almost anything can be accomplished concerning youth, at any age; it is only a question of imagination (what can we dream about?), anticipation (what kind of information is needed to support the project?), and capacity of modelling (where are the risks of mis-strategy?). In many fields and on essential topics, "Commercial Private Young Market Research" went ahead with what Public Laboratories and Universities were doing. France is a good illustration of that, with Institut de l'Enfant and Junium whose contributions have been determinant for understanding "New Adolescence = re-birth " and proposing relevant approaches.
- excellence in methodology (even if it costs more money and time than usual):
  - mastery about all technical approaches; from whom should we get the data we want, what are the provisions for getting the reliable information which is needed?
  - not only duplicate/adapt what is done with adults;
  - acknowledging the different levels of child development and capacities: attention span, measurement of time and frequency, cause/effect relation, egocentrism. . . (cf. D. Solomon and J. Peters (2005) "Measuring children's behaviour in a complex multimedia world" ESOMAR – Age Matters).
  - beware of the school environment: sensitivities of teachers, importance of school calendar. . .
- protection of investment: developing strategies that smoothly transit from one stage to the next. When developing a project for children we should think about the next step, when they will be teenagers. It's our interest as much as public's interest if we really want to establish a durable positive relationship!
- optimum application/"enforcement" of the results of research and recommendations: should be ready to use, lively, capable of being "staged" and even spectacular. What is essential is not "good research", it's "good decisions and successful action".

Speaking with young people is very rewarding and regular enlargement and deepening of this partnership should be our rule. Dynamic testing is the solution and astute research is the key!

Don'ts = Never Try to Manipulate the Youth Population

Based on our common experience, our main recommendations are as follows

- Do not stereotype the market; this population resents being pigeonholed: young people – and gatekeepers – agree: reject the idea of being considered as "a target" or "a market"

- Never impose opinions; only suggest attitudes and give evidence that you are only too eager to help these young boys and girls.
- Be "hip" only if it is acceptable: it is very tempting to use humour, slang or lifestyles references but boundaries of credibility should always be respected.
- And essentially "never rest":
  - o the public is continually evolving: getting older has nothing to do with being fickle or disloyal, it means "what's next" (i.e. new and dynamic!);
  - o the competition is fierce and "trade off" is permanent – between products of the same category or substitutes, within the portfolio of alternative brands, selection of distribution circuits...). Young consumer is only concerned with HIS/HER interest!
  - o cultural shifts can occur very quickly; what's cool today could be replaced by something else tomorrow. But fads are not always easy to distinguish from real fashion and steady trends!

CURRENT DEVELOPMENT AND THE NEAR FUTURE

Obviously one page is not enough to describe all "the good news" about Youth Research and the positive perspectives. Here are some aspects we consider as crucial!

Youth Research is constantly working on improvement in reliability. Even more than for adults, Young Consumer Insight is the major challenge; a better understanding of "the journey to adulthood", delving further into "what is cool?", conceptualising "platforms for action" about dynamic notions like luxury, cash rich or time poor...

Systematising the time flow – "relationship marketing", coaching – is the rule and will be of dramatic importance in the future.

We should aim for an Optimized Integration of Research into Strategic Plans and Teams; Market Research, R&D, Manufacturing, Marketing, Advertising, Sales, Finance, Human Resources should share the same objectives, use similar criteria and language... since they are in the "same boat". For everybody, to "be sharper" means being more inventive and more reactive.

There is no doubt about the rapid expansion of the World Youth Market; especially in developing countries in Asia and South America which are experiencing the "forces of modernisation" S. Bhosale and S. Gupta (2006) "Who is the future Asian Consumer? Youth and Women!" ESOMAR.

The concern about what's coming next will increase based on:

- securing the "attachment" from early adoption to loyalty; for products, brands, retailing...
- practising modelling: in 20 years from now, the two largest youth markets will be India and China. The two of them will be – are already – influenced by western references, but each will create its own way of progressing!
- Strong economic growth; 40 % of the Asian Pacific region consumers think their economies have improved over the past 6 months and 53 % expect further improvement within the next year (ACNielsen Online Confidence survey – 2005).
- Incredible "youth reserve power": in India 62 % of the population is under 29 years of age: "India is a young country; instead of an ageing population, here we have a case of reverse-ageing and the prognosis is the same over the next two decades" Statistical Outline of India 2005–2006/Tata Services Limited. Only 5 % of the Chinese 9 to 14 years old have a mobile phone... and 95 % dream about getting one!

- Social adaptation (urbanisation, universal connectivity, women's empowerment...) and open-mindedness to new products or services and open-heartedness to brands.

Besides the enormous opportunities offered by the take off of Young Countries, the world perspectives are presently favourable since there are no real reasons for "youth research" not to grow in its traditional markets, Europe and North America.

What precedes is not only based on our experience. An analysis of the 42 different papers concerning the youth population presented at ESOMAR events from 2001 to 2006 confirms the phenomenon of "youth globalisation" and the balance between "traditional youth markets" (Western Europe; 11 – North America; 4 – etc.) and "new youth markets" (South America; 11 – Asia; 6).

International studies will expand in the future. They will concern different countries or regions and will stress tracking opportunities for action and similarities, rather than description of specificities and differences.

Ethical issues will be more critical in the future and some regulations could appear; either at national or regional levels (Europe, North America...). There is nothing wrong with that since the Youth and the Future are logically major political issues. Our responsibility is to anticipate and "keep our noses clean".

CASE STUDIES

"Kandoo" for Procter & Gamble France – Research Conducted by Junium France

Who – what?

A new version of Kandoo flushable toilet wipes is about to be released: individual packages with a new scent. The objective of the test is to validate a dynamic "customer loyalty programme".

How?

Four focus groups: in Paris.

- 1 group of mothers with children aged between 3 and 7; regular purchasers of Kandoo;
- 1 group of mothers with children aged between 3 and 7; either no longer purchasers of Kandoo or, on the contrary, intending to try Kandoo;
- 1 group of children aged between 5 and 7; regular users of Kandoo;
- 1 group of children aged between 5 and 7; occasional users of Kandoo or non users.

Results?

The image of Kandoo is very positive, associated with values such as hygiene, softness and pleasure. Interviewees all liked the new scent and considered it coherent with the product. Mothers insisted on differentiation from food references. The test of a leaflet led the mothers to talk about the "ideal loyalty programme", and to imagine what type of actions would be appropriate for P&G. They outlined the criteria for acceptance: their child's pleasure when receiving gifts, the type of gifts they think their child would like and the ones they are ready to accept. The key is a combination of fun and educative information, providing greater autonomy for their children.

During graphic arts sessions we evaluated the ability of the children to play with the proposed gifts. They could imagine many others. They particularly like collections, if only for a short time, but they seem to favour a variety of gifts.

"Le Bioscope" for Grévin & Cie – research conducted by Junium France

Who – what?

Le Bioscope is an outdoor amusement park offering two shows, practical activities, encounters with scientists, explorers and navigators . . . The objective is to help the visitor understand not only the beauty of life, but also its fragility and the responsibility of mankind for the overall balance of the earth.

How?

Client wishes to test the concept of the park through various activities and with different types of publics:

- four focus groups lasting 2h30 for adults and 2h00 for young publics;
- one group of parents with children aged between 6 and 13;
- one group of grandparents with grandchildren of the same age;
- one group of children aged between 8 and 10;
- one group of "tweens" aged between 11 and 13.

We submitted the name Bioscope and encouraged the interviewees to express their understanding of the theme of the park and imagine a new language about the subject. We reviewed the various activities stimulating reactions, comments, offers for improvements, designs, information circulation throughout the park and between activities as well as shows. As a conclusion the participants constructed a short explanation of the purpose of the visit. We created the outline of a "discovery game": its mechanics, levels, results and rules.

Results

The focus groups stressed the necessity of improving the physical aspects of activities, and finding a balance between emotion, fun and information. For example, we created the game "Bioprofileur". Each visitor discovered his/her profile concerning environmental issues through answering amusing or informative questions. The children were excited and ready to make a commitment to protect the earth and life on a day-to-day basis.

Parents were concerned about their ability to be sufficiently knowledgeable about the subjects developed in the park, meaning answering the numerous questions of their children throughout the visit. The grandparents were very positive, motivated by the desire to transmit information, and ready for an emotional experience with their grandchildren. The "Tweens" were not positive about the park. They sought higher sensations and riskier activities than those offered here.

14
Researching Diverse
Individuals and Societies

Anjul Sharma

DEFINITION AND DESCRIPTION OF INTEREST

We live in multi-cultural and multi-ethnic societies. These are societies designed for the cultures of several different races or ethnicities. Some countries such as India and China have always been multi-ethnic and co-existed with the diversity that this brings. However, in other countries especially those in Western Europe and North America, such multiplicity is more recent. For them it is a widely acknowledged fact of life nowadays and evidenced by how the profile of countries has changed dramatically in the last 50 years. According to the US Census Bureau, the share of the US population that was foreign born doubled from 5 % to 12 % between 1967 to 2006. Their geographical dispersal also changed: in 1990, only 10 % of counties had 5 % or more populations that were "foreign-born" but by 2000, this figure had risen to 20 % of counties. And looking at one specific community, the Hispanic population rose by 50 % between 1990 and 2000. Taking the example of London, the 2001 Census showed that it housed people from 160 different countries: four out of 10 people living in London were from ethnic minority backgrounds. So far from being more mono-cultural and mono-ethnic, they have become more multi-cultural and multi-ethnic. Admittedly this has happened to a greater or lesser extent depending on the country in question but the overall trend is towards more fluidity across borders. Consequently, populations are becoming more heterogeneous and varied and this has concomitant effects on the ability to sample and research them easily and effectively as we shall see.

Several factors are responsible for such developments. First, the world wars saw countries recruiting soldiers from the colonies who then stayed on in the colonial parent country. Second, post war labour shortages encouraged workers from abroad to come over and fill these gaps in the labour market. Third, the reach of global media has meant that more people are now aware of the standard of living in other parts of the world. This is not to say that everyone who migrates to the USA expects to lead a glamorous life. Rather it presents people with an alternative to what they already have. Fourth, and related to this, greater economic prosperity and more opportunities in certain countries (especially in Western Europe, north America and the Antipodes) have encouraged people to seek a better life elsewhere. Fifth, warfare and instability in certain countries, e.g. Zimbabwe and the former Eastern Bloc countries, has meant these people are looking to increase their life chances and those of their children. And finally, the set up of common interest areas such as the European Union have made a significant

---

Market Research Handbook, 5th Edition. Edited by M. van Hamersveld and C. de Bont.
© 2007 John Wiley & Sons, Ltd.

contribution to encouraging migration within Europe. Striving to be one market, a central tenet of this belief has been free movement of people across borders.

However, multi-ethnic and multi-cultural communities are not without their problems. Riots in inner city areas of major capital cities such as Paris are a testament to this and symptomatic of the tense relations between host populations and those who have arrived or settled from abroad.

KEY STAKEHOLDERS WHO WANT TO UNDERSTAND ETHNIC COMMUNITIES

The key players in this area of research and marketing vary across countries. For example, in the UK, businesses, government and NGOs are often involved; in the USA it is likely to be businesses and in France it is also likely to be businesses. The reasons for these differences are often multi-faceted. However, a key differentiator is the way ethnicity relates to citizenship.

In France, everyone is assumed to be equal and French in the eyes of the law: they are all citizens of the republic. This approach overcomes the need to conceptualise any ethnic group or individual as anything other than French. Hence it is not legally possible to ask a direct question about ethnic background in research surveys. It also means that the government is unlikely to commission research in this area as that would contravene legislative boundaries. Thus it becomes the domain of businesses and their marketing and research agencies to find a way around this and target ethnic communities.

A similar set of circumstances applies in the USA. Everyone is American, albeit pre-fixed with African, Italian, etc. However, the key difference between France and the USA is that, whereas socialist France has heavy government involvement in civil society, the USA does not. The free market and more right wing slant of American politics and society means there is little reason for the government (national or federal) to be interested in different ethnic communities. It is again the domain of businesses to explore opportunities with ethnic communities.

By contrast, the situation in the UK is totally different. Falling somewhere between the socialist tendencies of France and the free market and right wing stance of the USA, the government in the UK has a key role to play. In the past, the government actively encouraged ethnic minorities to work in the UK either as soldiers or to join the labour market. As more and more citizens from the colonies settled in the UK, it created tensions with the indigenous population and eventually rioting. This led to the formulation of legislation to curtail migration and avoid civil unrest. The government also realised that they had to understand the needs of the communities and then meet or manage them. This is one of the reasons why the UK National Census carries questions about ethnicity. Such government involvement has opened the door on researching these communities and has benefited businesses, non-governmental organisations (NGOs) and other bodies.

IMPORTANCE IN CURRENT MARKET RESEARCH

Multi-ethnic communities and individuals are rapidly becoming an important part of market research and marketing. People are generally more aware of ethnic communities for several reasons. First, some communities have been established for many years and are beginning to be more visible and vocal in making their presence felt. Second, some members of indigenous communities are keen to replicate elements of diverse ethnic cultures through food and dress: this is one of the markers of living in a cosmopolitan society and being a cosmopolitan individual. Third, more recently arrived communities especially if they are asylum seekers, refugees and economic migrants are also likely to attract attention. This will tend to be either as the subject of negative portrayal or as a celebration of increased diversity. The need to research these communities can be gauged from the main audiences that are interested in multi-ethnic communities: businesses, government and NGOs.

Across countries, the interest of businesses in multi-ethnic communities can be for several reasons. They might want to promote a new product or service developed specifically for them. For example, Mecca Cola is a cola brand that specifically targets the Muslim community in a range of European, Asian and American markets. Alternatively it may be as a result of experiencing saturation in the core indigenous market. A good example of this would be the way the automotive market is trying to target ethnic communities to boost sales performance. Both of these could result in important changes to the service delivery, branding and communications offer leading to a need to test marketing literature in the mother tongue or other languages. A third reason could be because they have a multi-ethnic workforce and in order to provide facilities and policies that meet their needs, they might need to conduct some research.

Government interest in multi-ethnic communities stems from the need to have relatively harmonious relations between communities – an important responsibility particularly to maintain stability, quality of life and to be voted back into power. For example in Belgium, immigrant voters are undermining the strength of right wing extremists through their voting behaviour. And in the USA, the desire to court the Hispanic vote is strong given they represent a growing part of the population. But it also goes beyond this to providing public services for all and not just those from the indigenous host community. In some countries, the government has to provide schools, health facilities, housing and other amenities. To facilitate this, it needs to know how the needs for different services might vary according to ethnic community. In some countries, governments recognise the equality of all citizens in the eyes of the state but also acknowledge that some citizens will be different from others. To avoid penalising them for a difference that might not be in their control (such as their ethnic background), the government can institute legislation to prevent such discrimination: this may require primary research. For example, in the UK it is illegal to discriminate on the grounds of race, sexual orientation and disability. They may also want to celebrate diversity within their country and take into account the views of all citizens rather than just the indigenous population.

NGOs can also be interested in multi-ethnic communities. They can often have a link to governments or be independent charities who want to explore the potential for their "offer" amongst different ethnic communities. For example, VSO (Voluntary Service Overseas) conducted research to explore the motivations to become volunteers amongst the Black Caribbean, Black African and Indian communities. They decided to target the Black Caribbean and Black African communities for the immediate future as they were more public spirited and less concerned about working for free as volunteers.

RESEARCH QUESTIONS AND ISSUES

Conducting research amongst multi-ethnic communities is not a straightforward process and a number of factors need to be carefully considered before embarking on such a piece of research as Figure 14.1 demonstrates.

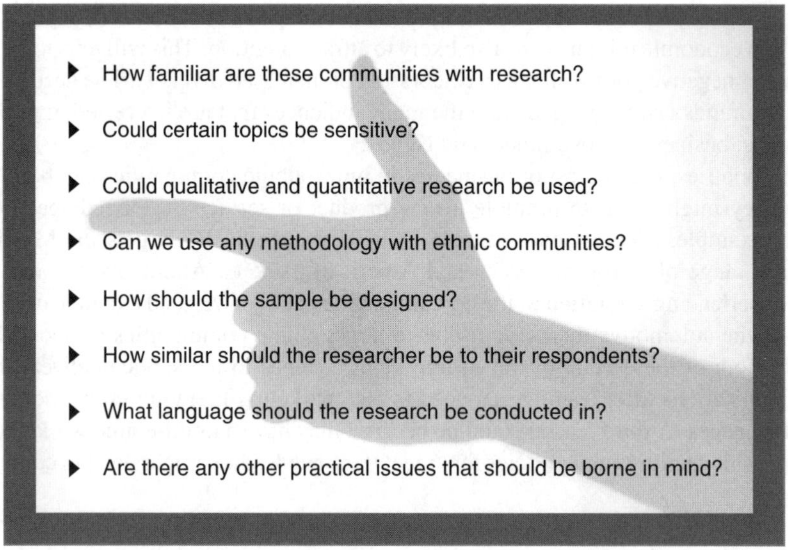

- How familiar are these communities with research?

- Could certain topics be sensitive?

- Could qualitative and quantitative research be used?

- Can we use any methodology with ethnic communities?

- How should the sample be designed?

- How similar should the researcher be to their respondents?

- What language should the research be conducted in?

- Are there any other practical issues that should be borne in mind?

Figure 14.1   Key research issues and questions

These Communities are not Always Familiar with Research

Whilst in some countries, indigenous populations are accustomed to taking part in research, ethnic communities may not be. In the countries where they originate, their views might never have been canvassed. Their views might not have been important enough. There was insufficient resource to do so, or it had never occurred to anyone to find out what ordinary citizens or consumers felt. Hence, arriving in a new country and being asked to take part in a street interview or a group discussion could come as a surprise or even a shock. For others who have not entered the country legally, there may be fear that they will be sent back home. Naturally, this would constitute a big barrier to taking part in anything that looks as if it is official.

This lack of familiarity with research means more time needs to be built into the process of conducting research especially at the recruitment stage. On average, for a qualitative project circa three weeks might be needed for recruitment: for a quantitative project, an extra three to four weeks may be needed to complete all the fieldwork. Of course, for more complex projects, more time could be added. Respondents from ethnic communities will also need to be reassured about what will be happening in the research, what will be expected of them and, if necessary, how the findings will be used. Emphasising confidentiality and anonymity will be paramount in some cases. They may wish to bring chaperones along and, in this case, the research team will need to gauge the feasibility of this.

However, there is a positive aspect to this lack of familiarity with research – it means that respondents are less cynical and jaded about being researched. And that is a pleasant experience for any researcher.

To increase confidence in the research process, it can often be useful making contact with key people in the ethnic community who have grass roots involvement with the population such as community workers, local nurses, doctors, priests, etc. They can often help recruit and snowball respondents and their involvement in the research can enhance its credibility as well as reassuring respondents that the research is bona fide. They are also particularly helpful if the recruiter or quantitative interviewer is not from the same ethnic background as the respondents.

Some Topic Areas Could be Sensitive

Certain topics can be sensitive in a multi-ethnic context. Some of these may seem obvious. For example talking to young Black youth about their feelings about the police is going to be a contentious issue given the often antagonistic relationship between the two. Others may seem less obvious. For example, when gauging reactions to marketing literature amongst Black Caribbean and Black African respondents, researchers failed to realise that they would pickup on images of White relief workers and hungry looking Black children and situate them in a framework reminiscent of colonial exploitation. There are also certain times when topics could be sensitive; for example, interviewing Muslims about food habits during Ramadan when they should be fasting. Part of this is related to the degree of assimilation into the host community but, more often than not, certain subjects can be sensitive *irrespective* of assimilation.

Quantitative Research Amongst Ethnic Communities can be Problematic

Given the complexity and heterogeneity of these ethnic samples, the need for robustness and the almost standard quantitative requirement for a minimum cell size of 75, it can often be more difficult conducting quantitative research with ethnic communities. Not only could it take an additional three to four weeks depending on the size and complexity of the questionnaire, it is often as much as one and a half times more expensive than quantitative research with mainstream audiences. But aside from resourcing there are also research design issues to bear in mind. Clients (and in some cases researchers) are not as familiar with these communities making it more difficult and dangerous to launch a quantitative stage prior to undertaking any qualitative research. After all, how will they be able to gauge the types of questions to ask, any sensitivities around topics, appropriate tone for that audience, etc?

Bearing these factors in mind, it is often more fruitful to conduct a larger, comprehensive qualitative stage to overcome the need to conduct a quantitative stage.

Not All Methodologies can be Used

Apart from the broader issues around using quantitative and qualitative methodologies, there are also deeper methodological considerations to bear in mind. Many of these stem from the lack of familiarity with research that seems to be the case amongst ethnic communities. Face to face methodologies tend to be favoured as they can go some distance in reassuring respondents about the researcher and the research. This level of engagement is much harder to achieve via telephone methodologies, hence, these tend to be used less often or not at all. Online approaches and other new technologies involving mobile phones and texting are likely to be even more problematic: not everyone is online, it may not be suitable for certain topics, it may not be appropriate for certain types of stimulus and techniques and the need to use mother tongue may be an additional barrier.

Likewise, certain creative and projective techniques may not be as fruitful with these audiences. In this case, it would be better to adapt these to the audience or re-evaluate if they are actually required at all.

Defining the Sample is a Complex Task

Sample definition is always crucial to research projects, but when conducting multi-ethnic research it is particularly complex as so many additional factors need to be taken into consideration. The key thing to bear in mind is that these populations are not homogeneous and differences exist at the level of country of origin, the region of that country they come from, religion, language and other ethnic criteria. These are all crucial in defining the sample, as shown in Figure 14.2.

All of these factors interweave and create a myriad of possible ethnic identities. To ensure that the research focuses on the specific audience required, samples have to be defined very, very precisely and clearly. The Indian sub-continent is a case in point. As a country, India is hugely diverse and this carries over into the populations that migrate abroad. So for defining the Indian sample, we first need to establish that they all originate from India (or at least their parents do). We then need to understand which part of the country they originate from as there are notable regional differences between populations from different parts: Punjab, Gujarat, Tamil Naidu, Karnataka or the large cities like Delhi or Mumbai. This is followed by capturing religious background: India has many of the world religions represented and has over 114 million Muslims making up 11 % of the population. However, most Indians abroad are Hindu and Sikh. And finally there is language to contend with: this acts as further control on ethnicity. Certain parts of the country speak certain languages so if a respondent appears in the sample as a Punjabee but speaks Tamil, this could signal a potential mis-recruit, or at least the respondents' details need to be re-checked. African samples would present similar challenges.

In addressing this area, there is merit in devoting time at the start of the project to think about the challenges in more detail. In the absence of a fully fledged ethnic research specialist, desk research can be particularly useful. This could involve calling up embassies and consulates to obtain population estimates for each community, looking at official statistics (although these

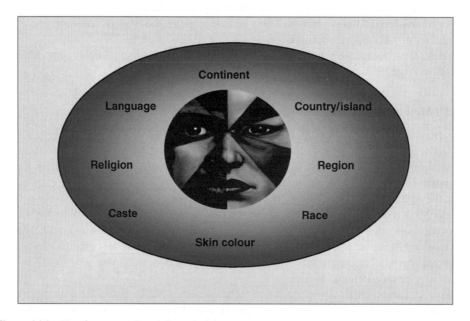

Figure 14.2   Key factors used to define ethnicity

may not be totally up-to-date or accurate), and searching on the Internet for additional sources of information.

There are Pros and Cons to Matching Researchers with Respondents

For certain types of projects and certain types of communities, there is merit in matching the researcher to the respondents. Using a female researcher to research Pakistani Muslim women means that gender barriers and taboos about mixing with the opposite sex can be overcome. Often with the Muslim community, gender matching is even more vital than ethnicity matching as female respondents will refuse to be interviewed by a male researcher even if they are from the same ethnic background. For other communities, e.g. the Black African community matching ethnicity may be more useful as it means the moderator can probe more incisively based on their knowledge of the culture. It also means respondents can be more open and frank in voicing their opinions especially if they do not fear they will be offending the researcher. For yet other communities, it may not matter at all, for example, talking to Australian ex-pats who live in Paris. Clearly these issues are likely to be more applicable to moderators for qualitative research, but they will also apply to quantitative research and interviewers used.

However, matching moderators is easier said than done. Traditionally, market researchers have tended to come from the mainstream indigenous community rather than from ethnic communities. Hence the pool from which to match a researcher with the ethnic community being researched is rather small. Thus there are limited numbers of researchers from Black, Asian or East European communities who work in research in countries in Western Europe, the Americas and the Antipodes. And it is likely that the reverse is also true, i.e. there aren't very many Americans practising market research in Africa who are researching Americans who live there. If such matched moderators can be found, they may not be available for the timings of any given project.

There is also another dilemma. Matching moderators is not always a good idea. In research conducted amongst Muslims, female respondents were openly talking to the female English moderator about how they engaged in taboo behaviour such as smoking, drinking, drugs and pre-marital sex. They claimed that Islam was a constraining and liberating force. However, their male colleagues spent less time talking about taboo topics with the female Asian moderator. They focused on how British society was degenerate, racist, discriminatory, anti-Islamic and how Islam was a force for liberation. So the ethnic background of moderators can impact on the data gathered and matching needs to be handled with care.

In deciding whether to match researchers with respondents, it is perhaps worthwhile reflecting on the objectives and target audience for each research project on a case by case basis.

Some Research may Need to be in Mother Tongue

We are accustomed to conducting research in the mainstream indigenous language. For ethnic communities, this may not always be possible if they are not confident in the language. To meet this need, the ideal solution would be to use mother tongue or another language. For example, Moroccans living in Italy could be interviewed in Arabic, but as there are very few Arabic speaking researchers, they could be interviewed in French if they are not confident in Italian. Other research materials such as questionnaires, pre-interview tasks and stimulus could also be translated.

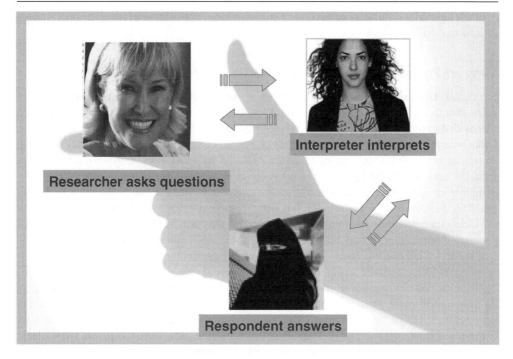

Figure 14.3   Conducting interviews via an interpreter

However, herein lies another issue. Not everyone who speaks their mother tongue can read and write in it. And that means that written translations are not as useful as they might first appear. Also some languages are spoken but not written. For example, Sylheti is spoken by some Bengalis but is not a written language. When Bengalis write, they write in Bengali using the Bengali script even though they speak Sylheti. To overcome these issues, it may be worth limiting the amount of written material required and using interviewer administered interviews.

For some ethnic communities, especially those that are more recent arrivals to the country, it may not be possible to have a mother tongue speaking researcher. In this instance, an interpreter could be used. Provided they are fully briefed on the requirements of the project, they would be part of a three-way conversation: the researcher asks the question in the indigenous language; the interpreter interprets into the mother tongue; the respondent answers in mother tongue; the interpreter translates this back into the indigenous language and then the researcher frames the next question. This is clearly a long winded process but sometimes the only viable option for more hard to reach ethnic communities. Figure 14.3 illustrates the process.

And finally, it is worth ensuring that all respondents in the same group discussion speak the same language. Bitter experience testifies to how difficult it is to conduct a group where not everyone can understand each other!

Practical and Logistical Issues can Affect Research Participation

Although they may seem trivial, researching ethnic communities often means being very aware of practicalities and logistics. Timing of research can be crucial as there are certain times of the year when it is more difficult to conduct research with certain communities. For example, interviewing Muslims during Ramadan can be more difficult. There are also certain times of the day that might be more problematic: more devout Muslims may ask permission to leave in the middle of a group or interview to pray. Similarly, certain venues can be problematic. Asking Black respondents to attend a group discussion in a pub frequented by White patrons in an area of the city that has racial tension would be a case in point.

To overcome these issues, it is also worth seeking out the advice of a researcher or local expert who has experience of dealing with ethnic communities and who can advise on practical matters.

COMMISSIONING RESEARCH WITH ETHNIC COMMUNITIES

Conducting research amongst ethnic communities may feel like a daunting task. Not only does it feel complex but there is the perennial fear of causing offence inadvertently. The need to apply best practice principles of research in general can often help overcome some hurdles. A skilled researcher should be thinking carefully about the suitability of certain methodologies on a project by project basis. They should be thinking hard about being precise in their sample definition. When in doubt, referring to good practice principles is always a good fall back position. However, there is also another way.

For clients buying ethnic research, it is always useful to question the research agency about how they plan to do the research. Some examples of the types of questions that could be asked are shown in Figure 14.4.

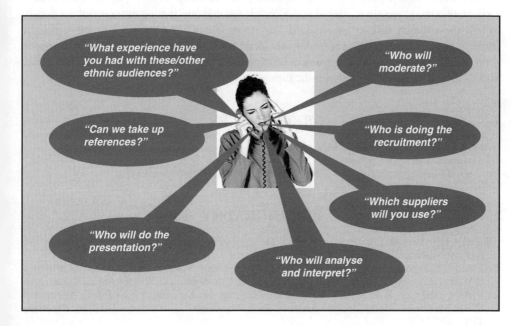

Figure 14.4 Questions to ask your agency

CURRENT DEVELOPMENTS AND THE NEAR FUTURE

Research into these communities is a source of constant fascination. The process by which the research is designed and implemented is fascinating; the people are fascinating and the findings are fascinating. It adds variety to mainstream market research. However, research into ethnic communities is still in its infancy and some countries are more au fait with these audiences than others. As with research in general, the UK and USA are probably near the forefront of understanding these communities, partly due to their hugely diverse ethnic make up and partly due to the weight of government and commercial interest respectively.

At present much research tends to focus on whether a product or service has sales potential or if marketing literature needs to be translated into mother tongue. Although opinions from these communities are canvassed for creative development, more sophisticated branding research and unusual methods such as semiotics are uncommon. Over time, as the marketing needs become more sophisticated and markets become more competitive, such methodologies and approaches will probably become more commonly used as brands come into play.

CONCLUSIONS

Modern societies are all the more interesting for the diversity of ethnicities and cultures that they now harbour. With the growth and increased prevalence of ethnic communities in countries comes interest from businesses, governments and NGOs who need to understand these communities. Researching ethnic communities is not straightforward and many factors need to be taken into consideration such as: bearing in mind lack of experience with research, designing the sample in the most precise way, using appropriate methodologies, considering language and practical details. However, a skilled and experienced researcher should be able to circumvent some of these issues by applying the principles of best practice in research. And clients should remain reassured in the knowledge that questioning agencies on the details of how the research will be conducted is a worthwhile pursuit. Although currently research amongst ethnic communities is at a relatively infant level, over time this will change to greater sophistication as markets and consumers become more complex. This should certainly be an area of research to watch closely for the future.

REFERENCES

National Statistics (UK) – www.ons.gov.uk
US Census Bureau – www.prb.org
http://www.london.gov.uk/gla/publications/factsandfigures/factsfigures/diversity.jsp

BIBLIOGRAPHY

Allahar, A.L. (ed.) (2001) *The Politics of Ethnic Identity Construction: A Special Issue of "Identity: An International Journal of Theory and Research" (Identity)*, Lawrence Erlbaum Associates.
Bell, M. and Sharma, A. (2002) "Beating the Drum of International Volunteering? Exploring Motivations to Volunteer Amongst Black and Asian Communities", Market Research Society, Annual Conference.
La Ferle, C. and Lee, W.N. (2005) "Can English Language Media Connect with Ethnic Audiences? Ethnic Minorities' Media Use and Representation Perceptions", *Journal of Advertising Research*, **45**(1), 140–153.
Fletcher, D. (2003) "Reaching the ethnic consumer", *Admap*, March 2003, Issue 437, 1–20.

Foxon, D. and Desai, P. (2004) "Targeting the kaleidoscope. Marketing in a multi-cultural age", ESOMAR, Qualitative Research, Cannes, November.

Gunaratnam, Y. (2003) *Researching Race and Ethnicity: Methods, Knowledge and Power*. Sage Publications.

Halter, M. (2002) *Shopping for Identity: The Marketing of Ethnicity*. Random House.

Leach, S. (2001) "Have you Woken up to the Benefits of Ethnic Targeting?", *Admap*, October, Issue 421.

Penninx, R., Martiniello, M. and Vertovec, S. (eds.) (2004) *Citizenship in European Cities: Immigrants, Local Politics and Integration Policies (Research in Migration & Ethnic Relations)*. Ashgate.

Rohde, L.V. (2005) "Multicultural Marketing: Just Do It!", *The Advertiser*, December, 40–44.

15

Opinion Polling

Kathleen A. Frankovic

Opinion polling is most often thought of as election polling – but there are more questions to ask of the public than simply how they will vote in an upcoming election. There are election-related items such as which issues affect people's votes, and how voters react to the candidates and critical issues in the election.

Outside of elections, opinion polls have become the voice of the people – the voice of democracy. They are the only way the public (by means of a representative sample of a country's citizens) can weigh in on critical issues and government assessments: examples include how well a regime is administering the government, whether or not critical needs are being taken care of, and what sort of activities the public wants the government to undertake. Opinion polling sometimes takes on a less substantive focus, as when it measures public reaction to particular events or scandals.

STAKEHOLDERS

We often think of opinion polling as part of news media coverage. For the news media, what matters most is timely information. Much of the time, in fact, we see opinion reported in news polls, but there are many other sources for opinion polls.

NGOs may commission opinion polls in support of their positions. Governments have an interest in opinion on policy issues; some government agencies may need to determine public concerns. For example, a government agency which manages elections may need to survey the public's confidence in election ballot counting, and the agency that is in charge of health care may want to conduct satisfaction studies of its customers. The collection of opinion data goes beyond the simple measurement of usage of services, or collection of information regarding the need for a service, or the compiling of demographic information. This use of opinion polling most closely resembles the work done for market research – learning the constituents' desires, needs and evaluations of existing products.

Political figures – and this sometimes includes government – may want to discover the public's desires in between elections. Just as business needs to know customer satisfaction with a product or service, an officeholder or a government would want to know its constituency's approval or satisfaction with its approach, and just as a company pursues discovering the desires of the consumer for a new product and guidance on how to market it, a political candidate may look to measure voters' desires and how to convince them that his or her positions are correct.

And of course, political figures also have a vested interest in assessments of themselves – and whether this assessment will permit them to seek further political office!

Market Research Handbook, 5th Edition. Edited by M. van Hamersveld and C. de Bont.
© 2007 John Wiley & Sons, Ltd.

Opinion polls are conducted by public interest groups as a way of discovering the public's views on matters important to the group. The results are then used in political debates and in presentations to decision makers. One caveat is that frequently the questions and the publicised results are in support of a political point of view. In Great Britain, the pro- and anti-fox hunting lobbies have used opinion polls as a way to try to convince government agencies that the public is on their side in the debate, and to convince the public that their group's position is that of the majority. The reason for the public relations angle may be the social science literature suggesting (although the evidence on the point is mixed) that those who know their opinion is in the minority may be less likely to be willing to express it publicly. The social sciences have developed opinion research as an academic subfield in sociology, communications research, political science and psychology.

But the main users of opinion research are news organisations. James Bryce, a British visitor to the United States in the 19th century, wrote in *The American Commonwealth* that newspapers had three functions. They were "narrators, advocates, and weathercocks". Newspapers (and now other media) narrate the story of what is happening, they advocate positions on important issues and as weathercocks, they tell readers what way the wind is blowing. George Gallup cited Bryce as he began his opinion polling career in the United States in the 1930s.

Although modern opinion polling, especially the pioneering work of George Gallup, may have begun in the United States, it quickly spread elsewhere, and surged in Europe and Japan after the end of World War II. Academic development was aided by government activities during and after that war. The United States even attempted studies of the impact of aerial bombing on morale in Germany. Later, but before the fall of Communism, sociologists in the Soviet Union were studying opinion, and in the 1980s Russian research firms were measuring public opinion there. Now, there are frequent opinion polls conducted for publication in nearly every country, as well as government and private studies of what the public thinks.

RELATIVE IMPORTANCE IN CURRENT MR

Opinion polling has frequently been used as a way for new market research firms to increase their public awareness and the awareness of potential clients. The public is believed to be interested in opinion poll results and especially election projections, so polling is frequently used as a way for new companies to make a name for themselves, by providing a public service, or by linking its name to a specific major news organisation, and of course by making a good projection of an upcoming election.

Market research companies, however, are also active in conducting opinion research for governments and private organisations. Most often these would be conducted by the custom research unit of a market research company.

Opinion research activity conducted in the public media and in academia is sometimes the source of research experiments in question order effects, scale measurements, and other studies in research methodology. Their findings may then be adopted by market researchers, and become part of standard research practice.

Research Questions/Issues

The most important research questions for polling are how one can truly measure an opinion, whether opinions are real, and whether attitudes affect behaviour. There is a long history of academic research on these questions.

The debate extends over a number of disciplines – sociology, psychology, communication and political science. In political science one of the research questions is how one can predict voting behaviour (and how to explain the voter's decision). A voter's group membership, his or her religious beliefs, friendships, what mass communications messages he receives, and his emotions all play a role. Obviously, one asks opinion questions to find out these characteristics.

The "art of asking questions" has been part of academic training in survey research since the 1930s. The debate covers many topics, including:

- Is it better to ascertain the salience of issues through open end questions (where the respondent answers in his or her own words), or through forced choices among specific topics? This was a debate that began in the 1940s. Rensis Likert, working with US agricultural surveys, conceived the "open interview", providing a general protocol, but allowing respondents to speak in their own words. Other researchers favored the limits of closed-ended questions. This debate continues, and there are examples that support each opinion. For example, when respondents are asked in an open-end format to name the most significant events of the twentieth century, few respondents mention the invention of the computer. However, when that is included in a pre-determined list, it is the most popular choice. When asked to name "the most important problem facing the country", Americans rarely volunteer "crime". But they often pick it from a pre-determined list. Similarly, in the 2004 US election, when voters were given a list of seven issues that could have affected their votes, "moral values" was selected by the largest number. That answer, at least in those specific words, was rarely given to open-end questions asked of likely voters before the election.
- How does one properly balance a question? Everyone understands that leading questions are inappropriate. But how much "balance" is required when presenting alternatives to a respondent? To evaluate political leaders, respondents are asked if they "approve or disapprove". But how much balance is required when presenting policy alternatives to a respondent? Should the number of words in each response be similar?
- When offering choices to a respondent, is there a response order effect? Some studies have found a primacy effect, with the first option favoured, others see a recency effect, especially in verbal questionnaires, where the last option is more likely to be remembered or chosen. Currently, when asking about voting preferences, the order of candidates is routinely rotated. Response order effects are occasionally surprising. There were primacy effects in pre-election polls for the 2000 US presidential election: George W. Bush and Al Gore (both non-incumbent candidates) did better in questions where their names were first in the two-way pairing. But there was little or no order effect in 2004 in pre-election polls asking voters to choose between George W. Bush (then the incumbent) and John Kerry. But primacy or recency order effects in two-response questions are rare. In long lists of response options, the response order can be even more of a factor. In spoken questions, as in a telephone survey, respondents tend to focus on the first and last responses, so those choices in the middle positions are least likely to be chosen.
- What is the impact of question order? Opinion questionnaires typically follow a pattern of beginning with general items ("What do you think is the most important problem facing the country today?") before moving on to questions about specific issues. To prevent assessments of one individual from influencing the assessments of another, the order can be rotated, just as answer categories are rotated. In addition, opinions that are perceived as most important are usually asked before other questions. In polling about a regime, respondents are usually asked to evaluate the performance of a chief executive before they are asked any questions

about specific issues. The principle is that respondents should give their assessment before being reminded of specific issues facing the country (in the US case, that means respondents should be asked their assessment of the performance of President George W. Bush before mentioning the war in Iraq).

- How real are opinions? Do respondents know what they are answering, or are they manipulated by the questioning itself? We know respondents will answer questions put to them, even if they have no real opinion. For example, both Stanley Payne and George Bishop, decades apart, found more than one third of Americans offered opinions on a non-existent "Metallic Metals Act", "Public Affairs Act", and a real, but unknown "Agricultural Trade Act". Some researchers use filtering questions to establish that respondents are following an issue before asking for opinions. Others, like Daniel Yankelovich, suggest that one needs several questions to determine when opinions are real. His "mushiness index" includes questions that ask how important a respondent thinks it is to have an opinion on an issue, how likely it is that they will change whatever opinion they expressed, and how long they have held their current opinion. That requires more questions to determine the reality of an opinion than to just ask the opinion. George Gallup had developed a similar procedure, which he called the "quintamensional plan of question design".

RESEARCH APPROACHES, METHODS AND WAYS OF WORKING

Most opinion polls for public consumption are conducted using probability samples, currently by telephone. Probability methods are applied by using either a variation of random digit dialling, or list-assisted methods. At the household level there is usually some method of random selection. However, some organisations use quota sampling methods, especially within a household.

In countries without near-universal telephone coverage, opinion polls are conducted in person, with random selection of sampling points and with random household selection or quota sampling at the individual level. There is relatively little opinion polling done using mail surveys, in part because of the recognition that certain opinions may be time-bound.

On election days, opinion polls are often exit polls, with interviewing conducted at selected polling places. In some countries, like the Philippines, conditions at the polls make it impossible to interview voters there, so day of election surveys at voters' homes are substituted for an exit poll at the polling place (voters there can be identified by an indelible mark on their hands).

The ESOMAR/WAPOR Guide to Opinion Polling notes that results of exit polls that indicate a winner must NOT be reported before the polls close. There is a complication in countries which have state and provinces that close at different times and report their votes separately.

Exit polling has been relatively accurate, but there are growing issues with it. In some places (like the United States), many votes are cast by mail well before Election Day, so any exit polls must collect the opinions and the votes of these individuals by telephone sampling. In addition, since interviewing is conducted in person, the interactions between the interviewer and the voter may create problems. In order to preserve confidentiality, exit polls are usually self-administered.

Opinion polls that are conducted for public consumption are meant to measure *current* opinion; consequently, surveys are done over a shortened field period. Typically, that may be between three and five days, although occasionally the field period is even shorter. One day surveys are not uncommon, especially during political campaigns or national crisis, when measurement of the impact of a particular event is deemed important. Those kinds of surveys are almost impossible to conduct in person.

The measurement of what people think has brought about an industry that pays attention to history. Specific questions have been asked for a long time. The rating of presidential approval in the United States, for example, goes back to the 1940s and the presidency of Franklin D. Roosevelt. The measurement of party identification has a similarly lengthy history.

Even if a particular question is wording has a certain bias in its construction, when the question is repeated over time, with that same bias, it is possible to measure changes in opinion over time. There is a premium in trend questions, and there are now accepted ways of asking about partisanship, candidates, and reactions to events. Searchable archives of those questions, most notably the Roper Center (now located at the University of Connecticut) make the process of gathering questions is with a history fairly easy.

Testing new questions sometimes involves the use of split-ballot experiments. A sample is divided into random halves, with each half asked a question a particular way. This is a method for testing whether wording changes affect the distribution of responses. If there is no difference, the two halves can be safely combined.

BENEFITS AND LIMITATIONS

The knowledge we get from opinion questions is critical for representative democracy. The information is used by governments, the media and private citizens.

But while the value of opinion polling is enormous, there are real limitations. Attempts to measure opinion at a specific time sometimes bring results that are unrelated to future behaviour and even future opinion. There are many hypothetical questions that are common in opinion research. The most famous is the one that asks "If the election were being held today". That question has proved a good indicator of election results, at least close to election day.

However, some hypothetical questions are much less predictive. And even questions about elections can get results that are way off the mark, if those questions are asked too early. The first US President George Bush trailed badly in 1987 against the then-most likely Democratic nominee: Mario Cuomo. And Bush had a dramatic lead over every possible Democratic opponent in 1991. Scarcely any Democratic challengers could even be found at the end of the Persian Gulf War when Bush had an approval rating near 90 %. In mid-1992, the independent businessman Ross Perot led the Republican and Democratic nominees; he eventually received 19 % of the vote.

There are even more examples. In 1983 and 1984, in the months before the Democrats named Geraldine Ferraro as the first major party nominee for vice president, much of the feminist campaign in support of her was based on a hypothetical poll question: "If the Democratic party nominated a woman for vice president, would you be more likely or less likely to vote Democrat?"

One of the more frequently reported results suggested that more than a quarter of the public would be more likely to vote for the Democratic candidate if a woman were on the ticket. But many if not most of those who said that putting a woman on the ticket would make them more likely to vote Democrat were already committed to voting Democrat.

In 1998, "what-if" questions dominated the polls. But these were about a president and a scandal that might result in his removal from office. Polls used questions like "What *if* Bill Clinton had an affair with Monica Lewinsky?" "What *if* he lied about it?" "What *if* he committed perjury?" and "What *if* he encouraged Monica Lewinsky to lie under oath?" By the middle of the year, the questions ran to things like: "What *if* Clinton had an affair with an intern?" "What *if* Clinton now publicly admits he did have an affair with Lewinsky?" "What *if* there is conclusive proof that Clinton lied under oath about having a sexual affair with Lewinsky?"

And to most of those questions, whatever the "if" was, majorities of respondents claimed that, *if* it were true, then Bill Clinton should leave office. Of course, as more and more real information came out, the poll results changed. The what-if questions early in 1998 seemed to show support for Clinton's resignation and impeachment under certain circumstances; but support for his removal from office disappeared as more and more Americans decided that in fact there had been a sexual relationship and that Clinton had, at the very least, misled and obfuscated under oath.

By the end of 1998, as the impeachment vote in the House of Representatives neared, polls asked what should happen if the President were impeached. There were wildly different responses – different from each other and different from opinions expressed after the fact. In a CBS News/New York Times Poll conducted during the week preceding the House vote, half the sample was asked: "If the President is impeached, would it be better for the country if he resigns?" 57 % said "Yes". The other half of the sample was asked: "If the House voted to send articles of impeachment to the Senate for a trial, would it be better for the country if the President resigns?" Only 40 % said yes to that. One reason for the difference is that, up until the time of the House's vote, nearly one-third of the public was under the mistaken impression that impeachment was the same thing as removal from office, in which case it was logical to them that Bill Clinton should just leave quietly, instead of being dragged kicking and screaming perhaps, from the White House. So support for resignation was much higher in the first formulation than in the second, when the two-step nature of the process was made explicit.

But after the impeachment vote was taken, fewer people said that resignation would be better for the country. The issue was no longer hypothetical: Bill Clinton had been impeached. Only 31 % at that point said that they wanted him to resign.

Besides the limitations of what one can truly learn from opinion polling, there are the limitations that come from the general difficulties of conducting research. Lower response rates are a matter of great concern in opinion polling because of the need for adequate representation of the population, and since opinion polls are mainly reported publicly, charges of unrepresentativeness are common from those whose opinions (or whose candidates) are in the minority. Those charges are particularly strong on topics of intense political conflict: the 2004 presidential election in the United States, and the issue of fox hunting in Britain.

DO'S AND DON'TS

The major issues for opinion polling have a great deal to do with the fact that opinion polls attempt to ascertain how the public feels about major issues of the day. That puts particular emphasis on questionnaire design and on transparency.

That means questions and methods come under increased scrutiny, especially when the subject matter is one of political consequence. So all of the rules for writing questions must be followed – balancing the question, not misrepresenting factual information, and ensuring that question order isn't biasing answers.

In recent years, poll results have become part of the public debate, with political candidates and parties much more likely to attack polls that suggest they are not popular. The extent of those attacks have become more intense, sometimes attacking poll methods and sometimes attacking the character of the pollster. In the US 2004 presidential election, the Republican

Party called on the Minneapolis Star-Tribune newspaper to fire its polling director, saying the paper's poll consistently interviewed "too many Democrats". Moveon.org, a left of centre website that encourages voters for the Democrats, personally attacked George Gallup, Jr. for his religious beliefs, claiming that this affected the results of the Gallup Poll.

There is evidence that while pre-election polls have had problems in the past, their accuracy in recent years has been good. In the United States, the story of the 1948 election, when pioneering pollsters like George Gallup, Elmo Roper and Archibald Crossley decided campaigns had little impact and ceased polling weeks before the election itself, has become part of polling lore. Their wrong predictions of an easy victory by Republican nominee Thomas Dewey over President Harry Truman threatened the entire research industry in the US and elsewhere, resulted in an industry inquiry, and moved polling methods away from quota sampling and towards probability methods. In addition, pre-election predictions knew that accurate measurements required surveys conducted much closer to the election.

There were outcries against the industry in the US and the UK in the mid-1990s, when pre-election polls underestimated the shares of the vote of the Republican and Conservative parties, giving rise to talk of "shy Tories" and "Republican refusers". In more recent elections, pre-election polls have been much closer to the mark.

Any public opinion pollster will have to be willing to accept attacks on findings as a matter of course. When opinion polls are conducted prior to elections, a further concern is the definition of likely voters. This is easier in countries with high voter turnout, but becomes more difficult in countries and in elections with lower turnout.

It is important to follow methodological guidelines so that the opinion polls are defensible, and to remember the importance of disclosure. The ESOMAR/*WAPOR Guide to Opinion Polls* contains all the relevant information.

CURRENT DEVELOPMENTS AND NEAR FUTURE

Recent developments in opinion polling mirror those in market research: researchers are trying to utilise new technologies while preserving representative samples. New technologies include using recorded questionnaires administered over the telephone and IVR (interactive voice recognition) or touch-tone entry to record answers, experimental sample of cell phone users, and using web panels of respondents, adjusted to resemble the entire population.

Web surveys are still controversial, since not all the relevant population is on line (with a bias against older and less affluent individuals), and there is, as of now, no way of drawing a representative sample of those who are. This is especially a problem for opinion polls, which are meant to show the opinions of all citizens or all voters.

We should expect that the near future will bring greater focus on web surveys and more stress on opinion polls. Researchers will be looking at response rates, as they do for all sorts of research. Opinion polling will likely come under increased attacks. The days of immediate belief in poll results may be over.

SUGGESTED READING

Asher, H. (2007) *Polling and the Public: What Every Citizen Should Know, (7th edn)*. CQ Press.
Schuman, H. and Presser, S. (1981) *Questions and Answers in Attitude Surveys: Experiments in Question Form, Wording, and Context*. Academic Press.
Tourangeau, R., Rips, L.J. and Rasinski, K. (2000) *The Psychology of the Survey Response*. Cambridge University Press.

16

Employee Research

Andrew Buckley and Richard Goosey

INTRODUCTION

There has been a significant amount of growth in the conduct, scope, application and sophistication of employee research since the 1990s. During the 1990s, most large organisations recognised the importance and value of obtaining regular feedback from employees, most commonly as a means of increasing staff retention and improving customer service delivery. In recent years, however, more organisations are beginning to understand and apply employee research in the wider context of the balanced scorecard, the service profit chain and in recognising the importance of employees as key stakeholders in terms of corporate social responsibility and reputation.

Figure 16.1 shows how thinking has evolved to link employee satisfaction to delivery of the organisations' service concept or brand, which generates customer satisfaction, customer loyalty and ultimately positive business outcomes.

The growing recognition of employees' potential impact on an organisation's performance has therefore lifted employee research up the senior management agenda. Equally, the type of organisations conducting employee research has proliferated; from the traditional sectors of retail, financial and the public sector to manufacturing, engineering and industrial sectors, from global organisations to SMEs.

Whilst the standard "employee opinion" or "staff attitude" survey still has an important role to play in supporting the HR strategy of many organisations, more sophisticated practitioners are attempting to measure and define concepts such as employee engagement, alignment and advocacy. Many organisations are also applying employee research more tactically (rather than just conducting an annual census survey), for example:

- Pre and post surveys following merger and acquisition activity or corporate restructuring (including temperature checking and tracking).
- Research to develop and implement vision and values based programmes.
- Internal communication surveys and audits.
- Exit interview tracking ("Leavers" Surveys).
- Needs analysis followed by measuring the impact of training programmes and other initiatives.
- Measuring the impact of both internal and customer-based initiatives.

Market Research Handbook, 5th Edition. Edited by M. van Hamersveld and C. de Bont.
© 2007 John Wiley & Sons, Ltd.

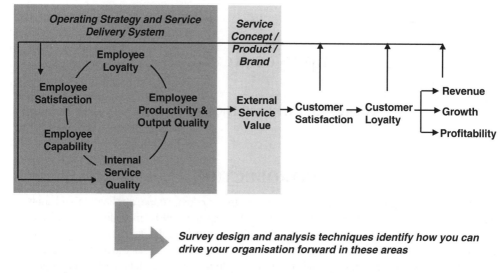

Figure 16.1   The Service Profit Chain (Heskett, Sasser and Schlesinger)

There has also been the growth of "Best Companies" type competitions sponsored by national newspapers or magazines, with the principal aim being to leverage the employer brand, both internally and externally. Examples of these include:

- Sunday Times 100 Best Companies to Work For – based on a sample of employees who complete a questionnaire containing 66 questions on eight workplace factors and a company based survey on their policies, processes, services and facilities.
- The Fortune 100 Best Companies to Work For – for US companies with more than 1 000 employees. Again based on a sample of at least 400 employees using both an employee attitude survey and company based survey about the companies workplace practices, philosophy, and work environment.

This chapter examines the latest thinking, development and implementation of employee research, including survey design, communications, data collection, maximising response rates, analysis, action planning and results dissemination.

THE GROWTH OF EMPLOYEE ENGAGEMENT

As previously mentioned, many organisations have started to go further than simply measuring and understanding what drives employees' job satisfaction and morale. At the time of writing the latest HR-driven concept in employee research is to *define, measure and identify the drivers of employee engagement.*

HR departments, management consultancies and market research agencies have developed different interpretations and models of employee engagement. However, most agree that engagement is essentially a measure of the strength of the personal relationship between the employee and employer; it is beyond both the formal and the psychological contracts of employment. Although there are different theories as to what drives engagement, almost all the

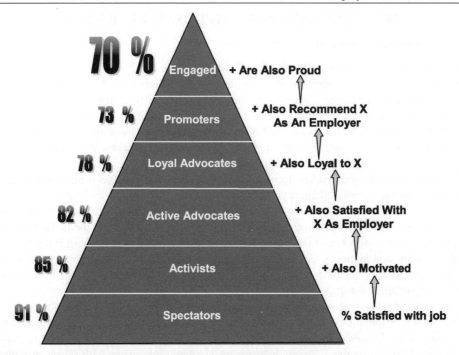

Figure 16.2   Level of engagement in company X, 70% are engaged

theories agree on the same principle – it is the sum of the emotional feelings and rational thoughts that an employee holds about their employer that determines their behaviour.

Engagement is, therefore, the result of a variety of factors which underpin the strength of the employer–employee relationship, including (amongst others) job satisfaction, motivation, advocacy, commitment and an employees' pride in their organisation. When employees are "fully" engaged with the organisation, it is essentially satisfying the employees' basic needs, facilitating their motivation and commitment, is honouring the employee–employer relationship and generates a sense of pride and purpose in the individual. In return, the employee intuitively understands how their personal role and behaviour impacts upon the overall vision and goals of the organisation. Employees' day-to-day decision making and behaviour is aligned to overall strategy, making the organisation a more powerful collective force.

Figure 16.2 shows how an engagement model is able to segment employees based on the level of commitment to the organisation. This moves from the lowest level of commitment ("Spectators" who are only satisfied with their job) to the highest level of engaged employees (those who are satisfied with their job, motivated, satisfied with their employer, loyal, would recommend and are proud to work for the company).

Critically, reciprocation and mutuality are at the heart of engagement. For engagement to be achieved, the employee must believe that they are valued, recognised, and that they will personally share in the success and achievement of organisational goals. Although employee engagement surveys are rising in popularity and have a slightly different focus from the standard "Employee Opinion Survey", the execution of such surveys is much the same. We will now examine the research techniques, approaches and best practices for conducting internal employee research.

THE EXECUTION OF EMPLOYEE RESEARCH

Obtaining Senior Management Commitment

For any organisation, the first critical stage of conducting an employee survey is to obtain the commitment of senior management. It is essential that the Chief Executive and other members of the senior team agree the objectives of the survey, commit to communicating the results back to employees and are prepared to take action on the findings. Although this may seem an obvious statement, in the experience of the author many organisations find it difficult to achieve this (for a variety of reasons), and can find themselves in a worse position at the end of the survey process than they were at the start.

It's at this stage that the first key decision is made of whether to conduct the employee survey in-house or to use an external agency who specialise in employee research (a market research agency or management consultancy). Generally, the fees associated with employee research are relatively low compared to other forms of research (because the sample is the company employees), and using an external agency has the clear advantage of portraying independence, confidentiality, and authority. A company would also expect an external agency to advise on issues relating to privacy of data, and codes of research practice (either legal or best practice industry regulation) within a country.

One of the first tasks for either the in-house resource or the external agency may in fact be to obtain senior management commitment by facilitating a workshop, allowing survey objectives to be discussed, mutually agreed and for any fears regarding the survey to be aired and allayed. An alternative is to conduct one-to-one depth interviews with senior managers, which have the advantage of providing a confidential environment where useful insight can be obtained regarding senior leadership politics. The interviews also allow an executive overview to be sought, giving the survey a "bottom down" as well as "top up" perspective, providing illuminating comparisons between top managerial views and those of other employees (e.g. effectiveness in communicating the vision and goals, alignment and understanding of them, perceived speed of change, etc.).

The interviews can be conducted ideally in person or over the telephone (given the difficulty in making and keeping appointments with senior managers), with interviews lasting around 30 to 45 minutes. As with all types of employee research, the maintenance of respondent confidentiality is essential.

Pre-Survey Planning

Employee surveys are more successful when employees from across the organisation have been involved and consulted in the process, in terms of setting survey objectives, being involved in questionnaire design (via focus groups, depth interviews, pilots) and in the feedback of results. Staff forums, communications groups and unions should be all involved in the initial consultation process; indeed, with effective consultation employee unions can become strong advocates of the survey process and be influential in improving response rates.

Some organisations set up systems of survey champions (which vary depending on the size, structure and culture of the organisation). For example, in multi-site organisations such as the retail and leisure industry, outlet managers are pivotal in pre-communicating, managing survey completion, cascading the results and taking actions on the survey. Survey pre-communications can be facilitated via issuing packs which contain detailed information about the survey, its objectives, FAQ's (e.g. how to field questions about confidentiality, the use of an independent agency), and explanations as to why obtaining a high response rate is important. This early engagement also involves managers in the process and enhances their involvement in the final communication and implementation of results. In other organisations, survey champions need not necessarily be of management grade – they could be staff representatives or hand picked internal "opinion leaders".

Other important tasks at the pre-survey stage are to plan survey logistics (i.e. distribution methods if using paper based questionnaires, or checking compatibility of systems and software for conducting the survey online). Another essential task is to plan the pre, during and post survey communications programme, which we will examine in more depth later.

Qualitative Research

As with many other forms of market research, qualitative research has a key role to play in ensuring that the right issues are measured in the main quantitative survey. The research also has a value in its own right, providing illustrative stories or "flesh on the bones" which helps interpretation of the statistics from the main survey. Qualitative methods are also effective in researching more abstract concepts, such as vision and values and organisational culture.

In repeat studies, qualitative research can be used to identify employees' detailed opinions of what has changed or improved since the last survey. Also, if response rates to the previous survey were low, qualitative research is an effective forum for obtaining feedback and insight as to the potential reasons (e.g. was the questionnaire too long, were there concerns over confidentiality, were employees given time to complete their questionnaires, etc.).

Qualitative research often takes the form of depth interviews with senior management (as previously mentioned) or focus groups with more junior staff. Focus groups have the following advantages and features:

- A group forum can stimulate spontaneous discussion on views that otherwise would not have arisen during personal interview;
- Group discussions mean that the role of interviewer or moderator is reduced in terms of guiding and influencing the process, i.e. employees are more likely to spend time discussing issues which are *most important to them*; and,
- The participation of employees in the focus groups will also help to raise awareness of the forthcoming quantitative survey, encourage higher response rates and demonstrate the commitment of the company to listen to the views of its employees directly.

A typically large organisation (say 5 000+ employees) would conduct six to eight focus groups, with eight to ten members of staff in each, comprising a range of staff from different departments and locations. However, it is important not to mix levels of seniority within the same focus group, so as not to inhibit the contribution of less senior employees. It is also advisable not to mix blue and white collar employees in the same groups.

The client organisation would typically conduct all recruitment and hold the focus groups at internal venues. However, it is advisable that an independent market research agency conducts the moderation so that the findings remain objective and that employees feel comfortable in giving their open and honest views of working for the organisation. The maintenance of employee confidentiality is essential throughout the process. For example, employees are reassured both at the start and the end of the focus group that none of their individual comments will be directly attributed.

Quantitative Research

Census or Sample?

Quantitative research is the most common vehicle used for employee research surveys, primarily because of the large numbers of respondents involved. The first key decision is whether to conduct a sample or census survey, although most organisations opt for the latter, for the following reasons:

- A census is a powerful demonstration of corporate commitment to listening to the views of all employees;
- This methodology avoids any groups of employees feeling excluded from the survey process;
- It allows more detailed statistical analysis of employee subgroups (e.g. by outlet, location, department, etc.);
- It overcomes the problem of having to set detailed sampling frameworks and then running the risk of having poor returns in some areas; and,
- The survey has greater validity, both politically and statistically.

A sample approach would be more appropriate where survey logistics become too difficult, if budget is an issue or if the organisation wishes to monitor employee opinion on a frequent basis (e.g. monthly or quarterly). A regular census would obviously lead to survey fatigue and extremely high costs.

Questionnaire Design

Employee survey questionnaires tend to be quite formulaic, but with good reason. They need to be easy to complete and simple to understand by employees at all levels of an organisation, and the questionnaire has to cover a wide range of topics in a relatively short time. Therefore, simple agree-disagree type rating scales are common (usually four or five point scales, but seven and ten point scales can also be applied).

The range of topics covered in an employee engagement or opinion survey typically include (this is by no means an exhaustive list):

- Key indicators: job satisfaction, motivation, advocacy, commitment or loyalty, pride, and likelihood to recommend the employer.
- Culture: job security, fair treatment, equality and diversity, social responsibility, health and safety.
- Job role: role design, whether the job makes a meaningful contribution, levels of empowerment.
- Leadership: understanding and support of the vision, whether feel able to contribute to vision, views of leadership team and style, trust.
- Management: views of immediate line manager's style (e.g. honesty, approachability, competence, communication skills, keeping promises, etc.).
- Communication: views of downward, upward and cross-organisation channels, strength of grapevine.
- Training and development: identifying training needs, effectiveness of delivery and application of training back into the workplace, opportunities for personal and career development.
- Reward and recognition: pay, benefits, whether feel valued, performance management.
- Working environment: physical conditions, tools and IT systems to do the job.

- Teamwork: within teams, across teams and departments, levels of internal customer service.
- Mirror questions: often questions can be inserted to obtain a mirror of customers' views from the organisation's customer satisfaction or brand tracking research, which then allows for gap or integrated analysis.
- Open ended question(s): where employees are given the opportunity to have their say on any issue important to them.
- Demographics: job role, length of service, contractual relationship and area of work are the most commonly asked questions. It is important not to ask too many or superfluous demographic questions as it raises employees' fears of being identified (e.g. age, gender, ethnicity, disability are usually only useful for equality and diversity monitoring).
- Note that both the questionnaire introduction and closing statement should reiterate the confidentiality of the exercise (preferably stating that the research is being carried out under the appropriate code of conduct, i.e. MRS Code of Conduct in the UK, the ESOMAR Code of Marketing and Social Research Practice, the Council of American Survey Research Organizations (CASRO), the Commission Nationale Informatique et Libertés (CNIL) – France – are all good examples). These organisations also publish Guidelines of how the codes should be interpreted when conducting employee research.

In terms of questionnaire length, it should really take no more than 10–15 minutes to complete or there can be a negative effect on response rates. In certain industries (e.g. 24 hour operations or shift based organisations, retail and leisure, engineering businesses) the optimum questionnaire length is around 5–10 minutes. A general rule of thumb is that if the employee sits at a desk or has a regular work-station, a longer questionnaire can be used.

It is always worthwhile piloting questionnaires with employees as part of the natural process of design. Piloting is useful in ensuring the right questions are asked, that questions are not ambiguous or that the language is not unnecessarily complex. Pilots can be conducted via self completion, whereby draft questionnaires are sent to say, 30–50 employees across the organisation. In addition to the normal questionnaire form, space can be left for employees to comment on individual questions, themes or the style of the questions and language used. Alternatively, pilot sessions can be invigilated by a market researcher and feedback can be given face-to-face in a group setting.

In terms of paper based questionnaires, they can be in A4 format, as an A5 booklet or even A6 pocket format (very useful for blue collar occupations). Many organisations print questionnaire internals black and white with colour front covers, which present a professional image without incurring too high a cost. The use of recycled paper for both questionnaires and return envelopes has also increased in popularity over the last ten years.

Survey Completion Methods and Considerations

There are several options for survey completion, the principal methods being:

- Self completion on paper;
- Self completion online (Internet, intranet or email);
- Telephone;
- Face to face.

Up until five years ago, the vast majority of employee surveys were self-completed on paper, although online surveys (particularly over the Internet) have seen a major increase for speed, cost, ease of distribution and completion and environmental reasons. Paper will continue to be used for many years yet, as many organisations have employees who do not have regular access to a PC, although hybrid paper-online surveys are common in organisations with a white and blue collar split. The advantages of self completion over interviewer-assisted interviewing are:

- Significantly lower costs;
- Employees can complete in their own time, at their own pace;
- Speed;
- Greater (perceived) anonymity.

The decision to run the survey by paper or online should be exercised on a case by case basis, depending on the culture and structure of the organisation. The advantages of paper-based completion to consider are:

- Access: by using personal hand-to-hand distribution, it could be argued that all employees should receive a questionnaire (it cannot be assumed that all employees would be allowed access or time to complete a PC-based survey in the workplace);
- Personal touch: mail is generally regarded as a more personal and engaging medium, making employees feel more comfortable about the survey process (and arguably more likely to respond);
- Quality: it could be argued that potentially better quality information may be obtained via a paper method; it could be argued that employees give more considered views when the questionnaire is completed at home, outside of the hustle and bustle of the working day (which could negatively skew responses);
- Choice: by using paper surveys, employees have the choice of where they would like to complete the survey, at home, at work or indeed anywhere else;
- Confidentiality: confidentiality is essential to the success of an employee survey, both to obtain the genuine, honest views of employees and to maximise response rates. With paper-based mailing, in the employees mind, confidentiality is assured for several reasons:
  o employees can complete the survey at home, and neither managers nor colleagues would be able to see the questionnaire or influence its completion. Again, from experience, employees have commented about feeling nervous that someone saw their screen/responses, particularly in open-plan offices;
  o despite repeated assurances, it is likely that some employees (particularly highly PC literate employees) would suspect that the survey is not anonymous (employees fear they can be identified from electronic survey completion, e.g. by time and date of completion or "electronic footprints" left on the data file).

However, there are also significant advantages to conducting surveys online:

- Potential cost savings: in terms of printing, envelopes, inbound postage and data processing.
- "Novelty" value: office based employees are likely to already work with a variety of paper based forms and documents. It is therefore possible that an online survey would be considered by some to be a "breath of fresh air" and thus encourage higher response rates.
- Faster turnaround of the survey: by approximately one to two weeks. The response to on-line surveys is also typically much quicker than paper, with a high proportion of employees responding within one to three days;
- The survey is always available: it is possible for paper questionnaires to be lost or thrown away (either on purpose or accidentally) and this can limit the potential response rate, particularly

if a reminder is sent to employees mid-way through the fieldwork period (to which they may have been persuaded to now respond but no longer have a questionnaire). The online method has the advantage of always being available and re-prints not being required.

- Data collection accuracy: in theory, web-based data collection and processing accuracy is 100 %. However, data collection of paper based questionnaires is only marginally behind if proper validation and quality control procedures are exercised.

Telephone interviewing is sometimes used for employee research, typically when a smaller or targeted sample is required, or a specific topic is being researched (e.g. views of internal communications, research regarding sales incentives, exit interviewing or retention research). Face to face interviewing is even less common, but can be used in potentially sensitive situations, particularly in manufacturing and industrial organisations (e.g. suspected bullying of staff, in employee union recognition and industrial relations situations).

Increasing Response Rates

One of the key measures of a successful employee survey is the response rate, and to a certain extent, it indicates the level of engagement employees have with the organisation. Typical response rates are around 55–60 %, although it varies widely both within and across industry sector. Not surprisingly, white collar occupations are far more likely to respond than blue collar (typical response rates are 60–90 % for white collar, 20–50 % blue collar). Note, there is a small school of thought that survey completion should be mandatory; some organisations have published achieved response rates of above 95 %. However, in the author's experience, such "forced" practices are ill advised and can result in poor internal publicity for the organisation and may affect the quality of data collected.

In terms of statistical validity, generally the data does not become negatively skewed until response rates drop below 25 %. However, politically, organisations (and senior managers) generally feel more confident taking action on the survey results when the response is over 50 %, regardless of the actual number of people who took part and how statistically accurate the data is.

Perhaps the biggest single driver of whether an employee responds to a survey is whether they feel action will be taken as a result. The rationale is quite logical; if an employee thinks nothing will be done with the results, they will simply not invest their time filling out the survey. The pre-survey communication must, therefore, convince employees that something will be done with the results and (at the very least) the results will be communicated back. Other suggestions for survey communications include:

- Early publicity for the survey (via workplace posters, articles in publications, employee briefings, etc.);
- Early briefing of line managers about the importance of the survey to the organisation;
- A communication from the CEO or Managing Director forewarning of the survey dates and stressing the importance of employee opinions to the organisation, then followed up by a communication from a more local manager to reinforce the timing issue;
- Setting up a specific site on the intranet. This could publish the objectives of the survey, its timeline, its outputs and could also allow employees to ask questions about the survey;
- Assurances of confidentiality to employees (verified by the use of an external research agency (if applicable), ideally bound by the appropriate code of conduct);

- Assurances to employees that data will only be reported for groups of a minimum size of 10 employees to retain anonymity; and, most importantly
- Assurances to employees of the intention to report back the results and act on the data along with a timetable for those actions.

Some organisations brand their survey, which can be helpful in raising awareness of the exercise amongst employees. For example, a retailer developed their own employee survey, branded "Hometruths". All materials and communications associated with the survey (posters, canteen table cards, articles in the in-house magazine, etc.) carried the branded logo. Subsequent research conducted for the communications department showed that the branding of the survey had raised awareness and had made employees more likely to respond to the questionnaire because of its higher profile.

Another major factor in achieving a high response is the monitoring of response rates throughout the fieldwork period. Survey champions or management would then be made responsible for chasing areas of low response. In many organisations, the introduction of targets and a little healthy competition between departments can be beneficial to increasing response rates without affecting the quality of information obtained.

Other techniques which can help organisations achieve a high response rate are:

- Allowing employees time in the workplace to complete the survey. This is critical for non-office based or shift working employees;
- The creation of special rooms at certain times of the day that have refreshments available. Again, critical for the reason given above, although completion should be voluntary;
- Creating 15 minutes at the end of a team brief or team meeting for the completion of the survey.

In conclusion, organisations should find the balance between proactively managing and encouraging employees and managers to promote the survey and complete it, without it becoming a witch hunt or three line whip. If an employee survey is to become a successful, long term tool which assists senior and line managers in making better decisions when managing their people, organisations need to be mindful of the survey's original spirit; it is intended to be a healthy exchange of information between employees and the employer, whereby both parties mutually benefit, come to understand each other a little better and strengthen the bond of their relationship.

Incentives

The culture of the organisation largely determines how successful an incentive is going to be. For example, a private sector organisation offered the incentive of an all-expenses paid holiday for two in San Francisco. The company had a population of 1 500 employees, so there was a relatively small chance of winning. However, fewer prize draw cards than completed questionnaires were received, and a final response rate below 30 % resulted.

However, in a transport organisation, a larger number of smaller cash value incentives were offered to teams with the highest response rate for their local area (£ 100). This scheme had a very positive impact on response rates amongst blue collar occupations.

Incentives which seem to work effectively in the public sector are charity donations (e.g. £ 1 for each questionnaire received). One organisation which was repeating its survey increased their response rates by around 20 % points using this incentive. Often, however, the majority of organisations do not offer incentives and healthy response rates are achieved, so judgement on a case by case basis should be exercised.

Analysis Techniques

Quantitative Analysis

The analysis of employee research data has also seen significant improvement over the last 10 years. The nature of employee research data lends itself to multivariate statistical analysis (i.e. use of rating scales, homogeneous respondents, a typically low margin of error from sampling a high proportion of the universe, high base sizes). The most common analysis techniques used are correlation, regression, factor analysis and segmentation, with typical analysis objectives being:

- To identify the drivers of employee satisfaction, advocacy or engagement (e.g. leadership, teamwork, communications, etc.).
- To identify the specific actions and issues to tackle (e.g. within leadership is it perceptions of leadership style, belief and understanding of vision or the way change is managed?).
- Via segmentation, to identify who are the apostles, mercenaries and saboteurs of the organisation, and to identify which attitudes, perceptions and demographics they possess.

More complex analysis techniques can be employed for certain organisations with multi sites (i.e. integrated or balanced scorecard type analysis). The organisation must have at least 50 discrete units (e.g. shops, outlets, sites) for which employee satisfaction, customer satisfaction and business information is available. It is then possible to model the relationships between the three sets of data and identify the drivers of business performance (e.g. sales, turnover, unit profitability, staff retention, absence and sickness rates, etc.). This is a major route forward for the growth and application of employee research, by statistically demonstrating the impact employees have on business performance.

It is also highly valuable to link the analysis to internal business KPIs for example, to demonstrate the correlation between staff turnover and employee satisfaction and engagement. This can be seen at the reporting stage by showing the staff turnover level by department, for example, against the employee satisfaction and engagement scores.

Benchmarking and Norms

Most organisations conducting an employee survey want normative data, so that they can externally contextualise the results. This is one of many reasons why organisations commission market research companies (who have large databases of previous clients' data) to conduct their survey. The larger agencies are usually able to provide norms by country and industry sector on most of the key metrics of an employee survey, giving both average and "best in class" or "top quartile" comparators.

However, whilst norms are useful in comforting and reassuring managers of their performance in comparison to other organisations, internal benchmarking is usually more productive and supportive to an organisation's development and progress. Therefore, the tracking of employee survey data over time, and benchmarking the organisation against itself (and the best performing areas of the organisation) should be given the most attention.

RESULTS COMMUNICATION AND ACTION PLANNING

Communication and Reporting

The most important stage of the employee survey comes at the end of the process – to take action on the findings. The first key task is to communicate the results back to employees and give them some indication about what the organisation plans to do about it. There are a number of ways an organisation can do this, including:

- Face to face briefings as part of a regular team meeting;
- Run some specially convened results briefings, often presented back by the independent agency for greater credibility;
- Publication of results in company newsletter or magazine;
- Publication of results via workplace posters or noticeboards;
- Presentation of results in a dedicated booklet;
- Videos;
- Roadshows by senior management;
- Display of results on the intranet.

The results are also typically presented back to senior management and often second line management by the agency. Action plans are then co-ordinated, agreed and communicated across the organisation.

Reports for teams, departments or units are then typically produced for local managers to take forward. Some organisations produce accompanying notes for managers, giving them advice on how to interpret the data and giving suggestions for action on the issues which the company as a whole has a relative weakness. This has the added benefit of managers then being more likely to take a more consistent approach to action across the organisation. For those who are PC based, again the intranet can be used, and part of the site could publish tips, hints and suggestions for areas of best practice.

Workshops

Some organisations help managers to produce action plans using workshops. Each workshop can involve between 12 and 20 managers, and ideally they should work in the same broad areas, so that they share common issues. For illustration, a typical workshop agenda (either full or half day) could be:

- Housekeeping, objectives of the session.
- An initial results presentation, to warm people up to the survey and help them understand how to correctly interpret the statistics.
- Issuing of managers' local reports and then go into group working sessions. Objectives would be set for each group.
- The groups report back their discussions and findings.
- The session could close with a round table discussion, or "next steps" and timeline for action, so that each manager takes a feeling of responsibility away with them.

- It is also important to send a follow-up summary or communiqué to participants following the workshop to maintain the momentum.

FREQUENCY AND TRACKING

As previously mentioned, an employee survey becomes of greater utility to an organisation when the survey is repeated and the results are tracked over time. Some organisations repeat annually and make the survey a calendar event. This is successful in making the survey part of the business cycle and planning process, and organisations which run annual surveys often input the metrics into a balanced scorecard or use them to support management bonuses or performance reviews.

Other organisations repeat every 18 months or two years, as they find it more difficult to implement actions and change; it can be disheartening and counter productive to repeat the survey annually for its own sake, if no significant changes can be effected and seen by employees.

Alternatively, some organisations run "temperature checks" on a monthly, quarterly or six monthly basis, whereby a sample of employees (representative of the organisation) are invited to take part, sometimes using a shorter questionnaire which includes just the key indicators and areas for action identified by the previous survey. These "temperature checks" can be either quantitative or qualitative (usually focus groups) in nature.

SUMMARY

Employee research is a very rewarding area of the market research profession. You are invariably researching people about matters which are very important to them, who enjoy taking part in the research, and the actions identified from the survey can significantly change their working lives.

REFERENCES

Conducting Research with Employees – Market Research Society Guidelines (revised 2005).
Goudge, P. (2006) Employee Research – How to increase employee involvement through consultation – Market Research in Practice Series.
McNeil, R. (2005) ESOMAR *Handbook of Market and Opinion Research* (4th edn), Chapter 26.

17

Mystery Shopping

Helen Turner

WHAT IT IS

Mystery Shopping is a term used to describe a form of research whereby individuals measure any type of customer service process by acting as actual or potential customers and in some way report back on their experiences, in a detailed and, as far as possible, objective way. The term can be a little misleading since the service under review may not in fact involve any form of "shopping", perhaps being a call to a Helpline or a check on a website for its user-friendliness. However, the term seems to have persisted over time but has come to cover a much wider context. For this reason, some clients choose to call any programmes they operate in this way Service Checks, Customer Checks, Customer First, etc., particularly if earlier projects, conducted under the name of Mystery Shopping, seemed to be viewed with suspicion by staff members – we will come back to that topic later.

It was developed from earlier methods used by private investigators checking up on staff misconduct such as theft or fraud, and the name "Mystery Shopping" was coined by Wilmark in the 1940s as the technique began to be used more widely to examine levels of customer service. The 1990s saw particular growth in the use of the technique as use of the Internet widened, leading to gains in the speed of reporting and economies of recruitment and data collection.

Mystery Shopping has been conducted within the Industry now for many years, following various debates in earlier years as to whether or not as a technique it was ethical, some seeing it as a form of industrial espionage not to be encouraged. However, the Market Research Society (MRS) and Mystery Shopping Providers Association (MSPA) developed Guidelines alongside ESOMAR to raise the quality of work done and now by embracing it within the industry we are able to apply these guidelines to its use to ensure it is correctly conducted, the results are not misused and that it is used to positive ends and not solely as some form of disciplinary tool. As the methodology continues to grow in importance globally this reassurance will become even more important.

The main distinguishing feature of Mystery Shopping is that the person undertaking the task does not declare the fact that they are conducting it. Any person involved in the transaction is therefore not alerted at that specific time to the fact that they are under review. However, ESOMAR Guidelines ensure that staff are alerted to the use of such techniques within their own organisation or are not adversely affected or identified when such checks are made on competitive organisations. The activity need not therefore be seen as threatening in any way.

Market Research Handbook, 5th Edition. Edited by M. van Hamersveld and C. de Bont.
© 2007 John Wiley & Sons, Ltd.

HOW IT IS USED

The objective of using a Mystery Shopping approach should be to increase customer service levels and to ensure that service is being delivered in the ways intended by an organisation.

Clients have at their finger tips so many forms of measurement these days – retail sales feedback from bar code systems, interactive voice recording (IVR) customer feedback surveys, online panel surveys, etc., etc. – but they must integrate all forms of information to get the total picture about their brand. Mystery Shopping can greatly add to this total picture as it gives a wealth of information about the actual service levels being delivered, whilst customer satisfaction surveys tell clients how such service is perceived by customers. Mystery Shopping programmes need to be targeted, actionable and an integral part of the company philosophy so all parties understand why they are being undertaken and how to use the results successfully.

It is an extremely useful methodology in the researcher's tool kit, particularly to use along-side Customer Satisfaction surveys in cases where customers may not take sufficient note of measurable aspects of service, such as the number of rings before a phone is answered or the number of days before a letter is replied to. However, such elements should only be measured if they are known to be of importance within service delivery, otherwise their inclusion is irrele-vant (parallel research projects can be conducted to examine their importance). Such measures often form the basis of contracts with sub-contractors, for example call centres, and therefore require accurate measurement to confirm service delivery covered by the contract. Mystery visitors may also be called upon to make observations of certain aspects, such as hygiene in washrooms or the quality of food, during their visit and to make comments on any particularly pleasing or unfavourable aspects. Again more detail will be recalled if the visitor has been briefed to report on such aspects before the event, rather than a "real" customer being asked about them some time after his/her visit.

Observations may also be required to check for presence of leaflets or posters in the correct places within a location; to check whether uniforms are being correctly worn and staff look smart and hence uphold the company image; to check the number of counters open or the length of queues. Staff knowledge may be checked by means of scenarios and set questions, and the manner of response also recorded – were staff friendly, efficient, professional, etc.? The Mystery Shopping programme can therefore act to link senior management of a concern with the actual shop floor or point of service delivery to reveal exactly what is going on in the day to day operation, and conversely can make junior staff members appreciate their importance in the delivery of customer service.

Mystery Shopping results can be used as inputs to the Balanced Scorecard, which utilises various forms of internal and external information, and is becoming more widespread as a management decision making tool. Similarly Quality systems set Standards which can be measured by means of Mystery Shoppers in many cases, and training needs can be identified or training initiatives monitored. Mystery Shopping agencies may also be called upon to conduct projects that compare prices or service levels across competitive offerings, for example to compare insurance quotes across different companies, or compare after-sales level agreements offered by different suppliers.

In recent years many major companies have linked staff bonus schemes to customer satis-faction levels and Mystery Shopping results. In these cases such results are very much exposed to critical examination and open to challenge by staff if they do not receive the rewards they anticipate, particularly if they perceive the checks as being based on observations of just a small number of staff contacts whereas the remuneration of all staff is affected by the results. It is crucial therefore that such work is carried out to impeccable standards. It is very important, particularly in such cases, that companies alert their staff to the programmes in a positive fashion, informing staff what will be happening, how the data collected will be used and issuing timely results in an easily assimilated format. It is good practice to include details of Mystery Shopping programmes in staff handbooks, including details of how the results of such studies may be used, e.g. links into bonus and commission schemes. By creating a certain amount of hype within a concern at the outset of a Mystery Shopping programme, perhaps by briefings, use of internal newsletters and other forms of communication, staff become alerted to the importance of customer service and performance may in fact rise as a result. It is also beneficial to involve frontline staff in the setting up of the project, perhaps pulling together a co-ordination team from across several departments who can oversee the project. Their views on aspects to include in the evaluation can be elicited by discussing the aspects that they feel contribute to good service, using workshops or brainstormings. This increases the acceptability of the project results since such staff members have been party to the project from its outset and can explain the necessary details to their colleagues as required, acting as champions for the project at "the coal face". Staff are also keen to see the first set of results rather than fearing their outcome.

In some cases it may be possible to set up a syndicated project so that several providers of a service can be party to results from their own checks in comparison to the average scores or results obtained across all participants. Using a syndicated survey may mean that you cannot include all the aspects you would like to but it should lead to a reduced cost. Similarly, if a supplier has norms that they have built up over time by conducting such projects in the same market sector, these will help to set the results in context.

The scope of the programme may be very widespread, covering all outlets or call centres internationally, or restricted maybe just to key areas or areas where poor service has been reported by customers so that corrective action can be taken.

Conducting a programme of Mystery Shopping contacts at periodic intervals provides a check over time on planned improvements or initiatives, perhaps in the staff training area, in turn providing feedback into such initiatives. The timing of such checks will depend on the speed of change and the type of business but they must not be so frequent that no time is left for the necessary corrective action based on the results to be taken and given time to take effect before the next check takes place.

THE INTERNATIONAL SCALE OF USAGE

The technique is used extensively worldwide and the MSPA has over 250 international member companies, including 70 in Europe, who conduct such research. This is the only specialist trade association in the Mystery Shopping industry and was founded in 1998 in order to establish standards and to aim to constantly improve service quality among the numerous agencies offering Mystery Shopping services. They estimate that the technique raises annual turnover of around $ 1billion (USD) worldwide currently. An enquiry among its members in 2005, to which over 50 % responded including responses from 28 different countries, gave an estimated market size of 210m Euros in Europe compared to 600m Euros in North America, with short-term growth forecast at 11 % per annum in both regions. From the same source, the estimated size of the market in Europe in 2010 is 360m Euros. The estimated growth for France, Germany and the UK in total showed just 8 % compared to 15 % for the rest of Europe, which is rapidly catching up in its usage of the technique. These growth estimates exceed those shown for market research as a whole, global market research being estimated to have grown by 4.3 % in 2005.

Growth in the developed countries of Europe and North America is coming not only from the traditional areas of retail, leisure and finance but also from increased usage by local and central government and by regulatory bodies.

Growth outside of Europe and North America is particularly being seen in the Asia-Pacific region. Growth from a small base is also being seen in Africa and South America. Estimates for 2007 suggest continued 11 % growth in North America and Europe, to 740m Euros and 260m Euros respectively with Asia-Pacific and the rest of the world estimated as possibly growing at 25 % to 94m Euros, giving a world total of around 1094m Euros.

In July 2006 the Dallas based headquarters of MSPA covering the United States and Canada announced that it had 50 000 certified Mystery Shoppers, built up since the inception of its certification programme, designed to improve the quality of work conducted, in November 2002. A fifth of these certifications had been awarded in the past eight months.

WHO USES IT?

The type of clients who use Mystery Shopping cover a wide spectrum within the public and private sector. Any business that provides a service of some kind could benefit from undertaking a Mystery Shopping programme. Many local and central government bodies are using the technique in the United Kingdom to monitor service delivery, particularly by helplines. This sits well alongside the Best Value customer satisfaction surveys being conducted among local residents and businesses to confirm whether or not the body is meeting its targets and being seen to be performing well. Such bodies compare their service delivery by means of Performance Indicators, some of which can be measured by means of Mystery Shopper evaluations. The financial industry similarly uses calls to its helplines to monitor service delivery both for the benefit of its customers and to monitor its contracts with suppliers, and visits where its services are offered through retail outlets. Retail outlets, hotels, restaurants and other leisure venues such as theme parks, bingo halls and casinos, use mystery visits to check they are maintaining their standards, whilst public transport providers including airlines use Mystery Shoppers to check all forms of service delivery, be it signage and information provision, punctuality, cleanliness, appeal of refreshments provided or the manner and knowledge of staff members. Car dealerships are often the subject of Mystery Shopping visits to check that the correct offerings are being made relating to price offers, after sales services, test drive facilities, etc. In fact any organisation that wishes to ensure that its "brand" is delivering its promise in terms of service should consider setting up a Mystery Shopping programme.

Regulatory bodies may seek to undertake Mystery Shopping projects in order to monitor the way providers operating within their remit are providing their services. (An example is the Financial Services Authority in the UK who conduct Mystery Shopping to check that financial services providers do adhere to financial regulations during such transactions as the selling of mortgages.) Here the relationship with those being observed while providing a service is a secondary one, but Guidelines do seek to cover such relationships and to suggest that staff be pre-warned that they may be observed in such a way.

Mystery Shopping can therefore take the form of visits to key sites, such as shops, Town Halls, Banks, Post Offices, etc., to check the knowledge of staff on key issues and the correctness of their actions, to record queuing times and numbers of counters open, to check the availability of literature or to observe aspects such as smartness of staff, cleanliness of location – the list is almost endless. Alternatively checks may be conducted by letter, phone or email in order to check the efficiency of the response, again in terms of knowledge, speed and manner. Call centres are particular recipients of mystery calls, checking the time waited at the start of a call, and the efficiency and ease of use of any IVR systems even before making any human contact. Websites are increasingly being Mystery Shopped to check for ease of access and efficiency of response. Some aspect of fulfilment of a request, say for a brochure, may be included in the measurement and the correctness and timing of the received material will then form part of the check. Any service delivery channel can be checked and any aspect that is thought to affect customer satisfaction can be considered for inclusion, the closer the observed experience is to that that would be encountered by a member of the public the better.

Mystery Shopping can be used in the Business to Business context as well as the Business to Consumer context as long as the evaluator is skilled enough to carry through the necessary scenario. In certain cases actual businesses may be recruited to provide feedback on actual service received, or it may be necessary for an agency to set up dummy company names so that certain aspects of service may be observed.

Within large concerns Mystery Shopping may be the responsibility of the Research Department who also commission other forms of market research, or it may fall under the remit of the Marketing, Sales or Customer Service Department who may seek to involve agencies in their monitoring directly.

Large multi-national companies based in Europe and North America, and to a lesser extent in Asia-Pacific, are fuelling the current growth in the market using Mystery Shopping to ensure that they are delivering their agreed customer service key performance indicators (KPIs) and to check that their staff are treating customers in the ways intended in order to maintain worldwide corporate images. Where the observed performance falls below expected levels, additional training or motivational schemes are put in place, whilst if expected levels are exceeded reward schemes are triggered to reflect this.

MAKING THE CONTACTS

This brings us on to the question of who is most likely to make the best Mystery Shopper. Some companies favour using research interviewers as they have been trained in questionnaire completion and used on previous projects where back-checking could be carried out. Because Mystery Shoppers do not make themselves known to the staff at the time of the contact, back checking is obviously not possible on such projects. Acting as a Mystery Shopper does call for certain skills of observation, memory and sometimes role playing so it does not appeal to all interviewers, but the tasks are often quite complex and we need to be sure that they have been performed and reported on correctly. However, many agencies train members of the public, who are not trained market research interviewers, to conduct Mystery Shopping projects, believing that this gives a truer picture of the experience a real customer does have. Such agencies operate large databases of contacts to draw on for any specific task. These "shoppers" or "evaluators" can be recruited and contacted online and return their work also online for speed and economy in terms of the removal of the need for postage, copying and data entry. Each agency has its own modus operandi and will be able to explain this to clients who are considering undertaking a project.

In any case the individual making a contact must fit the task, be it a teenager asking for careers advice, a mum booking a family holiday or someone playing the part of a business person. If the scenario relates to the purchase of a Porsche car the evaluator must look and sound as if they could afford it, or if it relates to commercial vans, the evaluator must again seem appropriate.

For some projects it is possible to use centralised telephone units to make Mystery Shopping calls, where call backs are not expected. This may be particularly appropriate in the case of calls across several competitors, collecting information about prices and service levels. The centralised nature of the fieldwork increases the level of control over the project and the handling of complex matrices in order to cover all options. However, computer assisted telephone interviewing (CATI) scripts should not be used at the time of making the Mystery Shopping contacts as the exact flow of the discussion cannot be predicted in advance.

The outcome of a contact must be recorded in some way. In most cases some form of questionnaire or evaluation sheet is used. In the case of visits this cannot be used during the actual visit so aspects have to be remembered for completion onto the required form as soon as is feasible. This may limit the number of aspects that can be covered at any one time. Some form of aide memoire, such as a "shopping list", may help the shopper recall key elements for later inclusion in the form – key aspects such as a given price may be jotted down in front of staff as it seems a natural thing a customer might do. Some agencies utilise tape or video recordings to aid recall of the contact. Such usage however is covered by the Guidelines (see later section) in order to protect the human rights of staff involved, and one must consider how the output from such recordings will be analysed and used as feedback. It is always advisable to pilot a type of contact at the outset of a new project to ensure that the evaluation sheet does reflect the experience and that the task can in fact be conducted in the way anticipated.

Whoever is used to conduct the task, the agency must ensure that they are fully briefed on what they are required to do and what may happen as a result. At the outset of a new project it may be advisable to conduct a centralised briefing, or a series of regional briefings, to ensure that the evaluator team fully understands the tasks required and the way to complete the records. Role playing may form part of such sessions to get them used to their tasks. Alternatively electronic material may be used to brief the team over the Internet, perhaps showing a dummy visit or call. Detailed information may need to be supplied to ensure that the "customer" can keep up their end of the story if asked questions in relation to their contact. Certain tasks may call for enormous complexity, for example where taking part in a mortgage interview to check that correct procedures are followed and correct information has being given at relevant stages. Here the "customer" needs to have complete financial information to hand in order to perform the task in a believable way. In such cases the agencies need to protect their Mystery Shoppers from any adverse effects that might follow such contacts – credit refusal being recorded against their name for example – and to ensure that those who conduct such work are aware of these potential problems.

The service being checked must be one that can be requested by someone merely role playing – one cannot, for example, Mystery Shop hospital waiting times unless one recruits patients with an actual need for such treatment. Role playing can be used widely to cover special scenarios, such as a "mother" asking about a holiday for her family of two adults and two children with special requirements for a baby. Although it is rare to do so as "normal" service is usually recorded, role playing can also be used to mimic certain types of customer, for example the awkward customer, one who fails to understand or one who is rude to staff, to see how they react. This might be used for example where a training initiative had been undertaken relating to handling certain difficult customers. Here the person conducting such a contact is being asked to act out a role, so again this calls for special skills.

Many scenarios these days deal with the question of disability since premises need to be adapted to allow access and assistance for those with all forms of disability, and staff need to be able to cope with enquiries by or on behalf of the disabled. Here the agencies may well recruit people with the necessary disabilities to conduct the contacts for them. It may be necessary to handle calls or visits by deaf customers; to ensure that wheelchair users can in fact easily access the premises; that those with guide dogs can access premises or means of transport, or that other partially sighted or blind people are being served in the correct manner.

Similarly it may be necessary to include various ethnic types among the evaluator team to check that service levels do not differ across the groups. Language problems may come into play here. Such issues are particularly important in the local government arena where service delivery to potentially less advantaged groups needs to be monitored.

In many cases it may be necessary to make a purchase or undertake some transaction that bears a cost, such as placing a bet. The client and agency must in these circumstances decide who is bearing the cost of these transactions and whether any items could be returned. For example if stamp books had been purchased in several post offices, there is potential for them to be returned to the client centrally, or larger items may be able to be returned for a full refund in store.

Evaluators should not be asked to perform tasks that are in fact illegal. For example, unless conducted under very controlled conditions and with the approval of the local Research Association, one should not ask teenagers who are under-age to attempt to buy cigarettes or drink if the law of their country prohibits it, or ask evaluators to try to buy pirated DVDs. Similarly evaluators must not be put in a situation that threatens their personal safety, for example asking female evaluators to check on illegal taxi touts late at night.

As far as possible the measures by "shoppers" should be able to be objective, such as the number of minutes queued measured on a stopwatch, or presence of certain signage – yes or no. However, when dealing with certain aspects, perhaps relating to manner of a member of staff or cleanliness of a washroom, we need to guard against totally subjective measurements, which would not be comparable across different Mystery Shoppers. Here detailed guidance on how to score aspects should be given in order to remove variability caused by personal perception. This again reflects a difference compared to Customer Satisfaction surveys, where subjective comments cannot be removed and where being willing to respond may reflect a polarised picture, those who have experienced particularly good service or particularly bad service being most keen to record this fact.

It can be very revealing to also include open ended feedback and hence provide verbatim comments covering the more subjective aspects, particularly if poor scores are being recorded, as these add depth to the findings and can bring them alive for clients in a way that simple scores do not. For example, evaluators may be asked to close their report by a short summary of how the contact went and how they felt about the experience. These comments often help to throw extra light on a bad experience or a particularly good one, and may expose new aspects that had not been considered worthy of specific inclusion in the evaluations. They may also expose examples of particularly good or bad practice by a team or branch that could be flagged up to other colleagues or to senior management.

In certain cases what starts out as a mystery visit may be turned into a declared presence visit once certain aspects have been covered. This might be used in the case of a promotion, say in a chain of service stations, checking if customers are told about the promotion correctly by staff. Where the correct actions are taken, the caller might declare their interest and congratulate the staff on their performance, maybe giving some immediate reward. In the case of incorrect actions, they might not declare their presence at all, merely reporting back on the experience, or they may inform the staff of what they should have done. There is obviously a danger where the presence is declared that outlets will warn other outlets of an impending visit so scheduling of visits should take this into account. This can of course also be the case if a Mystery Shopper has been detected if he or she has not performed the task very convincingly. Such "spotting" of the evaluators should be actively discouraged by management during the staff briefings as it is not helpful and could take the emphasis away from serving every customer well.

OUTPUTS AND SAMPLING

Because the feedback from any type of mystery contact is often at branch or outlet level where organisations are checking their own service levels, the correctness of all observations and measures is paramount as the managers of such outlets can become very defensive about the results. Many will have their own records, for example of queue lengths by time of day or number of counters open, so can dispute information that they feel is incorrect and hence undermine the whole programme. The briefing of managers about the objectives of any programme is therefore crucial and the project should be seen as being for positive rather than negative purposes. The aim should be for monitoring and retraining, not discipline or dismissal. In certain cases bonus schemes will depend on scores received in Mystery Shopping programmes so again the results will be under very close scrutiny. The day and time of any contact are therefore likely to be recorded alongside the results so that a trace against staff members and any problems affecting service levels that day can be undertaken if required. The use of branch codes affixed to records will greatly aid traceability.

In many cases all outlets will be covered by the checks but if not the sampling across the outlet database is crucial and must be agreed between the client and agency at the outset. It is likely that different waves will cover different outlets and detailed sampling frames will need to be produced across the checks, rotating the inclusion of outlets. Each wave should ideally be representative of a cross-section of outlets by type so that aggregated results are comparable wave on wave, but if results are being given by individual outlet this may be less important. Mystery Shopping projects are often based on smaller samples than traditional research projects and in many cases do not seek to be statistically significant in the traditional sense. It may not be economic to include all outlets, e.g. those in remote locations such as the Highlands and Islands of Scotland. Such aspects must obviously be agreed between the client and the agency prior to costing and commencing the project.

Beware that the collection of information at outlet level does not lead to identification of individual staff members by deduction where this level of detail was not intended. For example, if there is only one female member of staff in a branch, reference to contact with a female identifies her immediately.

Outputs are often provided at individual outlet/call centre, etc., level and aggregated data may also be required or not, depending on the objectives of the programme. Where levels are being compared over time it may be advisable to devise a scoring system for the key elements so that an index can be calculated for each wave for comparative purposes. For example the presence of crucial key aspects covered in the programme may each be given a score of 10, whereas less important aspects may score just 5. Certain "nice to have" aspects may not have any score affixed to them at all, being merely observed as being present or provided. In this way a maximum score for the ideal contact can be calculated and then each individual contact given its score, which can be compared to the ideal, and also aggregated by region, team etc., and up to a total index level if required by the project.

Ideally results need to be fed back quickly so that any necessary corrective action can be speedily undertaken. The need for minute detail across many aspects may need to be traded off against speed of reporting, or reporting done in stages, key aspects being reported first, followed by greater detail. In order to increase the speed of response shoppers may be required to phone in their findings immediately after completion of the contact or to send in electronic records of the results online or by use of IVR systems.

When considering whether to have presentations of results by the agency involved it is worth considering the level of staff to involve and hence pitch the level of findings to the specific needs of the chosen audience. Team leaders will want details about their own teams, but maybe not to have them revealed in open forum. Maybe smaller workshops for each team might be more productive. If attendees become too defensive in a presentation they may well make life very difficult for the presenter and fail to take in the results.

HOW PROGRAMMES CAN BE AUGMENTED

Mystery Shopping does not have to be covert and secretive, it can be used very openly in ways that can greatly increase staff acceptance of the findings and hence lead to more action oriented projects. Examples of this type of project are when staff members actually evaluate their own performance. This can be achieved by recording calls and allowing staff to listen to their own contacts and to evaluate them before discussing them with their line manager. This allows staff to hear the tone they adopted, the answers they gave and the manner in which they handled the call. There can be no argument as to whether they have been fairly judged – the recording speaks for itself. This can be a very revealing process. Often people are harder on themselves in these situations than evaluators might have been, and the lessons learnt are far more memorable when one has been involved in the evaluation. Remember the first time you saw a video of yourself presenting something? Quite a revealing process, remembered for a long time.

Actually getting the evaluators in to discuss the findings with the client is another way to increase the impact of the project. Some years ago my company undertook a project for a banking client which involved a regional programme of visits to key branches in city centres and to three competitor branches in each location. Workshop sessions were then held whereby the evaluators debriefed the bank managers one to one, in order to reveal any differences in service levels observed and to discuss "the nice touches" that can make all the difference to a visit. The managers felt fully involved with the process and were able to take actions immediately if change was needed.

Similarly this type of approach can be used in the retail context if an evaluator discusses the results of a visit with the store manager on completion. This can be achieved by declaring one's presence at the outset of the visit, but not giving prior warning, and then treating the visit more as a check on certain aspects, such as availability of certain items, as well as actual service levels. The manager can then put any findings into context by pointing out factors beyond his control, such as staff sickness, failure of leaflet deliveries despite their being ordered, etc. Again this allows staff to be party to the project and its findings rather than fear it or try to discredit it.

Outgoing calls from a call centre, perhaps for sales or service purposes, can be evaluated by recording them for later evaluation by a team of coders who look out for certain aspects within the calls to ensure that procedures are being followed. Again this is a type of Mystery Shopping.

At the outset of a project where the items to measure may not be fully known, or perhaps in a case where customer satisfaction research is probably going to be undertaken, it may be useful to conduct a totally qualitative type of Mystery Shopping where the evaluator starts with a blank sheet and records all aspects of the experience during the contact. An executive at the research agency might well conduct such a contact so that they experience it first hand, and can then discuss the results with the client one to one. This will certainly aid the development of the evaluation sheet or questionnaire and may well provide the client with unexpected insights into the service delivery provided by his/her concern. It may be useful to conduct similar contacts with competitors to look for points of difference, both positive and negative.

LIMITATIONS AND CONCERNS

Mystery Shopping does often operate using low sample sizes as even if all outlets within a concern are covered, one observation per outlet may be all that is conducted, but this should not be considered as a drawback as every contact is a snapshot in time and an observation in its own right, just as a series of depth interviews can be used to delve into a topic in more detail. A sample of outlets to be covered may need to be representative if aggregated data will be provided and comparisons drawn over time, but just a small sub-set of outlets may be covered for some specific reason, such as poor performance in sales terms, and then the nature of the project is not intended to be representative and statistical significance is not being sought. This more qualitative nature of the project may in fact help in global projects where it is necessary to reflect the diversity of retail models present in countries at different stages of development.

The technique did struggle under negative perceptions of being poor quality and bordering on industrial espionage in its early days, and was largely feared and misunderstood by members of staff but has managed to recover in recent years. Even industrial espionage is more acceptable these days – the competitor intelligence professionals now have their own association, the SCIP, and their own Code. It is up to all practitioners and users to ensure that the objectives of any project are clearly defined and are met by use of the technique, and that programmes are conducted responsibly and in accordance with the Guidelines relevant within each market. There are enormous numbers of agencies offering Mystery Shopping checks so do be sure you check out your supplier before commissioning a project. Evaluators need to be carefully selected and given the necessary training so that they correctly perform their tasks and record the outcomes. Buyers need to ensure that they are not bringing the technique into disrepute by asking their suppliers to perform unacceptable tasks. If a task is too complex the evaluators will simply not be able to conduct it satisfactorily and standards may slip.

Where global projects are undertaken it may be hard to devise the list of common elements to check and to agree the measurements for the more subjective elements. Translations must be carefully checked to ensure that identical aspects are being considered and measured across all countries. Alternatively the evaluations might be tailor made to each country to avoid this need, and comparison across countries made perhaps by use of a scoring system, as described in a preceding section.

The technique could become too subjective if steps are not taken to define levels for measuring aspects such as "professional", "friendly", etc., mentioned previously. Clients need to ensure that they define their KPIs fully and in a way that they can be meaningfully measured. It is the fact that we can aim to include such aspects at all that makes it such a useful tool alongside other customer related measures.

Back-checks cannot be conducted (or only in a limited way if recordings have been made) given the contacts are not made overtly so agencies must be able to trust the evaluators they use. Checks must be conducted in terms of the logical nature of the records made. Where possible evidence of a transaction should also be collected, e.g. tickets, invoices, proof of posting. The training of evaluators may include dummy projects so that the standard of their work can be assessed, and where any ambiguities occur in records for live projects the evaluator concerned may be contacted for further clarification.

Unfortunately the technique can easily be used to provide television footage that shows examples of poor service, usually extremely poor service, and hence this can bring ridicule and disrepute onto the technique. Reputable agencies should aim to guard against being party to such "bad press" if at all possible.

There is often debate as to just how much detail should be revealed following a Mystery Shopping contact. The Guidelines aim to protect individuals and clients should discuss with their agencies exactly how much detail is really required and how the results will be used. Where conducting competitor contacts we should bear in mind the principle of not unduly wasting the time or resources of a competitor – remember they may well do the same to you! Do not collect brochures if not necessary to do so, do not make a contact any longer than necessary, do not expect actions to be taken to follow up on an enquiry and do not record the contact by video or audio means. Also bear in mind the financial implications of certain contacts – is it fair to call out a financial adviser, who probably earns on a commission basis, to conduct a review that will lead to no sale? Put yourself in their shoes. The frequency of conducting competitor work should also be reduced in relation to checks on one's own concern.

GUIDELINES

Each country has its own laws particularly relating to data protection, privacy and human rights issues and users of Mystery Shopping and observational techniques must ensure that they do not fall foul of such laws. The local Research Associations also have their own Codes of Conduct, sets of Guidelines or Best Practice documents which should be closely adhered to. In the UK The Market Research Society (MRS) has a specific set of Guidelines relating to Mystery Shopping, as does ESOMAR for use across Europe (see www.mrs.org.uk and www.esomar.org).

The Guidelines aim to protect the individual's human rights and to ensure that staff are not harmed in any way because an organisation chooses to Mystery Shop their activities as such checks are not made overtly. They also aim to maintain certain standards of performance and behaviour so that the technique is not brought into disrepute. Disciplinary actions must not be taken as a result of Mystery Shopping. The aim should be to increase customer service levels and develop staff through training and motivation.

The first set of UK Guidelines for Mystery Shopping were drawn up in 1997 by the MRS but these are regularly revised to reflect the changing use of the technique. Similarly ESOMAR revised its Guidelines in this area only recently. The MSPA also has its own set of advisory Guidelines covering all aspects of good practice when conducting Mystery Shopping in Europe, revised in September 2003, which are very similar to the MRS Guidelines, and has agreements drawn up for its members and evaluators drawing on the key elements contained therein (see their website www.mysteryshop.org).

ESOMAR seeks to differentiate between projects where any personal data collected is treated with full confidentiality and is not used other than strictly for research purposes where such projects can be referred to as "Mystery Shopping research", and wider projects were personal data may not be treated as fully confidential and may be used for other purposes such as training or the operation of a bonus scheme, where the project must not be described as research but as a "Mystery Shopping project". This distinction originally led to debates within the industry as to whether differently named companies had to conduct such types of surveys if they cannot be called "research" and to whether reporting Mystery Shopping results side by side with other research results in order to aid assimilation for clients was possible, and discussions relating to these aspects are still taking place. Where "Mystery Shopper research" is being undertaken no individuals can be identified so results must not be disaggregated to a level where the identity of any staff member could be deduced, even if the staff work within your own organisation. Similarly recording by electronic means is prohibited as this identifies the staff members concerned.

In all three sets of Guidelines Mystery Shopping of one's own organisation means that staff must be alerted to such a project prior to its commencement. This can be done in fairly general terms and may be contained in staff documentation such as contracts, staff handbooks or Terms and Conditions. The objectives of the project and the way the results will be used as well as whether individuals will be identified should be communicated, but details of timings, locations and evaluation contents need not be given. The MRS allows the individual identity of a staff member to be revealed as long as the possibility of this situation has been previously communicated to staff. The use of electronic recording is therefore also permitted in this case, but remember this is only for own organisation Mystery Shopping exercises.

Where competitors are being covered in Mystery Shopping projects extra care should be taken since participating staff members cannot be warned in any way so all data must be kept to a non-identified level. Electronic recording of the contacts is therefore expressly prohibited. All data must be presented at aggregated level, again so that individuals cannot be identified. Where postal, fax or email evaluations are being undertaken, care must be taken to remove any staff identification from material forming part of the report. Only reasonable demands on time and resources should be made, in relation to the normal practices within a market. Any follow up work should also be kept to a minimum. Where a purchase is made the MRS Guidelines give greater leeway regarding the contact. Maximum time limits of 15 minutes for retail, manufacturing and leisure industry related contacts by phone or face to face, or 30 minutes in the case of automotive and financial sectors are recommended as best practice.

MRS Guidelines specifically mention projects conducted on behalf of Regulatory bodies. These have to be undertaken in the same way as those on competitors unless staff of the contracted body have been adequately warned that Mystery Shopping projects may be used and that data will be provided down to the individual level.

Where researchers use the Mystery Shopping technique for totally non-research purposes such as investigative journalism such Guidelines do not apply but obviously all appropriate legislation must be followed.

The MSPA is currently developing a certification programme to aid in the recruitment and efficient training of evaluators by providing online access to such training.

CASE HISTORIES

The intention here is not to give you named examples of projects since confidentiality must be respected, but to give you examples of the types of ways Mystery Shopping has been used in recent years, as follows:

- A financial institution used quarterly checks on its call centres across all its various teams with the two pronged objective of monitoring its service level agreements with its subcontracted supplier and also providing detailed feedback to its teams to expose any needs for retraining, monitor training initiatives and to look for examples of best practice. Summaries of results, in an easily read format, were therefore provided each wave, as well as periodic presentations being made, dwelling more on the overall trend data.
- One of the armed forces used contacts by coupon, phone, Internet, etc., to examine response times and correctness of fulfilment in relation to its recruitment drives being conducted across various ranks, in order to monitor the performance of a sub-contracted agency. This was a detailed programme, conducted across several waves and covering a large number of initiatives, delivery channels and ranks, with reporting at all levels. It revealed several weaknesses in the response system.
- A restaurant and pub chain commissioned a programme of visits across its various types of houses to monitor service provision and standard of food preparation with reporting at regional and house type level.
- A major supermarket required general service level checks throughout its various levels of stores on a continuous basis, covering observational, availability and knowledge based aspects with reporting at store level. This was extended to include brochure checking and interactive telling machine (ITM) checking in relation to financial aspects in later stages.
- A major utility required checks on its helplines to ensure that it was providing the correct information to its callers and despatching the correct material where necessary.
- A major high street bank instigated a large-scale project to feed into its general customer care programme involving business and consumer visits and calls to branches, competitor checks, mortgage interviews to check that legal requirements were being met, and self-evaluation by staff of tapes covering calls they had handled. The results of all these aspects helped to lift the service levels and to heighten awareness of the importance of customer service within the philosophy of the concern.
- A County Council used Mystery Shopping to examine its service delivery by means of contacts made by phone, email, online, letters and visits conducted to named departments, with specific scenarios being developed each wave to cover relevant issues, including ethnic aspects. Checks were made three times a year to allow time for actions to take effect between checks, the original schedule being that of quarterly checks but these were later deemed to be too frequent. Detailed results were provided to each department including detailed verbatim comments so that each scenario could be reviewed. Presentations majored on trend data at the total level across types of contact rather than on departmental differences. The project proved invaluable in highlighting key staff training needs particularly in relation to the handling of email communications, which were tending to get lost in the system and to be responded to too informally.

WHO OFFERS MYSTERY SHOPPING?

Many of the large agencies now have Mystery Shopping divisions and are able to offer programmes internationally, and can integrate data from such projects with other relevant projects,
such as customer satisfaction surveys. This is aiding the global utilisation and hence growth of
the methodology. Other specialist agencies also offer Mystery Shopping within certain countries and internationally. Many of the smaller agencies offer consultancy relating to the setting
up and reporting of Mystery Shopping projects but sub-contract the actual fieldwork. Clients
need to be sure they appreciate the nature of the services being offered. Agency listings should
reveal such specialisms and are available through ESOMAR or your local Association.

ESOMAR or The MSPA should be able to help you to locate agencies to consider for such
projects in specific countries if necessary.

THE FUTURE

The technique has come a long way since its inception in the 1940s and continues to show strong
growth globally, being likely to develop across even more countries as the major concerns
include it in the measures they utilise to monitor their businesses. As the global research
agencies and specialist Mystery Shopping agencies become even more sophisticated their
integrated offerings are assisting clients in this process, and they are able to conduct ever more
complex projects using the Internet for speed of recruitment, reporting and to provide cheaper
means of data collection. Confidence has grown in the technique as the service levels have
been improved under the various Guidelines set up within the industry, and the strength of the
tool now that it is being correctly utilised and correctly positioned to staff has been recognised.
There is no reason why the methodology should not develop even further as new uses are found
for it.

ACKNOWLEDGEMENTS

I would like to thank:

- Harvey Gilbert, President of MSPA Europe, for his input and MSPA figures relating to the
  size of the market.
- Jeanette Deetlefs, Global Director of Synovate Loyalty based in South Africa, for her inputs.
- Debrah Harding, Deputy Director General of The Market Research Society, for assistance
  re details, particularly relating to Guidelines.

POSSIBLE READING MATTER FOR FURTHER INFORMATION

Karlsson, V.B. and Horbec, K., Measuring Management and the Moment of Truth (see www.
    measuringmanagement.com).
Newhouse, I.S. (2004) Mystery Shopping Made Simple. Business Economics.
Raising Professional Standards – ESOMAR Retail Conference, April 2005.
Stucker, C. (2004) Mystery Shopper's Manual, 6th edn. Business Economics.
Szwarc, P. (2005) Researching Customer Satisfaction and Loyalty. Kogan Page.
Understanding Your Competitors – ESOMAR Asia Pacific Conference, March 2005.
Wilson, A. (2003) Marketing Research: An Integrated Approach. Prentice Hall.

18

Customer Satisfaction

Laurent Florès

CUSTOMER SATISFACTION: ORIGIN AND CURRENT MARKET

A Quick Background

Although customer satisfaction seems to have always been around, serious interest and the practice of measuring customer satisfaction is rather recent, at most about 20 years old. In fact, authors like Meyers (1999), for example, date serious US business interest in measuring customer satisfaction to the early nineties when several factors converged to produce an uncertain business climate made up of economic recession and hypercompetition from both domestic and foreign companies and demand shrinkage in many developed economies. Faced with increased competition US firms started to realise that in many industries foreign competitors were better able to understand and supply American consumers. In response, many businesses started to allocate more attention and investment to understanding their customers better, satisfying them better, improving products and services based on their feedback and increasing service quality in order to maximise their chances to better keep up with the competition.

The question is therefore to know what is the state of customer satisfaction practice nowadays, beyond its claimed popularity, what is its importance in the overall Market Research business? What are the trends, in other words, how serious have companies been and are being about becoming more customer centric?

THE MARKET OF CUSTOMER SATISFACTION RESEARCH

Although it may be a bit ambitious to summarise in a few paragraphs the current and past importance of customer satisfaction research, it is useful to gauge its real importance. In fact, the task appeared to be difficult because available data on the share of customer satisfaction research appears to be limited. Table 18.1[1] provides details of the relative importance of *"Stakeholder Measurement"* vs Other Measurements between 1997 and 2005. Please note that *"Stakeholder Measurement" includes customer, employee satisfaction and mystery shopping research.*

Quite clearly, the business of customer satisfaction is a big business representing from 1997 to 2005 the third largest market research segment in the US with about 9 % of total research

---

[1] We are specifically grateful to Larry Gold from Inside Research for providing this information. The findings come from a special questionnaire sent to the largest US MR firms (by revenue) asking for US-only revenue broken down by MR type. Information from all but two of the top 50 was provided (others do not keep records), or estimated. Identical questionnaires were previously sent for '03, '00 and '97 information.

Market Research Handbook, 5th Edition. Edited by M. van Hamersveld and C. de Bont.

Table 18.1   Revenue of Market Research Segments (97–05) (USA). (*Source:* Inside Research, May 2006)

Type of Research	% U.S. Revenue			
	'05	'03	'00	'97
Market Measurement (1)	29.0 %	30.2 %	31.4 %	34.7 %
Media Audience Research (2)	21.6	20.5	19.3	17.4
Stakeholder Measurement (3)	**8.8**	**8.2**	**8.9**	**8.4**
Market Modelling (4)	8.2	6.5	4.7	4.9
New Product/Service Development (5)	7.1	6.9	6.4	6.4
Usage & Attitude Studies (6)	4.8	5.8	6.0	4.5
Advertising/Brand Tracking	5.5	5.0	4.5	4.9
Qualitative/Focus Groups	3.4	4.7	4.2	3.5
Advertising Pre-Testing	3.4	3.3	2.9	2.9
Business-to-Business Studies	2.7	2.4	2.6	2.6
Omnibus/Shared Cost Surveys	0.9	0.8	1.1	1.4
Opinion Research/Polling	0.6	1.2	0.8	1.1
All Other	4.0	4.5	7.2	7.3
Total–%	100.0 %	100.0 %	100.0 %	100.0 %
Total–Revenue ($Mils)	$6,780	$5,488	$4,360	$3,198
Top 50 Companies Reporting	48	47	48	47
% Top 50 US Revenue	96.7 %	94.7 %	98.7 %	97.3 %

(1) Syndicated or custom retail/consumer panel/surveys for market size, share and tracking, including online
(2) Viewing, listening, readership, including online
(3) Customer/employee satisfaction and mystery shopping
(4) Including marketing mix and media modelling
(5) Testing of concepts, products, services, packaging, pricing, mix, etc., and volume forecasting
(6) Including segmentation studies and motivational research

expenditure. Similarly, and given that Europe is the second biggest research market in the world,[2] we can reasonably assume that Customer Satisfaction Research is certainly in the top five of expenditure for Europe as well.

The size and the stability of revenues over time demonstrate that since its early days back in the mid 80s customer satisfaction has matured to a point where it is a large and solid segment of the market research industry.

Nowadays, nearly all of the top ten market research companies in the world have a practice dedicated to customer satisfaction, and some small mid sized specialised companies continue to flourish proving further the sustainability of the customer satisfaction (CS) business. However, according to an Inside Research March 2005 letter, in the US "price pressure continues and several very large projects changed hands, perhaps driven by switch to Internet, purchasing departments increasingly involved" and "the trend continues, CS being too tied to customer database for CRM, loyalty, and impact on share/ROI and actionability". Although customer satisfaction research is facing increased price competition (like all research segments), it remains clear that it has matured to a leading position representing an important research spend for companies. The early days of customer satisfaction are now well over, and a strong, well established, and global practice has emerged. In the following paragraphs, we

---

[2] Source: Esomar Global Market Research Survey 2006.

will review the key concepts that played a role in shaping the Customer Satisfaction Research Business.

KEY CONCEPTS

As described briefly in our introduction, although it seems that customer satisfaction has always been around, serious interest in and the practice of measuring customer satisfaction is rather recent, at most about 20 years old. In fact, it appeared as a management necessity in response to increased competition. Competitive pressure further accelerated the adoption of customer satisfaction and a number of programmes and practices began to appear including:

- the famous TQM, Total Quality Management;
- Customer Satisfaction Programmes;
- in the early 2000: CRM, Customer Relationship Management;
- or more recently again, Relationship Marketing.

All these programmes share the same objectives, those of improving the desirability and quality of the firm's products and services in order to better fit customers' needs and in turn maximise their satisfaction. Eventually, the ultimate objective of all these programmes is that increased satisfaction leads to greater loyalty. In the present chapter, we will look specifically at opportunities and challenges surrounding customer satisfaction measurement and its implications for business and market research specifically. More specifically, the following paragraphs will provide a brief history of the concept and its origin, an overview of the business importance of customer satisfaction research, a brief overview of the most widely used methods for measuring customer satisfaction, a perspective on new methods for valuing customer satisfaction as well some final perspectives on the growing importance of a consumer driven world and its impact on marketing and customer satisfaction.

THE CUSTOMER ORIENTATION: A BRIEF BACKGROUND

As stated in the introduction, although serious interest in measuring customer satisfaction is only about 20 years old, interest in customers and the customer orientation of business dates back to the introduction of the "marketing concept" in business with authors such as Kotler and companies such as General Electric which stated in the 50s, "that customers should be at the center of any firm's activities, and that all resources should be aligned to serve customer needs". Back then, the objective was not to transform organisations from production operations into customer-satisfying operations. Indeed, faced with demand change due to increased availability of products (after the slow down of the post World War II rush for products), companies had to go beyond producing and delivering to adapting and selling following customer needs. In fact, as marketing leaders such as Professor Kotler (2003) from the Kellog's Business School stated clearly, the rise of the marketing concept within companies rested on:

- a need for a customer orientation;
- the establishment of a marketing department including areas of practice and functions such as market research or marketing research, brand/product management;
- the integration of all marketing functions (e.g. marketing, advertising, sales, merchandising) under a marketing director.

Many of these concepts were new to most firms in the fifties and the need for a customer orientation quickly boosted the adoption of "marketing" in most companies to the point where marketers became the new "stars" of organisations with some of them rising regularly to top management positions. However, the appearance of such practices and terms as TQM, customer satisfaction, CRM, etc., would not have appeared if marketing was really successful at satisfying customer needs. So the question really becomes, what ever happened to the original idea of marketing. In other words, what did not work as planned with the marketing concept?

Did Marketing Really Go "Wrong"?

Looking at what went or at what's "wrong" with marketing may seem a bit exaggerated. The purpose here is to highlight points of discussion that have been raised many times and that are still being discussed nowadays to challenge the real Return on Investment (ROI) of marketing. These points are usually raised by finance and accounting executives, and our purpose is not so much to contribute further to the debate but rather to summarise the issues that fuel most criticism surrounding marketing and show their connections to the concept of customer satisfaction.

The first issue is that initial enthusiasm towards marketing soon drove marketers to place more importance and emphasis on the marketing department rather than on customers or consumers. Indeed, even today, we are still puzzled about the fact that in an environment driven by open communication and consumer empowerment some marketers still know little about their customers. They do not talk to them, do not "live" with them enough and in fact do not really know them. As a result, rather than being customer centric, most companies became marketing centric. This may explain the so called rise of "CRM" or Customer Relationship Management, and even today most marketers are facing exactly the same trouble they faced back at the end of the eighties. However, they need to become more customer centric, why? Today the environment has changed dramatically and will further change with the rise of the Internet and the so-called web 2.0 that accelerates consumer empowerment.

The second issue, maybe a bigger one, is that marketing was and is still more about acquiring customers than retaining and expanding existing ones. Although it has been demonstrated many times that it costs much more, at least five times more to acquire new clients rather than to keep and expand current clients, most companies focus their efforts on acquiring new customers. In fact, most marketers and their agencies look primarily at acquisition strategies rather than retention strategies.

The third and fourth issues relate to a lack of ability for marketing to truly value its ROI specifically in the short term. Indeed, at a time where finance and numbers are running companies, and when marketing looks at building a brand and loyalty, it becomes easier to relate to new client acquisition rather than to retention or loyalty. It is indeed easier to count new clients and more challenging to count or rather estimate "kept" or "saved" clients. Unless you have a simple measurement system in place that tracks your current client base satisfaction and future intentions towards your company and brand, you may not really be able to track your marketing ROI. Marketing and marketing research tend to focus on insights that may help find out how to attract new customers rather than measuring and monitoring customer satisfaction and loyalty over time. Again, we are not suggesting that satisfaction is the best measure to track marketing ROI, we simply want to highlight the fact that without some type of "marketing measurement" in place no real marketing management can really take place. Indeed, *"you can't really manage what you can't measure"*.

THE CUSTOMER SATISFACTION ERA

Overall, the conjunction of the four issues described above provided an ideal framework for the rise and recognition of Customer Satisfaction as an important and well accepted business practice. Indeed, faced with increased domestic and foreign competition, companies needed to have a greater focus on customers, and their ability to serve them better and satisfy them appeared to be key to their survival strategies. The customer satisfaction trend offered marketers one good way to do this. Simple to understand, it represented a great way to picture the "customer voice" not only in the marketing function but across the whole organisation. It became a simple score card that everyone could refer to from the front line to the executive board room. The popularity and success of the concept even stepped out of the business world since it also entered the government and public world, most notably in the United Sates where initiatives such as the American Customer Satisfaction Index (ACSI)[3] brought *The Voice of the Nation's Consumer*™ to Washington. Established in 1994, the ACSI is a uniform and independent measure of household consumption experience. According to its inventors, the ACSI is a powerful economic indicator that tracks trends in customer satisfaction and provides valuable benchmarking insights into the consumer economy for companies, industry trade associations and government agencies. The point we are trying to make here is obviously to state that the importance of customer satisfaction that went beyond businesses to enter public administration; so clearly, thanks to customer satisfaction the marketing concept found its way back to the top.

Customer Satisfaction? Does It Really Relate to Customer Loyalty and Business Performance?

To most minds it sounds obvious that customer satisfaction is linked to company performance. In fact, as we will see briefly that what sounds obvious may not be as obvious as we think it is.

So let's start with the most plausible route: the one that supports the idea that customer satisfaction is linked to customer loyalty which in turn may be linked to a company's financial performance.

Of course, in every person's mind it makes a great deal of sense that someone who is satisfied will most likely be loyal to the brand or company. Now think about the many times you go to one gas station or another one based on convenience rather than satisfaction. You may indeed be very satisfied with your regular station, but you still go to the one that is the easiest for you to go to ... Still, I will not argue that satisfaction is not important as it helps minimise switching from one station to another. In this case, 100 % satisfaction does not guarantee your client 100 % business. The first early scientific proof of a direct relationship between satisfaction and loyalty relate back, for example, to Oliver (1999) followed by the popular work and practice of Claes Fornell[4] from the University of Michigan and its American Customer Satisfaction Index that we mentioned earlier. Again the key is to leverage the best available tools, proofs and methods to make them work for you. The question is of course, does satisfaction do enough for me to relate it to company performance, in other words is it a "nice to have" or a "must have" measure? Although the answer sounds simple, our experience shows that satisfaction became so popular that customer satisfaction programmes flourished everywhere with some

---

[3] For more information: http://www.theacsi.org.
[4] http://www.bus.umich.edu/FacultyBios/FacultyBio.asp?id=000120079.

of them forgetting to validate the ultimate goal: linking the satisfaction measure to company overall performance.

To this end a recent survey in France[5], for example, shows that satisfaction is not linked automatically to loyalty across a variety of different markets and that the dynamics of satisfaction vary across different product categories. For example, industry sectors that show high dissatisfaction rates are Internet Providers (17 %), Banks (13 %), Furniture Stores (10 %), Retail Stores (6 %), Internet Shopping Sites (4 %), CPG Products (3 to 5 %), Cultural Products Stores (3 %). According to the same study, on average and across different sectors, 17 % of satisfied customers may be tempted to switch to a competitor for a similar offer. This rate varies from a high 38 % for furniture stores to 4 % for car insurance. On the other hand, when customers are unsatisfied, 80 % are willing to change to another brand or provider, and 92 % will do so for an equivalent offer, not waiting specifically for a better deal. So, although satisfaction may not always translate into loyalty, satisfied customers are more likely to be loyal than unsatisfied customers. To this end, attempts to link satisfaction performance measures to loyalty or business impact measures may not be perfect, but they are at least instructive and can provide managers with a solid road map for monitoring business performance and directing company actions to produce better results. We will illustrate this point later by giving an example where website satisfaction is linked to website loyalty and business impact.

THE MEASUREMENT OF CUSTOMER SATISFACTION (CS)

Given the instructional nature of the present chapter on customer satisfaction, with its ambition to provide an overview, practice and way forward for the CS business, when it comes to measurement, it is worth reminding, that as in all sound market research initiatives, measurement is driven by objectives that in turn should be driven by a clear management perspective. Indeed, although simple and obvious, experience shows that a consistent ability to stick to the overall objectives of the CS measurement programme is key to getting ROI for the initiative. That being said, any CS programme needs to be structured around key determinants (see Figure 18.1) that relate to programme objectives, types of measurements and measures, frequency of measurement, types of delivery, etc.

Given the introductionary nature of this chapter and the available space, we will refer interested readers to specific authors such as Meyers (1999) or Hill and Alexander (2006) for thorough discussions and explanations. Here, we will focus essentially on key points of consideration when it comes to planning and drafting a measurement programme. This relates to questions surrounding the choice of methods to measure satisfaction, either direct or indirect methods, the characteristics of good performance sales, the development of summary metrics and models that both "explain" satisfaction and link it to company performance. We will then complete our exploration by looking at current and future developments that relate to customer satisfaction measurement. Let us then start with investigating "direct" and "indirect" methods for measuring customer satisfaction.

Direct and Indirect Methods for Measuring Satisfaction

Before entering the specifics of direct or indirect methods, it is important to remember that these methods relate to the measurement of *the relative importance of attributes, items that drive*

---

[5] Init Satisfaction Study, August 2006 as reported by Marketing Magazine article, October 2006, No. 107, pp. 74–75.

1 – What are the programme objectives?
(a) Retain customers
(b) Improve company operations and ROI
(c) Benchmark company to its competitors
(d) Track progress over time
(e) Compensate employee and management

2 – Who shall be measured?
(a) Customers
(b) Prospective customers
(c) Competitors' customers
(d) Lost customers
(e) Employees

3 – What measures are needed?
(a) Overall performance scales
(b) Descriptive items
(c) Summary measure such as Satisfaction Index
(d) How do we use open feedback?

4 – How do we source the measures?
(a) Existing research
(b) Market practice and consultants
(c) Interviews and focus groups with current and past customers
(d) Employee feedback

5 – How frequently do we measure?
(a) Continuous
(b) Semi-continuous
(c) Once to twice a year or less frequently

6 – How do we leverage the organisation natural point of contacts to conduct CS programme?
(a) We measure ourselves upon a service delivery
(b) We measure regularly based on a set timing
(c) We outsource

7 – Online/ Offline Data Collection?

8 – What do we deliver internally and to who?
(a) What measures shall we track and deliver (see point 4)
(b) Who receives our performance: management vs all company?
(c) How we deliver it? Balanced ScoreCard, Digital Dashboard, KPI, etc. '

Figure 18.1   The key determinants of a customer satisfaction programme

the overall satisfaction towards a company or a firm. Indeed, from a management perspective although it may be useful to know what the company's overall satisfaction performance is, it is just as important to be able to relate this performance to diagnostics variables or "hot buttons" able to "explain" and drive company improvements and objectives over time. In other words, a score card able to picture overall satisfaction and specific items that drive it is of crucial importance to track and set up goals to improve company performance over time.

Traditionally, two types of method have coexisted, direct and indirect methods of measurement.

In practical terms, direct methods are somewhat transparent for respondents since they ask them directly to rate how important a given attribute or product characteristic is to them. These methods are quite intuitive hence their success both with respondents and management as they are easily understood and are still largely used in companies nowadays. However, this practicality hides a number of weaknesses that relate to precision, reliability and sometimes the validity of the constructs measured.

Those criticisms opened the door to the development of a number of new methods, defined as "indirect", since it is unlikely that respondents will know that the market researcher will use these questions to relate them to overall satisfaction, for example. In this case, attributed importance is calculated using statistical analysis to *derive or infer* importance. As such, indirect methods are not as easily understood as their counterparts and therefore tend to be not as popular with management.

Within each group of methods, a number of specific methods exist, they are mentioned in Table 18.2.

We will not describe here the specifics of each method per se, but it is said that indirect measurement approaches offer the ability to measure perceptions "holistically" whereas direct measurement approaches tackle the measurement of specific perceptions well. As such, it is true to say that indirect measures require more statistical sophistication to infer the drivers of satisfaction than direct measures. To cover and further expand upon the subject we greatly encourage interested readers to refer to a "must read" for customer satisfaction research, namely the book of James H. Meyers (1999). Even today, as regular practitioners, we refer from time to time to Meyers' reference book, and we encourage readers to do so as well in order to gain the specifics of the description and explanation of methods.

The more important question for us is which types of method to prefer or select for your own measurement programme. Again, there is no universal answer, and the acceptable answer must rely on a set of questions that every company should ask before moving to a preferred method or way of working:

- Did we use specific methods in the past that are both sufficiently valid and well accepted internally?
- Are managers sufficiently aware and open to using indirect methods of attributing measures of importance?
- Which method best tracks company success and overall performance?
- Can the method be easily rolled out. In other words is it scalable to different markets and needs?
- Which method brings the best results in a cost effective manner?

Table 18.2   Direct and Indirect Methods for measuring attributes' importance

Direct Methods	Indirect Methods
Elicitation	Correlation/Regression Analysis
Importance Ratings	Structural Equation Models (PLS, Lisrel)
Constant Sum	Conjoint Analysis
Paired Comparisons	Extreme Differences
Determinance	Indifference level
Laddering or means-end chain analysis	Strategic cube analysis

Quite clearly, experience shows that the selected method needs to be both adapted to the company's needs and in line with market standards and practice in order to benchmark performance. As such, the key is to spend the right amount of time upfront in selecting the preferred method and remain relatively consistent over time in order to track and benchmark company progress. Rather than rushing into the implementation phase, it is therefore advisable to consult and gather vendors' experience, recommendations, and track records in order to favour one approach rather than another. Finally, once decided, the key is obviously to make the method work for you!

"Quality" of Performance Scales to Measure Satisfaction

This topic is obviously not specific to customer satisfaction but becomes of great importance to customer satisfaction as many programmes and company reviews are based on the scores that the company gets over time. Indeed, like any other marketing measures (Faris et al., 2006), whatever is the type of scale used the key is to have both valid and reliable measurement scales, in other words scales that actually measure satisfaction (*valid*) and that are sensitive enough to capture real changes over time while not too sensitive to provide consistently the same ability to actually measure the desired outcome (*reliable*).

Those scales may be nominal, ordinal, interval or ratio scales, it does not matter much, as long as they work for your company/brand measurements programmes and provide valid, reliable and sensitive and insightful results. However, it remains true to say that as is the case for other marketing research problems, interval and ratio scales offer more "robust" and more "nuanced" approaches to measure constructs and allow more sophisticated statistical analysis than nominal and ordinal scales. As such, they may be more suitable for advanced customer satisfaction programmes and refined consumer perceptions whereas nominal or ordinal scales may be more suitable to gather overall, or "rough" consumer perceptions.

As stated in the paragraph above, the key remains to have scales and measures work for you, so choose the ones that work best but do so in light of their ease of deployment and their ease of communication within the company. This last point is often underestimated but is often key to making a customer satisfaction programme work for and within your company. Indeed, you had best select scales that are easily understood by all in order to make them used and accepted by all.

So, as a simple rule of thumb, the key is and will remain to use something that works best for you and for your industry as well. To that end, review carefully the available options along with your suppliers, do not hesitate to call in specialists, as seen before the market for customer satisfaction research has grown so quickly that many research companies either made this business their core business or within the big research companies the chances are that you will find experts. Finally, feel free to call in experts from the academic world but make sure that they bear in mind the practical and business orientation of your venture.

Which Measures to Use?

This is a much debated topic, our objective here is not so much to solve it, but we will simply again re-state the importance of using measures that work well for you and your business. It could be Satisfaction, Intention to Recommend, or Intent to Repurchase, simply use the ones that track well with business growth over time.

Sound simple? Trust me, it is forgotten too often, the biggest mistake being to use as an indicator a measure that does not really relate back to business impact. Sooner or later, your customer satisfaction programme may lose value and credibility internally.

The reality shows that usually more than a single measure is used, indeed as we will see later, recent attempts to rely on one single indicator only, Intention to Recommend for example, is starting to be criticised just as Satisfaction only is. Along these lines, a smart move may be to gain experience of more than one measure and stick to the ones that work best for you. Ideally, you should also look at linking those measures together in some type of integrated model of business impact that links all the concepts together: satisfaction, loyalty and business performance. We will illustrate such an attempt in the following paragraphs where we provide a practical model linking satisfaction, loyalty and brand impact.

AN EXAMPLE: MEASURING WEBSITE SATISFACTION AND LINKING TO BUSINESS IMPACT

We describe here a practical example of measuring satisfaction with brand websites. Rather than looking only at satisfaction, we highlight specifically the link between satisfaction, site loyalty and brand impact. All data comes from the SiteCRM™ brand website effectiveness solution[6] and supports the idea that positive website experience impacts upon website loyalty and in turn brand perceptions and purchase intent (Florès, 2004) (see Figure 18.2).

In this example, the more satisfied visitors are with the overall website experience, the more inclined they are to revisit and recommend the site, and the more positive they are towards the brand. In this case, it therefore seems clear that satisfaction and loyalty towards the site are key mediating factors of brand impact and sales. In other words, the higher are satisfaction and loyalty towards the site, the higher should be the impact on the brand. This basic causal description is the foundation of a predictive model. When complemented by elements able to define and explain satisfaction, calibration work using PLS[7] analysis on the SiteCRM™ normative database provides a model of the impact of satisfaction on loyalty and branding.

As stated, the model confirms that satisfaction and site loyalty are mediating variables of brand impact and eventually sales. More specifically, satisfaction drives site loyalty (see Figure 18.3), which then drives brand impact (see Figure 18.4).

Furthermore, in this example satisfaction is best explained by four key latent variables that capture satisfaction towards specific site elements that are: Content Value, Navigation, Look & Feel and Site Performance. In addition, it is interesting to notice that although all four dimensions play a significant role in site ROI, it seems clearly that Content Value and to a lesser extent Navigation are key to any effect on site satisfaction and loyalty and therefore sales (Figure 18.5). This is clearly where the predictive ability of the model comes into play and provides decision makers with an ability to not only measure effect but also to predict which dimensions will offer the best leverage to drive sales. One of the benefits is that the approach is not "backward looking" only, but also offers managers the possibility to simulate and forecast which potential website changes will drive highest ROI.

---

[6] For more information: http://www.crmmetrix.com/en/sitecrmcopy.asp.
[7] PLS: Partial Least Square Analysis.

SALES IMPACT MODEL OF BRAND WEBSITES

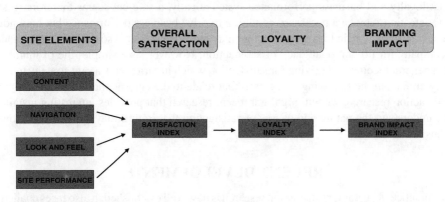

Figure 18.2   Branding impact model of brand websites

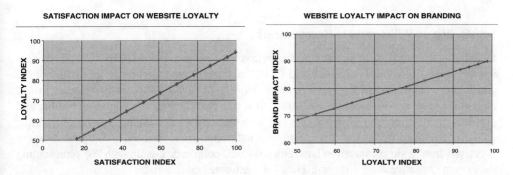

Figure 18.3 Website satisfaction impact on website loyalty

Figure 18.4   Website loyalty impact on branding

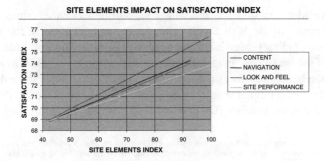

Figure 18.5   Website elements satisfaction impact on satisfaction

All in all, and although discrepancies may appear in the ability of satisfaction measures to impact loyalty and business performance systematically, a safe bet seems therefore to state that satisfaction may be a necessary condition to drive business performance but may not be sufficient to fully explain loyalty, a customer may indeed be satisfied sometimes but may leave the company for no "rational" lack of satisfaction. However, as a simple rule of thumb, we will in general recommend driving for satisfaction which in turn seems a safe strategy to foster loyalty. In fact, in the following paragraphs that relate to the current and future developments in satisfaction research, we will highlight recent research that provides interesting insights to better understand the nature and causes of satisfaction that in turn may better impact loyalty and business success.

RECENT DEVELOPMENTS

As the practice of customer satisfaction research is now well established, it also faces challenges and opportunities relating not only to the ability to predict and link measures to business success but also to relate measurement to a changing world, specifically with the rise of consumer empowerment well represented, for example, by web 2.0. Indeed, now more than ever consumers have easy opportunities to comment, criticise, praise products and brands and spread the word when they are happy or unhappy about them.

Satisfaction or Willingness to Recommend?

Leveraging the much criticised lack of connection between satisfaction measures and business impact, Bain consultant Fred Reichheld (2006) embarked upon the search for the holy grail and found what he called the *Net Promoter Score*®: "*a better indicator of revenue growth than other customer-satisfaction measures*". It is true that the measure sounds appealing and provides good supporting evidence of its fit with year after year revenue growth of multiple companies across different industries. Simple in nature, easy to collect and to compute, the score is derived from a simple question based on a 0-to-10 point rating scale with "0" representing the extreme negative and "10" representing the extreme positive end:

> How likely is it that you would recommend (Company X) to a friend or colleague?
>
> The "Net Promoter Score" or NPS, is simply the percentage of customers whose answers identify them as promoters minus the percentage whose response indicates they are detractors. Comparable to a financial net worth that takes the assets minus the liabilities, NPS provides a customer net worth by subtracting the liabilities (detractors) from the assets (promoters).[8]

Although Reichheld offers valuable and strong supporting evidence, critics have started to emerge most recently in the Wall Street Journal,[9] for example, where the reporter quotes multiple sources including professional and academic authors who find little evidence or no evidence at all of the measure's "magical" value (Keiningham et al., 2007; Morgan and Rego, 2006). Rather than building further on the criticism, we will say simply that all measures have value and provide at least reference points to implement programmes. To this end, for example, some market researchers at Philips (Otker et al., 2005), are already doing the key work to find

---

[8] *Promoters* (those who answer 9 or 10) are loyal enthusiasts who keep buying from a company and urge their friends to do the same. *Passives* (those who answer 7 or 8) are satisfied but unenthusiastic customers who can be easily wooed by the competition. *Detractors* (those who answer 0 through to 6) are unhappy customers trapped in a bad relationship.

[9] WSJ, 4 December, 2006 edition: "*One Question, Plenty of Debates*".

the measures that work best for you and your business. And in fact, in the case of Philips it seems indeed that recommendation measures correlate well "directly" and "indirectly" with business results.

In order to move beyond the limitations of the different measures, we decided recently with veteran researcher Larry Katz (2006) to reconsider what is actually measured in customer satisfaction research, trying to highlight the difference between what Dr Katz calls "*Deep and Surface Satisfactions*", and find potential explanations and reasons that may explain why current measures of satisfaction do not fully relate to churn rates in different sectors. We highlight below some of these initial findings and directions for future research.

Deep or "Surface" Satisfaction?

Our focus here is on customer satisfaction with services (banks, insurance, telephone, transport, etc.), a domain which, despite lively competition among providers in certain sectors, is characterised by an important degree of inertia in the customer base, especially when compared with fast-moving consumer goods. "Churners", while of utmost commercial importance, are a relative rarity, the majority of customers usually preferring to stay put and avoid the hassle of changing once they have chosen a provider. Relatively high levels of satisfaction and low levels of customer implication are thus common and, as we will discuss below, make both measuring and modelling satisfaction especially difficult. The problems that we discuss, however, are not unique to this domain but occur, in varying degrees, whenever measuring and modelling satisfaction are an issue.

Indeed, as most of our experienced readers will acknowledge, it is often true that correlations between two overall satisfaction ratings – one measured at the beginning of the questionnaire and the other towards the end of the questionnaire – do not show a high level of correlation. While those types of results raise a number of methodological issues, they also carry certain implications concerning the theoretical underpinnings of satisfaction research. Beyond judging the internal validity of the measures, the real insight is that the two questions may be in fact measuring different things. To us, this last point seems to be the most interesting one. Rather than saying (as most researchers do) that the two overall ratings are two imperfect measures that converge towards a common underlying construct of "overall satisfaction", we will argue in what follows that the two scales measure two things – "surface" and "deep" satisfaction – that are fundamentally different both with respect to the psychological processes upon which they depend and their relevance and utility for marketing. In fact, Katz (2006) argues correctly that the two different ratings of satisfaction may reflect two sorts of satisfaction, the first one reflecting what he calls "surface" satisfaction or spontaneous satisfaction, the second one "deep" or "thought" satisfaction. As discussed, this surface level of satisfaction is usually undervalued, underestimated by current methods of satisfaction measurement whereas it may explain a sudden churn from clients who until it happens (at least according to traditional satisfaction measures) never showed any desire to stop doing business with the company. What Katz (2006) offers here elegantly is a theoretical framework for understanding how these rapid, "surface" judgments are made.

According to Katz (2006), useful in this respect is the notion of "cognitive heuristic" proposed by Kahneman and Tversky (1973). According to these authors, many judgments (e.g. one's degree of satisfaction) made routinely in everyday life are based on a set of simple and efficient rules that they call "heuristics" which can be thought of as strategies or shortcuts that permit people to carry out what might otherwise require complex thought processes in simpler ways that economise cognitive effort.

Among the different heuristics described by the authors, one that they call "anchorage and adjustment" seems particularly useful for understanding spontaneous judgments of satisfaction. An "off the cuff" response to the question "How satisfied are you with X?" would, according this analysis, involve two steps: the first an "anchorage" phase in which the respondent formulates a preliminary response on the basis of the context in which he/she finds him/herself with respect to X ("I am presently a client and have not thought about changing, so I guess I'm satisfied"), and a second phase in which the person "adjusts" this first response as a function of any experiences with X that may be salient to his/her mind at that moment.

The differences with respect to the approaches discussed above are fundamental. Most important is that the heuristic-based approach takes as a given the superficiality of spontaneous judgments and does not make exaggerated claims concerning the cognitive basis upon which they repose. The anchoring of the preliminary response is assumed to be done with a strict minimum of introspection, the respondent *inferring* his/her degree of satisfaction from his current situation much as he would for a third person.[10] The response at this stage may, as a consequence, reflect the person's disposition and comparison levels more than it does the characteristics of the service in question. In the following "adjustment" phase, the things that modulate the preliminary judgment are not themselves abstract, more detailed judgments but rather simple perceptions or beliefs drawn from concrete experiences that the person has had (or has heard of) with the service.

And rather than an exhaustive review, the things that come to mind may mostly concern only a small number of the service's various components, and this with a high degree of thematic redundancy between the things cited.

By centering more the processes underlying spontaneous judgments than on the structure, the heuristic-based approach provides a simple, plausible model for understanding the determinants of spontaneous judgments of satisfaction. The central role accorded to salience, the allowance made for non-monotonic effects and the eventual interest in dispositional factors provide potential directions for making the monitoring of satisfaction more informative than just a simple tracking of satisfaction's fluctuations. And in fact, it does provide elegant and effective abilities to track spontaneous satisfaction regularly and relate it to loyalty changes. As such, the approach offers a promising future specifically when associated with "adaptive" open ended interviews algorithms such as brand Delphi™[11] (Katz, 2006) that offers the ability to generate and quantify simultaneously the importance of "spontaneous" feedback, thus being specifically useful in the case of measuring "surface" satisfaction.

From Questionnaire to Unsolicited Feedback: The Promise of Consumer Generated Media for Customer Satisfaction Research

As we mentioned very early on, customer satisfaction research has raised with marketers the need to "justify" or even demonstrate their ability to be customer centric. In this regard, the recent months have been especially interesting as they have shown clearly the rise of the customer as the centrepiece of any brand or business success. Indeed, as web 2.0 seems to

---

[10] A similar argument was advanced by Daryl Bem (Bem, 1967) with respect to the cognitive foundations (or lack of them) of attitudes in general.

[11] www.branddelphi.com.

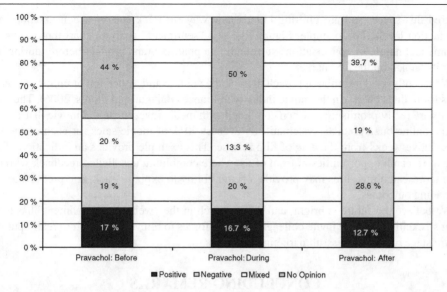

Figure 18.6   Sentiment analysis chart
Source: Nielsen Buzzmetrics, September 2004; *"When Trials go bad"*.
Note: Before (5/11/03–11/11/03): n = 100 messages, During (11/12/03–1/12/04) : n = 30 messages and
After (1/13/04–7/13/04): n = 63 messages.

remind us strongly, it is true that markets have always been customer driven (although the mass media have ruled the last 50 years), and today more than ever we have entered the era of a customer driven world, where satisfaction and word of mouth are key to any brand success or failure. Already, back in the late nineties, the authors of the Cluetrain Manifesto[12] stated beautifully that markets are "conversations" and that the Internet was going to change dramatically business, life and marketing. We are just entering this era, and we believe that the so-called social media offers huge opportunities for market researchers in general, and for satisfaction researchers in particular, to re-engineer their business for the 21st century.

For example, and as we highlighted previously, it seems clear that insights to prevent churn are usually found in "surface" satisfaction or "spontaneous" satisfaction or even better in unsolicited feedback from customers, the ones that usually arise in day-to-day customer "conversations". What a great opportunity to leverage for researchers specifically at a time when falling respondent cooperation rates are becoming a critical issue for the industry. As we have been arguing for a long time,[13] the real challenge lies in researchers' ability to move away from a pure "questioning process" that characterises most market research today to a "listening process" where unsolicited feedback becomes the gold mine for insights.

This is the promise of consumer generated media research or "research 2.0" as some authors named it.[14] The ability to learn and leverage unsolicited feedback and consumer conversations are certainly a big part of the future of market research. A number of companies[15] have already

---

[12] Visit www.cluetrain.com.

[13] Visit, for example, the "Customer Listening" blog: www.customerlistening.typepad.com.

[14] Look, for example, at Ray Poynter's blog: www.thefutureplace.typepad.com.

[15] Companies such as Cymfony, Brand Dimensions, Crmmetrix, Nielsen Buzzmetrics, Umbria, for example, are offering such services. For more information, look, for example, at Forrester research brief (Peter Kim): http://attentionmax.com/blog/2006/10/forrester_cgm_report_available.html.

entered this space, and are offering brands new ways to track customer conversations and satisfaction levels. For example, Figure 18.6 is a "sentiment" analysis chart that shows the volume and nature of conversations surrounding a pharma brand/product before, during and after its launch on the US market.

We recently used a similar approach to track the volume and dispersion of online conversations (or online "buzz") in the movie industry in France (Balagué and Florès, 2006). The early results are really promising as when combined with media investment and movie distribution levels, online buzz predicts systematically at least 90 % of movie sales for each of the five consecutive weeks from the date of film release. This example provides an indication of the type of research opportunities in front of us, where combining unsolicited feedback with traditional research measures may provide a better ability to explain, track, and predict specific marketing outcomes.

We believe the future is bright, and that research in the "web 2.0 environment" has never been so exciting, and we invite colleagues to join forces to reinvent research to really put it at centre stage of any successful marketing decisions.

CONCLUDING REMARKS

In the previous paragraphs we covered rapidly the key pillars of customer satisfaction research, of course our intention was not to be fully exhaustive but simply to provide key data and directions in order to state the importance of customer satisfaction as a key ingredient of marketing and firms' success today and in the future. To that end, we believe that market researchers have a key role to play to drive business success through innovative customer satisfaction research methods and practice. Indeed, our objective in this contribution was not so much to provide a detailed step by step approach on how to measure customer satisfaction, other very qualified authors have done so many times (Meyers, 1999; Hill & Alexander, 2006), but given the allocated space and the managerial perspective of the current book, our ambition has been to point readers towards key considerations when looking at implementing such measurement programmes as well as to provide directions for future developments in the customer satisfaction research industry. We simply hope that we achieved our goal and triggered enough interest to push readers to investigate further and go beyond the simple practical aspects of customer satisfaction research in order to consider new avenues that may impact upon the firm's overall performance. Now more than ever, we enter an era where customer satisfaction and firms' market orientation will be key to any company success and survival (Slater & Narver, 2000), so are you ready for those exciting times?

Tell us and let's continue the discussion at www.customerlistening.typepad.com.

REFERENCES

Balagué, C. and Florès, L. (2006) *Le Buzz on line comme écho des communications off line: quel impact sur les entrées des films de cinéma?* Working Paper.
Bem, D.J. (1967) Self-perception: an alternative interpretation of cognitive dissonance phenomena. *Psychological Review*, **74**, 183–200.
Faris, P.W., Bendle, N.T., Pfeifer, P.E. and Reibsetin, D.J. (2006) *Marketing Metrics: 50+ Metrics Every Marketer Should Master*. Wharton School Publishing.
Florès, L. (2004) 10 facts about the value of Brand Websites. *Admap*, February, 26–28.
Hill, N. and Alexander, J. (2006) *Handbook of Customer Satisfaction And Loyalty Measurement*, 3rd edn, Gower Pub Co.

Katz, L. (2006) *Rethinking and Remodelling Customer Satisfaction*, Working Paper.

Kahneman, D. and Tversky, A. (1973) On the psychology of prediction. *Psychological Review*, **80**, 237–251.

Keiningham, T., Aksoy, L., Cooil, B. and Andreassen, T.W. (2007) Net Promoter, Recommendations, and Business Performance: A Clarification and Correction on Morgan and Rego. *Journal of Marketing*, Forthcoming.

Kotler P. (2003), *Marketing Management*, Prentice Hall.

Levine, R., Locke, C., Searls, D. and Weinberger, D. (1999) *The Cluetrain Manifesto: The End of the Business as Usual*. Perseus Books Group.

Meyers, J.H. (1999) *Measuring Customer Satisfaction: Hot Buttons and Other Measurement Issues*. American Marketing Association.

Morgan, N. and Rego, L. (2006) The Value of Different Customer Satisfaction and Loyalty Metrics in Predicting Business Performance. *Marketing Science*, **25**(5), September–October, 426–439.

Oliver, R.L. (1999) Whence Consumer Loyalty? *Journal of Marketing*, **63** (Special Issue), 33–44.

Otker, T., Schellekens, M. and Harm Heutink, R. (2005) True loyalty. The predictive value of customer satisfaction indicators. *Esomar Annual Congress*, Cannes.

Reichheld, F. (2006) *The Ultimate Question*. Harvard Business School Publishing.

Slater, S. and Narver, J. (2000) Intelligence Corporation and Superior Customer Value. *Journal of the Academy of Marketing Science*, **28**(1), 120–127.

Part Four

Recent Developments – A Closer Look

19

The Changing Role of the Researcher

John Marinopoulos

INTRODUCTION

This chapter focuses on how a market researcher can have a greater impact on decision making within an organisation. To make this transition, market researchers should recognise that new methods and skills are required. Furthermore, new "delivery systems" are required to manage knowledge and intelligence within an organisation to extract maximal value. With all of these new methods, skills and delivery systems, the market researcher has in place a much stronger ability to influence business decision making in an organisation.

THE CHANGING MARKET RESEARCHER: WHERE ARE WE NOW?

In Chapter 1, David Smith has outlined the changing role of market research in today's world. This chapter puts the spotlight specifically on the new skills and operational methods needed for today's market researcher to transition into a market intelligence professional. In this chapter, we build on this overview by focusing on the following critical question: "As market research moves into an area of greater exposure within organisations, are we, as an industry and as researchers, *embedding* ourselves within organisations?" In many cases, we are not.

It is true that many organisations have recognised that market research is now an important component to their business knowledge. In those organisations, the language is about customer insights, innovation workshops, customer knowledge, data integration and on linking multiple information sets, and extracting a significant amount of combined value. However, in many other organisations, market research is seen as a quick validation and risk aversion tool. As market researchers, we need to focus within organisations to foster the former situation, not the latter.

In summary, market researchers are now expected to make a greater contribution to business. But are we capable of making this greater contribution? This is a question that has seen many answers over time, and invariably the answer should now be yes, but a conditional yes. Some areas of the market research industry will not be able to make this transition. As an industry, we have to accept that. As an analogy to another profession, not everyone can be a master chef in the catering industry. Some people are quite content to be the chef at the local café.

Market Research Handbook, 5th Edition. Edited by M. van Hamersveld and C. de Bont.
© 2007 John Wiley & Sons, Ltd.

THE PRESSURES ON RESEARCHERS TO ENHANCE THEIR CONTRIBUTION

Let's examine some of the specific ways in which organisations have greater expectations of researchers.

The "I Want It Now!" Syndrome

This issue is prevalent in many organisations around the world. Decision makers have less and less time to evaluate and assess market research. They want insights faster, better and quicker. A request many people have heard is "We have two weeks to write the business case. What can you deliver that will enable me to spend $x million on this project?" To deliver speed to the business, we need to: toggle between presenting the hard evidence and providing creative solutions; building the full picture of research from small fragments; and, have an awareness of the critical business issues.

A Need to Create Linkages to Other Parts of the Business and Not Just Report Data

The days of reporting on information surveyed and acting on that information alone are going. We need to understand any research in light of the implications for the business. Some of the questions we need to ask include: How does it affect the sales process? How does it affect the distribution channels? What impact does this have on the business process? Is the organisation capable of delivery? Market researchers need to bring in other areas of knowledge, such as secondary analyses and business frameworks to provide a greater context. By doing this, market research creates linkages to other parts of the business and increases its relevance.

New Methods to Tease Out Insights are Needed

Innovative methods are required to deliver greater insight and knowledge to business. Methods such as virtual workspaces, customer insight laboratories, segmentation houses, and story-telling add distinct flavour and colour to market research outcomes. Market researchers need to get into a businesses' mindset of how key insights need to be delivered. The more we can enrich market research and give it greater weight within business decisions, the better it will be for the industry.

A Need to Cut Data Finer than Ever Before

Businesses are asking for ever finer cuts of data to allow them to analyse particular market issues than ever before. With very large online panels and other large databases, we must be careful that the finer cuts meet our industry's stringent quality standards in place for elements of market research. This poses challenges where we must be aware of robustness of samples to evaluate answers to business problems.

Making Use of What We Know

We need to capture what knowledge is known today, what are the significant gaps in our knowledge sets, and understand how they are used. Key actions come from using significant linkages between market research and other parts of the business. From here, we can build "intelligence sets". These intelligence sets are linked and actionable sources which form the evidential basis for better business decisions. This allows us to deliver significant key actions that enables market research to transcend into marketing intelligence.

The Need to Start Understanding the Value of Evidence

Linked and actionable intelligence is critical to ensuring businesses have the appropriate evidence required to make better business decisions. However, as with all decisions, we need to assess the "power" and "risk" of the evidence at hand. This will be one of the more important areas of the market researcher's toolkit as the industry progresses forward.

Through all of these needs, we can summarise organisational requirements for market intelligence as: "Knowledge and insights that are finer cut, linked to other parts of the business and immediately actionable." This is a consistent theme in many of the organisational strategy-based articles from McKinsey & Co., IBM, Deloittes and other groups. The McKinsey Quarterly 2006 survey of global CEOs supports this point as "Greater ease of obtaining information and developing knowledge" is seen by CEOs as the biggest trend impacting profitability over the next five years.

In summary, we see that there is a very significant requirement to transition market research from its current focus of data, information, and knowledge delivery to market intelligence. This provides for a more integrated and impactful support of business process and strategy.

THE EMERGENCE OF THE EVIDENCE-BASED RESEARCHER

The changing needs of business are allowing market researchers to become an important component of how organisations understand customers and assist in driving business decisions.

Organisations now require a greater customer focus, which therefore highlights the need for greater measurement, understanding and the need to sustain competitive advantage in industry. However, business has focused primarily on assessing knowledge of customer behaviour rather than on customer expectations and needs.

For the market research industry to continue its growth as a relevant discipline within business, market researchers need to move away from low impact, time intensive data programmes to high impact, actionable and linked intelligence. This move will be the basis of the evidence-based researcher.

Many companies are already moving down this path. The specific areas of greatest change researchers should focus on are:

- market intelligence which delivers added value analysis;
- market intelligence which aggregates external knowledge with prior organisational knowledge in an actionable form;
- delivering the personal customer's voice into the organisation through actionable forms and tools;
- market intelligence which facilitates an organisation's need to have a shorter time span between the identification of an emerging customer need and the delivery of a new strategy meeting that need;

- identifying the business drivers and quantifying the impact of changes for an organisation;
- assessing the economic opportunity and potential to an organisation, and integrating business needs directly into outcomes.

There are a number of changes required to transition from traditional market research to market intelligence. Market research used to be a passive decision support tool which tended to see only part of the business. Market intelligence is a discipline that is an "active decision influencer".

In the next sections, we look at: new ways of working to enhance the knowledge and intelligence that we have available; new ways of thinking to meet new organisational needs; and, new systems to deliver market intelligence to organisations.

A NEW WAY OF WORKING

We now look at the new ways that market researchers are adapting their methods to enhance the knowledge and intelligence we have available.

Moving from Single Primary Knowledge Sets to Many "Imperfect" Knowledge Sets

These days, so many data sources have a significant profile higher than many market research primary knowledge sets. Market researchers need to integrate many sources as they provide a significant amount of additional knowledge to clients. Moreover, the additional knowledge sets are much more accessible than ever before and companies are much more likely to have accessed these knowledge sets (see Figure 19.1). As an example, in the reputation and corporate responsibility measurement field, there are public ranking scores from Interbrand, Reputation Institute, FTSE4Good Index, Dow Jones Sustainability Index, etc. that marketers can reference.

Using a single brand score from primary research alone seems pedestrian in comparison to many of these indexes as they are more global and encompass a greater number of competitors. However, most of the indexes and rankings are "imperfect" in their methodologies, simply due to the prohibitive economics of measurement and samples required in many countries.

Any imperfections in other less robust indexes and ranking systems does not mean they should be discarded. What the market researcher needs to do is to integrate the results and findings from external sources into primary research as greater evidence of primary research's direction. By doing this, the risk value of primary market research decreases due to the combination of multiple knowledge sources. In this way, results of primary market research are much more easily validated with less uncertainty of insights for clients.

Once the market researcher starts using multiple knowledge sets, the next stage is to extract a more advanced and combined form of integrated intelligence to clients. Return on investment increases as there is continual utilisation of knowledge resources.

Developing Linkages to Other Data Sets and Knowledge Sets to Build "Intelligence Sets"

Once the market researcher has started to use multiple knowledge sources, the next stage is to link the knowledge sets with other knowledge sets within an organisation. In this discussion, linkages are defined as the degree to which the primary market research is inter-linked with other decision-making issues being addressed in the organisation.

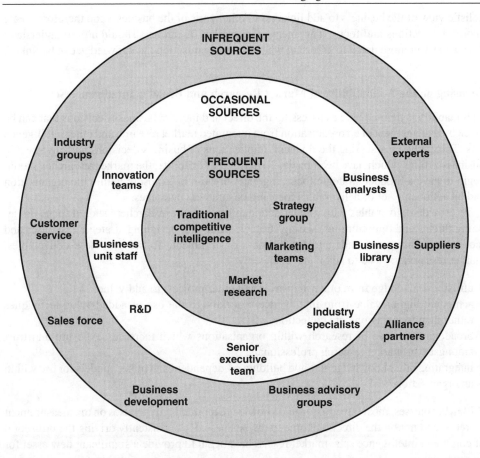

Figure 19.1   An example of multiple knowledge sources available to organisations

Creating linkages between different business units in an organisation is a vital new method as it embeds research knowledge into the fabric of an organisation, and increases the utilisation and revenue return from knowledge.

Organising linked knowledge into structured "intelligence sets" is the next stage of utilisation which provides further value to an organisation. These new intelligence sets are linked groups of knowledge aggregated to drive actions and decisions within organisations. Just as many business units in organisations need to increase the relevance and utilisation of systems, so do market researchers. The value of creating linkages is:

- to increase the value of information and knowledge to the organisation;
- to make the information and knowledge more robust as it "compensates" for imperfect evidence;
- moving linkages closer to building the full picture through small fragments of knowledge.

The imperative to develop links into other parts of an organisation can be discussed at length. However, it is very difficult to create linkages to other parts of the business with only a cloudy and unfocused view of the whole organisation. Therefore, market researchers need a full and holistic view of the business to add linkages to other parts of the business, and therefore create appropriate actions and focus. This means that market researchers should aim to understand the business in more detail to ascertain where in an organisation the knowledge can be linked.

Focusing on the Actionability of Market Research and Broader Intelligence Sets

Actionability is defined here as assessing the direct and indirect business decisions that can be taken by management of an organisation from integrated market research and other intelligence sets. This includes assessing the financial implications of business decisions and any specific business actions which have been made. To deliver actionability, the market researcher should begin to have a broader strategic focus, a greater breadth of exposure within the organisation and an actionable set of deliverables focusing on strategic outcomes.

To provide deliverables with greater actionability, market researchers should focus on defining threats and opportunities, setting strategic priorities, designing strategic responses and monitoring consumer trends and the business environment. To provide these deliverables, market researchers need to adapt and change by:

- utilising knowledge from other industries and other projects to add value;
- achieving higher value from intelligence sets through the use of added-value techniques rather than focusing on data collection;
- broadening the use of research within organisations which increases exposure and trust amongst non-market research professionals;
- integrating other knowledge sets and building co-dependent and linked models for use within an organisation.

Within businesses, most information and knowledge reported only focuses on the measurement systems, and not on the direct outcome to the business. By consistently driving the utilisation of combined intelligence sets, market researchers begin to provide a significant new asset for an organisation.

Ensuring There are Sufficient Financial Implications Coming from New Combined Intelligence Sets

Aggregating knowledge and insights into intelligence sets allows the market researcher to provide key measures which are now much more relevant to many parts of an organisation. If the intelligence sets are integrated with financial systems, organisations can now more easily define profit uplift, financial capital utilisation and other key financial measurements.

With financial implications coming from intelligence sets, we must test the decision impact on an organisation. Testing the "safety" and "influence" of the evidence in relation to business decisions includes applying frameworks that seek to combine an evaluation of the consumer evidence, but at the same time taking into account more intuitive management insights. Therefore, we need to know how these intelligence sets drive proposed changes, how they impact on the bottom-line profitability of the business and how they impact the financial capital of a business.

This is about getting to the kernel of the business drivers that will carry this idea forward. In short, market researchers need to understand how a potent insight is transformed into an actionable business process that will generate profit.

Power of Evidence Obtained and Used for Business Decisions

We as market researchers must now become the custodians of the knowledge and intelligence used for business decisions. Just as financial analysts, lawyers, mergers and acquisition advisers and other corporate advisory disciplines need to evaluate all the information that comes their way in making a business decision, so must we as market researchers. At this point we are moving into the realm of becoming market intelligence professionals.

Making a statement that market researchers are moving to deliver market intelligence is hollow without the beginning of a support framework to analyse the evidence in front of each of us in our everyday roles. A very good way, outlined in Smith and Fletcher (2004), is to use the constructs of the weight, power and direction of the evidence to assess its usability in business decisions:

- Weight of evidence: this is the idea of looking at quantitative support for ideas, coupled with the depth of feeling in support of the issues.
- Power of evidence: the strength of this genre of intelligence, coupled with what we already know about the topic.
- Direction of evidence: the internal consistency within intelligence sets, and the consistency across intelligence sets.

By utilising these three constructs to evaluate critical intelligence as evidence used in business decisions, market researchers are becoming much closer to being the market intelligence professional that organisations desire to support their business growth.

Focus on an Organisation in a Holistic Manner Rather than in a Singular Manner for Each Project

Having previously discussed integrated sets of intelligence, we now progress to the next stage of integration of knowledge and intelligence in an organisation. This is by working with an organisation in a truly holistic manner, where we now consider all the evidence in an organisation, rather than the currently available information provided within the market research programme.

Holistic analysis is much more about understanding all the influences on the decision-making process of an organisation. To be able to provide a more holistic view, market researchers must now be:

- business focused rather than research focused;
- proactive in solution and decision management;
- engaged in the overall business process;
- a generator of ideas for the organisation;
- comfortable with uncertainty;
- providing the full context of knowledge and intelligence.

In essence, holistic analysis is a move away from the classic hypotheses testing approach, to a much more fluid and pragmatic way of helping business decision-makers.

Ascertaining the Value of Intelligence Sets

Here we progress to the next stage of processes to ascertain the value of intelligence sets. This stage is important to ensure that the intelligence sets have an element of quality assurance, and provide a solid platform upon which to make informed decisions.

- Logic reviews: Logic reviews centre on the application of deductive and inductive ways of reasoning to arrive at an informed judgement on the quality of the intelligence set. This evaluative approach is used to ascertain if all the knowledge elements brought together in an intelligence set meld logically and allow for a coherent conclusion to be made.
- Knowledge filters: The ability to use our previous knowledge and norms to ascertain the value of the intelligence set we are using. For example, knowledge filters include all that we know about the way individuals will often act emotively, and then post rationalise this behaviour with a more rational account (see Smith and Fletcher, 2004).
- Validation analyses: The notions of validity, reliability and generalisability are important here. To adapt to this type of validation analysis, the market researcher should have a working knowledge of theories underpinning probability-based sampling and apply these to the intelligence set.
- Robustness: This is about how a particular genre of evidence is related to what we know about the "efficacy" of research. The evaluation includes applying "Bayesian thinking" to the intelligence set. We also need to take into account the popular practice of looking for "directional indicators" in the data which identify the overall pattern and shape of the intelligence set.

Strategic Tools to Allow Other Professionals to Integrate Linked Intelligence into Their Business Processes

Now that market researchers have integrated intelligence sets, have used holistic analysis to view the organisation on a broad basis and brought in the strength of indicators around the value of evidence available, it becomes a question of how these methods of working are used in an organisation.

At this point, we can turn to the vast body of knowledge that exists in the business literature around strategy tools. These tools are important in providing an interface between intelligence sets and the ability for business decision makers to integrate the intelligence into everyday operations. By successfully integrating intelligence into strategic tools, market researchers can deliver better insights to senior management and the ability to make better organisational decisions. There are many strategic tools that can be used. For a broader description, see Smith and Marinopoulos (2006). In this example, we will look at one of these methods in "Customer need-Business process mapping".

Customer Need–Business Process Mapping

This mapping method allows market researchers to provide a diagrammatical view of research outcomes. These maps are powerful in highlighting where important milestones occur within a business process which we know from the research. New strategy requirements can be overlaid onto maps providing insight into changes required by a business in a simplified manner. Actionable results are much easier to formulate as the process is easier to view and understand.

As an example, there are many cases where organisations seek to make significant changes to business processes. Quite often, the changes required by consumers are not linked to the new strategy. Therefore, many strategies fail as change in consumer behaviour does not eventuate. There are many cases of brand extensions such as Harley Davidson Cigarettes which would have benefited significantly from a customer need–business process map. In this case, Harley Davidson chose a brand extension into cigarettes as many of their customers were cigarette smokers. However, the change required to break brand associations primarily with Marlboro cigarettes was too ambitious. A customer need–business process map would have shown the difficulty with the required changes in customer behaviour.

A NEW WAY OF THINKING

So far, we have looked at the new way of working with research and intelligence to assist business decisions. However, what is required is the new thinking to transition market researchers who want to work as market intelligence professionals. Here are the types of skills required:

Developing the Problem Solvers' Mindset

Going beyond the skills needed to collect and report on intelligence and develop a "curious mindset" that allows the market researcher to "crystallise" the business problem. Furthermore, the market researcher should know exactly how their evidence will improve the bottom-line profitability of the organisation and identify that potent customer insight.

Thinking in a Holistic Way to Build the "Total Customer Experience"

Building on the holistic analysis, the market researcher needs to acquire the skills to integrate intelligence about customers and markets from a range of different sources. We must put ourselves in the position of explaining to the client the "total customer experience".

Having the Confidence to Use the Knowledge Filters

The market researcher needs to provide a more sophisticated account of what respondents are really trying to tell us when they take part in market research in order to understand a problem. In addition, we need to bring forward what the respondents were saying in the other knowledge sets integrated to a full intelligence set.

Using Our Creativity to Go Beyond the Research World to Identify Insights

This is about reading the contextual signals around our evidence and what is really happening. This brings a further dimension of intelligence and sophistication to our understanding of what our market research is really saying.

Bringing Our Marketing Intelligence Insights Alive within Your Organisation

Market researchers are getting much better at presenting their evidence, both verbally and in writing. But the bar keeps getting raised. In this skill, market researchers need to focus on new ways of making sure the evidence is brought to life, and about breathing understanding and insights into the client organisation.

Showing Good Judgement in Prioritising Potential Value

Drawing together the above skills and putting the spotlight firmly on the market researcher's ability to develop their confidence and expertise in identifying potent insights. The insights should be drawn to the attention of senior management prioritised by their potential value to the organisation.

Being Comfortable "Sparring" with Senior Management

On top of having the skills to ensure that organisations understand and utilise the intelligence sets, we need to make sure that the market researcher can have the correct dialogues with senior management of organisations. The market researcher needs to integrate the evidence in the wider context of business models and frameworks that are likely to add impact to our evidence-based argument.

Being Engaged with and Not Detached from the Decision-Making Process

This skill is about helping with the process of evidence-based decision-making. How can market researchers help guide decision-makers by framing choices for the organisation, and outlining the "safety" underpinning each choice? In addition, market researchers need to take presentations to the next level by knowing how to influence the way in which intelligence can be constructively used to the advantage of the organisation.

A NEW WAY OF DELIVERING MARKET INTELLIGENCE

In the previous two sections, we have discussed new ways of market researchers making a bigger impact on organisations. Firstly, there are new ways of working on how to integrate intelligence, and then there are new ways of thinking in how we work with organisations to embed market intelligence. The third area is the new way of delivering market intelligence into an organisation.

The delivery of market intelligence is where market researchers need to be most diligent as it is where the assessment of significant value is possible, but also the potential risk of incorrect judgments are also prevalent. Even with understanding the types of skills and approaches required, we need a governing set of systems to ensure that the delivery is pragmatic and practical to clients, and can be constantly assessed for value.

Here, we will focus on three areas of delivery: firstly, "systems" for managing and integrating multiple intelligence sets. Defining a "system" relevant to an organisation which shows how knowledge and intelligence can be used is extremely important to increasing the relevance and value of intelligence in an organisation. In this case, we will look at one system of "portfolio management" of intelligence sets.

Secondly, intelligence "value systems" that assess the value of insights and integrated intelligence to organisations, and provide evidence-based outcomes for organisations. In this case, we will look at an "Integrated Customer Intelligence" system to assist an organisation's decision-making process.

Thirdly, there should be company level "decision systems" in place to evaluate the success of evidence-based decisions against organisational target objectives. There are many potential systems that can be adapted here. This area is more about evaluating the aggregation of doing, thinking and delivering market intelligence as outlined in the last three sections.

Management of Intelligence Sets in an Organisation

Managing multiple intelligence sets for an organisation is important as it starts to link the businesses' intelligence base, and allows integration of intelligence into actions. The management and integration of intelligence sets depends very much on the power of evidence obtained and used. It also depends upon the logic review assessment, the application of knowledge filters, and assessing the validity and robustness of knowledge as outlined earlier.

One method of integrating intelligence sets is "portfolio management". This is similar to financial portfolio analysis where the best business portfolio is one that fits the company's strengths and helps focus on the most attractive opportunities. Here, "intelligence portfolios" are brought together to assess which intelligence sets provide the maximum value to an organisation's strategic direction.

The portfolio management uses "standardised templates" to assess multiple intelligence sets in an organisation. From there, performance metrics aligned to an organisation's strategy are used to evaluate which "intelligence portfolios" are important to consider.

To correctly build the performance metrics and align the portfolio to organisational strategy, the market researcher requires an understanding of the business "landscape" such as business issues and risks, the strategic direction of the organisation, and also the ability to assess the current organisational targets. From here, the market researcher can define performance metrics to evaluate the best "intelligence portfolio" for use within an organisation.

Valuing Multiple Intelligence Sets

Organisations can suffer from not knowing which of a number of plausible customer insights and possible strategies are the ones that represent the greatest economic opportunity. The ability to ascertain the market opportunity and understand these strategies in light of an organisation's capabilities is of significant value. Thus, market researchers must be comfortable in the role of valuing different customer propositions and prioritising their potential in the context of the organisation's current strengths and weaknesses.

An example of a system to value new business opportunities from multiple intelligence sets is "Integrated Customer Intelligence" as outlined in Marinopoulos and Laffin (2006). In this system, the focus is on integrating customer intelligence, strategic initiatives, and an organisation's internal intelligence and financial goals. A diagram of the system is in Figure 19.2.

Once the three elements of knowledge and intelligence are brought together, the system then focuses on extracting the value from integrated intelligence and creating material, distinct and optimal business value outcomes.

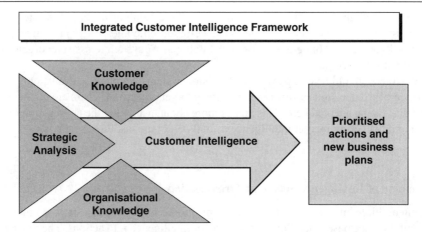

Figure 19.2   Diagram of the integrated customer intellgence framework (See Marinopoulos and Laffin, 2006)

Evaluating the Use of Intelligence Delivery

At this stage, the market researcher has defined certain delivery steps for the use of market intelligence. Overall, we have now defined and created a significant "intelligence asset" for an organisation. And just like any asset in an organisation, we should assess the value of the intelligence and its impact in an organisation.

To assess the impact, we should ensure there are company level "decision systems" in place to utilise the intelligence asset. Furthermore, we should evaluate the success of evidence-based decisions from the intelligence asset against target objectives of the organisations.

To encourage the maximal utilisation of intelligence assets, there is significant value in educating organisations in the use of integrated intelligence and the assessment of the value of the intelligence. This creates a "virtuous circle" of intelligence utilisation.

CONCLUSION

The transition of market research from a discipline delivering information and knowledge to a discipline delivering market intelligence cannot be achieved immediately. There are barriers due either to previous activity of market research and perceptions of what market research has previously delivered. In addition, market researchers themselves will provide barriers through their unwillingness to move past current practices into an uncertain territory.

Even with these barriers in place, market research is transforming. Market research is becoming more accountable for the investment made in research, and also for the decisions made from research. This will become an even wider trend as market researchers eventually transition into market intelligence professionals.

As this transition occurs, we will see the market intelligence outcomes will provide significant business outcomes that are much more focused, directed and actionable than pure research alone. At that time, the market research/market intelligence industry will have found a position of sustainable competitive advantage over many other knowledge disciplines.

REFERENCES

Almquist, E. and Pierce, A. (2000) Customer Knowledge and Business Strategy. *Marketing Research* **12**(1), 8.

Davenport, T.H. and Glasser, J. (2002) Just-in-time Delivery Comes to Knowledge Management. *Harvard Business Review*, July, 107.

INSEAD and Booz Allen Hamilton (2006) Innovation: Is Global the Way Forward?: A joint study by Booz Allen Hamilton and INSEAD. Fontainebleau, France.

Institute for the Future (2004) Toward A New Literacy Of Cooperation In Business: Managing Dilemmas In The 21st Century. SR-851A, Menlo Park, California.

Institute for the Future (2003) A New Era of Diagnostics. SR-821B, Menlo Park, California.

Kaplan, R.S. and Norton, D.P. (2004) *Strategy Maps: converting intangible assets into tangible outcomes.* Harvard Business School Press.

Lesser, E., Mundel, D. and Wiecha, C. (2000) Managing Customer Knowledge. *Journal of Business Strategy*, December, 35–37.

Marinopoulos, J. and Laffin, D. (2006) Integrated Customer Intelligence. Excellence 2006, ESOMAR, Amsterdam.

Marinopoulos, J. and Hill, W. (2003) How corporate reputation measurement can be a part of every CEO's KPI's: A financial services case study. Proceedings of the ESOMAR Congress, Prague.

Oliver, R.W. (2002) The Strategic Sweet Spot. *Journal of Business Strategy*, April, 6–9.

Pitt, L.F., Ewing, M.T. and Berthon, P. (2000) Turning Competitive Advantage into Customer Equity. *Business Horizons*, October, 11–18.

Porter, M.E. (1985) *Competitive Advantage.* Free Press.

Smith, D.V.L. and Fletcher, J.H. (2004) *The Art and Science of Interpreting Market Research Evidence.* John Wiley & Sons, Ltd.

Smith, D.V.L. (2004) Consolidating The Role Of Market Research In Business Decision-Making By Extending Our Skill Set Into Business Consultancy. Proceedings of the ESOMAR Congress, Lisbon.

Smith, D.V.L. and Marinopoulos, J. (2006) How to be a "Future Shock Absorber": The integration of market intelligence into the business strategy process. Proceedings of the ESOMAR Congress, London.

Voss, B.L. (2002) The McKinsey Mind: Understanding and Implementing the Problem Solving Tools and Management Techniques of the World's Top Strategic Consulting Firm. *Journal of Business Strategy*, April, 44–45.

20

Main Developments and Trends

Ray Poynter

Research is changing, and changing fast. Whilst some of these changes are as the result of endogenous causes such as better training, improved accreditation and the development of techniques such as ethnography and semiotics, many changes are the result of an exogenous cause, technology. This section reviews how the rapid changes in technology are impacting, and will impact in the future, market research.

When technologies change the market researcher needs to change and adapt. New technologies need to be assessed to see whether they are likely to have an impact, to assess the threats they may create for research and review the opportunities they will offer.

This section looks at a range of technologies that are already here, but which have not yet fully impacted market research. Experience has shown that new technologies take at least eight years to make a major impact on the world of market research, so we can reasonably assume that the technologies that will impact market research over the next five years or so are already here. As William Gibson has said "the future is already here, it is just unevenly distributed".

Some of the changes mentioned in this section will be dealt with more fully in other parts of the Handbook, for example online research. This section covers the key technologies and their likely impact on research, in particular the threats they may create and the opportunities they present.

THE ELECTRONIC WAKE

The electronic wake is the trail we all leave behind us as we travel through the modern world, every ATM usage, every smartcard swipe, every web access, every CCTV recording, each product with an RFID (Radio Frequency ID tag) in it, every mobile phone call, every Wi-Fi and Bluetooth connection adds to the amount of information we leave about ourselves (Poynter, 2002). We can see the full power of this electronic wake in action when there is a bombing or a security threat as the police and security services inspect this wake for clues or possible suspects.

Market researchers have been slow to capitalise on this wake and have to some extent left the field to others. Web metrics companies have specialised in collecting and producing data about website usage and are increasingly having key conversations with brand managers. CRM consultancies and database specialists have concentrated on the data provided by electronic transactions, loyalty cards and smart cards. Category management consultancies have specialised in scanner data and have started using CCTV and shopping carts fitted with RFIDs to measure and map shopping behaviour.

Market Research Handbook, 5th Edition. Edited by M. van Hamersveld and C. de Bont.
© 2007 John Wiley & Sons, Ltd.

The recording and analysis of the electronic wake raises a large number of privacy and legislative concerns. Most data protection laws and most codes of conduct are based on informed consent. But too often the consent that is obtained is not informed consent. Paradoxically, when most people are asked for their consent they agree, particularly if they are offered some small benefit.

The electronic wake is of growing value to companies, but its usefulness depends on the public's willingness to co-operate, which in turn depends on companies behaving sensibly. One useful case to consider is the loss in public support suffered by AOL when it accidentally released the complete search records of 658,000 of its users to the public. In August 2006 somebody at AOL put the 658,000 logs, containing some 21 million searches, onto an academic research website. The idea was to help with genuine academic research. However, on the web nothing stays secret very long and there was uproar when people became aware that this information was publicly accessible. AOL quickly removed the logs, but by this time the site had been copied to several other locations.

AOL, like most of the big search companies such as Google and Yahoo, saves all of the searches entered into its search engine and associates them by unique user. In the logs that were released by AOL the IDs had been replaced by random strings to protect users' anonymity. However, it soon became apparent that this still left concerns, for example many people search for their own name or for their home town.

News.com (7 August 2006) reported that "it's possible to guess that AOL user 710794 is an overweight golfer, owner of a 1986 Porsche 944 and 1998 Cadillac SLS, and a fan of the University of Tennessee Volunteers Men's Basketball team. The same user, 710794, is interested in the Cherokee County School District in Canton, Ga., and has looked up the Suwanee Sports Academy in Suwanee, Ga., which caters to local youth, and the Youth Basketball of America's Georgia affiliate.

That's pretty normal. What's not is that user 710794 also regularly searches for 'lolitas,' a term commonly used to describe photographs and videos of minors who are nude or engaged in sexual acts."

The New York Times (9 August 2006) went one step farther and ran a story showing how it had identified a woman from Georgia, USA, just from her "anonymised" search logs. The New York Times asked the lady for her views about what had happened and reported "Ms. Arnold says she loves online research, but the disclosure of her searches has left her disillusioned. In response, she plans to drop her AOL subscription. 'We all have a right to privacy,' she said. 'Nobody should have found this all out.'"

Threats

The first threat to market research is the potential for a popular backlash against this sort of data collection. Privacy groups and citizens could take a range of action such as boycotts, lawsuits, or lobbying politicians to legislate in order to eradicate or limit the ability of service providers to record or utilise details of their activities.

The second threat is that these sorts of techniques could reduce customers' and respondents' confidence in what companies, brands, and researchers are doing.

The third threat is that this sort of activity will enmesh researchers in the activities of the state. For example, in the US several court cases were lodged as a result of companies such as Yahoo handing search logs over to the US Government, and of phone companies handing over phone records, so that the Government could try to profile suspected terrorists.

Finally, there is the threat that market researchers will not engage with this information, ceding this area of business information to others.

Opportunities

If market researchers develop better synergies and strategies for working with the electronic wake, then there is the chance to create much fuller descriptions of what people do. As analysis of the wake provides more information about what people are doing, market researchers will have an opportunity to meet the growing challenge of explaining why people do the things they do, and of working out how they will react to new stimuli. One example of this type of synergy is provided by website surveys which pop up when specific browsing actions, for example an abandoned shopping cart, are witnessed by the metrics software. Another example is single source data which combines sales information with media data.

THE INTERNET AND ONLINE PANELS

The Internet is well on its way to being the dominant data collection medium, something which has changed, and is changing, research. Compared with telephone and face-to-face research, the Internet has opened up a raft of new possibilities such as sound, video, dynamic randomising, adaptive questionnaires and the collection of paradata, such as the length of time to answer each questions, the number of corrections, etc. (Jeavons, 2001).

There are three main modalities for the Internet medium: Website Surveys, Customer Lists, and most importantly Online Panels.

Website Surveys

Website surveys are triggered by people who visit websites, usually via pop-ups. Although website surveys were initially conducted by market researchers, they have more recently tended to become more the provenance of website specialists and in-house teams.

Customer Lists

In the mid-1990s most clients' lists of customer email addresses were in a sorry state, full of errors, ambiguities, and lacking the proper permissions to make them both practical and useful. Surveys conducted by emailing invitations to customers generated large numbers of bounce-backs and frequent accusations of spamming. However, customer lists were quickly recognised as a valuable way of researching customers, in particular for customer satisfaction studies.

Since the turn of the millennium, customer databases have improved substantially, largely because of their use in direct marketing. However, this change has created its own challenges. Most brands make heavy use of their email lists for marketing communications and many marketing managers see an invitation to a market research survey as a lost opportunity to market. Increasingly, customer lists are being used for hybrid research, where marketing, database collection and research co-exist together.

Online Panels

Online access panels, usually provided by third-party panel companies, are the main method by which Internet research is conducted, and are becoming the dominant method globally.

Globally, most economically developed markets are well supplied with access panels, which provide fast and reliable services.

Some online panels provide a sample only service, where the research agency is responsible for scripting and hosting the survey, other panels provide full service options, including scripting, hosting and sample provision.

In addition to consumer access panels there are growing numbers of companies offering B2B panels and specialist panels, for example doctors, life-style and sexual orientation.

There have been several studies into online panels and these have shown that panel members are very willing to do surveys, that they are motivated in a variety of ways, including: enjoying surveys, wanting to help, wanting their views to be heard and wanting to earn rewards and incentives. Research has shown that many panel members are on multiple panels, and that it is not unusual for people to do 50 or more surveys a year (Comley, 2005).

Threats

If we only research people who are online, particularly people on panels, and if we interview the same people more than 50 times a year, then we cannot automatically assume that our sample will be representative of anything other than regular responders to surveys. There is a risk that the way panels are developing, and the way costs are falling, will transform most research into commodity research. The growth of Internet research is likely to increase the integration of market research with direct marketing and database building.

Opportunities

The Internet and panels have numerous opportunities, including: increased speed, reduced costs and meeting clients' needs in terms of giving them what they want in time to aid decisions. The Internet also provides an opportunity to integrate with direct marketing and database building.

ADVANCED ANALYTICS

This section looks at a number of advanced techniques that have been enabled or developed by technological changes and the impact they are having on market research.

Bayesian Revolution

Bayesian statistics provide a good illustration of how a good idea needs the right context in order to blossom. The Reverend Thomas Bayes published his statistical technique in the 18th century, but it has only been over the last 20 years that advances in computing power have enabled the power of the Bayesian approach to be used. In many ways, the key to the Bayesian approach is a philosophical rather than a mathematical issue. Bayesians believe in using what we already know about a problem to improve our estimates about the data. In the jargon of statistics, they use the data to condition the hypothesis, classical statistics, by contrast, uses the hypothesis to condition the data.

The most common application of Bayesian statistics is Hierarchical Bayes (HB), particularly when applied to Choice Modelling. The basic approach is to collect a sparse data set, where each respondent answers perhaps 12 to 18 choice tasks. In total this data is enough to create an aggregate solution to the Choice Model, but there is not enough information to provide a solution at the individual respondent level. HB uses computing and statistical power to generate hundreds of thousands of possible solutions, sampling from the generated distributions. The output is an estimate of what each respondent would have said, if they had answered more questions.

HB is a very good fit with the Internet methodology. Each respondent is asked a limited sub-set of questions, and HB is then used to calculate a complete set of responses for each respondent. However, the maths used in HB means that it is beyond the capabilities of most researchers to understand the mathematics involved. The problem is somewhat compounded by the almost evangelical fervour of most Bayesian experts.

Discrete Choice Models

DCM's, Discrete Choice Models, have grown out of traditional Conjoint techniques which were often based on rank order or rating techniques. The key element of DCMs is that respondents are presented with a set of tasks where they are offered two or more (usually three or more) options and asked to pick or "choose" one.

The choices that are offered comprise different levels of different attributes. The aim of the analysis is to establish the additive value of each attribute and each level. Advances in computing power and statistical models have allowed more complicated DCMs to be designed and fielded, increasingly via the Internet.

Proponents of DCMs like the fact that the respondent task is straightforward and replicates the real world. In the real world people choose products (as in a DCM), they do not rank or rate products. The design of DCMs requires an in-depth knowledge of choice modelling, and the analysis tends to require a good understanding of things like orthogonality and interactions (Poynter, 2006).

BYO Surveys

Build Your Own surveys are becoming increasingly popular, particularly with clients. BYOs tend to replicate the real world where, increasingly, consumers are given a chance to configure their own product, be it a PC, a holiday, or even just a pizza.

In a typical BYO the respondent is given different sets of constrained choices and is able to select their most preferred configuration. The constrained choices and the choices made are then used as the input to the modelling software.

BYO studies are becoming more sophisticated using ever more realistic representations of products. The key problem with BYOs is that although they look as though they are providing plenty of information, they actually provide a poor level of data, because people are not forced to trade-off elements they want. The key to rich data lies in obliging respondents to make difficult decisions; in a BYO respondents tend to have more scope to pick items they like. Many researchers tend to use BYOs as a conditioning task in a DCM study, as it provides a good introduction to the attributes and levels for the respondent (Johnson, Orme & Pinnell, 2005).

Data Mining

As databases become larger and as the electronic wake provides an ever increasing quantity of information, the value of the data available increases. Data mining techniques are being developed that allow the information to be trawled more effectively, to discover the messages inside the data.

Although some market researchers have been pursuing data mining techniques, these approaches have been more extensively developed by CRM and database marketers (plus elements of the government). As the electronic wake of information grows and as the data mining techniques develop, market research will see an increased level of threat and competition from other data experts.

Other Advances in Mathematics and Advanced Analytics

In addition to the items above, there are a wide range of other techniques that are being developed in conjunction with the advances in technology. Examples of these approaches include Item Response Theory, Wavelets, Latent Class, Structural Equation Models and Artificial Intelligence. The key theme amongst these techniques is that they require an extensive amount of knowledge and training to apply them and that they usually take longer to utilise than conventional approaches.

Threats

One key threat arising out the advanced analytics is a narrowing of the base of those with the skills to use them. As techniques become more dependent on advanced mathematics, complex designs and more exacting assumptions about the nature of the measurements, fewer researchers have the knowledge and skills required to use them. As buyers and providers of market research understand less and less of the leading edge, they are tending to shy away from the more complex solutions, something that has been termed as "dumbing down", or the gathering of the low hanging fruit.

Another potential problem with advanced analytics is a temptation towards an assumption that complex behaviour can be reduced to equations. Frequently the arguments between proponents of rival techniques revolve around the theoretical underpinning of their approaches, rather than on their ability to easily and reliably provide useful information.

Opportunities

At a time when the Internet, online panels, reduced timelines and reduced budgets are turning most research into commodity research, advanced analytics provides an opportunity for researchers to provide value-added solutions. Just as qualitative researchers have used ethnography, NLP and semiotics to move into a more value-added sphere, advanced analytics provides an opportunity for quantitative researchers to move away from the commodity research business.

Many of the newer advanced analytics are focusing on the newer types of data; large, sparse data sets, often with longitudinal information at the individual level. Advanced analytics provide the opportunity for researchers to expand from their current core business into additional business information areas.

Finally, advanced analytics provide the opportunity to create surveys that are less "mind numbing" for respondents. Surveys can be more interactive, more adaptive, more contextual, and shorter for the individual respondent.

WORD OF MOUTH (WOM)

Word of Mouth is a collective term covering many different manifestations, from emails which are forwarded from reader to reader, to comments on product review sites, to the full-blown social interaction on sites such as MySpace. WOM recognises that increasingly people are acting more on personal recommendation and less on formal advertising (Marsden, 2006).

Although the term WOM usually refers to electronic discourses, the power of word of mouth is as old as society itself. The recognition of traditional word of mouth is evidenced by the power of scales such as the Net Promoter Score, based on whether people would recommend a brand or service, to predict future sales. The Internet did not create word of mouth it simply amplified it.

WOM is used as a marketing technique and the Word of Mouth Marketing Association has put together a really useful website for helping to understand WOM marketing (www.womma.org).

WOM research takes many forms, at one extreme the term covers analysts visiting discussion forums and potentially interacting with regular contributors (although there are ethical considerations if the posts the analysts are posting are misleading), through to automated software (bots) which trawl the net to look for references to brands, events, phrases, etc.

One of the key phrases used by the WOM advocates is "Why ask some of us when you can ask all of us?". However, here are two key problems with WOM; the first is that not everybody posts their views online. By listening to the online buzz there may be a risk that the message from the loud few will lead to the silent majority being ignored. The second issue is that it is hard to test hypotheses in the WOM world, it is more like astronomy than say physics. Researchers have to wait until an event happens before they can study it.

Threats

One threat to the research industry is that WOM research could replace large amounts of conventional research and the suppliers of the service may not be from the research industry. Potential areas that might be impacted are: brand and advertising tracking, customer satisfaction and U&As.

From a brand's point of view there is a risk that they will become increasingly driven by the vocal wishes of special interest groups and less focused on their core customers.

Opportunities

WOM research offers brands the chance to be completely up-to-date with what people are saying about them and about how their marketing is being perceived and responded to. As automation continues WOM research may provide much better value for money than conventional research.

WEB 2.0 AND RESEARCH 2.0

Just as the research industry was getting to grips with the Internet, the Internet has changed. Web 2.0 has created a whole new discourse, which is replacing the static, top-down nature of Web 1.0 and which will change power structures, business practices, and research in ways which dwarf previous changes (Trayner, 2006).

Web 2.0, also known as the participatory web, has changed the traditional unidirectional model of media, marketing and power, from monologue to dialogue. Customers are posting, reviewing, re-selling, discussing, sharing and creating via Web 2.0.

The term Web 2.0 was coined by O'Reilly Media in 2004 to describe the new web paradigm. As an example of the before and after, Tim O'Reilly (2005) offers the following table:

Web 1.0	Web 2.0
Mp3	Napster
Britannica online	Wikipedia
Personal websites	Blogs
Ofoto	Flickr
Publishing	Participation
DoubleClick	Google AdSense
Content management systems	Wikis
Stickiness	Syndication

The traditional research model is a top-down model based on a command and control paradigm:

- We contact respondents when we want to speak to them.
- We ask them our questions, in our order, and force respondents to pick answers from the set we consider to be the correct set.
- We rarely tell the respondent why we are doing the research, we rarely tell them the results of the research, and we rarely tell them the business decisions that have been made following them expressing their views.
- The statistics we use and many of the approaches we apply are more fitting of experiments with lab rats rather than with customers.

Research 2.0 is a response to the developing discussion that is Web 2.0. Research 2.0 adds new approaches to the traditional "lab rat" approaches. Examples of Research 2.0 approaches include:

- Creating advisor groups who not only respond to survey requests but can also initiate contact when they have something to say.
- Routing people at the end of survey to a discussion forum, where they can see what other people have said, where they can comment on the survey, ask questions of the client, or come back at a late stage to add additional thoughts.
- The ability to challenge the questionnaire, to add breaks, to add questions, to suggest amendments to questions.
- Blog based research where respondents are recruited to a specially created blog and are free to post a wide variety of pictures, comments, video clips to express their views about the brand and the research.

Co-creation

Brands as diverse as Boeing, Lego and Janet Jackson have discovered the merits of co-creation. Co-creation allows the brand to leverage the creative input of customers. In a typical example the brand opens a website and invites customers to contribute ideas, designs, code or graphics.

These contributions are assessed by the brand and by other customers and help shape the final product. For example, Lego have almost completely handed over the development of their Mindstorm product to the 75 000 members of the Mindstorm user group, whilst Boeing are working with "flyer and enthusiasts" to help design the planes of the future.

Co-creation creates two separate avenues of involvement for market researchers. Firstly, when brands are collecting consumer insight via co-creation, market researchers should be involved in the process, to help frame questions and to help interpret responses. The second opportunity for market researchers is to allow our respondents and customers to help design future research, if Boeing can admit it does not have a monopoly of aeronautical engineering know-how, perhaps market researchers can accept that respondents and customers could contribute to the design and interpretation of research.

Threats

For some research it is necessary to conform to certain methodological rules, such as respondents not being aware of the research context or objectives, and these could be compromised if too much research became participatory. A major threat is that Web 2.0 initiatives could render much of market research irrelevant. For example threadless.com is a website where people create and upload designs, vote and review designs, and the most popular are then outsourced to third-world factories and can be purchased via the web – cutting out the formal research process entirely. Chris Anderson's concept of The Long Tail (2006) suggests a future where in many areas a store no longer decides which products to offer, it offers a massive range, via the web, and dispenses with the old 80:20 rule. It was the 80:20 rule which explained why brands or stores tended to limit the range of products they offered, and therefore created the need to research options, without the tyranny of the 80:20 rule, some research will not be needed.

Opportunities

The greatest opportunity of Web 2.0 is the potential to leverage the creative power of hundreds or thousands of consumers. The "power of the many" to create better ideas, better methods, and better interpretations. Research 2.0 will also add greater validity to the researcher's claim to be the customers' voice in the boardroom.

NEUROMARKETING

Interest in neuromarketing has developed since the first few years of the current millennium. The key element is to use brain scanning tools such as fMRI to understand consumers' reactions to marketing stimuli and to use the information to improve and fine tune marketing and marketing communications.

Demonstrations of scanners have shown how they can produce images that show how consumers respond to commercials, marketing messages, and discussions about their shopping behaviour. However, practical usage of brain scanning techniques have been held up by their cost, the timescales involved in using them, and concerns about the atypical nature of the test environment. Indeed, very little credible work has been done on the validity of the outputs from Neuromarketing projects, although there have been some interesting first steps such as Penn 2005 and Page & Raymond.

Opposition to the general applicability of brain scanning as a research tool has centred on:

1. Do the responses of a subject immobilised inside scanners correctly reflect the responses of consumers when viewing communications in a more typical environment?
2. Concerns that the approach is too mechanistic; for example, can the workings of the brain be reduced to a simple cause and effect model?
3. Concerns that whether scanning a small number of consumers can adequately reflect the responses of a wide and varied population.

Threats

If brain scanning were to prove an effective and reliable way of assessing consumer reactions to advertising and marketing messages then there would clearly be a reduction in the amount of research that was required. Even if brain scanning techniques prove to be too expensive to roll-out for general research, they may ultimately show that some forms of research do not work.

Opportunities

If brain scanning proves to have some validity, it could prove invaluable in helping the research industry assess which research techniques work and in understanding how they work. The more researchers understand how the brain works, in relation to brands, marketing and markets, the more researchers can improve their tools and approaches to help clients.

CRM (CUSTOMER RELATIONSHIP MARKETING)

In the 20th century most marketing was mass marketing. Advertising was mass advertising, product ranges were narrow and designed to reach the maximum number of people with the minimum number of variations, and segmentation was seen as the high point of targeted marketing.

CRM, permission marketing, personalisation, bespoke production, mass customisation, loyalty and affiliate schemes are all beginning to treat each consumer as a segment of one. Brands are developing one-to-one relationships with their customers, where each transaction is seen as a conversation between the brand and the customer.

Brands, particularly services, are developing extensive databases of their clients and their transactions (part of the electronic wake created by customers). Techniques for utilising these databases are being developed. Initial techniques included statistical approaches such as Chaid and CaRT, but newer techniques have been developed to integrate marketing and communications with data mining and AI approaches.

Brands are beginning to see their relationship with their customers as a conversation rather than a monologue. Every communication with a customer is seen as a chance to build the relationship, to find out more about what the customer wants, and to offer relevant products and services to the customer.

One potential issue for market researchers is our long-established code of conduct, separating marketing and research. Traditionally, market researchers have avoided any form of market research which is used for direct marketing or database building. The problem with this approach is that it does not make economic or business sense for many clients. Where clients are treating every communication as a conversation, conducted for the mutual benefit of the brand and the customer, the market research paradigm does not fit. With classic market research there is no direct benefit for the customer, they can't buy anything, their answers won't improve their personal service from the brand, the points they raise (praise or criticism) won't often result in replies to that customer. For the brand an email invitation to conduct a survey can be a lost opportunity, many brands limit themselves in terms of their communications, to avoid annoying customers, for example they may limit emails to one per month. If emails are limited to one per month, then an invitation to a survey will block the "conversation" for that month.

Many types of research require the classic, independent type of market research, conducted by independent researchers, with traditional codes of conduct (for example comparisons between providers), but most research does not require the traditional codes of conduct and pseudo-scientific procedures.

Threats

The main CRM threat to the market research industry is that research becomes bypassed. As brands develop their conversations with customers, many aspects of research will be conducted as part of that process, but not necessarily by market researchers. Even those aspects of market research not conducted as part of the conversation with clients could suffer as they will look relatively expensive when compared with research which has been integrated into the brand/customer conversation process.

Opportunities

The main opportunity for market researchers is to seek to own large parts of the brand/customer conversation process. The core competencies of market researchers include asking the right questions, creating the correct contexts, and understanding consumer responses (for example by reading below the surface). If market researchers can update their codes of conduct, CRM related research could be one of the largest parts of their business.

NEW MEDIA

Although the term media is a plural, for many years it covered relatively few channels, there was print, radio, movies, TV and external (e.g. billboards, sides of buses, inside trains, etc.). Over the last 20 years there has been an explosion of media, including new channels, new uses of old channels, and hybrid combinations of forms, including Internet, video, mobile, digital and participatory media.

One of the key features of new media is that it is increasingly not broadcast, it is becoming more narrowcast. The days when all the family would sit down to watch a narrow range of TV programmes are long gone. Houses have multiple TVs, tuned into multiple delivery platforms including cable, satellite and Internet. People load movies onto their PC, their PDA, their iPod or their mobile. Devices such as TIVO and play on demand free people from the tyranny of schedules allowing people to increasingly watch what they want, when they want.

User generated media (UGM) is fast replacing programmed media as the first choice for viewing. A hit clip on YouTube will get many more viewers than the next blockbuster from Hollywood. Millions of people around the world are becoming citizen journalists, some by blogging, but most are doing it by sending photos and video clips to regular news suppliers, by chatting online, or by posting comments.

One of the earliest forms of the new media was email. Marketers quickly realised that viruses, sick jokes and funny pics could circle the globe in minutes, providing a vehicle for a new form of marketing, viral marketing.

Brands are experimenting with ways to use this new media to their advantage. Product placement, that great standby of 1950s US TV, is making a comeback with brands appearing in social networks such as MySpace and in virtual worlds such as Second Life, as is targeted advertising using techniques such as Google Adsense.

Threats

One problem with new media is that it is hard to draw sensible samples. People who have seen A but not B are hard to pin down. A highly targeted campaign may only reach 10 000 people, interviewing 100 of them might be too expensive and too slow.

In many cases brands may find it is more effective to apply a "trial and learn" approach where activities are tried and modified, rather than being refined by market research.

How are researchers going to work with issues such as opportunity to view in this multi-modal, time-shifted, on demand, new media world?

Opportunities

On opportunity for market research is to be fully engaged in the "trial and learn" process. Ensuring the right questions are asked and the correct inferences drawn. Researchers can cement their role as the representative of all the customers, not just the vocal minority, a group sometimes referred to as the chattering classes.

MOBILE 24/7 SOCIETY

One of the most visible technological changes over the last few years has been the arrival of the mobile, 24/7, always connected society. The most ubiquitous aspect of this phenomenon is the mobile phone. In most developed markets the number of mobile phones exceeds the number of land lines, and users increasingly have more than one mobile phone. In emerging markets, such as Pakistan and China, mobile phones greatly outnumber the number of land lines.

There have been several attempts to utilise the mobile society for market research, but they have only provided limited rewards, some interesting, early work was reported from Japan (Cattell, 2001). The key reason seems to be that at present methods of using mobile phones only produce small amounts of information per respondent (even though the number of respondents can be large). This small amount of information does not match the needs of most clients. Research tends to be about customer satisfaction, concept testing, U&A, brand and ad tracking. All of these require answers to 20 or more questions, often with long answer lists. This does not fit with mobile methodologies to date.

As mobiles get smarter, as marketers increasingly use geo-targeting to aid their marketing, and as the use of the electronic wake takes off, there will be new and significant ways of using mobile technologies in research.

Moblogging, Downloads, and Video Uploads

People use their mobile phone in a variety of ways in connection with the Internet: to download games, ringtones, video clips and music. These low barrier activities have created far more connectivity than attempts to get people to use their mobile as a browser. Research is needed to find out what the next mass activity will be and how to leverage it.

Sites such as YouTube.com survive largely on video clips that have been uploaded from people's mobiles. People compete to get the attention of their peers by uploading. This could be leveraged to help promote a brand or to help research a brand.

Moblogging is a form of blogging where the entries to blogs are uploaded via SMS text messaging, rather than via a browser. Researchers are beginning to explore this as a method of capturing views and attitudes during the day.

Beyond the Mobile Phone

Being mobile and connected is much more than just having a mobile phone. Laptops, phones and PDAs all routinely have Bluetooth, some have WiFi and there are promises of MaxFi (wide area wireless networking). As people become more connected they will create increasing amounts of electronic wake that can be analysed, and will present an ever more attractive target to brands attempting to geo-target them. All of these initiatives will require research to ensure that they are either welcomed or at least accepted.

Threats

So far most attempts to utilise the mobile/connected technologies have been relatively unsuccessful. However, somebody will come up with a "killer app" at some time, and those who do not see it coming will be in serious trouble.

Opportunities

The opportunity for research is to find a way to leverage the mobile revolution. Most people in developed economies have at least one mobile, many have more. Laptops, phones, PDAs are increasing fitted with Bluetooth and WiFi. This is an almost completely untapped area for modern research.

THE ROLE OF VIDEO AND ONLINE-VIDEO IN RESEARCH

Video has been around for years, but better, cheaper tools, and faster, cheaper streaming have fundamentally changed the way it is being used in research.

Ethnography has greatly increased in popularity and part of the reason is probably connected to how easy it is for researchers to collect hundreds of hours of videos of real lives, how easy it is to edit it, and how easy it is to create a DVD showing the most salient 30–60 minutes of the material. The whole process has also been made much more acceptable by the growth of reality TV, which appears to make more people comfortable with being videoed.

Conventional qualitative research has discovered the benefits of including video clips in the presentation, and usability researchers are developing techniques to combine images of the respondent with the task being undertaken. For example, researcher testing websites will often display a video showing the screen and mouse, with a picture-in-picture showing the person doing the browsing.

Focus groups are increasingly being viewed remotely, particularly via systems like FocusVision. Not only does this remote viewing allow more people to watch consumers talk about brands, but it creates databases that can be referred back to. Companies such as P&G are building a database of hundreds of focus groups, each session being tagged and reviewed by many viewers. The tagging process means that the images do not remain unused, but can be searched and accessed by people using the tagging system.

Many people, especially young people, are using webcams as part of their online world, particularly when they are combining chat with an online society such as MySpace. These webcams represent another way for researchers to interact with respondents, and to collect images of people talking about their life and their relationship with brands and services.

Threats

The two main threats raised by the increased use of video are data privacy/security and the convincing nature of video images. In conventional face-to-face encounters it is very easy to control the privacy and security of data subjects. For example, researchers and clients are told that if they recognise somebody in a focus group they are viewing they must leave. The protections are much harder to create and police when the images are online. In a company with hundreds of focus groups in the database, with possibly thousands of potential viewers, who will ensure that the sessions are only viewed for the correct purposes and that the privacy of the subjects will be protected?

The second problem arises out of the very success and power of video. One 30 second clip of a customer having a disaster with the product is likely to convey a stronger impression than a quantitative report based on 1000 people which says only 0.5 % of people have any problem with the product. Image makers and spin doctors have a long history of using the power of images to create a powerful, false impression. There is clearly a risk this could happen with market research, either deliberately or inadvertently.

Opportunities

The opportunities for researchers to use video are almost endless. We might see a world in the future where all quantitative interviews include video images as stimuli and as part of the data collected. Perhaps we will see houses wired like Big Brother, with cameras in every room capturing every detail of subjects' lives. Respondents can use their devices to capture images and upload them as part of research, presentations will include video and be themselves videoed, tagged, and added to a database of insight.

PRESENTING THE RESULTS

Most presentations are now facilitated, shaped and constrained by one particular combination of technology, namely PowerPoint, the laptop and a large screen or projector. Indeed some writers have started writing about "death by PowerPoint" to express their concern that this one-size-fits-all approach is reducing our ability to communicate insight, a particular critic being Edward Tufte (2006).

In terms of face-to-face presentations, the main impact of technology since 2000 has been the increased use of videoclips, in particular clips of customers articulating some view, or clips showing real lives (a cross between ethnography and reality TV). This trend is likely to continue, but care must be taken to ensure that very powerful persuasion in the video-clip adequately reflects the insight uncovered by the research.

Webinars, Web-ex, and Podcasts

The Internet is increasingly being used to conduct remote meetings, to conduct remote seminars and to create downloadable broadcasts (videocasts and podcasts). Most of the development in this area is taking place in the area of entertainment, sales and education. A number of market research companies make use of webinars and podcasts to tell prospective clients about new techniques and services.

Remote presentations and downloadable presentations tend to be used when a face-to-face presentation is not possible. In the future this could however be the preferred medium for many presentations. A remote presentation has the advantage of saving time (i.e. reducing costs) and of being captured electronically. Across time, clients will be able to tag the presentations they have received, allowing them to search and access the insight embedded in the presentations.

The DVD or the Book?

Until the 1980s the default format for market research insight was a written report. During the 1980s, 1990s and into the new millennium the default format became the PowerPoint presentation, perhaps annotated, perhaps accompanied by a management summary, often accompanied by copies of the data tables (in the early days on paper, later electronically).

As the use of video developed, and in particular with the rise of ethnography, a small but significant number of researchers started providing a DVD which captured the key elements of the research. For example, McPhee and Chrystal (2006) reported how they provided their client with a 30 minute DVD which captured the key elements of 200 hours of video, collected as part of an ethnography study into the daily lives of osteoarthritis sufferers.

What does the future hold? More video is clearly going to be part of the picture, but so will more journalistic approaches such as those shown by blogs and collaborative approaches based on wikis.

Threats

The appeal of the PowerPoint presentation is waning, fewer clients want to attend a traditional presentation, and few can find the time for extended presentation formats such as the workshop presentation. As a "leave behind", a PowerPoint presentation is not very effective (even when annotated) and market researchers risk becoming marginalised, or even replaced, by something with more instant appeal such as video clips.

Opportunities

The death of privacy, the growth of web cams, mobile phone video clips, video uploads, videoconferencing, webinars, etc., mean that market researchers can find better ways to pass on their insight to clients. The significance of the one-off meeting will reduce, and a piece of insight, captured on video, stored, tagged and multiply-linked will be better communicated and have a longer shelf life.

REPORTING OPTIONS

The story so far about the impact of technology on the reporting of market research results has been mixed, a few small successes, one transformational event and many half-successes and failures. The transformational event was the rise of email, which has facilitated faster delivery of results, reduced the barriers for additional analysis and has promoted a push method of distributing results.

The Pull/Push Dichotomy

One of the biggest differences between reporting methodologies is whether they are push or pull. A push technology is one where the vendor pushes information to the client, an approach which tends to result in more of the information being read. The classic push approach is email, where the vendor sends the results, or a link to the results, to the client, with an expectation that it will be acted on.

A pull technology is one where the client collects the information when they wish to. Examples of a pull technology include reportals, FTP sites and the online reporting built into many Internet based data collection systems. Systems which deliver the power to search and trawl the data, such as Quanvert, are also examples of pull techniques.

At first glance, the pull approach seems more client friendly, and likely to be more useful. The client knows what he or she needs, they can collect exactly the data or analysis they want, and they are not burdened with reports, tables or data streams which are not relevant to their current needs.

However, most pull systems have been fairly unsuccessful. One problem is that many clients do not have the time to visit a number of different provider sites to access the various elements they might need. Clients are often unsure of exactly which bits of large data systems they need to access, they do not want to learn several different procedures (nor do they want to store a raft of passwords) in order to answer an urgent question. Off the record, many vendors have commented that when they have provided their information in a pull environment, some clients never access it, rendering it very poor value and making the project less likely to be funded in the future.

Push systems, such as emailing results to clients, are based on vendors wanting clients to access information. The vendor tends to know what is interesting in the information and has a financial interest in ensuring that the client is aware of, and reads, interesting things in the data/information.

Pull systems seem to be most effective when they are delivering access to data rather than insight, where the information is necessary to the client (as opposed to desirable) and where the amount of information is so large that the client might be over-burdened if the information was sent straight to them. Examples that work well with pull systems are sales audit data (such as that provided by AC Nielsen), news services (although even here people are starting to use things such as RSS to simulate a push service) and process information (such as accounts, sales, and transactional data such as number of visitors, number of page views, etc.).

Push systems appear to have a distinct advantage over pull systems when the material being delivered is more insight focused rather than data driven, and in cases where the information is "nice to have" rather than essential – something which is often the case with market research data.

Some services provide a hybrid of pull and push. The underlying data might be made available via a reportal (i.e. a pull modality) but key findings are automatically emailed to the client, or pulled up via a dashboard.

Intelligent Tables

A number of tabs packages provide a cut-down version which allows clients to run additional queries on their data, perhaps the most well known being Quanvert from SPSS. The main player in making conventional tables more accessible is E-Tabs. The main difference between a tabs package and E-Tabs is that E-Tabs is a more attractive and powerful way of accessing tables that have been created in a tabs package. Amongst the various advantages offered by E-Tabs are the facility to put the tabs online and to automate the production of charts and reports.

Although products such as E-Tabs can make the life of a researcher easier, they have not fundamentally improved the life of the end client, because they provide better data, but do not provide insight. Future improvements in intelligent tables will help analysts, and anybody who needs to search data for answers, but are unlikely to help users of information greatly.

Dashboards and RSS

Inside the world of research a number of companies have been experimenting with dashboard reporting systems. In a typical manifestation, the supplier gives the client an application to store on their system, in effect and agent or bot. The agent scans the reported data and initiates an action if certain criteria are met, for example if the data indicate unusual values (good or bad) these will form a message sent to the client.

An alternative format of a dashboard is a resident reviewer which monitors a data stream from one or more agencies and indicates the status of various criteria, either with single number reporting or simple colour coding.

Outside of research one popular method of converting pull systems into push systems is the growing use of news aggregators, for example systems using feeds such as RSS (Really Simple Syndication). These products monitor a range of data feeds and feed excerpts to the user. Systems such as these could/will be applied to market research results as a way of ensuring that key insights reach clients.

Semantic Web

The semantic web is a new generation of the World Wide Web being promoted by such luminaries as Tim Berners Lee, the man credited with inventing the current World Wide Web. The semantic web is based on data which is tagged and capable of identifying itself. In the Semantic Web data will contain information about how that data should be used. For example, a research study would contain information about the methodology, the questions, the answers and existing analysis. Other users and programs will be able to access the tagged data and interrogate it, adding the information to other data collected at other times by other parties.

The Semantic Web holds the promise of not repeating studies unnecessarily and the prospect of analysts being able to conduct meta-analyses by aggregating a range of studies to draw out insight that may not be apparent within any one study.

Threats

The main problem with the current reporting trend is that clients are drowning in ever larger amounts of data. Most clients receive more data in a month than they could ever read in a year.

Opportunities

The main opportunity for researchers is to find a way of separating the signal from the noise. In particular to find ways of reporting insight, rather than simply reporting data.

OUTSOURCING

For many years market research seemed impervious to the global business trend towards outsourcing. Large and even medium sized companies often employed their own field forces, their own telephone interviewers, and usually owned and operated their own IT systems. A brief reading of Friedman's "The World is Flat" quickly shows that outsourcing is set to increase.

Market research is now more ready to adopt outsourcing, and the key driver has been the Internet. Online panels are largely a third-party option rather than an in-house option, and many projects are scripted by the panel companies rather than the research agencies. Companies in India are offering scripting and tabulation services that are catching the eye of companies from small to large. In the early days of online interviewing many companies developed or intended to develop proprietary systems, but the trend now is to third-party solutions, according to a study by Cambiar (2006).

As face-to-face and CATI decline as a share of the business, and as the use of third-party outsourcing increases, the headcount in market research companies will fall, in ways that will mimic other services and professions.

Upsourcing

The term upsourcing describes an alternative approach to using external services. Upsourcing provides expert advice to an organisation allowing it to extend the range of its capabilities. One essential element to upsourcing is knowledge transfer, something which sets it apart from typical consulting.

Threats

One threat of outsourcing is that it lowers the barriers to entry, if a new agency can simply pay the marginal cost of sample, software and analysis, then the start-up costs are greatly reduced.

Opportunities

The biggest opportunity with outsourcing is reduced costs, but almost as significant is the opportunity it creates for researchers to concentrate on their core competencies. The core competences of researchers are skills such as understanding clients' needs, framing questions, qualitative interviewing, ethnography, semiotics, quantitative analysis, interpreting what respondents say, drawing insight. The core competences do not include running DP departments, scripting surveys, running IT departments or running call centres.

WHY TECHNOLOGIES SUCCEED OR FAIL IN MARKET RESEARCH

A new technology will tend to have an impact if it matches the following criteria:

1. Can it replace something else and make it significantly better, cheaper or faster?
2. Can it meet a known or recognised unmet need at an acceptable cost and with an acceptable turnaround?
3. Can it satisfy a need that was not previously recognised at an acceptable cost, with an acceptable turnaround speed and in a way that makes enough people realise they have the need?

In addition techniques will tend to fail if they are only available from a single supplier or if the need they are meeting is not sufficiently prevalent in the market. Standardisation is a key factor; in general, strength of support for a standard will drive industry wide acceptance. A technique will have a better chance of succeeding if it can build on existing technologies, for example if it is compatible with existing protocols and procedures.

By these tests it can be assumed that neuromarketing will not be making a major impact on the market research world in the near future, it is not available from a wide range of suppliers, it is not cheap and it tends not to be fast.

Another example of a technology that has failed so far is mobile phone based research. The technology can produce large sample size, relatively cheaply, very quickly. However, the sort of information that is produced only rarely matches the sorts of needs that brand managers have. Mobile phone research has proved very weak for U&As, concept testing and even for satisfaction surveys.

Another factor that can also have an impact on the success or failure of a technology is legislation. Legislation can promote or more typically inhibit a new technique. Legislation about the Internet, RFIDs, data secrecy and data protection all have the potential to affect the usefulness of new technologies.

THE IMPACT OF TECHNOLOGY ON RESEARCH – SUMMARY

Some technologies simply allow research to be conducted faster, cheaper or more accurately; for example the introduction of scanning machines to make punching faster, cheaper and more accurate. However, many technological changes result in significant or even transformational change in research. The changes that are likely to have the strongest impact are those which mesh with other changes that are also happening. An example of this synergy is the way that advances in ethnography are dependent on changes in the technology of video, and are being expanded by techniques such as tagging and image based searches.

This review looks at current technologies with a view to assessing how they will impact research. In addition there will be new technologies which will burst on the scene. These new arrivals will have some impact, but the lesson of the past is that new technologies take about eight years from their first introduction until they make a significant impact on the research world.

REFERENCES

Anderson, C. (2006) *The Long Tail*, Hyperion.

Cambiar (2006) *The Online Research Industry*.

Cattell, J. (2001) The mobile internet revolution and its implications for research, ESOMAR, Internet Conference, Barcelona.

Comley, P. (2005) Panel management and panel quality issues – understanding the online panellist, ESOMAR, Conference on Panel Research, Budapest.

Friedman, T.L. (2005) *The World is Flat*, Penguin.

Jeavons, A. (2001) Paradata, ESOMAR, Internet Conference, Barcelona.

Johnson, R., Orme, B. and Pinnell, J. (2006) Simulating Market Preference with 'Build Your Own' Data, Sawtooth Software Conference, Delray Beach, Florida.

Marsden, P. (2006) Measuring the Success of Word of Mouth, Market Research Society Annual Conference, London.

McPhee, N. and Chrystal, G. (2006) Truly, Madly, Deeply – Ethnography illuminates pharma, ESOMAR Congress, London.

New York Times (2006), downloaded from http://www.nytimes.com/2006/08/09/technology/09aol .html?ei=5090&en=f6f61949c6da4d38&ex=1312776000&adxnnl=1&pagewanted=print&adxnnlx= 1162812190-JF1jai80xxoVBgt3N8jJcg, 6 November 2006.

News.com (2006), downloaded from http://news.com.com/2100-1030_3-6103098.html 26 September 2006.

O'Reilly, T. (2005) *What is Web 2.0*, downloaded from http://www.oreillynet.com/pub/a/oreilly/tim/news/ 2005/09/30/what-is-web-20.html, 22 November 2006.

Page, G. and Raymond, J. (2006) Cognitive Neuroscience, marketing and research, ESOMAR Congress, London.

Penn, D. (2005) Brain science . . . that's interesting . . . so, what do I do about it?, Market Research Society Annual Conference, London.

Poynter, R. (2002) The future is already with us – just unevenly distributed, ESOMAR Internet Conference, Berlin.

Poynter, R. (2006) The Power of Conjoint Analysis and Choice Modelling in Online surveys, Market Research Society Conference, London.

Trayner, G. (2006) The future of market research lies in open source thinking, *Market Leader*, Summer 2006, Issue 33.

Tufte, E. (2006) *The Cognitive Style of PowerPoint*. Graphics Press.

21

Online Market Research

Pete Comley

Online market research covers all research that is conducted in some way using the Internet. Typically it takes the form of online surveys on web pages (although other forms of online market research exist, e.g. email surveys, online discussion chat rooms, research blogs, etc.). A key characteristic of online surveys is that they are self-completion interviews where questions are presented automatically to respondents. Although initially regarded as inferior to more traditional methods, like face-to-face interviews and telephone research, recently attitudes have been changing to become much more positive.

ADOPTION OF ONLINE RESEARCH

The history of online market research spans just over a decade now, with the first commercial surveys being conducted in the mid 1990s (Comley, 1996). In such a short period of time, this area has grown from nothing to dominate data collection in many of the main worldwide research markets.

According to "Inside Research" (Inside Research, 2006), a third of all market research in the US was conducted online in 2006, and that figure is by value. In terms of the number of interviews conducted, it may well have approached a half already (Table 21.1).

Table 21.1 Online research spending in the USA

	Spend ($ millions)
2006 (est)	1408
2005	1184
2004	1011
2003	824
2002	651
2001	401
2000	253

Source: Inside Research, 2006.

In other countries such as the Netherlands, adoption has been even greater, with some suggesting that more than a half of all research was carried out online by 2005. Around the world and particularly in other key European markets (e.g. UK, Germany) there has been marked growth of online (Table 21.2), although adoption rates are currently not as high.

Market Research Handbook, 5th Edition. Edited by M. van Hamersveld and C. de Bont.
© 2007 John Wiley & Sons, Ltd.

Table 21.2   Online research spending in Europe

	Spend (millions of euros)
2006 (est)	288
2005	205
2004	137
2003	101
2002	87
2001	77

Source: Inside Research, 2006.

It is useful to understand a bit of the history of why online took off so quickly in the USA. There were probably four specific factors that contributed to this (Table 21.3).

In contrast to the USA, many European researchers appear much more conservative and have not had the benefit of the dot.com money, nor the benefit of established panels.

Interestingly though, the Dutch were a major European exception and it is useful to examine why this was the case. There are three reasons that are often cited for online taking off so quickly. First is the fact that research costs had increased markedly due to extra social security payments required by employers. The other reasons were declining response rates and a government very keen to develop its IT infrastructure (i.e. high Internet penetration). However, it is my view that the deciding factor in the Netherlands was probably the attitude of the research agencies. A number of top agencies embraced online wholeheartedly and then sold the idea to their clients.

In contrast to many other more conservative countries, agency researchers were quick to point out all the potential methodological problems and issues – these are discussed more fully below. However, another factor was undoubtedly the fear that if online research did take off, it would have a major impact on their company, the way it did business and eventually on their profitability (and in some cases even their viability).

Online research has been very successful in cannibalising research within customer satisfaction and concept/product testing arena. It has also been used highly in other areas such as ad/brand tracking, sales tracking and for usage and attitude studies, see Table 21.4. Its adoption however, for qualitative research to date, has been low and this is discussed more later in the chapter.

Table 21.3   Why online research took off so quickly in the USA

1. Prior to the Internet, a number of mail panels existed, so many research buyers had already accepted that a panel approach was suitable for many projects. Add to this that the mail panels were slow, expensive and of poor demographic quality. Therefore it was a bit of a "no-brainer" to switch surveys online. Overnight, they became faster, cheaper, and had a better sample representation.
2. Most of the main online access panels in the USA were set up in the dot.com boom when money was no object and in many cases those investments have now long since been written-off on balance sheets.
3. Attitudes of researcher buyers in the US were much more open to change and particularly to one where they could get surveys cheaper.
4. Response rates for traditional research were declining.

Table 21.4   Online research by type of research 2005

	Europe	USA
Usage and attitude studies	10 %	11 %
Advertising/brand tracking	13 %	10 %
Concept/product testing	24 %	30 %
Copy testing	6 %	6 %
Customer/employee satisfaction measurement	19 %	8 %
Qualitative/focus groups	2 %	1 %
Opinion polling	7 %	3 %
Sales tracking	7 %	20 %

Source: Inside Research, 2006.

THE ARGUMENT FOR ONLINE RESEARCH

So why have people been rushing to embrace online so quickly? The main reasons are now fairly obvious to us all, i.e.:

- *Cost.* Online can be significantly cheaper. It can often cost a quarter of the price of offline research such as telephone or face-to-face interviewing. Although many have taken this opportunity to increase sample size or to adopt more robust research designs, there is no doubt that online has contributed to a significant decline in research prices.
- *Speed.* The data collection part is undoubtedly very efficient, so much so that there are many online services offering 24 hour turnaround of projects. Just a decade ago, this would have been almost unheard of.
- *Quality.* This aspect is often forgotten. The lack of an interviewer tends to result in more honest data and with fewer "social desirability" effects. It can also generate more open-ended comments, allowing a greater understanding of quantitative surveys.
- *Other issues.* In addition to these, there are other benefits to running online projects. It is significantly cheaper and easier to carry out repeat projects. In projects where there is the need to present concept materials or adverts, there can be enormous savings in printing and copying (and also time). There are many other benefits too that are often overlooked, e.g. better geographical spread of samples, ease of interviewing minority samples; and as most panels are highly profiled, ease of conducting longitudinal studies, etc.

There is now a broad consensus that online research delivers *valid results*. Numerous validations (Hunter, 2005) have shown this. Companies like YouGov have consistently published surveys that accurately predict real life voting – be it at elections or TV show competitions (Table 21.5). Similarly, Harris Interactive have published similar successes in the US elections and moreover, the online polls have been usually more accurate than their offline counterparts.

THE ARGUMENT AGAINST ONLINE RESEARCH

The main issue that held back online research initially was *sample representativity*. This is still an issue that concerns people, although, even here, anxieties have declined. For example in the UK they reduced when Internet penetration reached 60 % in 2005. (Interestingly, the "magic level" of 60 % was the point at which telephone research became accepted by people in the 1970s/1980s.)

Table 21.5   Examples of validations from YouGov election polls (YouGov website)

Country/Election	Online Poll Result	Actual Result
UK – 2001:		
% Conservative	33 %	33 %
% Labour	43 %	42 %
% LibDem	17 %	19 %
% Other	7 %	7 %
Australia – 2001:		
% Coalition	45 %	43 %
% Labour	39 %	38 %
% Other	16 %	19 %

However, for some target groups, the representativeness of the sample is still a problem and the Internet cannot currently always deliver an acceptable sample – for example, the old and socially disadvantaged are much less likely to be online. This is a key fact that should not be forgotten by online researchers. When researching samples such as these, any online bias should be carefully thought about and the use of hybrid approaches considered.

Sophisticated weighting schemes also helped with sample representatively when penetrations were lower, but their usage is now declining in countries with high Internet usage. Moreover, weighting cannot fully rectify the differences caused by low penetration – especially amongst the older population.

Also, remember that sample representativity is much less of a problem for certain types of online research. Surveys conducted with customer databases (particularly of online users) can provide a 100 % representative sample frame. Surveys of website users similarly can also provide good samples. However, both will still have a response bias.

There are a number of other issues raised against online surveys and these are discussed in more detail later in the chapter. However, what has happened is that most of these issues have either been reduced, or we as an industry have become more tolerant of them. But that is not to say that they are not important and these factors still need to be considered carefully:

- Professional respondents.
- Never being sure of the true identity of respondents.
- Issues with asking open/spontaneous awareness questions.
- Difficulty in asking traditional long (and boring) surveys without dropouts/quality declines.
- Concern that online norms are different (and lower).
- Security concerns for online materials.
- Low barriers to entry and hence proliferation of non-market research trained people offering poorer quality survey services.
- A general concern that cheap price must equate to low quality.

ONLINE RECRUITMENT METHODS

There are four broad methods that have been adopted for online research.

Pop-up Surveys

These were a very popular method for recruiting for online surveys by the pioneer online researchers. They involve triggering a survey to a sample of users of a website and are so called because they typically appear in a new browser window that appears to pop out of the screen to the user. They can be triggered either by the site as a way of sampling their users to determine profiles and/or satisfaction, or from online advertising. In the latter case, they typically covered surveys unrelated to the triggering website.

Response rates varied greatly dependent on the method used. Furthermore, their usage declined markedly following the widespread adoption of pop-up blocking software (although technical solutions do exist to get around this issue). Companies still use this method for website satisfaction research and regularly get response rates over 20 %. They therefore probably are one of the more representative forms of survey that takes place nowadays, as their real effective response rate is significantly higher than both online panel surveys (when you take into account response to initial panel recruitment surveys), and also offline surveys like telephone and face-to-face.

Initially when pop-up advertising was used for recruitment, response rates were around 5 %. However, this has declined so much that it is no longer a feasible or reliable recruitment method for general research. Note though, it is still used and works best when a broad range of websites are used to recruit from.

Website Recruitment/Fun Polls

Many websites these days include links to fun polls to encourage interaction with their users. Initially it was thought that this would also be a simple method to recruit for surveys. However such techniques not only have very low response rates but also typically have very poor control over sampling. Unlike pop-up surveys, there is no control over who is selected for interview, nor a reliable method to stop people filling them in more than once. As such, placing open links on websites is now rarely ever used for professional research surveys.

Customer Email Surveys

Increasingly more surveys are being conducted directly with customers by emailing them a direct link to a survey. This is because, at last, companies have been prioritising the collection of email addresses to their databases. It has also been supported by increases in overall Internet penetration which is now over 50 % in most key worldwide research markets.

Not only is this quite a secure way of sampling, it can get good response rates. These very much depend on the relationship with the sample and type of survey, but typically vary between 5 % and 50 %.

Online Panels

The main hurdle that held back online research initially was the lack of sample. There never was (and probably never will be in the near future) any reliable database to sample from. It therefore became clear to pioneer researchers (Comley, 1996) that online panels would need to be created. In the space of less than 10 years, these have been created and now offer sample

Table 21.6 Recruitment methods used by online panels

- Recruitment from an existing (postal) panel
- Recruitment at the end of offline surveys, e.g. at the end of omnibus surveys
- Bespoke recruitment by telephone, personally or postally for the panel
- Recruitment from existing email marketing databases
- Recruitment using web advertising/pop-ups
- Recruit using alliances with sign-ups on portals/Internet service providers/sales websites
- Open recruitment on panel websites
- "Member get member" scheme recruitment

coverage of most developed markets. Moreover, specialist panels have been set up to allow research in such areas as doctors and business people.

In the USA for example, there were many companies that had panels with over 1 million respondents even before the start of the 21st century. Panel provision in other countries has increased markedly since then. For example in the UK in 2006, there were more than a half a dozen organisations with panels between one quarter to half a million participants.

Recruitment to online panels has used a variety of techniques (and indeed the best online panels are the ones that have used a combination of them).

Of these methods (see Table 21.6), those used most frequently by worldwide panel owners have been the use of marketing databases and alliances – driven primarily by their lower typical cost per acquisition rates.

The following sections describe the issues related to online panels in more detail.

ONLINE PANEL QUALITY

Online panel quality is increasingly becoming a concept that matters to buyers, according to a recent survey by Cambiar (2006) of 247 worldwide research professionals. Although it should be a "hygiene" factor for panels, there have been marked differences in the standards adopted by leading players.

Panel quality is important at all stages; from recruitment to panel management, through to survey execution, and then data delivery. It does not appear correlated with panel size. Some have argued quality can be gauged by *response rate*; although as you'll see, the data does not support this.

It has been reported that some of the large US panels, now, regularly deliver less than a 5 % response rate. (The issue here is probably not so much their large size, but the fact that they are probably some of the oldest panels too.) The reason for their low response rate is probably mainly due to panel owners being very reticent to remove inactive panellists, as it reduces their claims about panel size.

An unpublished study (in 2005) compared the response rate of six different US panels and their data quality versus a random telephone sample. It found that although response rates of the panels varied from 2 % to 47 %, the results were very similar between them all (and to the telephone sample). In fact the company with the highest response rate actually showed the most divergence from the mean.

A similar study was conducted in the Netherlands (Willems, van Ossenbruggen and Vonk, 2006). This compared 19 research suppliers and again all fielded an identical survey and

Table 21.7   ESOMAR 25 question checklist

1. Is it an actively managed panel (nurtured community) or just a database?
2. "Truthfully" how large is it?
3. What is the percentage of "active" members and how are they defined?
4. Where are the respondents sourced from and how are they recruited?
5. Have members clearly opted-in? If so, was this double opt-in? *(See Tip No. 2 in next section for a definition of "double opt-in".)*
6. What exactly have they been asked to opt-in to?
7. What do panel members get in return for participating?
8. Is the panel used solely for market research?
9. Is there a Privacy Policy in place? If so, what does it state?
10. What research industry standards are complied with?
11. Is the panel compliant with all regional, national, and local laws with respect to privacy, data protection, and children, e.g. EU Safe Harbour, and COPPA in the US?
12. What basic socio-demographic profile information, usership, interests data, etc. is kept on members?
13. How often is it updated?
14. In what other ways can users be profiled (e.g. source of data)?
15. What is the (minimum and typical) turnaround time from initial request to first deployment of the emails to activate a study?
16. What are likely response rates and how is response rate calculated?
17. Are or can panel members who have recently participated in a survey on the same subject be excluded from a new sample?
18. Is a response rate (over and above screening) guaranteed?
19. How often are individual members contacted for market research or anything else in a given time period?
20. How is the sample selection process for a particular survey undertaken?
21. Can samples be deployed as batches/replicates, by time zones, geography, etc.? If so, how is this controlled?
22. Is the sample randomised before deployment?
23. Can the time of sample deployment be controlled and, if so, how?
24. Can panel members be directed to specific sites for the survey questionnaire to be undertaken?
25. What guarantees are there to guard against bad data, i.e. respondent cheating or not concentrating/caring in their responses (e.g. click happy)?

compared results. Response rate varied from 19 % to 80 %. Again there was no consistent evidence of response rate being correlated with quality. Instead that survey suggested that quality was most affected by recruitment and that as diverse recruitment as possible should be adopted by all panels (including offline methods such as recruitment by an interviewer).

An alternative way of judging quality is to determine whether a prospective panel provider really does understand market research, sampling techniques and response rates; and indeed if they really understand why quality really matters. Thankfully, ESOMAR (ESOMAR Guidelines) has made this exercise easier by compiling a checklist of *25 questions* (Table 21.7) which it suggests research customers should ask of any panel company they wish to use.

SETTING UP AN ONLINE PANEL

Setting up an online panel is a complicated activity requiring a lot of market research knowledge as well as a thorough understanding of the online world. Indeed recruitment of the panel is probably the most important factor affecting overall panel quality.

Although setting up a panel has become easier recently with the development of companies offering third party hosting of panels (e.g. www.cint.com), it should still not be undertaken lightly. Before embarking on one, it is important to consider if:

- you really need your own panel;
- you know what you want to achieve; specification of outcomes and benefits;
- you understand the issues surrounding the implementation of panels, in particular their limitations;
- you have the resources and personnel;
- you have properly costed it.

The last point is particularly important. Set-up costs for panels are high, as are acquisition costs for respondents. Add to this the decline in costs for samples from third-party access panels, and it is difficult to see it being economical to set up new general online panels in many countries. However, that is not to say there is not merit for more specialised panels and indeed this is an area which may still see quite a bit of growth.

The following list of tips will hopefully help in ensuring that future money is not wasted.

Tip No. 1: Use a Wide Variety of Sources

Table 21.6 highlighted some of the most frequent sources used for the recruitment to online panels. Some of these can be quite cheap to use, e.g. recruiting from email databases or even recruiting at the end of conventional surveys (if you still conduct lots of them).

However, each source has its own bias and sometimes this bias can be quite marked, even though it might not appear biased when you inspect the basic demographics, such as age and gender. For example, would you want a panel solely made up of people who liked doing competitions? In many instances it may not matter, but there will be some cases where it will.

The other benefit of multiple source recruitment is to obtain as broad a demographic profile as possible. A number of the most frequently used recruitment sources (e.g. email databases) can often result in insufficient numbers of younger and older respondents.

Tip No. 2: Use a "Double Opt-In" Approach

"Double opt-in" means that you verify twice with your prospective new panellists that they really do want to join. This is particularly key when an online method of recruitment has been used. Only by mailing to the email address given at the initial sign-up and checking that that person really did sign-up can a system be safe from potential abuse. The verification email can also be kept by respondents to verify what they have agreed to sign-up for.

Tip No. 3: Try to Avoid Abuse at All Stages

Double opt-in is a system to reduce abuse, but there are many other ways that can and should be employed. This is particularly important in the online environment, where fraud is easy and can be conducted on a large scale.

One of the biggest issues is to ensure you have some way of verifying people are who they say they are and, from this, ensure that they cannot join your panel more than once. A good solution to this, adopted by some panels, is to collect bank details and pay respondents for interviews. However, even if you are running a panel with a prize draw incentive, you can set up systems to search for potentially duplicate registrations.

Another key element of potential abuse is people lying about eligibility questions in order to take part. Some argue (e.g. Stevens et al., 2005) that a simple solution is to give no clue to the survey topic in the invite and ensure that respondents cannot re-post answers to questions (after they have been screened out). Although this works, it can also have a negative effect on your panel's motivation (and retention rate), as people really dislike "wasting their time" getting screened out of surveys, often for no reward. A practical solution to this problem can be to give some rough idea of likely survey topics and broad ideas of eligibility in the invite. That at least reduces the annoyance rate whilst still maintaining control over recruitment criteria.

The other key abuse point is during the survey itself, with people not reading questions fully and inserting "rubbish" answers to complete the survey quicker. These people can often be spotted with simple data processing checks (e.g. all same answers in a grid). A better solution is to make sure that surveys themselves are interesting and are not repetitive. Sending out regular panel newsletters with results of recent surveys also probably helps in this respect.

Tip No. 4: Do a Detailed Registration Survey

It is a common mistake with panels to try to make sign-up too easy, as the panels strive to grow quickly and recruit large numbers of panellists. Although this will undoubtedly increase acquisition rate, it will also increase drop-out rate. If a person is not willing to answer a number of demographic questions to sign-up, the chances are they will not fill out a market research survey – which usually lasts over 10 minutes!

There are other benefits related to obtaining greater profiling information. Clearly, as a panel owner, the value of your panel is increased if you have profiling information. However, it also benefits respondents, as you'll need to do less screening and less likely to annoy people by inviting them to surveys they are not eligible for.

Tip No. 5: Make Sure You Use Them Quickly

When people take the time and effort to sign-up to a panel, they expect in return to do surveys immediately, or at least within a few days. In an attempt not to abuse panellists nor to overuse them, some companies may not invite new panellists to surveys for a long time. This can result in a significant decline in response rates. (It can also end up with them signing up with other panels in the meantime.)

Solutions to this issue can include sending out profiling surveys initially or to create some surveys that are specifically available just to new respondents.

Tip No. 6: Continually Recruit/Top Up

Panels suffer attrition and declines in response rates continually and so there has to be a policy to continually refresh them. There also needs to be a positive policy to review existing members and officially remove inactive members who have stopped responding to panel invites.

The exact replacement rate will depend on many factors but can be from 10 % to 40 % per annum. Some of the key variables are: the incentive scheme used, the sense of community created, the types of survey asked, the degree of screening exposed to, and the frequency of survey invites.

RUNNING AN ONLINE PANEL

In order to run an online panel there is the need for a combination of good procedures, people and technical hardware/software. There is also a requirement to understand something about panel motivation and likely "panellist lifestage".

A good *panel manager* is the most essential requirement for controlling an online panel. Even for a small panel (or a client panel), this is often a full-time job, see Table 21.8, and one that is often forgotten in the excitement to set-up a new online panel.

There is currently a wide variety of *survey software* available for online research. In 2006, these varied from the nearly free (e.g. Zoomerang.com) to expensive business enterprise products (e.g. Confirmit.com). Although some can be run on your own server (e.g. SPSS), many are offered in an ASP environment (e.g. GMI-MR.com) where you create the survey online and it is deployed immediately on their servers. For smaller panels, these online ASP solutions are viable, but most big panels run and host their own survey servers.

Disappointingly, there is not as much choice when it comes to *panel management software.* Some survey packages have this built in, but it may be necessary to seek some bespoke software (although in 2006, there were only a few options available). A good independent source of information about all the software options is www.macer.co.uk.

One thing that helps in running an online panel is to recognise and be aware of a *typical panellist's lifestage.* Like many relationships these days, they often go through five stages – see Table 21.9.

The better the panel motivation scheme and the way you treat your panellists, the longer you can keep them "involved" with you at stage 3. A key formula here is:

Total Respondent Worth = (Income per survey * Number of surveys) − Cost of acquisition

Table 21.8   Checklist of a panel manager's responsibilities

- Sampling, including ensuring that no-one is over/under surveyed
- Checking surveys prior to implementation
- Responding to queries from panellists, either about surveys or more generally about the panel (and its incentives)
- Communicating news and results to panel members (e.g. with newsletters)
- Monitoring response rates and then compiling a summary of statistics at the end of each project
- Compliance, e.g. ensuring that the panel complies with both industry rules (e.g. ESOMAR) as well as those of other legal requirements, e.g. data privacy laws.

Table 21.9   Panellist lifestage model

1. *Dating* – excited, enthusiastic, fresh, response rate is high.
2. *Getting married (or not)* – decide they like taking surveys or they decide they do not – response either increases/decreases fast.
3. *Stable relationship* – everything is going well, both parties are communicating and developing together.
4. *Having an affair* – it is fast becoming time to move on and response rate falls, no matter what it was before.
5. *Divorce* — the relationship ends, the respondent stops taking your email.

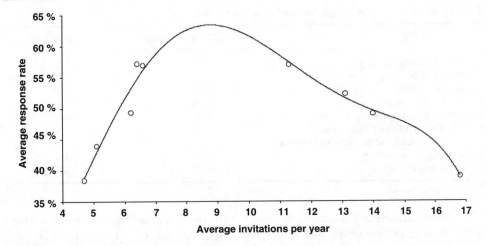

Figure 21.1   The effect of the number of invitations on response rate
Source: Stentbjerre, 2005.

Some panels have shown that you can double a panellist's active life by treating them well. The key things that need to be provided are:

- good incentives;
- variety of survey topics;
- good/honest communications;
- reduced screened surveys;
- sending optimum number of invitations/year;
- not sending them "poor" surveys.

Work has been done to investigate what is the *optimum number of surveys* that are sent to respondents in a year (Stentbjerre, 2005). This showed that when a respondent receives between six and twelve invitations a year, response rate is highest. It also showed that it declined if not enough were sent and when too many were (Figure 21.1).

Other surveys have shown that many respondents say that they'd like to receive more surveys than this – sometimes even weekly or more often (Comley, 2005). It is likely that this may be a function of the lifestage of respondents, the incentive scheme and possibly even culture.

Given these attrition factors, *panel maintenance* is a key issue. All panels need a strategy to continually recruit new members to replace those being lost. In addition they need clear procedures to remove inactive people from their databases.

If you ask people why they take part in online surveys, the results are sometimes surprising. The most important reasons mentioned are actually that people enjoy doing surveys or that they want their opinions to be heard. Some people do it primarily for the money or to try to win the prize draw, but these are not the only *motivations*, as Table 21.10 shows.

Given this variety of motivations, *segmentation* work has been carried out to look at this further (Comley, 2005). This showed there to be four different groups – see Table 21.11.

Table 21.10   Main reasons people take part in online surveys

	Total mentioned	Most important
I enjoy completing surveys	69 %	17 %
I want to win the competition/prize draw	62 %	12 %
To get free offers/vouchers/products	61 %	10 %
I want my views to be heard	60 %	17 %
I like looking at new ideas/products	58 %	10 %
I collect the incentives/points offered	57 %	7 %
I'm curious to see what the surveys are about	54 %	5 %
I find the topics interesting	51 %	4 %
I want the money	40 %	14 %

Source: Comley, 2005.

In the original research (Comley, 2005) on the UK opinion panel, the proportions of those in the altruistic or intrinsically motivated groups (Helpers/Opinionated) were split with those seeking a more materialistic or extrinsic motivation (Incentivised/Professionals). This broad finding has since been replicated for other panels – see Table 21.12. However the exact proportions probably depend to some extent on how the panel was recruited and to some extent

Table 21.11   Motivation segments for online panellists

Helpers
- Enjoy doing surveys and happy to do them without any payment
- Like being part of the "online community"
- Happy to do longer surveys than other groups – a third will do 30+ minutes
- More willing to answer open questions
- Do the most conventional offline surveys
- Older profile
- More likely to want to see results of surveys/have panel newsletters, etc.

Opinionated
- Particularly motivated by having their views heard and actually enjoy doing surveys and finding out about new ideas/products
- Will sometimes do surveys without reward
- However, more likely to be selective on which surveys they are willing to do based on topic area
- More likely to want to see results of surveys/have panel newsletters, etc.
- More willing to answer open questions
- More likely to be late responders to surveys

Incentivised
- Particularly motivated by competitions and offers
- Will sometimes do surveys without reward
- Younger profile
- Do lots of surveys (but less than professionals)
- More likely to be late responders to surveys

Professionals
- Motivated most by financial reward from surveys
- Will only complete surveys if there is a reward (and one they want)
- Not concerned about the topic of a survey
- Do the most surveys (often a number each day) and work with the most companies
- Nearly a half want to do surveys daily
- Like shorter surveys
- More of a male profile

Source: Comley, 2005.

Table 21.12   Motivation segments in various European panels

Motivation Segments	Norway Norstat	Netherlands Bloomerce	France Bloomerce	UK Bloomerce	UK UKopinion
Helpers	20 %	**27 %**	17 %	10 %	15 %
Opinionated	32 %	**42 %**	28 %	36 %	35 %
Incentivised	10 %	7 %	6 %	20 %	20 %
Professionals	38 %	24 %	**49 %**	34 %	30 %

Source: Comley, unpublished 2005.

on culture. Indeed, in the panel tested in the Netherlands there were more altruists whilst there were more materialists in the French one.

Given these findings, it would appear that the ideal panel needs to have a combination of *incentive schemes*. This needs to include so called "extrinsic" incentives (e.g. cash, prizes) as well as "intrinsic" ones (e.g. newsletters, feedback, communities, etc.). Although, ideally, each person should be motivated by their own scheme, practically this is difficult. Moreover, many in the altruistic segments still also believe that they should be paid for doing surveys and there is a good argument that all panels should pay everyone something – even for screenout interviews.

However, with downward pressure on prices for samples provided by access panels, the concept of paying all respondents has not been universally adopted. Indeed many panels currently often run prize draws (which are much cheaper and also easier to administrate). There is also evidence (Willems, van Ossenbruggen and Vonk, 2006) that paying people (versus running prize draws or even offering nothing) makes very little difference to apparent results. This is in spite of the fact that studies have shown that paying cash incentives tends to increase overall response rate (and so may be cost effective, if they can prolong the lifespan of a panellist).

One of the best methodological investigations was conducted by Van Hessen (2005). They recruited three different sub-panels in Germany and throughout recruitment and the first three surveys either offered them: cash incentives, a prize draw or a charity donation. The results showed that paying for each survey increased response by over a half compared with a charity donation (Figure 21.2). Note though, that the best incentive may well be country specific and this research was conducted in Germany.

So, should we be worried by the professionals' segment and the so called "*professional respondents*"? It can be worrying when you put a phrase like "paid surveys" into a search engine and see what results. In 2006, you would have found many sites and portals dedicated to help people become professional respondents – usually for a fee, of course. These provide guides to the market research companies, what incentives they offer and how to sign-up with them.

Comley (2005) has also published results showing that the *overlap in UK panels* was considerable, with most respondents being on at least two panels and sometimes many more. These results were mirrored in a Dutch study (Comley, 2005). Moreover the latter also showed that although panellists appeared to demographically match the population, they did appear to be psychologically different in some ways, e.g. more extreme in their voting behaviour.

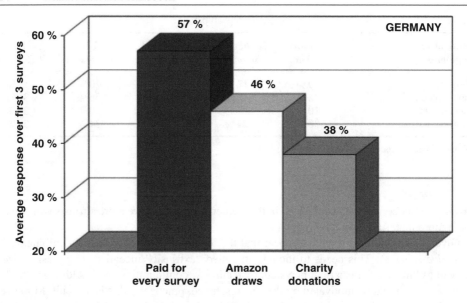

Figure 21.2   Effect of incentive on response rate
Source: Van Hessen, 2005.

Professional respondents' survey response behaviour can also be slightly different. They are more likely to recall brands (probably as they have more experience of doing surveys and have a heightened sensitivity to brands). However, they are less likely to answer open questions and say they recall advertising (as they know we'll ask them more questions and/or the survey will take longer to do).

Included within the professional respondents segment, are a hard core of people who aim to defraud surveys – either by lying in screening questions, filling out a survey a number of times under parallel identities, or by completing them out so quickly that they do not fully read the questions and/or answers. Some panel companies have procedures set up to try to identify these people and remove them from their databases. Furthermore there is currently an initiative to pool this information between companies – see puresample.com. Indeed, others (Comley, 2005) have suggested that what is needed is a register of all panel respondents in each country run by an independent organisation.

However, there are counter-arguments about the wider group of professional respondents. Some think that they add to the online research sample and improve it by allowing the inclusion of people who are only willing to offer their opinions in surveys for money. Indeed, this group is probably often excluded from most traditional (unpaid) quantitative research with a personal interviewer.

CLIENT ONLINE PANELS

It is perhaps worth looking with a little more detail at this specific genre of online panels which we expect to increase markedly.

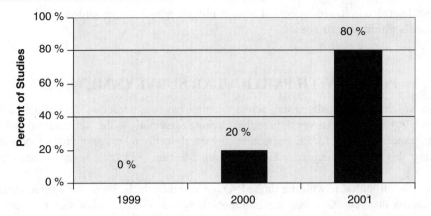

Figure 21.3   General Mills transition to online panels
Source: Hunter, 2005.

There had been some well publicised successes with them. For example in the US, *General Mills* (Hunter, 2005) had been running one since 1999 and it was used for a wide variety of its projects. They set it up not only to improve cost savings and speed of feedback but also to leverage greater customer insight, by developing a direct relationship with them. They also invested in the idea because conventional research was showing increasing problems in the US with representativeness, response rate and costs.

Interestingly, having made the switch (Figure 21.3), they also found it to have a number of other benefits they did not expect. The first was the ability to easily revisit respondents – either to carry out longitudinal studies or to recruit samples for follow-up focus groups. They also were able to carry out extensive strategic work at virtually no cost that would never have happened without the panel.

Another publicised example (MacQuire, 2005) was that of the TV company in the UK called *GMTV*. They converted their postal user panel to an online one. Like many others, GMTV found it not just a great way to run simple quick topical surveys, but also found it suitable for a wider range of surveys from concept development work for programmes, to pre-post ad checks to creative development testing. GMTV found that converting their postal panel online also significantly increased response rate (from 40 % to 60 %) and the reduced costs allowed them to run even more surveys for their advertisers.

Another separate motivation for setting up a client panel is to be seen to be customer facing and responding to feedback from users. Indeed there is currently a vogue for setting up *customer forums* where panellists become more than people we send surveys to. Instead they can have a full two way relationship with companies and offer comments directly to them on any issues of the moment.

So, with all these benefits, are there any *issues*? The main ones are cost and time. The amount of investment required for doing it properly should not be underestimated. It may well involve the recruitment of extra staff (e.g. panel manager), plus there will be web servers, interviewing software, database/sample management, provision/maintenance of websites, incentives, etc. It will also be a major time commitment on existing key research staff.

One way to reduce this, which many companies adopt, is to run the panel in partnership with a research agency/existing online access panel provider. They can help not only in managing the panel but also in its recruitment. They can provide non-customer samples and even create sub-panels within their databases.

ISSUES WITH PARTICULAR SURVEYS/METHODS

Techniques that have translated well across to online have included: concept testing, customer research (e.g. post sales surveys), brand/ad tracking (especially in the Netherlands) and mini-U&As (especially those for PR companies). Research involving usage of visual media is also growing; this includes communications and ad pre-testing, packaging research, and conjoint tests.

There is still an issue with the limited *screen size* though. In 2006, one-in-five users still had screens that are 800×600 pixels and even a 1024×768 pixel screen has very little space to display images (by the time you have allowed for a browser window and the survey header/footer). Indeed it is very difficult to do justice to testing press adverts that have small print or examining competitive displays with many products on them. There are also bandwidth restrictions, although online panellists are particularly likely to use broadband, so testing video online is less of an issue than it was even a year or so ago.

Although some have converted their brand and advertising *trackers* online, there is still concern over doing this amongst others, despite the major cost savings. One of the issues is with asking spontaneous awareness in a self-completion interview, particularly the difficulty of doing it well. There is also concern that the different media consumption habits of the heavy Internet users that comprise most panels, may not be representative of the total population. The long interview length of the average tracker has also not helped those migrating surveys as have concerns over discontinuities with the data.

Indeed, there is evidence that *long boring surveys* do not work well online. This has not been helped by the fact that many researchers try to field traditional questionnaires online, without thinking about the questions being used in a self-completion situation. The biggest issue is that if people get bored online, they give up. With an interviewer present they are usually "persuaded" to finish the interview.

This problem can have a big effect on *concept research*, as it means that people who dislike the concept are forced through seemingly irrelevant questions/grids and many just give up. It also means that running sequential monadic/paired comparison style concept tests can be fraught with problems. Figure 21.4, published by Miller (2005) at the ESOMAR Panels Research conference in 2005 illustrates this well.

It is also worth noting which *types of questions* people like responding to and which they don't. Not surprisingly this shows a marked bias towards those that are easiest and simplest to do – see Table 21.13.

Finally, one sector of research has not translated well online to date. That is "traditional" *online groups and qualitative*. Typically these take place in chat rooms and bulletin boards online. The main issue with them has been the lack of non-verbal communication and in-sufficient depth of comments. They have however been used more in the US, where the greater distances mean that they can offer significant cost savings (which do not apply within other smaller countries).

Note though that more recently there has been a bit of revival of online qualitative with the advent of *Web 2.0*. The more interactive and participatory nature of today's Internet has meant that interest in running research blogs, online forums and bulletin boards has been stimulated.

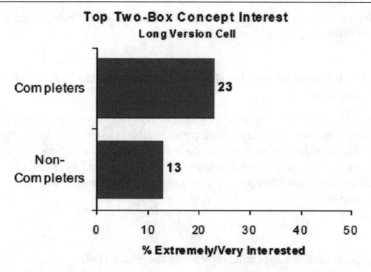

Figure 21.4   Concept interest amongst completers and non-completers of surveys
Source: Miller, 2005.

Table 21.13   Opinion of types of survey question

	Questions like	Questions dislike
Yes/No questions	76 %	4 %
Questions with pictures	71 %	6 %
Rating scales questions	69 %	7 %
Lists with answers to tick	67 %	4 %
Dropdown questions	59 %	10 %
Questions with slider scales	53 %	16 %
Agree/disagree questions (dropdown grid)	49 %	14 %
Agree/disagree questions (radio grid)	44 %	31 %
Questions where you type in numbers	27 %	28 %
Questions where you type in text	19 %	54 %
Grids with many questions	18 %	53 %

Source: Comley, 2005.

They certainly offer a way of collating customer feedback, although their usage as ad hoc data collection methods is still currently limited.

FUTURE PREDICTIONS FOR ONLINE RESEARCH

The following predictions were made about online research in 2006.

Prediction No. 1: Online Research will Increase

Although worldwide online research is still increasing at a great pace, it has always been difficult to predict the speed of adoption of online in particular countries. However, the switch to online now seems unstoppable and is very likely that we'll see it being at least 30 % of all research worldwide by 2010 (and probably sooner).

Prediction No. 2: Online Sample Provision will Increase but the Number of Companies may Decrease

Linked with this growth, there will be an increase in online access panel sample provision. Although short term this may mean more panel companies in each country, the increased competition will squeeze margins and some companies will fold and others will be taken over. Indeed, it is likely that most samples will end up being provided by a few very big access panels. Smaller sector specialist panels, local country experts and client panels will remain though and increase.

Prediction No. 3: Online Costs will Decrease in the Short Term

The competition between the growing online panels will force prices down as some seek to recoup investments (or price others out of the market). However, longer term pricing is less clear.

Prediction No. 4: Online Research Quality will Decrease

These changes towards sample being a commodity resource, supplied at the lowest price, could well lead to lower quality recruitment standards, unless great care is not taken to avoid this.

Prediction No. 5: Online Research will Face Competition from (Cheaper) Non-traditional Research Suppliers

The industry will face more competition from companies with large online databases, which they want to leverage to a wider audience. Some of these organisations which have a technical background may even offer other benefits (apart from cheaper prices).

Prediction No. 6: Online Response Rates will Continue to Decline

Response rates in all areas of market research are declining, which is largely a reflection of societal changes. Online is no panacea for the issue of declining response, even though some thought initially it might be. Indeed we are likely to online panel response rates decline particularly swiftly, although this may not affect quality greatly.

CONCLUDING COMMENTS

Online research has evolved from nothing to being the most important sector of research in less than a decade. It is not without its issues, as this chapter has shown. However it is here to stay and we all need to fully understand it in order to adapt our business fully to the new research world of the 21st century.

REFERENCES

Cambiar Survey of The Online Research Industry, May 2006.

Comley, ESOMAR/EMAC Symposium, November 1996.

Comley, ESOMAR Panel Research Conference, April 2005.

ESOMAR Guidelines to Conducting Market and Opinion Research Using the Internet – http://www. esomar.org/web/show/id=49859.

Hunter, ESOMAR Panel Research Conference, April 2005.

Inside Research, Vol 17, No 7, July 2006 see http://www.insideresearch.com.

MacQuire, MRS Online Panels Course, November 2005.

Miller, ESOMAR Panel Research Conference, April 2005.

Stentbjerre, ESOMAR Panel Research Conference, April 2005.

Stevens et al., ESOMAR Panel Research Conference, April 2005.

Van Hessen, ESOMAR Panel Research Conference, April 2005.

Willems, van Ossenbruggen and Vonk, ESOMAR Panel Research, November 2006.

22

Data Mining and Data Fusion

Colin Shearer

INTRODUCTION

The term "data mining" was first used to refer to certain types of data analysis in the early 90s, as people began to address the problem: *"How do we get value out of our data assets?"*

Of course, analysing data was nothing new. Statistical approaches had been around literally for centuries, and the first "machine learning" techniques from artificial intelligence were developed in the 1950s. What was new was the realisation that the valuable information held in large bodies of historical data – for example on past customer behaviour – could, with the right tools, be extracted and applied to current and future cases.

Data mining wasn't the only term used to describe this approach. "Knowledge Discovery in Databases" or KDD was favoured by many academics, and is still used today mainly among those focusing on underlying theory. Some practitioners talked about "distilling" knowledge from data, like whisky from barley. Others even described the process as "torturing the data until it confesses"! "Data mining" isn't a perfect analogy – data is what is mined *through*, so it implies people who dig for gold should be "rock miners" – but it has remained the most popular and familiar label for this type of analysis.

Today, data mining is used extensively in all sorts of organisations in the private and public sectors. Banks, mobile phone companies, casinos and many others use it to acquire, grow and retain customers. Credit card companies use it to identify and intercept fraudulent usage. Tax authorities find who is under-declaring their tax, and use predictive models to prioritise collection from debtors. Medical researchers are identifying new ways to diagnose and treat brain cancer. Police forces are anticipating crime levels and deploying their resources pre-emptively. Data mining can be used anywhere there is a business problem which has a body of data associated with it.

DATA MINING

In simple terms, data mining means "finding patterns in data that enable business improvement". The data that is "mined" is historical or current. The business improvement comes from applying the discovered knowledge about significant patterns to new or future cases, enabling better decisions to be made. Outcomes can be anticipated, and in many case influenced to give desired results – for example, persuading a customer who was on the point of switching to a competitor to stay loyal.

Market Research Handbook, 5th Edition. Edited by M. van Hamersveld and C. de Bont.
© 2007 John Wiley & Sons, Ltd.

Other types of analysis could also be said to "find patterns": querying and reporting techniques; crosstabs; Business Intelligence tools such as OLAP (On-Line Analytical Processing); traditional statistical techniques; and visualisation or graphing.

There are several key characteristics that distinguish data mining from these other approaches:

- The other techniques are "user driven" – that is, the user specifies what they want to see or investigate. In data mining, algorithms automatically explore and model the data with little or no guidance from the user.
- Traditional techniques are best suited to analysing small numbers of variables at a time, and exposing relationships simple enough to be easily spotted by users. More complex relationships might be discovered by the user following up what they see – for example, "drilling down" into an OLAP cube – but patterns found in this haphazard way are very unlikely to be the most significant and valuable ones that exist, and many will simply be missed. In contrast, data mining algorithms automatically identify patterns which are significant. These may include many variables, and will often be so complex or subtle that there is virtually no chance of them being stumbled upon by manual exploration.
- Most traditional statistics focus on verification, i.e. proving or disproving something the user suspects may be true. Data mining enables true discovery, unearthing relationships and patterns which are valid and significant but which may not even be suspected by users.
- The results of traditional techniques are information – reports, tables and graphs. While data mining can deliver extremely useful information, its greatest value comes from being able to produce models – a distillation of the patterns in the historical data, which can be applied to any new case to predict an outcome. This outcome might be a "score" – a number giving the likelihood that, say, someone will behave in a particular way or have a particular attitude – or a classification into one of several categories – for example classifying customers into "very likely to defect", "at risk if dissatisfied" and "unshakeably loyal". Because these models can be used directly in business applications, they can be thought of as "actionable knowledge".

This doesn't mean the traditional techniques listed here don't have a role to play in data mining. On the contrary, data mining tools often incorporate advanced visualisation capabilities to allow users to explore the data alongside the computer-controlled algorithms, and reporting functions to present the discovered knowledge in easily consumable formats. But these techniques *on their own* can never be classified as data mining. True data mining must involve algorithms to analyse the data, and be able to deliver the results as actionable models.

DATA MINING ALGORITHMS

Many algorithms have been developed to analyse data automatically. These have originated from research in areas including statistics, artificial intelligence and database technologies. Many are very specialised or are still largely at a research stage, and most commercial data mining is done using a relatively small number of tried and tested algorithm types.

All data mining algorithms can be thought of as "learning" from historical (or "training") data. They can be split into two families depending on the types of task they are used for: "supervised learning" and "unsupervised learning".

Supervised Learning Algorithms

In supervised learning, the algorithm has a "target" which the model must try to predict. Target variables can be categorical or continuous. With categorical targets, the aim is to predict which of two or more categories a new case belongs to – say, "service-driven" or "price-driven". Continuous targets are used to estimate where a new case falls on range given in the historical cases – e.g. satisfaction on a scale 0 to 10 – or to estimate a propensity score to indicate the likelihood of an event or an outcome. For example, the historical cases might include a variable "Intention" which can either be "leave" or "stay"; a scoring model can be trained to give a "Defection" score for new cases in the range 0.0 to 1.0, where 1.0 indicates "certain to leave" and 0.0 means "certain to stay", with the values in between interpreted as the likelihood of defection for each case.

Decision Trees

Decision trees (see Figure 22.1) are built by a fundamentally simple process:

1. Pick a variable to use as the "root" of the tree
2. Divide the training data according to values of that variable
3. For each subset of the data:
   o If it is "pure", containing only one value for the target variable, then stop.
   o Otherwise, pick another variable as a root and continue the process from step 2 to build a sub-tree.

The process continues until all the "leaves" of the tree are pure. For any new case, starting at the root, its path through the tree is determined by the values of its variables; when it reaches a leaf, the resulting class is delivered as the result.

In building a tree, the "intelligence" is in the choice of which variables to select and in what order. Algorithms try to select variables which give the maximum information about the target, so the tree will be compact, and also will be more likely to produce accurate predictions.

Most tree algorithms are designed to work with categorical targets, though some ("regression trees") can handle continuous targets.

Rule Induction

Decision trees give a clear, explicit view of the decision-making process. When a tree model is large and complex, though, trying to understand the rules it applies can be difficult. Rule induction is an alternative approach that produces rule-based models which are often simpler to understand.

Rule induction produces models consisting of a set of rules, of the form:

IF   <condition 1>
AND   <condition 2>
AND   ....
THEN   <conclusion>

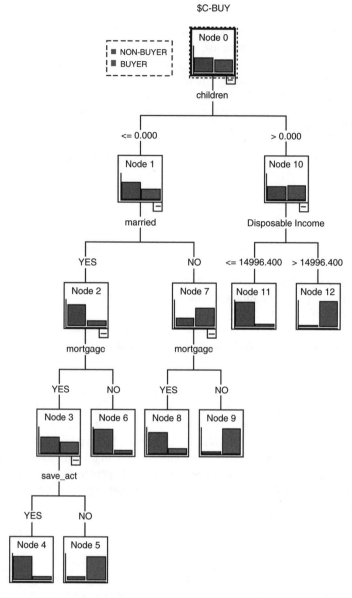

Figure 22.1 A typical decision tree

These are almost English-like, and can be interpreted very easily. For example:

IF   Times_used_per_week > 4
AND   Time_per_session > 25
AND   Top_priority = 'Reliability'
THEN   Satisfaction_level = 'Moderately Satisfied'

Rule induction is used for categorical targets, and is particularly useful when the user needs to understand the model in terms of "profiles" or descriptions of groups of examples which are described by the rules.

Regression

Statistical regression techniques build equations to estimate a target variable. The equations apply weights to the input variables, summing them and adding constants.

Linear regression estimates continuous outputs. An equation produced might be:

$$\begin{aligned}
\text{Projected\_Spend} = {} & \text{Years\_as\_customer} * 111.71 \\
& + \text{Other\_banks\_used} * -4.78 \\
& + \text{Satisfaction\_rating} * 2.24 \\
& + 1211.2
\end{aligned}$$

Logistic regression extends the technique to work with categorical targets. An equation is built for each possible outcome, and evaluated to give a score for each and select the most likely.

The term "regression" is also sometimes used in a more general sense to mean prediction of a continuous target. For example, when decision trees are used to predict a continuous target they are called "regression trees".

Neural Networks

Neural networks are a form of modelling inspired by the way the nervous system operates. The basic unit of operation – the neuron – receives one or more inputs, sums and weights these, and outputs the result. In the most commonly used type of neural network – a "multi-layer perceptron" – units are organised in connected layers. The overall structure or "shape" of a neural network is referred to as its topology (Figure 22.2).

Initially, the weightings on the connections between units are random. When a training case is presented to the untrained network's input layer, the values are propagated and a result produced at the output layer. This result is compared to the known value of the target, and information on the error is "back propagated" through the network, adjusting weights slightly

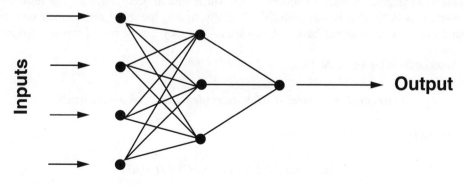

Figure 22.2 A typical neural network topology

to bring the result closer to the actual value. In training, the network is shown many training cases, over and over again; gradually, the network learns to replicate the values of the training cases and to generalise what it has learned to new cases.

Neural networks can be used with categorical or continuous targets. They have some important strengths – for example, they are very useful for fine-grained scoring, giving a unique value for each case. (Contrast decision trees, where there are only a fixed number of paths through the tree, and all cases following the same branch get the same score.) A common issue, however, is that neural networks are opaque and hard to understand; except for the most trivial cases, it is impossible to look at the connections and internal weights of a neural network and understand exactly how it makes its decisions.

Unsupervised Learning Algorithms

In unsupervised learning, there is no target variable for prediction. Instead, the algorithms are simply asked to find any significant patterns or relationships that occur in the data.

Clustering

Clustering techniques group together cases which are similar. Clustering is often referred to as segmentation, though this differs from how that term is often applied in marketing. Marketing segments are often defined manually, based on human knowledge or accepted wisdom. Clustering algorithms, by contrast, discover "natural" segments based on what is actually in the data.

Techniques used for clustering include statistical ones (e.g. k-means) and neural net-based ones (e.g. Kohonen nets, see Figure 22.3). Note that as well as being able to discover clusters, it is important to be able to understand the profile of each cluster. This information is not automatically produced by most clustering algorithms – at least, not in an easily understandable form – but many products which include clustering algorithms also provide very good tools for viewing or describing clusters.

Association Detection

Association techniques discover sets of things which tend to occur together. The most well known use is in "market basket analysis" – literally, finding the set of items which are often found in the same shopping basket at checkout – but they can be used for many different purposes.

Association rules are of the form:

$$consequent \Leftarrow antecedent1 \ \& \ antecedent2 \ \& \ldots \ \& \ antecedentN$$

For example:

$$beer \Leftarrow snacks \ \& \ newspaper \ (10697, 0.63)$$

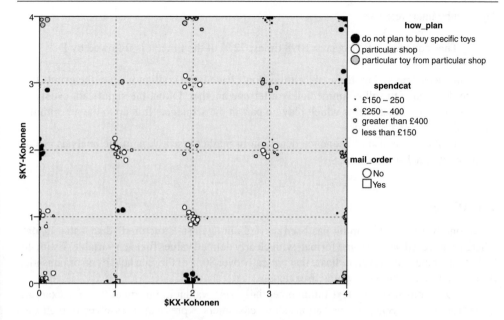

Figure 22.3   A cluster map with selected variables overlaid

This can be interpreted as:

"Customers who buy snacks and a newspaper are also likely to buy beer"

The numbers indicate that 10 697 people bought snacks and a newspaper, and 63 % of these people also bought beer.

Association rules do not indicate a *causal* relationship – the customers probably didn't buy beer *because* they bought snacks and a newspaper – just that certain things occur together. It is easy to see how association models can be used to drive marketing activities. For example, a rule revealing that people who own Product C and Product F also tend to own Product X suggests a cross-sell campaign to sell Product X to all customers who do not yet have it but who hold the other two products.

Association algorithms are unsupervised because they don't require a specific target variable, but are free to predict any attribute in the dataset. However, they can also be configured to focus predictions on one or more variables, making them "semi-supervised".

Sequence Detection

As the name suggests, sequence detection algorithms find common recurring sequences. These may be over any timescale, ranging from pages hit in a web visit lasting 30 seconds to financial products acquired from a bank over a lifetime relationship.

The sequences are in the form:

$$A, B, X \Rightarrow D \; (1098, 0.72)$$

This can be interpreted as:

"The sequence A,B,X occurs 1098 times; 72 % of the time, it is followed by D."

The sequences detected by these algorithms don't have to be contiguous, i.e. the events they include don't have to follow immediately after one another. Often, the significant events are interspersed with other events which play no part in the sequence. It is up to the algorithm to extract the relevant sequences.

The most obvious use of sequence detection in market research is in the analysis of data from longitudinal studies.

Text Mining

Traditionally, most data mining has been carried out against "structured" data – that is, data where each record has the same format, with clearly defined values for each variable. Estimates by IDC and others, however, indicate that typically over 80 % of the data held by an organisation is "unstructured" – in other words, free text.

Obviously, much of this text holds potentially very valuable information – for example, notes from service centre conversations show customers expressing themselves in their own words. Until recently, however, the only way to extract that value from the text was by reading it – not feasible for, say, a million service centre notes per year.

In the last few years, technologies have emerged which automatically analyse bodies of text. These "text mining" algorithms extract relevant information, translating it to a structured format which can be analysed like any other data.

The first generation of text mining techniques were statistical. They treated documents simply as "containers of words", and identified "important" words based on how often they were seen, or how often pairs or sets of words occurred in the same document. But by completely ignoring the language in which the document was written, they ignored everything that gave the words context and meaning.

More advanced text mining algorithms have emerged which are based on Natural Language Processing (NLP) techniques. These algorithms extract key "concepts" – significant words or phrases – based on a knowledge of language grammar and syntax. For example, based on its context, they could determine that in a particular sentence "JFK" represents a place (the New York airport) rather than a person (the late US President). NLP-based text mining algorithms can also find relationships and linkage between concepts, and can automatically recognise positive and negative sentiments.

Working with survey data, text mining is a powerful tool for analysing verbatims. Rather than using manual or semi-automated coding approaches, which merely sort responses into pre-chosen categories, text mining can automatically discover new topics and issues raised in open-ended responses.

THE DATA MINING PROCESS

There is more to data mining than simply building predictive models. In fact, it is generally accepted that only about 20 % of the time and effort in a data mining project is used on the core task of model building.

Data mining is a broader process. It involves analysts and usually business experts, covering business issues as well as technical steps. Viewed at a high level, the process flow is:

- Define the business objectives
  - Map the business objectives to data mining goals
    - Use data mining techniques to solve the data mining goals
  - Map the results back up to the business level to assess their value
- Deploy the results to meet the business objectives

In 1996, an initiative was launched to produce a standard methodology for data mining. CRISP-DM, the Cross-Industry Standard Process for Data Mining (Figure 22.4), was intended to be vendor-neutral and tool-neutral, and to fit any application type.

CRISP-DM was partially funded by the European Commission. A core consortium of companies (Integral Solutions, NCR, Daimler-Benz and OHRA) created the methodology, supported by a Special Interest Group (SIG). The SIG included data mining vendors, consultancies,

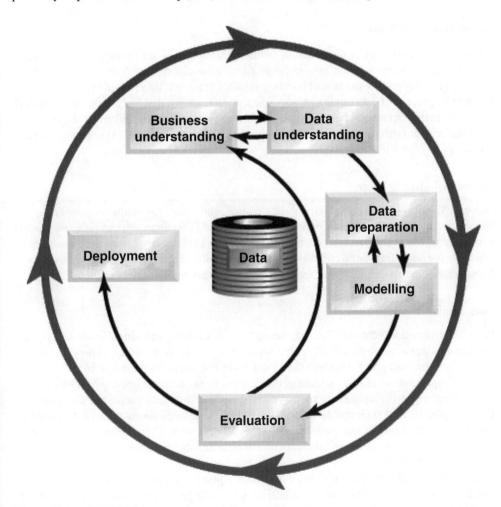

Figure 22.4   CRISP-DM phases and process flow

data warehouse vendors and large-scale data mining end users. SIG membership grew to over 200, and the SIG helped steer the development of CRISP-DM by providing their ideas and reviewing and critiquing drafts of the process model.

CRISP-DM 1.0 was published in 1999, and rapidly established itself as a de facto standard in the data mining industry. A poll in 2002 showed over 50 % of data mining practitioners using CRISP-DM; the majority of the others used approaches developed by themselves or by their company, or didn't use a methodology.

In July 2006, a "CRISP-DM 2.0" initiative was announced to update CRISP-DM to cover new developments in data mining (for example, text mining) and to bring it into line with the latest best practice.

SELECTING DATA MINING TOOLS

There are several types of data mining tool on the market. The tool selected for any specific company will depend upon their objectives, resources and requirements for analysis.

Single Algorithm Tools

These tools support a single algorithm or family of algorithms – for example, decision trees. They usually provide excellent implementations of these algorithms, with rich functionality and very good support for the task of building a model. However, they provide little support for the broader process of data mining. Also, experience has shown that there is no "silver bullet" algorithm that provides the best possible result for every business problem. If the optimum solution for your problem can't be found by the algorithm type that the tool supports, you have no way to explore alternatives.

Automated Mining Tools

Automated tools hide the complexity of data mining, and make it as simple as possible to just connect the tool to a data set and have a model produced. This approach can generate models very quickly, but at the cost of reducing the process to a "black box", with little visibility of what is being done, little or no control over the model building, and no involvement of business knowledge. If the model built isn't satisfactory, there is no opportunity to improve it.

Data Mining Workbenches

Workbenches pull together all the tools needed for data mining in a single environment, and include multiple algorithms and algorithm types. It isn't usually possible to know in advance which algorithm will give the best results for any given data set and business problem, so having multiple algorithms available maximises the chances of producing a good result. Models can also be combined – like a panel of experts – or used together to address each other's weaknesses. For example, a neural net might be trained to provide fine-grained scoring, then a decision tree built to give some insight into how the net makes its decisions. Clusters could be discovered using a k-means algorithm, then rule induction used to find the profile of each cluster in a clear and understandable form.

As well as a rich set of algorithms, workbenches provide support for the full data mining process; they usually include tools for accessing data, manipulating it, visualising it, reporting on it and exporting models in a variety of forms for deployment.

Workbenches are very powerful and flexible, and some provide very high productivity. However, some are aimed solely at expert users and are inaccessible to novice or non-technical users.

Packaged Applications

In the last few years, applications have emerged which package data mining algorithms to tackle specific business problems. The algorithms are pre-configured, and their complexity is hidden from the business end user. The user interface supports a business workflow rather than general analysis, and all results of modelling are presented in business terms rather than with technical measures of accuracy.

Most of the applications on the market are for CRM or fraud detection. So far, the only packaged applications that have emerged for Market Research are products that use text mining algorithms to handle verbatims. These tools provide a discovery-based approach to enhance and automate the creation and execution of coding schemes. Text mining concept extraction and clustering help the user to find the best coding categories, which can then be automatically applied to the current data set or future cases.

DATA FUSION

Data mining can provide higher value analysis than, say, crosstabs by discovering more complex or subtle patterns. Based on responses to a set of questions, it can predict how someone will respond to another question – for example, that people who say they care very much about service and care moderately about value for money are very likely to say they are dissatisfied.

Applying data mining to survey data alone, though, has limitations.

In the context of market research, data fusion means combining survey data with other sources of data. This dramatically increases the possibilities for benefiting from data mining.

The data most usually combined with survey data are behavioural and descriptive data. If the survey respondents are customers, descriptive data might include some mix of self-declared information and bought-in geodemographics based on postal code. Behavioural data, in its simplest form, may simply be transactions: what they bought and when. In the case of a telecom company, it could include details of calling behaviour. For credit card users, it could record how they spend on their card and how they pay off their bill.

In some cases, more esoteric data types may be included in the "holistic" view of the customer. These can include text from various sources – such as call centre notes and customer emails – which is processed by text mining to extract concepts to include in the customer data. For companies that provide web facilities for their customers, data from web visits can also provide very rich behavioural insights. Specialised "web mining" techniques are used to process the click-level "web log" data and extract high level descriptions of the "events" which happen during visits. These trails of events can then be integrated with other customer data.

Data fusion enables two main types of application:

Providing Proxies for Attitudinal Profiles

Analysing survey responses using clustering or rule induction techniques can discover groups of people who have similar attitudes. One cluster might represent people who value service and personal attention above everything else; another might be value-seekers who don't feel strong loyalty and would be quick to move elsewhere if made the right offer; and so on.

These profiles can be very valuable: among other things, they can drive marketing actions and product design. But they can only be applied directly to people who have responded to surveys. Using data fusion, other sources of data are used to re-profile the discovered clusters in terms of behavioural and/or descriptive elements which are available for any customer. The resulting clusters are "proxies" for the attitudinal ones. They can be applied to any current or future customer regardless of whether they have been surveyed or not, and used to predict their attitudes.

Predicting Customer Behaviour

The second type of application is to use attitudinal data, often combined with other data, to predict some aspect of customer behaviour – for example, defection or purchase of a particular product. These predictive models can be used directly in CRM, driving customer interactions by recommending cross-sell/up-sell offers or retention incentives. Again, because attitudinal data will not be available for all customers, it is usually necessary to build models which use "universal" behavioural/descriptive profiles as proxies for the attitudinal data.

PRIVACY

There has been much publicity around governments' activities in analysing citizens' data in the cause of "national security", and other related topics. This has given the impression that data mining, by definition, infringes privacy.

This is far from true in most applications of data mining. On the contrary: the results of data mining – rules, decision trees, cluster profiles, predictive models – are *abstractions* that do not include any identification of an individual. Whether derived from survey data or combinations of data integrated through data fusion, they can be built from anonymous data records. The understandable knowledge they contain – for example, profiles – describe groups of similar people, rather than identifiable individuals.

CASE STUDY: CABLECOM

Cablecom's combined use of satisfaction surveys and predictive models to improve customer retention illustrates many of the concepts discussed in this chapter.

Cablecom, a leading Swiss provider of cable television, telephony and Internet services, wished to reduce customer "churn" (defection) for their broadband Internet product. From initial analysis, they discovered a peak in service disconnection at the thirteenth month after the start of the contract, corresponding to a termination notice being submitted in month nine. Cablecom aimed to reduce this termination rate.

Trying to reach customers before they made the decision to leave, and with time for marketing offers to influence them, Cablecom sent all customers reaching the seventh month of their contract an invitation to participate in an online survey. The survey comprised ten straight forward 1–10 rated questions on satisfaction-related issues, plus one question inviting free text comment. Approximately 2000 customers responded, a response rate of approximately 20 %. The responses were converted to a single score for each customer in the range 0 to 100, where 0 means "Perfectly satisfied" and 100 means "Totally dissatisfied".

Cablecom combined the respondents' scores with other data held on their customers, including other product holdings, product usage behaviour and externally-sourced geodemographics. Using the overall satisfaction score as a target variable and non-survey data as inputs, they built predictive models to estimate the dissatisfaction level of any customer.

These models were then applied to all customers reaching the seventh month of their contract, and retention offers were made to those with highest predicted dissatisfaction scores. In the group treated in this way, churn was reduced from 19 % to 2 % – a dramatic illustration of the value that can be gained by combining data mining and survey data.

DATA MINING APPLIED TO THE MARKET RESEARCH PROCESS

As well as using data mining to extract value from survey data, alone or combined with other data sources, there are also opportunities for applying data mining to improve the process of market research.

One is the imputation of missing responses using predictive models. For example, most respondents to a survey may happily answer fifteen questions on aspects of their lifestyle, but then many of them choose to leave a final question – *"What is your income?"* – blank. Using the data from respondents who did provide an income figure, it is possible to build a model that will take the other lifestyle data as inputs and predict the income; this can then be used to fill in the income field in the cases where it was left blank. Clearly such imputed values are not as reliable as data provided directly by the respondents, but they can still help give a more complete picture.

Another application area is in panel management. Data mining is used to help manage "churn" (defection) in industries including telecom and banking. It can also be used effectively to predict churn among panel members, so that panel recruitment can be scaled accurately to match requirements.

THE FUTURE

Data mining has shown its value, with many organisations reporting substantial ROI from investing in advanced analysis. In many sectors, such as banking and telecommunications, it has been a "must have" for years, and its use in many other areas is growing steadily.

The breadth, depth and quality of algorithms for data mining continues to grow, though no single new algorithm is likely to have a revolutionary effect. Rather, the future data mining market is likely to see much more emphasis on *automation* and *integration*.

Many data mining tasks such as ongoing monitoring and upgrading of deployed models are labour intensive. As the use of data mining spreads within organisations, it's increasingly common to see tens or hundreds of models applied in many different areas across the business. Systems are emerging which organise and manage these models, and which automate repetitive tasks to free the analysts for more skilled work.

Integration with business applications will become more and more prevalent; many people will be using data mining in their daily work without being aware of it. Models produced by data mining are already being embedded in operational systems – for example, for making recommendations to call centre agents. So far, having the modelling algorithms themselves embedded to "learn" in the course of using an application is rare, but with advances in automation this is an area that is likely to develop rapidly in the next few years.

REFERENCES

Berry, J.A. and Linoff, G.S. (2004) *Data Mining Techniques* (2nd edn). Wiley Computer Publishing.

Berson, A., Smith, S. and Thearling, K. (1999) *Building Data Mining Applications for CRM.* McGraw-Hill.

Chapman, P., Clinton, J., Kerber, R., Khabaza, T., Reinartz, T., Shearer, C. and Wirth, R. (1999) *CRISP-DM 1.0 Step-by-step Data Mining Guide.* Published electronically by the CRISP-DM Consortium – can be downloaded from www.crisp-dm.org.

Delmater, R. Jr, and Hancock, M (2001) *Data Mining Explained.* Digital Press.

Hand, D.J., Mannila, H. and Smyth, P. (2001) *Principles of Data Mining.* The MIT Press.

23

Ethnography and Observational Research

Hy Mariampolski

INTRODUCTION

Ethnography rose to the top of the market research agenda in the late-1980s as naturalistic inquiry began to be perceived as forward movement for market research practice. Statistical surveys were growing in importance, despite compromises in reliability caused by diminishing response rates and such devices as answering machines and do-not-call lists; however, corporate users were craving for a more complete picture of customers.

Qualitative techniques in use at the time, such as focus groups, offered closer engagement with customers but these, too, only whetted marketers' appetites. Many clients felt that encountering consumers in laboratories dominated by conference tables and one-way mirrors could be improved through contact with people during actual buying and usage situations. Going to where products and services were purchased and used by consumers, watching and speaking with real people in their own surroundings, alongside other household members, using their own machines and devices suddenly yielded insights that no other research approach could match. Ethnography became entrenched in the market research armamentarium.

DEFINITION AND HISTORY OF ETHNOGRAPHIC PRACTICE

Marketing ethnography is a subfield of applied anthropology and sociology that uses the direct experience of consumers' everyday reality to stimulate the innovation process and the intensive understanding of purchase and usage dynamics. Through direct behavioural observation, usually supported by video recording, still photography, diaries and in-depth interviewing, researchers can gain insights into people's desires and aspirations as they adapt through the life course, and technological, ideological and socio-economic changes. This consumer understanding leads to the creation, differentiation and modification of products and services offered in the marketplace.

An in-home observational study of consumers' interaction with major appliances, for example, demonstrated a wide array of marketing opportunities. Such factors as dietary shifts toward greater consumption of fresh foods, modifications of interior living space design preferences, a movement toward increased home-based socialising, and other forces were found to have profound implications for the design of refrigerators, stoves and dishwashers.

It is somewhat ironic that in reverting to ethnography, marketers began relying upon a set of tools and techniques that were not "new" but rather well established in the academic realms of anthropology and sociology. The principles of ethnography, and their related ideas

Market Research Handbook, 5th Edition. Edited by M. van Hamersveld and C. de Bont.
© 2007 John Wiley & Sons, Ltd.

about culture and naturalistic immersion as a methodological approach, were set by such early practitioners as Franz Boas (1940, 1969) who studied family forms among the Native First Peoples of British Columbia, and by Bronislaw Malinowski (1922) who studied economic exchange rituals among Pacific Islanders. Margaret Mead (1961, 1972) a student of Boas at Columbia University, created a scandalous sensation in the 1920s through her reports of girls' sexual awakening in *Coming of Age in Samoa*. The fact that she lived among the natives as a single Western woman, sharing their diet and rituals was greeted with a mixture of fascination and outrage at the time.

Ethnographic principles and techniques became standardised tools for cultural analysis. Culture, the conscious and unconscious behavioural and symbolic patterns that are consequences of living in groups (Geertz, 1973; Hall, 1959, 1977), and related ideas about cultural causation, cultural relativism and ethnocentrism, in turn, became major organising ideas underlying all the social sciences.

As campuses became embroiled in the protest movements of the 60s and 70s, the science of culture was confronted and criticised. On the one hand, dissidents challenged the very existence of objective and dispassionate cultural description. On the other side of the spectrum, many activists objected to ethnography's detachment, demanding that it become more actively involved in the formation of social policy and other efforts to salve the human condition (see Lewis, 1966; Liebow, 1967). This debate revived earlier efforts by ethnographers (e.g. Park, 1952; Warner, 1941; Wirth, 1956 and Zorbaugh, 1976) to confront the reality around them and stimulate improvements.

During the late 70s and 80s, sociological and anthropological practitioners became determined to go beyond social amelioration. Influenced by yet another group of innovative thinkers such as Amos Rapoport's *House Form and Culture* (1969), William H. Whyte's *The Social Life of Small Urban Spaces* (1980) and Donald Norman's *The Design of Everyday Things* (1990) researchers started to promote ethnography's basic tools of observation and *in situ* interviews outside of academia. The objective became improving the texture of everyday life – to make the ways we buy goods, clean our homes, diaper our babies and navigate our environments more sensible, satisfying and humanistic.

Everyday life and the role of quotidian consumption are intrinsic though sometimes overlooked aspects of culture. The relationship between buying and using everyday goods and the underlying culturally-based patterns of meaning creation that those objects stimulate and sustain, according to several analysts (e.g. Desjeux, 2006; McKracken, 1988) become the foundation of identities and social relations in post-capitalist societies.

Ethnography, consequently, provides a holistic way of studying people during the purchase and usage of goods and services and also provides the framework for analyses of evolving human ideals, culturally constructed needs and social trends. It is different from simply conducting an "at-home interview" or producing a video recording of consumers using products because it seeks a deeper level of both engagement with people and cultural understanding.

PRINCIPAL APPLICATIONS OF MARKETING ETHNOGRAPHY

Ethnographic principles and methods are used nowadays when marketers wish to go beyond the conventional wisdom yielded through other knowledge-generation approaches. Marketers may want a closer approximation to reality by observing their products being used in a natural everyday setting. Ethnographic description and analysis are particularly appropriate when marketers seek cultural insights into people's daily routines and lifestyles or wish to analyse behavioural processes and transactions. As a prospective, rather than a retrospective method, ethnography can be very powerful as an idea generation resource. It can help marketers understand deep symbolic meanings behind communications as well as patterns of behaviour; in Clotaire Rapaille's (2006) words, deep cultural understanding can help reveal the "code" underlying people's wishes and desires.

On the other hand, like other qualitative approaches, ethnography is inappropriate when validated quantifiable parameters, such as pricing structure or sales projections are required. Conducting ethnographic assignments for businesses requires an investment of time and resources. Collaborative client–researcher teams commonly need to be mobilised; consequently, this approach may not be optimal when a rapid decision turnaround is demanded.

Here are several examples of areas that have benefited the most from the applications of ethnographic tools and perspectives:

Ethnic and Regional Cultures

Understanding the subtleties of human differences and similarities calls for cultural insights produced through ethnography. Whether the focus is a country's minority communities, such as America's Hispanics or England's Asians, or lifestyle differences among age segments, a country's regions or across national boundaries, ethnography is the method of choice.

Ethnographers have also called attention to new subcultural forms common in contemporary societies. As ties of blood and belief have weakened, marketers have noted a turn to *brand communities* as an emerging form of interpersonal affiliation. Muniz and O'Guinn (2001) point out that despite an absence of geographic cohesiveness, brand communities, nevertheless, coalesce around "shared consciousness, rituals and traditions, and a sense of moral responsibility". Consumers of many iconic brands, such as Apple, Harley-Davidson, Gibson guitars and Saab, have a sense of loyalty and commitment to other customers that can be studied at road rallies, music conventions and within Internet blogs. When a brand is strong enough that it becomes an identity tag, marketers possess a resource that needs to be nurtured.

New Product Discovery and Development

Being involved directly in consumers' everyday experience of product usage provides ethnographers with first-hand encounters with their frustrations, problems, joys and satisfactions. These yield surprising behavioural or cultural insights that can produce innovations. Besides generating new product discovery ideas, ethnographic insights also yield guidance for improving product formulations and brand communications.

A.G. Lafley, CEO of Procter & Gamble became the leading spokesperson for this form of ethnography when he told the *Wall Street Journal* (Ellison, 2005) about his excursions around the world talking with women about how they use his products. "So much of what they want is unarticulated", he said; consequently, it takes watching their behaviour to figure out what they really want. For example, although women claimed that opening their laundry boxes was "easy", after watching them jabbing the boxes with screwdrivers, Lafley understood that observed behaviours can betray unrealised and unspoken needs. Moreover, his insight resulted in the design of an easy-to-use package opener for detergent boxes.

Retail Navigation

Ethnographic insights have produced a "science of shopping" that advances our understanding of purchase dynamics at various types of retail outlets. Paco Underhill (1999) has shown how systematic analysis of shelf locations, adjacencies (which products are next to each other) and signage can produce profitable sales turnarounds for retailers. For example, based on the finding that shoppers tend toward the right – walking and looking rightward – merchandisers can advantage new offerings by placing them to the right of known top sellers.

Retailing studies may take advantage of passive videotaping of in-store locations. Alternatively, it is also useful to accompany consumers during "shop-alongs" to probe their inner thoughts, wishes and feelings while they navigate supermarkets and chain stores.

Retail ethnography has been particularly effective at making in-store promotions more effective and in structuring a better match between store patrons and environmental characteristics. For example, through a more judicious selection of in-store music and olfactory cues, such as fresh bread or vanilla scents, retailers can "invite" shoppers who are more likely to purchase their own unique product mix.

Usability Studies

The growing science of usability involves the application of ethnographic research techniques that analyse interactions between people and their low to high tech tools. The primary goals of this sub-discipline are to better understand consumer/user problems, barriers, and facilitators while using various technologies. The ways in which objects and spaces in our everyday lives are designed – from our home and workplace interiors, to the simple tools we use to solve daily problems of personal care, meal preparation, or household maintenance, the familiar geography of our routines, such as entryways and signs – can thwart or support our intentions and ideals.

As a discipline for developing technology products, structured usability observations also can improve the usefulness, enjoyment and effectiveness of web sites (Nielsen, 2000).

Norman (1990) has shown that the principles of usability lie in peoples' mental models, their understandings of how things operate based on their experience or learning. Consumers come to product usage with a natural sense of themselves and others, feelings about human capabilities, ways of perceiving the environment, ideas about causation, cultural habits and so on. Product designers can either leverage these fundamental principles to improve usability or ignore them at their peril. Although consumers may accept poor product performance and inattention to usability for some time, eventually, businesses that follow the rules will gain a competitive edge. Usability studies consistently find that consumers expect that the functionality of technology has some level of visibility; that is, they will be able to understand the operation of a product without referencing external sources. In essence, users anticipate clues to the way things work and expect feedback from the machines they are navigating following actions they may take.

Communications Development

Strategic communications through a range of media – words and images distributed through print, electronic or interpersonal means – are the currency of contemporary marketing. Ethnographic research provides insights into the people that are targeted by these messages and traces the process of person-to-person influence in situations where word-of-mouth is operative. In a textured and granular manner, ethnography shows how messages are heard and processed in real life. For example, QualiData's ethnographic work was responsible for repositioning a client's insect control products from "bait" to "nest killers", thereby providing customers with information that adjusted their mental image of how these products work.

Commercial and Corporate Culture

Ethnographic approaches are also useful in studying commercial environments. Work groups of any size develop unique corporate cultures, representing the collective character and personality of the organisation. Culture provides the basis of values, ideals and norms that may shape internal dynamics such as communications, hierarchy and mobility. Corporate cultures define the ways companies think about customers: as objects to be manipulated, with mistrust, or as valued partners.

Applying ethnographic research in commercial organisations may impact the profitability and success of the enterprise. For example, ethnography can help the organisation integrate new technologies or manage a change in workflow. It can also reveal factors that are facilitating or complicating communication between and among employees. Outcomes of studies have led to programmes that promote cultural diversity and the retention of employees who differ in racial, ethnic, gender and linguistic traits.

The June 2005 edition of *Fortune Small Business* (Murphy, 2005) describes how Microsoft is using ethnographic marketing research methods to develop products targeted at entrepreneurial businesses. By sending out experts to explore a range of companies, Microsoft researchers were able to understand a variety of distinct types of small businesses. Using the study's insights, they then designed a new financial management programme that solved problems encountered by each user segment.

Ethnography and Other Information Sources

Consumer immersions and observational research can complement and benefit from the utilisation of other qualitative research tools, including depth interviewing of individuals and groups, semiotics and content analysis. Sometimes, ethnography as a form of market research practice is contrasted as a single monadic approach versus these other methods. This is a false dichotomy. All qualitative research is, to some extent "ethnographic". Using a range of tools provides cumulative learning. Despite currently being in vogue, ethnography is not a "new" or "alternative" method. It is simply an approach to taking research from the laboratory and into the real world.

COLLECTING AND ANALYSING ETHNOGRAPHIC DATA

This section highlights a select group of procedures that should be used in the proper conduct of ethnographic research (for further detail, see: *Ethnography for Marketers: A Guide to Consumer Immersion*).

For the most part, being an effective researcher requires a high level of ease and comfort among people from all walks of life and an ability to quickly cultivate relationships of confidence and trust. Accepting a high level of ethical responsibility is another serious requirement because we are entering spaces and life worlds that people ordinarily consider private and restricted. Ethical concerns are heightened when we are working with vulnerable groups, such as patients suffering from various health conditions, members of racial and cultural minorities and people of low socio-economic status.

Ethnographers must also minimise their expectations and bracket their own cultural patterns and behaviours in order to observe respondents with fresh eyes. The sin of ethnocentrism – believing that your own cultural practices are singularly proper, correct and normal – must be strenuously avoided in all forms of ethnographic practice.

There are several other practical problems that must be managed in each ethnographic market research study:

Access to Respondents' Environments

"How do you get people to let you into the privacy of their homes and spend days watching them?" is the first question that usually comes up at cocktail parties when an ethnographer tells someone about his or her profession. Everyone involved in market research has to deal with getting respondents to reveal things about themselves in various situations; however, among ethnographers this is a heightened issue.

"To address this challenge, we advocate turning respondents into valued partners in the research process" (Mariampolski, 2006). This involves empowering them with as much information as possible without biasing them in one way or another. This means telling respondents in advance about the study's auspices and goals; explaining who will be coming to the site; and what will be done with the information they provide. Another important point to be shared in advance is describing what it takes to be a "helpful" respondent while carrying out the study's purposes. For example, our participants are instructed not to clean their homes in advance if we're interested in home cleaning; to wear the clothes they normally use for cleaning rather than dressing for guests; and not to change their usual practices and routines.

Nevertheless, the "politeness barrier" is a huge hurdle that needs to become part of the discussion with prospective respondents well before we arrive to conduct the site visits.

Market researchers of all stripes know that respondents arrive within our sphere seeking a range of both intrinsic and extrinsic rewards. Commonly, people receive generous incentive payments commensurate with the time and tasks involved in the site visit yet they are seeking something more. Many appreciate participating in activities designed to yield better products and services. Those less altruistic may be slightly exhibitionistic or narcissistic; they enjoy being the "star" with people watching every stroke of their hand and hanging on every word they speak. Others simply delight in the experience and diversion. Regardless of the respondents' inner drives and motives, we need to value their commitment and concern with being "good" participants. We also need to maintain constant vigilance that people may seek to idealise their behaviours and minimise their confusions when being accompanied by a friendly stranger. Time is on our side, however, as respondents commonly lose inhibitions and controls as they become more familiar with the task and more comfortable with the visiting team.

Cultivating Rapport

Rapport, a sense of common purpose, a strong feeling of connection expressed through words, eye contact and gestures, is an essential ingredient for useful ethnographic outcomes. This cannot just be left to chance. It must be nurtured through every moment of the encounter. Cultivating rapport sometimes involves sharing yourself with the respondent, cultivating authentic human bonds by discussing your common leisure pursuits or family commitments; by talking about pets, children, sports, travel and collecting, perhaps.

Showing constant interest and reinforcing cooperation with positive but non-judgmental words and gestures – a smile or nod, "uh-huh", "your explanation is helpful", "thank you for showing me that", are necessary features of all ethnographic encounters. We do this not to manipulate but to mobilise the features of everyday language that sustain intimacy and confidence in any encounters between strangers.

Our hosts at the site often expect us to be the experts and sometimes solicit advice and approval. Best practices require ethnographers to avoid being placed in the authority role, politely and generously. Acting as though you are the expert biases the situation because respondents may now subconsciously engage in behaviours that only seek your approval and may hesitate to do anything without first waiting for the go-ahead.

Client Co-participation

Executives, managers and researchers from sponsoring companies often insist upon accompanying ethnographers on consumer encounter sites. They are welcomed graciously most of the time. Indeed, a principal benefit associated with ethnography is the ability of internal marketers to learn about their targets directly through interaction with customers. On the other hand, client co-participants are often guilty of making frequent interruptions, questioning in a direct and aggressive manner and drawing false conclusions on the basis of incomplete observations.

For the benefit of preserving the integrity, quality and validity of information gained from consumer encounters, it is necessary for non-researchers to undergo some level of technical training, particularly if they have had no prior experience participating in ethnographic research. It is critical to teach client observers to avoid making egregious errors such as asking leading questions or requiring respondents to carry out tasks they do not normally perform. Authority relations at the site also must be carefully managed – for example, it is not helpful for the lead ethnographer to be publicly challenged or reprimanded by client observers. Establishing protocols and defining roles necessary for cooperation at the site beforehand are steps that will preempt problems during research execution.

Internal vs. External Execution

Nowadays, as many individuals with graduate training in ethnographic methods have joined the ranks of corporate research or consumer insights groups, a debate has arisen about the relative benefits of using internal vs. external support in executing field studies. The main benefits of working with outside ethnographers include the breadth of experience they bring to the study and their freedom from the client company's internal political dynamics which enables them to generate objective and fresh insights. The main value of using an internal expert is their relatively stronger familiarity with the workings of their own corporate culture, as reported by Intel's Ken Anderson (Kenyon, 2005) – a characteristic that may promote an easier implementation process and wider internal communication of findings.

Making Observations

Watching someone engaging in routine tasks over some length of time is not an uncomplicated activity. Acting as the proverbial "fly on the wall" by keeping all of one's senses and perceptual faculties continually engaged is not easy. The normal human restraints, like fatigue, boredom and disinterest kick in over time; furthermore, every ethnographic encounter is also susceptible to bias through selective attention, avoidance, repression, rationalisation, and other expectable phenomenological complications. Moreover, moving from perception and experience to description and discourse creates another level at which bias, misperception and mistakes may produce invalid conclusions.

As a pragmatic though partial antidote to these kinds of problems, we normally recommend using multiple observers and otherwise providing internal validation of findings by asking about behaviours and feelings in multiple ways during the course of the ethnographic encounter.

Recording Observations – Notes and Video

Creating a record of site visits is essential to data analysis; however, this process also entails complicating considerations. Handwritten notes, sketches as well as documentary records produced by the respondent, through diaries, collages and other forms of expression, have usually been sufficient to produce excellent documentation of ethnographic sites. Still photography became another important component following the availability of inexpensive digital cameras. Nowadays, as video photography has become as cheap and convenient as still photography, it has also found its place as an essential part of the ethnographer's toolkit.

Contrary to the expectations of many clients, video ethnography is neither more objective, complete nor comprehensive than note taking. It brings its own set of biases and misperceptions (Pink, 2001). A key area of potential bias comes into play if respondents see their role as performers for the camera rather than as typical consumers. Nevertheless, visual ethnography has grown in popularity because it appeals to the contemporary obsession with image-laden media (McPhee, 2004) and the corresponding nexus of voyeurism and exhibitionism fuelling phenomena such as reality television and the YouTube web site.

Video recordings of consumer encounters are effective in communicating ethnography-driven insights with immediacy and emotional intensity. Video reports of findings are particularly impactful in communicating key findings to senior executives as well as throughout the client organisation. A variety of new reporting formats that simplify communicating findings broadly have gained appeal, including searchable databases of consumer behaviour videos, standalone video reports and PowerPoint presentations with embedded video.

Quality, Validity, Reliability

Regardless of the flash and glitter that can be produced by ethnographies, it would indeed be tragic if researchers failed to address the need for quality, validity and reliability in the execution of studies. Both users and providers of ethnography need to establish quality assessment parameters and challenge their performance at every stage of the process.

Like most other forms of professional services, there is a relationship between quality and the budget allocated to ethnographies. There is no such thing as a "quick and dirty" ethnographic study. It is a form of research that requires senior researchers working in real time throughout the process. In addition, a critical mass of respondent cases needs to be built in order to provide comprehensive coverage of consumer segments and opportunities for meaningful comparisons among equivalent cases. There needs to be some parallelism between the number of cases studied and the level of generalisation expected from the findings.

Researchers attempting to generalise from fewer than ten cases in a study may be leading themselves astray. We recommend a minimum of 15 cases per study assuming that the scale of generalisation is proportionate to the activity being studied.

Adequate budgets also provide some assurance that corners are not cut during respondent recruitment and orientation. Depending on the topic of interest, ethnographers sometimes need to spend one or several days to thoroughly understand consumer lifestyles. It is a mistake to limit time spent at a site on budgetary considerations when this may cause failures in gaining clear insights.

Finally, if mission-critical decisions will be made on the basis of ethnographic findings, for example, if an observation leads to a new product concept, marketers should invest in further research to establish sales projections and other quantifiable parameters of future success in the marketplace.

INSIGHTS AND IMPLEMENTATION

The experience of consumer immersion is so compelling for practitioners and clients alike that it is sometimes easy to forget that our primary purpose is not real world engagement for its own sake. Commercial ethnographers are committed, first of all, to advancing their sponsors' businesses by stimulating the creation and adaptation of new or improved products in the marketplace and by enhancing customers' everyday satisfactions. We are also challenged to not only be innovative but to communicate our findings effectively and to help shepherd our ideas from concept to implementation.

Fieldwork studies typically generate massive amounts of data – video recordings, observational notes, photos, interview transcripts, respondent diaries, etc. – by teams of researchers working relatively independently against the same guidelines. This body of raw background detail must be organised, compiled and evaluated for their inherent transcendent truths. This can be achieved by integrating all data into site case reports, which can then be compared by topic and across consumer segments. The information management function can also be systematised and automated through any of the many qualitative data analysis (QDA) software packages available today, some of which are customised for ethnographic fieldwork data.

Our main purpose in completing all the data sifting, however, is to move beyond behavioural observations to cultural understanding and to insights about goods and services that will win consumer hearts and wallets in the marketplace. The well-publicised study of showering behaviour that QualiData completed for the Moen Corporation (ElBoghdady, 2002) for example, went from observing that people spend most of their time in the shower luxuriating and relaxing playfully with water to the cultural understanding that showers had gone beyond utilitarian cleanliness to a place for indulgence, escape and sensual pleasure. We used this idea to plan and develop a showerhead engineered and positioned as the perfect tool for luxurious interaction with water, the Moen "Revolution" shower.

Insight generation is partially process-driven but it is mostly an art. The process can be advanced by the mutual stimulation of practitioner–client teams collaborating in brainstorming sessions. Various tools for symbolic or functional analysis can educate this process (Arnould and Wallendorf, 1994; Mariampolski, 2006; McKracken, 1988); however, ultimately, it requires inspiration and imagination to create innovative concepts based on cultural insights.

CURRENT DEVELOPMENTS IN ETHNOGRAPHY

As a form of practice, ethnography is alive and vital, not restrained by rigid orthodoxies. New challenges and opportunities stimulated, for example, by technological advances, theories and organising concepts drawn from the social sciences, and emerging cultural and political forms will continue to inspire practitioners to push the field beyond its current complexion.

Here are several directions that ethnographic practice is taking:

Triangulation

Ethnography benefits from being integrated with complementary data collection approaches. Consequently, we are seeing the application of multi-method studies (sometimes called "bricolage") that use ethnographic site visits among other tools. The work that we completed for Alimentare Barilla, the leading Italian food products company (Mariampolski & Wolf, 2006) for example, applied semiotic analysis, depth interviews with experts and lead users, street intercepts, group interviews in addition to in-home observations to produce findings leading to innovative new products and a new positioning platform.

Auto-ethnography

Most of the time, ethnographers enter consumers' life worlds as presumed outsiders and carry out studies by direct engagement. An alternative model sometimes used is to arm people with video cameras and ethnographic tools and empower them to bring back depictions of their world from the inside. This has turned out to be a valuable way to study youth markets, for example, and other worlds with strong impermeable boundaries.

Netnography

The Internet has created a truly alternative format for human communities. The World Wide Web is a new marketplace, a new kind of library, a new town square and an alternative context for various forms of relationships all resident at any computer desktop. Since people are increasingly living within the web for a large share of their lives, it is becoming a new source for analysing the human condition. By studying text and images on personal blogs (or weblogs) and web communities such as YouTube, MySpace, Slashdot and BlackPlanet, researchers can discover how consumers and professionals live with various brands in cyberspace (Mariampolski, 2005). Internet communities create and sustain unique cultures, complete with rules, roles and relationships.

CONCLUSIONS

Ethnography today is at a watershed, moving from an incipient to an established form of qualitative market research practice. It is gaining more and more adherents, specialists and supporters each year. The ethnographic approach will be increasingly challenged to sustain its creativity, authenticity and quality standards in a business context that sometimes devalues ideas through popularisation and commoditisation. In the years to come, ethnographers will have to prove their unique significance to the marketing enterprise. This can only be accomplished by sustaining its strong heritage in the social sciences, by maintaining ethical relationships among clients, practitioners, respondents and the larger community and by taking steps to assure continuous enhancements of client value.

REFERENCES

Arnould, E.J. and Wallendorf, M. (1994) Market-oriented ethnography: Interpretation building and marketing strategy formulation. *Journal of Marketing Research*, **31**, 484–504.

Boas, F. (1940) *Race, Language and Culture*. Free Press.

Boas, F. (1969) *The Ethnography of Franz Boas*. Compiled and edited by Ronald P. Rohrer. University of Chicago Press.

Desjeux, D. (2006) La consommation, PUF, Que sais-je.

ElBoghdady, D. (2002) Naked truth meets market research: Perfecting a new shower head? Try watching people shower. *The Washington Post*, 24 February, H1, H4–H5.

Ellison, S. (2005) P&G Chief's Turnaround Recipe: Find out what women want. *Wall Street Journal*. 1 June, 2005, 1.

Geertz, C. (1973) *The Interpretation of Cultures*. Basic Books.

Hall, E.T. (1977) *Beyond Culture*. Doubleday.

Hall, E.T. (1959) *The Silent Language*. Doubleday.

Kenyon, M. (2006) "Interview with Ken Anderson at IIR's Market Research Event in San Francisco in November 2005". Downloaded from www.mrweb.com on 17 February.

Lewis, O. (1966) *La Vida; A Puerto Rican Family in the Culture of Poverty – San Juan and New York*. Random House.

Liebow, E. (1967) *Tally's corner; a Study of Negro Streetcorner Men*. Little Brown.

Malinowski, B. (1922) *Argonauts of the Western Pacific; an Account of Native Enterprise and Adventure in the Archipelagoes of Melanesian New Guinea*. Dutton.

Mariampolski, H. and Wolf, S. (2006) What Does Italian Mean to You? *Quirk's Marketing Research Review*, **20**(6) June, 66–71.

Mariampolski, H. (2006) *Ethnography for marketers: A Guide to Consumer Immersion*. Sage.

Mariampolski, H. (2005) *Innovate!* Research World. Vol. 13. April.

Mariampolski, H. (2001) *Qualitative Market Research: A Comprehensive Guide*. Sage.

McKracken, G. (1988) *Culture and Consumption*. Indiana University Press.

McPhee, N. (2004) Reality TV and the growth of Ethnographic/Qualitative Research – coincidence, or context? ESOMAR Insight Conference, Vienna.

Mead, M. (1961) *Coming of Age in Samoa; a Psychological Study of Primitive Youth for Western Civilization*. Morrow.

Mead, M. (1972) *Blackberry Winter: My Earlier Years*. Morrow.

Muniz, A. and O'Guinn, T.C. (2001) Brand Communities. *Journal of Consumer Research*, March.

Murphy, R.M. (2005) Getting to Know You: Microsoft dispatches anthropologists into the field to study small businesses like yours. Here's why. *FORTUNE Small Business*, **15**(5), June, 1,

Nielsen, J. (2000) *Designing Web Usability: The Practice of Simplicity*. New Riders.

Norman, D. (1990) *The Design of Everyday Things*. Doubleday.

Park, R.E. (1952) *Human Communities; the City and Human Ecology*. Free Press.

Pink, S. (2001) *Doing Visual Ethnography*. Sage.

Rapaille, C. (2006) *The Culture Code*. Broadway Books.

Rapoport, A. (1969) *House Form and Culture*. Prentice-Hall.

Underhill, P. (1999) *Why We Buy: The Science of Shopping*. Simon & Schuster.

Warner, W.L. and Lunt, P.S. (1941) *The Social Life of a Modern Community*. Yale University Press.

Whyte, W.H. (1980) *The Social Life of Small Urban Spaces*. Conservation Foundation.

Wirth, L. (1956) *The Ghetto*. University of Chicago Press (original work published in 1928).

Zorbaugh, H. (1976) *The Gold Coast and the Slum*. University of Chicago Press (original work published in 1929).

24
Semiotics: What it is and What it Can Do for Market Research

Virginia Valentine

INTRODUCTION

Semiotics has been part of era of tumult and acceleration in the development of new techniques and methodologies in the Market Research universe.

However, despite, as we shall see, taking a radical approach to the influences that shape and drive consumer thinking and, indeed, behaviour, the semiotic approach is gaining ground, respect and recognition throughout the industry.

Whereas in 1988 the UK could muster only one MR company offering semiotics, today's directory lists forty.

ESOMAR Conferences are also testament to the importance of semiotics in spearheading new thinking particularly in the area of the understanding of popular culture and its critical role in consumer lives and lifestyles.

We are seeing the growing application of semiotics across the research board. In fmcg, retail design, advertising, brand development – and multi-national company research philosophy. Alongside this comes the recognition, not just by the market research industry, but by commerce, communications and even governments, that this powerful methodology offers a new, and effective tool to analyse the giant paradigm shifts we are experiencing throughout the global marketplace.

In the chapter that follows, Part 1 describes the semiotic approach and summarises its value for marketing and social research. Part 2 will gives the reader an overview of the theory and the methodology – and what the semiotician actually does in practice. Both parts contain examples and case histories showing flashes of semiotics in action and I've also included a substantial selection of papers and articles which I hope will be useful for readers who want to dig deeper.

PART 1. WHAT SEMIOTICS IS – AND WHAT IT CAN DO FOR MARKETING RESEARCH

What It Is

Semiotics is the theory of the production of meaning: it is a fascinating and powerful analytic tool and brings to market research a unique perspective on how information is encoded and decoded in everyday life. Its findings are based on state-of-the-art cultural and communication theory, not on consumer opinion.

Market Research Handbook, 5th Edition. Edited by M. van Hamersveld and C. de Bont.
© 2007 John Wiley & Sons, Ltd.

In cultural theory, consumers are not independent spirits, articulating their own original opinions and each one making individual buying decisions. Instead, consumers are products of the popular culture in which they live.

They are "constructed" by the communications of that culture (the discourse of television, films, newspapers, books, magazines, PR, advertising, retail spaces, websites, etc.).

Consumers are thus not prime causes; they are cultural effects. So to find out what's really going on in the marketplace, the semiotician begins by looking beyond consumers into the cultural context that surrounds and informs them, in order to evaluate all the forces at work.

In effect, the cultural context is made up of dozens and dozens of different "languages". That means verbal language of course, but also the language of images, music, colour, shape and form – and in this context, the complex language/s of products, goods, services and brands.

Effectively these languages are "sign systems" through which marketers encode cultural beliefs and values into marketing messages – and consumers decode them, according to their own deep-seated cultural drives and passions.

The problem is that both of them do it unconsciously.

Unconscious Encoding: The Great Airline Miscommunication

Take, for instance, an ad that ran for one of the world's biggest international airlines.

Aimed at women business flyers, the visual showed a shapely female leg stretched out and relaxing. So relaxed, in fact, she'd kicked off her high-heeled red shoes. The copy promised superb technically advanced seating that would give the business passenger

"comfort and support, whether you're an imposing 6'5" (*just under 2 metres*) or a modest 5'6" (*around 1.68*)"

A perfectly valid claim one might think, but, hang on a minute. When did you last see a woman who was nearly 2 metres tall? To be that height wouldn't be "imposing" for a woman. It would be extraordinary! And 1.68 isn't "modest" in female measurements. It's a rather good, confident stature. The creatives had been unconsciously working to male cultural norms in the values of "tall" and "short".

Importantly, these cultural norms can have a profound effect on consumer decoding. In the case of the airline ad they automatically gendered the "*you*" the ad was addressed to as male. The assumed reader was not the female business market at all, but a male passenger. So all the symbolism in the ad was semiotically "on offer" to the male reader. And that includes the woman with her shapely leg and her red shoes (red garments are culturally the colour of the harlot). No wonder the ad failed miserably to appeal to its intended target audience.

But if the creative team had been working to male norms, so indeed had everybody on the client side that had read and vetted and approved it. In a huge establishment-led patriarchal organisation, it had simply not occurred to anybody to question that tiny, but massively important signifier. As the late, great French semiotician, Jean Marie Floch, elegantly demonstrated in his analysis of the Apple logo, the communication devil is truly in the detail.

We'll return to the theory and how these sign-systems actually work as this chapter progresses, at least as much theory as anybody needs to know to optimise the value of semiotics in the daily life of brand and social marketing.

For the moment let's turn to the all-important issue of what semiotics can do for the market research industry.

What It Does for Marketing Research

On the practical level of marketing (or social) research and strategic planning, semiotics provides a unique tool for analysing what one might call "the body language" of advertising and packaging.

This body language leaks out through all the signs and symbols that go to make up marketing messages. It acts like two-way mirror. On the one hand, it reveals the psycho-cultural make-up of the brand, what the brand thinks, its beliefs and value systems – and, on the other, it constructs a hidden image of the consumer it assumes will share these values as they look into the brand mirror.

Using semiotics it is possible to decode the cultural structures behind all marketing messages (product, advertising, packaging, websites, retail merchandising, etc.) and see whether or not they really fit with the values of the consumer. (Remember the hidden "male" in the female flyer airline ad.)

By putting brand communications under the semiotic microscope planners and marketers can see the codes and rules the market is playing by. From this, they can then make truly informed judgements about which rules to obey and which rules they can break to achieve cut-through and impact.

Breaking the Rules: New World Wines

> New World wines have virtually re-written the rules of wine labelling by replacing the traditional medals and other symbols of authenticity and provenance with impressionistic imagery of the pleasures of wine-drinking. Moreover, the New World has also created new idyllic "myths of place" to break the stranglehold of wine heritage. Instead of the revered areas of "terroir" and the great winelands such as Bordeaux, Tuscany or Penedes, we have Echo Falls, Jacobs Creek or Blossom Hill; names which have a romantic mystique that owes as much to the holiday brochure as it does to the world of wine.
>
> In this they have not only recoded wine iconography but have brought a whole new generation of consumers into the market, people who might have been intimidated by being constructed as a fine wine connoisseur, but who readily identify with the joys of Bacchus and the delicious pull of faraway places. A new hidden consumer is revealed, not so much an expert wine buff as an everyday wine drinker. It doesn't take rocket science to calculate the relative sizes of these two market segments

Semiotics brings another value to market research and planning: that of futurology. One of the frustrations of consumer research has often been the inability of ordinary men and women, as respondents, to look into the future and guide our marketing strategies on the basis of their forecasts. That, after all, is not their job.

But what consumers cannot do, semiotics can.

By applying semiotic techniques over a longer time frame than the immediate present world of the consumer (what's going on their lives now) it's possible to map the cultural paradigm shifts that will generate new trends and behaviours. By analysing symbolic movements in the language and imagery of a market – or even a single brand – across time, the semiotician can pinpoint emerging cultural changes which signal shifts in attitudes and beliefs. The car market shows this paradigm shift in action.

> As a symbol of success, the automobile was like the sword of the knight – the heavier, the more expensive, the more covered with jewels, the more eloquently it expressed the power of the warrior. (Ernest Dichter)

Paradigm Shift: Automotive Design

Over the past decade there has been a profound change in the design of motor cars. Along with the exponential growth of the female car market has come a whole new range of smaller, bubbly, curvy girl-shaped models. Yes, driving is still about speed and power, and, of course, safety, but driving is now also about an existentialist pleasure – think of Renault Megane's "*Shake it*" campaign where the technology of the design of the rear of the car is expressed through the metaphor of beautifully rounded, sexy, wiggling human bottoms. And the Clio catchline "*vavavoom*" is a gentle dig at the boy racer for so long beloved of car advertising.

The car market has had to rethink its use of warrior power as a metaphor in line with cultural change. And, indeed, it has. Instead of Dichter's knight with his jewelled sword, we have the burly hulk of the 4×4, a close semiotic cousin to the military tank. Often these extreme vehicles are driven by women, in towns and cities, under the rubric of protection for themselves and their children. We should all be asking ourselves the significance of this cultural change.

There are two important points to make here.

Firstly, we have to recognise that cultural change comes at different speeds in different parts of our global marketplace. Semiotics is also uniquely equipped to monitor these relative cultural movements because it can analyse all marketing communications in the context of their own specific popular culture. Styles of advertising are often very important indicators of cultural difference.

Secondly, paradigm shifts and movements in culture are often paralleled in different markets. The pleasure of driving signified by *vavavoom* and the bubbly, sexy little cars is echoed in the impressionistic wine label with its hedonistic, sensual imagery. Because semiotics looks across the whole cultural context it can pick up these correspondences. Thus code-changes in one sector are corroborated in another – and we begin to get hard evidence of big cultural swings at work.

One of the changes that analysts have noticed across global popular culture recently is the phenomenon of "celebritisation" – the insatiable appetite for celebrity news, pictures and gossip. This goes hand-in-hand with the worldwide rise in reality TV, and it has clearly had enormous implications for brands that rely on famous faces to sell their product. On the one hand, celebritisation is creating Warhol's "15 minutes of fame", for more and more people – and on the other fame is inevitably becoming commoditised.

What the Semiotician Actually Does

The semiotic market research methodology is based upon, and adapted from, modern communications and cultural studies. Its focus of attention is communications, consumption environments and popular culture. Semioticians, as it were, ask questions of communications rather than of consumers. All the analysis is desk-based.

Advertising, packaging, websites, retail environments and cultural contexts are analysed by a team of experts, using specially developed techniques.

The reason for this is at once very simple, and extremely complicated. Simple to say, it is because communications are in code.

As culturally sentient human beings, we acquire the ability to encode and decode as we learn the ability to communicate through language, we become a part of culture. Complicated because you have to be able to crack the code in order to understand what's actually going on.

As Roland Barthes had it the coded sign is "the way men and women make sense of their world". In other words, the way we respond, both as human beings and as consumers is a "natural" semiotic technology.

Perhaps, then, we can say that the semiotician works on two simultaneous levels. On one level, mining the big cultural context for all the forces that are shaping and driving consumer opinion, but which consumers cannot articulate, because they simply take these forces for granted. And, on another, closely analysing all the little details of brand communications to reveal the hidden consumer "constructed" by the message.

The Uses of Semiotics

Over 20+ years of practising, semiotics has inevitably been involved with every kind of (qualitative) research study, but in our experience the technique is at its unique best in the following research areas:

Change of strategy and relaunch. Semiotics is among the best diagnostic tools available to marketers to understand the big picture. Its ability to draw a cultural map of the marketplace and the brand's potential within it is second to none.

NPD and the introduction of new brands. For all the reasons outlined above, but also because looking at a market (or potential market) across time enables the semiotician to highlight "cultural gaps" that are simply waiting for a product to be created which will fit that gap. (Interestingly, the technological masters of product research and development seem to find it really exciting to be given a cultural model for NPD rather than a consumer model. It's simply much easier to use.)

Reinvigorating great old brands. When a brand which is still much loved by consumers and whose advertising is quoted in every focus group is simply not delivering on the bottom line, more often than not, this occurs because the brand has fallen out of tune with culture. Semiotics can show how the misalignment has happened and provide relevant recommendations for re-alignment, by retuning the core values, the DNA, in line with contemporary cultural perceptions.

A note on finding the brand DNA: where consumers can obviously talk to us about their feelings for a brand, they are usually inarticulate about why they loved it so – and even projective techniques will often yield no more than a replay of its former glory. By digging in the archives of historical brand communications, a semiotic analysis will uncover the symbolic meanings that once made it great and which can be reinvigorated to connect with the culture of the day: brand building blocks that will also underpin a modern strategy.

Creative development. Another important illustration of the difference between semiotic analysis and consumer research. Consumer research (particularly qualitative) is designed to uncover people's thoughts and feelings, the psychology of the mass market, if you like. And it does superb work in that area. However, crucial though it is that creative work should *connect* with consumer psychology, ads and packs are not made out of thoughts and feelings. They are made out of concrete, material signs and symbols: words, images, plot, characters, lighting, photography, music, product look and feel, colour, materials, pack shapes, dispensing mechanisms, etc., etc.

Semiotics deals in exactly these same "units", analysing the very cultural commodities from which ads, packs, products, websites, etc., are made. As the Euro is instantly translatable across economies, semiotic findings can be instantly translated into the creative process. Consumer research findings, on the other hand, have to be "converted" into creative action. The report has to be converted into the creative brief and the brief into the idea.

A semiotic analysis of advertising, for instance, involves close reading of the plot, the characters, the voice-over, the music and the narrative strategies.

It can therefore show if and how the script is (a) performing coherently within the original basic idea and (b) staying true to the creative and advertising strategy and its brand objectives. Semiotics also gives us the tools to be able to create models that can capture the structure of successful advertising so that creatives have a framework (but certainly not a cage) to work within. Such models also provide planners/clients with a soft guide for evaluating whether individual executions are adhering to that framework. And, where they have moved away, whether or not it is strategically a good move.

The following case history for a campaign for the agency handling recruitment for Teacher Training in the UK provides a fine example. (The case history won a bronze medal for advertising effectiveness, one among many winners for semiotically powered advertising development.)

Teacher Training Agency: Creative Development

(Taken from the submission by Julie Neilson, IPA Area Effectiveness Awards, 2003)

> Sound strategic insight and fascinating use of semiotics led to an advertising campaign which successfully reduced the response rate from the previous campaign. Yes, you did read that right! The Teacher Training Agency needed to change the way response was handled and laid down the task of reducing the volume of expensive to handle calls to the Teaching Information Line and increasing the use of the web as a response

channel. Crucially, this reduction in volume of calls had to be accompanied by a significant increase in the quality of those calls – in terms of callers' eligibility for initial Teacher Training, and in the proportion of callers with qualifications in key priority subjects. Achievement of these objectives needed a fresh approach and diligent implementation of a new strategy. The (semiotic analysis) research was designed to elicit exactly how the existing campaign resonated with the audience and precisely where its strengths lay.

Results of the research concluded that the use of metaphor and the multi-layered structure of the advertising allowed prospects to open their minds to the possibilities of what teaching could now offer them, as opposed to presenting them with a scenario which could be accepted/rejected on the basis of existing prejudices and preconceptions.

The double meanings and tangential references set up their own intellectual challenge which implicitly conferred an intellectual status onto teaching itself. Furthermore the highly creative structure imagery and approach directly connoted the creativity you need to have as a teacher.

In short, the sort of people who instinctively responded positively to the ad were likely to self-select in terms of their own intellectual standards, and their likelihood to have some of the key qualities needed to make it as a good teacher.

The end results surprised everyone. Call volumes decreased by 41 % while web visits rose by 216 %, with the crucial measure of quality – eligible enquirers – going up by 37 %. All of which puts the TTA firmly on track for ensuring a continuing supply of appropriately qualified teachers in our schools.

The same use of semiotics in creative development holds good for packaging and even retail design. When Tesco moved from a predominantly red corporate identity to the now familiar blue, plus red and white, they used semiotics to establish both the cultural meanings of the new colour scheme and how much of the symbolic values of the original red the brand would be unwise to jettison.

Market mapping. This is a critical precursor to many kinds of brand development activities from NPD to repositioning to new advertising or packaging. Semiotics offers a unique cultural map of the marketplace, setting the brand (or potential product) in the context of not just the competition, but of other categories that are competing for share of purse and, of course, the role and place of the product field in popular culture. It would be difficult, for example, to ask consumers to talk about the cultural relations between the purchase options of snacks, confectionery, cakes, deli, a Starbuck's latte or a soft drink. They would say, naturally, "it depends what I feel like". In contrast, a semiotic sweep of all these categories, will show how the "feeling" or "fancy" is culturally organised, where the products symbolically overlap and where the brand or category in question can open up a space for gaining share.

Cross-cultural Research. All cultures are different. Yet all of culture works to the same set of rules and systems. Semiotics, as we have shown, is one of research's most powerful technologies for understanding these cultural rules and for also harnessing them in the service of developing relevant communications across the diversity of the global marketplace. That's why many major multinationals[1] now regularly use semiotic insights to help them achieve brand saliency in today's fragmented and ever-evolving consumer universe. Cross-cultural semiotic research uses two major models. The first is perhaps the most familiar: selling a global brand across the diversity of local culture. The World Gold Council, for instance, commissioned a seven-country study to understand how gold jewellery could connect with the deep symbolic values of gold in cultural contexts as different as the ancient rituals of India, the emergent mindset of China and the fashionistas of Italy. The other model comes from the opposite pole and has to do with the way cultures integrate in the modern world. Such integration is tellingly described in the results of a semiotic project on the acculturation of the USA Hispanic consumer:

> Against the backdrop of earlier historical patterns of assimilation, with their assumption of a linear transition from being, say, Italian, Irish or Polish to being an American, US Hispanic culture today embodies a major shift towards more complex and multidimensional patterns of acculturation. (*Emerging Patterns in US Hispanic culture, ESOMAR Congress 2006*)

Semiotics also brings values of economics and speed to cross-cultural research. To study a market across countries or regions could involve a costly and administratively horrendous project, comprising multiple groups or interviews in several locations. In many instances, however, the answers you need can be found in popular culture, advertising, packaging, retail spaces and websites. These can be assembled quickly and relatively cheaply, compared with recruitment and studio costs – and they can be analysed at a surprisingly quick pace.[2] To make the project even more cost and time effective many studies work to this highly efficient formula: the project kicks off with a pilot, either in one location or in the two most culturally diverse areas. The pilot then raises a set of hypotheses which can be verified or adjusted, according to the cultural beliefs of all the other countries.

Semiotics and Consumer Research – Do's and Don'ts

Of necessity, this chapter has made much of the difference between semiotic analysis and qualitative consumer research methods such as focus groups and interviews. That's an important part of clarifying what the techniques are and how they can be best used. However, it is equally important to state here that it is not in any way meant to imply that semiotic analysis should replace consumer research, although, as described above, there are some types of project for which it is much better suited. Rather the two methodologies should be used synergistically to achieve strategic marketing and business objectives. In other words, semiotics and consumer research make up the two halves of the insight equation. Having said that, semiotics cannot be used to record behaviour as ethnography does, although it can help to explain it. And, of course, it won't provide empathetic consumer quotes for debriefs.

A semiotic analysis, on the other hand, can help to illuminate those quotes. Semiotician Rachel Lawes suggests that: "semiotics can be used following consumer research to explain

---

[1] The semiotically-based brand consultancy Space Doctors has been developing an internal semiotic capacity for Procter and Gamble, which has just such a remit. See Evans/Maggio-Muller, *Culture, Communications and Business: the Power of Advanced Semiotics*, MRS Conference, 2006.

[2] This is well illustrated in Evans and Harvey, *Decoding Competitive Propositions. a semiotic alternative to traditional advertising research*, IJMR, Vol 43, 2001. During a question and answer session on the original paper at the MRS Conference, 2000, Michael Harvey described how an international semiotic analysis for whisky actually came in ten times cheaper than the qualitative quote.

(the cultural drives behind) interesting or unusual responses". In my experience it is extremely useful to understand and explain *consistent* use of verbal and body language.

Using Semiotics to Explain Consumer Response: Peperami Case History

In a joint semiotic/qualitative project on the Peperami sausage, the word "Spicy" was consistently used to describe the product as it was being eaten quite aggressively in the groups. Even small children were biting and tearing into it, while talking about its spiciness. At the same time, all respondents always remarked on the bright green confectionery-like wrapper. Taking this behaviour in conjunction with a cultural analysis of meat and its macho symbolism, we could see that the bright childlike snack pack controlled the symbolic aggression of the meat. This was paralleled by the kind of comic violence pioneered by the "Terminator" cult and developed in oriental martial art movies. The spicy taste and aggressive eating behaviour signified a "hot", almost violent experience that could be legitimised because it was not real

In the majority of cases where semiotic analysis and consumer research can be used in harness, however, it is recommended that the semiotics should come first. For NPD, brand relaunch, strategic and creative development and cross-cultural studies, a semiotic analysis will create a valuable and focused basis for going to the consumer.

Strategic and/or creative concepts can be easily developed from the semiotic study. These can then be tested and refined in subsequent consumer research. That will also by definition verify the semiotic findings through consumer evaluation. It's also extremely cost-effective as concept development is already quite far advanced before consumer research starts.

A semiotic analysis will sharpen and refine objectives for any consumer research. If you know the cultural influences surrounding consumers in the product area, you can better interrogate (a) their effect on different segments of the target market and (b) see if and how any consumer groups resist the influences and depart from the prevailing wisdom.

PART 2. THE THEORY AND THE PRACTICE – METHODOLOGICAL OUTLINE

It is not the purpose of this section to attempt to "teach" the reader how to become a semiotician, but to provide an overview of the key theoretical precepts behind the methodology – and of the most important elements in the analytical process.

The aim is to enable users, buyers and researchers who are interested in developing a semiotic capacity, to broadly understand the actual process and the way it works to produce actionable results, different from other forms of research, but providing a complementary – and necessary – cultural perspective. It will, hopefully, both guide the briefing of a semiotic project and outline the major deliverables an expert analysis can be expected to produce. By the same token, its objective is to add a practical slant to academic explanation and study.

The Theoretical Background

It's a fundamental semiotic premise that culture works to a set of rules and systems. One could describe these rules as the technology of culture. This technology lays the ground for a rigorous and sound semiotic analysis. It was first brought into the intellectual and philosophical field in the late 19th and early 20th century by two founding fathers, Ferdinand de Saussure a Swiss linguist and American philosopher Charles Sanders Pierce.[3] Both Saussure and Pierce were concerned with the nature of the sign. Saussure, in particular developed his "life of signs in society" into the nature of language itself – and, ultimately the structures of language and communication. While it's neither appropriate, nor possible, to detail Saussure's work here, three key theoretical precepts inform all semiotic analysis.

The first is that the connection between a word and the thing it designates is arbitrary. The word d-o-g has no unbreakable connection between the letters and the animal with four legs and a tail. If it did then you couldn't have the words c-h-i-e-n or p-e-r-r-o or the Chinese ideogram designating the same thing. It follows then that these words are coded so that everyone knows what they are designating without having to see a picture of a dog (what Pierce called an iconic sign). But the code doesn't stop with the simple designation. We understand d-o-g in relation to a whole set of complex meanings – what one might call "dogness". Dogness is not a property of the actual four-legged creature, but of its place in culture. The sign therefore encodes cultural meanings which are not intrinsic but are put there by the decoding process. "Dogness" in Antarctica is entirely different from dogness in Paris.

Secondly, Saussure argued that no sign exists in isolation, but in relation to all other signs. Dogness you see is only understood in relation to catness or horseness or fishness. If we narrow the possibilities down to paired opposites, then the relationship becomes even more forcefully clear. We know about *clean* because we know about *dirty* (think of detergent advertising). We know about *day* because we know about *night*. The switch between our "day" and "night" selves carries immensely complex connotations to do with work and leisure, seriousness and fun, waking and sleeping . . . and on and on. And, despite all the changes in our perceptions of the place and role of men and women in society, "male" is still mainly understood as "not female" and vice versa. Importantly, for a semiotic analysis, the opposite of any sign is always there, hidden behind it, a bit like the thin person trying to get out of the fat body in slimming product claims. When marketers talk about "comfort", for instance, they are at the same time invoking the spectre of "discomfort".

The Grey "Other" in Persil "Whiteness" Advertising

> For all its early life Persil showed a child in a sparkling white dress (good mother) skipping past another in a dingy grey dress (bad mother, they'll take your child away from you if you don't use our product to eliminate evil dirt). It's interesting that today Persil has caught up with child psychology and loudly proclaims "*dirt is good*". (Subtext, as opposed to the "dirt is bad" ideology we used to subscribe to.)

Finally and most radically, Saussure insisted that our world is constituted by language. It does not merely label or record it. There is no "truth" in the world which can exist outside language, so consumers aren't telling us the "truth" about their lives, they are constructing it in language. Cultural theorist Peter Barry gives the example of different colours made into

---

[3] The reader will note that the references at the end of this chapter do not include the works of the "fathers" of semiotics: Saussure, Pierce, Lacan, Greimas et al. This because the writing/reading is difficult and highly formalised by the disciplines from which they come. Instead, I have listed some further reading which, hopefully, has summarised their initial thinking in a helpful, accessible way.

reality by language; in the spectrum all the colours run into one another. Likewise the year is continuous, but we make four seasons – a way of seeing, not an objective truth. How we complain when "the Spring was really cold this year". And what will our way of seeing do to the effects of global warming?

What Saussure's work did was to posit a model of language as a system which is self-contained in which individual items relate to other items and thus create ever-widening and larger systems. And all languages can be read in the same way. We read the language of fashion, flowers, colour, music, shape (think of big square-shouldered "male" toiletry bottles, curvy feminine ones).

Peter Barry writes:

> The culture we are part of can be "read" like a language, using these principles, since culture is made up of many structural networks which . . . operate in a systematic way. These networks operate through "codes" as a system of signs. They can be read or decoded by the semiotician.

Practical Application. The Decoding Process

Codes make themselves felt in patterns, repetition of certain images and structures across the brand, the category and culture itself.

Patterns, or Codes, in Bottled Water

Bottled water codes almost all use these patterns: transparent glass; soft blue graphics and typography; often some symbol of a mystic origin or source (a mountain, a sacred spring, a primitive rune) perhaps echoed in the name, Volvic, Highland Spring, Ty. These are the codes of purity and purification (as opposed to the implied impurity to be found in many other, non-water, drinks such as carbonated soft drinks – or alcohol).

To see patterns such as these a semiotic analysis must look at both breadth and depth of material. (And just to be very clear, in analysis one is not talking at all about consumer research: no groups, no interviews, only desk analysis of communications and culture.)

So let's start with the corpus of materials to be analysed. That will comprise:

- brand communications (ads, packs, product, websites);
- competitive context (as above);
- category communications;
- the product in popular culture (retail space, TV, magazines, the net, etc.).

The codes or patterns we find will signify the cultural beliefs and values around the product field, what semioticians call "the cultural referent".

Cultural References: Whisky Advertising

Whisky advertising has for decades referenced an ideology about the drink as reward at the end of the working day, there are endless images of Scottish cottages in the fading light or expensively shod executive feet reclining on the managerial desk as the sun sets over

the skyscraper. It's the same with all dark luxury spirits. An American ad for Hennessy brandy once showed a group of young businessmen gathering in the train station bar under the headline *"When the 7.30 isn't leaving till 8.15"*.
The ad didn't even feel the need to explain it meant 7.30 at night!

Codes and Discourse

The grouping of codes and cultural references creates the phenomenon of discourse.

Discourse is the collective coding system of a cultural grouping, the particular sets of language and imagery, used by:

- a group of people (think of youth discourse, political discourse, agricultural discourse, marketing discourse);
- a product field (the discourse we use to describe fragrances, for instance is quite different from that of do-it-yourself or financial services);
- a brand (McDonald's discourse vs Starbuck's; Calvin Klein's discourse as opposed to Chanel's).

The importance of discourse is that it is, if you like, the voice of culture. Culture is secret, silent, running through our socio-psychological bloodstream. It is the iceberg that lies underneath all our beliefs and thinking. Discourse is the tip of that iceberg. If you open up the discourse you can listen to the voice of culture.

Moreover, discourse structures our thinking. We do not have a fully-formed thought that comes into our mind and then searches for the right language and image in which to communicate that thought. The thought itself is made by the discourse. In the UK, for instance, thinking about food preparation has been radically changed by a shift in the cooking discourse from "measurements" such as *250 gms of Crème Fraiche* to supermarket units: for instance, *"1 pot of Crème Fraiche – or 6 skinless, boneless chicken breasts"*. Alongside this, the language of cookery *"gently pour, blend in"*, etc. is being replaced by a kind of cooking nonsense slang – *"bung in the oil, whoosh it all up"*. Cooking itself then moves from serious expertise to a playful activity. It takes knowledge to pour gently and blend ingredients. Anyone can bung it all in and whoosh it all up.

Focused discourse analysis is one of the newest developments of semiotic marketing research. It is described by practitioner Gill Ereaut thus:

> Discourse analysis might mean looking in forensic detail at some key word or phrase that is central to a brand – a sharp tool with which to dissect some knotty brand issues
>
> Or it might mean looking in the broadest possible way at a "linguistic landscape". Language analysis gives access to the cultural environment in which your brand or organisation operates. (*Linguistic Landscapes* website)

So, to recap. A semiotic analysis starts with mining a large body of materials to look for patterns and the cultural beliefs that are being referenced by repeated instances of images and language, the discourse.

But there is something else that can be revealed in the patterns of cultural communications. Changes in codes over time.

Tracking Code Changes Over Time

Culturalist Raymond Williams has shown that code changes can be tracked by using three simple classifications: *residual, dominant* and *emergent*. (Marxism and Literature.) Semiotican Monty Alexander has explained the process masterfully.

> *Residual* codes are leftovers from an earlier set of cultural values and usages. Looked at from today, although still in existence, residual codes are steadily weakening as they become increasingly outdated and either disappear altogether or get replaced by newer codes. Brands that are passing their sell-by date are often using some if not all, residual codes. (Codes and Contexts, MRS Conference 2000)

Residual to Emergent Codes: A Brand Recovery

An interesting example of a famous British food brand using a residual code was its lovingly photographed imagery of English traditional fare being carefully produced in English pastoral scenes, when all around, the British consumer was experiencing and enjoying every kind of *world* cuisine. People loved the imagery but in a nostalgic, abstract way. They'd stopped buying the brand because it had fallen out of line with culture. Only when the packaging started to use modern "food porn" photographic codes in line with the explosion of world food visuals that flooded contemporary media, did the brand begin a magical recovery and find a new relevance. The semiotics of nostalgia were replaced with contemporary greed – and the privileging of long slow food production gave way to the immediate gratification of consumption.

> *Dominant* codes are the codes of the present day, and often difficult to spot as codes because they are all around us (*"That's not a code, that's what is"*). The bottled water packs are a good example of a dominant code.

> *Emergent* codes are of particular interest to the analyst (and to the client!). Because they are not yet fully formed, so to speak, they are signposts to the future as it is now appearing over the cultural horizon. As such, emergent codes tend – at this point in time – to be a more mixed bunch than the other two classifications. All candidates for the future; they are today still experimental, often tentative, sometimes outrageous when seen through "dominant eyes". But each of them is currently jockeying for a pole position – and one of them at least is set to achieve dominance tomorrow (*op cit*).

In order to actually see code changes – and to map them against the shifts in popular culture they are mirroring, a semiotician must analyse over time. So our universe of analysis now looks like this:

- brand communications (ads, packs, product, websites);
- competitive context (as above);
- category communications;
- the product in popular culture (retail space, TV, magazines, the net, etc.). *All over as long a period as practical.*

The historical time frame requires some clarification. How far back do you need to go – and where do you get hold of the historical material?

In a semiotic brand audit, it is really helpful to go into the client/agency archives and look as historically far back as possible. Often companies will also have a wealth of historical competitive advertising. Category communications can be accessed through the commercial archivists. And for anybody seriously entering the semiotic field, it is sensible to subscribe to the regular "new commercials" reels created by the archive companies. Arguably this would be hugely beneficial to academic institutions. The Internet is also a superb resource.

Contemporary packs in the category can be obtained either from company collections – or just bought in. And historicial pack designs will show up as the pack shots on the advertising of the time. The semiotician needs to be as resourceful as any recruiter in the gathering of material. But you simply cannot do the job without it. Semiotics looks and analyses concrete material. It doesn't guess!

In other projects, the historical material needed is a matter of judgement. In NPD for instance, a sweep of the current state of the cultural context may be sufficient. Brand development will always need the brand's history, but maybe not all the competition.

It is probably true to say that, by their very nature, brand leaders will play by the dominant codes: they set the norms that all other brands live by. But more often than not, they broke the codes and rose to become leaders on the tide of an emergent wave.

One more point on code-change: emergent codes are the raw material of brand and market cultural forecasting. To turn them into reliable strategic guidelines, they should be developed into concepts which can then be fed into consumer research. Consumers, as has been said earlier, cannot easily forecast emergent trends themselves, but they are certainly able to assess the value and relevance of concepts based on changing cultural codes.

Some Deeper Semiotics: (1) Rational and Emotional Language

This final part of the section on the semiotic methodology, provides an opportunity to touch on a few of the other great theoretical principles that lie behind much of the development of Saussure's work into contemporary semiotics. These principles deal with the way semiotics understands that communications actually interact with the subconscious.

In this, the chapter is absolutely not making any biological neurological or neuro-scientific claims. This is an explanation of the mechanisms of language, not a study of the functioning of the brain.

The first explanation concerns the way language/s work to trigger emotional and responses. This owes to the linguist Roman Jakobson who identified two axes of language, metaphor (the "emotional" axis) and metonymy (the "rational"). Mythic discourse, lyric poetry, symbolism, Surrealist painting, music, colour, shape, and folkloric are all metaphorical – as is film montage (juxtaposition of images generating meanings in excess of the sum of the parts). And, of course, advertising devices and brand properties, think of the Sure/Rexona tick, the Nike Swoosh, McDonald's Golden Arches. The key point here is that we cannot find a perfectly right, provable answer to the meanings of these metaphors. We think we can understand what Beethoven meant with the famous da-da-da-daa opening to the 5th symphony, but we cannot be sure. We can guess about the swoosh, but we don't truly know. We have to decode on the level of the imagination, feel the meaning rather than articulate it – and so respond with our emotions.

Metonymic forms of expression, on the other hand, predominate in scientific discourse and in "clear" or "transparent" prose generally – also in literary and photographic realism . . . and in positioning statements, concept boards and helpfully explanatory voice-overs. Measurements are metonymic, as are ingredient lists and nutritional statements. Metonymy, in the main, demands to be decoded with the head.

Metaphor and metonymy are key pointers to the relationship brands and categories are setting up with their marketplace. Chocolate works largely on metaphor in order to stimulate and encourage a more emotional relationship, often so that deep feelings of guilt and sensuality can be brought into play. Fragrance exists almost entirely in a metaphorical world. Financial services rely heavily on metonymy, playing to the need for the expert "knowledge" of the financier.

From the point of view of semiotic findings, it is often invaluable to be able to see just where each of these two axes are in the foreground of communications – and how they are interacting. P&G's Pampers communications have for most of the brand's history shown real diapers with metonymic absorbency channels, etc., so we all know what we're on about – but the mother and baby has always been bathed in a metaphorical golden light that we could feel has some sacred symbolic significance. The interaction can be extremely important in packaging and in retail design where a lot of information has to be processed within a more emotional context, or some emotion needs to be injected into an information-heavy base.

Changing a brand position will often involve rethinking the levels of metaphor and metonymy in communications, they are after all, also coding systems, norms that can be exploited or broken.

For the way metaphor and metonymy can provide a useful input into projective techniques and the analysis of consumer response in focus groups and interviews, see The Dark Side of The Onion (Evans and Valentine).

Deeper Semiotics: (2) Contradiction and Reconciliation – The Power of Myth

Conventionally, we tend to think of "a myth" as a tall tale, a legend, a story that is powerful, appealing and enduring but not true. Structural anthropologist, Claude Levi-Strauss, however, thought not of myths as a collection of stories, but of myth as a cultural mechanism all humankind uses to reconcile the difficult and disturbing contradictions we all have to live with. In his words:

> *The purpose of a myth is to provide a logical model capable of overcoming a contradiction* (Claude Levi-Strauss, Structural Anthropology 2)

Monty Alexander enlarges on this and shows its relevance for marketing:

> Translating this definition into modern marketing language means that a *brand's* myth is the belief by consumers that that brand offers them a way of resolving a problem or situation that hitherto represented some kind of contradiction. Or, from the perspective of the marketer, that the brand holds the power to reconcile a cultural opposition. (Alexander, The Myth at the Heart of the Brand, ESOMAR Qualitative Seminar, 1996)

Alexander's paper provides a detailed explanation of how successful brands embody myths and offers a technique for how this brand myth can be identified, evaluated and exploited. In our view it is required reading for everyone seriously interested in pursuing semiotics as a research methodology.

In the time and space available here, however, it would enough to show how important the reconciling myth is to all mega products and brands – and how the analysis of such myths fits into the semiotic scheme of things.

A Megabrand Reconciliation of Oppositions: The iPod

The iPod reconciles the public and the private space. On any bus, metro, plane, street or any other public space you can see iPod man or woman (girl or boy) lost in their own private world of listening.

The logical model that explains how this can be is the technology that is capable of "fitting" 10 000 tunes (the contents of stacks and stacks of CDs) into a machine so small and slim it will fit into a pocket. And, while the Sony Walkman, of course, is the precursor to this, the pod goes much further in its paradoxes. Its randomness constantly surprises the listener, even though he/she is the architect of the material on the software. It collapses time with its "podcasts" ... and on and on ...

Diagrammatised, it looks something like this:

Many tunes	Few tunes
Lots of disks	One disk
Large area	Small area
Not portable	Portable
Private space	Public Space
Ordered download	Random upload
Fixed Time	Moveable time

This harks back to Saussure's notions that we understand what a thing is by what it is not. We define reality in oppositions, but the most powerful cultural elements bring those oppositions together. Think of the wicked stepmother in "Snow White", beautiful but bad, a logical model that overcomes the contradictory, and ambivalent, feelings that children have towards their parents. According to child psychologist Bruno Bettleheim, fairy tales, "represent in imaginative form what the process of healthy human development consists of ... (and) make great and positive psychological contributions to the child's inner growth" (Bettleheim, The Uses of Enchantment). Another contradiction that fairy stories help the child to live with is the opposite to that of the wicked stepmother, the goodness in ugliness – an explanation for "Beauty and the Beast", the "Frog King" and the enormous modern success of "Shrek".

In methodological terms, these oppositions hold the key to uncovering the brand myth. Alexander uses the following demonstration:

As an example, let us use scotch whisky. For the purposes of this paper, we'll consider a (fictional) mid-market, old-established, *declining* whisky brand, called *Black Sporran*.

Let us further suppose that its owners are searching for an exciting new, *younger* positioning in the marketplace. In our terms, they are searching for *a new scotch whisky myth*.

So we can list each of the properties and perceptions of *Black Sporran*, (good and bad) and at the same time we can also list its opposite to form a "rival" column

smooth	rough
dark	light
heavy	light
formal	informal
drunk neat	drunk diluted
serious	fun
"sacred"	"profane"
respectful	flippant

older men	younger men/women
sincere	ironic
strong	mild
deserved	undeserved
reward	stimulus
private	social
"traditional" label	"modern" label
men's club	cafe bar
heritage	instant
authentic	phoney
pedigreed	illegitimate
hierarchic	egalitarian
upper class	lower class
cliché Scotland	real Scotland
national	international

It is interesting in this particular listing – and in the light of the whisky company's declared objective of going for a younger market sector – to see just how many *"opposites"* of the traditional world of scotch whisky-drinking are also discriminators of today's younger end of the drinks market.

Using these lists of oppositions we can see that our "young Scotch whisky" might embody any number of myths:

- sincere phoney-ness;
- serious irony;
- formal modernity;
- strong fun, etc., etc.

"Strong fun", indeed, might mount quite a forceful challenge to the myth of Bacardi Breezer.

The Bacardi Breezer "Myth"

Awarded the accolade of the "most successful launch of the decade" (UK Advertising Effectiveness Awards) Breezer revelled in the myth of "outwardly innocent, inwardly wicked", embodied in the logical model of the candy-coloured fruit drinks concealing the kick of the big bad Bacardi bat.

Some Other Important Semiotic Models

It is not possible to detail here all the models the growing community of semioticians in marketing research will bring to the analytical party. It would be wrong, however, not to mention, if nothing more, a few of the most important ideas which have influenced the development of semiotics and its practice. Interested readers can seek fuller explanations from the references and reading lists at the end of the chapter.

The models include that of *A.J. Greimas* who developed the notion of oppositions into the well-known "semiotic square". The square contains not only oppositions, such as "life" and "death", but further oppositional breakdowns, i.e. "not-life" and "not-death". One can see from this how Greimas can be used to unpack the complexity of any given term and to explain the structure behind such narrative mechanisms as plots or stories in advertising.

Other seminal work on narratology (developed by Greimas) has come from *Vladimir Propp*. Propp's "Morphology of the Folk Tale" explained how all stories actually perform to the same structure of heroes and villains, donors, helpers and magic agents. These characters fulfil the dreams of the hero/heroine (usually by the "magic agent" plugging some identified lack, such as poverty or orphan status, and, along the way, dispatching of the villain). Problem/solution advertising has been working to this structure forever. We have also identified a new post-Proppian model in which the hero or heroine does not lack anything but simply wants more. The task of the magic agent is therefore to deliver self-enhancement.

French psychoanalyst *Jacques Lacan* has also been hugely influential with his work on the relation between the unconscious and language, cf. his famous dictum, "the unconscious is structured like a language". From this Lacan goes on to show how the "subject" (the perceived person) is constructed in language and only exists in and through communications. (His theory of "the mirror stage" demonstrates that babies learn their selfhood as they see themselves in a mirror and become aware that this is "me" – or "not you").

Moreover this subjectivity, in Lacanian theory, is unstable and can change itself as the occasion demands. For a further discussion of the importance of Lacanian theory to the brand-consumer relationship, see Gordon and Valentine, *The 21st Century Consumer*, MRS 2000).

It would be remiss to conclude this key-thinkers roundup without reference to the marvellous cultural idea of "Carnival", largely brought to notice by *Mikhail Bakhtin* and finely described here by Raman Selden.

> The festivities associated with Carnival are collective and popular; hierarchies are turned on their heads (fools become wise, kings become beggars); opposites are mingled (fact and fantasy, heaven and hell); the sacred is profaned. The "jolly relativity" of all things is proclaimed. Everything authoritarian or rigid is subverted, loosened and mocked. (*A Reader's Guide to Contemporary Literary Theory*)

In Carnival we find the semiotic and cultural root of so much playful modern advertising, the interactivity of websites, the naughty disregard of grammar and spelling in SMS – and the compelling unpredictability of reality TV.

Other ideas that will be brought into play as we seek to understand the consumer in the contemporary marketplace and the overarching cultural context, include deconstruction, post-modernism, feminism and intertextuality (alluding or quoting one text within another). Testimonial advertising, using a personality made famous in another sphere is an example of intertextuality. Borrowing the genre or style of films, or using a pop song soundtrack as the creative idea is another.

The UK school of semiotics (now spread all over the world) owes much to modern cultural studies, developed from the radical input of semiotic theory and sociology to literary and film criticism. A recent American development has pursued Pierce's classification of the three types of sign – iconic, where the sign resembles the thing (e.g. a picture of a dog); indexical, where the image points in the direction of the thing (e.g. a collar and leash points towards the idea of a dog) and symbolic, where the sign has an arbitrary relationship with the object (e.g. d-o-g) – and used it to analyse consumer response. This is explored in a paper by Kent Grayson and David Shulman, *Journal of Consumer Research*, volume 27 (2000).

Semiotics continues to develop, as the world becomes more complex and culture morphs yet again to accommodate this complexity.

In that context, of course, semioticians are all too well aware of the need to adapt old theories and forge new thinking to understand the virtual world of the Internet. Here, if anywhere, the

Lacanian subject is truly in evidence, switching identities – from blogger to banker, to auction-eer – at the drag of a mouse. It will take all our ingenuity to get on top of that semiosphere.[4] But, at least, with semiotics we have a head start.

A Concluding Note – from the Macro to the Micro

On the macro level, there is no doubt that semiotics has properly penetrated the world of market research and marketing, but it is also having an influence on the wider world of business, management and organisational development. In academic terms, many disciplines beyond cultural studies now recognise both the importance of the cultural context and of interrogating "truth" or "facts" as constructions of language. And clients are certainly becoming much more semiotically literate, partially as many more of them graduate from courses which have included some semiotic studies and partially simply as the word has spread.

On the micro level of methodology, it would be foolhardy to try to summarise everything covered in this chapter, but hopefully those of you who have come this far will take with you these fundamental semiotic concepts.

1. The "consumer" is not an independent being making free and individual choices. He or she is a cultural construct, set up in communications by a system of signs, which create a hidden image of the assumed reader/viewer. This is why the semiotician looks beyond consumers to the wider cultural world to find out what's going on.
2. The sign systems are in code, referring to cultural assumptions, values and beliefs. They are encoded and decoded largely unconsciously in everyday life, including, of course, marketing messages. To know what consumers are doing with brands you have to crack the code.
3. We have three coding systems present in culture: residual, dominant and emergent. Residual codes represent fading cultural beliefs, Dominant codes, the present thinking and Emergent codes point the way towards a possible future philosophy.
4. Language/s and discourse constitute our world. There is no objective "truth" out there recorded by language, it is made in the text.
5. The unconscious is also structured like a language. We become aware of our identity when we discover our self as an "I", but the "I" is not stable, it can assume many, many different identities. That is why we can have so many shifting relationships with brands.
6. All humankind lives with contradictions. Culture has invented the mechanism of myth to reconcile these contradictions. Brand myths perform exactly the same function and thereby connect with consumers on the deepest level of cultural belief.
7. All cultures are different. Yet all of culture works to the same set of rules and systems. Semiotics is the technology of culture, using the rules and systems to uncover the deep similarities and differences across the global marketplace.
8. All methodologies have their parameters and boundaries in relation to other marketing research approaches. Semiotics cannot be quantified, although it can produce hard evidence of corroborations and correspondences across the sweep of culture. Nor can it record either the behaviour or the spoken "thoughts and feelings" of consumers, but it can, and does, explain both in terms of the unconscious cultural forces and drives that lie behind them. In this sense, semiotics is the hidden half of the consumer equation.

---

[4] The word semiosphere was actually coined by Alex Gordon to describe the post-modern world of brands. In true semiotic spirit I've borrowed it to describe the identity of the post-modern consumer constructed in the texts and Intertexts of the Internet (Signs and Wonders, the transformative power of International Semiotics).

REFERENCES

Alexander, M. (1996) The Myth at the Heart of the Brand, ESOMAR Qualitative Seminar.

Alexander, M. (2000) Codes and Contexts, MRS Conference.

Anderson, M.E. (2006) Malcolm Foresight semiotics – Emerging patterns in US Hispanic acculturation, ESOMAR Congress.

Barry, P. (1996) *Beginning Theory. An Introduction to Literary and Cultural Theory*. Manchester University Press.

Barthes, R. (1972) *Mythologies*. Wang and Hill.

Bettleheim, B. (1989) *The Uses of Enchantment: The Meaning and Importance of Fairy Tales*, Vintage; Reissue edition.

Dichter, E. (1964) *Handbook of Consumer Motivations. The Psychology of the World of Objects*. McGraw-Hill.

Evans, M. and Valentine, V. (1993) The Dark Side of The Onion, MRS Conference.

Floch, J.M. (2001) *Semiotics, Marketing and Communication Beneath the Signs, the Strategies*. Palgrave Macmillan.

Gordon, W. and Valentine, V. (2000) The 21st Century Consumer: a new model of thinking, MRS Conference.

Gordon, A. (2004) Signs and Wonders, the transformative power of International Semiotics, ESOMAR Qualitative Seminar.

Levi-Strauss, C. (1968) *Structural Anthropology*. Doubleday Anchor Books.

Selden, R. (1985) *A Reader's Guide to Contemporary Literary Theory*. Harvester Wheatsheaf.

Williams, R. (1977) *Marxism and Literature*. Oxford University Press.

USEFUL FURTHER READING

Chandler, D. (2002) Semiotics for Beginners, Routledge. Online: Chandler, Daniel (1994): *Semiotics for Beginners* [WWW document] **URL** http://www.aber.ac.uk/media/Documents/S4B/semiotic.html December 2006 (Chandler's online site contains a comprehensive reading list).

Johnson, M. and Lakoff, G. (1980) *Metaphors We Live By*. University of Chicago Press.

SELECTED FURTHER PAPERS AND ARTICLES ON SEMIOTICS AND MARKET RESEARCH

Alexander, M. (1999) Which Comes First: The Consumer Chicken or the Cultural Egg? How Semiotics Can Improve the Speed, Validity and Reliability of Qualitative Research, ESOMAR, Qualitative Research, Athens.

Alexander, M. (2004) As above, so below, Market Research Society, Annual Conference.

Alexander, M. (1996) Big talk, small talk. British Telecom takes a look at British telephone culture, ESOMAR, Telecommunications, Athens.

Beasley-Murray, J., Griffiths, J., Rowland, G. and Siamack, S. (2004) The Qual remix Market Research Society, Annual Conference.

Bitoun, C. and Legris-Desportes, C. (2002) Semiotics and internet communications, ESOMAR, Internet Conference, Berlin, 281–298.

Bitoun, C. and Maïer, C. (1999) ESOMAR, Semiotics for Strategic Forecasting Marketing Research Congress, Paris, September.

Brown, S. (1995) Postmodern Marketing Research: No Representation Without Taxation, *International Journal of Market Research*, **37**(3), 287–310.

Caillat, Z. and Mueller, B. (1996) The Influence of Culture on American and British Advertising: An Exploratory Comparison of Beer Advertising, *Journal of Advertising Research*, **36**(3), 79–88.

Callow, M. and Schiffman, L. (2002) Implicit Meaning in Visual Print Advertisements: A Cross-Cultural Examination of the Contextual Communication Effect, *International Journal of Advertising*, **21**(2), 259–278.

Camillo Furio, M.F. and Traldi, T. (2005) From Marketing To "Societing" – Reading ethnographic material through the use of digital matrix and Semiometrie, ESOMAR, Innovate! Conference, Paris.

Ceriani, G. and Furlanetto, P. (1999) The Value of Women's Magazines for Advertisers: Supporting Print Peculiarity in the Internet Age, ESOMAR, Strategic Publishing, Milan.

Davies, A. (2003) Pot Noodle – The "Slag of all Snacks", Account Planning Group (UK), Highly Commended, Creative Planning Awards.

Elliott, R. and Wattanasuwan, K. (1998) Brands as symbolic resources for the construction of identity, *International Journal of Advertising*, **17**(2), 131–145.

Evans, M. and Harvey, M. (2001) Decoding Competitive Propositions: A Semiotic Alternative to Traditional Advertising Research, *International Journal of Market Research*, **43**(2), 171–180.

Evans, M. and Maggio-Muller, K. (2006) Culture, Communications and Business: The Power of Advanced Semiotics, Market Research Society, Annual Conference.

Frank, B. and Stark, M. (1995) Semiotics and entertainment: A marriage made in Heaven, *Journal of Advertising Research*, **35**(5).

Fletcher, J. (2003) A data factory in the middle of storyville? Market Research Society, Annual Conference.

Glaros, E. (1997) A constructive approach to advertising testing: shifting from the content to the form of representation in advertising, ESOMAR, Qualitative Research, Singapore.

Grafton-Small, R. and Linstead, S. (1989) Advertisements as artefacts: everyday understanding and the creative consumer, *International Journal of Advertising*, **8**(3), 205–218.

Higie, R.C. and Zaltman, G. (1995) Seeing the Voice of the Consumer: Metaphor-based Advertising Research, *Journal of Advertising Research*, **35**(4), 35–51.

Petitimbert, J.-P. (1998) Managing a Portfolio of Brands: A Semiotic Approach to Multibrand Policies, ESOMAR, Brand Management, February.

Khanwalkar, S. (2001) When is a coconut not a coconut? ESOMAR, Qualitative Research, Budapest, 187–197.

Lawes, R. (2002) Demystifying semiotics: some key questions answered. *International Journal of Market Research*, **44**(3), 251–265.

Leech, C. and September, K. (2004) Semiotics and narrative congruence. Leveraging consumer insights through product placement, ESOMAR, Consumer Insight Conference, Vienna, April.

Manning, P. K. (1987) Semiotics and Fieldwork, Qualitative Research Methods Series 7, Sage, California.

Marion, G. and Hetzel, P. (1995) Contributions of French Semiotics to Marketing Research Knowledge. Part I, ESOMAR, Marketing and Research Today, January.

Marion, G. and Hetzel, P. (1995) Contributions of French Semiotics to Marketing Research Knowledge. Part II, ESOMAR, Marketing and Research Today February.

Neilson, J. (2003) Teacher Training Agency – Less is more: how a reduction in call volumes spelt success for the TTA, Institute of Practitioners in Advertising, Bronze Winner, IPA Area Effectiveness Awards.

Okin, G. (1999) Electrolux, Account Planning Group (UK), Creative Planning Awards.

Origlia, C. (2003) Sensory semiotics: culture sensitive, holistic research approaches to explore sensory complexity, ESOMAR, Fragrance Conference, Lausanne, March.

Rowland, G. (2003) The slag of all semioticians, Market Research Society, Annual Conference.

Ryan, L. (2004) Life beyond the focus group, ESOMAR, Asia Pacific Conference, Shanghai, March.

Stuart, J. (1994) Chicken Tonight: Advertising that Dares to Come Out of the Closet, Institute of Practitioners in Advertising, IPA Effectiveness Awards.

Valentine, V. (1995) Opening up the black box: Switching the paradigm of qualitative research, ESOMAR, Qualitative Research, Paris, December

Valentine, V. (2002) Using semiotics to build powerful brands for children, *Young Consumers*, **4**(2), 9–16.

Valentine, V. (2002) Repositioning Research: a new language model, *International Journal of Market Research*, **44**(2), 163–192.

Valentine, V. (2002) What is webness? ESOMAR, Internet Conference, Berlin, February, 265–280.

Vallance, C. (1995) Account Planning Group (UK), Creative Planning Awards.

Vilhalemm, T. (1997) Construction of otherness via cross-cultural advertising: "we" versus "other" semiotic dichotomy in east European markets, ESOMAR, Qualitative Research, Singapore.

White, R. (2005) Semiotics deciphered, *Admap*, September, Issue 464, 16–17.

25
Creative Approaches for the Fuzzy Front End

Lucile Rameckers and Stefanie Un

INTRODUCTION

Seizing Today's Challenges in Innovation

Companies are continually on the look out for new opportunities for innovation and innovation is set high on management agendas. Companies can no longer rely on technological break-throughs and incremental product development solely for innovative solutions. Companies are forced to explore the territory of innovation beyond today, moving from a traditional linear innovation process towards a creative innovation process to be able to anticipate the changeable consumer in order to create new solutions. In this chapter, we will discuss this from the perspective of Philips Design, part of Royal Philips, a healthcare, lifestyle and technology company, aimed at delivering products, services and solutions that improve the quality of people's lives.

Philips Design translates technology into human-focused solutions, from products to interfaces and communications as part of the total brand experience, for today and the future. Exploring the future implies a different approach to design and innovation as well as a different way of conducting market research, in which people rather than solutions are put at the core. We will discuss in this section:

- a non-linear approach to innovation beyond today that leaves more space for exploration and creativity;
- a "people" research approach that is aimed at engaging people in design and innovation processes, rather than market research which is aimed at gathering data about customers, competitors and the market; and
- the implications for research conducted at the early phases of innovation.

The core focus of this section is on process and practices around *innovation within an organisation*, rather than the adoption of innovation by users or the rate of the adoption once a solution is on the market (Rogers, 1995).

WHY INNOVATE?

For companies it becomes increasingly challenging to maintain, grow and sustain profits in their current line of business. Opportunities are sought in unmet customer needs, new market segments or new market directions. Innovation has become a complex activity in which products,

Market Research Handbook, 5th Edition. Edited by M. van Hamersveld and C. de Bont.
© 2007 John Wiley & Sons, Ltd.

services, user needs and technologies need to be integrated, while bringing a lot of different stakeholders together, which isn't easy to achieve. Most companies are walking along the same path to meet a common aim: to ensure growth and profit through continuous innovation. They encounter similar challenges in achieving successful innovation: dealing with the *complexity* of innovation within an organisation, as well as the *convergence and commoditisation* in different markets and industries.

Complexity of Innovation within Organisations

In many organisations, the innovation process is translated conventionally into a so-called innovation funnel, see Figure 25.1, through which ideas are gathered, steered and controlled. First, a broader perspective is taken to come up with a multitude of creative ideas. These creative ideas are then later assessed with criteria, as set up by the business to come to a smaller selection of ideas. Eventually these ideas are steered towards more specific "best in class" ideas that should be further developed into marketable solutions. In reality, such an approach steers outcomes according to specific criteria that are set up beforehand, and leaves little room for true creativity, exploration or out-of-the-box-thinking.

Convergence in Industry and Commoditisation in Innovation

Looking at the different industries, they have become more homogeneous than ever before. Whereas in the past each industry had its specific products and customers, today these industries target the same customer with similar solutions. As an example: entertainment in the living room is no longer connected solely to the industry of Consumer Electronics. Feared competitors for the living room who offer multi-functional solutions come from industries such as computing, telecommunications and automation. At the same time, people feel overwhelmed by the offerings available to them. Throughout the past, a vast number of innovations entered the market; people own, have or use all the possible solutions that one can think of. Where in the past, new and not-yet-existing products were introduced, room for truly new solutions

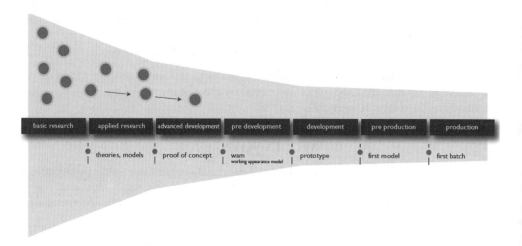

Figure 25.1   Conventional innovation funnel

has become scarce, as most imaginable solutions already exist or are being replaced by better fitting options. Think of, for example the diminishing interest in physical encyclopedias, due to the growing number of people who have access to digital online encyclopedias such as Wikipedia.

NEW WAYS TO INNOVATE: INCORPORATING CREATIVITY AND PEOPLE

Faced with the challenges of innovation within corporations today, we can no longer treat innovation as a singular process. Many companies acknowledge that innovation goes beyond technology development in itself. Anticipating people, exploring future possibilities and thinking out-of-the-box is valued within many companies and is seen as a creative source for idea generation and in the end innovation, but not one that is easy to realise. Innovation is a complex process in which different elements have to be brought together in the right mix to find new areas for innovation. Innovation requires a new way of thinking or new structures. In that regard, creativity in the process of innovation becomes of increasing importance, as it enables companies (a) *to look beyond today*; to explore and to imagine what innovative possibilities for the future might be, as well better understand how companies can (b) *anticipate people and their lives* in a future context.

Imagine the Future

The process of innovation should allow room for unintended innovative ideas. These innovative ideas should be explored for their immediate as well as future potential. Innovation processes should be focused on "breathing life into delicate ideas", in which there is room for both "failures" and successes, to turn these eventually into potential tangible solutions, today, tomorrow or in the distant future (Gardien, 2006).

In this view, innovation is not solely about managing innovation into a process. The innovation process should be seen as a network of options, rather than a traditional "innovation funnel". This network of options needs to be developed, allowing for creativity and exploration and taking into account different time horizons; see Figure 25.2. (Baghai et al., 1999). Organizations have to manage the three different time horizons simultaneously in order to be able to innovate effectively. Innovation at "horizon 1" is aimed at defending and extending a company's core business, which is related to innovation for today, e.g. product improvements. Innovation at "horizon 2" is aimed at developing and building new business, whereas "horizon 3" is about creating viable options for the further future. Recognising and anticipating different time horizons for innovation purposes enables a specific focus on new opportunities either in line with or beyond current business.

Provide People with Meaningful Solutions: Today and in the Future

It is not only differentiating in innovation for today and the future that is crucial. Creating innovative solutions that matter to people is of as much importance. Understanding what people really want and need in their lives and taking the different time horizons into account on which innovation is realisable is key in creating solutions that add value to people's lives.

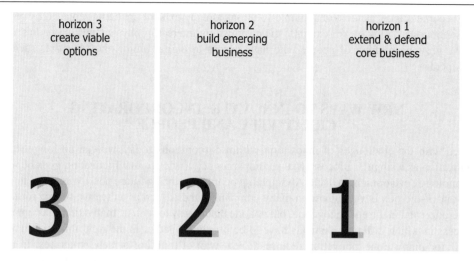

Figure 25.2   Horizon model

The future is a difficult topic to study via conventional consumer research methods, as it's almost impossible for people to talk about their potential or even latent future needs. It requires an approach that goes beyond typical quantitative and qualitative market research, as this type of research refers to the status of today. To create a better understanding of which and how possible *future* solutions can add value to people's lives, a research approach has been set up that *engages* people over time. Besides engaging them, people are invited to *co-create experiences* in the form of experience prototypes. These experience prototypes are possible physical embodiments of a future solution and create a way to uncover the future together with people. They help people to imagine and experience, in a tangible manner, potential future solutions that are in many other aspects no more than vague descriptions (Gardien, 2006). These potential future solutions, based on insights and co-created user experiences, can be used to validate a possible value proposition. The following three sections will go more in depth into respectively how we can engage people in innovation; its implications for research and how experience prototypes help to make tangible and understand what people might value in the future.

ENGAGING PEOPLE IN INNOVATION

To put people at the heart of creation and innovation – beyond tomorrow – "The Four Principles of Engagement" are created to guide the research process with the aim of engaging end users in the entire creation and innovation process, from the early stages onwards. The main aspects of the Four Principles of Engagement are:

- understanding people in the context of their everyday lives;
- involving people early in the creation and innovation process;
- creating a "continuous dialogue" with people;
- regarding people as co-creators.

The Four Principles of Engagement

> It is not about understanding people's opinions on specific products, brands or technology only. It is more about understanding people's everyday routines and rituals, their experiences and the lives they live that tells us how future solutions can add value.

Principle 1. Understand People in the Context of Their Everyday Lives

Understand Daily Life and Its Dynamics

In conventional market research, research is often done in one-off settings. Striving to take conventional market research further, we aim to understand people's daily lives including its dynamics of everyday life that goes beyond technology or specific products. For example, what are people's routines and rituals, how do they interact with others, etc.?

Understand the Personal, Cultural and Social Context

As in traditional market research the focus lies on the individual and his/her personal motivations. It is necessary to establish knowledge on how people and their needs are connected to the communities, the groups, the environment they live in and its object therein. Understanding this broader societal and cultural context increases our understanding of what people tell us about their personal context.

Towards an Understanding of Experiences around Needs

Whereas in conventional market research the main emphasis lies in evaluating, tracking or testing of specific needs, the experiences around these needs are of interest as well. The experiences that people go through are processes that happen over time and have many aspects that make them much more complex to investigate than solely needs.

> How can people be part of innovation? Through involving them early in the innovation process, rather than solely at the end.

Principle 2. Involve People Early in the Process

In many cases end users are involved at the end of an innovation process to, for example, test and evaluate a prototype that is as good as ready to be marketed. We aim to integrate end users as early as possible in the innovation process – ideally the fuzzy front end of innovation – to use this in the direction setting of solution development. In these early phases of innovation the needs and values of a person's life need to be taken along.

> How can we keep people involved in innovation? Through creating a "continuous dialogue" over a period of time.

Principle 3. Create a Continuous Dialogue with People

Besides involving people in early stages of the innovation process, we also aim to create a dialogue with people in various encounters. A dialogue enables one to build further on specific issues, collect additional feedback on ideas and clarify things that were misunderstood. Through a dialogue, iterative loops are created throughout the entire process that feed the interaction between end users, designers and researchers; as every insight and every action can lead to another insight and another action and in the end another direction for solutions.

> How can we create solutions that add value for people? Through involving people as experts of their own lives and see them as co-creators, rather than participants.

Principle 4. People are Co-Creators

Rather than merely perceiving people as passive respondents, people are considered as partners who are engaged in research and creation: they become co-researchers as they are invited to research and explore their own lives. End-users become co-designers as well, creating their own relevant and meaningful experiences. It testifies to an interest in their personal life rather than confronting them with specific concepts, product ideas, brands or technology, or any other business issue.

Summarised, the principles have to be reflected in research methods that:

1. Understand people in the context of their lives and not so much solely the products, services, brands or technology they use;
2. Involve people already in early phases in the research and creation process;
3. Creating a dialogue with people;
4. Consider people as co-creators, rather passive respondents;

in order to feed and inspire the creation and innovation process.

PUTTING IT INTO PRACTICE: IMPLICATIONS FOR RESEARCH

Engaging and co-creating with people requires specific methodologies, techniques and tools that go beyond those used in conventional market research. Methodologies should be able to incorporate creative elements in order to obtain a better understanding of people and ultimately engage with end users. Therefore we propose to:

- use multi-disciplinary techniques to collect insights;
- adapt research and creation processes to engage people;
- use creative tools to communicate with multiple stakeholders.

Using Multi-Disciplinary Techniques to Collect Insights

Beyond Traditional Research

In-depth interviewing and focus groups by themselves are no longer sufficient to understand and engage end users. These techniques are based on pre-set questions that generate answers that only skim the surface (Atkinson, 1998). They are too fixed to explore beyond existing interpretations and explanations and find new and relevant meanings. Looking for personal meanings and experiences, we need to focus on techniques that allow for more openness and flexibility, taking people and their perspectives as the main source of information. The techniques and tools should be based on both Ethnographic approaches as well as Design research approaches, in which analytical and creative aspects are combined into one approach.

Combining the *analytical, structured and "objective"* conventional research approaches with the more *intuitive, flexible and "subjective"* design research approaches brings an enriched and better understanding of people and the context of their lives. Therefore, involving designers more in the research process is of importance and makes researchers more aware of how to make sense of data specifically for the sake of innovation and design (Beyer & Holtzblatt, 1997). Combining methods from both a research as well as design discipline helps to understand and engage users better in the design and development of new products. Core techniques used for this are for example, participatory design, user-centred design, ethnography, contextual design (Kujula, 2002) storytelling and enactment of activities. These techniques allow us to follow the participant's life, capturing the richness and broadness of how people experience their world, and integrating on-going experiences with memories from the past and aspirations for the future (Atkinson, 1998).

Adapting the Research and Creation Process to Incorporate Insights and Engagement

To put the Principles of Engagement in practice, the Multiple Encounter Approach has been developed (see Figure 25.3). This approach is characterised by its multiple encounters with people over a period of time throughout the entire innovation process in order to involve them early and continuously. The different and multiple encounters create an ongoing dialogue and two-way interaction with people. The encounters focus on capturing the dynamics in everyday life rather than observing the facts. This provides deeper insights as well as a larger social context about people's lives and the interactions and changes in it.

The nature and objective of each encounter is different, depending on the particular phase of creation and innovation. Therefore, encounters with end users can be either face-to-face or online; in a generic or specific context; built around their "values and needs" or their feedback

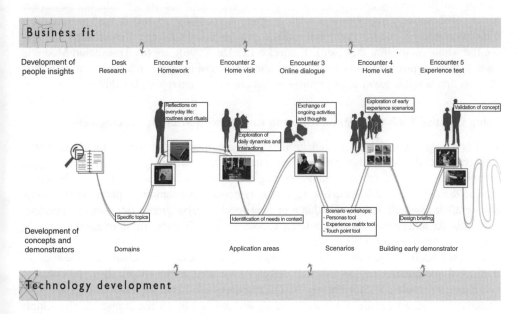

Figure 25.3 Multiple encounter approach

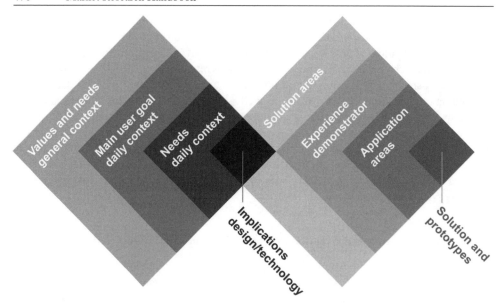

Figure 25.4   Translation model

on conceptual ideas. Whatever the core or nature of the encounter, each encounter has its specific aim and builds upon the previous encounter.

Translating Intangible Research Outcomes into Tangible Solutions

Throughout the creation and innovation process, researchers and designers translate values and needs collaboratively into solutions while keeping the personal context in the forefront. This translation is not a one-off event, but rather a process consisting of different steps throughout the whole innovation trajectory (Rameckers & Un, 2006); see the Translation Model in Figure 25.4. It moves from general values and needs towards specified needs in daily life, towards first tangible experience prototypes and ultimately into tangible solutions.

Using Creative Tools to Communicate and Engage with Multiple Stakeholders

The knowledge and insights gathered through the engagement of end users should be kept alive and brought to life for stakeholders involved in innovation. A creative tool to inspire and trigger professionals from different disciplines on insights, beyond traditional reporting, is "Personas" (Bueno & Rameckers, 2003). Personas are archetypical representations of people created from ethnographic research with people that represent specific target groups or segments. Personas have, just like real people, names, preferences, occupations, friends, life stories, values, needs, fears, aspirations, etc. (see Figure 25.5).

The methodology used to create Personas is based on a complementary combination of traditional and creative research, which makes Personas an enriched and illustrative way to communicate results. Within Philips Design research-based Personas are used as a tool to communicate about people, their lives, needs and wishes in an illustrative, lively, simple manner and ultimately create solutions beyond today and for tomorrow.

Figure 25.5   Example of Personas tool

MAKING THE FUTURE TANGIBLE

Creating a User Experience through Experience Prototypes

Through engagement creative ideas can be made tangible: user experiences can be better attuned to people in Experience Prototypes. Based on insights and the translations of them into design and technology specific user experiences are identified that come to life in a so-called experience prototype, which embodies a possible future solution. The primary goal of an experience demonstrator is to bring across the specific experience build around specific user needs, rather than the presentation of specific product features and the technology behind it. They are not necessarily fully workable prototypes, as the technology behind the demonstrator is often still in development (Andrews, Geurts & Kyffin, 2005). That said, they must have a reasonably "finalised" execution, and as such are particularly suited to involving the end-user in exploring both the medium-term and distant possibilities. In that sense, Experience Prototypes refer to a new way of thinking about innovation, leaving room for adjustment throughout the innovation process.

There are several advantages in developing an Experience Prototype. One is that in conventional market research it is almost impossible for people to talk about their potential or even latent future needs; these experience demonstrators create a way to uncover the future together with people. A second advantage is that an experience demonstrator acts as a tool to help R&D departments clarify what type of technology developments and applications make sense in people's everyday life. Thirdly, an experience prototype serves as a developmental aid to help the business organisation imagine and understand the concept behind the demonstrator, stimulate the innovation and development discussion between designers and business and create food for thought that permeates throughout the organisation and/or industry to become a marketable product (Rameckers & Un, 2006). For these reasons, the creation of early experience demonstrators will become a crucial step in the innovation process where different parties collaborate to develop ambient, system-based solutions for the future.

Case Study: Lifestyle Home

Shaping your own connected experiences

The Future Connected Living

"Lifestyle Home" presents a vision for the future of connected living that embraces a diversity of tastes, habits and needs. It proposes that people will value solutions they can easily adapt to match as closely as possible their personal requirements. This is vividly illustrated by a set of three experience prototypes they can adapt to match their personal requirements. Each prototype targets a different type of person, and illustrates how a family of solutions can be adapted to support many lifestyles. People are free to select, tailor and enjoy their digital media and connected experiences to best suit their unique situation.

The aim of Lifestyle Home is to show that the future can be experienced today with the help of experience prototypes. It embodies a future vision, and makes it possible for people to imagine and understand possible future solutions.

Applying Future Technologies to Shape People's Experiences

The starting point for Lifestyle Home was a clear focus on user experience, and was based on the complexities and dynamics of potential users' lives. Using an approach called "Multiple Encounters", we involved and engaged people more fully throughout the fuzzy front end of innovation, so helping to develop solutions that were better attuned to people's needs and abilities and that make sense in their everyday lives. The experience prototypes are developed around three Personas: Alexandra, Simone and Justin. They focus on the three key user experiences of easy personalization, intuitive use and content-free flow.

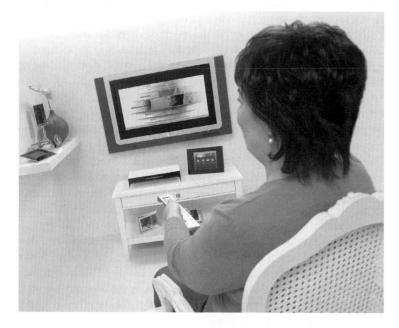

Figure 25.6   Lifestyle Home Personas: Alexandra, Simone, Justin

Figure 25.6   (*Continued*)

Each of the prototypes makes use of a host of new and emerging (Philips) technologies. And wherever possible, standards have been used to increase the chances of innovations being more widely adopted.

Source: Lifestyle Home, Shape your own connected experiences, 2006, Philips Design.

CONCLUSION: INNOVATION BEYOND TODAY

Sustaining as well as growing profits is crucial for organisations to be able to play the game. For companies it is essential to explore the territory of innovation, beyond the current scope of one to three years that most companies operate on today. To conclude, we would like to recap some of the implications of exploring innovation.

Firstly, innovation should not be seen as a linear approach, but as a much more complex process, non-linear surely, where creative ideas need to be nourished and developed. In such a process, creativity plays a crucial role as well, as it looks beyond the conventional lines of thinking and allows for future exploration. Secondly, exploring innovation through creativity has implications for the way research for innovation is conducted. Rather than focusing on the conventional *market* research approaches, we focus on *people research* in which people are considered as co-researchers and co-creators who are engaged in the innovation process. Thirdly, through engaging people in innovation, researchers, people and designers work together to co-create tangible future solutions, so-called Experience Prototypes. These Experience Prototypes enable the exploration of specific future experiences in an explicit and physical manner, both by potential future end-users as well as professionals from the business.

Any organisation that is exploring new ways to innovate has to take into account that new ways imply adaptation in ways of working on innovation and conducting research. Creativity and engagement of people are crucial to exploring future solutions and identifying new business opportunities that result in solutions that make sense to people and their lives.

REFERENCES

Andrews, A. et al. (2006) Lifestyle Home, shaping your own connected experiences, Philips Design Positioning Paper.

Atkinson, R. (1998) *The Life Story Interview*. Sage Publications Inc.

Beyer, H. and Holtzblatt, K. (1997) *Contextual design: A Customer-Centered Approach to Systems Designs*. The Academic Press.

Baghai, M., Coley, S. and White, D. (1999) *The Alchemy of Growth, Kickstarting and Sustaining Growth Within Your Company*. Texere.

Bueno, M. and Rameckers, L. (2003) Understanding people in new ways, Personas in context: forging a stronger link between research and its application in Design. Proceedings of Esomar conference.

Gardien, P. (2006) Breathing life into delicate ideas, Developing a network of options to increase the chance of innovation success, Philips Design Positioning Paper.

Kujula, S. (2002) User Involvement: a review of the benefits and challenges. In: Soininen, T. (ed), Preprints, Software Business and Engineering Institute, Helsinki, University of Technology, Report number: HUT-SoberIT-BI. Espoo, Finland.

Kyffin, S., Geurts, L. and Andrews, A. (2005) TO:DO, Technical Objectives: Design Objectives – Integrating design, technology and business for rapid, people-driven innovation, Philips Design Positioning Paper.

Rameckers, L. and Un, S. (2006) People insights at the fuzzy front of innovation. How to achieve human-centered innovation?, Philips Design Positioning Paper.

Rogers, E.M. (1995) *Diffusion of Innovations*. The Free Press.

26
Brain Science: In Search of the Emotional Unconscious

David Penn

INTRODUCTION

If you have attended a market research conference in the last few years, you will have noticed an increased emphasis on the brain, with research practitioners looking to exciting new insights from the brain sciences to help them explore emotions and unconscious responses. It is a rapidly developing area, and one which has already spawned a new offshoot from conventional research: *neuromarketing*, which uses new brain imaging technology to observe response inside the brain.

Brain science draws from a range of academic disciplines – mostly from cognitive neuroscience, but also from philosophy, biology and evolutionary psychology – and the aim of this chapter is to build a bridge between academic theory and practice, and help research professionals understand both the technology and the philosophy that underlies brain science. If we know better, we can do better.

We might not realise it, but market research grew up under the influence of mid 20th century cognitive science, with its *"mind as machine"* metaphor, and many (particularly quantitative) researchers feel more at home with the *cognitive* aspects of behaviour than with the unconscious and emotional. This is particularly so in advertising and communications research, which has placed a lot of emphasis on conscious, rational measures such as recall and persuasion.

In the last two decades, brain science has challenged our view of the human mind and how it works and, by doing so, has challenged the emphasis which market researchers place on conscious and rational response – bringing the unconscious and emotional aspects of the mind into focus.

Increasingly, we've come to understand that unlocking the mystery of consciousness actually depends on figuring out the *unconscious* functions of the brain. Not Freud's unconscious – a repository for repressed memories – but rather the many things the brain does that are *not* available to consciousness. Unconscious processes include most of what the brain does – we can often be aware of what we're doing when these things happen, but much of the time consciousness is informed after the fact. So, when we ask someone *why* they made a particular brand choice, is their answer just a post-rationalisation of an unconscious or emotional reaction?

Understanding the emotional unconscious is the biggest challenge facing conventional market research, because it is becoming clear that researchers cannot understand the consumer mind adequately unless they understand its unconscious and emotional aspects. The possibility that so much of what we know about brands is absorbed unconsciously, and that choice

Market Research Handbook, 5th Edition. Edited by M. van Hamersveld and C. de Bont.
© 2007 John Wiley & Sons, Ltd.

between brands is driven by emotional processes, requires us to revisit our techniques (built mainly on rational choice models and verbal response) and acquire a new skill set to interpret and understand what consumers tell us.

WHAT IS "BRAIN SCIENCE" AND HOW DOES BRAIN IMAGING WORK?

What we call brain science is actually an amalgam of many different disciplines, the dominant one being *cognitive neuroscience*: the study of how cognition and emotion are implemented, either consciously or unconsciously, in the brain. It seeks to understand how the biology and neurochemistry of the brain relate both to behaviours (such as buying a product in a supermarket) and mental states (such as brand loyalty).

It is important, at this stage, to make clear the distinction between cognition and emotion, because, in brain science, the words are used differently from how most market researchers interpret them. Cognition refers to any mental event, either conscious or unconscious; i.e., any mental event more complex than a reflex. It encompasses all forms of "thinking" and "reasoning", either high level problem solving (so-called complex or cold cognition) or low level mental activity. It thus includes attitudes and beliefs about brands and products, as well as habitual purchasing, e.g. when we buy things "on automatic pilot".

Emotion is different from cognition in that it is an *embodied* rather than a mental state; thus emotions are brain and body states that arise in response to certain external stimuli or to certain internal need or goal states. Emotions are, by definition, not thought-through responses; they are involuntary impulses toward or away from a stimulus. Emotions *give rise* to feelings, because feelings are the conscious component of emotion.

In practice, the dividing line between emotions, feelings and cognition is so hard to draw that most neuroscientists accept that all cognition has an emotional component. It is this belief that fundamentally differentiates brain science from mid 20th century cognitive science, which pursued the functional organisation of the mind without too much reference to the brain: seeing the mind as essentially *disembodied*, or floating free of the biological constraints of mind and body. Because cognitive science defined the mind by its functions, it paid little or no attention to the brain structures which underlie it. Brain science takes the reverse view that we cannot understand the mind without understanding the brain.

Thus the single big idea that underpins brain science is that of the embodied mind, and from this flows three propositions:

1. Unconscious processes account for most of what we think, feel and do.
2. Conscious reasoning accounts for only a small part of our 'thinking'.
3. Emotion precedes our conscious feelings and works in tandem with rational thinking to help us make (better) decisions.

The implications of this new thinking for market research are enormous. If the "handed down" wisdom (from mid 20th century cognitive science) is that consumers make rational choices and, moreover, can *explain* those choices, then brain science suggests, more or less, the opposite. In this alternative view, unconscious processes *mediate* cognitive rational decision making, leading to a choice, which can only be half understood (at best) by introspection. In other words, we can't always say with any reliability, *why* we made a particular choice. Sometimes, we just "do it", because "we always do it".

Brain Imaging Techniques and the Birth of Neuromarketing

Over the last decade, the development of brain imaging techniques (such as functional magnetic resonance imaging, or fMRI, and electroencephalography (EEG) has made the neuroscientific search for the unconscious and emotional especially fascinating. The significance of these imaging techniques for market research is that they allow us to link a certain behaviour not only to its mental counterpart (as in traditional psychology or cognitive science), but to specific brain structures or activities.

The availability of brain imaging techniques has given rise to an entirely new discipline: *neuromarketing*, which attempts to explain buying behaviours and attitudes to brands by correlating them with observed responses in the brain. The applications (and limitations) of neuromarketing are explained in more detail below (see "Is neuromarketing the answer?").

The two techniques that have so far been most widely deployed for marketing purposes (neuromarketing) are fMRI and EEG:

Functional MRI (fMRI) shows the areas where brain activity is greatest, i.e where there is most oxygen. Because neuronal firing is fuelled by glucose and oxygen which are carried in the blood, when a part of the brain fires up, these substances flow toward it. As the latest scanners produce up to four images a second, and the brain takes about half a second to react to a stimulus, this technique has the potential to show the ebb and flow of activity in different parts of the brain as it reacts to stimuli or undertakes tasks.

fMRI is proving to be one of the most rewarding techniques for brain imaging, but is phenomenally expensive and brain mappers often have to share with clinicians who have a more pressing claim on it. It also requires that the subject lies extremely still within a large circular drum that makes a loud rhythmic thumping sound. A large magnet is placed around the subject's head that measures the blood flow throughout the brain. They can view stimuli through a small mirror, listen to sounds and touch things. In short, not a "normal" experience!

fMRI is good for finding out *where* activity is taking place, but not very good for telling us the *sequence* of things that happen in the brain. For this we need to use EEG, which works on the principle that mental experience, even when below our normal level of consciousness, has a corresponding electrical signature capable of detection. EEG measures changes in the brain's systematic electrical potential during different activities. Essentially it measures brainwaves – the electrical patterns created by the rhythmic oscillations of neurons – by picking up signals via electrodes placed in the skull, The latest version takes readings from dozens of different spots and compares them, building a picture of the varying activity across the brain. Brain mapping with EEG often uses Event-Related Potentials (ERPs), which simply means that an electrical peak (potential) is related to a particular stimulus. For example, Steve Luck at the University of Iowa has found that certain ERPs are correlated with visual attention.

THE THEORETICAL PRINCIPLES OF BRAIN SCIENCE

This section discusses some of the key hypotheses of brain science.

The Interconnectedness of the Brain Facilitates the Joint Operation of Rationality and Emotion

A brief tour of the brain's physiology makes plain the interconnectedness of emotional and cognitive functions (Figure 26.1).

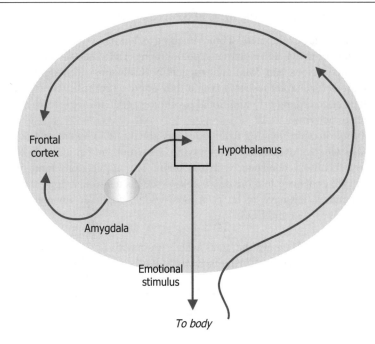

Figure 26.1   The interconnectedness of the feeling and thinking parts of the brain
(*Source*: Carter, Rita *Mapping the Mind,* 1999, p. 82)

Everything we see, hear, taste and touch comes in through the thalamus, which controls the flow of sensory information throughout the brain. A large part of information ends up in the frontal cortex, the "intelligent" part of the brain, where we make plans and decisions. The bottom of the thalamus is fused with the hypothalamus, which regulates important bodily functions such as changes in heartbeat and breathing, which are coupled with emotional reactions. The thalamus is located close to the limbic system, which contains the *amygdala*, responsible for analysing every incoming signal and evaluating its emotional meaning (Figure 26.1).

The key point is, that there is constant *two-way traffic* between the limbic system and the frontal cortex. Any information processed by the conscious brain is sent to the limbic system to be evaluated emotionally. The reaction goes back to the frontal cortex, where it is interpreted as feeling.

From Think, Feel, Do to Feel, Do, Think

In cognitive science, the most prevalent explanation of emotion was *appraisal theory*, which argued that for a stimulus to produce an emotional response, the brain must first appraise (consider) its significance. Basically, this sees emotion as a "thought" response (think – feel – do). But leading neuropsychologist, Joseph Le Doux, believes that the interconnectedness of thalamus and amygdala enables us to react first, *before* the stimuli that provoke an emotional response have been analysed by the thinking brain. Thus with an emotion like fear, the conscious feeling of fear is only part of a bodily reaction that includes sweating, pounding heart, etc. According to Le Doux, the system that sets this process in train acts unconsciously, before we even know we're in danger.

This replaces the traditional cognitive model of *think – feel – do* with one of *feel – do – think*. The new model's significance for market research is huge, because it suggests that what we *think* is happening (e.g. when we respond to a marketing message) is only the end result of an unconscious process that we are actually unaware of.

Emotions Precede Feelings and Help us Make Better Decisions

One of the most enduring "dualities" in western thought is the separation of emotion, or passion, from reason.

It was the neuropsychologist Antonio Damasio who reconnected emotion and reason by showing what goes wrong when we have reason but not emotion, and lose their inter-connectedness. His observations, of patients whose emotional capacity is impaired, show that, without emotional "connectedness", we make very poor decisions, even if we retain the cognitive ability to "solve" a given problem.

Damasio is in little doubt about the power of unconscious emotional motivation: "We do not need to be conscious of the inducer of an emotion and often are not. Nor can we control them wilfully. You may be in a happy or sad state, but can't say why. We are about as effective at stopping an emotion as stopping a sneeze."

Thus, emotions are not the same as feelings, because emotions come first and feelings second.

How do Emotions and Reason Work Together?

The world is so complex that we almost never make wholly rational decisions – we simply do not have the time or the capacity to consider every choice we make. Operating unconsciously, emotions act as *heuristics*, basically a way of making a decision where no "logical" solution is available. We use heuristics all the time to help us navigate the multiplicity of brand choices offered to us, particularly in markets where there is little or no functional product differentiation.

Over our lives, we gain factual and emotional experience and associate emotions with objects that might otherwise be neutral in emotional terms. Over time we do more than just respond automatically: we create *emotional associations* with courses of action, and when a similar situation arises we activate the appropriate emotions. In other words, a gut feeling may lead you to refrain from a choice, which previously had negative consequences, or guide the adoption of an alternative positive choice. Hence, we often buy things which make us *feel* good, and then rationalise our choice afterwards.

The Unconscious Explains Most of What We Feel, Think and Do

Until quite recently (in historical terms) the mind and the conscious mind were seen as synonymous. It was not until the mid 20th century, when the idea that computers had parallels with human problem solving gave birth to cognitive science, that we came to accept the existence of *internal* mechanisms that process information. Cognitive science hypothesised that, while we can have conscious access to the outputs of cognitive processes, we often work in ignorance of the processes themselves.

Cognitive science sees the mind as being both *implicit and explicit* – terms borrowed from the study of memory, where it is now widely accepted that there are two distinct brain systems:

- The one engaged in forming consciously accessible explicit memories.
- Another that is capable of learning and storing information *implicitly*, i.e. without us being consciously aware of it.

By breaking the equation of consciousness with mind, cognitive psychology opened the door for the study of cognition and consciousness *in* the brain.

Working Memory

Working Memory is like a temporary storage mechanism where thinking and reasoning take place. The stuff in Working Memory is what we're currently thinking about or paying attention to and it is tempting to equate consciousness with focused attention. However, consciousness and working memory are not exactly the same.

If you are reading a book, you ignore things around you, yet if something meaningful occurs in the background like someone calling your name, you stop reading and turn to the caller. Thus while your conscious mind is ignoring everything apart from the book, your brain is not.

Philosopher Daniel Dennet described the conscious and unconscious aspects of thought in terms of serial or parallel functions – a theory which influenced the development of the *Low Attention Processing model* of advertising, which we will discuss later. Basically, this model makes the distinction between the brand information that we consciously process in our working memory, and other information that is processed either at very low levels of awareness or *implicitly* (below awareness). The implication being that, whilst we may have been affected by advertising, and other brand communication, we may well not recall having seen it.

The Cognitive Unconscious

Higher level cognitive reasoning exists to help us make considered choices, and cope with the complexity of the world, while much of the day to day stuff is taken care of by our *cognitive unconscious*, working through the lower level processors.

The cognitive unconscious takes care of the mind's routine processes. It's thinking, but not as we know it: it's what enables you to avoid obstacles when walking or driving a car, etc. The brain can process information below awareness and store it implicitly or unconsciously and it can influence our thought at a later date. Thus when we buy things on "automatic pilot" (i.e. without thinking) that's the cognitive unconscious at work.

HOW DO WE BUILD A BRIDGE BETWEEN THEORY AND PRACTICE?

We could say there are two brains:

- a cognitive one that knows, analyses, reflects, calculates and makes decisions;
- and an *emotional brain* that reacts spontaneously, immediately and intuitively to perceived stimuli.

The picture of emotions that is merging from brain science is largely one of automaticity: the initial response to most marketing messages appears to be automatic and does not require conscious awareness of the stimuli. Whatever the exact truth of this, what is certain is that the

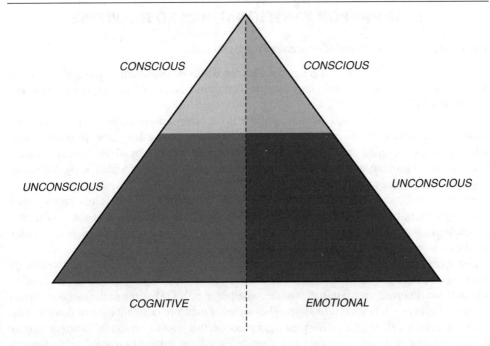

Figure 26.2   The Conscious and Unconscious Mind

choices made by the emotional brain are quick, automatic and certain. The emotional brain believes its judgements to be true and that's why, whenever emotions conflict with thinking, emotion wins.

This has two fundamental implications for market research:

The Most Important Brand Response is Emotional

Brain science suggests that emotions powerfully influence much of our brand choice. We have seen that, in neuroscientific terms, emotions are *not* the same as feelings – they are simple, unconscious and non-verbal responses: shortcuts, that help us to make choices in ever more crowded markets. It follows that, to fully understand a brand, research needs to *drill down* – to the emotional unconscious. If we concentrate only on expressed feelings, we run the risk that emotions are disguised or (post) rationalised by the respondent.

Most of Our Decisions are Unconscious

Because we are bombarded with information, there simply isn't time to think through everything we do. Brain science suggests that much of our behaviour, and our response to brands, is not thought-through: it's unconscious and intuitive; furthermore, that there is no need to think it through, particularly if the messages are emotional. A lot of our "thinking" about brands and advertising may not, therefore, be accessed easily via standard (conscious) questioning.

LOOKING FOR EMOTIONAL BRAND RESPONSE

The Problem: Conventional Research only goes so Far

The problem for market research is that the traditional way of examining "emotion" is usually by asking subjects to reflect back (i.e. introspect) on some past emotional experience: *How did it make you feel?*

Yet this doesn't make much theoretical sense if we believe unconscious mental processes pre-date conscious ones (in evolutionary terms) and also pre-date language. In other words, asking people to describe or reflect on their emotional states is beset by a basic methodological contradiction: How can we consciously access and explain something which is, by definition, unconscious and non-rational?

Introspection and verbal self-reporting (for example through qualitative research) cannot *explain* emotion, but can tell us how emotion *feels*, and indeed, are some of the only means available of knowing this. Feelings tend to come with a colouring of cognition, because they are the conscious representation of emotion in our thoughts.

The term "emotional brand response" is often used with little consideration given to its meaning. Generally it is used to connote a non-rational, and usually positive, response to a brand, and Franzen and Bauman wonder whether most of what we call emotional brand responses goes much beyond a (non-specific) sense of pleasure or likeability. In other words, what is normally called *affect*. This means, in practice, that a lot of "emotional" response may be encapsulated in simple measures that capture overall favourability toward, or preference for, a brand. In fact, preferences, or simple choices, replicate how simple emotions manifest themselves behaviourally.

Because we generally see a high correlation between brand preference and positive brand image, we like to think that it's the positive beliefs and feelings that drive the preference, whereas it's just as likely that the reverse is true. Memories linked to positive feelings are more easily accessed because they make brand choice easier and these positive feelings may act as heuristics – they become the dominant choice criterion. Thus in relatively risk free decisions, like frequent purchases, consumers are likely to let their feelings dominate: the brand choice *preceding* the rational consideration of a brand's attributes. Furthermore, consumers tend to protect their positive brand emotions – they do not want to hear anything negative about the brand they love, which would help to explain why those with a favourable brand disposition also have a positive brand image.

The idea that consumer decision-making is rational and linear with each stage causing the next, only really takes account, at best, of *one* of our two brains – the cognitive one. The alternative model overturns conventional wisdom by putting effect (or more specifically, *affect*) before the cause. Adoption of this alternative model frees us from the constraint of having to seek the explanation of affect in (conscious) verbal response and allows us to concentrate on the *manifestation* of affect. Once identified (as a dependent variable) we can then seek out the independent variables that might influence affect, be they in advertising, product or service factors.

The gap between what brain science hypothesises and the "handed down wisdom" indicates the need to bridge theory and current practice. In market research we often default too easily to the conscious and rational, simply because its easier to think that way and to frame questions that way. For example, in a marketing mix test, it's tempting to load the survey with questions about the relative contribution of various elements to eventual brand choice: *"How much did the pack influence you ... and what about the advertising ... ?"*

Is Neuromarketing the Answer?

We have seen that new brain-imaging techniques, such as fMRI and EEG have allowed scientists to record brain activity when participants carry out perceptual, cognitive and motor tasks. Among these developments, one of the most fascinating is the emergence of *neuromarketing*, which can be defined as the neurological study of a person's mental state and reactions while being exposed to marketing messages.

This nascent science is beginning to capture headlines, but so far there's not a lot of solid evidence on which to base an assessment of neuromarketing. The few published studies in neuromarketing have used fMRI only, although, in time, the use of EEG may enable us to have information both about brain localisation and the time course of brain processes.

The most famous, and indeed the only widely circulated study was conducted in the US at Baylor College in Houston, however. Using fMRI, researchers monitored brain response during a test of taste and brand preferences for Pepsi vs. Coke amongst 67 volunteers. On the blind test, stated preferences were balanced, but when told *what* they were drinking, sensory preferences were over-ridden, with a significant preference for Coke. None of which is particularly surprising, but the really interesting thing is the results of the brain imaging. Essentially, when subjects used their sense of taste alone, part of the prefrontal cortex lit up. But when subjects were then scanned, while a picture of a Coke can preceded their sips, the memory region called the hippocampus and another part of the prefrontal cortex lit up. The same was not true when they were told they were drinking Pepsi – indeed no brain areas showed a significant difference to Pepsi delivered with brand knowledge vs. Pepsi delivered without brand knowledge.

Both the brain regions affected by Coke branding have been previously implicated in modifying behaviour based on emotion and affect. "Our finding suggests that the hippocampus may participate in recalling cultural information that biases preference judgements . . . We hypothesise that cultural information biases preference decisions through the dorsolateral prefrontal cortex (DLPFC), with the hippocampus engaged to recall associated information."

This is brain science in action: with fMRI actually observing the neurological basis of a brand response. Not surprisingly, excited journalists were soon writing articles like "In Search of the Buy Button" or even "Pushing the Buy Button". Now, it is certainly true that this study identified the areas correlated with different mental tasks, but what exactly does it tell us? It is, in fact, open to a number of interpretations: we could have identified a part of the brain which is strongly associated with Coke, or with brands in general, or with affective response to brands, or to advertising. Alternatively, we might conclude that it is an area of the brain that is activated when people are certain of what they are drinking, or one that gets activated when taste and words are combined.

Moreover, it's also true that, from a simple blind vs. branded product test, we could have *inferred* that the change in preference scores (when Coke's branding was revealed) was due to the unconscious (emotional) impact of its branding. However the results of the brain imaging make this a much more robust hypothesis and, moreover, also appear to locate the response *specifically in a part of the brain*.

We have to admit that, when we first read about this experiment, it was like revisiting a familiar place, or looking again at a familiar painting and seeing it in a different way. After all, what we're observing in the prefrontal cortex and hippocampus is a reaction brought about by decades of *implicit learning*. A stimulus triggers a deep unconscious emotional response, which *automatically* generates a brand choice.

Neuromarketing – For and Against

It is important to distinguish between brain science, which is a new way of understanding the consumer mind, and neuromarketing, which seeks to supplant conventional market research. What brain science suggests is, that verbal response may mislead – particularly for emotional/ affective response – but neuromarketing seems to take this a stage further and says that we could use brain imaging to dispense with verbal response entirely.

If we accept that all that matters is brain, and that the mental world is an illusion, then it follows that all we need to do to understand the mind is to correlate mental activity with response in specific parts of brain. Then, after a while, there may be no need to *ask* the subject anything at all – just *look for* the correct brain response via fMRI, EEG, or similar. For example, Clint Kilts, of the Brighthouse Institute, argues that if the medial prefrontal cortex fires when you see a particular product, you are more likely to buy, because that product clicks with your mental self-image.

Yet, ironically, the discovery of the *interconnectivity* of the different parts of the brain and the reestablishment of the link between brain and mind (i.e. the rejection of Descartes' dualism), should lead us to challenge this sort of reductionism, not blindly accept it. Just because you *see* a brain response doesn't mean you can *explain* it; because the brain functions as an interconnected system, not a set of components, we can never see the complete picture, particularly at the higher level where meaning is constructed.

The (philosophical) problem is this:

1. We can introspect on our own feelings and thoughts, but *we can't see into* our own brain processes. That window is closed to us except through the third party route of brain imaging.
2. We can "look" into the brain using fMRI/EEG etc. and observe the neural correlates of mental activity, but we can't "see the mind" – how it feels to the person experiencing it. These experiences are usually categorised as *qualia*. Only conventional research permits this.

This means that all brain imaging is, by definition, completely correlational in that it can tell us that a part of the brain *is* active – whenever a subject is experiencing, or tells us they are thinking, a particular thing – but it cannot tell us *what* part of the mental process is actually being fulfilled, or *why* that particular part of the brain is active. A huge amount of (subjective) interpretation is required to make sense of brain imaging data, simply because of the huge number of possible interrelationships and possible causal links that exist between mental events and brain imaging output. It is therefore not as "objective" as it appears.

Neuroscientist Steven Rose goes so far as to suggest that brain imaging (and, by implication, neuromarketing) commits a category error by assuming that we can *locate* thought, affect or emotion in the brain at all, because (he argues) "such processes are not held in one location but in a pattern of dynamic interrelationships between multiple brain regions . . . ".

Leaving aside the philosophical debate, what is certainly true is that, beyond the Baylor Institute study discussed earlier, there is a dearth of objective case studies to conclusively demonstrate the effectiveness (or otherwise) of neuromarketing. This is mainly because brain imaging of all types is quite expensive – because of the technology and the high level of training needed to make sense of the output – and it also takes much longer than a conventional survey. A Google search on the subject throws up a few news articles (often from those concerned about the ethics, rather than the scientific objectivity, of neuromarketing), some excited, others sceptical, but little concrete evidence of progress.

There are, on the other hand, plenty of claims made by various start-up companies about the effectiveness of their particular approach to neuromarketing, be it through EEG or fMRI. However, almost none of the client companies who have used brain imaging techniques are willing to comment on results.

Douglas Rushkoff, writing in the NyPress, has this to say of neuromarketing:

> A decade or so from now, I suspect we will regard neuromarketing researchers and their techniques the way we regard phrenologists or blood-letters today. And we'll realize that the only people who ended up being hypnotized by their wares were the daft corporate executives who paid for them.

We wonder who will be proved right.

Making Retrospective Sense of Old Intuitive Practices

Often brain science makes retrospective sense of some old MR practices, particularly those based on inference rather than direct questioning.

We visit the unconscious every time we run a conjoint exercise, or a blind vs. branded test, or observe consumer behaviour (rather than simply asking questions); because, in each case, we're trying to infer the impact of unconscious motivation rather than relying on what people – consciously – tell us. The "test and control" approach, borrowed from experimental science, provides a good template because, by holding constant everything except the affective stimulus (such as a pack or an ad), we can identify the impact of that stimulus on a dependent measure of affect, such as brand preference.

There are three principles that we need to remember when trying to research unconscious, particularly affective, responses. These are *implicit, inference and indirect*.

Implicit

Implicit learning is the process by which we absorb a wealth of associations about a brand, some of which may be linked with affective response and others with emotions proper. Most of what we know about brands is not consciously learned, or processed in our working memory: there simply is not the time and, frankly, we have more important things to attend to. It has been described as a process by which we absorb (but do not interpret) emotional/affective associations which become linked to the brand over time via a low-level cognitive process called passive learning.

The evidence that feelings and attitudes can be influenced by experiences that cannot be (consciously) recalled is well established. This is why Graf and Schacter coined the term *implicit memory* to cover such phenomena. Schacter hypothesised the existence of a perceptual representation system (PRS) specialised in the recognition and processing of the exterior characteristics of objects and phenomena (visual forms, colours, etc.). These representations work outside our consciousness and cannot be brought into consciousness. Nevertheless, they exert subtle effects on the way that we feel about and react to the same objects represented to us.

In explicit memory, a learning experience is always required. In implicit memory, it is not. However in implicit memory, it is not essential for the learning experience to have also been unconscious (implicit). It may have been conscious but forgotten, i.e. it may have featured in Working Memory but not been consolidated into long-term memory. Arousal, repetition and recency all play a part in determining the process of consolidation, as do the hippocampus and amygdala.

Thus, in the Baylor study, referenced earlier, it can be argued the affective response triggered by Coke branding was the result of decades of implicit learning, by consistent and repetitious association of the Coke packaging and logo with pleasant and pleasurable experiences. Acceptance of the value of the principle of implicit, as opposed to explicit, learning (which involves our Working Memory) leads us to the second and third principles.

Inference

The second principle is that verbal self-reporting will not identify affective response as accurately as an *inferential technique*. In the Coke vs. Pepsi example, the actual brain process by which a sensory preference got converted into a brand preference could only be observed via brain imaging, because it is an unconscious (and hitherto invisible) mental process, way below the mental radar that we call awareness. (Although, it was actually not brain imaging per se, but the division of the test into blind and branded cells that allowed us to infer the affective response to Coke branding.) Had we *asked* respondents to explain why they preferred the taste of Coke it is likely the responses would have been "I just like it", "Coke just tastes better", etc. Probing further would not have helped, because respondents cannot describe a process that they're unaware of.

Indirect Questioning

Which brings us to the third principle: *indirect questioning*. We were able to learn more about affect by focusing on the *object* of the stimulus, i.e. brand favourability, rather than on the stimulus itself – the pack. In other words, asking respondents directly about their feelings about the pack would have been much less helpful than concentrating on the ultimate objective – creating a more favourable disposition toward the brand. Even when we use techniques such as logistic regression to identify the brand attributes or clusters of attributes that drive brand disposition, it is frequently the case that the most powerful driver is an attribute like "it's a brand for me". Frequently, this finding is dismissed as an auto-correlation or straight tautology, but it is just as likely that it shows how difficult it is to locate affect in specific verbal response. "I like it because I like it" may be a tautology, but it also may explain a lot about the nature of affect.

And even when our brand choices are not driven by affect, self-reporting does not always work that well, because we often use our cognitive unconscious to navigate a way through the vast choices of brands available. Essentially, this may be a simple habitual behaviour ("what I always do") rather than a resort to an emotionally underscored or patterned behaviour. It's analogous to the same unconscious cognitive behaviour that enables us to do everyday tasks without consciously considering what we're doing.

CHANGING THE WAY WE EVALUATE ADVERTISING

All of these issues and debates come together in the world of advertising research. It's no great surprise that many of those who have written about brain science and its implications have come from advertising backgrounds.

The earliest models of how advertising worked often assumed a simple linear relationship between attention (impact) and action. Models such as AIDA (Attention – Interest – Desire – Action) hypothesised that, through the medium of a persuasive message, information is *consciously processed* and can be accessed via conscious or Working Memory (the conscious, mental workspace that we use to solve our day to day problems).

Three of the academic theories we discussed earlier have proved particularly influential in challenging conscious, rational models of advertising.

The first is Le Doux's belief that the direct link between thalamus and amygdala enables the brain to react emotionally, prior to conscious awareness of stimuli, creating the possibility that emotional information might be processed independently of attention.

The second is Damasio's assertion of the primacy of *affect* over cognition (thinking). This, more or less, turns the cause and effect of AIDA on its head, because it suggests that emotions (not thinking) drive behaviour, and hypothesises that when emotion and cognition come into conflict, emotions win.

Finally, Daniel Dennet's notion of *parallel processing* of information, at high and low attention levels, creates the possibility of learning about brands via information processing at either no, or very low, levels of conscious awareness.

And two new models have emerged to challenge the conventional wisdom of how advertising works:

- Tim Ambler's MAC (Memory – Affect – Cognition) model hypothesises that it is the affective content that drives advertising effectiveness and our "thinking" merely supports a decision which may have already been made.
- Robert Heath's LAP (Low Attention Processing) model is heavily influenced by all the above, and hypothesises that *implicit learning* is probably much more important than explicit (conscious) processes – particularly for ads with high affective content, which is probably the majority of ads these days, at least in the UK and in other developed markets.

Yet the model that still implicitly (and often explicitly) underpins much of contemporary advertising research pre-dates this revolution. It still assumes a rational consumer who cognitively and consciously processes information received from advertising and is able to play it back to interviewers, through the medium of recall. This model probably made sense in the 50s and 60s, but, nowadays, with many more brands, more choice, yet fewer genuine differences to communicate, it seems improbable, to say the least, that this explains how most modern advertising works.

Can Affect *be* Processed Independently of Attention?

Because Heath believes that emotive advertising can be processed independently of attention, he argues that what's in our Working Memory (WM) will not reveal the emotive content of the advertising we process. He hypothesises that the more emotive an ad is, the less attention will be paid to it, citing work by Christie Nordheilm, who found a U-shaped relationship between favourability and repeated exposure to a message. On the other hand, with shallower processing there is enhancement of evaluation, with no subsequent downturn.

Millward Brown's Erik Du Plessis asks why emotive advertising should be processed at low level of attention. The role of emotion, he argues, is to drive our attention and to "shape and feed our conscious thought". We seek out the positive – the pleasurable rather than things which make us anxious or unhappy. Thus we pay attention to ads we like, and what we pay attention to we remember. This view comes somewhere close to the controversial "appraisal" theory of emotion discussed earlier, and tends to contradict the feel – do – think model which has, in most neuroscientists' view, superseded it.

Attention is necessary, Du Plessis argues, to impart new information, although he accepts that ads can work at low attention *"if there exist memories available to be refreshed"*.

Perhaps then, we need to make a distinction between "old news" (being told what we know already) and receiving new information about a brand. Even if the new information is affective (rather than rational) it is probable that it needs to be (cognitively) appraised in some form. Thus, for example, if Coca-Cola makes an advertisement, which transmits the same emotional messages that consumers have received countless times before, it may by-pass the conscious mind completely – simply because there is no need to process it and retain it in Working Memory (WM). If, on the other hand, the information is new, or disruptive of accepted beliefs, it is likely that it will be processed consciously and may well show up in WM as a sort of "work in progress", en-route to long-term memory.

Thus, whilst it seems likely that *previous* affective/emotional responses to advertising (created through long-term repetition of an affective message) *will* probably reside in long-term memory and not in WM, it is unclear whether they by-pass WM completely on their way there. In fact, it is likely that they pass through WM and may be accessible to recall questions for the (relatively) short while that they reside there.

Do we Need a New Way of Accessing Advertising Memories that Lie Beyond Working Memory?

If it *is* true that the effects of emotional advertising linger beyond the disappearance of the advertising itself from WM, it follows that more people will have seen such ads than will claim to remember them. That is why some argue that we need a way of accessing advertising memories that lie beyond WM.

Recognition (via visual or aural prompts) might be the way forward, because it seems to have a number of advantages over claimed ad awareness/recall.

Recognition is a completely different type of process from recall. Firstly, unlike recall, it is quick and semi-automatic. Perhaps more importantly, it doesn't seem to be constrained in any way. Whereas recall is finite, limited by the capacity of our WM, recognition seems to tap into our long-term memory, which is almost inexhaustible.

Furthermore, recognition brings with it an instantaneous, automatic and involuntary flow of emotion, provided that the object identified has emotional significance. Recognition thus taps into something much deeper than recall, because the latter is essentially a cognitive process of searching conscious memory. If you were shown pictures of past lovers, you would almost certainly recognise them and have an automatic emotional response toward them – even if you did not remember their names!

Recognition thus certainly seems much more enduring than recall and is clearly less dependent on attention, since advertisements that are poorly recalled may well achieve good recognition scores. Essentially, recognition seems capable of tapping into both the short-term and long-term memories of advertising.

In 2005, Conquest Research Ltd conducted a case study to test the following hypotheses:

- that TV commercials with a high affective/emotional content are most likely to work though implicit rather than conscious processes;

- that memory of such advertising is unlikely to be accessible through conscious recall, but may be accessible via recognition;
- that affective response to such advertising should, therefore, correlate with recognition rather than recall.

The results of the case study strongly suggest that:

- A lot of our memories of advertising lie beyond the reach of conventional recall questions (i.e. outside WM), and that an over reliance on recall could mislead us about the true impact of advertising.
- That those memories that lie beyond recall may be just as powerful in influencing the way we *feel* toward brands.

However, the study challenges the view that affective ads work mostly though implicit mechanisms. It suggests something more complex than this. Firstly, that whilst affective memories may not be susceptible to recall, their mode of acquisition is not necessarily implicit. In other words, new emotional information may be processed in WM and be accessible via recall, in the short-term, en-route to long-term memory.

The belief that advertising *has* to be consciously recalled to work is a very persistent one, at least amongst marketing professionals. Advertising awareness is still perceived as a key metric, because it's easy to measure, simple to understand and makes intuitive sense; but, it clearly does not tell the full story. It would seem that those advertising researchers who rely exclusively on conscious recall may do their clients a disservice. The key point is, you may make different (and potentially worse) decisions if you rely on recall alone.

OTHER APPLICATIONS OF THE 3i PRINCIPLE

Packaging and Ad Pre-Testing

One area of research where the application of the "3i" principle (implicit learning, inference and indirect questioning) could improve research practice is packaging, where traditional research techniques tend to rely too much on a "show and tell" approach, with respondents asked to say what impressions they derive from a pack design, why they like it, etc. The problem with this approach is, quite simply, that consumers do not normally use their cognitive conscious capabilities to evaluate pack designs. Response is generally unconscious and triggered by certain embedded visual cues. It is noticeable, for example, in the case of very well established brands, that brand favourability rarely increases as the result of a pack change, for the simple reason that if the visual cues are altered, the affective response may be triggered less effectively until the new packaging cues become familiar. In newer, less well-established brands, the potential for improvement is greater.

In advertising pre-testing too, the idea that advertising has to be consciously recalled to work is still a guiding principle, and it would seem sensible to apply some of the lessons learned here to take account of unconscious processes. In particular, an approach based on the three principles of implicit learning, inference (test and control) and indirect questioning, may prove far more useful than "show and tell".

FOCUS GROUPS AND THE UNCONSCIOUS

The new hypotheses offered by brain science challenge any research method that relies on mainly verbal response. However, one particular qualitative methodology – the focus group – has excited attention in recent years.

Many of us grew up with the assumption that focus groups somehow dig deeper, and can tell us about emotional response. But many practitioners now question the premise that we can "bring to the surface", particularly in a group, something which is, by definition, buried and unconscious. Put simply, there is always a risk in a focus group of building elaborate and *cognitively derived* explanatory structures on top of simple affective or non-rational responses.

According to Valentine and Gordon, "focus groups hothouse the marketing and research agendas (that rely on the consumer model of control) thus failing to reflect the reality of brand and cultural ambiguity". Others have suggested that the focus group method may prompt respondents to find "things to say" and "fill-out" the discussion, and that one-to-one interviews may be preferable.

The Harvard business professor, Gerald Zaltman, is an arch critic of focus groups who argues that focus groups fail to deliver because they are not based on any well-founded insights from either the biological or social sciences – group therapy is perhaps the closest model. He also argues that one-to-one hour interviews are preferable because:

- They are more likely to allow moderators to build trust and give a greater depth of understanding.
- The optimal number for group interaction is three, and incremental respondents add little.
- The average "air-time" per respondent in a group is 10 minutes, which is too short to achieve real depth of mutual understanding.
- Worse, the 10 minutes has to cover multiple topics.

However, qualitative research is not just about focus groups, and it is fair to say that there's a quiet revolution going on in qualitative research. New approaches are much more eclectic, embracing *ethnography*, as well as integration with other disciplines and sources, including quantitative data. Increasingly, groups are being used alongside other methods, or are being replaced by non-group methods. One commentator remarks that "we are emerging from two decades of 'let's do some groups' and re-embracing what's really possible with qualitative thinking".

WHAT SHOULD WE DO ABOUT BRAIN SCIENCE? SUMMARY

Use brain imaging *only* in conjunction with conventional research, and in a balanced experimental design. Remember that brain imaging can only tell you that a response is taking place, not why it is happening.

Use inference to determine the effect of unconscious motivation through a matched control sample, who are unexposed to the marketing message.

Use indirect questioning to move the focus away from testing the marketing message (the stimulus), and start concentrating on the *object* of stimulus – an affective/emotional response to the brand.

Accept that what people know about brands may be implicit as well as explicit, and stop relying so heavily on conscious recall (particularly in advertising research). Use recognition, as well as recall, to understand the relationship between communication and affect.

Treat verbal self-reporting with extreme caution as a means of *explaining* affect. Brands often evoke an affective response: people feel more or less positive, warmer or colder toward them. This is generally unconscious and non-rational and may not, therefore, be readily apparent in expressed reasons for liking a brand.

Remember that preference (if it's made instantaneously and non-reflectively) is not the same as considered choice. Simple (heuristic) choices often tell us more about the operation of the unconscious than expressed *reasons* for choice. So, avoid asking people to explain or justify decisions, particularly those they have made automatically, through simple habit (cognitive unconscious).

Because emotions are simple, unconscious impulses toward behaviour, qualitative research should also encourage an intuitive, emotional response. In other words, the more "thought-through" the response, the further from the emotion it's likely to be. We do not understand emotions better if we build elaborate cognitive structures on top of them.

Observe as well as ask, because emotions are public, feelings are private. (Yes, that is the right way round!) Ethnography has much to offer research, as has the integration of qualitative with behavioural and other quantitative data.

AND FINALLY . . .

The importance of brain science is that it has brought consciousness and emotion back into focus; and provides an explanatory model of mind that is too powerful to ignore.

Yet the theoretical basis of market research still seems to derive mainly from cognitive science, and we have some way to go in integrating the hypotheses of brain science into our thinking about marketing, advertising and research. If we do, I am convinced that we will emerge with a model that challenges our methods, whilst making retrospective sense of some old intuitive practices.

REFERENCES

Addison, T. (2005) *Admap*, May.
Carter, R. (1999) *Mapping the Mind*. University of California Press, Ltd.
Damasio, A. (1994) *Descartes' Error*. GP Putnam's Sons; (1999) *The Feeling of What Happens*. A Harvest Book, Harcourt Inc.
Dennet, D. (1991) *Consciousness Explained*. Little Brown and Company.
Du Plessis, E. (2005) *The Advertised Mind*. Millward Brown.
Fletcher, J. and Morgan, B. (2000) New directions in Qualitative Brand Research. MRS Conference Paper 2000.
Franzen, G. and Bauwman, M. (2001) *The Mental World of Brands*. WARC.
Gordon, W. (2004). Consumer Decision Making. *Admap*, Oct.
Heath, R. (2001) *The Hidden Power of Advertising*. Admap Publications; (2004) Measuring the Hidden Power of Advertising. MRS Conference Paper.
Le Doux, J. (2002) *Synaptic Self*. Penguin Books, London; (1996) *The Emotional Brain*. Touchstone, Simon and Schuster.

McClure, S.M., Li, J., Tomlin, D., Cypert, K.S., Montague, L.M. and Montague, P.R. (2004) Neural Correlates of Behavioural Preference for Culturally Familiar Drinks. *Neuron*, **44**, 379–387. Cell Press.

Page, G. and Raymond, J. (2006) Cognitive Neuroscience, Marketing and Research. ESOMAR Congress paper.

Penn, D. (2005) Brain Science, That's Interesting, What do I do About It? MRS Conference Paper 2005; (2006) Looking For The Emotional Unconscious in Advertising. *IJMR*, Issue 5.

Rose, S. (2005) *The 21st Century Brain*. Jonathan Cape.

Valentine, V. and Gordon, W. (2000) The 21st Century Consumer. MRS Conference Paper.

Zaltman, G. (2003) *How Customers Think*. Harvard Business Press.

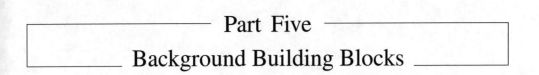

Part Five
Background Building Blocks

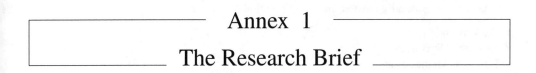

Annex 1
The Research Brief

C. Frederic John

INTRODUCTION

This chapter deals with the information exchanged between research buyer, or client, and supplier before consummating the agreement to initiate a project. As used here, the term "brief" or "briefing" encompasses both the request for proposal (RFP) issued by a buyer to one or more research suppliers, as well as the proposal prepared by the firms in response to the request. For clarity's sake, the terms "RFP" and "proposal" will be used to distinguish between the two.

Moreover, while primarily devoted to the preparation of written documents, the subject is treated very broadly here to cover all relevant communications, including phone discussions, meetings and correspondence back and forth between the parties.

Wide variation can be found in current practices for both RFPs and proposals, reflecting accepted norms in different countries and across various industries, the expectations of individual companies, research firms and their personnel, and the nature of the assignment.

Other variables that shape both content and form include the formality required in the bidding and/or purchasing processes – for example, to assure that all bidders receive the same information – and the degree to which the proposal serves as a legal contract.

No single "best practice" model can suit all these situations, and would inevitably be considered insufficiently rigorous by some and overkill by others. The emphasis, then, is more on the *nature* of the information to be exchanged than on the structure of the two types of documents. At the same time, a basic format will be suggested with the understanding that individual companies and firms will shape this to meet their own requirements.

Readers may also wish to consult the ESOMAR guidelines on "How to Commission Research".

The remainder of this section will be devoted to the two types of briefs, considered in turn, and then provide some additional guidance on the quality of the on-going information exchange. Hypothetical examples will also be provided to illustrate the points made.

FOCUS ON THE CUSTOMER BRIEF (RFP)

The request for proposal functions as a statement of *expectations* of the supplier. It provides a meaningful context and details requirements regarding both the process (beginning with the proposal and continuing through the project) and outcomes. As such, it should provide all the necessary and relevant information for the supplier to be able to design a response that will indeed fulfil these expectations.

Market Research Handbook, 5th Edition. Edited by M. van Hamersveld and C. de Bont.
© 2007 John Wiley & Sons, Ltd.

The sections generally covered in the RFP include:

- Background
- Research Objectives
- Proposed Methodology
- Deliverables
- Timing Requirements
- Budget (sometimes)
- Other requirements

Background

The background and objectives sections represent the most critical components of the proposal. The background should provide the historical context of the request, which might include the following:

- Brief description of the company, including primary lines and/or brands.
- Recent developments, such as a new acquisition, change in management, rise of a new competitor, etc.
- Relevant issues confronting the company, such as loss of share, commoditisation of the category, low brand recognition, poor coverage in business press, etc.
- The specific issue or circumstances that have led to the need to do research.
- Any prior research or consulting work related to the topic, and their conclusions.

Two things should be readily apparent from this list. The first is that in many circumstances, much of this background information will be unnecessary, either because the company is well known, or the supplier has worked with the company before. The second is some of this information may be quite confidential, and the customer is not willing to broadcast it, at least not at this stage.

Addressing the first concern is relatively simple – the depth of general information about the company provided depends on the audience. If the RFP is sent to suppliers with whom the client has not worked before, providing more of a general backdrop is reasonable and helpful. If, however, the RFP is only circulated among suppliers with prior experience of working for the company, much of this information can be trimmed back or eliminated completely.

The second concern is far trickier to deal with. Eventually, the successful bidder needs a detailed understanding of the objectives (see the discussion on the Continuous Briefing below). The question is, how much do the firms need to know to prepare the proposal, and at what stage of the process? As a general rule, the amount of "confidential" information imparted will depend on how widely the RFP is distributed (number of companies) and whether or not all of these companies have an established relationship with the client.

It will also depend on the stage of the process. In the initial stages a company may be screening through a larger number of firms and may want to limit the amount of information it provides. However, after selecting a few to submit more formal proposals, it may choose to provide a more detailed briefing to these "survivors". This need not necessarily be in writing, but more likely take place in a meeting with the supplier agreeing to respect the confidentiality of what he/she learns.

In fact, in may be good practice for companies to insist on a signed confidentiality agreement before sending any such information to potential suppliers. This need not be onerous or overly legalistic – just a form that states that suppliers will not divulge any information imparted by the company in preparation of the proposal to others, limit its distribution internally to those who need to know, and destroy or return any materials received if the contract is not awarded.

While the background section might well include some fairly general information about the company, its history, business and current situation, the thrust of the section should be on identifying the question, issue or need that has generated the desire for research. In some cases, this may mean delineating a real problem (such as declining share); in others, simply a pro forma statement of usual practice for that company. For example, an agency that always outsources copy tests for new creative does not have to spend much ink explaining this need, only state that it plans to launch three new 30-second ads in the coming season and requires copy tests be conducted on a certain schedule.

Research Objectives

Objectives should flow directly from the background – knowing the need. What does the company expect to learn from the research? While the single most critical aspect of the RFP, this section is often treated as if the answers were obvious or even redundant with the background section of an RFP. Without an accurate sense of what the research is intended to accomplish, the supplier can only really focus on the more mechanical/methodological aspects. Neglecting to clarify these objectives can even lead to serious consequences if the supplier takes an abbreviated version too literally and builds a design to address what he/she thinks the objectives are, only to learn in the end that the buyer really was getting at something else.

For example, a client asking for research to test a new product concept should explain the stage of development and expected output. This will have a profound impact on whether the appropriate method is a concept screen, concept test, conjoint or discrete choice optimisation, or a forecast.

In some cases, a flaccid objectives section may actually reflect the buyer's lack of clarity about the purpose of the project, or may serve as a cover for multiple agendas among internal stakeholders that have failed to form consensus before issuing the RFP, and are, in effect, dumping their failure in the lap of an unsuspecting supplier.

What *is* required is a clear and concise description of the expected *impact and output* of the research. Ideally, this should be presented as a series of statements or questions organised as a funnel, beginning with the broadest and ending with the most specific. This description should include, or even begin with, a statement of what decision(s) might be made on the basis of the research.

The emphasis should really be on *learning* rather than on answers to specific questions, and the buyer should avoid the temptation to start writing the questionnaire in the process.

An objectives section might be structured as follows:

- Decision to be made on the basis of the learning.
- Learning/understanding required to make that decision.
- Types of information required to achieve that learning.
- Scope of the inquiry (specific informational needs).
- Examples of questions that need to be answered.

ILLUSTRATION OF A HYPOTHETICAL OBJECTIVES SECTION

[Note: The Background section of this hypothetical RFP has already explained ABC Company's desire to introduce a new product in to the market that it hopes will reverse recent customer losses, and its decision to develop the "X-Thing" for that purpose.]

- ABC must decide whether or not to continue developing X-Thing or identify an alternative.
- To make that decision, it must understand basic unmet needs in the category, and the degree to which X-Thing is seen to address these needs.
- To get there, it must have a firmer grasp of the marketplace situation, dynamics, and motivation.
- Also, an objective reading of basic appeal of X-Thing in its current form:
  - If basically sound, can it be improved?
  - If basically weak, can the idea be salvaged or should it be abandoned?
- This requires in-depth information on:
  - key reasons consumers own this type of product;
  - penetration of current offerings;
  - drivers of selection and loyalty;
  - satisfaction with current offerings;
  - identifying areas of opportunity – dissatisfaction with current offerings;
  - interest in the X-Thing solution;
  - drivers of interest in X-Thing;
  - profile of acceptors.
- Among the questions that should be answered by the research are:
  - How involved are consumers in this category?
  - What brands do they own, prefer, know about?
  - How long have they owned their present brand?
  - What features or benefits resonate most with various target audiences?
  - How satisfied are they with what they own? What might they change?
  - How appealing is the X-Thing concept? Likes, dislikes?
  - How could the concept be improved?
  - Likelihood of acquiring at different price points?

Methodology

Many RFPs include a methodology section, either as a suggested approach or a mandatory guide. In fact, many documents contain considerable detail on anticipated method. Typically included in a methods section are:

- study design;
- analysis;
- universe definition (sample frame);
- sample size, structure, incidence, and source;
- means of data collection;
- location and language (sometimes).

As noted earlier, many factors may influence the complexity and flexibility offered in this section of the brief. These include the following:

- *Uniqueness vs. generality of the project.* A buyer may be more open to suggestions for a one-off ad hoc project as opposed to one that conforms to many done in the past.

- *Need to compare.* Far less flexibility in design may be allowed if the results of this study have to be compared to others done in other markets, or tracked with earlier studies.
- *Desire to maintain a level playing field.* A buyer may wish to have everyone bid on the same specs in order to be able to compare the proposed budgets on an apples-to-apples basis. This desire may also be affected by company policies.
- *Sophistication of the research buyer.* Some buyers are experienced research professionals who have a strong understanding of various approaches and informed opinions on what really serves their needs best. Others may be less experienced or not research professionals at all and may not even be aware of alternative approaches.

Study design refers to the overall structure of the research, such as the proposed number of cells or focus groups, the general nature of the inquiry (concept test, awareness and usage study, ideation session, etc.), and will inevitably flow into other aspects such as sample, analysis and data collection method. Examples:

> We envision a concept test among three monadic cells, two seeing the two new products under consideration, the third a control cell evaluating our current offering...

> The study involves a series of two-dozen in-depth interviews among recent or likely visitors to our theme park regarding their general desires for a family destination; sources relied on in selecting a family vacation; and experiences and/or expectations of our park...

> To meet the objectives stated above requires a segmentation study of the entire Columbian market for recorded classical music, with the various segments distinguished by their relative profitability... A sample of at least 1200 such consumers is envisioned...

An RFP may list *analyses or procedures* desired, either in general terms or more specifically. For example, the brief may simply state that the research will determine the drivers of usage in a category, anticipating each supplier will recommend their own approach or model – or suggest an alternative. Or the brief may list specific multivariate analyses expected to meet this end.

In many cases, it is probably best to limit the analytic requirements to a general statement incorporated within the design description, and focus on the desired output of the analysis in the discussion of deliverables discussed below.

Universe definition or sample frame. Suppliers should be told what audiences are to be included in the study, precisely how they are defined, and what their estimated incidence is among the general population.

Buyers often mistake descriptions or profiles of target audiences for definitions. For example, they may say something like, "Prior research indicates the target audience for this study is predominantly male, between 40 and 45 years old, mid- to upper income, with a strong interest in the latest technology." While an accurate description of the "typical" target, the actual audience to be included in the study may be much broader and has to be spelled out. In this case it might be, "Adults 30–65, full-time employed with at least $ 50K annual income who have purchased at least one of the following high-tech products within the past 3 years...".

For B2B studies it is necessary to define both the qualifications of companies to be included as well as those of the respondents. For example, "Executives of mid-sized businesses, defined as having annual revenues of $ 10–100 million, have more than one facility, and have been in business for at least one year. Qualified respondents will have primary company-wide responsibility for the purchase or lease of telephone systems."

Incidence is often a critical aspect of pricing, so data on the proportion of qualified respondents within a population, whether as broad as the general population or as narrow as customer lists, should be shared. (Where not available, suppliers will provide bids based on either their or the client's estimates, but will probably include a contingency in case these estimates are off the mark.)

Sample Structure. If the client wishes to establish any *sample quotas*, these should be clearly spelled out in the brief. This is true both for straight quota samples (to make sure specific groups actually are captured in the final sample in their true proportions) as well as stratified samples in which over-samples or augments of specific groups are desired.

The brief should also state that the final sample should be weighted to match the specified sample universe.

Desired *sample source* may or may not be left to the supplier, unless the client intends to provide lists, such as those of customers (see below). Some buyers may choose to specify the specific source or type of source to be used, such as an Internet panel with certain characteristics, random phone numbers for RDD or published lists of businesses or professionals for B2B studies.

In the case where the client is providing list sample, the nature, origin, size, accuracy and other relevant information about the list should be provided, along with the relevant fields available. Key is contact information, including name, address, phone number(s) and email addresses. Any other information that might relate to screening criteria, such as how long someone has been a customer, size of purchases, number of times called customer service, etc., should also be included if known.

Besides the types of fields available on the list, the supplier should get a sense of the presumed incidence of qualified respondents, and an honest sense of the "goodness" of the list. This would include information regarding the proportion of cases in which specific fields are actually populated (for example, while a field for email address is provided, it may only be filled in one of four cases); and the recency of these data (for example, phone numbers may be collected when a customer relationship is established, but rarely updated).

The proposal should also make clear who will be pulling the actual list to be used for sample from the data source, and whether any efforts would be made before providing the list to increase its effectiveness, such as only providing listings with complete contact information. If phone numbers are to be matched to published phone records, the responsibility for that should also be clear.

In all cases, but especially in those using customer lists, the RFP should clearly state whether or not the survey will be blind.

The RFP may specify or suggest the *data collection method* to be used, which generally stems from the overall design. The expected length of the interview or focus groups should also be provided, since that too can have a significant impact on cost, and should be tied to the data collection method. In many countries a personal interview can last far longer than a phone interview, while the maximum length of an Internet survey may be even shorter.

Location. Qualitative and quantitative studies requiring personal interviews will generally specify the cities in which research is to be conducted. Some studies may even require more precise information, such as in-home interviews, store or mall intercepts, recruitment to a downtown central-location, or secret shopping locations.

For international studies or those among ethnic groups, *language* requirements and translation responsibilities should also be clearly spelled out for survey instruments, stimuli, and deliverables. For example, an RFP for a qualitative study in the US might specify that six focus groups are to be conducted in English and two in Spanish; that the client will provide stimuli in both languages but the supplier will have to translate the English versions of the final screeners and guides into Spanish; and that transcripts of the Spanish audiotapes will have to be translated into English.

In general, it might be said that too many companies overemphasise certain methodological requirements in their RFPs, especially when it comes to ad hoc studies conducted to address what might be termed "occasional" issues or larger strategic questions. But these are precisely the areas in which good suppliers can make substantial contributions to the impact of a research effort, delivering the "added value" so often demanded.

This applies most particularly to the research design. In cases where the solution is not bound by the need to conform to other research, inventiveness should be encouraged. Thoughtfulness in designing a study to meet the stated objectives can, in fact, be a major differentiator among bidders. It may also challenge a buyer to re-think the nature of the inquiry or some of the underlying assumptions. At the very least, having the option of evaluating a number of competing approaches provides the buyer with the best thinking of a number of experienced, outside professionals as opposed to that limited to internal participants.

Other aspects where companies tend to over-prescribe include the number and size of sample cells, data collection methods and questions to be asked. These, of course, may be determined by the overall approach under consideration, but an individual supplier may also have recommendations to make in these more specific areas as well. For example, an RFP may cite 200 online interviews among small business owners using an Internet panel. A supplier may believe that none of the small business panels currently available in that country are truly representative, and recommend an alternative method.

The issue of the hallowed "level playing field" may still have to be dealt with in many companies. While conceived to ensure fairness and equal opportunity in the bidding process, this policy practically forces a decision on price. It can be held chiefly responsible for the mediocrity in output, as well as the over-reliance by firms on branded products. The underlying assumption of this policy is that research is essentially a commodity and fails to recognise that suppliers are anything but equal. It makes no allowances for the wide variation in quality of sampling, field, tabulation, and coding activities, and provides no space for the intellectual and creative contributions suppliers can make to the success of a project – and the larger enterprise which it serves.

Buyers are strongly urged to place sufficient weight in their RFPs on the methodological input of the bidders even when required to adhere to a totally equitable bidding process. The simplest solution is to provide a suggested method and ask all suppliers to provide a bid for that design, but also encourage them to offer alternatives and the opportunity to express the reasons for these.

At the same time, there are methodological aspects that should be more carefully delineated than is often the case, particularly those that relate to universe definition and sample structure, incidence and source.

Deliverables

Deliverables refers to the entire range of materials and other things the supplier is expected to deliver. Often suppliers and buyers may find themselves divided by a common language without hard definitions, where terms such as top-lines, reports, presentations, tables, findings, etc., may convey different meanings. It is essentially up to the buyer to state what he/she wants, and clarify exactly what the terms used imply. And this must be done in the RFP, since price, among other things, will be significantly affected by this.

Deliverables may include:

- Survey instruments including screeners, questionnaires, and moderator's guides;
- Sample plans;
- Field reports;
- Cross-tabulations (tables);
- Multivariate analyses;
- Qualitative output;
- Preliminary or top-line reports;
- Final reports;
- Presentations.

Some of these items may be generated by the supplier but not desired by the client.

The brief should specify the number of *survey instruments* and expected variants or versions. For example, a study among three separate audiences may require a very similar questionnaire with 80 % overlap among them. On the other hand, a study that involves interviews with both customers and prospects might require two relatively distinct questionnaires with a completely different line of questioning and only a 20 % overlap.

The number of open-ended questions that have to be coded should also be specified.

Sample plans include both source and type of sample as discussed above, but also may require more specific documentation once the study has begun. For example, a B2B study in Brazil may require a detailed plan indicating the number of businesses to be interviewed in three specific regions broken into cells by company size and industry category.

Field reports are generally provided by field departments or services to the supplier team. Buyers should indicate their desire to receive them as well if interested.

Most quantitative studies generate *cross-tabulations*, and the decisions regarding these data are generally left to the supplier. (Cross-tabs are often referred to as "tables", but should not be confused with those shown in a report document.) However, it is good practice for a buyer to indicate the anticipated number of banners to be produced, since this not only affects cost but indicates the amount of "slicing and dicing" desired. Some buyers may also wish to specify the level of statistical testing or other features.

In addition, if a client expects to review materials that may not be common practice, such as the tab or banner plan, coding frame, or receive a hard or soft copy of the raw data or tabs, this too should be clearly stated in the brief. This also applies to the raw output of *multivariate analyses*.

Essentially, a client's request to receive such data is a strong indication of the desire to be directly involved in the analytic process.

For *qualitative* projects, a different set of potential deliverables arise, and the desire to receive these should also be spelled out. These include audio and videotapes, and whether a stationary or manned camera is preferred; transcripts; need for remote access (via videoconferencing, video streaming, telephone, or other media); and whether video clips from the groups are to be inserted into the report. (There are also legal and ethical restrictions in many countries concerning the use of films of groups or individual respondents. Buyers should make themselves aware of these restrictions before finalising a brief.)

If interviews or groups involve more than one language, or another language from that spoken by the research buyer, the need for simultaneous translation and possibly the translation of all deliverables should be specified.

Reporting. The terms top-line report, final report, and presentation can mean different things to different professionals and are best clearly spelled out in the RFP. The brief should indicate the preferred format, nature and even expected length of these documents. Format includes type of file (Word, PowerPoint, etc.). Nature is a more general term that should indicate the relative extent of non-verbal materials (tables, charts, graphs, etc.), the degree to which verbiage is desired and the preferred form (full sentences or simple bullets), and the relationship between verbal and graphic elements.

(Since there is such a wide diversity of practice and preference, a buyer is well served by providing actual examples to the supplier after the project is awarded, especially if they haven't worked together before.)

- A *top-line* or *preliminary report* is generally an initial assessment of key findings, often restricted to total. It may or may not offer any interpretation or summary judgments.
- A *final report* is usually the most comprehensive statement of the research findings and implications, and may include tables, charts, graphs, and explanatory text. It often includes a summary of findings and some kind of assessment of the meaning of the findings to the client.
- A *presentation* can refer either to the act of the supplier presenting the results to the client, the document that is presented, or the final report itself (which is often but not always the same as the document presented).

Timing, Budget, and Other Requirements

Buyers should provide realistic parameters for both timing and budget in their briefs so the suppliers can build designs appropriate to both. Unfortunately, these are often the areas of the brief where open communication breaks down.

Schedule. Clients often set stringent timing requirements quite arbitrarily, to avoid giving the supplier too much latitude, in the process potentially eliminating better approaches that might require a longer duration to complete. If there is no hard deadline, it is best if the RFP suggest a timeframe for completion but keep it open for discussion.

In fact, timings often reflect the eagerness to receive the results rather than a true understanding of the time it may require to "do it right" or even at all. If the buyer takes too strong a stand on the time allowed, less than optimal sample sizes, data gathering methods and analyses may be used, and quality controls may slip.

If, in fact, timing is linked to a fixed delivery date, such as the need to present the findings at a meeting already scheduled for a specific date, or to launch a campaign at a certain time, that deadline should be clearly indicated in the brief. In such cases, the anticipated awarding of the project should also be provided, so the supplier knows how much time he/she has to finish the project.

There is generally no need to dictate a detailed schedule for the supplier, which could border on micromanagement, unless there are, again, real milestones before the end of the project that have to be observed, such as a review of preliminary findings by senior management by a certain date.

Budget. Many buyers hesitate to provide any budgetary parameters, even if the budget is already fixed, out of fear that all the bidders will simply put this price tag on their proposals regardless of true cost or value of what they propose. This is short-sighted and often self-defeating. A set of objectives can be met at different levels of completeness or rigour and it does no one any good if the supplier proposes a comprehensive solution to the research purpose which far exceeds the (hidden) budget. In fact, stated objectives may be overly ambitious for the monies allowed, and a supplier may come back with a suggestion that the objectives be pared back in order to fit the budget.

It is generally far better for a proposal to state the anticipated budget range, and also indicate how much, if any, flexibility there might be. This way suppliers can build their best designs within the budget allowed, but also know whether it is worthwhile to suggest a more costly alternative.

Other requirements. The brief should provide a clear statement of basic information that the suppliers should be aware of in preparing the document. This should include contact information, the delivery due date, acceptable or required form of delivery (electronic file, mail, courier, etc.) which may be fixed in terms of a sealed bid, number of copies required, and anticipated date of awarding the contract. It may also be a good idea to let the bidders know what the selection process involves, and if an in-person presentation of the proposal is anticipated.

In addition, the client may wish to spell out the decision criteria to be used in evaluating the proposals received. This is a good way of letting the bidders know if their offerings are going to be judged primarily on originality of design or on cost, for example.

ILLUSTRATION OF A COMPLETE RFP

The following is a hypothetical example of a fairly extensive RFP for a large-scale ad hoc study sent to suppliers not expected to be very familiar with the company, if at all:

Background

JHF Corp. is a leading Canadian manufacturer of hardwood furniture. Founded in 1923 by Jack Hudson, Sr., the company has grown from a small family-based operation employing less than a dozen craftsmen and serving the local Calgary market to a global player with plants in six countries employing over 10 000 people. The company remained a fairly small enterprise until after World War II, when demand for quality furniture, especially in the US, jumped dramatically. Global expansion was fuelled in subsequent decades by a rising world economy, reduction of tariff and other trade barriers, and the development of machinery that allowed the widespread reliance on workmen in cheaper labour markets without sacrificing product quality.

Today the company enjoys a leading position in the high-end furniture market in North America, and is increasing its share of the market in Western Europe, South America, and the Far East. Historically, it has relied on independent furniture stores as its primary distribution channel. A number of its lower-priced lines, however, have been available in a few Canadian furniture chains since the 1940s.

The company remained family-owned and managed through three generations, until Jack Hudson III decided to bring the company public in 2003. He still serves as CEO and is the majority shareholder. Going public has, however, brought the company a new set of stakeholders, including the financial community, an expanded business press, and investors and consumers in over 30 countries.

Some recent press coverage and analyst assessments of the company have not been particularly positive. A few questioned the long-term strategy of the company and the current leadership's ability to abandon its traditional ways and adapt to a rapidly changing global environment.

In 2003, JHF engaged Booz-Allen to assess the company's position vis-à-vis competitors around the world. Their findings indicated that while the company was well regarded within the category and among the furniture trade press, it was hardly known among many other key audiences. BA also suggested that the traditional distribution system might become increasingly outmoded with the increasing dominance of mass market outlets.

Objectives

In light of these findings, JHF wishes to carry out a large-scale multi-country quantitative research programme among professional and consumer audiences. The primary objective of this initiative is to provide a sound basis for a number of decisions regarding the company's corporate positioning and communications efforts to multiple audiences, as well as the viability of the company's channel strategy. Decisions likely to be made based on the research include:

• Whether or not to develop a new corporate positioning strategy, and if so, what key messages should be emphasised.
• How best to meet the needs for information about the company and its products of specific audiences.
• Whether to place greater emphasis on consumer vs. professional audiences in marketing the company's products.
• Whether to continue the historic reliance on the independent high-end retail channel, or develop alternative channels, especially outside of North America.

Specific objectives include:

• Determine the overall reputation of the company among key audiences.
• Evaluate the impact of the company's current communications in terms of building brand awareness and associations with quality.
• Evaluate the relative position of the brand vis-à-vis competitors on a market-by-market basis.
• Evaluate the perceived effectiveness of its reliance on independent retailers.

Areas of inquiry are likely to include:

• Awareness, familiarity, and specific knowledge about the company and its competitors.
• Reputation of the company and competitors in general and on a battery of attributes.
• Sources of information about the company, including advertising recall.
• Among professional audiences:
  o awareness/perceptions of the recent public offering;
  o experiences with the company, its products, and with those of competitors;
  o key trends affecting the industry.

- Among buyers:
  - where they shop for furniture;
  - sources of information relied on in the process;
  - pieces/brands purchased recently and why chosen.

Proposed Methodology

The research will consist of a series of quantitative surveys among multiple audiences in five countries – Canada, the US, the UK, Germany, Japan and Brazil. The audiences include the investment community (both buy-side and sell-side), general business media, furniture trade press, furniture retailers and recent buyers of high-quality furniture.

Each audience will be analysed separately and, wherever possible, compared to the others. For larger groups, responses will also be analysed on a country-by-country basis. Inherently smaller groups, such as the trade press, will be evaluated in aggregate with only directional differences among countries reported.

Sample description:
The proposed sample for each country is as follows:

- Analysts – 100
- General business media – 100
- Furniture trade press – 25
- Independent furniture retailers – 50
- Recent purchases of high-quality furniture – 200

(One-quarter of the Canadian interviews should be conducted among the French-speaking population, and at least some of the interviews among the professionals should also be conducted in French.)

Suggested descriptions of each audience follow. However, local variants will arise, and recommendations from the supplier are welcomed:

- Analysts – professionals employed either by investment firms or institutions to evaluate manufacturing stocks.
- General business media – editors, reporters, and columnists employed in the print, electronic, and online media with primary responsibility for business.
- Furniture trade press – editors, reporters, and columnists employed by publications targeted to the furniture and allied trades.
- Furniture dealers – a cross-section of owners, managers, and buyers for wholesale and retail outlets primarily devoted to furniture.
- Recent purchasers – Consumers who have purchased at least one piece of high-quality furniture costing at least US $1000 including a bed, chest, table, chair, sofa, breakfront, etc. within the past 12 months.
  - Incidence will vary across the countries but is expected to range from 5 to 8 % based on trade data

Sample sources: Suppliers are expected to generate their own sources of sample for each audience. JHF will provide lists of trade publications and major wholesale and retail outlets, but these should not be considered exhaustive.

Data collection method: It is suggested that all interviews be conducted by phone, but alternative methods, especially for the professional audiences, may be suggested. Interviews are expected to last about 20 minutes and contain six to eight open-ended questions requiring coding.

Deliverables

The study is expected to require two basic questionnaires – one for the professional audiences, with about an 80 % overlap among the four groups, and another for the consumers that will have only about 30 % overlap with the other versions.

It is suggested that a basic English version be developed and then modified for individual countries if necessary before being translated into Portuguese, French, German and Japanese.

The supplier will be expected to develop a sample plan for each country, noting the source(s) used for each audience, which must be approved prior to commencing field work. The supplier will also provide a weekly summary of the status of field work by audience by country, and report on any issues that may arise during the interviewing.

Each audience will have its own set of cross-tabulations with at least two banners including breaks for the individual markets. No weighting of the data is expected.

Reporting: The agency will provide top-line reports for each audience as all the interviews are tabulated. These will consist of summaries of key findings based on totals in word format without charts or tables approximately eight to ten pages in length.

The final report will consist of a full analysis of the entire data, broken down by audience and, where possible, by country within audience. The report will contain charts, tables, and graphs and explanatory text in a PowerPoint format, along with an executive summary, and a set of implications and recommendations.

The supplier will be invited to present the results at JHF Headquarters in Calgary.

Timing, Budget and Other Information

We assume the study will last between four and five months considering the number of audiences and countries involved. The proposal should contain a detailed timetable as well as any efficiencies that might speed up the timing required.

The proposal will also provide a budget break down of costs by country and audience, as well as indicating the approximate proportion of the total accounted for by direct or out-of-pocket costs and those accounted for by professional time and other fees including overhead and profit.

JHF envisions this project will cost approximately $ 300,000 Canadian.

Besides the information cited above, proposals should contain the following:

- Age and size of the firm (in terms of full-time employees).
- Relevant experience and references.
- List of key members of the team who will be handling the project and their respective roles.
- Relationships with field services in the various countries (whether owned by the firm, part of a preferred network, or independent sub-contractors).
- Full description of any proprietary models recommended.

Responses to this RFP are due by 25 November 2006. Any questions should be directed to Sheila Jones, Research Director, at the contact information listed below. JHF expects to award the project by year end.

FOCUS ON THE SUPPLIER PROPOSAL

The proposal generally serves two overlapping needs – as the response to a specific request and as a sales piece. Balancing these purposes is one of the greatest challenges facing the supplier, and will, of course, be affected by the degree to which the buyer already knows the supplier.

As noted at the start of this chapter, tremendous variation exists in terms of the length, style, detail and content of proposals, reflecting both the common practice of the firm as well as the expectations for a specific project. It can be said, however, that many proposals over-emphasise certain aspects, tending to lean too heavily on the sales side while failing to focus sufficiently on the project at hand.

A few general principles that should guide the writing of proposals are writing to the audience, relevance, responsiveness, clarity, brevity, organisation and accuracy.

- **Writing to the audience**. As much as possible, the proposal should be customised to the primary reader(s) of the document. If the supplier has not worked for a client before, it is a fair question to ask the buyer's preferences in terms of length, format, etc., as well as the level of research sophistication of the recipient. Some buyers will judge a proposal on their originality, others on the graphics.
- **Relevance**. As much as possible, the proposal should focus on the project in question. Establishing the credentials of the firm is important, but should relate as much as possible to what is being requested. For a French firm, proposing on four food product focus groups in Paris on behalf of a French client, it is hardly necessary to cite the agency's 20 overseas offices, expertise in eight product categories, or list of proprietary quantitative models.
- **Responsiveness**. Remember that the proposal is a response to a request, and all the elements requested should be addressed. Err on the side of completeness. If certain aspects cannot be answered, that should be stated. Similarly, if the supplier decides to offer an alternative approach, the original idea should be acknowledged before it is rejected. ("While the RFP calls for an evaluation of the equity of a series of brands, we believe the objectives really call for a line optimization study...")
- **Clarity**. The buyer is looking for specific information, often to compare one proposal to another, and these are best communicated in straightforward statements without ambiguity.
- **Brevity**. Relevance and clarity should lead to shorter sections and (hopefully) shorter proposals.
- **Organisation**. The structure of a proposal can not only support its persuasiveness, but also assist the buyer's ability to evaluate and compare it to others. Less critical sections can often be placed in an appendix rather than interrupt the flow.
- **Accuracy**. While speed may often be required to prepare a proposal, there is no excuse for misstatements, typos, misspellings (especially of the client's brand names) or other errors. If cutting and pasting from an earlier document, make sure no inadvertent baggage is carried over – such as a sudden mention of dog biscuits in a banking proposal.

The sections most often included in a more formal proposal include the following:

- Introduction and overview of the company.
- Understanding of study background and objectives.
- Proposed methodology.
- Deliverables.

- Supplier and team credentials.
- Timing and budget.

Introduction and Overview of the Company

A proposal often begins with a brief statement declaring exactly what it is, referencing the specific request to which it is a response.

Illustration

> ABC Research is pleased to present this proposal in response to Halfwit Corporation's Request for a Research Proposal dated 31 October, 2006. Our proposal is based on that document and on follow-up discussions with Jill Knowles, Halfwit VP for Intelligence.

While this may appear to be a statement of the obvious, it may eliminate any ambiguity in case the client has more than one RFP outstanding, or if the RFP in question has been amended a number of times. In addition, it establishes the precise basis for information and puts assumptions governing the proposal clearly in the client's court.

A brief description of the supplier often follows which should serve to establish its basic credentials and a meaningful context for the proposal that follows. It is generally *not* the best place to pitch the company itself. Remember, the primary subject of a proposal is how best to meet the needs of the client, not the curriculum vitae of the supplier. Forcing a prospect to read through pages of self-praise before getting to the matter at hand may create a dissonance.

Key topics that may be included in this part of the introduction are age, size, and relevant experience of the firm; special or unique capabilities; and something about the character of the firm. The last item is often the most challenging since so many agencies today make such similar claims to adding value, providing insights or actionable results, shaping decision-making, etc., that differentiation has become exceedingly difficult.

ILLUSTRATION OF A HYPOTHETICAL INTRODUCTION AND OVERVIEW SECTION

> ABC is a well-established Swiss firm serving the pharmaceutical industry globally since 1978. Based in Basle, the firm offers a highly experienced professional staff of 25, complemented by a support staff of 18. In addition, ABC owns and operations its own physician panel and multi-lingual field operation dedicated to interviewing hard-to-reach healthcare professionals, as well as consumers and patients.
>
> ABC prides itself on designing and executing research studies customised to meet the objectives of our clients, and delivering concrete recommendations for marketing, product, and communications decisions.

Understanding of Study Background and Objectives

This section generally comprises a level-setting exercise, demonstrating that the supplier understands the task at hand, often repeating verbatim the comparable sections in the RFP. While parroting back objectives is almost inevitable, suppliers should remember their audience when reviewing the background information. A buyer hardly needs to be told what business they're in or other facts about their own company. The only background information worth citing is that directly related to the research request, such as a problem that has emerged or a decision that has to be made. A quick summary should suffice.

Since this section is nearly totally derivative, it is best introduced with words to the effect, "As we understand it, . . . ". However, if the supplier wishes to (diplomatically) question any assumptions underlying the objectives, these should follow a recap of those stated in the RFP. (It is assumed that any unintentional ambiguities or omissions in the objectives will have been clarified before drafting the proposal.)

For example

> The objectives as provided in the RFP appear to assume that the loss of market share is directly attributable to the rise of a new competitor. While certainly possible, we recommend testing this hypothesis directly in the research, making the identification of the cause of brand erosion one of the primary objectives of this effort.

Proposed Methodology and Analysis

This is the first section in which suppliers can truly shine, and they should take this opportunity to demonstrate their creativity, methodological sophistication, and understanding of the larger business issues at stake – assuming the buyer allows this.

If the RFP recommends or even mandates a study method, that must be acknowledged and at least considered. If the supplier essentially agrees with this solution, then opportunities to elaborate on specific aspects covered in less detail should be taken, demonstrating thought-fulness by filling in the blanks. For example, a supplier might offer a more precise definition of the sample frame, offer a specific sample source, offer a questionnaire outline, etc. Slight modifications might also be offered in this vein – "While the RFP calls for balanced cells of 150, we believe the minimum size should be at least 200 per cell to allow for a comparison of male/female responses within each cell."

More radical departures from what was requested require more elaborate explanations, especially if the supplier is, in effect, not only rejecting the buyer's approach but refusing to bid on what was asked.

Illustration

> While the RFP calls for a series of focus groups with former customers, we do not believe this approach can effectively meet the primary objective to provide concrete guidance to build retention. We believe that meeting that goal requires a full understanding of why most customers remain loyal while others decide to leave. The real task is to identify the key expectations and how well they are being met among the customer base as a whole, including recent attriters. We believe this can only be done through a large-scale quantitative survey . . .

This is also the section where suppliers can explain the benefits of their proprietary models. Firms can be justifiably proud of the tools they have developed to address specific research needs, and buyers are often beneficiaries of the work that has gone into these models. Suppliers should take care to link them to the objectives and keep the discussion relevant. A proprietary system may be able to do five things, but if only two are really called for in this study, those two alone should be addressed. The point is to customise the boilerplate or at least delete unnecessary sections. (This can be especially true if the standard presentations have been developed with a particular audience in mind. For example, some model descriptions are written to convince statisticians that they are technically superior to competing approaches. But that may be totally inappropriate for a general marketing or even research audience not versed in the technicalities of the issue.)

Deliverables

This section, like Background and Objectives, often entails repeating what has been requested. If is often worthwhile to elaborate these items to prevent any misunderstanding around expectations at a late stage in the process, stating what the supplier means by terms such as top-line, presentation, etc.

The primary exception, of course, is the output from any proprietary models, or other material that may not be called for in the brief. Model output may best be incorporated in the prior section in which the models are introduced, and the same might be true for other ways of illustrating findings, such as perceptual maps or profiles of segments. Providing illustrations with clear descriptions can be very helpful.

Supplier and Team Credentials

While the firm generally introduces itself early on, it is recommended that a more detailed description be held until later in the proposal. Primarily, this shifts the weight of the sales pitch toward the back, when the buyer will hopefully be more inclined to hear it based on the preceding sections. It also produces a better flow: "We understand what has to be done, now we'll tell you why we are the right people to do it" often works better than "We really are terrific, now we'll review your assignment".

Often included here are a more detailed profile of the company, its philosophy or mission, history, principals, relevant experience, clients served, case histories, awards received and credentials of the team if the project is awarded. The great bugaboo is irrelevant boilerplate. Many buyers *do* want assurances that their suppliers are not only legitimate but can claim a solid position and enjoy a reputation within the research profession. (This can be especially true if an in-house researcher has to "sell" a supplier to a non-research audience unfamiliar with all but a handful of supplier names.)

But while conveying some sense of the breadth of the firm's activity is appropriate as a means of establishing its size or stature, long descriptions of specialties, tools or geographies not called for in the proposal should be avoided. Additional information on a firm can always be slipped into an appendix.

Perhaps more relevant, this is the place to refer to the firm's adherence to international or other ethical codes of conduct, and to meeting other standards, such as ISO. Such statements underscore the professionalism of the firm and the seriousness with which they take their responsibilities – to their clients, their respondents and to their profession itself.

Experience – particularly that with the client itself or in the category – can be very persuasive, since one of the biggest concerns buyers have is a supplier's lack of understanding for their business. Experience with a similar kind of assignment in another category can (or at least should be) equally compelling, since it demonstrates the proven ability to address a similar marketing or other problem successfully. Case histories are often powerful tools in demonstrating both understanding as well as ability to solve problems.

Providing lists of clients within or outside the category has become widely expected, but alone may not be as impressive as suppliers often think and may connote little more than name dropping. On the other hand, a description, however brief, of what was done for a specific company, the size of the project and results take on a whole new dimension. (Suppliers must, of course, obtain a company's permission to provide such details.)

A list might include items such as the following:

> **Ergo Frozen Foods**. Carried out a major brand equity evaluation of an entire line of frozen potato products, leading to the consolidation of existing brands and the company's development of an entirely new area of frozen snacks.

Providing former client names as references is sometimes done but not mandatory unless requested.

The purchase of research is similar to that of many other professional services, where clients often buy the services of a person or persons, not the organisation for which they work. Including the names and credentials of the key team members who will handle the project can personalise the proposal while adding substantially to its credibility. It is most valuable to list not only the people but their roles within the team. It is especially important for the client to know who the primary or day-to-day contact will be, and who has ultimate responsibility for the success of the project.

Presenting the team in the proposal also creates an obligation on behalf of the supplier too often ignored. If the individuals are important enough to cite in the sales process, they are certainly important when the project is awarded. Substituting personnel to meet the supplier's needs amounts to little more than "bait and switch". (This practice raises even more ethical issues when carried out during the project itself.)

Timing and Budget

This section – often the first read by the buyer – should be kept brief and to the point. A detailed schedule by stage is recommended. Often it is best to write this in terms of duration – elapsed time from authorisation in days or weeks – than calendar days, since a schedule tied to a specific start date will immediately become outdated if the project start is delayed.

If the time required is different from that anticipated in the RFP, the reasons for the longer time required should be spelled out.

It is customary in many cases to provide only the total costs for a project, or totals for various scenarios. For example, if the RFP requests bids on two sample sizes, both numbers would be given. Many firms resist providing detailed breakdowns of their costs since it opens them up to pressure to cut non-direct costs such as professional costs, overhead, or profit. If clients insist on a more detailed breakdown of costs, suppliers have to consider whether or not they wish to provide this.

ILLUSTRATION OF A PROPOSAL

The following is a hypothetical, somewhat abbreviated example of a fairly formal proposal:

Introduction

Insights Unlimited GmbH, is pleased to present this proposal in response to the RFP issued by Sauber Plus for a New Kitchen Product Test dated 1 October, 2006. We appreciate being given this opportunity and believe we are particularly well suited to carry out this project.

Since its inception 25 years ago, Insights Unlimited GmbH (IUG) has devoted its energies to wedding the most sophisticated research techniques to the practical marketing requirements of its clients. Above all, the firm is committed to the success of its clients where it really counts – the marketplace.

Originally established in Munich, IUG now has offices in London, New York, and Seoul. Despite its growth as a leading supplier in three continents with over 75 full-time research professionals, the firm retains the same high standards of client service and customised attention that it did when it was a five-person operation.

Background and Objectives

As we understand it, Sauber Plus, a leading manufacturer of kitchen cleaning products based in Düsseldorf, is in the process of developing a new scouring pad product. Historically, the company has dominated this category in the Northern German market and has, over recent years, made sizeable inroads into the rest of Germany, France, Spain, and Poland.

However, competition from leading US, British and Italian brands has intensified in these markets and even begun to challenge Sauber Plus's primacy in its core area. Moreover, low-cost products from former members of the Soviet bloc countries are starting to win share, especially among lower-income households.

In response to these circumstances, Sauber Plus has decided to develop a new generation of products that offer greater durability and more effective cleaning agents without increasing retail prices. The first of these innovative items likely to be launched is a new scouring pad for heavy-duty cleaning of cast iron and stainless steel pots and pans.

Before investing more heavily in R&D, the company wishes to conduct quantitative research to confirm its hypothesis that this type of product will be well received by German housewives and other buyers.

The primary objective cited in the RFP is to provide an objective basis for the development of this new product. Specifically, the research will:

- Determine the level of interest in the product among a broad cross-section of German housewives and others;
- Identify the features, benefits, and product attributes that drive appeal;
- Identify any potential ways in which the product could be improved, or aspects that take away from its appeal;
- Establish a hierarchy of needs when it comes to kitchen cleaning products in general, the satisfaction with current product offerings, and the degree to which the new pad is expected to meet critical needs;
- Identify and profile the most attractive target(s) for this new pad.

Study Method and Analysis

The RFP calls for a concept test carried out in a number of central locations (hall test) throughout Germany. Sample size and markets (with the exception of Düsseldorf) are left to the supplier. Stimuli provided would consist of printed descriptions of the product and illustrations showing its use, but no prototypes would be available.

Based on the RFP and subsequent discussions with Jörg Finsster, Director of New Product Marketing, we recommend the following study design:

General – A concept test using personal interviews conducted in five central locations across Germany – Düsseldorf, Berlin, Frankfurt, Munich and Freiberg.

Sample size and description – 500 interviews, 100 in each location, consisting of house-wives, single men and single women. Specifically, in each market:

- 60 housewives aged 25–65, currently married;
- 20 single, divorced, or widowed women, 20–65;
- 20 single, divorced, or widowed men, 20–65;
- No quotas for size of household or presence of children are needed.

Additional qualifications:

- All respondents will be in the scouring pad category and the primary purchaser of kitchen cleaning products in their household.
  - To be in the category, respondents must buy at least one box of scouring pads a year.
  - Incidence estimated at 80 %.
- Minimum annual household income of 12 000 Euros.
- All interviews will be conducted in German, but no ethnic qualifications will be established.

Respondents will be recruited by phone and/or street intercept depending on the city.

Questionnaire length – the interview is expected to last 40 minutes using a CAPI system. At least six open ended questions are expected to be asked and coded.

IUG has developed a highly successful method for concept testing that combines certain qualitative techniques with rigorous quantitative measures called CapSize. This approach begins with a less structured inquiry focused on the feelings surrounding the tasks involving a specific type of product type, associations with the products themselves and the current brand offerings before collecting more concrete usage data. This process increases the engagement of the respondent in the interview before being exposed to the new concept and other stimuli.

All the data will be cross-tabulated using two banners.

Deliverables

The deliverables will consist of a top-line report, based on total only, to be provided two weeks after the end of the field work. This brief document will summarise key findings in no more than ten pages, and will contain at most four to five tables.

The final report, in PowerPoint format, will consist of a full description of the findings using charts, graphs, and tables with explanatory text relying on bullets rather than full paragraphs. The report will also contain an executive summary of findings and a set of conclusions and recommendations.

We will be pleased to present the findings in the Sauber Plus headquarters at your convenience.

Company Profile

Insights Unlimited GmbH was founded in 1978 by Prof. Hermann Deutsch of the Economics Dept. of the University of Munich and Philip Dreiser, then serving as head of research for a leading German confectionery firm. Both believed there was a pressing need to bridge the gap between the highly sophisticated but "ivory tower" statistical tools being developed in academia and the practical, business-oriented demands of real-world marketing organisations. IUG was established to fill this gap, and soon became well-known as a proponent of innovative solutions to packaged goods companies throughout Germany.

Over the next decade, the firm expanded its range of services into other categories, including pharmaceutical, durables, financial services, and telecommunications, at the same time extended its activities to all of Western Europe and North America. Thirty years later it boasts offices on three continents but proudly maintains its independence and dedication to customer service.

IUG has pioneered a number of innovative solutions for positioning, copy-testing, ad tracking, new product development, and brand equity. Of particular relevance for this proposal is our CapSize model for new product evaluation cited above. A more complete description follows...

***

If awarded this project, IUG would assign a team of professionals including Rolf Jäger, head of our FMCG division; Susan Dwight, VP, who heads one of our FMCG groups; and Lori Cohen, Coordinator. In addition, members of our sampling, field, and data processing sections would be assigned to the project.

Mr. Jäger would have overall responsibility for the project and would be instrumental in designing the study and interpreting the findings. Ms. Dwight would be the day-to-day project manager and primary contact. She would be supported by Ms. Cohen who would serve as a back-up contact.

Credentials of all three individuals can be found in the Appendix.

Timing and Budget

We estimate the project will take about 12 weeks to complete and is expected to follow this series of steps:

Task		Elapsed Time
Finalise project design and sample specs	1 week	1 week
Draft screener and questionnaire	2 weeks	3 weeks
Program CAPI questionnaire, receive final stimuli	1 week	4 weeks
Pre-test, recruit, and conduct interviews	3 weeks	7 weeks
Coding and data processing	1 week	8 weeks
Analysis and report presentation	3 weeks	11 weeks
– Delivery of top-line report (1 week)	1 week	
– Delivery of final report (2 weeks)	2 weeks	
Presentation	1 week	12 weeks

The total cost of this project, based on the assumptions expressed in the RFP and this proposal, is € 57 000, and comes with a 10 % contingency. This figure includes all fees and expenses including travel, incentives, and other out-of-pocket expenses.

Payment terms are 40 % upon authorisation, 30 % upon completing field work, and the remaining 30 % upon submission of the final report.

THE CONTINUAL BRIEF

As noted at the beginning of this chapter, the degree of variation in both RFPs and proposals is huge, and the only things that are really critical is that the client communicates its needs clearly and the supplier's response meets the expectations of the buyer. Most of the chapter has been devoted to written documents between the two sides, and has emphasised completeness and a somewhat formal style as might be exchanged between parties that have never worked together before. In many cases where the company and firm know each other well, certain sections might be omitted or greatly abbreviated and shorthand bullets be substituted for sentences. Content, not form, should be the ultimate guide.

But the term "brief" can also be extended to the entire interchange between client and prospective supplier, much of which will be verbal such as phone discussions and meetings, or informal notes or e-mail messages passed back and forth. Here, too, the quality of information exchanged is far more critical than the form, and can be as important if not more so than the formal documents to the ultimate success of the project.

The underlying assumption is that the best research results from true partnerships between buyers and suppliers, and that open communications are an essential ingredient in establishing and maintaining such a relationship. Open dialogue between client and supplier before the project is awarded can initiate the partnership (with the winning supplier) early on, and provide the buyer with an additional method for evaluating all the bidders. This dialogue (or series of dialogues between buyer and various bidders) may be initiated before the proposals are delivered – maybe even before the RFP is sent out – and may last until the project is awarded.

Each party has one primary type of information to impart. If the background and objectives are the most important part of the RFP, these represent the most meaningful insights the client can convey. For the supplier to deliver a solution that truly meets the needs of the client, he/she really has to understand what those needs are. Often this requires an understanding of developments in the business, internal politics or other confidential situations that the buyer may be reluctant to put in writing. However, since this knowledge may affect the execution of a project in terms of its focus, analysis, interpretation, and even tone, the in-house researcher or commissioning agent may wish to fill the supplier in ahead of time – at least as soon as a project is awarded.

But it can even be helpful to make such information available before that, assuming a genuine need and level of trust in the supplier(s) since "hidden" agendas can also impact study design. For example, a supplier may bid on what appears to be a straightforward new product test assuming standard cell sizes and margins of error. However, if he/she learns that the test in question is anything but straightforward but a showdown between a brand manager who has already invested heavily in the idea and a marketing manager who doesn't believe in it, the design may be upgraded. Understanding the stakes, the test may become far more rigorous.

Suppliers in turn can utilise these less-formal channels to enhance the quality of their solutions by asking probing questions and making constructive suggestions. The buyer will benefit from a genuine give-and-take with his suppliers, even learning things that can improve the study from those not selected. And the supplier will be able to enhance his/her credibility by demonstrating how well they can think "on their feet" and get on the same wavelength as the client.

Ultimately, the goal of the entire briefing process is a smooth transition into the next stage – the project itself – with as little of a disconnect as possible. Continuous interchange between the two parties is often the best way of achieving this goal.

REFERENCE

Esomar (2005) World Research Codes & Guidelines "How to Commission Research".

Paul Harris and Ken Baker

Statistics may be defined as "the collection, analysis and interpretation of numerical data". As market research is concerned mostly with counting and measuring, it is not surprising that the theory of statistics can play an important part in assisting researchers to collect valid samples of data, and in helping them to draw correct conclusions from those data. In this chapter, the emphasis will be on the "analysis and interpretation" aspects of statistics dealing mainly with simple descriptive measures calculated from survey data and the testing of hypotheses about those data. The techniques and significance tests described below are those which have been found most useful in interpreting survey tabulations. This is not an exhaustive list, by any means, and the reader who wishes to know more about statistical analysis in market research may consult the texts given in the references at the end of the chapter.

TYPES OF MARKET RESEARCH DATA

Classified Data

This is defined as data which have been collected using only different classifications or categories as the measuring scale. Much of the demographic data collected on market research questionnaires, for example, are of the type consisting of groups of respondents who fall into one of a number of classifications. Two obvious examples are sex and marital status, where the categories would be:

Sex	Marital status
Male	Single
Female	Married
	Widowed
	Divorced

The numerical data are simply obtained by counting the frequency of occurrence of respondents in each classification. The various classifications used form a type of measurement scale known as a *nominal* scale. The basic property of this weakest form of measurement scale is that items or people that fall into one classification are different in some way from those falling in the other classifications. When the frequency counts for each classification are each divided by a base figure, such as the total number of respondents in the survey, and are multiplied by 100, a percentage is obtained for each classification. A frequency count and a percentage for

Market Research Handbook, 5th Edition. Edited by M. van Hamersveld and C. de Bont.
© 2007 John Wiley & Sons, Ltd.

a number of classifications is one of the most commonly occurring formats of market survey tabulations. The statistical treatment of these counts and percentages will form a large part of this chapter.

Ranked Data

Data are often collected by classifications which are not only different, but where some classifications are "higher" or "lower" than other classifications in some sense. A common example in market research is where purchasers of various amounts of a product are classified as:

(a) heavy buyers (e.g. ten or more packets);
(b) medium buyers (e.g. five to nine packets);
(c) light buyers (e.g. one to four packets).

Another example is where respondents are asked about their attitudes towards a product on semantic scales such as:

• very sweet;
• sweet;
• neither sweet nor bitter;
• bitter;
• very bitter.

In all these examples the classifications on the scales have a natural ordering, which distinguishes them from the previously defined classified data. Numerical data are obtained from the count of respondents for each classification and its associated percentage. The natural order of classifications for ranked data gives the researcher more scope in analysing data of this type, which are often referred to as *ordinal* scale data.

Measured Data

Under this heading are included all data where the scale of measurement consists not of labelled classifications, but real numerical values. Obvious examples are height (in metres), age (in years), and number of packets of "brand B" bought last week. Measured data include the two types of measurement which are known as *interval* scales and *ratio* scales. In the former, the distance between two positions on the numerical scale is known and is interpretable numerically, and in the latter the ratio of two positions on the scale is independent of the unit of measurement. The ratio scale has the further property that its zero point is known and meaningful. An example of interval measurement is temperature which can be measured on Fahrenheit or Centigrade scales. Height is a good example of the use of ratio measurement, where the ratio of two heights is the same, irrespective of whether they are measured in feet and inches or in metres.

A further distinction between types of measured data is that of *discrete* (or *discontinuous*) data and *continuous* data. Discrete data occur when the measurement scale consists of a number of distinct numerical values such as "the number of times a certain advertisement has been seen in the last month". The values on the scale must be 0, 1, 2, 3 ... etc., with intermediate values such as 1.5 being impossible. No such restriction is applicable to continuous data where the measurements may be taken to any number of decimal places, depending only on the accuracy of the measuring instruments being used. In practice, continuous data such as height are usually collected to distinct values such as two decimal places of metres.

Under the heading of measured data are included data obtained from semantic rating scales, to which simple discrete numerical scores have been attached. An example of two such scoring systems commonly used is given below:

	Score	Score
A preferred to B very much	5	+2
A preferred to B a little	4	+1
No preference	3	0
B preferred to A a little	2	−1
B preferred to A very much	1	−2

This practice of taking an ordinal or ranked measuring scale and giving the various classifications a numerical score is widespread in market research. By doing so the researcher is assuming that underlying the semantic scale is a continuous numerical scale which it is not possible to measure accurately, and that the numerical values given correspond approximately to positions on that scale. If such assumptions can be validly made, then a lot more can be done with the data statistically.

SIMPLE DESCRIPTIVE STATISTICS

In this section a number of summarising features of measured data will be given.

Frequency Distributions

If data have been collected on the number of one kilo bags of flour bought by 200 housewives each month, it would be confusing to list all 200 values obtained. It is much better to display the data in the form of a *frequency distribution* as below:

Number of one kilo bags bought	Frequency of occurrence = number of housewives buying
0	12
1	15
2	20
3	40
4	60
5	30
6	15
7	5
8	3
Total	200

In this form, the data can be more easily understood and interpreted, especially as this frequency distribution (or "distribution" as it is often simply called) may be represented pictorially as in Figure A2.1. This graphical representation of a frequency distribution is known as a *histogram*. In the above example the data are given for a discrete distribution, but these two ways of displaying data are equally useful for continuous data. All one has to do is group the continuous

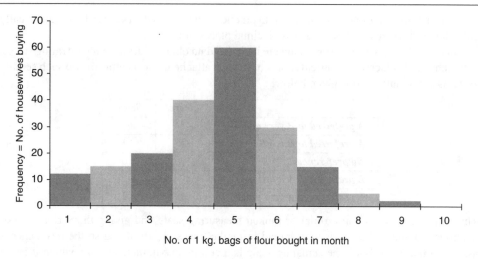

Figure A2.1   Histogram of frequency distribution of flour purchases

data values into convenient groupings or class intervals and count the number of observations in each class. A number of classes between eight and fifteen is usually adequate.

If data on height were collected in metres, part of the frequency distribution might be as follows:

Height (m)	Frequency = number of people
1.51–1.55	20
1.56–1.60	27
1.61–1.65	34
1.66–1.70	46
etc.	etc.

Continuous data that have been grouped into class intervals may also be represented by a *frequency curve*, which is obtained by drawing a smooth curve through the mid-points of the top of each bar on the histogram. An example of a frequency curve derived from a histogram is shown in Figure A2.2.

The Mean, Variance, Standard Deviation and Standard Error of a Distribution

Although the frequency distribution and histogram describe a set of data in simple terms, an even more valuable condensation of the data may be obtained by calculating a single value which summarises the distribution. Such a value is the *arithmetic mean* or just simply the *mean* of the distribution. It is often referred to as the *average*, but this is not strictly correct as the mean is only one of a number of averages that may be calculated from a distribution. Other averages are the *mode* defined as the data value with the highest frequency, and the *median* defined as the middle value when all the data values are arranged in order of magnitude.

To show how to calculate the mean of a distribution the previous data on bags of flour will be used. It is customary to denote the data values by 'x' and the frequency of occurrence by those values by 'f'. The mean, which is usually denoted by $\bar{x}(x - bar)$, is calculated by using

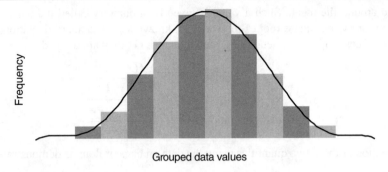

Figure A2.2   Frequency curve

the formula:

$$\overline{x} = \frac{\Sigma fx}{\Sigma f} \text{ where } \Sigma = \text{the sum of}$$

Putting the formula into words we have: multiply each data value (x) by its associated frequency (f), add up the multiplication and divide their total by sum of the frequencies. This has been done below for the data on flour.

Number of one kilo bags bought	Frequency	
x	f	fx
0	12	0
1	15	15
2	20	40
3	40	120
4	60	240
5	30	150
6	15	90
7	5	35
8	3	24
Total	$\Sigma f = 200$	$\Sigma fx = 714$
$\overline{x} = \dfrac{\Sigma fx}{\Sigma f} = \dfrac{714}{200} = 3.57$		

Reference to Figure A2.1 shows that the value of the mean of the distribution lies near the middle of the data values. Both the median and the mode of this distribution are equal to 4. To calculate the mean of a continuous distribution it is necessary to take the midpoints of the class intervals as the data values (x). In the height example given above the values would be:

Height (m)	Midpoint (x)	Frequency (f)
1.51–1.55	1.53	20
1.56–1.60	1.58	27
1.61–1.65	1.63	34
1.66–1.70	1.68	46

Not only is it useful to have a summarising value such as a mean for a distribution but it is also of interest to have another value which indicates how much the individual data values are spread around the mean. Such a value is given by a quantity called the *variance* of the distribution, or by the square root of the variance, known as the standard deviation. In terms of the data values (x), the frequencies (f) and the mean ($\bar{x}$) they are defined as:

$$\text{Variance} = s^2 = \frac{\Sigma f(x - \bar{x})^2}{\Sigma f - 1}$$

$$\text{Standard deviation} = s = \sqrt{\frac{\Sigma f(x - \bar{x})^2}{\Sigma f - 1}}$$

The calculation of these two quantities using the data on bags of flour, is demonstrated below:

Number of one kilo bags bought x	Frequency f	$x - \bar{x}$	$(x - \bar{x})^2$	$f(x - \bar{x})^2$
0	12	−3.57	12.74	152.88
1	15	−2.57	6.60	99.00
2	20	−1.57	2.46	49.20
3	40	−0.57	0.32	12.80
4	60	0.43	0.18	10.80
5	30	1.43	2.04	61.20
6	15	2.43	5.90	88.50
7	5	3.43	11.76	58.80
8	3	4.43	19.62	58.86
	$\Sigma f = 200$			$\Sigma \mathbf{f}(x - \bar{x})^2 = \underline{592.04}$

$$\text{Variance} = s^2 = \frac{\Sigma f(x - \bar{x})^2}{\Sigma f - 1} = \frac{592.04}{199} = 2.98$$

$$\text{Standard deviation} = s = \sqrt{\frac{\Sigma f(x - \bar{x})^2}{\Sigma f - 1}} = \sqrt{2.98} = 1.73$$

It is quite usual to replace Σf by the symbol n, i.e. $n = \Sigma f$. Figure A2.3 shows two hypothetical distributions, each with the same mean of $\bar{x} = 5$ units. For distribution A, which has data values ranging from 3 to 7 units, the variance and standard deviation would both be smaller than that for distribution B, where the data values range more widely from zero to 10.

In the case where we do not have a frequency distribution but only individual data values (x), then the formulae for the mean ($\bar{x}$) and the standard deviation (s) simplify to:

$$\bar{x} = \frac{\Sigma x}{n}$$

$$s = \sqrt{\frac{\Sigma(x - \bar{x})^2}{n - 1}}$$

The value n is, of course, the sample size.

There is a further important statistic that can be calculated from a distribution, namely, the *standard error of the mean*. Suppose it is known that in a certain town the true average number of persons per household (based on *all* households) is $\bar{X} = 3.12$ with a standard deviation of

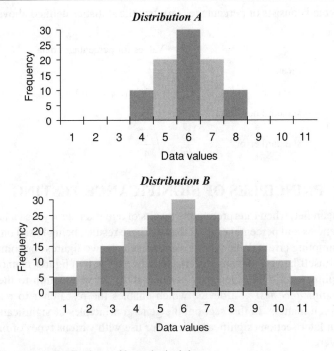

Figure A2.3   Frequency distributions of hypothetical data

$S = 1.00$. The values are denoted by capital X and S as they are population values and not sample values. If a random sample of 250 households is selected from the town it would be possible to calculate the mean number of persons per household for this sample. Let the mean of this sample be denoted $\bar{x}_1$. Putting this value to one side, a second random sample of 250 households is selected and the mean ($\bar{x}_2$) is calculated.

Similarly, a third sample of 250 is selected, giving $\bar{x}_3$, and so on, until 100 samples have been collected. The resulting 100 values of $\bar{x}$ may then be grouped into a frequency distribution. In general the 100 values of $\bar{x}$ will all be fairly close to the population mean, $\bar{X} = 3.12$. In fact, their distribution should have a mean, i.e. the mean of all the 100 means, which is indistinguishable or nearly indistinguishable from the value 3.12. Certainly, if all possible samples of 250 households were selected from the town, then the mean of the frequency distribution of all possible sample means would be exactly 3.12. The distribution of sample means will have a bell-shape distribution, which is known as the *normal distribution*. The standard deviation of the distribution of 100 means may be calculated and it is usually called the *standard error of the mean*. Fortunately it is not necessary to draw a large number of samples to estimate the standard error, as its value may be calculated from the single sample that is normally selected. If a sample of n members is selected and the standard deviation (s) calculated for some data values (x) then the standard error of the mean ($\bar{x}$) is given by:

$$\text{Standard error } (\bar{x}) = \frac{s}{\sqrt{n}}$$

If the data collected consists of percentages (p) then the statistics defined above take a simple form:

Values for percentages data

mean	$\bar{x}$	p
variance	s^2	pq, where $q = 100 - p$
standard deviation	s	$\sqrt{pq}$
standard error	$\dfrac{s}{\sqrt{n}}$	$\sqrt{\dfrac{pq}{n}}$

PRINCIPLES OF SIGNIFICANCE TESTING

The market researcher, when interpreting the results of a market survey, has a large number of tables of frequencies and percentages to examine. These results, being based on a sample, will be subject to sampling errors. When the researcher selects two figures for comparison he/she has to assure himself/herself that any difference between the two figures cannot be explained solely by sampling error. Only then may he/she validly draw attention to the difference in figures. The *significance test* is a device which enables the researcher to reach a decision objectively in such matters. In this section, the general principles of significance testing will be described. In later sections significance tests for use with various types of market research data will be given.

The Null Hypothesis and the Alternative Hypothesis

A significance test is used to decide whether to accept or reject hypotheses concerning the sample data that have been collected. The first step in a significance test is to set up a special hypothesis known as a *null hypothesis* (usually denoted by H_0). It is so called because it is quite often expressed in null or negative terms. A typical one in market research, not in negative terms, would be "The percentage of men in the population who smoke is $P = 50\%$". Next, the researcher must define an *alternative hypothesis* (H_1) which may be accepted if the null hypothesis is rejected. The corresponding alternative hypothesis to the null hypothesis stated above might be "Percentage P is not equal to 50 %". A significance test based on this alternative hypothesis would be of the type known as a *two-tailed test*, as it states that P may be either higher or lower than 50 %. Two examples of alternative hypotheses each of which lead to a separate *one-tailed test* are given below.

(a) P is greater than 50 %;
(b) P is less than 50 %.

Both of these predict a difference in *one* direction only.

Testing the Null Hypothesis

The steps employed in conducting a significance test are best explained in the context of an example. In this section the hypothesis concerning the percentage of men who smoke will be tested using the two-tailed alternative hypothesis. To test the validity of the null hypothesis a random sample of n men, e.g. $n = 250$, is selected from the population of all men, and from

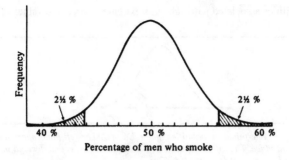

Figure A2.4   Sampling distribution of a test statistic

the data values the statistic to be tested (p_1) is calculated, p_1 being the proportion of men who smoke. This is the result from just one sample. It would be possible in theory, as described in the previous section on the standard error of the mean, to draw all possible samples of size $n = 250$ from the population to produce a large number of estimates p_1, p_2, p_3 ... etc. If these estimates were formed into a frequency distribution it would be a normal distribution. If the null hypothesis is true, this distribution, which is called the *sampling distribution of the test statistic*, will have a mean of $P = 50\%$ and a standard error of:

$$\sqrt{\frac{PQ}{n}} = \sqrt{\frac{50(100 - 50)}{250}} = \sqrt{10} = 3.16\%$$

Figure A2.4 shows this particular distribution, from which it can be seen that, if the null hypothesis is true, then a sample value of p_1 lower than 40% or higher than 60% is very unlikely.

Of course, it is possible that a sample of $n = 250$ will give $p_1 = 40\%$ even when the null hypothesis of $P = 50\%$ is true; but this would probably not occur. What the researcher has to decide now is where to place cut-off points on this distribution beyond which he is not prepared to accept that the null hypothesis is true but that an alternative hypothesis is true. These cut-off points are normally referred to as critical values in the statistical literature. To assist in this decision a valuable property of the normal distribution may be used. In any normal distribution the area of the distribution outside the limits, arithmetic mean $\pm z$ standard deviations (where z is any number), can be calculated.

Three examples are given below:

(a) only 5% of the area is outside the limits, mean ± 1.96 standard deviations;
(b) only 1% of the area is outside the limits, mean ± 2.58 standard deviations;
(c) only 0.1% of the area is outside the limits, mean ± 3.29 standard deviations.

Tables of the areas of the normal distribution have been calculated and one version is given in Table A2.1. It gives the area of the distribution beyond certain multiples of the standard deviation for one tail of the distribution only. The value corresponding to $z = 1.96$, for example, is 0.025 on one tail and, therefore, as stated above, 0.05 or 5% of the area of the curve is outside 1.96 standard deviations.

Figure A2.4 shows the critical values for the men smokers, giving the limits outside which 5% of the area of the distribution lies ($2^1/_2\%$ on each tail). As this is a distribution of a mean,

Table A2.1   Probabilities associated with values as extreme as observed values of z in the normal distribution

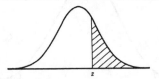

The body of the table gives one-tailed probabilities under H_0 of z. The left-hand marginal column gives various values of z to one decimal place. The top row gives various values to the second decimal place. Thus, for example, the one-tailed p of $z \geq 0.11$ or $z \leq -0.11$ is $p = 0.4562$.

z	0.00	0.01	0.02	0.03	0.04	0.05	0.06	0.07	0.08	0.09
0.0	0.5000	0.4960	0.4920	0.4880	0.4840	0.4801	0.4761	0.4721	0.4681	0.4641
0.1	0.4602	0.4562	0.4522	0.4483	0.4443	0.4404	0.4364	0.4325	0.4286	0.4247
0.2	0.4207	0.4168	0.4129	0.4090	0.4052	0.4013	0.3974	0.3936	0.3897	0.3859
0.3	0.3821	0.3783	0.3745	0.3707	0.3669	0.3632	0.3594	0.3557	0.3520	0.3483
0.4	0.3446	0.3409	0.3372	0.3336	0.3300	0.3264	0.3228	0.3192	0.3156	0.3121
0.5	0.3085	0.3050	0.3015	0.2981	0.2946	0.2912	0.2877	0.2843	0.2810	0.2776
0.6	0.2743	0.2709	0.2676	0.2643	0.2611	0.2578	0.2546	0.2514	0.2483	0.2451
0.7	0.2420	0.2389	0.2358	0.2327	0.2296	0.2266	0.2236	0.2206	0.2177	0.2148
0.8	0.2119	0.2090	0.2061	0.2033	0.2005	0.1977	0.1949	0.1922	0.1894	0.1867
0.9	0.1841	0.1814	0.1788	0.1762	0.1736	0.1711	0.1685	0.1660	0.1635	0.1611
1.0	0.1587	0.1562	0.1539	0.1515	0.1492	0.1469	0.1446	0.1423	0.1401	0.1379
1.1	0.1357	0.1335	0.1314	0.1292	0.1271	0.1251	0.1230	0.1210	0.1190	0.1170
1.2	0.1151	0.1131	0.1112	0.1093	0.1075	0.1056	0.1038	0.1020	0.1003	0.0985
1.3	0.0968	0.0951	0.0934	0.0918	0.0901	0.0885	0.0869	0.0853	0.0838	0.0823
1.4	0.0808	0.0793	0.0778	0.0764	0.0749	0.0735	0.0721	0.0708	0.0694	0.0681
1.5	0.0668	0.0655	0.0643	0.0630	0.0618	0.0606	0.0594	0.0582	0.0571	0.0559
1.6	0.0548	0.0537	0.0526	0.0516	0.0505	0.0495	0.0485	0.0475	0.0465	0.0455
1.7	0.0446	0.0436	0.0427	0.0418	0.0409	0.0401	0.0392	0.0384	0.0375	0.0367
1.8	0.0359	0.0335	0.0344	0.0336	0.0329	0.0322	0.0314	0.0307	0.0301	0.0294
1.9	0.0287	0.0281	0.0274	0.0268	0.0262	0.0256	0.0250	0.0244	0.0239	0.0233
2.0	0.0228	0.0222	0.0217	0.0212	0.0207	0.0202	0.0197	0.0192	0.0188	0.0183
2.1	0.0179	0.0174	0.0170	0.0166	0.0162	0.0158	0.0154	0.0150	0.0146	0.0143
2.2	0.0139	0.0136	0.0132	0.0129	0.0125	0.0122	0.0119	0.0116	0.0113	0.0110
2.3	0.0107	0.0104	0.0102	0.0099	0.0096	0.0094	0.0091	0.0089	0.0087	0.0084
2.4	0.0082	0.0080	0.0078	0.0075	0.0073	0.0071	0.0069	0.0068	0.0066	0.0064
2.5	0.0062	0.0060	0.0059	0.0057	0.0055	0.0054	0.0052	0.0051	0.0049	0.0048
2.6	0.0047	0.0045	0.0044	0.0043	0.0041	0.0040	0.0039	0.0038	0.0037	0.0036
2.7	0.0035	0.0034	0.0033	0.0032	0.0031	0.0030	0.0029	0.0028	0.0027	0.0026
2.8	0.0026	0.0025	0.0024	0.0023	0.0023	0.0022	0.0021	0.0021	0.0020	0.0019
2.9	0.0019	0.0018	0.0018	0.0017	0.0016	0.0016	0.0015	0.0015	0.0014	0.0014
3.0	0.0013	0.0013	0.0013	0.0012	0.0012	0.0011	0.0011	0.0011	0.0010	0.0010
3.1	0.0010	0.0009	0.0009	0.0009	0.0008	0.0008	0.0008	0.0008	0.0007	0.0007
3.2	0.0007									
3.3	0.0005									
3.4	0.0003									
3.5	0.0023									
3.6	0.0016									
3.7	0.0011									
3.8	0.0007									
3.9	0.0005									
4.0	0.0003									

Note: The blanks in the lower part of the table indicate that the values do not differ appreciably from those in the column headed "0.00".

the standard error of the mean must be used in place of the standard deviation to calculate the critical values. These are given by:

$$\text{mean} \pm 1.96 \text{ standard errors} = P\,\% \pm 1.96\sqrt{\frac{PQ}{n}}$$

$$= 50\,\% \pm 1.96(3.16)$$

$$= 50\,\% \pm 6.20\,\%$$

$$= 43.80\,\% \text{ and } 56.20\,\%$$

If all possible samples of size $n = 250$, therefore, were drawn from the population and the null hypothesis were true, 5 % of these samples would give a value less than 43.80 % or greater than 56.20 %. If the calculated value of p_1 from the one sample actually selected is outside these two limits, then the null hypothesis is rejected and the alternative hypothesis is accepted. Alternatively, if p_1 is within the limits, then the null hypothesis is accepted. When such a decision is made in practice there is a chance that an error will be made. There is a 5 % chance that the null hypothesis may be rejected when, in fact, it is true because the sample just happened to be one of the 5 % of all possible samples that will always fall outside the specified limits. This chosen value of 5 % is known as the *significance level* of the test and is often stated in the form $\alpha = 0.05$. In other words, it is often stated as a probability of 5 in 100, i.e. a one in twenty chance, that an error will be made. The significance level is often referred to as the *type I error*. Of course, there is nothing to stop the researcher using the 10 % or 1 % or any other significance level; it depends on the error he is prepared to accept when making the decision. If the calculated value of the test statistic p_1 obtained from the sample is found to be outside the calculated limits it is said to be *significant* at the chosen level of significance. If it was found from the sample, for example, that 42 % of men smoke, this result would be significant as the difference 50 to 42 % is greater than 1.96 standard errors, and the null hypothesis that the population percentage is 50 % would be rejected.

It is important to note that, although $P = 50\,\%$ has been rejected, nothing has been said in this significance test as to the true value of P, except that it is different from 50 %. In this case the best estimate of P is given by the sample estimate $p_1 = 42\,\%$. This estimate will be subject to sampling error and it is not possible to state categorically that $P = 42\,\%$. All that can be done is to give limits known as *confidence limits* within which the true value of P will lie.

These limits are based on the areas of the normal distribution and are given by:

$$p_1\,\% \pm Z\sqrt{\frac{p_1\%(100 - p_1)\%}{n}}$$

When $Z = 1.96$ standard errors, then 95 % of the area of the normal distribution is covered by these limits which would then be known as 95 % confidence limits. In the present example for sample size $n = 250$ and $p_1 = 42\,\%$, the 95 % limits are given by:

$$42\,\% \pm 1.96\sqrt{\frac{42 \times 58}{250}}$$

$$42\,\% \pm 6.12\,\%$$

$$35.88\,\% \text{ to } 48.12\,\%$$

The type I error (or significance level) is not the only error that can be made when doing a significance test. Whereas the type I error is the error of saying a result is significant when it is not, the *type II error* is the error of saying a result is not significant when it is. To explain this new concept the previous null hypothesis H_0 will be tested against the one-tailed alternative hypothesis (H_1) that "P is greater than 50 %". The assumption will now be made that, unknown to the researcher, in fact the alternative hypothesis is true and that $P = 54\%$ in the population of all men. Just as it is possible to have the sampling distribution for the null hypothesis, so it is also possible to construct a theoretical sampling distribution for when the alternative hypothesis is true. This distribution will also be a normal distribution based on the principle of selecting all possible samples from a population where $P = 54\%$ and its standard error will be given by:

$$\sqrt{\frac{54\,\%(100-54)\,\%}{250}} = \sqrt{9.94} = 3.15\,\%$$

The sample size is assumed to be $n = 250$ as before and a 5 % significance level will be used. Figure A2.5 shows the sampling distribution of samples of $n = 250$ when the null hypothesis (H_0) is true and beneath it is the sampling distribution for samples $n = 250$ when the alternative hypothesis (H_1) is true, and in particular when $P = 54\%$. As the alternative hypothesis only specifies values of P greater than 50 %, only the right-hand tail of the null hypothesis sampling distribution is used in the significance test. Table A2.1 of the area of the normal distribution can be used to find the cut-off point, beyond which 5 % of this distribution will lie. This value is given by:

$$\text{mean} + 1.645 \text{ standard errors} = 50\% + 1.645\,(3.16\,\%)$$
$$= 50\% + 5.20\%$$
$$= 55.2\%$$

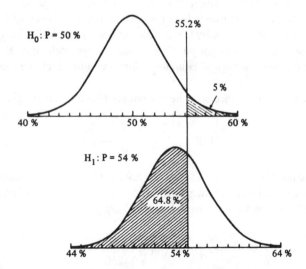

Figure A2.5   Sampling distributions of the null and alternative hypotheses

If, in the one sample actually selected, it is found that the proportion of men who smoke is $p_1 = 55.2\%$ or greater, then the null hypothesis that $P = 50\%$ in the population is rejected. If p_1 is any value less than 55.2% then there is no reason to doubt the null hypothesis, as 95 % of all possible samples will give a result less than 55.2 % when the null hypothesis is true. However, if the latter decision is made in the present example where, unknown to the researcher, P is actually equal to 54 %, there is a 64.8 % chance that the decision will be wrong. This can be seen by referring to the bottom distribution of $P = 54\%$ in Figure A2.5. The area of the distribution to the left of the significance criterion (55.2 %) may be calculated using Table A2.1 of the normal distribution. It is the area shown shaded, and is found to be 64.8 %. This chance of error is known as the type II error. It is quite often denoted by β and is sometimes expressed, like the significance level, as a probability. The present example would give $\beta = 0.648$.

If the chances of reaching a correct decision in a significance test are to be high, then both the significance level and the type II error ought to be kept to a minimum. This can be done by increasing the sample size, as this reduces the standard error and the spread of the sampling distributions of the null and alternative hypothesis. To make $\alpha = \beta = 0.05$ in the present example, when testing H_0 against the specific alternative hypothesis that $P = 54\%$, would require a sample size of approximately $n = 1680$.

SOME USEFUL SIGNIFICANCE TESTS IN MARKET RESEARCH

This section will be concerned with giving examples of a number of the most frequently used significance tests in market research. Some tests are more suitable for use on certain types of data than others. For this reason the tests most suited to the three types of data previously defined will be given under those three headings below.

Tests on Classified Data

Testing the Difference between Two Independent Percentages

Very often, the researcher wishes to judge whether two independent percentages from different samples are significantly different. He may wish, for example, to know whether a percentage $p_1\%$, based on a random sample of size n_1 selected in 1970, is significantly different from an equivalent percentage $p_2\%$ based on a sample size n_2 selected in 1968. The null hypothesis is that there is no difference in the percentages and that the two samples were selected from the same population in which the true percentage is $P\%$. The alternative hypothesis is that the two samples come from different populations in which the two percentages P_1 and P_2 are different, giving a two-tailed test. If the null hypothesis is true, then $p_1\%$ and $p_2\%$ are both estimates of $P\%$. To find out whether the difference $p_1\% - p_2\%$ is significant, the standard error of $p_1\% - p_2\%$, when the null hypothesis is true, is needed. This is given by the formula:

$$\text{Standard error } (p_1 - p_2) = \sqrt{p(100 - p)\left[\frac{1}{n_1} + \frac{1}{n_2}\right]}$$

where

$$p = \frac{n_1 p_1 + n_2 p_2}{n_1 + n_2}$$

is the best estimate of the unknown population percentage P %. Tables giving the value of this standard error for various values of n_1, n_2, and p are available (Stuart 1963). If the difference $p_1 - p_2$ is greater than 1.96 times its standard error then this observed difference can be declared significant at the 5 % level.

Example. In 1968 a random sample of $n_1 = 400$ men showed that $p_1 = 42.5$ % of them regularly read a certain newspaper. Two years later, in a random sample of $n_2 = 200$ men, it was found that $p_2 = 35.0$ % of them read that newspaper. Is the difference significant or can it be explained as the random fluctuations of sampling? The first step in this test is to calculate:

$$p = \frac{(400 \times 42.5) + (200 \times 35.0)}{400 + 200} = 40.0\,\%$$

The standard error of $(p_1 - p_2)$ is then:

$$\text{Standard error } (p_1 - p_2) = \sqrt{40 \times 60 \left[\frac{1}{400} + \frac{1}{200} \right]} = 4.24\,\%$$

Dividing $p_1 - p_2$ by its standard error gives:

$$\frac{p_1 - p_2}{\text{standard error } (p_1 - p_2)} = \frac{42.5\,\% - 35.0\,\%}{4.24\,\%} = \frac{7.5\,\%}{4.24\,\%} = 1.77$$

The observed difference is less than 1.96 times its standard error and, therefore, it is not an unusual value to obtain from the sampling distribution when the null hypothesis is true. Accordingly, the conclusion is reached that these data do not give any reason to reject the null hypothesis that there has been no change in the percentage of men reading the newspaper.

Testing the Difference between Two Correlated Percentages

(a) Mutually Exclusive Classifications

Questions to which the respondent may give only *one* of a number of answers occur frequently in market research questionnaires. The analysis of such questions results in a series of percentages adding up to 100 % based on a sample of size n. The testing of the difference between two such percentages is complicated by the fact that if one of the percentages goes up, then one or more of the other percentages must go down, as they all must add up to 100 %. The test differs from the previous one on independent percentages by having a different formula for the standard error:

$$\text{Standard error } (p_1 - p_2) = \sqrt{\frac{1}{n}(p_1 q_1 + p_2 q_2 + 2 p_1 p_2)}$$

where

$$q_1 = 100 \text{ minus } p_1$$
$$q_2 = 100 \text{ minus } p_2$$

Example. From a random sample of $n = 400$ housewives the following results were obtained in answer to the question "Which brand of coffee do you buy most often?":

Brand A	$p_1 = 40\%$
Brand B	$p_2 = 30\%$
Brand C	$p_3 = 12\%$
Brand D	$p_4 = 11\%$
No regular brand	$p_5 = 7\%$
	100%

The null hypothesis to be tested is that there is no difference between brand A and brand B and that the observed difference in percentages can be explained as sampling variations. The alternative hypothesis is that there is a difference in the percentage share held by these two brands. The standard error of the difference is given by

$$\text{Standard error} = (p_1 - p_2) = \sqrt{\frac{1}{400}[(40 \times 60) + (30 \times 70) + 2(40 \times 30)]}$$
$$= 4.15\%$$

The observed difference $p_1 - p_2 = 10\%$ is 2.41 times this standard error and is significant at the 5% level. The data, therefore, suggest that there is a real difference between these two brands.

A quick alternative approximate way of calculating the significance criterion value z is to use the actual numbers of housewives choosing brand A and brand B. Denote these by n_A and n_B and the criterion is

$$z = \frac{n_A - n_B}{\sqrt{n_A + n_B}}$$

In the above example, $n_A = 160$ and $n_B = 120$, giving

$$z = \frac{160 - 120}{\sqrt{160 + 120}} = 2.39$$

(b) Overlapping Classifications

With some market research questions the respondent may give more than one answer. The result of analysing such a question will be in the form of a number of percentages adding up to more than 100%, being based on the sample size n. As an example consider the question, "Which brands of soap did you buy in the last seven days?" The housewives asked this question could possibly have bought more than one brand. To test the difference between two brand percentages a different standard error formula is needed to account for the overlap between brands.

$$\text{Standard error} = (p_1 - p_2) = \sqrt{\frac{1}{n}[p_1 q_1 + p_2 q_2 + 2(p_1 p_2 - p_{12})]}$$

where $p_{12} =$ the overlap proportion, i.e. the proportion buying both brands.

For arithmetical reasons it is best to convert all the percentages in the above standard error formula to proportions when doing the calculation and multiply the answer at the end by 100 to give the standard error as a percentage.

Example. The following data were obtained from a sample of $n = 2000$ men who were asked which brands of petrol they had used in the previous three months:

Brand 1	$p_1 = 25\%$
Brand 2	$p_2 = 20\%$
Brand 3	$p_3 = 18\%$
Brand 4	$p_4 = 18\%$
Brand 5	$p_5 = 11\%$
Brand 6	$p_6 = 13\%$
Brand 7	$p_7 = 12\%$
	117%

The difference between brands 1 and 2 is to be tested for significance, the null hypothesis being that there is no difference between the two percentages p_1 and p_2 in the population from which the sample was drawn. The alternative hypothesis is that the two brands have different shares of the market. The survey results also show that $p_{12} = 8\%$ of men had bought both brands 1 and 2 in the previous three months. To calculate the standard error the three relevant percentages, $p_1 = 25\%$, $p_2 = 20\%$ and $p_{12} = 8\%$, are converted to the three proportions 0.25, 0.20, and 0.08 respectively.

$$\text{Standard error } (p_1 - p_2) = \sqrt{\frac{1}{2000}[(0.25 \times 0.75) - (0.2 \times 0.8) + 2(\{0.25 \times 0.2\} - 0.08)]}$$
$$= 0.0120 = 1.20\%$$

The actual difference p_1 minus p_2 = 25% minus 20% = 5% is 4.17 times its standard error. The ratio is higher than the value 3.29 needed to be significant at the 0.1% level, and it can be concluded that a real difference exists in the population from which the sample of $n = 2000$ men was selected.

As before with mutually exclusive classification there is a quick approximate way to arrive at the significance test criterion value z. This is calculated using the number of men using Brand 1 and not Brand 2 and the number of men using Brand 2 but not Brand 1. Denoting these by n_1 and n_2 respectively, the z value is given by:

$$z = \frac{n_1 - n_2}{\sqrt{n_1 + n_2}}$$

In the above example the proportion using both brands is 8% and the following two-way table may be formed:

		Brand 1		
		Used	Not used	Total
Brand 2	**Used**	160	**240**	400
	Not used	**340**	1260	1600
	Total	500	1500	2000

Thus $n_1 = 340$; $n_2 = 240$

$$\text{and} \quad z = \frac{340 - 240}{\sqrt{340 + 240}} = 4.15$$

TESTS ON RANKED DATA

Testing Rating Scales

1. The Kolmogorov-Smirnov Test for Two Independent Samples

Semantic rating scales are extensively used by market researchers. An example of such a scale would be:

(a) very good quality;
(b) good quality;
(c) neither good nor bad quality;
(d) bad quality;
(e) very bad quality.

This scale represents a non-numerical ranking of the attribute "quality". The Kolmogorov-Smirnov test assumes that underlying this scale is a hypothetical numerical measuring scale, to which the five statements approximate. In a later section actual numbers will be attached to each position on such scales, and more powerful statistical tests will be carried out, involving assumptions about the underlying numerical scale.

The Kolmogorov-Smirnov test may be used to compare two sets of percentages on the same rating scale obtained from two independent samples. The test consists of cumulating the percentages for each sample separately, and finding the maximum difference between any two cumulative percentages at any of the positions on the scale. This maximum difference may be compared against known theoretical values to judge its significance.

Example. A random sample of $n_1 = 200$ men and an independent random sample of $n_2 = 200$ women were asked to assess a new brand of sherry in terms of its sweetness/dryness. The result of the test were as follows.

	Men (%)	Women (%)
Very sweet	18.5	15.0
Sweet	22.5	17.5
Neither sweet nor dry	29.0	25.0
Dry	20.0	22.5
Very dry	10.0	20.0

The null hypothesis to be tested is that there is no difference in assessment by men and women, against the alternative hypothesis that there are some differences. This gives a two-tailed test. Denoting the percentages for men by p_1 and for women by p_2 the calculation of the maximum difference D between the cumulated percentages proceeds as follows:

p_1	p_2	*Cumulative* $p_1 = A$	*Cumulative* $p_2 = B$	$D = |A-B|$
18.5	15.0	18.5	15.0	3.5
22.5	17.5	41.0	32.5	8.5
29.0	25.0	70.0	57.5	12.5
20.0	22.5	90.0	80.0	10.0
10.0	20.0	100.0	100.0	–

In a two-tailed test the maximum positive difference $D = |A - B|$ is taken as the test criterion irrespective of whether the difference is positive or negative. In this example, $D = 12.5$. The significant values of D for two samples of size n_1 and n_2 are shown below. The sample value of D must equal or exceed these values to be significant at a given level.

Significance level (%)	Significant value of D
	$\sqrt{\dfrac{n_1 + n_2}{n_1 n_2}}$ times:
10.0	122
5.0	136
1.0	163
0.1	195

Using the 5 % significance level it is calculated that D must equal or exceed the value,

$$D = 136\sqrt{\frac{200 + 200}{200 \times 200}} = 13.6$$

The sample value of $D = 12.5$ is less than this, and therefore these data lead to the conclusion that there is no difference in the assessment of the new sherry by men and women.

For this particular significance test a one-tailed test will also be given, as the significance testing procedure differs from that of a two-tailed test. The null hypothesis will now be tested against the alternative hypothesis that men rate the product sweeter than do women. The calculation of the test statistic D is the same as for the two-tailed test, except that the sign of D in the last column of the above calculation is retained. If A is greater than B, then D is positive, and if B is greater than A then D is negative. The maximum value of D, in the direction predicted by the alternative hypothesis, is taken as the test statistic. In the present example this means considering only *positive* values of D, which would indicate men rating the product sweeter. In the one-tailed test the calculated value of D must be equal to or greater than:

$$\chi^2 = 4D^2 \left[\frac{n_1 n_2}{n_1 + n_2} \right]$$

a quantity which has the chi-square distribution with two degrees of freedom, when D is expressed as a proportion and not as an percentage. In the example $D = 12.5\,\%$ or 0.125 as a proportion and χ^2 is found to be equal to:

$$\chi^2 = 4(0.125)^2 \left[\frac{200 \times 200}{200 + 200} \right] = 6.25$$

Table A2.2 of the significance points of the chi-square distribution shows that for two degrees of freedom $\chi^2 = 5.99$ would be significant at the 5 % level. The calculated value of $\chi^2 = 6.25$ is greater than this and it may be argued that the data support the alternative hypothesis that men judge the new sherry to be sweeter than do women. This result is different from that obtained previously by using a two-tailed test, and illustrates the point that a one-tailed test is always better at rejecting the null hypothesis than a two-tailed test.

Table A2.2   Table of Significant Values of Chi-Square*

df	0.99	0.98	0.95	0.90	0.80	0.70	0.50	0.30	0.20	0.10	0.05	0.02	0.01	0.001
							Probability under H_0 that $X^2 \geq$ chi-square							
1	0.00016	0.00063	0.0039	0.016	0.064	0.015	0.46	1.07	1.64	2.71	3.84	5.41	6.64	10.83
2	0.02	0.04	0.10	0.21	0.45	0.71	1.39	2.41	3.22	4.60	5.99	7.82	9.21	13.82
3	0.12	0.18	0.35	0.58	1.00	1.42	2.37	3.66	4.64	6.25	7.82	9.84	11.34	16.27
4	0.30	0.43	0.71	1.06	1.65	2.20	3.36	4.88	5.99	7.78	9.49	11.67	13.28	18.46
5	0.55	0.75	1.14	1.61	2.34	3.00	4.35	6.06	7.29	9.24	11.07	13.39	15.09	20.52
6	0.87	1.13	1.64	2.20	3.07	3.83	5.35	7.23	8.56	10.64	12.59	15.03	16.81	22.46
7	1.24	1.56	2.17	2.83	3.82	4.67	6.35	8.38	9.80	12.02	14.07	16.62	18.48	24.32
8	1.65	2.03	2.73	3.49	4.59	5.53	7.34	9.52	11.03	13.36	15.51	18.17	20.09	26.12
9	2.09	2.53	3.32	4.17	5.38	6.39	8.34	10.66	12.24	14.68	16.92	19.68	21.67	27.88
10	2.56	3.06	3.94	4.86	6.18	7.27	9.34	11.78	13.44	15.99	18.31	21.16	23.21	29.59
11	3.05	3.61	4.58	5.58	6.99	8.15	10.34	12.90	14.63	17.28	19.68	22.62	24.72	31.26
12	3.57	4.18	5.23	6.30	7.81	9.03	11.34	14.01	15.81	18.55	21.03	24.05	26.22	32.91
13	4.11	4.76	5.89	7.04	8.63	9.93	12.34	15.12	16.98	19.81	22.36	25.47	27.69	34.53
14	4.66	5.37	6.57	7.79	9.47	10.82	13.34	16.22	18.15	21.06	23.68	26.87	29.14	36.12
15	5.23	5.98	7.26	8.55	10.31	11.72	14.34	17.32	19.31	22.31	25.00	28.26	30.58	37.70
16	5.81	6.61	7.96	9.31	11.15	12.62	15.34	18.42	20.46	23.54	26.30	29.63	32.00	39.29
17	6.41	7.26	8.67	10.08	12.00	13.53	16.34	19.51	21.62	24.77	27.59	31.00	33.41	40.75
18	7.02	7.91	9.39	10.86	12.86	14.44	17.34	20.60	22.76	25.99	28.87	32.35	34.80	42.31
19	7.63	8.57	10.12	11.65	13.72	15.35	18.34	21.69	23.90	27.20	30.14	33.69	36.19	43.82
20	8.26	9.24	10.85	12.44	14.58	16.27	19.34	22.78	25.04	28.41	31.41	35.02	37.57	45.32
21	8.90	9.92	11.59	13.24	15.44	17.18	20.34	23.86	26.17	29.62	32.67	36.34	38.93	46.80
22	9.54	10.60	12.34	14.04	16.31	18.10	21.34	24.94	27.30	30.81	33.92	37.66	40.29	48.27
23	10.20	11.29	13.09	14.85	17.19	19.02	22.34	26.02	28.43	32.01	35.17	38.97	41.64	49.73
24	10.86	11.99	13.85	15.66	18.06	19.94	23.34	27.10	29.55	33.20	36.42	40.27	42.98	51.18
25	11.52	12.70	14.61	16.47	18.94	20.87	24.34	28.17	30.68	34.38	37.65	41.57	44.31	52.62
26	12.20	13.41	15.38	17.29	19.82	21.79	25.34	29.25	31.80	35.56	38.88	42.86	45.64	54.05
27	12.88	14.12	16.15	18.11	20.70	22.72	26.34	30.32	32.91	36.74	40.11	44.14	46.96	55.48
28	13.56	14.85	16.93	18.94	21.59	23.65	27.34	31.39	34.03	37.92	41.34	45.42	48.28	56.89
29	14.26	15.57	17.71	19.77	22.48	24.58	28.34	32.46	35.14	39.09	42.56	46.69	49.59	58.30
30	14.95	16.31	18.49	20.60	23.36	25.51	29.34	33.53	36.25	40.26	43.77	47.96	50.89	59.70

Table A2.2 is abridged from Table IV of Fisher and Yates: Statistical tables for biological, agricultural and medical research, published by Oliver and Boyd Ltd., Edinburgh by permission of the authors and publishers.

2. The Sign Test for Two Matched Samples

The "sign test" may be used in a number of market research contexts, but here it is demonstrated in the situation where two matched samples of respondents rate two items, or where the same sample of respondents rates both items. The results are often presented in survey reports in a form which gives the impression that the Kolmogorov-Smirnov test for two independent samples is appropriate. An example of this would be where $n = 200$ men were asked to rate two improved versions, X and Y, of an existing after-shave lotion. The data would probably be presented as below, in terms of frequencies and percentages.

	Version X (%)		Version Y (%)	
Like very much	82	(41.0)	50	(25.0)
Like	57	(28.5)	70	(35.0)
Neither like nor dislike	29	(14.5)	40	(20.0)
Dislike	18	(9.0)	30	(15.0)
Dislike very much	14	(7.0)	10	(5.0)
	200	(100.0)	200	(100.0)

As the samples are matched a different approach is needed, which involves presenting one rating analysed by the other in the form of a two-way table. The sign test is then applied to some of the cells of this two-way table.

Rating on version Y ↓	*Rating on version X* →					
	Like very much	*Like*	*Neither like nor dislike*	*Dislike*	*Dislike very much*	*Total*
Like very much	**20**	20	4	4	2	50
Like	30	**20**	10	5	5	70
Neither	18	10	**8**	3	1	40
Dislike	10	7	5	**4**	4	30
Dislike very much	4	0	2	2	**2**	10
Total	82	57	29	18	14	200

Example. The data above show the results obtained by analysing version X ratings against version Y ratings in the example on after-shave lotion.

The null hypothesis is that there is no difference in the ratings for the two versions, and this will be tested against the alternative hypothesis that one or other of the two new versions is better liked. If the null hypothesis is true then the number of men rating X more favourably than Y on the scale ought to be the same as the number of men rating Y more favourably than X. Usually those rating X above Y are denoted by a + sign and those rating Y above X by a − sign, and this is how the sign test gets its name. The test consists of comparing the observed numbers rating X above and below Y with their expected frequencies.

	Observed	*Expected*
Number rating X above Y(+)	f	$\dfrac{f+g}{2}$
Number rating X below Y(−)	$\dfrac{g}{f+g}$	$\dfrac{f+g}{2}$

$\chi^2 = \frac{(|f-g|-1)^2}{f+g}$ with one degree of freedom.

In the example the number rating X above Y is obtained by summing the frequencies in the lower triangle of the above two-way table and the number rating Y above X is obtained from the sum of the frequencies in the upper triangle. Those men giving equal ratings are not used in the test, but the size of this group should be taken into account when interpreting the result of the significance test. Two summations give $f = 88$ and $g = 58$.

$$\chi^2 = \frac{(|88-58|-1)^2}{88+58} = 5.76$$

From Table A2.2 of the chi-square distribution with one degree of freedom it can be seen that a value of 5.76 is significant at the 2% level. The observed differences in the two ratings do not appear to be due to sampling fluctuations, and the data suggest that version X is the better product.

TESTS ON MEASURED DATA

Testing the Difference between the Means of Two Independent Samples

A frequent comparison, which is needed when assessing the results of a market research survey, is that between the means of two rating scales, where the scales have been given simple numerical scores. As explained earlier, if one is prepared to assume that the scores represent meaningful values on an underlying continuous distribution, then the test about to be described, which is applicable only to measured data, may be used. As an example of how more than one type of significance test may be used on the same set of data, the data previously used in describing the Kolmogorov-Smirnov test will be examined again for significance. This time a scoring system will be attached to the scale positions, and the frequencies are used in place of the percentages.

Rating on New Brand of Sherry

	Score	Men	Women
Very sweet	+2	37	30
Sweet	+1	45	35
Neither sweet nor dry	0	58	50
Dry	−1	40	45
Very dry	−2	20	40
		$n_1 = 200$	$n_2 = 200$

The main assumption being made is that the scoring system is an interval scale and that the numerical distances between the scale positions are valid. The Kolmogorov-Smirnov test makes no such assumptions.

To test the difference between two means $\bar{x}_1$ and $\bar{x}_2$ based on two independent samples of size n_1 and n_2 it is necessary to calculate the variance of each set of data. From the two variances s_1^2 and s_2^2 the standard error of the difference between two means is calculated as:

$$\text{Standard error } \bar{x}_1 - \bar{x}_2 = \sqrt{s^2 \left[\frac{n_1 + n_2}{n_1 \times n_2} \right]}$$

where s^2 is a pooled estimate of the variance based on both samples

$$s^2 = \frac{\sum f_1(x_1 - \bar{x}_1)^2 + \sum f_2(x_2 - \bar{x}_2)^2}{(n_1 - 1) + (n_2 - 1)}$$

This average value of the variance is used as this test assumes that the two samples come from populations where the variance is equal. The null hypothesis usually states that there is no difference in the means. If this is true then the quantity:

$$Z = \frac{\bar{x}_1 - \bar{x}_2}{\text{standard error } (\bar{x}_1 - \bar{x}_2)}$$

will have the normal distribution (except when the sample sizes are very small). Tables of the normal distribution may, therefore, be used to test the significance of Z calculated from the two samples.

Example. The data on sherry are used in the example calculations given below. Subscripts 1 and 2 in the formulae refer to the sample of men and women respectively.

Score

$(x_1$ or $x_2)$	f_1	f_2	$f_1 x_1$	$f_2 x_2$	$(x_1 - \bar{x}_1)$	$(x_1 - \bar{x}_1)^2$	$f_1(x_1 - \bar{x}_1)^2$
+2	37	30	74	60	1.805	3.2580	120.5460
+1	45	35	45	35	0.805	0.6480	29.1600
0	58	50	0	0	−0.195	0.0380	2.2040
−1	40	45	−40	−45	−1.195	1.4280	57.1200
−2	20	40	−40	−80	−2.195	4.8180	96.3600
	200	200	39	−30			305.3900

$(x_2 - \bar{x}_2)$	$(x_2 - \bar{x}_2)^2$	$f_2(x_2 - \bar{x}_2)^2$
2.150	4.6225	138.6750
1.150	1.3225	46.2875
0.150	0.0225	1.1250
−0.850	0.7225	32.5125
−1.850	3.4225	136.9000
		355.5000

$$\bar{x}_1 = \frac{\Sigma f_1 x_1}{n_1} = \frac{39}{200} = 0.195 \quad \bar{x}_2 = \frac{\Sigma f_2 x_2}{n_2} = \frac{-30}{200} = -0.150$$

$$s^2 = \frac{305.39 + 355.50}{199 + 199} = 1.661$$

$$\text{Standard error } (\bar{x}_1 - \bar{x}_2) = \sqrt{1.661 \left[\frac{200 + 200}{200 \times 200} \right]} = \sqrt{0.01661} = 0.1288$$

$$Z = \frac{\bar{x}_1 - \bar{x}_2}{\text{standard error } (\bar{x}_1 - \bar{x}_2)} = \frac{0.195 - (-0.150)}{0.1288} = 2.68$$

Table A2.1 may be used to determine the significance level obtained by a difference in means which is equal to $Z = 2.68$ standard errors. Such a value is greater than the 2.58 standard errors needed for the result to be significant at the 1 % level but less than 3.29 standard errors needed for 0.1 % significance. It is actually significant at the 0.74 % level. The conclusion which leads from this significance test is that men rate the new sherry to be more sweet than do women.

When scores are attached to the semantic rating scales used in market research and the data are assumed to have the properties of measured data, significance tests such as the one just described may be used to evaluate differences. The gain in doing so may be seen by considering the results of the present significance test on the sherry data along with the analysis of the same data using the Kolmogorov-Smirnov test. This latter test was unable to detect any significant differences between men's and women's ratings, whereas the present test between the two means was able to show that a real difference was present. On the debit side the two-means test requires a lot more calculations than does the Kolmogorov-Smirnov test. However, most modern computer programs for survey analysis have facilities for automatically calculating means, variances, standard deviations and standard errors for scales which have been scored.

Testing the Difference between the Means of Two Matched Samples

When the same sample of respondents rates two separate items, or rates the same item on two separate occasions, the ensuing data are often presented in a form which may suggest that the test for two independent means may be employed. The test, if applied to such matched sample data, would give too few significant results due to the matching. The correct test for this situation will now be described using the data on after-shave lotion previously analysed by means of the sign test. These data consisted of a sample of $n = 200$ men rating two new versions, X and Y, of an existing after-shave lotion, by means of a semantic scale. It will give another example of how ranked data may, if certain assumptions are made, be treated as measured data by attaching a numerical scoring system to the scale positions. The scoring used in the example will be:

	Score
Like very much	5
Like	4
Neither like nor dislike	3
Dislike	2
Dislike very much	1

The matched sample test uses the two-way table, presented previously, of version X's score (denoted by x_1) analysed by the score for version Y (denoted by x_2). From this table the difference in scores, $d = x_1 - x_2$ may be calculated and a frequency distribution of the d value can be formed. If the null hypothesis that there is no difference in the ratings of the two versions is true, then the expected or mean difference score $(\overline{d})$ would be zero, with a standard error of:

$$\text{Standard error } (\overline{d}) = \frac{s_d}{\sqrt{n}}$$

where s_d = the standard deviation of the difference scores,

$$d = x_1 - x_2$$

The null hypothesis that $\overline{d} = 0$ may be tested by calculating the criterion:

$$Z = \frac{\overline{d} - 0}{\text{standard error }(\overline{d})} = \frac{\overline{d}\sqrt{n}}{s_d}$$

Z will follow a normal distribution, when the sample is not too small, and Table A2.1 may be used to evaluate the significance level.

Example. Scoring the two-way table of version X's ratings against the ratings on version Y gives the following table.

Rating on version Y (x_2 score)		*Rating on version X (x_1 score)*					
		5	**4**	**3**	**2**	**1**	**Total men**
	5	20	20	4	4	2	50
	4	30	20	10	5	5	70
	3	**18**	10	8	3	1	40
	2	10	**7**	5	4	4	30
	1	4	0	2	2	2	10
Total men		82	57	29	18	14	200

From this table a frequency distribution of difference scores is easily obtained; for instance, the score $d = x_1 - x_2 = +2$ is obtained from the cells in bold in the above table.

$d = x_1 - x_2$	f	f_d	$(d - \overline{d})$	$(d - \overline{d})^2$	$f(d - \overline{d})^2$
+4	4	16	3.725	13.876	55.504
+3	10	30	2.725	7.426	74.260
+2	27	54	1.725	2.976	80.352
+1	47	47	0.725	0.526	24.722
0	54	0	-0.275	0.076	4.104
−1	37	−37	−1.275	1.626	60.162
−2	10	−20	−2.275	5.176	51.760
−3	9	−27	−3.275	10.726	96.534
−4	2	−8	−4.275	18.276	36.552
	200	+55			483.950

$$\overline{d} = \frac{\Sigma f d}{\Sigma f} = \frac{+55}{200} = +0.275$$

$$s_d = \sqrt{\frac{\Sigma f(d - \overline{d})^2}{\Sigma f - 1}} = \sqrt{\frac{483.950}{199}} = \sqrt{2.432} = 1.56$$

$$\text{Standard error }(\overline{d}) = \frac{s_d}{\sqrt{n}} = \frac{1.56}{\sqrt{200}} = 0.110$$

$$Z = \frac{\overline{d}}{\text{standard error }(\overline{d})} = \frac{+0.275}{0.110} = 2.50$$

The calculated mean $\overline{d} = 0.275$ is 2.50 standard errors distant from the hypothesised mean of zero. Such a deviation is almost equal to the 2.58 standard errors needed to be significant at the 1 % level. It is, in fact, significant at the 1.24 % level. The sign test applied to these data gave a result which was just significant at the 2 % level according to Table A2.2 of the chi-square distribution.

SOME GENERAL POINTS ON SIGNIFICANCE TESTING

Significance Tests on Small Samples

When the data collected are based on small samples, many of the significance tests given in this chapter need modifying or replacing by special alternative tests. As a rough rule it is recommended that, if the sample size is $n = 50$ or larger, the tests given may be all applied without serious error. On this point, it is worth mentioning that the first two tests given for measured data are often referred to as "the t-test for two independent sample means" and "the paired t-test for two matched sample means". This is because the significance test criteria Z, in both cases, will follow a statistical distribution known as the t distribution. This distribution which is applicable for small samples becomes more and more like the shape of the normal distribution as the sample size increases. The convergence may be illustrated by considering the number of standard errors difference that are needed between two means to achieve a 5 % significance level. In the case of large samples, where the normal distribution is appropriate, the value is 1.96. For small samples leading to the t distribution, a value of 2.04 is required for $n = 30$ and 2.00 for $n = 60$. This shows that the normal distribution may be used for samples of $n = 50$ or more in such significance tests.

Interpretation of Significant Results

The fact that a survey result is found to be significant, by carrying out a statistical significance test, often leads to confusion when such a result is presented to people unfamiliar with recent methodology. The layman, when told that something is significant, often assumes that the researcher considers the result to be "important". As explained in this chapter, such an inference is not necessarily true. In statistical terms, if, for example, a difference between two percentages is declared significant, it simply means that this difference, no matter whether it is a *large* or *small* difference, cannot be explained by sampling errors. With very large samples, where the sampling distributions of the null and alternative hypotheses will have small standard errors, small differences in percentages will be significant. Whether these small differences are important to the researcher and his client depends on the subject matter of the survey, previous survey results and any number of other practical considerations. The example that follows gives some idea in one particular case how small differences in percentages may be viewed. A random sample of 1000 housewives owning washing machine brand A is found to contain 48 % who claim to be "very pleased" with the machine. A further random sample of 1000, who own brand B, contains 56 % who are "very pleased". The difference in percentages 56 % − 48 % = 8 % is comparatively small and might be regarded as unimportant, even though it is a statistically significant difference. However, if it is known from previous surveys with samples of 1000 that differences between brands of washing machine are always insignificant, then the observed difference may be thought of as being an important finding.

This chapter has been presented in terms of simple random sampling. Most surveys use more complicated sampling methods where the standard errors are usually larger than the standard error formulae given here. The amount by which they are larger is known as the *design factor*. In those cases above where a standard error has been given, this standard error should be increased by the design factor of the survey being analysed, when carrying out a significance test.

On this point about simple random sampling it is difficult to give much advice to users of quota samples. Strictly speaking, it is not possible to calculate sampling errors and, therefore, carry out significance tests on data from quota samples. In practice, researchers quite often assume that the data are as if they had come from a random sample and proceed to carry out significance tests as described above. The limited research that has been done on quota sampling methods indicates that, in some cases, the sampling errors may be higher than for random sampling. For this reason, some researchers increase the standard error by an arbitrary factor such as 1.5 or 2.0 when carrying out significance tests on quota sample data.

Use of Computers in Significance Testing

With the advent of powerful desktop computing placing a personal computer on most market researchers' desks, most or all of the drudgery of calculation in significance testing has been removed. In some ways this is a retrograde step in the sense that one cannot really understand, say, the chi-square test without actually doing one by hand. Readers are strongly advised to work through the examples given earlier before relying on the computer to automatically spew out reams of significance testing results. Most survey analysis packages and statistical analysis packages (e.g. SPSS) now offer a range of significance tests. Most of the tests given in this chapter are available in SPSS and other similar packages. Even spreadsheets (e.g. EXCEL) offer some of them. With this increased power and flexibility come attendant problems. More than once in this chapter we have referred to the dangers of multiple comparison significance testing on the same set of data. Almost inevitably many of our so-called significant results will include those that are occurring by chance.

MULTIVARIATE ANALYSIS OF SURVEY DATA

Having discussed methods of estimating the likely accuracy or statistical significance of data obtained from sample surveys, we now examine how statistical science can help us analyse survey results. This section of the chapter is concerned with techniques of multivariate analysis looking beyond the cross tab. There are a wide variety of such techniques, of which the traditional forms have an underlying statistical basis. More modern techniques involve artificial intelligence and iterative processes of reasoning and include neural networks and genetic algorithms. There is much debate amongst practitioners as to the relevance of these techniques to market research, and it is fair to say the jury is still out on these matters. Limitations of space will restrict this section to concentration on some of the traditional statistically based techniques.

A chapter such as this can only scratch the surface in terms of informing the reader of the available techniques, what they do, how they do it, and what the pitfalls are, so it must be seen as purely introductory.

Multivariate analysis is broadly concerned with the relationships between a set of variables. How similar are they? Are they correlated? Can they be summarised effectively? Are they predictive of outcomes in any sense? Are there groups of respondents with similar behavioural or attitudinal patterns as measured by these variables? Multivariate techniques attempt to answer questions such as these. Traditionally multivariate techniques are classified into two groups:

(a) *Interdependence.* Here we are only interested in the interrelationship between variables and not in their power of influence on the value of other variables. Correlation analysis and techniques summarising the correlation structure of a series of variables such as the various forms of factor analysis are typical statistical techniques for examining interdependence.
(b) *Dependence.* Here the value of a variable, usually termed a dependent variable, is assumed to be influenced in some sense by the value of a series of other variables, usually termed independent variables. The most commonly used statistical techniques for handling the concept of dependence include regression analysis – producing regression equations of the form

$$Y = b_1x_1 + b_2x_2 \text{---} + b_nx_n + C$$

and the "tree drawing" techniques such as AID and CHAID.

INTERDEPENDENCE TECHNIQUES

Correlation Analysis

Consider the following data set. Two variables A and B are collected for five respondents. The values of each variable can vary between 1 and 5. Consider the following set of raw data.

Respondent number	A	B
1	1	1
2	2	2
3	3	3
4	4	4
5	5	5

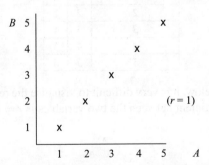

The values of A and B follow each other exactly for each respondent. For respondent 1, A has a well below average value of 1, and so does B. Respondent 5 has well above average values of both A and B. In this data set A and B are moving in the same direction with a relationship so clear that if we plotted the data on a scatterplot as above we can see a clear and perfect linear relationship between the two variables. In this case the data set is completely explained by the relationship $A = B$, and the correlation coefficient, usually depicted as r, has the value +1.

A similar case occurs if the raw data look as follows:

Respondent number	A	B
1	1	5
2	2	4
3	3	3
4	4	2
5	5	1

In this case respondent 1 has a value well below average for variable A and well above average for variable B, and conversely for respondent 5, and the same pattern occurs for all respondents. A and B are moving in opposite directions, but in a way which can be perfectly explained by the relationship $A = 6 - B$. The correlation coefficient between A and B is now -1, indicating a perfect but negative relationship between the two variables, as shown in the diagram below.

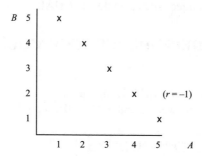

The third case involves a very weak relationship between the variables A and B. The raw data set now becomes

Respondent no	A	B
1	1	4
2	2	2
3	3	1
4	4	5
5	5	3

As can be seen in the plot below, it is very difficult to visualise the relationship between A and B. Here the correlation coefficient between the two variables is $r = 0.1$, quite close to zero.

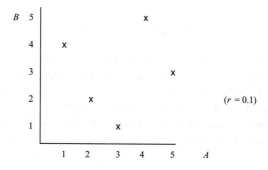

Thus the correlation coefficient r is used to depict the strength of the inter-relationship between any two variables. The stronger the relationship the closer will be the correlation coefficient to 1 (although the sign of the relationship can be negative as well as positive). The weaker the relationship the closer will be the correlation coefficient to 0. The correlation between more than two sets of variables may be depicted by the correlation matrix, which looks as follows

	Variable				
	A	B	C	D	E
A	1.00	−0.05	0.75	0.20	0.14
B	−0.05	1.00	−0.40	0.80	−0.28
C	0.75	−0.40	1.00	−0.20	0.14
D	0.20	0.80	−0.20	1.00	−0.14
E	0.14	−0.28	0.14	−0.14	1.00

From the correlation matrix we can see that there is a strong relationship between A and C (0.75), between B and D (0.80) but E is very weakly correlated with any of variables A to D. If we wished to summarise these data in any sense, we may describe them as the three concepts A and C, B and D, and E.

Correlation analysis is particularly useful for examining broad patterns in the data set with a view to reducing the data dimensionality, and if there is a key survey variable, e.g. weight of use of product field, likelihood of recommending the product to a friend, it is very useful to correlate variables such as those with all other survey variables to produce hypotheses about possible influences on these key variables. However, some caution should be observed when interpreting the results of correlation analysis when the data being correlated consist of data of variable form. It is easier for a variable A consisting of five possible values to correlate with a variable B consisting of five possible values, than to correlate with a variable C consisting of nine possible values. Hence the size of the correlation coefficient may be influenced by the "scaling effect". Data in binary form can present peculiar difficulties here. Nevertheless correlation analysis can be an extremely useful preliminary analysis to aid understanding of the results of survey data. Statistical tests are available to show the probability of the true correlation between any two items being greater than zero, and these can help guide the analysis through the quantity of numbers generated.

Factor and Principal Component Analysis

Consider the correlation matrix depicted above. We have already noted that A is highly correlated with C, B is highly correlated with D, and E is not really correlated with any of A to D. Intuitively, instead of the five dimensions we have measured, a reasonably accurate summary of this data could be made in three-dimensional space. Summarising the underlying correlation structure of multidimensional space has traditionally been the task of a series of techniques broadly classified as factor analysis, of which the most widely used in market research is principal component analysis. Principal component analysis involves mathematical techniques attempting to summarise a data set such that each component extracts successively as much explanatory power as possible, and as such provides a straightforward mathematical transformation of the data. Classical factor analysis is model-based – it assumes that within a data set, each variable has at least something in common with other variables, and something which is unique to itself, and factor analysis is concerned with the communality in the data set. However, although the mathematical procedures are different, results tend to be interpretably similar. The terms factor or principal component will be used interchangeably.

Principal component analysis of the data set which generated the correlation matrix has produced the following set of factors. Factors should be interpreted by their loadings e.g. Factor 1 below has a loading of 0.89 with variable B, 0.98 with variable D and only 0.12 with variable A. Factors loadings represent the level of correlation between the factor and the original variable so clearly Factor 1 is highly associated with variables B and D, and not with variables A, C and E.

Variable	Factor 1	Factor 2	Factor 3	Factor 4	Factor 5
A	0.12	0.98	0.08	−0.15	−0.02
B	0.89	−0.15	−0.17	−0.06	0.39
C	−0.25	0.86	0.04	0.44	−0.04
D	0.98	0.08	−0.04	−0.05	−0.18
E	−0.11	0.08	0.99	0.01	−0.02
Variance explained	39 %	35 %	20 %	4 %	3 %

Examining the factor solution further we see that Factor 2 is describing A and C, Factor 3 is associated with E and no other variable and Factors 4 and 5 have at best moderate loadings and do not seem to be describing very much at all. As we have observed by eye, the data may be adequately summarised by taking the first three components. The degree to which the summarisation is adequate is described by the row "variance explained", when if we add the percentages for the first three factors we can see that 94 % of the variance in the data is explained. (Variance explained is a measure of the ability of the principal component or factor analysis to recreate the original data set.) Factors are interpreted by their loadings and a typical market research factor analysis may look as below.

Factor 1 above has clearly something to do with healthy eating, and Factor 2 with modern eating. The statements above are based on five-point scales where agree a lot $= 5$, and disagree a lot $= 1$, so it is not surprising that a person with a score of 5 on "I try to include plenty of fibre in my diet these days" tends to give a score of 1 on "I think health foods are only bought by fanatics", and vice versa. Hence these two items are negatively correlated, and this is reflected in the opposite signs of the factor loading.

	Factor 1	Factor 2
I enjoy eating food from other countries	0.02	−0.84
I make sure my family eats a balanced diet	0.87	0.21
I always think of the calories in what I eat	0.74	0.14
I try to include plenty of fibre in my diet these days	0.92	0.23
I think fast food is all junk really	0.41	0.89
I like to try out new food products	0.13	−0.78
I often buy take away meals to eat at home	−0.07	−0.30
I think health foods are only bought by fanatics	−0.82	0.04

Factors or principal components may be activated for individuals by means of factor scores. A person who is a healthy eater will tend to score 5 very often on statements highly loaded on

Factor 1 (and only 1 for the negatively loaded item). If we think conceptually of factor scores as the product of the individual's raw score for a variable multiplied by the factor loading and summed across all variables (in reality factor score calculations are rather more complex), we can see that a healthy eater will have a high score on Factor 1 and a person whose diet consists mainly of fast foods and ready-made foods will have a low score. This single analysis has reduced dimensionality from the eight items contained in the attitudinal battery to two items, health and modernity, and via factor scores eight sets of numbers per individual may be reduced to two. This can be extremely useful in data interpretation and as input into further types of analysis, e.g. cluster analysis.

Factor and principal component analysis involve a series of complex mathematical procedures which are well beyond the scope of this article. However sophisticated the mathematical procedures, usage of such analysis mainly involves the art of market research. When analysing data via such analysis the main tasks of the analyst are:

(a) Which factor solution to choose. As a summary of say twenty variables do we choose the 7-factor solution, the 8-factor solution, or the 9-factor solution ... and so on? The major statistical guides which can help us are:
   o Variance explained – the higher the better within the realms of practicability.
   o Which if any of the original variables are not being adequately summarised by the chosen factor solution, and if they are "lost" in some sense, does it matter?
(b) Interpretation of the factors. Do they make sense? Are they useful for marketing purposes?

The arts of factor analysis can only be learned by experience but this form of analysis has enormous benefit in understanding the underlying dimensions by which respondents answer questions, and as such can greatly reduce the task of data analysis. Ideally factor analysis is conducted on scaled data, and the analyst should be wary of mixed scale data.

Mapping Techniques – Correspondence Analysis

Techniques of correlation and factor analysis may greatly aid interpretation of a data matrix. Consider the following matrix where the data involve the level of association in percentage form for each brand (in this case football teams) with a series of statements presented to the survey respondent. It should be noted here that this data set is purely hypothetical.

	Team A	Team B	Team C	Team D	Team E	Team F
Efficient	90	50	70	80	70	70
Stylish	60	50	90	80	60	70
Improving	50	60	60	60	50	60
Successful	90	60	60	80	60	60
Entertaining	60	60	80	90	60	70
Imaginative	50	50	70	70	60	70

It is easy to see that team A is perceived to be the most efficient, team D the most entertaining and so on, but what about team B? Does it have any merit at all? If we look along the row "improving" we note that it has an equal highest score of sixty with three other teams. But, given that it tends to score lower than other teams on most other dimensions can we not infer that in relative terms team B is the most improving side? Perhaps the data matrix would be clearer if we looked at the relative performance of each team on each of the dimensions, i.e. given the total size of a brand's image, what share is taken up by each of the attributes. Obviously here we are dealing with the "personality" of a brand. We may now want to answer questions such as "which brands have similar personalities?" and "Which attributes tend to measure similar things across brands?" One method of doing this is by setting up a chi-squared expected matrix. For each data cell we would obtain, from the row and column marginal totals, the value which each brand would be expected to have if it behaved averagely on each dimension. We now look at the 'deviations from expected' values for each data cell. The table now looks like this:

	Team A	Team B	Team C	Team D	Team E	Team F
Efficient	18	−10	−8	−3	5	−2
Stylish	−9	−7	16	1	−2	1
Improving	−7	13	−1	−6	−1	3
Successful	21	3	−14	1	−2	−9
Entertaining	−11	2	4	9	−4	−1
Imaginative	−12	−1	3	−2	4	8

Looking at the pattern of the deviations we can see that for the dimensions "efficient" and "successful" the teams with big deviations on these dimensions (teams A and C) have the same pattern of deviations i.e. team A being relatively efficient and successful, and team C being relatively inefficient and unsuccessful. For these brands efficiency and success are correlated. Similar logic applies to the correlation between brands A, B and C and the variables stylish, entertaining and imaginative. Elsewhere the pattern is a little more confusing. However, the pattern within the data becomes clearer if we re-order the table putting together rows (attributes) which are correlated and similarly for brands. The final table looks as follows:

	Team A	Team C	Team F	Team B	Team D	Team E
Efficient	18	−8	−2	−10	−3	5
Successful	21	−14	−9	3	1	−2
Stylish	−9	16	1	−7	1	−2
Entertaining	−11	4	−1	2	9	−4
Imaginative	−12	3	8	−1	−2	4
Improving	−7	−1	3	13	−6	−1

We can now see clearly that team A sacrifices style for success and efficiency, team B seems to be improving although lacking efficiency or style (perhaps sheer team spirit is dictating here). The imaginative/stylish teams C and F, alas, are relatively unsuccessful. Team E's attempts to model themselves on Team A have not proved successful and Team D's brand of entertaining football has resulted in success, but they are perceived to have peaked and "improving" is not a major feature of their brand personality.

This form of analysis, looking at the relative structure of a data matrix and using the concepts of correlation/factor analysis to represent the data, is the basis of the most widely used of graphical "mapping" techniques, namely "correspondence analysis". The two-dimensional correspondence analysis representation looks as follows:

Team B*	
*Improving	
	*Successful
Entertaining*	
*Team F	
*Imaginative	
Team D*	Team A*
	*Team E
*Team C	
	*Efficient
*Stylish	

Correspondence analysis involves the use of angles to represent correlations. If a line (vector) is drawn from the point representing "imaginative" to the origin (intersection of the axes), and a similar line from the point representing "entertaining", it will be noted that the angle between the two vectors is small. The smaller the angle, the nearer the "cosine" of that angle is to 1 (or perfect positive correlation). There is little correlation between the concepts "stylish" and "improving" and the angle between the two vectors tends towards a right angle – and the cosine of a right angle is zero indicating no correlation whatsoever. It should be noted that the angle between the vectors "stylish" and "successful" is approximately 180° and the cosine of an angle of 180° is −1 (perfect negative correlation). As we have seen, in relative terms style and success are very highly negatively correlated.

The correlation between teams is similarly represented by angles. In terms of the relationship between teams and attributes the representation is directional. The eastern sector of the map includes the attributes "efficient" and "successful", and we are not surprised to find Team A dominating this sector. Conversely Team C is to be found in the western section of the map, surrounded by attributes such as "stylish", "entertaining" and "imaginative", and a long way from the attributes "successful" and "efficient". Team B is in the northern section, close to the attribute "improving".

Correspondence analysis thus examines the relative structure of a data matrix. It is particularly useful for brand attribute matrices where brand personalities can be examined in some detail, but can be used for any type of data matrix. It is a form of analysis which can be considered as a brand of the factor family. However we know that the world is not purely two-dimensional. It is unlikely that, say, a twenty brand by thirty attribute matrix can be represented efficiently by two factors. Correspondence analysis generates as many factors as are needed to recreate the original data matrix – but to represent even three-dimensional space graphically three diagrams have to be shown (Factor 1 with Factor 2, Factor 1 with Factor 3, and Factor 2 with Factor 3) and few of us have sufficient mental agility to interpret data formed by a series of maps. Thus, if a two-dimensional map does not provide an adequate representation of the original data set, it is probably "unwise" to use this form of analysis. As with all forms of the factor family the variances explained attributed to Factor 1 (the horizontal axis) and Factor 2 (the vertical axis) are calculated in correspondence analysis. In the case of the map presented above, 89 % of the variation in the data has been explained by the first two factors, and we are safe in presenting the information in the form of a map. When two-dimensional mapping produces adequate representation the ability to recreate a data matrix in graphical form has enormous advantages. A map presents the notion of a market gap clearly. In our map there is no team which is both relatively efficient and stylish – there is room for a team with both those attributes. Within the breakfast cereal market there has been traditionally a gap between the brands appealing to children, and the brands appealing to the health conscious. Is there room in the market for a healthy children's brand – and would it sell? The major power of mapping techniques lies in their idea generation ability and data are presented in a way that no purely mathematical technique can match.

Correspondence analysis is only one of the many forms of mapping technique available to the analyst. Other techniques produce maps with greater emphasis on the size of the brand's image as opposed to the structure of the brand's image. The most commonly used of this form of map is the biplot. Some forms of mapping involve the perception of closeness or similarity between objects, and this generates maps by techniques such as multidimensional scaling. It is beyond the scope of this article to give more than a broad introduction to mapping techniques, and in particular correspondence analysis, but the golden rule of presentation of a data set in two dimensions, whatever form of map is used, is simple.

Do two dimensions form an adequate representation of my data matrix for practical marketing purposes?

If the answer is yes to this question, then the scope for idea generation which a map offers has huge advantages over other methods of analysing a data matrix.

Cluster Analysis

We now move away from techniques based on correlation and address ourselves to the inter-relationship between objects formed by distance, or similarity. Cluster analysis is usually concerned with the similarity or distance between respondents across a series of measures. Cluster analysis attempts to form groups such that:

I. within each group each individual is as similar as possible (minimise within cluster variance);
II. the difference between groups is as great as possible (maximise between cluster variance).

There are many forms of cluster analysis, in part depending on how similarity or distance is calculated, and within this framework there are two major typologies.

(a) Hierarchical techniques – starting from all individuals in their own individual cluster and proceeding to group individuals on a stage-by-stage basis. These techniques are most suitable for small sample cluster analysis.

(b) Iterative techniques – starting by selecting a series of respondents randomly and allocating all other respondents to these originally selected respondents on the basis of least distance. Successive iterations increase the accuracy of the clusters. By far the most widely use of this form of cluster analysis is the technique known as k-means or iterative relocation, and this is the technique we shall be describing in this section.

The most common form of distance measure used in k-means cluster analysis is squared Euclidean distance. Let us assume that three respondents are measured on four characteristics A, B, C and D, as in the table below.

		Respondent		
		1	2	3
Measure	A	36	40	38
	B	112	196	124
	C	22	34	24
	D	35	42	36

The distance between respondents 1 and 2 via squared Euclidean distance is given as the sum of squared distances for each dimension. In our case this becomes $(36-40)^2 + (112-196)^2 + (22-34)^2 + (35-42)^2 = 7265$. A distance matrix may now be formed for each respondent which looks as follows:

	Respondent		
Respondent	1	2	3
1	n/a		
2	7265	n/a	
3	153	5324	n/a

So if we wanted to form two clusters from these three respondents, clearly we would group together respondents 1 and 3.

Observation of the original row scores, however, shows that the distance measure is dominated by measure B, which varies to a much greater extent than the other measurements because it is on a different scale. In fact these measurements are to do with bodily shape – measurement B is weight in pounds and the remaining measurements are in inches. In order to get over this problem the data are entered in "standardised" form, deducting from each observation the mean of that set of observations, and dividing by the standard deviation of those sets of observations. By this means the "standardised score" is formed. Each measurement now has a mean of 0 and variance 1, and the distance measure will not be biased.

It should be noted that factor scores are standardised and are frequently used as the input into cluster analysis.

Given that we now have a suitable distance measure, how do we proceed with the task of computing the distance between large numbers of respondents on a large variety of measures? The major method is known as k-means clustering. If the 6-cluster solution is required, six respondents are selected to represent six initial cluster centres. In some programs these respondents are selected randomly, in others they are selected to be as far apart as possible. Using these six respondents as the first basis for calculating distance, the most similar respondents are added to the initial members to increase the size of the clusters. As new members are added the cluster centres change, and eventually, at the first iteration, all respondents are allocated to one of these six clusters. However, since the cluster centres have been changing throughout the process, there may be some respondents allocated to a particular cluster who are now close to another cluster. Thus iteration two begins and reallocates respondents. Eventually, after a finite number of iterations, the program determines that it has reached the maximum possible level of "variance explained", i.e. it cannot further reallocate respondents in such a way that it would increase the discriminatory power of the cluster analysis on the cluster variables.

Once a cluster analysis has been produced, we now have to examine how good it is. If we could visualise points in n-dimensional space, we might hope that we could detect "natural" clusters, i.e. thickly populated areas of data points surrounded by relatively clear areas of space. In reality, many market research cluster analyses are formed from data which produce continuous sets of points in space – i.e. there are no natural clusters in the data. A little thought will tell the researcher that there are a large variety of ways of carving up such a data set, of which the cluster analysis performed is one of the many which could have been formed.

A highly recommended technique for testing the presence of natural clusters if sample sizes permit is to split the sample into two random halves and to conduct a series of cluster analyses on each half of the data (perhaps all solutions from the 4-cluster solution to the 10-cluster solution).

If a particular cluster analysis reproduces itself on both halves of the data, it is likely that some evidence of natural clusters has been found. However, one should be very wary of any cluster analysis solution when little or no resemblance between the solutions in the two sub-samples can be discovered.

A further useful diagnostic is the proportion of variance explained by the analysis. The closer the respondents within clusters and the further apart the clusters, the greater the variance explained. Let us assume that we have produced all possible cluster solutions from 2 to 10. The table below shows the variance explained by each of these analyses:

No. of clusters	Variance explained (%)
2	11
3	19
4	25
5	30
6	34
7	37
8	39
9	40
10	41

The diagnostics suggest that the 7-cluster solution could be considered optimal, because after that the increase in efficiency is relatively small. But this set of information should be used in conjunction with split-sample comparison techniques where possible.

Cluster analysis is a very popular segmentation technique, but the most important question is how well it discriminates in a sense useful for marketing purposes. It can produce a set of stereotypes which describe only a handful of people, and hence care must be taken when using this technique. Nevertheless, at its best it can produce outstandingly useful results. Perhaps the best known example of cluster analysis in Britain is the original ACORN geodemographic classification of residential neighbourhoods, by which small areas were clustered on a series of 1971 census variables; similar systems have been employed in the United States and other countries. A 36-cluster solution was formed, which could be described in terms of eleven broad groups as follows:

Rural areas	Areas with high proportions of workers in agriculture
Modern housing for young families	Predominately areas of recent settlement with young middle class owner occupier families
Areas of older housing and settlements	Traditional market towns with population a cross section
Areas with poor quality older housing	Houses lacking basic amenities such as fixed baths
Local authority housing in areas of recent settlement	In particular inhabitants of new towns with low unemployment
Traditional local authority housing	Poorer areas with high unemployment
Local authority housing in areas of high stress	The most deprived communities in Britain, with huge levels of unemployment
Inner city ethnic areas	Areas with high proportions of Afro-Caribbean or Asian residents
Fashionable inner city areas	Areas with high proportions of young professionals and students
Traditional high status suburbia	Older more conservative areas with high proportions of middle class
Seaside and retirement resorts	Areas with high proportions of older residents

Since 1971 Britain has changed, and so of course has the ACORN solution shown above. Nevertheless ACORN revolutionised marketing, and in the late 1990s in Britain there are many geodemographic systems formed by cluster analysis, and a variety of marketing applications are produced. So ACORN is an example of a cluster analysis which spawned an industry.

DEPENDENCE TECHNIQUES

We now turn our attention to techniques measuring dependence. As stated previously, we assume that a dependent variable is influenced in some way by a series of independent variables, and usually a model revealing this dependence is formed. There are many forms of such models, some based on correlation, others based on techniques of sums of squares, and another set based on model building via statistical tests such as chi-square analysis.

Automatic Interaction Detector (AID)

AID is a grandfather of methods of data analysis involving the generation of data trees which attempt to maximise the explanatory power of each branch of the tree. Consider the following set of eight observations based on the daily smoking consumption of eight respondents:

40

35

25

20

20

15

5

0

The data sums to 160, and hence average consumption is twenty cigarettes. If a single count such as this is the only analysis conducted, the only conceivable prediction we could make about the daily smoking habits of an individual is that he or she smokes twenty. In most cases we would of course be wrong. The extent to which we are wrong can be determined by what we predicted minus what the survey respondent actually smokes. Since these errors will sum to zero, the best method of expressing the extent of the error is by squaring the individual errors and summing for the population. In this example the sum of squared errors is 1300, as is shown in the table below:

Cigarette consumption	Prediction	Error	Error squared
40	20	−20	400
35	20	−15	225
25	20	−5	25
20	20	0	0
20	20	0	0
15	20	+5	25
5	20	+15	225
0	20	+20	400
			1300

However, suppose we now start to classify respondents. The first four respondents are male, and the last four respondents are female. We now recalculate average consumption amongst males to be thirty and females to be ten. Now, we improve our prediction. For every male the prediction is now thirty, and for every female the prediction is 10. The table below shows the new model and a recalculation of the error.

Sex	Cigarette consumption	Prediction	Error	Error squared
M	40	30	−10	100
M	35	30	−5	25
M	25	30	+5	25
M	20	30	+10	100
F	20	10	−10	100
F	15	10	−5	25
F	5	10	+5	25
F	0	10	+10	100
				500

The reduction in the error term can be calculated as $1300 - 500 = 800$. This reduction in the error term is often known as the between-group sum of squares. Basically, the larger the between-group sum of squares the greater the discriminatory power or predictive power of an independent variable – in our case sex – on a dependent variable – in our case smoking consumption. The calculation we have seen above is the basis of the AID algorithm. As with all models of this type the data input consists of a dependent variable and a series of independent predictor variables. At stage 1 the AID algorithm examines all possible dichotomous splits of all predictor variables and partitions the data using the variable with the greatest between-group sums of squares as its predictor. Let us suppose that the sample size for a survey on smoking consumption was 10 000 and that sex was the best predictor. The stage 1 algorithm would look as follows:

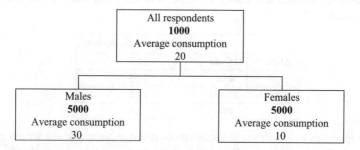

The algorithm now examines the 5000 males to see which variable produces the highest between-group sum of squares. Let us suppose that this is age 15–44 years versus 45+ years. The AID algorithm may now turn its attention to the 5000 females and again it may find the best possible split on age. However we may find a very sharp interaction in the data as can be observed by the stage 2 level of the AID tree below:

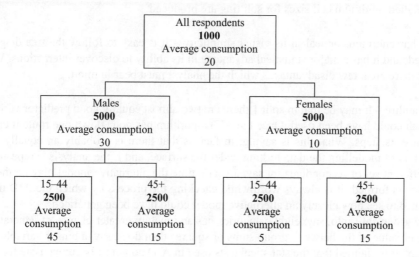

The diagram shows that amongst men, cigarette consumption declines steeply with age, whereas amongst women cigarette consumption rises steeply with age. What we have observed here is a somewhat extreme example of an "interaction" – age and sex do not react independently in terms of cigarette consumption; one needs to know what sex the respondent is before predicting his or her cigarette consumption from age.

The discovery of interactions is a key feature of model building. Looking at a simple two-way crosstab of cigarette consumption such as the raw data which went into this AID analysis can produce misleading results, as a perusal of the following data shows:

	Average cigarette consumption
All respondents	20
Male	30
Female	10
15–44	25
45+	15

If we fail to discover the interaction term we shall be in danger of inferring the following from the simple crosstabs:

		Cigarette consumption
Male	15–44	37.5
	45+	22.5
Female	15–44	12.5
	45+	7.5

Targeting of cigarettes to females will undoubtedly result in aiming at the wrong group.

AID thus finds significant interactions within the data set and this is undoubtedly its greatest strength in terms of model building. The process of creating a model by generating branches of a tree continues until some stopping rules are observed:

(a) No further dichotomous split produces statistically significant results in terms of differences in the value of the dependent variable.
(b) Specified minimum cell sizes for splitting are produced.

AID has enormous appeal in its visual simplicity – it is easy to follow the tree diagrams produced, and it has a major statistical advantage in its ability to discover interactions. When using it there are a few disadvantages which the analyst must bear in mind:

I. Instability – It may be that in split 1 there are two almost equally good predictor variables which could have been used. Once the AID algorithm has gone down one route it cannot retrace its steps. What this is saying, in fact, is that there is probably an equally good method of modelling the data lurking under the surface, and if the analysis is repeated on a different set of respondents in, say, a year's time the alternative model may be the one which is formed. It is always worthwhile checking the process by which the AID tree is formed to see how closely an alternative model could have been generated.
II. Any group split into, say, eight categories has an innately greater chance of generating a higher value of the between-group sums of squares than does, say, a binary variable such as sex. It is claimed that the statistical tests used in AID do not fully compensate for this.

One form of statistical test which would take into account the various levels of categorisation in the data is the chi square test via degrees of freedom. This is one of the reasons why the technique of chi square automatic interaction detector or CHAID was developed.

CHAID

CHAID differs from AID in the following ways:

I. The statistical test used, which results in a different method of tree generations.
II. It is not limited to splitting into dichotomies. Thus more branches of a tree can be generated.
III. It is recommended for use when the dependent variable is "categorical". It is particularly powerful when the dependent variable is a binary variable.

AID is recommended where the continuous variable is continuous, e.g. cigarette consumption. However, continuous variables can be categorised into groups and increasingly the CHAID technique seems to be more widely used.

The AID/CHAID techniques ultimately form groups which have considerable segmentation power on the dependent variable. Within the end cells formed by the algorithm we predict that all respondents have the same value. Perhaps alternative techniques can provide us with the ability to predict the behaviour of individuals and hence prove to have greater modelling power than tree generation algorithms. The next section examines one of these forms of model, namely regression analysis.

Multiple Regression Analysis

This form of analysis attempts to explain the values of a dependent variable in terms of one or more independent or predictor variables by means of an equation. The methodology is based around the concept of correlation. At its most basic the model produced is in the form of "simple least squares regression", producing an equation of the form:

$$Y = bX + c$$

where

$$b = \frac{\text{covariance } XY}{\text{variance } X}$$

c is a constant

Such a simple model may suffice well when the data are truly linear as shown below:

but if the data show some form of non linearity such as the following, a straight line will provide a less than optimal model of the data set.

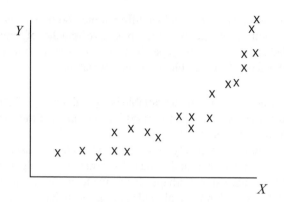

In the non linear case such as shown above perhaps a model of the form

$$Y = b_1 X^2 + b_2 X + c$$

may provide a better fit of the data points.

The purpose of regression modelling is to provide the best possible fit of the data relating to the dependent variable. The term least squares refers to the error term – the difference between the predicted value of the dependent variable and the actual value for an individual. The sum of squared differences is minimised when fitting the regression line.

It is usually unrealistic to assume that the value of a dependent variable is purely a function of a single independent variable. In most cases, for more realistic modelling we fit an equation based on multiple regression of the form:

$$Y = b_1 X_1 + b_2 X_2 + \ldots b_n X_n + c$$

There are many methods of producing multiple regression models, of which stepwise regression is the most popular form, and this is the method outlined in the following section.

Consider the following data set based on five time periods. The variables sales, advertising and marketing effort are measured in terms of volume of expenditure, and the variable income in terms of an index to base 100 for the first time period.

Sales	Advertising expenditure	Marketing effort	Income
100	30	30	100
130	60	10	95
120	60	5	105
160	70	20	105
200	90	30	110

We are now trying to build a model explaining sales in terms of three independent variables. The first stage is to examine the correlation coefficients of each of the independent variables with sales, as shown below:

	Correlation with sales
Advertising expenditure	0.94
Marketing effort	0.34
Income	0.70

Since advertising expenditure is the most highly correlated with sales, and the degree of correlation is statistically significant, this term enters the equation at stage 1 and a simple linear regression model is formed which is:

$$Sales = 1.69 \times advertising\ expenditure + 37.1$$

We now examine the stage 1 results. The model predictions are contained in the second column:

Observed sales	Predicted sales	Residual error
100	88	12
130	139	−9
120	139	−19
160	155	5
200	189	11

We now correlate the residual error with the two variables not in the equation forming the "partial correlation coefficient", i.e. the correlation with sales once the advertising effort has been removed. The partial correlations are as follows:

Marketing effort	0.98
Income	0.34

Because marketing effort is heavily correlated with the residual and is statistically significant, this term now enters the equation, and the new equation becomes:

$$Sales = 1.69 \times advertising\ expenditure + 1.14 \times marketing\ effort + 15.8$$

The stage 2 results read as follows:

Observed sales	Predicted sales	Residual error
100	101	−1
130	129	1
120	123	−3
160	157	3
200	202	−2

We now examine, as before, the correlation of the remaining term with the residual error. This is non-significant, so the procedure stops with the final model formed:

$$Sales + 1.69 \times advertising\ expenditure + 1.14 \times marketing\ effort + 15.8$$

The goodness of fit of the model is given by a statistic called the multiple correlation coefficient. In our case the fit of the model is extremely high, with a multiple correlation coefficient of 0.99.

The example is of course somewhat simplistic. Multiple correlation coefficients of 0.99 are rare indeed. In reality model building using regression requires a good deal of preparatory work from the analyst. In particular three stages must be carefully gone through.

(a) The search for non-linear relationships. This is usually done by scatterplots of each independent variable with the dependent variable and examination of the results.
(b) The search for interactions. As we have seen in the section on AID/CHAID modelling, making assumptions of independence can cause misleading results. An interaction between two independent variables, if discovered, can improve the model greatly. Traditionally statisticians looked for interactions between any two independent variables on the dependent variable using techniques such as analysis of variance, but increasingly there is a tendency to use AID/CHAID modelling first and enter key interactions terms into the regression model.
(c) The avoidance of multicollinearity. Multicollinearity infers a high degree of intercorrelation amongst the independent variables. It is good practice to examine the correlation matrix before committing variables to regression. The presence of multicollinearity can alter regression parameters to the extent where the results can appear nonsensical. If two or more terms are very highly intercorrelated it is sensible to remove at least one of them from the equation.

Regression techniques are also sensitive to the kind of data which are entered. Ideally continuous variables are used. However, if categorical data are used, the categories must be ordinal in some sense. If the categories are not ordinal, e.g. standard region, then the data should be entered as a series of dummy variables e.g.:

$$\text{Inner urban area} = 1$$
$$\text{Outer suburban area} = 0$$

Regression analysis requires a good deal of expertise, and inevitably with the proliferation of statistical packages for the PC there is a tendency to regard it as just another press button technique. At its best, and used wisely, it can outperform modelling techniques such as AID and CHAID, although this is not necessarily the case. Used unwisely, it can produce results which are at best misleading and at worst wrong. The reader is strongly recommended to study the literature carefully before embarking on regression analysis.

MULTIVARIATE ANALYSIS – CONCLUDING REMARKS

Inevitably, this chapter can only contain a brief outline of the vast range of tools of multivariate analysis available. With computing capabilities expanding seemingly without finite limit and with a host of software packages offering multivariate solutions to problems, it is vital that the analyst should be aware of the strengths and weaknesses of each alternative method of analysis. Alas, one cannot simply feed a set of data to a multivariate technique, press a button, and expect the perfect solution to emerge. Before using a technique it is vital that some basic understanding of the principles behind it are understood. Within our industry there is inevitably scope for misapplication of multivariate methods. In particular, regression-based techniques are sometimes abused leading to very misleading conclusions. Mapping techniques may hide more than they show. The cut-off point in factor-based techniques may be badly chosen, hence excluding a key variable. The cluster solution chosen may be a broad stereotype which describes no individual at all. So the interested reader is asked to explore the literature to examine the subject in much greater depth. A reading list is thus included. However, the use of multivariate analysis will doubtless continue to expand and the researcher is advised to gain experience with these techniques. Researchers should not just concentrate on conventional statistical methods, but keep an eye on alternative artificial intelligence systems. When attempting to solve a multivariate problem, they should try alternative methods of analysis – and above all remember that they are just tools. There is still no substitute for the human brain in selecting the correct tool for the problem to be solved.

REFERENCES

Alt, M. (1990) *Exploring Hyperspace: A Non-Mathematical Explanation of Multivariate Analysis.* McGraw-Hill.
Draper, N. and Smith, H. (1981) *Applied Regression Analysis.* John Wiley & Sons.
Everitt, B.S. (1980) *Cluster Analysis.* Gower.
Greenacre, M.J. (1984) *Theory and Application of Correspondence Analysis.* Academic Press.
Stuart, A. (1963) Standard errors for percentages. *Journal of the Royal Statistical Society, Series C. Applied Statistics,* **12**, 2.

SUGGESTED FURTHER READING

Aleksander, I. and Morcon, H. (1990) *An Introduction to Neural Computing.* Chapman & Hall.
Mood, A.M. and Graybill, F.A. (1963) *Introduction to the Theory of Statistics.* McGraw-Hill.
Quenouille, M.H. (1959) *Rapid Statistical Calculations.* Charles Griffin.
Siegel, S. (1956) *Non-Parametric Statistics for the Behavioural Sciences.* McGraw-Hill.

Annex 3

Demographic and Other Classifications

Mario van Hamersveld

INTRODUCTION

In the early stages of the development of modern market research, a lot of attention was paid to charting aggregated-demographic and socio-economic features of the population. Consumption and spending habits were presented by age, income and other physical characteristics, and so insight into the size of selected sub-groups set the direction for policymaking. In particular, use was made of the available statistics and secondary sources.

With the growth in primary research, especially face-to-face research, there was a growing need to know more about demographic and socio-economic variables in more detail, if possible on an individual level. The driving force here was not only the improvement in the quality of random sampling; the idea also grew that better segmentation would also be possible. As more research was carried out in several countries, the call for internationally comparable standards and classifications of respondents for robust international survey-research became stronger.

The harmonisation of tools became an important focus of attention across the industry. In recent decades, it also became clear that demographic and socio-economic features were no longer sufficient to provide an adequate level of explanation. For this reason, other classifications were developed, based on elements such as opinions, attitudes and behaviour. Powerful concepts for such international approaches were launched. However, comparability over countries is, of course, not just a matter of classification. Attention must also be paid to the quality of data collection and to models of analysis and interpretation as they may differ widely across cultures.

This chapter starts by looking at the importance of standards of classification. First, recent developments are highlighted. Next, two main directions are dealt with in brief: demographics and other approaches to classification, with other dimensions and indicators being placed in the foreground.

The point of view is international research, taking into account the complexity of harmonising instruments and measures. This is done using a global description of the state-of-the-art. For more detailed, methodological considerations, please see the references.

THE NEED FOR HARMONISATION

Central to this Annex is the division of a market (country) into its components by some scheme and the harmonisation of the division across different markets and/or countries. The dimensions of stratification that can be included in the scheme could refer to " socio-economic indicators,

Market Research Handbook, 5th Edition. Edited by M. van Hamersveld and C. de Bont.
© 2007 John Wiley & Sons, Ltd.

public influence, reputation, ethnicity – as determined by one's race, religion or national origin – style of life and intellectual level" (Olsen, 1968). In principle, a wide range of variables can be specified.

The objective of harmonisation is to achieve the comparability of information and statistics across different markets. Harmonisation usually begins with the setting up and putting into use of common definitions.

One can state that the quality of international research and the comparability of information across countries stands or falls by good information on demographic or socio-economic variables in the selected countries.

These "background" variables "contain necessary information to define homogeneous sub groups, to establish causal relations between attitudes and societal facts, and to define differences between scores on scales. In short, they allow us to define contexts in which respondents' opinions, attitudes and behaviour are socio-economically embedded" (Braun and Mohler, 2002).

The need for reliable standards and tools for cross-cultural comparison was prompted initially by considerations with regard to sample design and weighting for achieving representativeness and predictability. Experience existed primarily in defining national samples according to each local market's standard demographic and socio-economic classification. From the 1980s onwards, this resulted in problems for multinational research, as it was called initially, especially at the level of the providers of research. How could representativeness be guaranteed, given that surveys were being conducted in several countries simultaneously?

Above all, two questions were posed:

- "how to ensure the sub-sample in each market is comparable with all others;
- how to analyse the total sample effectively if the background variables on which sub-groups are to be formed differ from country to country". (Esomar, 1997)

The ideal solution would be to work with a demographic/socio-economic classification relevant to all countries, balancing national and international variables.

While international classification criteria aim to be fully compatible, national ones allow a deeper understanding of cultural identity.

However, the increasing need for the reliable cross-cultural measurement of all sorts of background variables cannot be viewed separately from the client's side. Characteristic to all of this was the process of internationalisation and increasing competition beyond national borders, which was becoming a deciding factor for international business. Users of research were orientated primarily towards obtaining better, comparable insight into regional markets for the sake of the possible standardisation of the supply of products and services, branding, marketing and segmentation. And this was done primarily to achieve economies of scale in a larger sales area.

Another motive must also be mentioned for the intensification of efforts in the area of harmonisation of international information and statistics. With the growth of supranational bodies and joint ventures, and the growth in the number of their member states or partners, there also arose a greater need for cross-national measurement at that level.

THE STAKEHOLDERS

In principle, activities in the area of demographics and other approaches to classification are shaped by four categories of players:

- **Industry organisations:** In the market research industry, Esomar has played a role in the development of a "Standard Demographic Classification" since the 1980s. Elaborating on the work of two earlier working parties, extensive data analysis was applied in seven waves within the scope of the Eurobarometer Surveys.

   This was reported on extensively in 1997. Based on this approach, activities were also developed in order to arrive at equivalent measures in other regions, such as Latin America.
- **Research providers:** the standardisation of background variables is a condition for success, especially for international chains. A lot of work has been done by the respective organisations in creating reliable cross-cultural roadmaps. Considerations of sampling were decisive. It seems that the attention paid to demographics/socio-economic data has declined a little, with other criteria increasingly being included in considerations. This should also be seen in the light of client pressure for tailor-made approaches or the demand for application-orientated or domain-specific segmentations.
- **Supranational authorities:** with the growth in scope and influence, bodies such as the EU (currently 450 million citizens in 25 countries) are showing themselves to be increasingly active in the harmonisation of relevant variables and statistics. Special mention here can be made of Eurostat. The task is not easy: there is a need to remove various methodological roadblocks and to develop common points of departure. An additional challenge is bringing the basic administration of the new participating countries up to the mark.
- **Universities/semi-governmental institutes:** social scientists, in particular, are increasingly occupied with comparative measurement in international research. Here as well, it is evident that the importance of this has grown with the process of internationalisation and globalisation which has coloured recent decades. The driving force for the scientist is the increasing demand for approaches that allow compatible measurement of background variables.

SOME RECENT DEVELOPMENTS

In this context reference should be made to the complexity of the object being researched. The simplification of definitions and features has been argued for on several occasions. However, there is no relatively static research scope or territory.

On the contrary: through, for example, changes in societal norms and values and, for instance, driven by mobility and immigration a dynamic – constantly shifting – picture of demographics and related features arises. Among other things, we are confronted with the increasing individualisation of behaviour and other developments that have created a "multi-dimensional consumer", who can no longer be so easily classified.

Market research has also changed recently. Clients have become more demanding.

Furthermore, an important part of research takes place online, which in turn places quite different demands on responsible classification and comparison than before.

In view of increasing non-response, many research companies started working with large consumer panels. This simplifies matters: questions on classification are only asked when a household (or individual) joins the panel. This enables the gathering of complete information on statistics without having to ask the same questions over and over again.

More than ever, there is a call for speed of delivery: in a number of cases speed of research seems to be the decisive factor in commissioning surveys. But, how good is the quality of data collection? How does the argument for simplification and the call for speed relate to the need to develop solid classifications that facilitate good cross-national measurement? The discussion on this is still at an early stage, so it seems.

DEMOGRAPHIC CLASSIFICATION: A CLOSER LOOK

Currently it may look as if small-scale research has acquired the upper hand in international research. However, if one is striving for solid, reliable research, it is necessary to quantify the hypotheses formulated in small-scale research by large scale survey projects.

Which variables are mostly taken into consideration? There are regional differences. For this reason, comparing across regions is frequently no longer possible. Within regions, there are also divergent national statistics. It is usually customary to differentiate according to the following characteristics: age, sex/gender, region in a country, size of town, household, family, education, employment/occupation, income, race and ethnicity and religion. Sometimes additional features are added for the construction of classifications, such as ownership of durables, languages spoken/understood and the like. Emphasis in most cases is obtained through a sharper, more discriminating classification through a combination of characteristics.

Let us have a closer look at the characteristics and review them one by one. The point of view – by way of illustration – is predominantly the situation in Europe.

In general, it is assumed that establishing age and sex/gender does not present any problems. However, there are varying definitions of "adult" or "child" from place to place. Classification by regions and size of towns is also mostly easy to do. In Europe the so-called NUTS clasification (Eurostat) was instrumental in resolving the harmonisation issue.

Over the years, increasingly divergent societal forms have arisen; consequently, more and more attention must be paid to the definitions of "household" and "family". Indicative for the demographic dynamism of recent decades are, for example, the possible descriptions as proposed by Jary and Jary (1991):

- **Household:** a single person or a group of people who have the same address as their only or main residence and who share one meal a day or share living accommodation.
- **Family:** a group of people related by kinship or similar close ties in which the adults assume responsibility for care and upbringing of their natural or adopted children; i.e. a group of at least two generations.

    When measuring these variables, differences in local culture, law and administration can play a role. So it should not come as a surprise that the approach shows considerable difficulties in practice.

It is known that education systems can vary a lot by country in terms of duration, content and certification. Classification is essentially related to the educational system in each country or region. The definition of the variable of education therefore requires a little hard thinking.

In the above-mentioned ESOMAR classification, emphasis was primarily placed on the Terminal Education Age (TEA). Classifying by age allows for an easy international comparison. Attention should be paid to the difference between "completed education" level and "non-completed" level.

When it comes to measuring the status in employment – as defined as any kind of regularly exercised activity that is compensated by an income – there are some problems too: part-time work, temporary leave, extra training offered by the employer. All these new employment schemes are in line with evolving national legislation.

However, the measuring of occupation in terms of the defining of jobs with a high degree of similarity with regard to their main tasks and duties is more complicated. Over the years, some efforts have been made to develop international standard classifications and indexes of occupations. The International Labour Organisation (ILO) did some groundbreaking work there. The ISCO classification is no doubt the best known effort to harmonise this intrinsically diverse reality.

Esomar, striving for the simplification of international survey research, presented a set of questions in order to harmonise the occupation across national boundaries. This information was subsequently used together with information on education and economic status information as measured by ownership of selected durables, to construct a "Social Grade": the so called Esomar Social Scale (ESS). In the case of ownership, the list appears dated in 2007 and an adjustment seems desirable.

For insight into how classification might look and especially the detailed construction of the ESS, please see the appendix, which also includes the questionnaire used.

The collection of comparable data regarding the variable of income is made slightly harder by the high percentage of non-answers with which the researcher is confronted, as well as the differences in payment, tax, income transfers and social security in the various countries. However, the introduction of the Euro in January 2002 solved the comparability issue to a large extent for the Euro-region.

Increasing attention is being paid to the measuring of race and ethnicity in international survey research. Questions on this aspect were not included in the above-mentioned ESOMAR classification. Was this measure less important at that time? The focus for this variable is on elements such as common citizenship, mother tongue, cultural background, country of birth, similar skin colour. The classification of groups from this point of view is still in its infancy, it seems.

The definition and recording of religion is also no easy task, given the divergent forms in which religion appears and the expressions of religious experience in the various countries.

The classification of groups from this point of view faces reluctance from both the public and the researchers. Some of these questions are considered to be rather delicate, and in some countries even forbidden.

This is as far as global reconnoitring has come. In order to make real progress on the structure of equivalent measures, nation-specific concepts and structures must be respected, as mentioned above.

In the search for common definitions, the similarities of the different structures are, in principle, a good point of departure. But it will be clear: a lot of energy must be put into defining indicators and – last but not least – into creating a research questionnaire that can be understood by the survey respondent.

OTHER FORMS OF CLASSIFICATION

In 2007, the description of markets according to demographic/socio-economic characteristics can be called a classical point of view.

With the further development of target marketing and related concepts such as, ultimately, "one-to-one" marketing, an extensive repertoire of approaches has recently been added.

Sometimes it is about creating fine, very precise descriptions of sub-groups based on a considerable number of criteria. With the arrival of "consumer generated media" and the influence that groups of consumers can exercise via the Internet, one may even state that some segments are self-defining. The aim of all efforts is for the most part to offer a different market- or target-group perspective, to obtain insight for innovation, better positioning and market approach.

We will review a number of classification schemes in outline below. The schemes overlap each other partly. This is not surprising: "mixed typologies" increasingly form the basis of tailor-made segmentation. Breakthroughs in the area of multivariate analysis, data mining and data fusion have played an important role in the growth of possibilities.

- **Product classification:** in a few companies, classifications are used in which product-related indicators form the source of inspiration and one's own product portfolio is the starting point. For example, one looks primarily at the physical aspects of the product (such as engine power, screen size of TV sets or LCD screens, fat content, packaging size, shoe size, price classes, etc.). In practice, these categorisations are insufficient – partly coloured by considerations of internal business orientation. Enrichment through the addition of other variables is desired in order to obtain meaningful segments.
- **Psychographics:** this looks primarily at shared attitudes, interests and opinions: how far can homogeneous clusters of consumers be differentiated on the basis of these characteristics? The market researcher is above all searching for the more psychological characteristics of individuals and groups, or factors which are important in the information, orientation and decision-to-buy process. One also labels this the study of lifestyles, with focus on core values of the people concerned, their norms and behaviours. Categorisation is often done on the basis of activities, interests, opinions and ideas, the amount of money or free time available, experiences, etc.

    One of the best known systems is VALS (Values and Lifestyles), created by SRI Consulting Business Intelligence. However, quite a number of providers currently offer services with "value compasses", "socio styles" and other typologies.

    It is important to note here that these systems claim to describe a reasonably consistent and characterising lifestyle of relevant consumer groups for a specific period of time, allowing marketing efforts to be tuned to them.
- **Behaviour:** how do consumers use a product, what do they actually do with it?

    This is the point of view for these types of classification. People use the same product for different reasons, for varying lengths of time and in various capacities. Naturally, use–non use is a predominant indicator here.

    The context and frequency of use – heavy, moderate, light – and duration of use can also play a role. When is the product used, on what occasion? One can think of in the home or outside, special occasions, times of the day and so on.

    Ultimately, loyalty is also an important variable for success in this approach.

    Is one so satisfied that a subsequent purchase of the same product of the same brand takes place?

    In particular, ethnography has an increasing role to play in establishing behaviour (see also Chapter 23). More accurate information on the actual use and the context of use can be obtained through systematic observation. Semiotic classification based on the meaning of words that are, for example, related to the different propositions in a product category, can also offer fruitful clues.
- **Other:** Some segmentations are primarily about consumer markets. Naturally, a great deal of energy is also expended in industrial markets searching for powerful classifications. In business-to-business, slicing up the pie means, among other things, the use of dimensions such as organisational characteristics (size, total sales, number of employees, type of business, production technology, etc.) as well as classifying according to fulfilled functions and benefit segmentations: what are the benefits customers get from the products and services in the category? In some concepts, the main focus is the decision-making process: who are the ultimate deciders, what are their characteristics and how can we reach them?

Is one technique of classification the best? In everyday practice, a combination of approaches is mostly followed, as already mentioned. For a defined product category, "a domain-specific" classification is developed, which integrates both the necessary information on the consumer's behaviour and lifestyle as well as detailed information that is characteristic to the product group. This is because product groups vary a great deal.

One can only move forward with a deep understanding of the unique character of the category – in terms of needs, demand patterns, engagement and involvement not realised, and one never succumbs to over-generally offered typologies. In some cases, one therefore sees that clients with MR providers as partners create jointly the desired – often exclusive – domain-specific schemes.

The ways of working to choose – and the extent of the analysis – also depend on the phase of development of a market. Thus, in several emerging markets Unilever uses a Living Standard Measure (LSM) with a strong accent on standards demographics.

Respondents are asked about ownership of durables, with additional questions about their education, the type of outlet they shop in most often for fast moving consumer goods and general readership of newspapers and magazines (Cir, 2004). However, this classification is less useful in the developed world – in other markets, Unilever therefore also uses supplemental methods and also looks, for example, at "fulfilling the need for an intense experience", "credibility of well being concepts", and so on.

CONCLUDING REMARKS

It seems that there is still a long way to go to obtain solid comparable information on demographic and socio-economic characteristics across countries.

Is it possible to state that given the status quo the MR industry may be characterised by stagnation and lukewarm interest in harmonisation? Is complexity of the subject matter an issue or do cost considerations play a role? One might argue that attention has shifted from sampling to understanding consumer behaviour.

Whatever the case, the subject at the moment is a bit lower down the agenda in the public industry debate. It remains to be seen whether only co-operation between governments and the academic world, possibly supplemented with initiatives from representatives of industry, can deliver greater progress.

In the meantime, classification by means of other indicators has become more dominant in the fight for the consumer and obtaining a competitive advantage.

The possibilities of classification have increased sharply. Precisely in the area of the classification of markets – delivering insight and foresight with respect to the development of meaningful categories, the market researcher, as the voice of the customer, can continue to play a decisive role like no other.

Note: The author wishes to thank Yves Marbeau (France) for his initial suggestions and Dominique Vancraeynest (Belgium) for review of a first draft. For more detailed information readers could contact bodies such as Eurostat (EU-Brussels), UNESCO (Institute for Statistics – Paris) and ILO (Bureau of Statistics, Geneva). Also very useful is the "Working Book" by Juergen H.P. Hoffmeyer-Zlotnik and Christof Wolf: "Advances in Cross-National Comparison", Kluwer Academic/Plenum Publishers 2003.

REFERENCES

Braun, M. and Mueller, W. (2000): "Background Variables" in *Cross Cultural Survey Methods*. John Wiley & Sons, Ltd.

Cir, J. (2004) "Consumer Segments in Central and Eastern Europe", *Research World*, February.
Cahill, D.J. (1997) *How Consumers Pick a Hotel*, The Haworth Press.
Esomar (1997) "Standard Demographic Classification", Esomar.
Jary, D. and Jary, J. (1991) *The Harper Collins Dictionary of Sociology*, Harper Collins Publishers.
Olsen, M.E. (1968) *The Process of Social Organisation*, Holt, Rinehart and Winston.

APPENDIX

Composition of the ESOMAR Social Grade variable

1 Determining the appropriate Social Grade category

The ESOMAR Social Grade is a composite variable constructed from:

- the Occupation of the Main Income Earner in the household (the M.I.E.), based on the questions developed by the ESOMAR working parties;
- the Terminal Education Age (T.E.A.) of the M.I.E., adjusted to incorporate any further education or professional training completed by the M.I.E. following a period of employment;
- and in the case of non-active M.I.E.s, the Economic Status of the household, based on the household ownership level of ten selected consumer durables.

For all M.I.E.s in active employment the appropriate Social Grade category is determined using a two-dimensional matrix incorporating the sub-variables: Occupation and Terminal Education Age.

For all M.I.E.s not in active employment an alternative two-dimensional matrix is used to allocate the respondents to the appropriate Social Grade category. In such cases the Occupation of the M.I.E. is replaced by the Economic Status of the household.

The cells of these two matrices are used to allocate the individual respondent to one of the eight ESOMAR Social Grade categories: ranging from A (high) through B, C1, C2, D, E1, E2 to E3 (low). This eight category classification represents the optimal solution to achieving a balance between the objectives of:

- obtaining fairly evenly sized sub-groups per market;
- making rational and meaningful groupings of occupations and education levels;
- ensuring reasonable homogeneity within the aggregated cells, based on the Economic Status scores within each cell.

An additional Social Grade category has also been introduced (N.A.) to which problem cases resulting from non-response are allocated.

For the definition of each of the M.I.E. Occupation categories on which the matrix is based (see the "Analysis Guideline").

It should be noted that the M.I.E.'s Terminal Education Age takes into account any professional training or education undertaken by the respondent even after completion of the main period of education. Five categories are defined for the T.E.A.: 21 years or older, 17–20 years, 15–16 years, 14 years, 13 years or younger. Again a "no answer" category is included for non-response.

The Economic Status Scale reflects the penetration of ownership of ten key consumer durable items at household level (see questionnaire). The original objective in compiling the Economic Status Scale was to construct a variable capable of representing the financial status of the consumer, without the inevitable problems associated with asking sensitive questions about income and having to cope with high non-response rates. Instead of attempting to determine household income, the focus is placed on the ownership of key consumer durables selected to reflect the level of disposable income in the household.

However, it is recommended that the Economic Status Scale should only be used to assess a respondent's Social Grade when it is impossible to obtain details of the M.I.E.'s occupation. The Economic Status should not be regarded as an easy alternative method.

For the purposes of the Social Grade analysis six Economic Status Scale categories are defined: households possessing 5 or more of the durables, 4, 3, 2, 1 and zero/those not answering the question.

2 Description of the Social Grade categories

In order to provide researchers with more tangible insight into the types of individuals to be encountered in each of the Social Grade categories a brief description of each category has been compiled:

A "well educated top managers and professionals": well educated top to middle level managers with responsibility for more extensive personnel; well educated independent or self-employed professional people;

B "middle managers": well educated smaller middle level managers or slightly less well educated top managers with fewer personnel responsibilities;

C1 "well educated non-manual employees, skilled workers and business owners": smaller middle level managers; well educated non-manual employees, supervisors/skilled manual workers and small business owners; less well educated managers;

C2 "skilled workers and non-manual employees": better educated supervisors/skilled manual workers; moderately well educated non-manual employees and small business owners;

D "skilled and unskilled manual workers and poorly educated people in non-manual/ managerial positions": less well educated supervisors/skilled and unskilled manual workers and poorly educated non-manual workers; poorly educated top/middle managers or smaller business owners;

E "less well educated skilled and unskilled manual workers, small business owners and farmers/fishermen":

- E1 comprises mainly poorly educated supervisors/skilled manual workers and better educated unskilled workers, with some poorly educated non-office non-manual employees and small business owners;
- E2 comprises mainly very poorly educated supervisors/skilled manual workers and small business owners plus very poorly educated non-office non-manual employees;
- E3 comprises poorly educated unskilled manual workers and farmers/fishermen.

For the purposes of everyday research these eight Social Grade categories can be aggregated to provide a more practical four-category classification:

AB "managers and professionals";
C1 "well educated non-manual and skilled workers";
C2 "skilled workers and non-manual employees";
DE "unskilled manual workers and other less well educated workers/employees".

3 ESOMAR Social Grade questionnaire

Shown below is the set of questions developed for the ESOMAR Social Grade classification in English. The occupation and education questions relate solely to the M.I.E., i.e. the person contributing most to the income of the household. The Economic Status Scale relates to the respondent's household and is therefore not specifically related to the head of household.

ESOMAR RECOMMENDED QUESTIONNAIRE   **ENGLISH VERSION**

Q.1   INT. RECORD SEX: ☐ male   ☐ female

Q.2   What is your age?   _ years

Q.3   How many people live in your household
       including yourself?

Q.4   How many children under 16 are there?

Q.5A   Are you, in your household the person who
       contributes most to the household income?   ☐ yes   ☐ no

Q.5B   Are you, in your household the person
       mainly responsible for ordinary shopping
       and looking after the home?   ☐ yes   ☐ no

Q.6   Are you...

       • married/living together   ☐

       • single   ☐

       • separated/divorced/widowed   ☐

INT.: IF RESP. ANSWERS "No" AT Q.5A, REPHRASE Q'S 7–12 IN THE THIRD PERSON ("He"/"She") AND ASK ABOUT THE MAIN INCOME EARNER (M.I.E.)

Q.7   At what age did you finish full-time education?   _ years

       M.I.E. is still studying (e10)   ☐   GO TO Q.13

Q.8   Any time after that, did you...
       • resume general education
         at a later stage in your life?   ☐ yes   GO TO Q.9

                                                           ☐ no   CONTINUE...

    • take any apprenticeship/professional
      training for your job?   ☐ yes   GO TO Q.9

                                            ☐ no   GO TO Q.10A

Q.9   How many months did your (further education/
        professional training) last in total?   _ months

Q.10A At present, are you . . . ?

    • self-employed   ☐   GO TO Q.11A

    • in paid employment   ☐   GO TO Q.11B

    • temporarily not working
      (unemployed, illness)   ☐   GO TO Q.10B

    • retired   ☐   GO TO Q.10B

    • not working/responsible for ordinary
      shopping and looking after the home (e13) ☐   GO TO Q.13

Q.10B And formerly, have you been . . . ?

    • self-employed   ☐   GO TO Q.13

    • in paid employment   ☐   GO TO Q.13

    • no former employment   ☐   GO TO Q.13

Q.11A SELF-EMPLOYED:
        • What kind of work do you do?
          (What position do you hold?)
          PROFESSIONAL (e.g. Doctor, Lawyer,
          Accountant, Architect) (e2)   ☐   GO TO Q.12

        • BUSINESS PROPRIETOR, OWNER OF
          COMPANY/SHOP, CRAFTSMAN,
          OTHER SELF-EMPLOYED PERSON:
          How many employees do you have?   ☐ 0–5(e9)   GO TO Q.12

                                             ☐ 6 or more (e7)   GO TO Q.12

        • FARMER/FISHERMAN (e12)   GO TO Q.12

Q.11B IN PAID EMPLOYMENT:
        What position do you hold?
        (What kind of work do you do?)
        • PROFESSIONAL (in actual profession) (e3) ☐   GO TO Q.12

        • GENERAL MANAGEMENT
          (Exec./Manag. Dir., Officer, Mgr.)   ☐   CONTINUE . . .

        How many employees are you responsible
        for?   ☐ 0–5 (e4)   GO TO Q.12

                                            ☐ 6 or more (e1)   GO TO Q.12

- MIDDLE MANAGEMENT
  (Dept./Branch Head, Junior Mgr.)
  How many employees are you responsible for?   □ 0–5 (e6)   GO TO Q.12

  □ 6 or more (e5)   GO TO Q.12

- OTHER NON-MANUAL EMPLOYEE
  Do you work mainly in an office?   □ yes (e8)   GO TO Q.12

  □ no (e11)   GO TO Q.12

- MANUAL WORKER
  Do you work as a foreman or in a supervisory
  capacity?   □ yes (e14)   GO TO Q.12

  □ no   CONTINUE...

  Have you received any formal training to
  acquire specific skills in the work you do?   □ yes (e14)   GO TO Q.12

  □ no (e15)   GO TO Q.12

Q.12 How many hours per week do you normally work?   _____

Q.13 Do you or does anyone else in your household, own ... ?
- a colour TV set   □ yes   □ no
- a video recorder   □ yes   □ no
- a radio-clock   □ yes   □ no
- a video camera/Camcorder   □ yes   □ no
- a PC/home computer   □ yes   □ no
- an electric deep fryer   □ yes   □ no
- an electric drill   □ yes   □ no
- a still camera   □ yes   □ no
- at least two cars   □ yes   □ no
- a second home or holiday house/flat   □ yes   □ no

Q.14 Your main home: do you ... ?
- rent it   □
- or own it   □

Q.15 Which foreign languages do you understand well
      enough to read a newspaper or listen to radio news?

□ Danish   □ Italian
□ Dutch   □ Portuguese
□ English   □ Spanish
□ French   □ Swedish
□ German   □ other
□ Greek

INT.: NOTE ADDRESS

Q.16 Region*
Q.17 Size of town*

*Based on address using the usual, local categories (as documented in available statistics on universe)

4 Analysis Guideline

Step 1: Determine the M.I.E. Occupation category as follows:

Category:

1. IF Q.11B is Employed General Management, responsible for 6 or more employees ... e1
2. IF Q.11A is Self-employed Professional e2
3. IF Q.11B is Employed Professional e3
4. IF Q.11B is Employed General Management, responsible for 5 or less employees e4
5. IF Q.11B is Employed Middle Management, responsible for 6 or more employees ... e5
6. IF Q.11B is Employed Middle Management, responsible for 5 or less employees e6
7. IF Q.11A is Self-employed Business Proprietor, owner of a company/shop, craftsman, other self-employed person, responsible for 6 or more employees e7
8. IF Q.11B is Employed Other Non-manual position, working mainly in an office e8
9. IF Q.11A is Self-employed Business Proprietor, owner of a company/shop, craftsman, other self-employed person, responsible for 5 or less employees e9
10. IF Q.7 is Non-active: Still studying e10
11. IF Q.11B is Employed Other Non-manual position, not working mainly in an office (e.g. travelling or in a service job) e11
12. IF Q.11A is Self-employed Farmer or Fisherman e12
13. IF Q.10A is Non-active: responsible for ordinary shopping and looking after the home, housewife e13
14. IF Q.11B is Employed Manual Worker: Supervisor or Skilled Manual worker e14
15. IF Q.11B is Employed Other (Unskilled) Manual worker, servant e15
16. IF Q.10A is Non-active: retired or unable to work through illness, unemployed or temporarily not working e16

IF don't know OR no answer the Occupation variable is replaced by the Economic Status variable (see Step 3).

Step 2: Determine the M.I.E. Terminal Education Age category as follows:

1. CONVERT all figures in months at Q.9 to years (rounding to whole numbers)
2. SUM Q.7 + Q.9 'summed T.E.A.' .... Category:
3. IF summed T.E.A. is >20 .... 21+
4. IF summed T.E.A. is 17, 18, 19 OR 20 17–20
5. IF summed T.E.A. is 15 OR 16 15–16
6. IF summed T.E.A. is 14 14
7. IF summed T.E.A. is <14 13–
8. IF don't know OR no answer .... N.A.
9. IF Q.7 is 'Still studying' .... N.A.

Step 3: Determine the ESOMAR Social Grade category as follows:

1. IF the Occupation of the M.I.E. category is NOT e10 or e13 or e16 or don't know or no answer, determine the ESOMAR Social Grade category on the basis of the matrix shown in Figure A3.1:

Base: active M.I.E.s	e 1+2	e 3+5	e 4,6+7	e 12	e 8+9	e 11+14	e 15
21+	A	A	B	B	C1	C1	D
17–20	A	B	C1	C1	C2	C2	D
15–16	B	C1	C2	D	D	D	E1
14	C1	D	D	E1	E1	E1	E3
13	D	D	D	E3	E2	E2	E3

Figure A3.1   Occupation of the main income earner →
↓ Terminal education age of the main income earner

2. IF the Occupation of the M.I.E. category IS e10 or e13 or e16 or don't know or no answer, determine the **Economic Status** category as follows:
   - SUM number of durables owned .... integer: max. 10–min. 1
   - IF don't know OR no answer .... N.A.
   - determine the ESOMAR Social Grade category on the basis of the matrix shown in Figure A3.2:
3. IF Q.10A/B AND Q.11A/B is don't know OR no answer AND Q.13 is don't know OR no answer, code Social Grade as no answer.
4. IF SUMMED T.E.A. is don't know OR no answer, code Social Grade as no answer.

Base: non-active M.I.E.s	5+	4	3	2	1	0/NA
21 or older	A	A	B	C1	C1	D
17–20	A	B	B	C2	C2	D
15–16	B	C1	C1	E1	E1	E2
14	C1	C2	C2	E1	E2	E3
13 or younger	D	D	D	E2	E3	E3

Figure A3.2   Economic status (no. of consumer durables owned) →
↓ Terminal education age of the main income earner

Annex 4
Professional Ethics and Standards

Véronique Jeannin

INTRODUCTION

Corporate ethics are of increasing importance for all industries that value their reputation. Integrity, fairness and transparency are central to most codes of conduct that aim to build and promote public trust. As market researchers depend on the good will of respondents, it is even more important that our profession maintains public confidence by demonstrating that we recognise our responsibilities in ensuring consumer protection to provide the assurance that market research is carried out honestly, objectively and ethically.

ESOMAR first published a professional code on market and social research in 1948. This demonstrates the importance that the market and social research profession has always placed on building public trust and its recognition of the ethical and professional responsibilities in carrying out market research.

In this Annex we would like to discuss why professional ethics and standards are so important to our industry, with a few examples of what has been achieved in recent years, and the latest challenges that are facing our industry.

WHY SO IMPORTANT?

Most major industries and professions now have a code of ethics. This will normally embody the ethical commitments of a profession, tell the world who you are, what you stand for, and what to expect when conducting business or when dealing with you. But what do we mean by "ethical"? "*In accordance with principles of conduct that are considered correct, especially those of a given profession or group*" says the Collins dictionary.

This means for instance, that no matter what their specialism or country, all medical practitioners should operate under the same ethical principles contained in the Hippocratic Oath. In the same way, all researchers wherever they are working, should comply with the same basic principles that ensure they respect the rights of respondents, and are transparent and objective in their work.

Ethical standards are particularly important for market research which depends, for its success, on public confidence to ensure that it is carried out honestly, and without unwelcome intrusion or disadvantage to its participants. These standards need to be clearly linked to business practice for credibility and transparency, and communicated in a concise and readable way that is also understandable to non-researchers.

Market Research Handbook, 5th Edition. Edited by M. van Hamersveld and C. de Bont.
© 2007 John Wiley & Sons, Ltd.

In addition to ethics, there are also professional standards. For instance, in medicine, there might be different guidelines for specific activities, but patients are at least assured that standards are defined in clear treatment protocols which improve over time, as science develops. This also applies to market research, where techniques might change, but common standards ensure validity and comparability of results.

Indeed, professional ethics and standards are vital for our industry. They build trust and credibility and enhance quality. They create differentiation and transparency in the market place. They foster professionalism and economies of scale by focusing on consistent policies and practices that are common to all operators worldwide.

With the introduction of data privacy regulations and do-not-call lists for marketing contacts in many regions, it is also increasingly important that we clearly differentiate our activities from commercial initiatives such as direct sales and marketing, which tend to attract heavier regulations.

We need professional standards to differentiate market research for the public, legislators and regulators. Professional standards build trust making further regulation of research unnecessary. Professional standards differentiate market researchers from other information providers, and help to demonstrate that our information and insights are more reliable and valid than others which helps to stimulate growth. Professional standards facilitate international work providing a common language and definitions to ease communication and reduce errors.

WHAT HAS BEEN ACHIEVED?

In 1977, ESOMAR and the ICC (International Chamber of Commerce) published the ICC/ESOMAR International Code of Marketing and Social Research Practice. There have been a number of updates since then to ensure that the Code remains relevant and in line with legislative requirements. Since then the Code has been adopted by over 100 associations worldwide and today is the only global market, opinion and social research code.

As it is so vital to take into account changes in the external environment to ensure that guidance is up to date and credible, ICC and ESOMAR initiated a key global project in 2006 to review the Code.

The Code was adapted to add clarity and transparency and to strengthen the section on data privacy to state more explicitly the legal obligations in collecting personal information from respondents. A clearer definition of market research was also developed to help us to communicate the unique character of our sector and to help to clearly differentiate market research from other activities.

It is increasingly important to ensure that the principles of the Code are communicated more widely than just within the market research industry, and we aim to ensure that respondents, legislators, and the general public are informed of the Code as a recognised means of providing an additional layer of consumer protection. The revised Code is built around these fundamentals which encapsulate the ethical essence of the profession:

1. Market researchers shall conform to all relevant national and international laws.
2. Market researchers shall behave ethically and shall not do anything which might damage the reputation of market research.
3. Market researchers shall take special care when carrying out research among children and young people.

4. Respondents' cooperation is voluntary and must be based on adequate, and not misleading, information about the general purpose and nature of the project when their agreement to participate is being obtained and all such statements shall be honoured.
5. The rights of respondents as private individuals shall be respected by market researchers and they shall not be harmed or adversely affected as the direct result of cooperating in a market research project.
6. Market researchers shall never allow personal data they collect in a market research project to be used for any purpose other than market research.
7. Market researchers shall ensure that projects and activities are designed, carried out, reported and documented accurately, transparently and objectively.
8. Market researchers shall conform to the accepted principles of fair competition.

The Code sets out the rules which must guide those who carry out or use market, social and opinion research whether provider or client. They should follow not just the letter but also the spirit of these rules.

A key requirement relates to transparency. ICC and ESOMAR believe that all information collection and handling activities must be transparent to avoid confusion, especially on the part of the public. For this reason, market research activities must be clearly separated from non-research activities such as direct sales or direct marketing, which are usually governed by different rules and regulations that are often more restrictive.

The Code also clearly states that researchers must abide by all relevant national and international legislation and regulations. In certain countries there are additional national requirements laid down by legislation or by the local professional association. These take precedence where they add to or differ from the Code, when carrying out research in that country.

ESOMAR has also published guidelines on conducting various types of research which are drafted by experts from research companies, client companies and national and international associations.

Some guidelines concentrate on researching sensitive samples and emphasise the need for a special responsibility for instance, in relation to seeking the opinions of children and young people. Others provide "how to" guidance such as ESOMAR's guidelines on how to commission research which includes selecting a market research agency, reaching agreement on a market research project and international research.

Opinion polls take a top priority because of debates about pre-election polls and the role of the media. Whilst ESOMAR champions the freedom to conduct and publish opinion polls as part of the public's right to information, and this right exists in most democracies, the publication of pre-election poll results is restricted in some countries, for instance in Greece, where they cannot be published up to 15 days before an election. The idea behind such prohibitions is that poll results can affect how people vote but, according to all studies, it is impossible to say accurately what the effects actually would be and selective rumours or leaks about the results of private polls can be much more damaging to the democratic process than full publication and public debate about of the quality and meaning of the results of a particular poll.

The Guide to Opinion Polls published by ESOMAR and WAPOR (World Association of Public Opinion Research) was reviewed in 2005 to reflect the latest developments in opinion polling, especially pre-election polls. Updates take account of the latest practices in online surveys and exit polls and also aim to improve transparency by encouraging research organisations to publish detailed information about the methodology and results on their company websites.

The Guide is divided into four sections each aimed at specific target groups: a text setting out the democratic value of opinion polls, aimed at politicians and the general public; FAQs that can be used to educate journalists on technical aspects; and an introduction and key principles based on the ICC/ESOMAR Code as well as guidelines on the practical aspects of conducting pre-election polls, aimed at researchers.

QUALITY STANDARDS

Clients not only want to compare results from cross-border research projects, they also want to feel confident about the professional quality of their research partners. Reliability, transparency and accountability are key requirements.

In 2005, international agreement was reached on ISO 20252 which sets global standards for carrying out market research. Promoted by EFAMRO (the European Federation of Associations of Marketing Research Organisations) these were developed by the 22 member countries of the technical committee and approved by the national standards bodies which are members of the International Standards Organisation (100 countries, including all the major economies).

The standards specify the processes in conducting research projects from proposal, through sampling, fieldwork and data analysis to the final report. External accreditation agencies check independently that the specified procedures are indeed followed by the company. They are the process and control aspects of market research just as doctors follow specific protocols when treating patients.

The standards require that researchers first tell clients what they will do and how they will provide that offer. The second step is that they implement the job as they said they would, and the third stage involves checking if everything is going as planned while working on the project. If there are errors or breakdowns in the process, these have to be recorded and adjustments and improvements have to be made to ensure that these failures are not repeated.

To become ISO certified, an agency has to ask an accredited auditor to assess whether it meets all requirements, such as having a quality system in place, keeping proper records, training and monitoring the performance of employees and interviewers, reporting to clients on project progress and key decisions and all other quality procedures. The company is then audited regularly to check that the procedures are being followed.

The ISO 20252 norm will be adjusted and updated on a regular basis as market research techniques evolve.

OTHER INITIATIVES

With the emergence of not only new techniques but also new entrants to the sector, some of whom do not join professional associations, clients find it more difficult to differentiate between good and bad research. Effective and publicised self-regulation in defending the industry from unprofessional operators, reassuring the public and maintaining standards is even more essential for the market research industry.

National trade organisations such as the ADM in Germany and the MRS in the UK have developed strong self regulatory systems, comprehensive complaint handling procedures and sanctions such as public warnings and reprimands to stress the difference between professional and unprofessional behaviour.

ESOMAR is working with associations all over the world to promote the adoption of templates based on effective national compliance systems. For instance the procedures developed in Germany involve a joint industry approach from all professional and trade associations as well as academics and clients. Sanctions can include for instance, publishing cases and company names to publicise the fact that the industry takes action if professional norms are not respected.

Professional standards and privacy programmes are of increasing importance worldwide. Developments in the US include work by associations such as CASRO (Council of American Survey Research Organizations) which for instance, has produced a Privacy Protection Program (CASRO 3P) that gives legal proof of research companies accountability and compliance via model policies, business contracts, and privacy language. The MRA (Market Research Association) has initiated a Professional Researcher Certification programme. Furthermore, the trade associations in Australia, Canada and Japan have all developed comprehensive privacy programmes on behalf of their members.

In recent years associations in the largest markets in Latin America such as Argentina, Brazil and Mexico, as well as in Asia Pacific have made huge strides in adopting and implementing professional ethics and standards.

ESOMAR is committed to working with national and international associations to develop and implement professional and ethical standards. This is not always easy, given the need to stay abreast of rapidly developing technologies in a complex legislative and increasingly global environment.

Recognising that every national and regional market has its own requirements, we aim to promote our professional ethics and standards to researchers, the public and to legislators all over the world in a clear and credible way, to make known the common fundamental principles on which we have built our profession.

LATEST CHALLENGES

There are many methods of gathering information, and the channels available are multiplying with the development and use of Internet-based technologies and other interactive media. In the last decade, technology has transformed market, opinion and survey research, making it possible for us to collect ever more detailed information about people's behaviour, habits and personal preferences. With the growing use of technology in the collection of information about people actively and passively, it becomes increasingly difficult to explain to respondents how we safeguard and protect their personal information.

In parallel, response rates have fallen dramatically. People are less willing to give up their time to answer our questions, they are more concerned about issues of data privacy, and they are less open to being contacted at home, in the street, or on the phone or online, for research purposes. Many are however, prepared to provide information about their views and preferences, if they have a more formal relationship with research companies and this explains the growth of research panels consisting of people who have agreed to participate in research interviews in exchange for incentives or rewards.

The Internet has opened new opportunities for collecting and disseminating research information worldwide. At the same time it raises a number of ethical and technical issues that must be addressed if the medium is to be used responsibly for market and opinion research purposes.

ESOMAR first published a guideline on Internet research in 1998 and this has been updated on a regular basis since then. The guideline combines an interpretation of the ICC/ESOMAR International Code as applied to Internet research with practical guidance on technical issues, privacy policies, data security, interviewing children and young people and unsolicited email. In 2005, a new section on access panels was added. The project team pushed for international agreement on how to help clients assess the quality of a panel through applying common definitions as until then there was no standard way to discuss quality issues. The guideline encourages transparency and stresses that respondents need to be treated fairly and in line with principles accepted by professional researchers worldwide.

Our professional standards must keep pace with new techniques and technology. For instance, the observation of human behaviour has always been an important component in qualitative research but recent technology has created new opportunities such as remote viewing from other locations including across borders as well as a resurgence of interest in ethnographic research which involves observing and filming people in natural settings, over an extended period of time.

The increasing use of CCTV in public places also enables researchers to, for instance, observe behaviour in a shopping centre and this can be done either overtly or covertly, where the observers are concealed. Furthermore, websites collect browsing data and there are other passive measure based on techniques such cookies and web bugs. Likewise, smart cards and scanners collect a wide range of consumer behaviour. The observation of online groups and bloggers, often linked with growing marketing methods such as WOM (Word of Mouth), relies upon observing how people interact with one another in both the face-to-face but also virtual environments.

ESOMAR is developing a guideline to include all forms of observation and passive research which aims to also take into account technology that is being developed, including brain scans, and eye-tracking. The guideline focuses on the need for transparency about the information that is being collected especially in view of data protection legislation.

The requirements for our industry are changing as researchers are increasingly being asked to provide consultancy services when interpreting their research findings to inform business strategies. Education and training play a key role in enhancing the skills, know how and expertise of market research professionals to meet the needs of business. ESOMAR is working with partners to enrich and harmonise market research training and education in academic circles, creating awareness within the market research industry of the importance of building new marketing intelligence skills and developing workshops and publications to provide researchers with the tools to build on their competences.

Both client companies and research chains are now operating on an international level and the market research industry is becoming increasingly global. Legislation has not keep pace with this development. For instance, the EU legal framework for data protection has not been implemented in a standardised way by the member states and there are also differences between the way this is handled in the EU and the USA, whilst some countries in Latin America or Asia have related laws and others do not.

CONCLUDING REMARKS

With the growth of international research and particularly research via the Internet it becomes increasingly important to develop internationally consistent rules, definitions and standards that apply wherever the respondent is located. The ICC/ESOMAR International Code for instance, provides respondents with data protection guarantees wherever they are based. National associations might add supplementary requirements that are specific to their markets or develop national approaches such as privacy programmes to implement these guarantees.

This exemplifies ESOMAR's key role as facilitator in aligning national and regional perspectives to create and promote industry-led professional ethics and standards on an international level. The legal environments and case law under which the industry has to operate may differ from country to country but the industry's principles that we respect and promote are the same. We will continue to depend on public goodwill to collect information about people's views, preferences and behaviour, and we need to reassure the public that we are honest and transparent in handling their personal data.

Given the increasing need for business and governments to stay closely in touch with consumers' preferences, we are convinced that developing and promoting professional ethics and standards and the value of market research services, ultimately safeguards and promotes both economic and societal growth and well-being.

REFERENCES

ICC/ESOMAR International Code of Marketing and Social Research Practice.
ESOMAR/WAPOR Guide to Opinion Polls.
Who's Afraid of Election Polls? Wolfgang Donsbach, University of Dresden. ESOMAR 2001.
ESOMAR Guideline on Conducting Marketing and Opinion Research Using the Internet.

ESOMAR World Organisation for Research www.esomar.org.
ICC International Chamber of Commerce www.iccwbo.org.
WAPOR World Association for Public Opinion Research www.unl.edu/WAPOR.
EFAMRO European Federation of Associations of Market Research Organisations www.efamro.com.
ADM Arbeitskreis Deutscher Markt- und Sozialforschungsinstitute e.V. www.adm-ev.de.
CASRO Council of American Survey Research Organizations www.casro.org.
MRS Market Research Society www.mrs.org.uk.

Index

Index compiled by Terry Halliday